"This excellent volume offers a much-needed multi-level perspective on creativity and innovation at work. Coverage ranges from individual level processes, abilities, and personality, to team climate and processes, to firm-level strategy, planning, structure, and capabilities. The volume examines a wide variety of topics yet is coherent in its emphasis on the importance of the broader context in which creative action and innovation takes place, and the dynamic processes that make creativity and innovation possible and successful. Together, the chapters provide an insightful and timely summary and integration of this rich literature. Highly recommended for scholars and professionals who wish to gain more insight into these important 21st century skills."

—Bernard A. Nijstad, *Professor of Organizational Behavior, University of Groningen, The Netherlands*

"*Creativity and Innovation in Organizations* is the go-to guide for anyone interested in understanding creative performance and innovation at work."

—Ronald A. Beghetto, *Editor,* Journal of Creative Behavior

CREATIVITY AND INNOVATION IN ORGANIZATIONS

This volume presents a distinctly multilevel perspective on creativity and innovation that considers individual-level, team-level, and firm-level factors. In illustrating these factors, this volume presents both theoretical and practical implications to guide researchers and practitioners alike in the continued study and advancement of creativity and innovation in organizations.

Chapter authors not only discuss the abilities, personality, and motivational attributes that contribute to employee creativity, but they also address the impact of leadership and climate on creative performance in teams. Subsequently, firm-level influences such as planning, learning, strategy, and professions that influence the success of creative and innovative efforts are examined.

With contributions from leading scholars around the globe, this book offers a comprehensive review of creativity and innovation to assist researchers and practitioners in their quests to understand and improve organizational creativity and innovation. This is an essential resource for scholars, researchers, or graduate students interested in creativity, innovation, and organizational behavior.

Michael D. Mumford is the George Lynn Cross Distinguished Research Professor and Director of the Center for Applied Social Research at the University of Oklahoma. Mumford is a recipient of the Society for Industrial and Organizational Psychology's M. Scott Myers Award for Applied Research in the Workforce and the Academy of Management's Eminent Leadership Scholar Award, as well as the Society for Aesthetics, Creativity, and the Arts Anaheim Award for Lifetime Contributions.

E. Michelle Todd received her doctoral degree in Industrial-Organizational Psychology, as well as a minor in Quantitative Psychology, from the University of Oklahoma. She has published research papers in multiple professional journals, including *The Leadership Quarterly, The Creativity Research Journal,* and *Accountability in Research,* and she has contributed book chapters on leadership, creativity, and ethics. In addition to academic work, she has worked in a variety of applied settings, including government agencies, tech start-ups, and nonprofit organizations.

SIOP Organizational Frontiers Series

Series Editors

Angelo DeNisi
Tulane University, USA

Kevin Murphy
University of Limerick, Ireland

Editorial Board

Derek R. Avery
Wake Forest University, USA

Paul Sparrow
Lancaster University, UK

Jill Ellingson
University of Kansas, USA

Hannes Zacher
Liepzig University, Germany

Franco Fraccaroli
University of Trento, Italy

Jing Zhou
Rice University, USA

Susan Jackson
Rutgers University, USA

Mumford/Todd: *(2020) Creativity and Innovation in Organizations*

Nye/Rounds: *(2019) Vocational Interests in the Workplace*

Ferris/Johnson/Sedikides: *(2018) The Self at Work*

Ellingson/Noe: *(2017) Autonomous Learning in the Workplace*

Ashkanasy/Bennett/Martinko: *(2016) Understanding the High Performance Workplace: The Line Between Motivation and Abuse*

King/Tonidandel/Cortina: *(2014) Big Data at Work: The Data Science Revolution and Organizational Psychology*

Finkelstein/Truxillo/Fraccaroli/Kanfer: *(2014) Facing the Challenges of a Multi-Age Workforce: A Use-Inspired Approach*

For more information on the series, please visit: https://www.routledge.com/SIOP-Organizational-Frontiers-Series/book-series/SIOP

CREATIVITY AND INNOVATION IN ORGANIZATIONS

*Edited by Michael D. Mumford
and E. Michelle Todd*

NEW YORK AND LONDON

First published 2020
by Routledge
52 Vanderbilt Avenue, New York, NY 10017

and by Routledge
2 Park Square, Milton Park, Abingdon, Oxon, OX14 4RN

Routledge is an imprint of the Taylor & Francis Group, an informa business

© 2020 Taylor & Francis

The right of Michael D. Mumford and E. Michelle Todd to be identified as the authors of the editorial material, and of the authors for their individual chapters, has been asserted in accordance with sections 77 and 78 of the Copyright, Designs and Patents Act 1988.

All rights reserved. No part of this book may be reprinted or reproduced or utilised in any form or by any electronic, mechanical, or other means, now known or hereafter invented, including photocopying and recording, or in any information storage or retrieval system, without permission in writing from the publishers.

Trademark notice: Product or corporate names may be trademarks or registered trademarks, and are used only for identification and explanation without intent to infringe.

Library of Congress Cataloging-in-Publication Data
A catalog record for this title has been requested

ISBN: 978-1-138-72310-8 (hbk)
ISBN: 978-1-138-72415-0 (pbk)
ISBN: 978-1-315-19259-8 (ebk)

Typeset in Bembo
by Nova Techset Private Limited, Bengaluru & Chennai, India

Printed in the United Kingdom
by Henry Ling Limited

CONTENTS

Contributors   *xi*
Series Editors' Foreword   *xvii*

1. Creativity and Innovation at Work   1
   Michael D. Mumford and E. Michelle Todd

2. The Assessment of Creative and Innovative Performance   17
   Alexander S. McKay and James C. Kaufman

3. What Is Needed to Think Creatively at Work? Knowledge and Skills   41
   Michael D. Mumford, E. Michelle Todd, Cory Higgs, and Robert Martin

4. Abilities that Contribute to Creativity and Innovation at Work   69
   Mark A. Runco

5. Personality and Creativity at Work   89
   Adrian Furnham

6. Temporal Dynamics of Creativity and Motivation: What We Know, What We Do Not, and a Few Suggestions for Filling the Gap   105
   Logan M. Steele

7 Integrating Creative Climate and Creative Problem-Solving *Samuel T. Hunter, James L. Farr, Rachel L. Heinen, and Julian B. Allen*	137
8 Cognitive and Social Processes in Team Creativity *Roni Reiter-Palmon and Paul B. Paulus*	161
9 The Leadership Role in Creative Problem-Solving and Innovation *Miriam Erez, Alon Lisak, and Raveh Harush*	191
10 Firm Strategy for Innovation and Creativity *Danielle D. Dunne and Kimberly S. Jaussi*	219
11 How Do Leaders Plan for Firm Innovation? Strategic Planning Processes and Constraints *Logan L. Watts, Kajal R. Patel, Ethan G. Rothstein, and Alessa N. Natale*	243
12 Creativity and Innovation in the Context of Firms *Kyriaki Hadjikosta and Tamara Friedrich*	271
13 Institutional Supports for Innovation *Leif Denti and Sven Hemlin*	315
14 Unleashing Creative Talent in Organizations – Linking Learning and Creativity through Creative Problem-Solving *Scott G. Isaksen*	339
Index	*393*

CONTRIBUTORS

Julian B. Allen is a doctoral student at the Pennsylvania State University, studying the impact of leadership on individual, team, and organizational creativity. In the past two years, he has contributed several chapters on the direct and indirect impact of leadership on creativity, as well as research articles on a multiple pathway approach to leadership.

Leif Denti is a Senior Lecturer at the Department of Psychology, University of Gothenburg. He is also a visiting lecturer at Chalmers University of Technology. He is a jury member of the national award Manager of the Year, staff writer at innovationmanagement.se, and founder of the Swedish innovation dissemination website tusentips.se. Currently, Leif is engaged in several state-funded action research projects directed toward increasing the innovation capabilities of the Swedish innovation system, on both the employee level and the top management level.

Danielle D. Dunne is an Associate Professor of Strategy in the School of Management at Binghamton University. Her research focuses on innovation management, collaboration in and across organizations, and organizational learning. She is particularly interested in how scientists work and learning and innovation in healthcare.

Miriam Erez is a Professor Emeritus, Vice Dean for the MBA programs, Faculty of Industrial Engineering and Management, Technion–Israel Institute of Technology and Chair of the Knowledge Center for Innovation, Haifa, Israel. Her research focuses on innovation and entrepreneurship, cross-cultural organizational behavior, and work motivation. She is a Fellow of the Society for Industrial and Organizational Psychology, the Academy of Management, and IAAP. She is the recipient of the IAAP Distinguished Scientist Award (2002) and the Israel Prize (2005).

James L. Farr is Professor Emeritus of Psychology at Pennsylvania State University. He has also been a visiting scholar at Sheffield University, United Kingdom, the University of Western Australia, the Chinese University of Hong Kong, and the University of Giessen, Germany. He is the author or editor of over 90 publications in journals and books, has served as editor or has been on the editorial boards of multiple professional journals, and has held prestigious positions such as President of the Society for Industrial and Organizational Psychology (SIOP).

Tamara Friedrich is an Associate Professor of Entrepreneurship and Innovation at Warwick Business School. She has worked on research grants with several funding agencies, including the Army Research Institute. Her work has appeared in several books and journals, including *The Leadership Quarterly*, *Creativity Research Journal*, and *Human Resource Management Review*.

Adrian Furnham has held scholarships and visiting professorships at the University of New South Wales, the University of the West Indies, the University of Hong Kong, and the University of KwaZulu-Natal. He has also been made Adjunct Professor of Management at the Norwegian School of Management (2009) and Honorary Professor at the University of KwaZulu-Natal (2014). He has served as the President of the International Society for the Study of Individual Differences and is also a founding director of the Applied Behavioural Research Associates (ABRA).

Kyriaki Hadjikosta is a doctoral student at Warwick Business School, the University of Warwick, studying the mechanisms by which play can promote creativity in the organizational context. Her PhD is funded by the Economic and Social Research Council Doctoral Training Centre (ESRC DTC). She has an undergraduate degree in Computer Science from the University of Cyprus and a postgraduate degree in Programme and Project Management from the Warwick Manufacturing Group, the University of Warwick.

Raveh Harush is a Lecturer and head of the Management and Organizations specialization at the Graduate School of Business Administration, Bar-Ilan University, Israel. He received his PhD in Industrial and Organizational Psychology from the Technion–Israel Institute of Technology. His research focuses on multiple identities, teams, leadership, and globalization.

Rachel L. Heinen, is an Industrial/Organizational Psychology doctoral student at the Pennsylvania State University. Her research interests fall under the broad realm of creativity, including the creative process and creative climate. Specifically, her thesis research examined the dimensionality of creative climate.

Sven Hemlin is Emeritus Professor of Psychology and Social Psychology at Gothenburg Research Institute, School of Business, Economics and Law. He has been a Visiting Research Fellow at the Science Policy and Technology Research Unit at the University of Sussex and Visiting Professor at Copenhagen Business School, Denmark, and the University of Tampere, Finland. He has published in multiple books and journals, such as *Creativity and Innovation Management*, *European Management Journal*, and *International Journal of Innovation Management*.

Cory Higgs is a doctoral student in the University of Oklahoma's program in Industrial and Organizational Psychology. His research interests include leadership, creativity, and ethics.

Samuel T. Hunter is an Associate Professor of Psychology and is head of the Industrial and Organizational Psychology program at the Pennsylvania State University. His research focuses on leadership and innovation management, and within those areas, he has published more than 75 papers, books, and book chapters in outlets such as the *Journal of Applied Psychology* and the *Journal of Organizational Behavior*. His work has been funded by agencies such as the National Science Foundation, and his research has been featured in a number of press outlets, including CNN, Fortune Magazine, Inc.com, Fastcompany, Yahoo, and MSN.

Scott G. Isaksen is a Professor of Leadership and Organizational Behavior at BI-Norwegian Business School. He has published over 200 articles, chapters, and books. He founded the Creative Problem Solving Group to help organizations meet their innovation challenges, and has worked with over 400 organizations in 30 countries. His research interests include taking a more systemic approach to creativity and innovation, improving the application of creative problem-solving through understanding and appreciating diverse problem-solving styles and the climate for creativity, innovation, and change within organizations.

Kimberly S. Jaussi is an Associate Professor of Organizational Behavior and Leadership in the School of Management and a Fellow at the Bernard M. and Ruth R. Bass Center for Leadership Studies at Binghamton University, New York. Her research focuses on strategic leadership for creativity and innovation, as well as identity processes, commitment, diversity, and women and leadership. Her work has appeared in leading journals, including *The Leadership Quarterly*, the *Academy of Management Journal*, *Group and Organization Management*, and the *Creativity Research Journal*. Her research on creativity and innovation has been noted in popular press outlets, including *The Wall Street Journal*.

James C. Kaufman is a Professor of Educational Psychology at the University of Connecticut. He is the author/editor of more than 40 books, and he has published more than 300 papers, which include theoretical contributions such as the Four-C Model of Creativity. James has won many awards, including Mensa's research award, the Torrance Award from the National Association for Gifted Children, and American Psychological Association's Berlyne, Arnheim, and Farnsworth awards.

Alon Lisak is a Senior Lecturer of Organizational Behavior at the Guilford Glazer Faculty of Business and Management, Ben-Gurion University of the Negev, Israel. He received his PhD in Industrial and Organizational Psychology from the Technion–Israel Institute of Technology. His research focuses on leadership, identity, culture, and innovation.

Robert Martin is a doctoral student in the University of Oklahoma's program in Industrial and Organizational Psychology. His research interests include creativity, leadership, and ethics.

Alexander S. McKay is an Assistant Professor of Management and Entrepreneurship at Virginia Commonwealth University, Richmond, Virginia. He earned his PhD in Industrial-Organizational Psychology from the Pennsylvania State University in 2018. His research focuses on creativity/innovation and person-centered research approaches. He has published book chapters and journal articles in a variety of outlets such as *Personnel Psychology*, *European Journal of Personality*, *Psychology of Aesthetics, Creativity, and the Arts*, and the *Journal of Creative Behavior*.

Michael D. Mumford is the George Lynn Cross Distinguished Research Professor of Psychology at the University of Oklahoma, where he directs the Center for Applied Social Research. He is a fellow of the American Psychological Association (Decisions 3, 5, 10, 14), the Society for Industrial and Organizational Psychology, and the American Psychological Society. He has written more than 350 peer-reviewed articles on creativity, leadership, planning, and ethics. Mumford has served as editor of *The Leadership Quarterly* and has been on the editorial boards of multiple other professional journals. He has also served as principal investigator on grants totaling more than $30 million. He is a recipient of the Society for Industrial and Organizational

Psychology's M. Scott Myers Award for Applied Research in the Workforce and the Academy of Management's Eminent Leadership Scholar Award, as well as the Society for Aesthetics, Creativity, and the Arts Anaheim Award for Lifetime Contributions.

Alessa N. Natale is a doctoral candidate in the Industrial and Organizational Psychology PhD program at Baruch College and the Graduate Center, City University of New York. She holds a bachelor's degree in Psychology from Boston College. Her research interests include leadership and diversity.

Roni Reiter-Palmon is the Varner Professor of Industrial/Organizational (I/O) Psychology and the Director of the I/O Psychology Graduate Program at the University of Nebraska at Omaha (UNO). She also serves as the Director for Innovation for the Center for Collaboration Science. She has received grants totaling over $7 million, and she has over 80 publications in leading journals such *Journal of Applied Psychology* and *The Leadership Quarterly*. In addition to serving on several journal editorial boards, she is the Editor of *Psychology of Aesthetics, Creativity, and the Arts* and an associate editor for the *European Journal of Work and Organizational Psychology*. She is also the recipient of multiple awards, including the UNO Award for Distinguished Research and Creative Activity.

Kajal R. Patel is a doctoral candidate in the Industrial and Organizational Psychology PhD program at Baruch College and the Graduate Center, City University of New York. She holds a bachelor's degree in Psychology from the College of New Jersey. Her research interests include leadership and selection.

Paul B. Paulus is a Distinguished University Professor in the Department of Psychology at the University of Texas at Arlington, where he serves as the Director of the Industrial/Organizational Psychology program. He has published over 140 papers and chapters and five edited volumes related to group processes. He has served as Chair of the Department of Psychology and Dean of the College of Science. He has been a visiting professor at multiple institutions, including the National Academy of Science in Beijing, and he has been a Visiting Fellow with the National Institute of Justice. His research has been supported by collaborative grants from the National Science Foundation for the past 11 years in conjunction with multiple other academic institutions.

Ethan G. Rothstein is a doctoral candidate in the Industrial and Organizational Psychology PhD program at Baruch College and the Graduate Center, City University of New York. He holds a bachelor's degree in Clinical Psychology from Tufts University. His research interests include workplace ostracism, the work-family interface, and assessment and selection.

Mark A. Runco has published over 300 books, articles, and chapters on creativity. He has held adjunct positions at Buffalo State University, Southern Oregon University, and the Norwegian Business School. Runco is a Fellow and Past President of Division 10 of the American Psychological Association and remains Distinguished Research Fellow of the American Institute of Behavioral Research and Technology. He is Founding Editor of the *Creativity Research Journal* and coeditor of the *Encyclopedia of Creativity*, each of which is being revised in 2019 (https://www.markrunco.com). He is currently Director of Creativity Research and Programming at Southern Oregon University where he organizes the annual SO Creativity Conference.

Logan M. Steele is an Assistant Professor of Information Systems and Decision Sciences in the Muma College of Business at the University of South Florida. He earned his PhD in Industrial and Organizational Psychology from the University of Oklahoma. His research interests are primarily in the areas of leadership, creativity, motivation, and ethics. Within these areas, Logan has published in outlets such as *Journal of Management*, *Journal of Applied Psychology*, *The Leadership Quarterly*, *Psychology of Aesthetics, Creativity, and the Arts*, and *Creativity Research Journal*.

E. Michelle Todd received her doctoral degree in Industrial-Organizational Psychology, as well as a minor in Quantitative Psychology, from the University of Oklahoma. She has published research papers in multiple professional journals, including *The Leadership Quarterly*, *Creativity Research Journal*, and *Accountability in Research*, and she has contributed book chapters on leadership, creativity, and ethics. In addition to academic work, she has worked in a variety of applied settings, including government agencies, tech start-ups, and nonprofit organizations.

Logan L. Watts is an Assistant Professor of Industrial and Organizational (I-O) Psychology at Baruch College and the Graduate Center, City University of New York. He received his PhD in I-O Psychology from the University of Oklahoma in 2016. He publishes on the topics of organizational leadership, ethics, creativity, and stories in outlets such as *The Leadership Quarterly*, *Journal of Business Ethics*, and *Psychology of Aesthetics, Creativity, and the Arts*. His research focuses on strategies for developing ethical leaders and enhancing innovation in organizations.

SERIES EDITORS' FOREWORD

The goal of the *Organizational Frontiers Series* if to produce volumes that pull together knowledge from a variety of disciplines, identify new concepts, methods and theories and extend the boundaries of the field. For over 25 years, this series has helped to define, shape and advance Industrial and Organizational Psychology and related fields concerned with understanding behavior in organizations. Mumford and Todd's volume, *Creativity and Innovation in Organizations*, exemplifies this set of goals, and helps to define and advance research and theory in this critically important area.

Many organizations claim to value and support creativity and innovation, but it is not always clear that they truly understand the challenges involved in fostering creativity and innovation or even the nature of the phenomena. Mumford and Todd have assembled a distinguished and talented set of authors who attack the problem of understanding creativity and innovation and the wide range of individual and organizational forces that sustain or that interfere with the behaviors, beliefs and motivations that underlie creativity and innovation.

These chapters tackle the Definition of creativity and innovation and relationship between them, the and the role requirements moderate the development and expression of creativity and innovation. Several chapters examine individual differences that influence creativity and innovation ranging from knowledge and ability to learning, cognitive and social processes and motivational states. Discussions of personality and creativity make the important point that highly creative employees can be particularly difficult to manage and even to work with; some of the personality characteristics that distinguish highly creative innovative employees from others include Psychoticism and divergent thinking. Managers who wish their employees were more creative might not always know what they are getting themselves into.

Other chapters examine organizational processes that foster creativity and innovation, including leadership, planning for innovation, firm strategy, institutional support for innovation, and organizational climate/climate for creativity innovation. These chapters make a strong argument that organizations can build conditions that support creativity and innovation, but that this requires the right combination of good luck, smart management and strong commitment to building and sustaining the right climate and culture.

Creativity and Innovation in Organizations is a timely volume that sheds light on topics that are increasing important to the success and even the survival or organizations. It brings together a growing body of research and theory and lays the groundwork for a science-based set of approaches for assessing, fostering and sustaining creativity in organizations. It is a very welcome addition to the *Organizational Frontiers Series*.

Angelo DeNisi
Kevin Murphy
Series Co-Editors

1
CREATIVITY AND INNOVATION AT WORK

Michael D. Mumford and E. Michelle Todd

When one mentions the word *creativity* or asks about people who do creative work, the images that come to mind are of the "great" scientist (Root-Bernstein & Root-Bernstein, 2013), the award-winning film director (Simonton, 2004), or the stunning new artist (Feist, 1998). As much as we might value the creative work done by scientists, directors, and artists, there simply seemed to be no place for these people in the modern firm. They were too individualistic, too nonconformist, and simply not conscientious enough to hold a job. Indeed, John D. Rockefeller, the founder of Standard Oil (today's Exxon Mobile) noted, "I have never felt the need for scientific knowledge... I can always hire them" (Chernow, 2007, p. 182). Many firms and many scholars interested in human behaviors in the workplace seem to have adopted the same attitude – creativity and innovation are not needed at work.

The evidence accrued over the last fifty years, however, indicates that creativity and innovation are critical to both the success of firms and the well-being of those who work in firms. The development and fielding of new products and services has been found to be the *key* determinant of the long-term survival of firms (Cefis & Marsili, 2005). Indeed, innovative new technologies often provide the basis for founding a firm in the first place (Audretsch, 1991). Firm growth and profitability appear tightly tied to a firm's ability to continuously field viable and new innovative products and services (Cohen & Levinthal, 1989).

The production of innovative new products and services, however, ultimately depends on someone formulating the new ideas that provide the basis for innovation. Put differently, innovation depends on worker creativity. Indeed, those workers who think creatively on their jobs are commonly held by managers to be their best performers (Ng & Feldham, 2008). Well-led teams composed of especially creative workers are more likely to meet schedule and budget performance goals for assigned projects (Keller, 2006). Moreover, creative workers seem happier and more satisfied with work when their jobs allow them to do creative work of interest (Shalley, Gilson, & Blum, 2000).

The impact of creativity on firm innovation, work performance, and satisfaction with work underscores the need to understand the forces that encourage creativity and innovation in firms. Accordingly, in this volume, we examine creativity and innovation at work and in firms. In this regard, however, it is important to bear in mind a point stressed by Mumford and Hunter (2005). Creativity and innovation in firms reflect an inherently multilevel phenomenon. Yes, people must be creative (Vincent, Decker, & Mumford, 2002). However, they must also be working in a field ready for innovation (Wise, 1992). Creative people must be effectively led if their work is to prove of value (Mumford, Scott, Gaddis, & Strange, 2002). The firm must support the creative efforts both institutionally (Dougherty & Hardy, 1996) and operationally (Jelnek & Schoonhoven, 1990). Creative people must work with others as they pursue new ideas – people who provide both support and criticism (Gibson & Mumford, 2013).

The manifold, often contradictory, interactions occurring within and across different levels of analysis underscore the complex nature of creativity, and innovation, in firms. In recent years, however, substantial progress has been made not only in understanding creativity and innovation at a given level of analysis, but also at the cross-level interactions that arise as one attempts to explain creative performance. Accordingly, in the present volume, we examine creativity and innovation in firms from a distinctly multilevel perspective. We examine not only the attributes of creative workers and creative work but also how creative work occurs in teams and in certain contexts. Additionally, we examine how creative teams should be led and how firms should plan for innovation, as well as how professions, and the fundamental nature of the industry, act to shape creative work in firms.

Creativity

Before turning to the influences on creativity and innovation, it would seem well advised to define exactly what is meant by the terms *creativity* and *innovation*. Perhaps the most common definition of creativity holds that the creative person generates many new ideas. Indeed, this basic concept – that creativity requires idea generation – provided the foundation for much of the early work on creativity. This proposition provided the basis for Guilford's (1950) work on divergent thinking measures. And, linking creativity to divergent thinking (the production of multiple ideas) provided the basis for many other scholars' work on creative thought (e.g., Kim, 2006; Torrance, 1972).

Over the years, the works of many scholars (e.g., Acar & Runco, 2014) have provided us with a better understanding of how divergent thinking measures such as the Consequences or Alternative Uses measures of divergent thinking should be scored. Divergent thinking tests occasionally have been scored for fluency (the number of ideas generated), flexibility (shifts in the categories of ideas provided), and idea originality (idea novelty). Broadly speaking, the optimal procedure for scoring these measures involves identifying the three most original ideas from the total pool of ideas generated and scoring the average originality of those ideas (Silvia, 2011). In this regard, however, the findings of Mumford, Marks, Connelly, Zaccaro, and Johnson (1998) suggest that scoring ideas for manifestations of originality within the performance domain at hand may yield especially valid measures for predicting real-world creative performance. Work by Zaccaro et al. (2015) has indicated that when measures of divergent thinking are scored in this way, they strongly ($R \cong 0.40$) predict not only real-world performance, but also real-world performance over substantial periods of time (e.g., career continuation among Army officers in an up or out system over a 20-year period). Divergent thinking measures result in the prediction of performance on jobs requiring creative thinking above and beyond more traditional predictors of job performance, such as intelligence and expertise (Vincent et al., 2002).

Although the evidence for the validity of divergent thinking measures is compelling – at least when appropriate tests are used – divergent thinking should not be arbitrarily equated with creative performance. The procedures used to identify divergent thinking are identical to the procedures used by Fleishman (1972) to identify key abilities underlying performance in various domains (Merrifield, Guilford, Christensen, & Frick, 1962). Thus, divergent thinking measures do not define exactly what is meant by the term *creativity*. Instead, they reflect an ability, one of many potential abilities, that might influence or contribute to creative performance in various domains of work where creative production is valued.

One early attempt to define creative performance was provided by Ghiselin (1963). He argued that creativity ultimately reflects an appraisal of performance. In his view, creative performance requires the production of a product evidencing two key characteristics – it must be original (something new and different), and it must be useful. Thus, production of a new drug, an Oscar-winning film, or a new business process may all be seen as creative work. Although students of creativity continue to debate exactly what the key characteristics of creative performance are (Weisberg, 2015), studies of creative products conducted by Besemer and O'Quin (1999) and Christians (2002) indicate that creative products evidence three key attributes: (a) originality, (b) usability or quality, and (c) elegance, which implies that the elements of the performance flow together seamlessly.

It is the person's capacity to produce original, high-quality, and elegant products that we refer to when we say someone's work is creative. Thus, creativity is defined with respect to a certain type of work product. Therefore, a journal article may be creative, a new business idea may be creative, and a new engineering design may be creative. Moreover, imposition of the term *creative* implies an appraisal of work, or work products, often by experts or supervisors. For example, actors and directors appraise films for the Academy Awards. Peers or supervisors might appraise the creativity of business reorganization proposals. Consequently, in studies of creativity, we must ask who is the judge being asked to appraise the creativity of the products provided (Redmond, Mumford, & Teach, 1993).

Although the attributes of a creative product (its originality, quality, and elegance) may seem clear, product attributes do not address a key issue: What are the characteristics of the tasks that allow people to produce original, high-quality, and elegant products? This issue has been addressed by Mumford and Gustafson (2007) and Mumford, Medeiros, and Partlow (2012). They note that original, high-quality, and elegant products emerge only when people are asked to solve novel complex, and ill-defined, or poorly structured, problems. Thus, creativity represents a form of complex, high-level cognition required to produce original, high-quality, and elegant solutions to novel, complex, and ill-defined problems people encounter in their work or day-to-day activities (e.g., hobbies).

Defining creativity as the production of original, high-quality, and elegant solutions to novel, complex, and ill-defined problems has several noteworthy implications. To begin, creative problems come in many forms. Thus, we see people speak of product versus process innovation, or radical versus incremental innovations (Anderson, Barker, & Chen, 2006). We also see people speak of social versus technical innovations (Mumford, 2002). These and other potential distinctions all reflect differences in the content of the novel, complex, and ill-defined problems people are attempting to solve to produce a problem solution of adequate quality, originality, and elegance.

The fact that creative performance is ultimately based on the solutions provided to a certain type, or class, of problem is noteworthy for four reasons. First, many types of creativity exist as people work on many different types of creative problems. Therefore, creativity is ultimately a domain-specific phenomenon (Baer, 2012). Accordingly, general conclusions about creativity across domains must be made cautiously and only after adequate evidence has been garnered. Moreover, assessments of creative production and creative potential should be made within a given domain.

Second, some jobs present many challenging, novel, complex, and ill-defined problems, while other jobs present very few of these problems. This observation may seem obvious. However, it implies that creativity can be studied effectively on some jobs (e.g., marketing, strategy, research and development) but not other jobs (e.g., accounting, logistics, customer service). Moreover, on any job when we study creativity, we must remember that we are studying only a part of a job – albeit a significant, high-value, part of a job – where people are presented with novel, complex, and ill-defined problems.

Third, in studying creative problem-solving, we must remember that we are studying complex, real-world performance. Yes, individual cognition is critical to the production of creative problem solutions (Mumford, Hunter, & Byrne, 2009). People, however, must also invest effort in creative problem-solving. Indeed, people choose to be creative, and so motivation is important to creative problem-solving (Tierney & Farmer, 2002). Additionally, the style by which people approach their world (i.e., their personality) may, in fact, influence whether they ever see a problem as calling for creative thought (Reiter-Palmon, Mumford, & Threlfall, 1998). Thus, multiple attributes of people, including their expertise and intelligence, will influence their ability to solve creative problems.

Fourth and finally, remember that creativity, or a creative product, should be appraised with respect to quality, originality, and elegance, and it should stem from a complex, novel, and ill-defined problem. Thus, creativity is intimately tied to innovation, or the development and fielding of creative problem solutions. What should be recognized here, however, is that the development and fielding of creative problem solutions occurs in a distinctly social context. Creative problem solutions must be criticized and refined (Gibson & Mumford, 2013), which is a distinctly social process. People must acquire information – often acquiring such information by scanning their professional/technical networks (Perry-Smith & Shalley, 2003). They must work with others to develop creative problem solutions into viable new products. Therefore, teamwork is often held to be critical to creativity and innovation (Reiter-Palmon, Wigert, & de Vreede, 2011). As a result, social processes may be as important, if not more important, to innovation as actual creative production and achievement.

Innovation

Our foregoing observations are noteworthy because they imply that creativity is not solely an individual-level phenomenon. Rather, creative achievement (i.e., the development and fielding of innovative new products and services based on creative problem solutions) depends on, and is influenced by, social context. Perhaps the first point to recognize regarding innovation is that innovation and creative problem-solving occur within the context of a profession. To clarify, impressionism as an art form, in part, was driven by a response to the emergence of photography. More centrally, as Wise (1992) notes, innovation in the electrical industry came in waves as a function of the technological readiness of the profession.

Along somewhat different lines, Gordon (2017) notes that the production of creative problem solutions and the fielding of innovative new products and services is not an isolated activity. To ensure automobiles functioned, creative problem solutions were required with respect to road design, fueling (gas stations), and automotive repair (tow trucks). Thus, innovations and creative problem solutions unfold in chains where one innovation serves as a stimulus for future chains of innovation and creative problem-solving. Technical innovation may require chains of process and institutional innovations to support the given technical innovation. Consider, for example, the imposition of traffic lanes to support the adoption of automotive technical innovations.

In this regard, however, it is important to recognize that innovative new products and services rarely enter the world fully formed. The implications of a creative problem solution must be explored – a time-consuming and costly effort (Chandy & Tellis, 1998). The products and services flowing from creative problem solutions must be prototyped and tried out – again a rather costly effort. Procedures for production and fielding of a new product or service must be formulated and institutionalized – yet again, a costly venture. The many varied costs associated with the development and fielding of innovative new products and services must be borne by someone – the government, firms, teams, and individuals. As a result, innovations typically occur in an institutional context.

What must be recognized here, however, is that many creative ideas can be generated to solve a problem or a set of problems. Unfortunately, the bulk of these problem solutions will fail. Thus, for institutions, innovative efforts present real risks as well as real opportunity. One way institutions seek to manage these risks is to rely on institutional expertise formulated with respect to a limited set of key fundamentals (Hounshell, 1992). Consider DuPont's focus on the properties of long-chain polymers. Another way institutions attempt to manage this cost-benefit tradeoff is to focus on the value of learning with respect to a given set of fundamentals (Cohen & Levinthal, 2000). Still another way institutions seek to manage these cost-benefit tradeoffs is through the formation of strategic alliances (Osborn & Marion, 2009).

These observations are noteworthy, in part, because they indicate institutions seek to create structures, processes, and decision frames that will help them manage the cost-benefit trade-offs associated with the development and fielding of innovative new products and services. Frames for planning creative efforts and appraising the success of these efforts are institutionalized (Hunter, Bedell-Avers, & Mumford, 2009). Procedures for allocating resources to innovative efforts are formalized (Nohari & Gulati, 1996). And, managers both direct creative efforts with respect to organizational strategy and seek to champion innovations to other key constituencies in the firm (Howell & Boies, 2004; Mumford, Scott, Gaddis, & Strange, 2002).

These observations point to a broader conclusion. Creative work, work we hope will result in the fielding of innovative new products and services, occurs in an institutional context. Thus, any attempts to understand creative work cannot consider the creative person unto themselves; they must also consider the institutional context in which creative work is occurring. With this point in mind, in this volume, we examine both the attributes of creative people and the attributes of the institutional environment that contribute to creative work.

People and Performance

The second chapter in this volume, by McKay and Kaufman, examines what we mean when we use the term *creativity*. They begin by arguing that at work, creativity occurs in jobs, or in roles, where people are presented with tasks that are unique or nonroutine. This observation is consistent with the definition of *creativity* provided earlier. Perhaps more critically, they summarize a number of studies indicating that when people are presented with nonroutine tasks, creative performance is very strongly related to overall job performance. These observations are noteworthy because they suggest that to understand performance on high-level jobs – or jobs where people are presented with nonroutine tasks – we *must* understand creativity.

McKay and Kaufman, however, note that this observation also implies that we must be able to assess creative performance at work. Although it may seem desirable to assess creative products (e.g., awards won), this is not always either possible or feasible for many jobs. Subsequently, they examine the major procedures used to appraise creativity on jobs, noting that self-appraisals and supervisor appraisals might both be used to appraise creativity – although the value of both measures is open to question. This observation led them to argue for the use of multiple measures in assessing creative performance, especially measures that focus on performance in executing nonroutine tasks.

Mumford, Todd, Higgs, and Martin (Chapter 3) describe an ongoing series of studies examining how people work through the problems presented by nonroutine tasks. One key point they make is that creative performance requires substantial knowledge and expertise within the task domain. Mumford and his colleagues, however, note that if only extant knowledge would suffice to allow people to solve a problem, creative thinking would not really be required. Rather, people in creative problem-solving must reshape, or reform, extant knowledge to formulate the new understandings that allow people to generate original ideas.

Based on this observation, Mumford, Todd, Higgs, and Martin examine the key cognitive processes people must execute to allow them to generate new ideas and new understandings using extant knowledge to produce creative problem solutions. They provide evidence indicating that eight key processes are involved in most incidents of creative problem-solving: (a) problem definition, (b) information gathering, (c) concept/case selection, (d) conceptual combination, (e) idea generation, (f) idea evaluation, (g) implementation planning, and (h) adaptive monitoring. They show that effective execution of these processes contributes to the production of creative problem solutions in multiple domains and that certain strategies are needed to execute each process effectively, including some general strategies, or skills, contributing to effective execution of multiple processes, such as causal analysis skills, error analysis skill, and forecasting.

Runco (Chapter 4) examines the basic abilities that contribute to creative problem-solving and effective process execution. He notes that divergent thinking is a key ability contributing to performance on many tasks that call for the production of original problem solutions. Notably, however, Runco notes that creative problem-solving requires convergent, as well as divergent, thinking abilities. As a result, he notes that intelligence, at least to a point, is needed for performance on most creative problem-solving tasks. Runco, however, reminds us that in addition to divergent thinking ability and intelligence, several other abilities exist that contribute to both divergent and convergent thinking in different task domains. Thus, creative performance should not be understood in terms of a single ability (e.g., divergent thinking), but rather it should be understood in terms of a pattern of underlying abilities.

Creative performance, however, does differ from other forms of performance in a noteworthy way. Creative performance does not occur in an automatic fashion. People must decide if they want to be creative, and they must invest effort in process execution. Thus, motivation is commonly held to be critical to people's success in creative efforts. As a result, one often finds creative people evidence substantial achievement motivation and an intense, personal interest in the problem at hand (Feist & Gorman, 1998).

Furnham (Chapter 5) examines one set of variables that contribute to motivation for creative work: people's personality. He notes prior research points to the need for openness (over inclusive thinking) and extraversion in creative work. He notes, however, that neuroticism, agreeableness, and conscientiousness all tend to be negatively related to creativity. Put differently, creative people are often a bit disagreeable, although as Furnham reminds us, they are not necessarily psychologically unstable (i.e., an instability that acts to disrupt creative thinking).

In studies examining the impact of personality on creative work, however, scholars often fail to distinguish between attraction to the field where creative work is required and performance on creative tasks within this field. In this regard, Furnham's work is noteworthy. He finds that two key dimensions of personality seem to be uniquely related to performance when working on creative tasks within an occupation field – imaginativeness (i.e., the desire to do things differently) and productive obsessionality (i.e., the obsession with getting things right). Both imaginativeness and productive obsessionality clearly warrant more attention as we seek to understand how personality shapes creative performance, and nonroutine performance, on jobs at work.

Imaginativeness and productive obsessionality are noteworthy, in part, because they encourage people to invest resources in creative thinking and development of creative problem solutions. And, creative efforts differ from other efforts, because people must decide to invest resources, often substantial resources, in developing creative problem solutions. This observation, of course, suggests that motivation, perhaps intrinsic interest in certain nonroutine creative tasks, will contribute to creative performance.

Steele (Chapter 6) examines one motivational variable known to contribute to creative performance: creative self-efficacy. Prior work by Tierney and Farmer (2002) has shown that confidence in one's ability to do creative work is a powerful influence on creative performance. Steele, however, reminds us that there is both between- and within-person variation in creative self-efficacy. This observation is noteworthy because it suggests we need studies expressly intended to identify the conditions of work that will serve to maximize within-person, as well as between-person, creative self-efficacy.

Context and Teams

Studies of the environmental conditions that motivate creative work are traditionally subsumed under the rubric of climate (i.e., people's perceptions of their work environment). Drawing from earlier work by Hunter, Bedell, and Mumford (2007), Hunter, Farr, Heinen, and Allen (Chapter 7) provide a new taxonomy describing the key contextual (i.e., climate) variables contributing to creative work: (a) perceptions of work autonomy and stimulation, (b) perceptions of positive peer exchange, (c) perceptions of leader direction and engagement, (d) perceptions of organizational resources and support, and (e) perceptions of organizational integration and extension. This model is noteworthy, in part, because it implies that people appraise their environment at multiple levels with respect to multiple issues when deciding if they will undertake, or invest in, creative work. Indeed, Hunter and his colleagues suggest that actions must be taken with respect to the individual, the team, team leaders, and the organization to establish favorable climate perceptions. They argue, moreover, that certain climate perceptions are especially important to encourage people to invest resources in certain creative thinking processes – an idea worthy of future investigation.

Hunter and colleagues' (Chapter 7) discussion of creative climate points to the importance of the team in which creative work occurs. Reiter-Palmon and Paulus (Chapter 8) examine how team process variables influence creative performance in group or team settings. They examine how perceptions of psychological safety and trust contribute to creative performance in team settings. They note the importance of information access, and they note it may not be desirable for creative teams to avoid conflict – at least technical conflict. Perhaps more centrally, however, Reiter-Palmon and Paulus tie these observations with respect to team processes to effective execution of three key individual creative thinking processes: problem definition, idea generation, and idea evaluation. Although the question remains as to how team processes might contribute to other creative thinking processes (e.g., conceptual combination), such cross-level integration is an important step forward in studies of creativity and innovation (Scott, Lonergan, & Mumford, 2005).

The need for cross-level integration is evident in Erez, Lisak, and Harush's (Chapter 9) discussion of leadership of creative efforts. In recent years, it has become clear that leadership is a powerful influence shaping the nature and success of creative efforts in firms (Mumford & Licuanan, 2004). What has been lacking are well-developed theoretical models identifying the key behaviors to be exhibited by those asked to lead creative efforts. Erez, Lisak, and Harush propose a model of requisite leader behaviors by referencing these behaviors to the key creative thinking processes identified by Mumford, Medeiros, and Partlow (2012). Notably, they argue that these behaviors must consider not only the team doing the creative work, but also the strategy and business processes of the firm in which the team is working.

Firms and Institutions

The impact of firm strategy on creativity and innovation in firms is examined in greater detail by Dunne (Chapter 10). She argues that firm strategy with respect to innovation must be grounded in firm resources and the firm's established capabilities. She argues, however, that innovation in firms also depends on more subtle features, or structures, that have been developed to support firm strategy, including firm information search strategies, network building, adaptation of organizational routines, and abductive reasoning by top management teams. The notion that top management teams need abductive reasoning (i.e., thinking about something that may be rather than something that must be) points not only to the need for top management teams to envision the future, but also that they must have the expertise allowing them to envision the future.

Mumford, Schultz, and Van Doorn (2001) note the mental simulation of future actions and outcomes of those actions provide the basis for planning. Although traditionally the need for planning innovative and creative efforts has been discounted, Watts, Patel, Rothstein, and Natale (Chapter 11) provide a compelling argument that firm-level planning for innovation is a critical determinant of institutional capability for creative work and successful fielding of innovative new products and services. They argue that innovative firms (i.e., firms deploying successful new products and processes) plan and plan extensively, using plans not only to establish goals for creative work, but also to provide a basis for relocating resources to creative projects and appraising the success of those projects. Notably, however, they argue that planning for innovation is not an open-ended, unconstrained exercise. Instead, they argue that firms in planning for innovation must take into account multiple external and internal constraints.

In firms, internal constraints, extant processes, norms, and structures all can act as significant constraints on innovation. Various organizational units, ranging from purchasing to marketing, may take actions that undermine or delegitimize an innovative effort. In this regard, the work of Hadjicosta and Friedrich (Chapter 12) is of importance. They examine how various key functions in firms (e.g., purchasing, finance, resources) all act to contribute to innovative capabilities of firms. For example, they argue that human resources, by stressing training and appropriate rewards for creative work as well as building firm knowledge management capabilities, may become a key facilitator (as opposed to an inhibitor) of creative and innovative efforts in firms.

Hadjicosta and Friedrich make a broader point that innovative efforts are not isolated but *live* in the broader sociotechnical environment of the firm. Denti and Hemlin (Chapter 13) extend this argument noting that creative and innovative efforts in firms exist in a broader socioprofessional context. They argue that firms must be ambidextrous in working with professional expertise, both separating, and integrating, themselves with other institutions as they seek to create and profit from new professional knowledge developed for the creative and innovative efforts they pursue. These observations are noteworthy because they suggest, in our attempts to understand creativity and innovation in firms, that we cannot see the firm as an isolated entity. Instead, the firm is a player, one player, in an active exchange among people, firms, professions, and academia seeking to create new knowledge and new technologies.

One implication of Denti and Hemlin's observations is that firms, like teams and individuals, must engage in ongoing learning if they are to develop and maintain their capability for creative and innovative work. Isaksen (Chapter 14), in fact, stresses the importance of ongoing learning to creativity and innovation in firms. He extends this argument, however, noting that developing the creative thinking skills of all employees working in a firm is one critical component of this learning enterprise. Firms that explicitly seek to develop the creative potential of their employees are, more often than not, the firms that continuously produce successful creative work and the fielding of innovative new products and services.

Conclusions

The development and deployment of viable new products and services – new products and services ultimately based on someone's creative thinking – provide the foundation not only for firm success, but also firm survival as new competitors enter the picture. The value of creativity and innovation at work, however, is not just a matter of concern for the firm. Creativity at work contributes to an employee's sense of well-being and his or her commitment to the firm. Creative and innovative efforts in firms allow for integration of the diverse functions in a firm. Creativity and innovation in firms tie firms to the broader world of professions, government, and academia, integrating firms in a quest to produce something new and make our world a better place. We have iPhones due to creative work. We have yellow sticky notes due to creative work. We have self-driving automobiles due to creative work. These examples underscore a key point: creative work in firms gives us our world – a better world today than yesterday.

In recent years, scholars have begun to focus on what makes creative work in firms possible. We now know creativity is not simply a matter of generating ideas. Creativity involves producing original, high-quality, and elegant solutions to novel, complex, and ill-defined problems. We now know far more about the key requirements for creative problem-solving. We have begun to understand how creative problem-solving unfurls in teams and how leaders can encourage creative problem-solving by team members. We have begun to understand how firms formulate strategies and plans for pursuing creative efforts.

Although we now know far more about the nature of creative work in firms, far more research is needed. We need to know what the critical creative thinking processes within different occupational fields are. We need models that will help us integrate diverse forms of expertise as teams pursue work on a creative project. We need to know more about how firms build strategies and workforce capabilities to pursue certain fundamentals. Although we do not have complete answers to these and a host of other questions about creative work in firms, we hope the present volume provides a foundation for future work along these lines.

Acknowledgments

We would like to thank Cory Higgs, Robert Martin, Samantha Elliott, Yash Gujar, Colleen Standish, Tanner Newbold, Samantha England, and Mark Fichtel for their contributions to the present effort. Correspondence may be addressed to Dr. Michael D. Mumford, Department of Psychology, the University of Oklahoma, Norman, Oklahoma 73019 or mmumford@ou.edu.

References

Acar, S., & Runco, M. A. 2014. Assessing associative distance among ideas elicited by tests of divergent thinking. *Creativity Research Journal*, 26, 229–238.

Andersen, H., Barker, P., & Chen, X. 2006. *The cognitive structure of scientific revolutions.* Cambridge, England: Cambridge University Press.

Audretsch, D. B. 1991. New-firm survival and the technological regime. *The Review of Economics and Statistics,* 73, 441–450.

Baer, M. 2012. Putting creativity to work: The implementation of creative ideas in organizations. *Academy of Management Journal,* 55, 1102–1119.

Besemer, S. P., & O'Quin, K. 1999. Confirming the three-factor creative product analysis matrix model in an American sample. *Creativity Research Journal,* 12, 287–296.

Cefis, E., & Marsili, O. 2005. A matter of life and death: Innovation and firm survival. *Industrial and Corporate Change,* 14, 1167–1192.

Chandy, R. K., & Tellis, G. J. 1998. Organizing for radical product innovation: The overlooked role of willingness to cannibalize. *Journal of Marketing Research,* 35, 474–487.

Chernow, R. 2007. *Titan: The life of John D. Rockefeller, Sr.* New York, NY: Vintage.

Christiaans, H. H. 2002. Creativity as a design criterion. *Communication Research Journal,* 14, 41–54.

Cohen, W. M., & Levinthal, D. A. 1989. Innovation and learning: The two faces of R & D. *The Economic Journal,* 99, 569–596.

Cohen, W. M., & Levinthal, D. A. 2000. Absorptive capacity: A new perspective on learning and innovation. In R. Cross, & S. Israelit (Eds.), *Strategic learning in a knowledge economy: Individual, collective and organizational learning process* (pp. 39–67). Woburn, MA: Butterworth Heinemann.

Dougherty, D., & Hardy, C. 1996. Sustained product innovation in large, mature organizations: Overcoming innovation-to-organization problems. *Academy of Management Journal,* 39, 1120–1153.

Feist, G. J. 1998. A meta-analysis of personality in scientific and artistic creativity. *Personality and Social Psychology Review,* 2, 290–309.

Feist, G. J., & Gorman, M. E. 1998. The psychology of science: Review and integration of a nascent discipline. *Review of General Psychology,* 2, 3–47.

Fleishman, E. A. 1972. On the relation between abilities, learning, and human performance. *American Psychologist,* 27, 1017.

Ghiselin, B. 1963. Ultimate criteria for two levels of creativity. In C. Taylor, & F. Barron (Eds.), *Scientific creativity: Its recognition and development* (pp. 30–43). New York, NY: Wiley.

Gibson, C., & Mumford, M. D. 2013. Evaluation, criticism, and creativity: Criticism content and effects on creative problem solving. *Psychology of Aesthetics, Creativity, and the Arts,* 7, 314–331.

Gordon, R. G. 2017. *The rise and fall of American growth: The U.S. standard of living since the Civil War.* Princeton, NJ: Princeton University Press.

Guilford, J. P. 1950. Creativity. *American Psychologist,* 5, 444–454.

Hounshell, D. A. 1992. Continuity and change in the management of industrial research: The DuPont Company 1902–1980. In G. Dosi, R. Giannetti, & P. A. Toninelli (Eds.), *Technology and Enterprise in a Historical Perspective.* Oxford, UK: Oxford University Press.

Howell, J. M., & Boies, K. 2004. Champions of technological innovation: The influence of contextual knowledge, role orientation, idea generation, and idea promotion on champion emergence. *The Leadership Quarterly,* 15, 123–143.

Hunter, S. T., Bedell, K. E., & Mumford, M. D. 2007. Climate for creativity: A quantitative review. *Creativity Research Journal,* 19, 69–90.

Hunter, S. T., Bedell-Avers, K. E., & Mumford, M. D. 2009. Impact of situational framing and complexity on charismatic, ideological and pragmatic leaders: Investigation using a computer simulation. *The Leadership Quarterly*, 20, 383–404.

Jelnek, M., & Schoonhoven, C. B. 1990. *The innovation marathon: Lessons learned from high technology firms*. Oxford, England: Blackwell.

Keller, R. T. 2006. Transformational leadership, initiating structure, and substitutes for leadership: A longitudinal study of research and development project team performance. *Journal of Applied Psychology*, 91, 202–210.

Kim, K. H. 2006. Can we trust creativity tests? A review of the Torrance Tests of Creative Thinking (TTCT). *Creativity Research Journal*, 18, 3–14.

Merrifield, P. R., Guilford, J. P., Christensen, P. R., & Frick, J. W. 1962. The role of intellectual factors in problem solving. *Psychological Monographs: General and Applied*, 76, 1–62.

Mumford, M. D. 2002. Social innovation: Ten cases from Benjamin Franklin. *Creativity Research Journal*, 14, 253–266.

Mumford, M. D., & Gustafson, S. B. 2007. Creative thought: Cognition and problem solving in a dynamic system. In M. A. Runco (Ed.), *Creativity research handbook: Vol. 2* (pp. 33–77). Cresskill, NJ: Hampton.

Mumford, M. D., & Hunter, S. T. 2005. Innovation in organizations: A multi-level perspective on creativity. In F. J. Yammarino, & F. Dansereau (Eds.), *Research in multi-level issues: Volume IV* (pp. 11–74). Oxford, England: Elsevier.

Mumford, M. D., & Licuanan, B. 2004. Leading for innovation: Conclusions, issues, and directions. *The Leadership Quarterly*, 15, 163–171.

Mumford, M. D., Hunter, S. T., & Byrne, C. L. 2009. What is the fundamental? The role of cognition in creativity and innovation. *Industrial and Organizational Psychology*, 2, 353–356.

Mumford, M. D., Marks, M. A., Connelly, M. S., Zaccaro, S. J., & Johnson, J. F. 1998. Domain-based scoring in divergent-thinking tests: Validation evidence in an occupational sample. *Creativity Research Journal*, 11, 151–163.

Mumford, M. D., Medeiros, K. E., & Partlow, P. J. 2012. Creative thinking: Processes, strategies, and knowledge. *The Journal of Creative Behavior*, 46, 30–47.

Mumford, M. D., Schultz, R. A., & Van Doorn, J. R. 2001. Performance in planning: Processes, requirements, and errors. *Review of General Psychology*, 5, 213–240.

Mumford, M. D., Scott, G. M., Gaddis, B., & Strange, J. M. 2002. Leading creative people: Orchestrating expertise and relationships. *The Leadership Quarterly*, 13, 705–750.

Ng, T. W., & Feldman, D. C. 2008. The relationship of age to ten dimensions of job performance. *Journal of Applied Psychology*, 93, 392–423.

Nohari, K., & Gulati, S. 1996. Is slack good or bad for innovation. *Academy of Management Journal*, 39, 799–825.

Osborn, R. N., & Marion, R. 2009. Contextual leadership, transformational leadership and the performance of international innovation seeking alliances. *The Leadership Quarterly*, 20, 191–206.

Perry-Smith, J. E., & Shalley, C. E. 2003. The social side of creativity: A static and dynamic social network perspective. *Academy of Management Review*, 28, 89–106.

Redmond, M. R., Mumford, M. D., & Teach, R. 1993. Putting creativity to work: Effects of leader behavior on subordinate creativity. *Organizational Behavior and Human Decision Processes*, 55, 120–151.

Reiter-Palmon, R., Mumford, M. D., & Threlfall, K. V. 1998. Solving everyday problems creatively: The role of problem construction and personality type. *Creativity Research Journal*, 11, 187–197.

Reiter-Palmon, R., Wigert, B., & de Vreede, T. 2011. Team creativity and innovation: The effect of team composition, social processes and cognition. In M. Mumford (Ed.), *Handbook of Organizational Creativity* (pp. 295–326). New York, NY: Academic Press.

Root-Bernstein, R. S., & Root-Bernstein, M. M. 2013. *Sparks of genius: The thirteen thinking tools of the world's most creative people*. New York, NY: Houghton.

Scott, G. M., Lonergan, D. C., & Mumford, M. D. 2005. Conceptual combination: Alternative knowledge structures, alternative heuristics. *Creativity Research Journal*, 17, 79–98.

Shalley, C. E., Gilson, L. L., & Blum, T. C. 2000. Matching creativity requirements and the work environment: Effects on satisfaction and intentions to leave. *Academy of Management Journal*, 43, 215–223.

Silvia, P. J. 2011. Subjective scoring of divergent thinking: Examining the reliability of unusual uses, instances, and consequences tasks. *Thinking Skills and Creativity*, 6, 24–30.

Simonton, D. K. 2004. *Creativity in science: Chance, logic, genius, and zeitgeist*. New York, NY: Cambridge University Press.

Tierney, P., & Farmer, S. M. 2002. Creative self-efficacy: Its potential antecedents and relationship to creative performance. *Academy of Management Journal*, 45, 1137–1148.

Torrance, E. P. 1972. Can we teach children to think creatively? *The Journal of Creative Behavior*, 6, 114–143.

Vincent, A. S., Decker, B. P., & Mumford, M. D. 2002. Divergent thinking, intelligence, and expertise: A test of alternative models. *Creativity Research Journal*, 14, 163–178.

Weisberg, R. W. 2015. Toward an integrated theory of insight in problem solving. *Thinking and Reasoning*, 21, 5–39.

Wise, G. 1992. Inventors and corporations in the maturing electrical industry. In R. J. Weber, & D. N. Perkins (Eds.), *Inventive minds: Creativity in technology* (pp. 291–310). New York, NY: Oxford University Press.

Zaccaro, S. J., Connelly, S., Repchick, K. M., Daza, A. I., Young, M. C., Kilcullen, R. N., ... Bartholomew, L. N. 2015. The influence of higher order cognitive capacities on leader organizational continuance and retention: The mediating role of developmental experiences. *The Leadership Quarterly*, 26, 342–358.

2

THE ASSESSMENT OF CREATIVE AND INNOVATIVE PERFORMANCE

Alexander S. McKay and James C. Kaufman

Creativity is one of the most sought after abilities in the 21st century. Indeed, the World Economic Forum (2016) asked people in charge of hiring and top management at 371 organizations across multiple industries to report the abilities that jobs required in 2015 and will require in 2020. In 2015, creativity was ranked as the tenth most required ability, but it was ranked third for 2020, a clear indication that creativity is seen as growing in importance. Further, the first and second ranked abilities for 2020 were complex problem-solving and critical thinking, respectively, which are closely related to creativity (Sternberg, Kaufman, & Grigorenko, 2008). More recently, the World Economic Forum (2018) found that the three most important abilities predicted for 2022 are as follows: (a) analytical thinking and innovation, (b) active learning and learning strategies, and (c) creativity, originality, and initiative. These findings again indicate that organizations see creativity and innovation as critical factors in their survival in a constantly changing and competitive economic landscape. However, an important question remains: How do organizations measure creativity to ensure employees are meeting these needs?

Assessment and measurement of creative and innovative performance make up the backbone of organizational creativity research. However, organizational scholars and practitioners are often left with a difficult decision to make: What is the best way to measure creativity? This difficulty is similar to discussions about the "criterion problem" in organizational behavior and management research (Austin & Villanova, 1992), which is and continues to be a discussion within the creativity and organizational creativity literature (Hughes, Lee, Tian, Newman, & Legood, 2018; Montag, Maertz, & Baer, 2012; Simonton, 2018).

The goal of this chapter is to focus on the assessment and measurement of creativity and innovation. To accomplish this goal, the chapter is split into three general sections. First, we discuss and review different definitional considerations with regard to creativity and innovation. In doing so, we focus on whether task/routine performance and creative performance are distinct concepts and frameworks that differentiate various types of creative contributions identified and discussed in the research literature. These conceptualizations are important given that they influence how creativity is measured. Second, we review different measurement approaches used to assess creative and innovative performance. We then provide a critique on these different approaches. Last, we focus on practical considerations for assessing creativity within organizations and organizational creativity research. Across the chapter, we attempt to stay agnostic with regard to level of analysis. As discussed elsewhere, creativity can (and does) occur across multiple levels of analysis (Mumford, Hester, & Robledo, 2012; Mumford & Hunter, 2005). This chapter, however, focuses both implicitly and explicitly on individual- and team-level creativity but does mention organizational-level measurement of creativity and innovation when relevant.

Defining Creativity and Innovation at Work

Although similar and often used interchangeably, creativity and innovation reflect two different stages of an idea's journey. According to Anderson, Potocnik, and Zhou (2014):

> Creativity and innovation at work are the process, outcomes, and products of attempts to develop and introduce new and improved ways of doing things. The creative stage of this process refers to the idea generation, and innovation refers to the subsequent stage of implementing ideas towards better procedures, practices, or products. (p. 1298)

This definition reflects the link between the two concepts. Creativity precedes innovation: Creative ideas must be generated for innovation to occur, and creativity can occur without innovation, but innovation cannot occur without creativity. This definition is also agnostic to levels of analysis. As stated, creativity can and does occur at individual, team, and organizational levels of analysis (Mumford & Hunter, 2005; Mumford et al., 2012).

An important distinction previously raised is between creative and noncreative performance. For example, Amabile (1983) distinguished between noncreative and creative work behaviors based on tasks that are algorithmic versus heuristic. As she notes, "algorithmic tasks are those for which the path to the solution is clear and straightforward – tasks for which an algorithm exists" and "heuristic tasks are those not having a clear and readily identifiable path to solution – tasks for which algorithms must be developed" (p. 360). These heuristic tasks often present novel, complex, and ill-defined problems

(Mumford & Gustafson, 1988). This distinction indicates that creativity arises from heuristic tasks that require breaking already existing scripts for solving problems. However, it also raises questions regarding how to distinguish between tasks/routine performance and creative performance.

Are Task/Routine Performance and Creative Performance Distinct?

The previous definitions distinguish between creative and innovative performance and noncreative and creative performance. They do not, however, deal with creative performance's relationship with task/routine performance. Before diving into these distinctions, we need to define different types of work performance with an emphasis on task and nontask performance. Borman and Motowidlo (1997) define task performance as "the effectiveness with which job incumbents perform activities that contribute to the organization's technical core either directly by implementing a part of its technological process, or indirectly by providing it with needed materials or services" (p. 99). The same definition has also been used for the term *routine performance* (Madjar, Greenberg, & Chen, 2011). Nontask performance often encompasses behaviors that are not part of one's formal work role. These may be positive, such as contextual performance (Borman & Motowidlo, 1997) or organizational citizenship behavior (OCBs; Wildman, Bedwell, Salas, & Smith-Jentsch, 2011), or more negative, such as counterproductive work behavior (CWB; Wildman et al., 2011). Although OCBs are positive in nature and CWBs are negative in nature, they do not reflect two ends of one continuum but rather two separate dimensions (Sackett, Berry, Wiemann, & Laczo, 2006).

Some creativity theorists have argued that task and creative performance are specifically different. For example, Ford (1996) noted differences between routine and creative performance. When choosing which tasks to do, people must choose between more routine, habitual tasks or creative behaviors. Expanding on this view, Madjar and colleagues (Gilson & Madjar, 2011; Madjar et al., 2011) distinguished between routine, incremental creativity, and radical creativity. Routine performance is defined using Borman and Motowidlo's (1997) definition of task performance. Incremental or "adaptive" creative ideas are those that "imply few changes in frameworks and offer only minor modifications to existing practices and products" (Madjar et al., 2011, p. 731). Radical creative ideas are "ideas that differ substantially from an organization's existing practices" (Madjar et al., 2011, p. 731). Taking this view, creative and innovative performance would be categorized as nontask rather than task performance.

Rather than view task/routine and creative performance as distinct, we argue that the relationship between routine and creative performance is moderated by role requirements for creativity, which is the extent to which jobs or roles require creativity (Shalley, Gilson, & Blum, 2000). Some distinction has been made for role and job requirements in that role requirements (what is expected/required for that role) are not the same as job requirements (a perceptual-based assessment of a person being expected to generate work-related ideas; Unsworth, Wall, & Carter, 2005). For this chapter, we focus more on the "objective" role requirements rather than perceptual-based job requirements for creativity. Indeed, self-assessments of creative job requirements are influenced by other factors that might be unrelated to role requirements (Unsworth et al., 2005).

We argue that as role requirements for creativity increase, the relationship between task/routine and creative performance increases. Consider roles or professions that have high role requirements for creativity, such as designers, scientists, or performing artists. For these roles, the generation and implementation of creative ideas are central to the organization's technical core. In other words, their task/routine performance is creative performance. For example, a scientist's primary responsibility to meet the organization's or university's mission is to engage in knowledge creation and creativity/innovation. Although some tasks for that role (e.g., answering standard emails) might be uncreative, such work is peripheral to their primary goal and would be better classified as nontask performance.

Alternatively, when role requirements for creativity are low, the relationship between task/routine performance and creativity is low and essentially zero. For example, consider postal carriers, plant operators, or transcriptionists, where role requirements for creativity are low. It is less likely that engaging in creativity is required or going to contribute to the organization's technical core (indeed, in some cases creativity may be specifically an impediment). Thus, task/routine and creative performance would be distinct, supporting views that these behaviors fall into distinct categories (Ford, 1996; Gilson & Madjar, 2011; Madjar et al., 2011).

When examining prior research, this distinction becomes clearer. For example, Janssen and Van Yperen (2004) examined the relationship between in-role job performance and innovative job performance. Employees in their sample "performed a wide range of different jobs in different functions, including customer service, meter reading, front office work, back office work, invoicing, collection, accounting, and call center work" (p. 373). These roles have lower requirements for creativity, and a weaker correlation should exist between task and creative performance. Indeed, the relationship between the two factors was $r = 0.17$ in their study. Alternatively, Oldham and Cummings's (1996) study examined employees in roles that had high requirements for creativity. Employees in their sample were from a variety of jobs including "design engineer, manufacturing engineer, design drafter, toolmaker, and technician" (p. 614). Because creativity is central to these roles' requirements, there should be a stronger correlation between task and creative performance, and there was: The relationship between job and creative performance was $r = 0.75$. It is important to note that in both studies, ratings were obtained from a single source (i.e., supervisors), indicating that common method bias is not the sole driver of this effect (see also Harari, Reaves, & Viswesvaran, 2016).

A meta-analysis recently summarized the relationship between task and creative performance quantitatively. Harari et al. (2016) found the uncorrected relationship between job performance and creative performance was $r = 0.49$ (corrected $r = 0.55$). Their results highlight that two performance dimensions were distinct, yet always positively related. However, they also noted, "there was a great degree of variability left in these estimates once accounting for statistical artefacts (i.e., sampling error, measurement error), suggesting the likely presence of moderator variables" (p. 503). As we argue, a primary moderator for this relationship is job requirements for creativity.

Although our view of task/routine and creative performance being identical in some situations might seem odd, especially given previous conceptualizations of task/routine performance, it aligns with specific definitions of task/routine performance (Borman & Motowidlo, 1997) and does not conflict with definitions of tasks being algorithmic or heuristic (Amabile, 1983). It also does not conflict with recent critiques of creative performance as a criterion (Montag et al., 2012). Montag and colleagues distinguished between creative performance behaviors and creative outcome effectiveness. Creative performance behaviors are "the set of interdependent observable and unobservable activities that occur in response to a nonalgorithmic task or project and that purportedly constitute the creative process" (Montag et al., 2012, p. 1365). Creative outcome effectiveness is "the extent to which the outcomes (idea, prototype, product, etc.) of non-algorithmic task or project completion are judged by relevant stakeholders to be both novel and useful" (Montag et al., 2012, p. 1365). Rather, our argument simply clarifies that role requirements for creativity are central when making judgments about the distinctiveness of task and creative performance.

This alternative conceptualization might provide a better understanding of why leader-reported ratings of job performance are strongly related to leader-reported ratings of creative performance (Gerhart & Fang, 2015; Madjar et al., 2011). Although this connection has been viewed as a potential confound of leader-reported performance, it might actually be an indication of the overlap between task/routine and creative job performance. This strong correlation might be due to the roles and organizations studied in creativity research rather than leader biases or methodological artifacts.

It is, however, important for us to clarify that we are not saying the high correlation between task and creative performance is absolutely nonproblematic. Indeed, we are unfamiliar with any empirical study that has thoroughly and theoretically addressed the overlap between these two performance dimensions. We believe this to be an important area for future inquiry. Such investigations would need to treat role requirements for creativity as a factor in the same space as creative performance, rather than an antecedent or a moderator of the relationship between other antecedents with creative performance (Unsworth et al., 2005). Next, we shift our attention and discuss theoretical arguments for distinguishing types of creativity.

Types of Creative and Innovative Contributions and Ideas

Separate from the distinction between task/routine performance and creative performance, creative and innovative contributions can be classified as different types. Sternberg's propulsion model of creative contributions argues that there are eight types of creative contribution (Sternberg, 1999; Sternberg, Kaufman, & Pretz, 2003). These eight types are split up into two overarching categories. The first category of creative and innovative ideas, which includes four types, focuses on contributions that move a domain in the direction it is already going. These four types are as follows: (a) replication, (b) redefinition, (c) forward incrementation, and (d) advance forward incrementation.

First, replication is when there is no change from currently existing practices. For example, a web developer has a tried and true approach to creating a website. They apply this approach across multiple projects. This type of creative contribution might seem odd; however, it indicates that the current state of a domain represents a useful approach and change is not needed for a basic contribution to be made.

Second, redefinition is when the domain stays as it currently is, similar to replication, but the domain is viewed using a different perspective or lens. An example of redefinition might be aspirin. Aspirin's primary purpose following development was for pain relief. Creating a generic version of aspirin to be used for this purpose would be replication; the product works well and needs minimal change. However, aspirin has a second use – preventing heart attacks. This second use has since become one of the primary uses for aspirin. This alternative use was simply a change in understanding of the product's usefulness.

Third, forward incrementation is when a domain is moved forward in the direction it is already heading in. Most creative ideas likely fit into this category. It is also a form of creativity that is least threatening to stakeholders and product users. These creative contributions do not make large changes to existing practices or products and do not threaten currently existing products that a company produces. Amazon's original concept as a bookstore is an example of forward incrementation. Initially, Amazon's goal was to create an online bookstore, where people could have greater access to many different books. In other words, they were moving a bookstore onto the Internet, which is what was occurring for other businesses.

Fourth, advance forward incrementation is when a domain is moved forward in the direction it is already heading in, but faster than people are ready for it to move. Whereas forward incrementation takes one step forward, advance forward incrementation takes two or more steps forward. Although forward incrementation is often successful, advance forward incrementation is typically less successful at first because stakeholders and users are not ready for such extreme changes. An example are Xerox's personal computers. At the time, they were rejected and had limited success. However, Apple then took this technology and was successful a short time in the future.

The second category of creative contributions, which includes the remaining four types, focuses on contributions that move a domain in a different direction than it is already heading. These four types are (a) redirection, (b) reconstruction, (c) reinitiation, and (d) synthesis.

First, redirection is when a domain is moved in a different direction than the one in which it was heading. This might be a company changing what product it primarily sells or its approach to selling products. For example, in the 1930s, Mattel changed the way it sold toys to save itself from going out of business. Prior to this shift, Mattel sold directly to wholesalers and toy stores. If the wholesalers and toy stores did not want to buy the toy, it would not sell. However, Mattel started advertising directly to children. Thus, wholesalers and toy stores had to buy the toys children wanted. This redirection of the domain changed who the primary motivators were to toy sales. Blockbuster Video and Hollywood Video also failed to redirect their businesses when faced with challenges from Redbox and Netflix. This failure was detrimental to the future success of Blockbuster Video and Hollywood Video but was beneficial to Redbox and Netflix for redirecting the domain of video rentals in a different direction.

Second, reconstruction is when a domain or organization attempts to move back to a point in the past and then move forward from that point. This creative contribution is similar to redirection, but there is first a shift backward before moving forward in a new direction. For example, this might be watch manufacturers creating mechanically powered watches in addition to battery-powered ones. Mechanically powered watches are an old technology, but there is a new twist when using this old technology in new watches with a modern design.

Third, reinitiation is like starting a domain from scratch – that is, the domain does not rely on an already existing starting point. Rather, the contribution starts a new domain. This is arguably the most radical form of creativity given that it completely changes a domain or the direction in which an organization is heading. For example, the Wright brothers developing an airplane would be in this category. Rather than developing a new form of ground transportation, they developed a completely new form of transportation that created a new domain, air flight.

Last, synthesis is when ideas across multiple domains or ways of thinking are integrated together. These ideas were likely seen as unrelated or even in conflict before their integration. When combined, however, the concepts create something entirely new. An example within this domain might be seaplanes, which is a combination of a plane and a boat.

More recently, Litchfield, Gilson, and Gilson (2015) developed a type-based model for creative ideas within the organizational creativity research domain. Their model focuses on a mix between novelty (originality) and two types of usefulness: feasibility (quality) and value (contribution). They defined feasibility as ideas that are easy to implement or practical and value as a subjective judgment based on an idea's "potential effectiveness, worth, or success in facilitating goal attainment along a scale that may not include an actual or directly implied monetary exchange" (p. 243). The primary difference between the propulsion model and the current model is that Litchfield and colleagues use a different, unidimensional definition of novelty that focuses on an idea's distance from a currently established idea. As stated, Sternberg and colleagues distinguished between two types of contributions that differ in novelty (i.e., novelty that moves a domain in a forward direction versus novelty that moves a domain in a different direction). Litchfield and colleagues argue there are eight types of ideas, including one where ideas are not creative/innovative and seven types ideas that are creative.

First, the type of ideas that are not creative are those low in novelty, feasibility, and value. They call these types of creative ideas "bad ideas likely to stay bad." These ideas might be those already being done (similar to "replication" in the propulsion model) or ideas that are not novel, are expensive to implement, and would not provide any return on their investment (or a negative return). These ideas are those an organization would like to avoid.

The first three types of creative and innovative ideas are those that are all low in novelty but have varying levels of feasibility and value. These types include "easy incremental ideas," "hard incremental ideas," and "low-hanging fruit." Easy incremental ideas are low in novelty and value but high in feasibility. These ideas would provide a small return for an organization but are cheap and cost little for an organization to develop and implement. Hard incremental ideas are low in novelty and feasibility but high in value. These ideas provide a higher return for an organization but are difficult and costly to develop and implement. Litchfield and colleagues provide an example of developing software across multiple computer operating systems (e.g., Windows, Mac, Linux). This would be difficult to implement given different computer languages used but would provide a greater return on the number of users. Because the software is merely being developed across operating systems, it would not be a novel contribution. Low-hanging fruit are low in novelty but high in feasibility and value. These ideas might not be particularly transformative within or for a company, but they require minimal resources to implement and have a high return on investment, which means they are worth pursuing.

The next four types of ideas are all high in novelty but have varying levels of feasibility and value. These four types are "worthless follies," "disruptive ideas," "radical ideas," and "breakthrough ideas." Worthless follies are those that are high in novelty but low in feasibility and value. These ideas are referred to as "foolish" and are the least promising type of novel ideas. These ideas are often ridiculous, as they are difficult to implement and would provide no return or a negative return. For example, having a troupe of ballet dancers come out and give a one-hour performance for a customer's or client's birthday would not be an effective way to retain customers/clients unless there was an already expressed high interest in ballet. Although these ideas are not useful themselves, the act of generating and sharing ridiculous ideas might help spark other ideas given that the nature of the environment supports the sharing of ideas (Ekvall, 1996; Litchfield, 2008).

Disruptive ideas are high in novelty and feasibility but low in value. Although they might be high in novelty and easy to implement, they might not provide a large return for an organization or stakeholders. These ideas challenge and could potentially negatively affect an organization's long-term goals, which means they are often the least preferred type. Radical ideas are high in novelty and value but low in feasibility. As their name indicates, these ideas are a form of radical creativity. They are high in novelty and would provide a large return but are difficult to implement. Like the example for reinitiation in the propulsion model, a radical idea would be the Wright brothers developing a motorized plane. It took years to develop and implement but created radical changes in the modern world. The last type, breakthrough ideas, are high in novelty, feasibility, and value. They are extremely new to a domain or organization, require minimal resources to implement, and would provide a large return on investment.

Summary

Scholars continue to publish articles further refining the definition of creativity (Simonton, 2018) and differentiating types of creative contributions (Litchfield et al., 2015; Sternberg & Kaufman, 2012). We further refine these definitions by considering how creativity relates to task/routine performance and how role requirements for creativity impact this relationship. This has important implications for assessing creativity in organizations because it impacts how employees and supervisors view and judge creativity and innovation. We also reviewed two models of creative contributions. These models offer ways to think about and classify creative and innovative ideas. These frameworks might be useful for classifying existing creative ideas and better understanding what antecedents might differentially impact and relate to types of creativity.

Observing and Assessing Creativity in Organizations

Management scholars and organizations have assessed creativity and innovation in variety of ways. These approaches overlap to some extent, but there are also notable differences. To gain a better understanding of what approaches organizations used, The Boston Consulting Group surveyed senior management members of *BusinessWeek*'s Market Advisory Board and obtained responses from nearly 1,600 executives across the world (Andrew, Manget, Michael, Taylor, & Zablit, 2010). These executives reported various ways their organizations measure innovation. Across the executives, the most common two ways their organizations measured were customer satisfaction and overall revenue growth. Other methods included percentage of sales from new products or services, higher margins, new-product success ratios, return on innovation spending, projected versus actual performance, number of new products or services, time to market, and patents. In this section of the chapter, we discuss these measures and how they relate to other measures of creativity and innovation. Before discussing some of these alternative and "objective" measures, we discuss the approach more commonly used within the management research literature: survey-based measures of creative and innovative behaviors. We then provide a critique of current and relevant issues regarding these assessment methods.

For management scholars, survey-based measures are the most common approach to measuring creative and innovative performance (Hughes et al., 2018). When using these measures, people obtain survey responses from one or more sources. These sources can be self-report and leader/other-report. Self-report surveys are completed by the target person. They are used to assess whether someone perceives themselves or their work to be creative. Leader/other-report surveys are those completed by another person or supervisor for a target person. Leader-reported creativity is the most common survey-based approach used in top-tier management journals (e.g., Baer & Oldham, 2006; Liu, Gong, Zhou, & Huang, 2017; Zhu, Gardner, & Chen, 2018). Other-report performance might also come from colleagues/peers who have knowledge of a target's creative performance (e.g., Grosser, Venkataramani, & Labianca, 2017; Jaussi & Randel, 2014; Jaussi, Randel, & Dionne, 2007). Both self-report and leader/other-reported measures can be split up into different categories, including person, process, and product/evaluation (Hughes et al., 2018; Kaufman, 2019). When used as self-report measures, researchers often adapt a creative performance measure typically completed by supervisors for the targeted individual to complete (see Carmeli & Schaubroeck, 2007; Hsu, Hou, & Fan, 2011; Vinarski-Peretz, Binyamin, & Carmeli, 2011).

First, person-based measures typically focus on creative self-beliefs, such as how efficacious a person feels about his or her creativity (Farmer & Tierney, 2017; McKay, Lovelace, & Howard, 2018; Tierney & Farmer, 2002) or to what extent someone views creativity as part of his or her identity (Farmer, Tierney, & Kung-Mcintyre, 2003; Jaussi et al., 2007; Karwowski & Kaufman, 2017). Notably, these measures do not measure creative performance and are rarely, if ever, used for such purposes. Doing so would be inappropriate, particularly in any high-stakes situation. This is not to say these measures should not be used in research – in fact, they can illuminate important motivational mechanisms underlying creative performance (Liu, Jiang, Shalley, Keem, & Zhou, 2016).

Second, process-based measures ask people to report on the types of behaviors that lead to creativity. These measures are primary antecedents to creative performance (Montag et al., 2012; Zhang & Bartol, 2010a,b). An often used measure for assessing the creative process in organizational research is the Creative Process Engagement Scale (CPES; Zhang & Bartol, 2010a,b). This scale measures three creative process stages: problem identification, information searching, and idea generation. Researchers also use it as a single, higher-order factor of creative process engagement (Zhang & Bartol, 2010a,b). This measure has been used in experience sampling methodology studies to assess how frequently people engage in creative activities. For example, To, Fisher, Ashkanasy, and Rowe (2012) asked participants to complete the CPES and measures of momentary mood three times per day for 10 working days. They found that roughly 60% of the variability in creative process engagement was within-person, indicating there is meaningful variance worth studying in the amount of time spent in the creative process.

Although the creative process engagement scale is well developed and frequently used, it lacks subscales for later creative process stages such as idea evaluation. There are, however, other process-based measures focusing on later creative process stages. For example, Holman et al. (2012) developed a process-based measure focusing on later stages. Their measure includes three factors: idea generation, idea promotion, and idea implementation. Taken together, the two measures could be combined and refined to capture multiple stages of the creative process from problem identification to idea implementation.

The third category of measures for creative and innovative performance includes product- or evaluation-based measures. Product- or evaluation-based measures ask a person to report on his or her or another target person's creative performance with an emphasis on the creativity produced. An example is Oldham and Cummings's (1996) three-item measure that focuses solely on evaluating people's work rather than them as a creative person or the process-related behaviors they engage in (Hughes et al., 2018).

Issues with Survey-Based Measures of Creative and Innovative Performance

The use of surveys for assessing creative and innovative performance has its advantages and disadvantages. A clear advantage is that such measures are easy to use and take little time for an employee or supervisor to complete. However, ease of use does not always translate to the reliable and valid measurement of creative and innovative performance. We discuss three issues with using survey-based measures of creative and innovative performance: survey source, survey content, and expertise of source.

Survey Source

For self-report measures, there are two different views on whether they are valid measures of creativity. The first view argues that self-report measures of creativity are biased and measure creative self-beliefs like creative self-efficacy (e.g., Reiter-Palmon, Robinson-Morral, Kaufman, & Santo, 2012). Indeed, self-report outcome measures of creativity are strongly correlated with creative self-efficacy (Liu et al., 2016). The relationship between creative self-beliefs with other measures of creative performance increases concerns as to whether people are distinguishing their actual creative performance from their creative self-beliefs.

A second reason self-reported creativity might be less effective is due to concerns with common method bias. The relationship between any two variables might be larger simply because they were measured by the same person, at one time (Podsakoff, MacKenzie, & Podsakoff, 2012). To partially deal with this issue, researchers have separated data collection across two or more time points (e.g., Carmeli & Schaubroeck, 2007) or statistically determined whether common method bias is an issue (e.g., Zhou, Shin, & Cannella, 2008).

The alternative view argues that self-report creativity measures might be valid. For example, Janssen (2000) argued that self-reported innovative work behavior is potentially more valid because (a) employees might be able to more easily recall a greater number of instances where they used creativity in their work that the supervisor is unfamiliar with, (b) supervisors may be influenced by other rater characteristics rather than the primary construct of interest, and (c) supervisors might base their judgments on employees' appeasement to supervisors. Thus, based on this view, people are able to better report on their creative behaviors than their supervisor. There is also some evidence that self- and leader-reported innovative behavior scales are moderately ($r = 0.35$; Janssen, 2000) to strongly ($r = 0.62$ for a "suggestions" scale and $r = 0.42$ for an "implementation" scale; Axtell et al., 2000) correlated.

Taking both views into consideration, we argue the decision to use self- or leader-/other-reported measures should depend on two important factors. First, researchers should determine what facet of creativity they would like to assess: person, process, or product. We believe that person-based measures of creativity are best assessed via self-report, process-based measures can be measured via self- or other-report, and product-based measures should ideally be assessed solely via other-report in organizational settings. We believe that people likely have a better grasp on their own confidence in or value of their creativity than do others. For process-based measures, we agree with Janssen (2000) that people's own accounts can be a good source of their actual creative behaviors. The issue of self-efficacy being strongly related to engaging in creative behaviors is due to their temporal precedence. In other words, creative self-beliefs are likely the most proximal predictor of engaging in creative behaviors and would align with results in empirical research and meta-analyses (Liu et al., 2016; Reiter-Palmon et al., 2012). For product-based measures, we believe that other people (e.g., peers, colleagues, supervisors, stakeholders) are the best source, with peers rather than leaders likely being the ideal source (see Berg, 2016; Mumford, 1983). This basis aligns with the consensual assessment technique (Amabile, 1982, 1996), which argues that domain experts are a good source for assessing creativity, a discussion we return to in the section, "Expertise of Source."

The second factor deals with the content specification of the scales being used. A notable issue with various measures is that they may encompass multiple content areas rather than one area (Hughes et al., 2018). However, if measurement is focused solely within one content area, the potential confounds of self-report process/behavior measures might be theoretically meaningful. That is, creative self-beliefs impact whether people are willing to work on and engage in creative performance behaviors, which in turn influences a person's creative outcome effectiveness as judged by relevant others (Liu et al., 2016; Montag et al., 2012). We discuss this issue next.

Survey Content

As mentioned, survey measures can be split into three facets: person, process, or product (Hughes et al., 2018). Additionally, definitions for creativity and innovation have distinguished between the two concepts. However, many scales used to measure creative and innovative performance confound creativity and innovation. They also often confound person, process, and product facets. This confounding leads to an inability to determine what is exactly being measured when these scales are used as self- or other-reported assessments of creativity and innovation.

We believe the validity issues with survey-based assessments of creativity/ innovation have likely played a critical role in the lack of theoretical advances within the organizational creativity scholarship (Anderson et al., 2014; Hughes et al., 2018). When results are reported, it is nearly impossible to tease apart the implications for creativity versus innovation research and whether the results have implications for the creative process or product. Notably, the only commonly used measure that taps solely into the product facet is Oldham and Cummings's (1996) three-item scale. Yet one item in this scale captures creativity, the second and the third innovations cover both creativity *and* innovation. Despite this limitation, it remains the only scale that exclusively focuses on the creative product facet, making it ideal for examining creative/innovative performance (Hughes et al., 2018). However, we agree strongly with Hughes et al. (2018) that one of the most important next steps for management creativity scholars is to develop new tools to distinguish creativity from innovation and between person, process, and product facets. Ideally, these measures should differentiate creative process behaviors and creative outcome effectiveness and ensure that neither measure taps into the other content area (Montag et al., 2012) and would likely tap into the multidimensional space that makes up creativity and innovation. Once creative and innovative assessment is based solely within single content facets, we can gain a better understanding of what specific factors lead to creativity and subsequent innovation.

Expertise of Source

When obtaining creative and innovative performance ratings from others, rater expertise is an important issue (Kaufman, Baer, & Cole, 2009; Kaufman, Baer, Cole, & Sexton, 2008; Kaufman, Baer, Cropley, Reiter-Palmon, & Sinnett, 2013). Amabile's (1982, 1996) consensual assessment technique argues that creativity and innovation should be assessed independently by experts within a domain, and those experts should agree on whether an idea/product is or is not creative. This research has distinguished between three types of raters based on expertise: novices, quasi-experts, and experts (Kaufman & Baer, 2012). Novices have minimal or no domain expertise; quasi-experts have some domain knowledge, expressed ability, or relevant training in creativity; and experts have lots of domain knowledge and expressed ability. This research has shown that there is stronger agreement among experts and quasi-experts across many domains, whereas novices do not usually agree on the assessment of creative performance with each other or with experts (Kaufman et al., 2008, 2009, 2013). The more technical a domain is (e.g., engineering), the more expertise is typically needed in raters (Kaufman et al., 2013). Because leaders and colleagues/peers are either experts or quasi-experts, they would be a valid source for assessing a person's creative and innovative performance within their area of specialty (i.e., someone in research and development may not have the same insight into creative performance within human resources).

Alternative and "Objective" Creativity/Innovation Measures

Aside from survey-based measures, a number of alternative and "objective" measures of creativity and innovation are often studied. However, these assessments are often based on implemented ideas, meaning they are more likely to tap into innovation as opposed to creativity. We focus on the relationship between different factors in research in conjunction with the results from the Boston Consulting Group's survey mentioned earlier.

First, customer satisfaction is one of the primary measures used by organizations for assessing creativity (Andrew et al., 2010). Thus, creativity can be a way to attract and retain customers. Although research shows that creativity and customer satisfaction are related (Dong, Liao, Chuang, Zhou, & Campbell, 2015; Martinaityte, Sacramento, & Aryee, 2016), they are not synonymous. Even when both creativity and satisfaction are assessed by the customer, they are highly correlated ($r = 0.60$) yet still have distinct factors. Additionally, customer judgments might be more strongly influenced by a product's usefulness (Kornish & Ulrich, 2014) rather than its creativity. Biases against creative ideas (Mueller, Melwani, & Goncalo, 2012) and preferences for the status quo (Eidelman & Crandall, 2012) indicate that ideas low in novelty are preferred over those high in novelty. In fact, particularly new ideas are often underestimated (Licuanan, Dailey, & Mumford, 2007). As mentioned, it is important to identify the mental processes novices use when assessing creativity and how this relates or does not relate to their satisfaction.

Second, other studies have examined other "objective" and "macro" innovation factors such as sales effectiveness (e.g., Kornish & Ulrich, 2014; Martinaityte & Sacramento, 2013), projected versus actual performance (see Kahn, 2014), number of new products or services (e.g., Liu et al., 2017), and time to market (e.g., Hansen, 1999). Similar to creativity/innovation and customer satisfaction, these studies indicate that creativity/innovation (often measured via survey measures) are highly related to such factors, but not synonymous with them. This type of close relationship does not mean they should not be used. Rather, determining how and in what ways survey-based creativity assessments are related to "objective" and organizational-level outcomes is important. For example, it might be useful to examine the relationship between factors such as creative performance behaviors or creative process engagement with factors such as time to market using experience sampling methodology. This approach would help tease apart how more subjective, survey-based measures are related to more objective measures. Moreover, researchers could examine how different individual- and team-level factors impact organizational-level outcomes using alternative multilevel modeling approaches (e.g., Croon & Van Veldhoven, 2007).

Third, a large body of research has focused on patent applications and patents as a measure of creative/innovative performance at various levels of analysis (e.g., Audia & Goncalo, 2007; Oldham & Cummings, 1996; Rost, 2011; Stuart, 2000; Tortoriello & Krackhardt, 2010). These studies have utilized different aspects of patents as measures of creative and innovative performance. For example, a number of studies have focused on the number of patents or patent applications (e.g., Audia & Goncalo, 2007; Oldham & Cummings, 1996; Stuart, 2000). This usage might be akin to measures of fluency, albeit much more complex than a rudimentary divergent thinking task (i.e., generate uses for a brick). Notably, research shows leader ratings of employee creativity are moderately related to the number of patent applications or patents/research reports submitted by employees (Oldham & Cummings, 1996; Tierney, Farmer, & Graen, 1999). This modest correlation is likely due to contaminating factors in both survey and "objective" assessments of creativity and innovation.

Alternative research has focused beyond the number of patents, by examining the impact of patents on future patents. For example, Rost (2011) utilized forward patent citations to determine how much a given patent impacts future patents. Thus, it could be conceptualized as the usefulness of an idea for the development of creative/innovative ideas that further build on and refine current ideas/products. Although neither the number of patents nor the number of patent citations are complete measures of innovative performance, they reflect two potential ways that patents can be used as a measure of creativity that might have different antecedents.

Last, awards have also been used to assess the impact of creativity and innovation in both ideas and people (e.g., Aadland, Cattani, & Ferriani, 2018; Cattani & Ferriani, 2008; Cattani, Ferriani, & Allison, 2014; Rossman, Esparza, & Bonacich, 2010). These studies focus on whether creative/innovative ideas are well regarded by stakeholders within a given domain, akin to the consensual assessment technique (Amabile, 1982, 1996). Ideally, researchers could examine different factors that lead to people being nominated and whether or not people receive an award within a domain. This research can better understand how factors like the originality of the idea (e.g., Kornish & Ulrich, 2014), social/political support (e.g., Kanter, 1988), and other factors impact recognition.

Although the measures listed are alternative and "objective" indicators of creative and innovative performance, they present other biases that might not be inherent in survey-based measures. Creativity/innovation assessments are difficult or impossible to attribute fully to one person or team making them difficult metrics to assess at the individual and even team level. In today's world, multiple people across multiple creative process stages play important roles in the generation and implementation of an idea (Perry-Smith & Mannucci, 2017). Additionally, other factors beyond creativity are important in the success or failure of ideas. We believe these measures are important to examine but should be treated as complex factors.

Summary

There are multiple approaches to measuring creative and innovative performance. Each method has its advantages and disadvantages; some methods are better for certain types of creativity, in certain domains, and when assessing specific aspects of the creative process. We provided an overview of approaches used within the research literature and organizations. Now, we provide two issues that should be addressed moving forward.

First, a notable issue across many studies and measures is whether creativity or innovation is the focal outcome. Often, the term *creativity* is used when the measurement is more focused on innovation (and vice versa). The interchangeable usage of these terms creates ambiguity in determining what is being studied and makes it difficult to categorize and identify the "big picture" of the research literature. Thus, creativity and innovation researchers must ask themselves whether differentiating creativity and innovation actually matters if we do not adhere to these distinctions. If the two terms are not operationalized in different ways, then the literature will likely continue to be stagnant with few meaningful theoretical advances (Anderson et al., 2014; Hughes et al., 2018). If differentiating them does matter, then it is time to do so in our measures. Authors should clearly specify whether their measure is designed to assess creativity or innovation – and why. Editors and reviewers should hold strict standards to ensure this information is included. A notable exemplar of this distinction is Baer's (2012) study using creativity as a predictor and implementation as the outcome.

Second, it is time to move beyond the study of what factors predict the antecedents of creativity and innovation. A quick perusal of the creativity research literature shows that the majority of studies focus on antecedents predicting creative process behaviors as the outcome and do not include product-based measures or any measure of creative outcome effectiveness (Montag et al., 2012). McKay et al. (2018) could not identify a single organizational study examining the relationship between creative self-efficacy with an objective creativity measure (e.g., patents or research reports). The limited nature of the criterion space examined narrows our knowledge of creativity and innovation. We know much about what factors will lead people to engage in behaviors that *might* lead to creativity and innovation, but we know very little about what factors *actually* aid in those behaviors leading to creativity.

In order to accomplish both goals, it is not enough to develop and validate measures of creative outcome effectiveness. We also need to determine which sources of information can and cannot provide valid and predictive information. More likely than not, it might be useful to obtain assessments from multiple sources and identify mechanisms that differentiate when and how these sources differ in their judgments. Examining multiple measures, especially longitudinally, can help organizations identify potential roadblocks in a person's or team's creativity or in the organization as a whole. This information can help determine where and how to target creativity training programs to increase creativity (Valgeirsdottir & Onarheim, 2017).

Additionally, if possible, it would be useful to include both subjective and objective measures of creative performance. However, in doing so, researchers should be mindful of the theoretical linkages between those measures. As mentioned, how does creative process engagement impact time to market? Or, how does time to market impact the success or failure of ideas? These are important questions that will help tease apart critical creative process aspects that draw on both survey-based and objective-based measures of creativity and innovation.

We should also consider if the true goals of assessments of creativity and innovation are to simply be accurate as outcome variables or if they are ultimately primarily of use as predictive or moderating variables for a larger outcome such as annual profit, employee retention, company growth, or whatever else. Do we actually care about creativity or innovation stripped of its ability to impact the bottom line, or is it a means to an end? The scope, depth, and nuances of measures would vary based on their intended usage.

Practical Implications

Throughout this chapter, we discussed a number of factors that influence how creativity/innovation is conceptualized as a performance dimension and the utility of current approaches to measuring creativity/innovation. We offer a number of practical implications for assessing creativity and innovation.

First, those interested in measuring creativity and innovation should be mindful of the extent to which these constructs are part of a person's formal role. If creativity were measured as an extra-role behavior among employees working in research and development, it might lead to inaccurate measurement. A similar situation would occur if creativity were measured as an in-role behavior among postal service employees. It is important to determine whether creativity is part of one's formal role requirement, as this influences how creativity and innovation can be measured. It is easier to find more objective measures of creativity and innovation in domains where creativity is part of one's formal role as opposed to those domains that do not include creativity as part of one's formal role.

Second, it is necessary for researchers and practitioners to improve the measurement of creativity. Creativity is often measured differently by organizations (Andrew et al., 2010) compared to how it is measured in research studies (Hughes et al., 2018). Further, like many other fields, organizational scholarship often ignores work done in adjacent domains, such as psychology or education (Reiter-Palmon, Beghetto, & Kaufman, 2014). The history and breadth of creativity assessment (e.g., Plucker, Makel, & Qian, 2019) are quite larger than that represented in the organizational literature. Not all aspects are relevant (indeed, measures of imagination may be negatively related to positive work outcomes), but there are many other occasions where many existing and validated measures are available to be used or adapted but remain undiscovered.

Last, taking a role-based view for measuring creativity indicates that a better way to measure creative performance might be to ask others to appraise whether and how well people execute specific creative tasks embedded in their job roles. Although more difficult to create than global creativity and innovation ratings, this approach would take a more role- and domain-specific approach to studying creativity (Amabile, 1996; Baer, 2010). It is straightforward to make the argument that someone's creativity in visual art would differ from their creativity in nuclear physics. It is more nuanced to suggest that someone working in advertising might be more creative at generating an idea for a slogan or advertisement than at pitching that concept to a prospective client. Recent research indicates that even within divergent thinking tests, different types of tasks and even prompts may be measuring distinct things (Barbot, 2018).

Conclusion

We are at a point where the next steps lead in multiple directions. Some go inward as we refine, specify, and narrow our definitions, whereas others will go outward as we consider additional facets, interactions, outcomes, and input from other fields. To advance to the next stages, we will ultimately need to do both and forge a path driven by better overarching theory, grounded in firmly established practices, and ultimately better serving the needs of organizations seeking continued growth.

References

Aadland, E., Cattani, G., & Ferriani, S. 2018. Friends, cliques and gifts: Social proximity and recognition in peer-based tournament rituals. *Academy of Management Journal*, 62. doi: https://doi.org/10.5465/amj.2016.0437

Amabile, T. M. 1982. Social psychology of creativity: A consensual assessment technique. *Journal of Personality and Social Psychology*, 43, 997–1013.

Amabile, T. M. 1983. The social psychology of creativity: A componential conceptualization. *Journal of Personality and Social Psychology*, 45, 357–376.

Amabile, T. M. 1996. *Creativity in context: Update to the social psychology of creativity*. Boulder, CO: Westview Press.

Anderson, N. R., Potocnik, K., & Zhou, J. 2014. Innovation and creativity in organizations: A state-of-the-science review, prospective commentary, and guiding framework. *Journal of Management*, 40, 1297–1333.

Andrew, J. P., Manget, J., Michael, D. C., Taylor, A., & Zablit, H. 2010. *Innovation 2010: A return to prominence and the emergence of a new world order*. The Boston Consulting Group. Retrieved from https://www.bcg.com/documents/file42620.pdf

Audia, P., & Goncalo, J. 2007. Past success and creativity over time: A study of inventors in the hard disk drive industry. *Management Science*, 53, 1–15.

Austin, J. T., & Villanova, P. 1992. The criterion problem: 1917–1992. *Journal of Applied Psychology*, 77, 836–874.

Axtell, C. M., Holman, D. J., Unsworth, K. L., Wall, T. D., Waterson, P. E., & Harrington, E. 2000. Shopfloor innovation: Facilitating the suggestion and implementation of ideas. *Journal of Occupational and Organizational Psychology*, 73, 265–285.

Baer, J. 2010. Is creativity domain-specific? In J. C. Kaufman & R. J. Sternberg (Eds.), *The Cambridge handbook of creativity* (pp. 321–341). New York, NY: Cambridge University Press.

Baer, M. 2012. Putting creativity to work: The implementation of creative ideas in organizations. *Academy of Management Journal*, 55, 1102–1119.

Baer, M., & Oldham, G. R. 2006. The curvilinear relation between experienced creative time pressure and creativity: Moderating effects of openness to experience and support for creativity. *Journal of Applied Psychology*, 91, 963–970.

Barbot, B. 2018. The dynamics of creative ideation: Introducing a new assessment paradigm. *Front. Psychol.* 9,2529. doi: 10.3389/fpsyg.2018.02529

Berg, J. M. 2016. Balancing on the creative highwire: Forecasting the success of novel ideas in organizations. *Administrative Science Quarterly*, 61, 433–468.

Borman, W. C., & Motowidlo, S. J. 1997. Task performance and contextual performance: The meaning for personnel selection research. *Human Performance*, 10, 99–109.

Carmeli, A., & Schaubroeck, J. 2007. The influence of leaders' and other referents' normative expectations on individual involvement in creative work. *The Leadership Quarterly*, 18, 35–48.

Cattani, G., & Ferriani, S. 2008. A core/periphery perspective on individual creative performance: Social networks and cinematic achievements in the Hollywood film industry. *Organization Science*, 19, 824–844.

Cattani, G., Ferriani, S., & Allison, P. D. 2014. Insiders, outsiders, and the struggle for consecration in cultural fields: A core-periphery perspective. *American Sociological Review*, 79, 258–281.

Croon, M. A., & Van Veldhoven, M. J. P. M. 2007. Predicting group-level outcome variables from variables measured at the individual level: A latent variable multilevel model. *Psychological Methods*, 12, 45–57.

Dong, Y., Liao, H., Chuang, A., Zhou, J., & Campbell, E. M. 2015. Fostering employee service creativity: Joint effects of customer empowering behaviors and supervisory empowering leadership. *Journal of Applied Psychology*, 100, 1364–1380.

Eidelman, S., & Crandall, C. S. 2012. Bias in favor of the status quo. *Social and Personality Psychology Compass*, 6, 270–281.

Ekvall, G. 1996. Organizational climate for creativity and innovation. *European Journal of Work and Organizational Psychology*, 5, 105–123.

Farmer, S. M., & Tierney, P. 2017. Considering creative self-efficacy: Its current state and ideas for future inquiry. In M. Karwowski, & J. C. Kaufman (Eds.), *The creative self: Effects of beliefs, self-efficacy, mindset, and identity* (pp. 23–47). London, UK: Academic Press.

Farmer, S. M., Tierney, P., & Kung-Mcintyre, K. 2003. Employee creativity in Taiwan: An application of role identity theory. *Academy of Management Journal*, 46, 618–630.

Ford, C. M. 1996. A theory of individual creative action in multiple social domains. *Academy of Management Review*, 21, 1112–1142.

Gerhart, B., & Fang, M. 2015. Pay, intrinsic motivation, extrinsic motivation, performance, and creativity in the workplace: Revisiting long-held beliefs. *Annual Review of Organizational Psychology and Organizational Behavior*, 2, 489–521.

Gilson, L. L., & Madjar, N. 2011. Radical and incremental creativity: Antecedents and processes. *Psychology of Aesthetics, Creativity, and the Arts*, 5, 21–28.

Grosser, T. J., Venkataramani, V., & Labianca, G. 2017. An alter-centric perspective on employee innovation: The importance of alters' creative self-efficacy and network structure. *Journal of Applied Psychology*, 102, 1360–1374.

Hansen, M. T. 1999. The search-transfer problem: The role of weak ties in sharing knowledge across organization subunits. *Administrative Science Quarterly*, 44, 82–111.

Harari, M. B., Reaves, A. C., & Viswesvaran, C. 2016. Creative and innovative performance: A meta-analysis of relationships with task, citizenship, and counterproductive job performance dimensions. *European Journal of Work and Organizational Psychology*, 25, 495–511.

Holman, D., Totterdell, P., Axtell, C., Stride, C., Port, R., Svensson, R., & Zibarras, L. 2012. Job design and the employee innovation process: The mediating role of learning strategies. *Journal of Business and Psychology*, 27, 177–191.

Hsu, M. L. A., Hou, S. T., & Fan, H. L. 2011. Creative self-efficacy and innovative behavior in a service setting: Optimism as a moderator. *Journal of Creative Behavior*, 45, 258–272.

Hughes, D. J., Lee, A., Tian, A. W., Newman, A., & Legood, A. 2018. Leadership, creativity, and innovation: A critical review and practical recommendations. *Leadership Quarterly*, 29, 549–569.

Janssen, O. 2000. Job demands, perceptions of effort-reward fairness and innovative work behaviour. *Journal of Occupational and Organizational Psychology*, 73, 287–302.

Janssen, O., & Van Yperen, N. W. 2004. Employees' goal orientations, the quality of leader-member exchange, and the outcomes of job performance and job satisfaction. *Academy of Management Journal*, 47, 368–384.

Jaussi, K. S., & Randel, A. E. 2014. Where to look? Creative self-efficacy, knowledge retrieval, and incremental and radical creativity. *Creativity Research Journal*, 26, 400–410.

Jaussi, K. S., Randel, A. E., & Dionne, S. D. 2007. I am, I think I can, and I do: The role of personal identity, self-efficacy, and cross-application of experiences in creativity at work. *Creativity Research Journal*, 19, 247–258.

Kahn, K. B. 2014. Solving the problems of new product forecasting. *Business Horizons*, 57, 607–615.

Kanter, R. M. 1988. When a thousand flowers bloom: Structural, collective, and social conditions for innovation in organization. *Research in Organizational Behavior*, 10, 169–211.

Karwowski, M., & Kaufman, J. C. (Eds.). 2017. *The creative self: Effect of beliefs, self-efficacy, mindset, and identity*. San Diego, CA: Academic Press.

Kaufman, J. C. 2019. Self-assessments of creativity: Not ideal, but better than you think. *Psychology of Aesthetics, Creativity, and the Arts*, 13(2), 187–192.

Kaufman, J. C., & Baer, J. 2012. Beyond new and appropriate: Who decides what is creative? *Creativity Research Journal*, 24, 83–91.

Kaufman, J. C., Baer, J., & Cole, J. C. 2009. Expertise, domains, and the consensual assessment technique. *Journal of Creative Behavior*, 43, 223–233.

Kaufman, J. C., Baer, J., Cole, J. C., & Sexton, J. D. 2008. A comparison of expert and nonexpert raters using the Consensual Assessment Technique. *Creativity Research Journal*, 20, 171–178.

Kaufman, J. C., Baer, J., Cropley, D. H., Reiter-Palmon, R., & Sinnett, S. 2013. Furious activity vs. understanding: How much expertise is needed to evaluate creative work? *Psychology of Aesthetics, Creativity, and the Arts*, 7, 332–340.

Kornish, L. J., & Ulrich, K. T. 2014. The importance of the raw idea in innovation: Testing the sow's ear hypothesis. *Journal of Marketing Research*, 51, 14–26.

Licuanan, B. F., Dailey, L. R., & Mumford, M. D. 2007. Idea evaluation: Error in evaluating highly original ideas. *Journal of Creative Behavior*, 41, 1–27.

Litchfield, R. C. 2008. Brainstorming reconsidered: A goal-based view. *Academy of Management Review*, 33, 649–668.

Litchfield, R. C., Gilson, L. L., & Gilson, P. W. 2015. Defining creative ideas: Toward a more nuanced approach. *Group and Organization Management*, 40, 238–265.

Liu, D., Gong, Y., Zhou, J., & Huang, J. 2017. Human resource systems, employee creativity, and firm innovation: The moderating role of firm ownership. *Academy of Management Journal*, 60, 1164–1188.

Liu, D., Jiang, K., Shalley, C. E., Keem, S., & Zhou, J. 2016. Motivational mechanisms of employee creativity: A meta-analytic examination and theoretical extension of the creativity literature. *Organizational Behavior and Human Decision Processes*, 137, 236–263.

Madjar, N., Greenberg, E., & Chen, Z. 2011. Factors for radical creativity, incremental creativity, and routine, noncreative performance. *Journal of Applied Psychology*, 96, 730–743.

Martinaityte, I., & Sacramento, C. A. 2013. When creativity enhances sales effectiveness: The moderating role of leader-member exchange. *Journal of Organizational Behavior*, 34, 974–994.

Martinaityte, I., Sacramento, C., & Aryee, S. 2016. Delighting the customer: Creativity-oriented high-performance work systems, frontline employee creative performance, and customer satisfaction. *Journal of Management*. https://doi.org/10.1177/0149206316672532

McKay, A. S., Lovelace, J. B., & Howard, M. C. 2018. The heart of innovation: Antecedents and consequences of creative self-efficacy in organizations. In R. Reiter-Palmon, V. L. Kennel, & J. C. Kaufman (Eds.), *Individual creativity in the workplace* (pp. 223–244). San Diego, CA: Academic Press.

Montag, T., Maertz, C. P., & Baer, M. 2012. A critical analysis of the workplace creativity criterion space. *Journal of Management*, 38, 1362–1386.

Mueller, J. S., Melwani, S., & Goncalo, J. A. 2012. The bias against creativity: Why people desire but reject creative ideas. *Psychological Science*, 23, 13–17.

Mumford, M. D. 1983. Social comparison theory and the evaluation of peer evaluations: A review and some applied implications. *Personnel Psychology*, 36, 867–881.

Mumford, M. D., & Gustafson, S. B. 1988. Creativity syndrome: Integration, application, and innovation. *Psychological Bulletin*, 103, 27–43.

Mumford, M. D., Hester, K. S., & Robledo, I. C. 2012. Creativity in organizations: Importance and approaches. In M. D. Mumford (Ed.), *Handbook of organizational creativity* (pp. 3–16). New York, NY: Academic Press.

Mumford, M. D., & Hunter, S. T. 2005. Innovation in organizations: A multi-level perspective on creativity. In F. J. Yammarino & F. Dansereau (Eds.), *Multi-level issues in strategy and methods* (pp. 9–73). San Diego, CA: Emerald Group Publishing.

Oldham, G. R., & Cummings, A. 1996. Employee creativity: Personal and contextual factors at work. *Academy of Management Journal*, 39, 607–634.

Perry-Smith, J. E., & Mannucci, P. V. 2017. From creativity to innovation: The social network drivers of the four phases of the idea journal. *Academy of Management Review*, 42, 53–79.

Plucker, J. A., Makel, M. C., & Qian, M. 2019. Assessment of creativity. In J. C. Kaufman & R. J. Sternberg (Eds.), *Cambridge handbook of creativity* (2nd ed.). New York, NY: Cambridge University Press.

Podsakoff, P. M., MacKenzie, S. B., & Podsakoff, N. P. 2012. Sources of method bias in social science research and recommendations on how to control it. *Annual Review of Psychology*, 63, 539–569.

Reiter-Palmon, R., Beghetto, R. A., & Kaufman, J. C. 2014. Looking at creativity through a Business-Psychology-Education (BPE) lens: The challenge and benefits of listening to each other. In E. Shiu (Ed.), *Creativity research: An interdisciplinary and multidisciplinary research handbook* (pp. 9–30). New York, NY: Routledge.

Reiter-Palmon, R., Robinson-Morral, E. J., Kaufman, J. C., & Santo, J. B. 2012. Evaluation of self-perceptions of creativity: Is it a useful criterion? *Creativity Research Journal*, 24, 107–114.

Rossman, G., Esparza, N., & Bonacich, P. 2010. I'd like to thank the Academy, team spillovers, and network centrality. *American Sociological Review*, 75, 31–51.

Rost, K. 2011. The strength of strong ties in the creation of innovation. *Research Policy*, 40, 588–604.

Sackett, P. R., Berry, C. M., Wiemann, S. A., & Laczo, R. M. 2006. Citizenship and counterproductive behavior: Clarifying relations between the two domains. *Human Performance*, 19, 441–464.

Shalley, C. E., Gilson, L. L., & Blum, T. C. 2000. Matching creativity requirements and work environment: Effects on satisfaction and intentions to leave. *Academy of Management Journal*, 43, 215–223.

Simonton, D. K. 2018. Defining creativity: Don't we also need to define what is not creative? *Journal of Creative Behavior*, 52, 80–90.

Sternberg, R. J. 1999. A propulsion model of types of creative contributions. *Review of General Psychology*, 3, 83–100.

Sternberg, R. J., & Kaufman, J. C. 2012. When your race is almost run, but you feel you're not yet done: Application of the propulsion theory of creative contributions to late-career challenges. *Journal of Creative Behavior*, 46, 66–76.

Sternberg, R. J., Kaufman, J. C., & Grigorenko, E. L. 2008. *Applied intelligence*. New York, NY: Cambridge University Press.

Sternberg, R. J., Kaufman, J. C., & Pretz, J. E. 2003. A propulsion model of creative leadership. *The Leadership Quarterly*, 14, 455–473.

Stuart, T. E. 2000. Interorganizational alliances and the performance of firms: A study of growth and innovation rates in a high-technology industry. *Strategic Management Journal*, 21, 791–811.

Tierney, P., & Farmer, S. M. 2002. Creative self-efficacy: Its potential antecedents and relationship to creative performance. *Academy of Management Journal*, 45, 1137–1148.

Tierney, P., Farmer, S. M., & Graen, G. B. 1999. An examination of leadership and employee creativity: The relevance of traits and relationships. *Personnel Psychology*, 52, 591–620.

To, M. L., Fisher, C. D., Ashkanasy, N. M., & Rowe, P. A. 2012. Within-person relationships between mood and creativity. *Journal of Applied Psychology*, 97, 599–612.

Tortoriello, M., & Krackhardt, D. 2010. Activating cross-boundary knowledge: The role of Simmelian ties in the generation of innovations. *Academy of Management Journal*, 53, 167–181.

Unsworth, K. L., Wall, T. D., & Carter, A. 2005. Creative requirement: A neglected construct in the study of employee creativity? *Group and Organization Management*, 30, 541–560.

Valgeirsdottir, D., & Onarheim, B. 2017. Studying creativity training programs: A methodological analysis. *Creativity and Innovation Management*, 26, 430–439.

Vinarski-Peretz, H., Binyamin, G., & Carmeli, A. 2011. Subjective relational experiences and employee innovative behaviors in the workplace. *Journal of Vocational Behavior*, 78, 290–304.

Wildman, J. L., Bedwell, W. L., Salas, E., & Smith-Jentsch, K. A. 2011. Performance measurement at work: A multilevel perspective. In S. Zedeck (Ed.), *APA handbook of industrial and organizational psychology, Vol 1: Building and developing the organization* (pp. 303–341). Washington, DC: American Psychological Association.

World Economic Forum. 2016. The future of jobs: Employment, skills and workforce strategy for the fourth industrial revolution. Available from: http://www.weforum.org/reports/the-future-of-jobs [last accessed 06 August 2019].

World Economic Forum. 2018. Readiness for the Future of Production Report 2018. Geneva: World Economic Forum.

Zhang, X., & Bartol, K. M. 2010a. Linking empowering leadership and employee creativity: The influence of psychological empowerment, intrinsic motivation, and creative process engagement. *Academy of Management Journal*, 53, 107–128.

Zhang, X., & Bartol, K. M. 2010b. The influence of creative process engagement on employee creative performance and overall job performance: A curvilinear assessment. *Journal of Applied Psychology*, 95, 862–873.

Zhou, J., Shin, S. J., & Cannella, A. A. 2008. Employee self-perceived creativity after mergers and acquisitions: Interactive effects of threat – Opportunity perception, access to resources, and support for creativity. *Journal of Applied Behavioral Science*, 44, 397–421.

Zhu, Y. Q., Gardner, D. G., & Chen, H. G. 2018. Relationships between work team climate, individual motivation, and creativity. *Journal of Management*, 44, 2094–2115.

3

WHAT IS NEEDED TO THINK CREATIVELY AT WORK? KNOWLEDGE AND SKILLS

Michael D. Mumford, E. Michelle Todd, Cory Higgs, and Robert Martin

Both product (e.g., powered flight) (Crouch, 1992) and process (e.g., worker efficiency) (Kanigel, 2005) innovation make, and reshape, the world we live in. The social impact of innovation (the development and fielding of new products or new processes) has long been recognized (Mumford & Van Doorn, 2001). More recently, however, it has become apparent that long-term success and survival of firms depend on sustained patterns of innovation by the firm (Audretsch, 1995; Cefis & Marsili, 2005). Recognition of this point has led firms to seek and encourage innovation through a variety of mechanisms – mechanisms ranging from resourcing systems (Engel & Keilback, 2007) and cannibalization policies (Chandy & Tellis, 1998) to planning processes (Mumford, Bedell-Avers, & Hunter, 2008) and cross-functional teaming (Majchrzak, More, & Faraj, 2012).

Although these, and a number of other actions, can contribute to the innovative capacity of firms, production and fielding of any new product, or products, however, necessarily depend on employee creativity – typically the production of not one, but many, creative ideas (Gordon, 2016). Accordingly, firms have begun to seek ways to encourage employee creativity. Efforts along these lines, however, must begin with an explicit definition of exactly what is meant by the term *creativity*. Although many definitions of creativity have been proposed over the years – creativity as idea generation (Osburn, 1954), creativity as originality (Weisberg, 2015), and creativity as eminent achievement (Simonton, 1997) – in recent years a consensus definition has emerged as to what precisely is meant when we use the term *creativity* (Amabile, 1996; Mumford & Gustafson, 1988; Sternberg, 2011). More specifically, creativity is held to be reflected in the production of original, high-quality, and elegant solutions (Besemer & O'Quin, 1999; Christiaans, 2002) to complex, novel, ill-defined, or poorly structured, problems (Mumford & Gustafson, 2007). Thus, creativity represents a specific form of performance applying to a certain class, or type, of problems.

As with any form of complex performance, many factors contribute to creative problem-solving, including motivation (Tierney & Farmer, 2002), active engagement (Baas, De Dreu, & Nijstad, 2008), openness (Batey & Furnham, 2006), and psychological safety (Carmeli, Reiter-Palmon, & Ziv, 2010), to mention a few. Nonetheless, as a form of problem-solving performance, one would expect that creativity is most appropriately understood as a form of expertise (Ericsson, 2007). Put differently, to produce original, high-quality, elegant solutions to complex, novel, ill-defined problems in the "real world," people must possess knowledge and know-how to work with this knowledge in producing viable, creative, problem solutions. In this effort, we examine how people work with the knowledge and the skills they need to produce original, high-quality, and elegant solutions to complex, novel, ill-defined problems. Moreover, we consider certain contextual variables that shape effective application of creative thinking skills.

Processes

Process Model

For many years, scholars have sought to identify the key processes to be executed as people work with knowledge in creative problem-solving efforts (e.g., Dewey, 1910; Finke, Ward, & Smith, 1992; Sternberg & O'Hara, 1999; Wallas, 1926). Mumford, Mobley, Reiter-Palmon, Uhlman, and Doares (1991) reviewed the various attempts made over the years to identify the key processing activities involved in incidents of creative thought. This review led to the identification of eight critical processing activities commonly held to be involved in incidents of creative problem-solving: (a) Problem-definition, (b) Information Gathering, (c) Concept Selection, (d) Conceptual Combination and Reorganization, (e) Idea Generation, (f) Idea Evaluation, (g) Implementation Planning, and (h) Adaptive Solution Monitoring. Figure 3.1 illustrates Mumford et al.'s (1991) model of creative problem-solving processes.

With regard to this model, a number of points should be noted. First, the products flowing from execution of an earlier process (e.g., problem definition) influence, or shape, execution of subsequent processes (e.g., information gathering). Second, if products generated in process execution are found to be inadequate, people will typically cycle back one step in an attempt to resolve this deficiency. This observation implies *both* generative and evaluative activities are involved in the execution of each of these processes (Cropley, 2006; Parnes & Noller, 1972). Third, creative problem-solving involves, and

What Is Needed to Think Creatively at Work? 43

```
Problem Definition
        ↓
Information Gathering
        ↓
Concept Selection
        ↓
Conceptual Combination
& Reorganization
        ↓
Idea Generation
        ↓
Idea Evaluation
        ↓
Implementation Planning
        ↓
Adaptive Solution
Monitoring
```

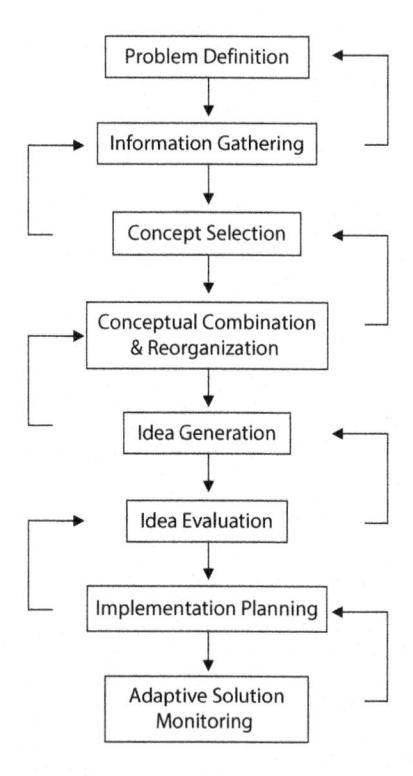

FIGURE 3.1 Creative thinking processes.

emerges from, more open early cycle activities (e.g., concept selection and conceptual combination and reorganization) and more contextually driven late cycle activities (e.g., idea generation and idea evaluation). Thus, creative problem-solving is *always* context, or "real-world," driven. Fourth, each process is a complex operation in its own right. This observation implies that creative problem-solving will require not only substantial resources, but it will often fail (Huber, 1998) due to both the complexity of the processes involved and the resources required for effective process execution.

The question that arises at this juncture is what evidence is available to support this model. Mumford, Medeiros, and Partlow (2012) summarized the available evidence pointing to the plausibility of this model. The first line of evidence has sought to demonstrate that more, or less, effective execution of each of these processes contributes to production of more original, high-quality, and more elegant solutions to various novel, complex, and ill-defined problems. For example, Redmond, Mumford, and Teach (1993) asked undergraduates to formulate advertising campaigns for a new product, the 3-D holographic television, where the resulting advertising plans were appraised for quality and originality by marketing experts. A manipulation intended to encourage better problem definition, a manipulation requiring listing important considerations and restating the problem in their own terms, was found to result in higher-quality and more original advertising campaigns. In another study, Baughman and Mumford (1995) asked undergraduates to formulate and define new categories after reviewing three categories (e.g., birds, sporting equipment), defined by four exemplars (e.g., robin, owl). The new categories produced were appraised by judges for quality and originality. More centrally, a manipulation in stimulus category similarity was made through the categories presented, and, as expected, based on resource requirements, it was found that those presented with more similar categories produced the most original and highest-quality new concepts. In still another study, Osburn and Mumford (2006) provided undergraduates with training in implementation planning. They found that such training contributed to the production of educational plans for leading a new experimental secondary school on higher quality, originality, and elegance.

Other studies have provided evidence pointing to the impact of other processes on the quality, originality, and elegance of peoples' solutions to complex, novel, ill-defined problems. For example, Mumford, Baughman, Supinski, and Maher (1996) have provided evidence for the impact of information gathering; Mumford, Supinski, Threlfall, and Baughman (1996) have provided evidence for the impact of concept selection; Licuanan, Dailey, and Mumford (2007) have provided evidence for the impact of idea generation; Lonergan, Scott, and Mumford (2004) have provided evidence for the impact of idea evaluation; and Marcy and Mumford (2010) have provided evidence for the impact of adaptive solution monitoring. Thus, evidence is available indicating that effective execution of each of these processes contributes to creative problem-solving. Moreover, because these studies employed a number of different tasks, marketing problems, educational leadership problems, and public policy problems, it seems that effective execution of these processes influences creative problem-solving in a number of domains.

Although these experimental studies provided evidence for the impact of effective execution of each specific process in the quality, originality, and elegance of peoples' creative problem-solutions, the question arises as to how well these processes predict above and beyond more basic abilities, such as intelligence and divergent thinking. This issue has been addressed in a study by Vincent, Decker, and Mumford (2002). They measured intelligence, divergent thinking, and expertise, along with appraising more or less effective execution of each of these processes, in a sample of military officers who were asked to solve a set of novel, complex, ill-defined military problems. It was found that divergent thinking, intelligence, and expertise influenced processing capacity, but that skill in executing these creative processes had a unique and stronger, more direct, effect on officers' production of novel, high-quality, and elegant solutions to these problems. Indeed, other studies, for example, Lonergan et al. (2004) and Osburn and Mumford (2006), have shown that these processing skills account for variance in creative problem-solving above and beyond other relevant constructs.

These observations, however, broach a new question: how effective are aggregates of these skills in predicting performance? An initial answer to this question has been provided by Mumford, Supinski, Baughman, Costanza, and Threlfall (1997). They asked 137 undergraduates to solve problems, problems drawn from two different domains (e.g., public policy, business) that judges appraised for quality and originality. Skill in problem definition, information gathering, concept selection, and conceptual combination and reorganization were assessed through a set of measures administered prior to problem-solving. It was found not only that effective execution of each process contributed, contributed uniquely, to creative problem-solving performance in both domains, but that the observed prediction was, in fact, impressive. More specifically, the multiple correlations lay in the mid to low 0.50s for both solution quality and solution originality. In fact, this prediction becomes especially impressive when it is borne in mind the reliability of these quality and originality appraisals lay in the high 0.70s.

Moreover, this prediction is not apparently an artifact of the laboratory. For example, Connelly et al. (2000) assessed effective execution of each of these processes through a modified think-aloud protocol where answers to probe questions intended to elicit processes were appraised by judges for effectiveness of process execution. When those process execution measures were correlated with and regressed on appraisals of leaders performance in resolving critical incidents, multiple correlations in the mid 0.40s to mid 0.50s were again obtained. In another study on eminent achievement in the sciences, Mumford et al. (2005) found that evidence of effective execution of these processes over the course of scientists careers was strongly, positively related ($r = 0.35$) to indices of eminent achievement (e.g., publications, citations) among 499 20th-century scientists. In still another study, Mumford, Antes, Caughron, Connelly, and Beeler (2010) found that effective execution of these processes was strongly related to professional performance across multiple different disciplines (e.g., physical sciences, social sciences). Members of a discipline, moreover, displayed exceptional performance on those processes known to be particularly critical to effective performance in this work domain.

Perhaps the most compelling evidence for the validity of this model has been provided by Friedrich and Mumford (2009). They asked 250 undergraduates to solve a marketing problem calling for creative thought. As participants worked through this problem, prompts were presented to induce application of various creative thinking processes – prompts presented in the sequence suggested by Mumford et al. (1991). When participants encountered a prompt, they might, or might not, be presented with conflicting information as they worked through a given process – this manipulation was based on the proposition that presentation of conflicting information would disrupt process execution. The effectiveness with which participants executed each process was assessed. It was found that disruption of earlier processes, for example, information gathering, disrupted execution of subsequent processing activities, for example, concept selection, even when conflicting information was not presented in concept selection. Thus, in accordance with Mumford et al.'s (1991) model, errors flow through this system of processing activities held to contribute to creative problem-solving. In fact, this finding has been confirmed in another study by Mederios (2016).

Taken as a whole, it appears we now have a model that accurately describes the key thinking processes people need to execute as they seek to solve problems of the sort that call for creative thought. Each process has been shown to make a unique contribution to the production of original, high-quality, and elegant solutions to creative problems. These processes operate on problems drawn from multiple different task domains. Effective execution of these processes is strongly positively related to both incidents of creative problem-solving and "real-world" creative achievement – producing strong, sizable, multiple correlations in the 0.50s. Moreover, this prediction is maintained even when one controls for other variables such as intelligence and divergent thinking. Finally, these processes appear to operate in the fashion one would expect given Mumford et al.'s (1991) model.

Process Execution Strategies

If it is granted that the model by Mumford et al. (1991) provides a viable and valid description of key creative thinking processes, then a new and critical question comes to fore: What strategies should be employed in executing any given process to result in the production of more creative problem solutions? Put somewhat differently, what should people *do* as they attempt to execute these processes and formulate creative problem solutions? This issue has been addressed in a series of experimental studies examining "within process" execution strategies.

In one investigation along these lines, Mumford, Baughman, Threlfall, Supinski, and Costanza (1996) presented undergraduates with a task where they were asked to select their preferred restatements, redefinitions, of a series of problems where 16 redefinitions for each problem were presented. Problem redefinitions reflected high-quality or original redefinitions with respect to goals, procedures, restrictions, or key information. Subsequently, they were asked to solve a marketing problem and a public policy problem calling for creative thought where judges appraised problem solutions for quality and originality. It was found the highest quality and most original problem solutions were produced by people who defined problems with respect to solution procedures and restrictions but not goals or information. Thus, in problem definition, creative people use strategies that allow them to define their approach rather than presume information or seek a particular outcome.

Although it is not surprising that creative people define problems with respect to the procedures or approach to be employed in problem-solving, it may, at first glance, be surprising that they define problems with respect to constraints. This finding, however, has been confirmed in a series of studies by Medeiros (2016) and Medeiros, Partlow, and Mumford (2014). More centrally, the findings obtained in these studies indicated that in problem definition, creative people define problems in terms of constraints in a balanced fashion using neither too few nor too many constraints in problem definition.

Mumford et al. (1996) sought to identify the strategies creative people employ in information gathering. They asked 137 undergraduates to formulate advertising campaigns for a new product, the 3-D holographic television, where judges appraised problem solutions for quality and originality. Before working on this creative problem-solving task, participants were presented with four other creative problems and a series of cards reflecting information bearing on these problems. The cards presented (a) key factorial information, (b) anomalous information, (c) principles, (d) goal-relevant information, (e) information bearing on restrictions, or (f) diverse information. Time spent reading each card was recorded as an index of processing time. It was found that those producing the most original and highest-quality problem solutions were those who spent time gathering information bearing on key facts and anomalies or information inconsistent with these key facts.

In a study of concept selection strategies, Mumford et al. (1996) asked undergraduates to provide solutions to a set of creative problems where judges appraised solutions for quality and originality. Prior to working on this task, however, participants were presented with another set of creative problems, and for each problem, a set of concepts that might be used in problem-solving were presented. Participants were asked to indicate which concepts should be employed in problem-solving. It was found the highest-quality and most original problem solutions were produced by people who preferred to employ concepts, flexible organizing concepts, which might be applied in a number of different ways in problem-solving.

To produce new ideas, new knowledge, or new understandings, of the problem must be formulated. In other words, concepts must be combined and/or reorganized to provide a basis for creative problem-solving. Mumford, Baughman, Maher, Costanza, and Supinski (1997) asked undergraduates to provide solutions to a marketing problem calling for creative thought where judges appraised solution quality and originality. Prior to working on this task, however, participants were asked to work on a series of conceptual combination problems drawn from Mobley, Doares, and Mumford (1992). On these problems, people are presented with three categories (e.g., birds, sporting equipment, vehicles) where each concept is defined by four exemplars (e.g., owls, balls). In the Mumford et al. (1997) study, people, in solving these problems, were asked to label their new category and list additional members of this new category – products evaluated by judges for quality and originality. Manipulations were made to encourage identification of similarity in the features of the categories presented – for example, use metaphors or higher-order structures to identify shared or similar features. It was found that performance on these conceptual combination problems was positively related to prediction of creative problem solutions, especially when participants searched for shared features of the categories. In other studies, Baughman and Mumford (1995) and Scott, Lonergan, and Mumford (2005) have shown it is not only a search for shared and nonshared features of categories that contributes to creative problem-solving, but also elaboration, contextually based elaboration, on emergent features that contribute to creative problem-solving.

Although idea generation has long been studied, strategies employed in effective idea generation have received less attention. In one exception to the rule of thumb, Mumford, Marks, Connelly, Zaccaro, and Johnson (1998) asked a sizable sample of army officers to work on Guilford's (1950) consequences measures where people are asked to generate ideas about the outcomes of unexpected events (e.g., what would happen if gravity was cut in half?). Judges were asked to appraise the ideas generated with respect to whether they reflected thinking about positive consequences, thinking about negative consequences, the time frame over which ideas unfolded, the realism of ideas, the complexity of ideas, and the use of principles (e.g., mass) in generating ideas. These ratings of idea attributes were then correlated with performance on a set of military problems calling for creative thought. It was found that the most creative problem solutions were produced by those who generated ideas using principles. Other work by Finke et al. (1992) indicates that idea generation is especially likely to contribute to creative problem-solutions when people think about principles with respect to application. Thus, idea generation appears to require both abstract and practical generative activity where practical ideas are embedded in a system of abstract features, or principles, emerging from prior conceptual combination efforts.

In creative problem-solving, it is useful to generate multiple ideas using multiple emergent features and multiple potential applications. However, clearly many of the ideas generated will prove of limited value. Thus, idea evaluation is considered critical to creative problem-solving. Lonergan et al. (2004) in a study of idea evaluation, asked undergraduates to formulate marketing campaigns for the 3D holographic television task of Redmond et al. (1993), where judges appraised the advertising campaigns produced for quality, originality, and elegance. In working through this task, participants were asked to assume the role of a senior manager reviewing ideas produced by teams working for them – ideas to be used by participants in formulating their advertising campaigns. What is of note is that the ideas presented were either of known high quality or known high originality given the findings obtained in earlier studies. Moreover, in evaluating these ideas, instructions indicated that ideas should be evaluated with respect to either innovative potential or operating efficiency. The highest quality and most original problem-solutions, were obtained when high-quality ideas were evaluated with respect to innovation potential *and* when highly original ideas were evaluated with respect to operating efficiency. Thus, it appears that creative people do not evaluate ideas in a "go-no-go" framework. Rather, they approach idea evaluation as an active process where they seek to compensate for deficiencies in ideas. In fact, other more recent work by Gibson and Mumford (2013) points not only to the value of compensation in idea evaluation but also deep analysis of potential deficiencies in ideas. Thus, a deep analysis of ideas coupled with compensation for identified deficiencies appear to contribute to creative problem-solving.

After ideas have been selected and refined, people must formulate plans for acting on and implementing their ideas (Latham & Arshoff, 2015). This impact of implementation planning strategies on creative problem-solving has been examined in studies by Marta, Leritz, and Mumford (2005) and Osburn and Mumford (2006). In the Osburn and Mumford (2006) study, undergraduates were provided with self-paced instruction bearing on key strategies contributing to effective planning. These strategies were penetration, or the identification of critical causes in plan execution, and forecasting, or the projection of downstream consequences. Not only was it found that training in these planning skills resulted in production of more creative solutions to an educational leadership problem, developing a curriculum for leading an experimental secondary school, but that this instruction was especially valuable for people with substantial creative ability as evident in scores on a divergent thinking measure. In the Marta et al. (2005) study, undergraduate participants were asked to formulate plans for turning around a failing automotive firm. Plans were appraised for quality, originality, and elegance. Prior to starting work on this task, a team task, all participants completed a measure of planning skills that provided scores measuring identification of key causes, identification of emergent restrictions, identification of downstream consequences, opportunistic implementation, and environmental scanning. It was found that when team leaders evidenced these planning skills, the teams provided turn-around plans of higher quality and great originality.

Clearly, a complex array of planning strategies appears to contribute to creative problem-solving, including strategies seen as backup planning (Giorgini & Mumford, 2013). However, plans must be executed in real time and in the real world, with plans being adapted to changing conditions. Caughron and Mumford (2008) conducted a study bearing on the strategies contributing to effective execution of the adaptive monitoring process. They asked 219 undergraduates to formulate solutions to three educational problems calling for creative thought – solutions appraised by judges for quality, originality, and elegance. Prior to beginning work on these problems, participants were trained in three planning techniques: (a) Gantt charts, (b) case-based planning, and (c) critical path analysis. It is of note that critical path analysis requires identification of potential disruptions of plan execution and identification of markers for monitoring disruptive influences. It was found that training in critical path analysis resulted in production of the most creative problem-solutions – a finding pointing to the value of employing active monitoring strategies, as well as potentially contextually based adaptive strategies in creative problem-solving.

Knowledge

Our foregoing observations are noteworthy because the studies described earlier have provided us with an initial understanding of the key strategies contributing to effective execution of each creative thinking process. Creative people define problems in terms of procedures and restrictions – not goals. They search for information bearing on key facts and anomalies. They select viable concepts for understanding these facts and anomalies. And, in conceptual combination, they search for and identify shared features of these concepts, elaborating on the new features emerging from these concepts to generate ideas – ideas generated by taking principles and applications into account. Deep criticism of the ideas generated and compensation for deficiencies leads to selection of ideas for implementation planning. In implementation planning, people seek to identify key causes shaping successful idea development and project downstream consequences of executing their ideas, thus implementing ideas in an active fashion where idea implementation is monitored and tailored to context. These observations are noteworthy, in part because they also indicate creative thought is a complex, demanding activity. In part, however, they indicate that creative problem-solving requires substantial procedural knowledge – procedural knowledge acquired as a function of expertise (Ericsson, 2009).

By the same token, one must also recognize the strategies used in process execution are executed with respect to declarative, factual, knowledge. Thus, one would expect the value of various strategies for creative thought would vary as a function of the type of the declarative knowledge being employed (Bink & Marsh, 2000). Although many types of knowledge exist (Costanza, Fleishman, & Marshall-Mies, 1999), scholars typically distinguish among three key types of knowledge in discussions of complex, or high-level, cognition (Lord & Shondrick, 2011; Mumford, Todd, Higgs, & McIntosh, 2016): (a) conceptual knowledge (symbolic abstract concepts), (b) associational knowledge (correctionist overt linkages), and (c) case-based knowledge (contextually based abstracts of past experiences).

Hunter, Bedel-Avers, Hunsicker, Mumford, and Ligon (2008) examined how these three types of knowledge are used in creative problem-solving. In this study, undergraduates were asked to formulate plans for leading a new experimental secondary school with judges appraising these plans for quality, originality, and elegance. Prior to starting work on this task, participants were asked to complete a series of training exercises that illustrated the value of employing conceptual, case-based, and associational knowledge in problem-solving. Participants were then asked to apply this instruction in solving three complex, ill-defined problems. This training intervention was intended to prime application of certain knowledge structures. It was found the highest-quality, most original, and most elegant solutions to the educational creative problem were obtained when people employed conceptual and case-based knowledge in problem-solving, or alternatively, when associational knowledge was employed along with case-based or conceptual knowledge. This led Hunter et al. (2008) to conclude that the basis for creative thinking lay in conceptual and experiential knowledge with associations simply proving of value as "value-added" information.

The impact of conceptual knowledge on creative problem-solving has also been demonstrated in a study by Scott et al. (2005). They also asked undergraduates to formulate plans for leading an experimental secondary school, where plans were appraised for quality, originality, and elegance. They presented participants with 8 or 28 concepts, concepts drawn from the extant technical literature, which had been found to influence the performance of educational institutions. It was found the most creative problem solutions emerged when people worked with a larger number of more viable, or effective, concepts in formulating their plans for leading the experimental secondary school.

Other studies by Barrett, Vessey, and Mumford (2011) and Vessey, Barrett, and Mumford (2011) have provided evidence for the use of case-based knowledge in creative problem-solving. Vessey et al. (2011), for example, asked undergraduates to assume the role of an upper-level leader in a marketing firm. They were asked to formulate solutions to three marketing problems calling for creative thought, where problem solutions were appraised by judges for quality, originality, and elegance. Prior to preparing these problem solutions, participants were asked to work through a series of self-paced instructional exercises where they were provided with better strategies for working with case-based knowledge structures. Cases provide information about causes as well as information about resources, restrictions, contingencies, actors, actor affect, and systems (Hammond, 1990). Study participants were instructed to work with causes that had large effects and causes that affected multiple outcomes. It was found that training people to work with various elements of case-based knowledge resulted in more creative problem solutions – solutions of greater quality, originality, and elegance to these complex, novel, ill-defined problems.

These studies are noteworthy because they point to a key fact bearing on creative problem-solving. Creative problem-solving apparently depends strongly on the depth and extensiveness of peoples' knowledge bearing on the types of problems encountered in a given domain. Weisberg (2011) has shown how knowledge, specifically knowledge of constraints and resources, was critical to emergent real-world creative achievement – Frank Lloyd Wright's design of Fallingwater. Other work points to the impact of expertise on other creative achievements such as the development of nuclear weapons (Bird & Sherwin, 2005) and task/time systems of management (Kanigel, 2005). Expertise, however, is not simply a matter of having concepts and experience. It also depends on how the knowledge is structured. Thus, Connelly et al. (2000) found that Army officers produced more creative solutions to military problems as they began to acquire not only more knowledge but also better organize knowledge with respect to the requirements for military leadership.

Our foregoing observations point to the importance, at least the potential importance, of mental models, which are structures for knowledge organization, in creative problem-solving. At a minimum level, mental models may be defined as case-goal linkages (Goldvarg & Johnson-Laird, 2000). Mental models, however, may be more complex, far more complex, entities with models specifying when and how case-goal linkages operate, along with moderators and mediators of these relationships. Such models may take into account not only the expected strength of relationships, but also more complex considerations, such as lags in the effects of actions on a cause vis-à-vis their impact on goal attainment (Rouse & Morris, 1986). It is held that viable mental models arise from deliberative practice (Ericcson, 2002) and self-reflection on the causes of performance (Strange & Mumford, 2005).

In a recent series of studies, Mumford and his colleagues examined the impact of mental models on creative problem-solving (Mumford et al., 2012). In an initial study, they provided some 450 undergraduates with a self-paced training program. This training program taught students how to illustrate their mental models for understanding complex problems in terms of structural equations. Following training, training based on management of a sports team, participants were asked to illustrate their mental models for understanding two creative problems – one involving marking a new high-energy root beer and one involving leading a new experimental secondary school. After illustrating their mental model, participants were asked to provide their solutions to these problems with judges appraising the resulting problem solutions for quality, originality, and elegance. A separate panel of judges appraised objective (e.g., number of causes, number of outcomes, number of moderators, number of mediators) and subjective (e.g., novelty, elegance, workability) attributes of the model provided. When quality, originality, and elegance ratings were regressed on these appraisals of objective and subjective features of mental models, it was found that peoples' mental models accounted for variance in creative problem-solving above and beyond that which might be accounted for by intelligence, divergent thinking, and personality. More centrally, it was found that those who provided creative solutions to these problems evidenced more coherent, systematic, and complete mental models with people whose mental models were based on high importance, critical concepts, being those most likely to produce creative problem solutions. Indeed, the inclusion of a large number of novel attributes in peoples' mental models seemed to undermine creative problem-solving. Thus, creative people structure knowledge in a coherent, viable, fashion, not in an especially unique way.

Mental models, conceptual knowledge, and experiential knowledge, however, unto themselves do not give rise to creative problem solutions. Rather, as noted earlier, how people work with this knowledge is what gives rise to creative problem solutions. By the same token, the types of knowledge people are working with will condition the nature of the strategies that can, or should, be employed in creative problem-solving. This point is underscored in the Scott et al. (2005) study cited earlier. In this study, participants were presented with either concepts or cases reflecting the same concepts. Prompts provided as people worked through this problem were provided to encourage the application of different strategies. It was found that when people worked with conceptual knowledge, feature search and mapping strategies contributed to production of more creative problem solutions. When, however, people worked with cases, analysis of case strengths and weaknesses in context, resulted in production of more creative problem solutions. Moreover, due to the complexity of case-based knowledge, people provided more, not less, creative problem solutions when working with fewer cases.

In another set of studies examining how people work with mental models in creative problem-solving, Barrett et al. (2013), Hester et al. (2012), Mumford et al. (2012), Peterson et al. (2013), and Robledo et al. (2012) examined how various general cross-process strategies influenced the application of mental models in creative problem-solving. Cross-process strategies might prove of value in executing a number of discrete processing operations. For example, focusing on critical causes might prove of value in information gathering, conceptual combination, idea generation, and idea evaluation. Similarly, because the aspects of all processing operations must be appraised, error analysis would seem of value in the execution of virtually all of the creative thinking processes. The findings obtained in these studies, all studies where people were provided with training in strategies for executing certain cross-process skills, specifically causal analysis, error analysis, applications analysis, and constraint analysis, indicated that application of these strategies interacted with mental model viability in such a way as to result in the production of more creative problem solutions. Moreover, application of viable strategies in working through creative problems appeared to contribute to acquisition of better, stronger, mental models, as indicated in a pre-post design, for those tackling relevant problems.

Cross-Process Strategies

These observations, however, bring to fore another new question: What are the cross-process strategies likely to facilitate application of relevant knowledge and execution of necessary processes in creative problem-solving? In fact, Mumford, Todd, Higgs, and Elliott (2018) have argued that multiple cross-process strategies, or skills, will contribute to peoples' creative problem-solving efforts: (a) causal analysis, (b) forecasting, (c) error analysis, (d) constraint analysis, and (e) wisdom. In the following section, we examine some of the evidence bearing on the relevance of these five cross-process skills to the success of peoples' creative problem-solving efforts.

Causal Analysis

In executing the various creative thinking processes, people have available multiple strategies for process execution. Moreover, multiple pieces of knowledge are available that might, or might not, be relevant to the creative problem-solving effort. One implication of these observations is that creative problem-solving will depend on the capacity to identify critical considerations or critical causes. Some support for this argument has been provided in a set of studies by Marcy and Mumford (2007, 2010).

Marcy and Mumford (2010) asked 180 undergraduates to solve six social innovation problems calling for creative thought. Three problems were drawn from the business domain and three problems were drawn from the educational domain where judges appraised problem solutions for quality and originality. Before working on these problems, participants were, or were not, asked to complete a set of self-paced instructional modules. These instructional modules taught people to employ potentially viable strategies for thinking about causes. More specifically, instructional modules encouraged people to think about causes that (a) can be manipulated, (b) influence multiple outcomes, (c) have large effects, (d) can be controlled, (e) have synergistic effects, (f) work together, and (g) have direct effects. Marcy and Mumford (2007) found that use of these causal analysis strategies resulted in production of higher-quality and more original solutions across both the business and educational problems. Thus, causal analysis seems to contribute to creative problem-solving.

In a related study, Marcy and Mumford (2010) asked undergraduates to work on a university leadership simulation exercise with the goal of improving research performance. This novel, complex, ill-defined task, a task calling for creative problem-solving, allowed performance to be assessed with respect to "objective" outcomes of performance on the simulation exercise. It was found not only that causal analysis training contributed to better performance on the simulation exercise, but also that causal analysis skill contributed to better performance regardless of either the cases or mental models that were to be employed in problem-solving. In still another study, Hester et al. (2012) asked some 230 undergraduates to produce advertising campaigns appraised for quality, originality, and elegance. Prior to starting work on this task, participants were provided with training in techniques for illustrating their mental models, as well as training in causal analysis strategies – both through self-paced instructional modules. It was found that training in causal analysis skills contributed not only to the production of higher-quality, more original, and more elegant problem solutions but also to the acquisition of stronger mental models for understanding the problem. Thus, causal analysis skills contribute to knowledge acquisition along with creative problem-solving.

Forecasting

Execution of each creative thinking process (e.g., problem definition or conceptual combination) requires appraisal of the downstream implications of the products produced in process execution for execution of subsequent processes. Put differently, forecasting skill is likely critical to the appraisal of process outputs. Although peoples' skill in forecasting has been questioned (Pant & Starbuck, 1990), it appears that when people have domain expertise and implementation intentions, forecasts are often of adequate accuracy – they are in the range of actual outcomes. Thus, Dailey and Mumford (2006) asked undergraduates to assume the role of a member of a proposal review board and forecast likely outcomes and resource requirements. Actual outcomes and resource requirements, obtained from historic data, were within a fifth of a standard deviation of participants' forecasts when they had relevant expertise and believed recommendations would be acted on. Thus, people can, apparently, forecast.

The issue that arises at this juncture is whether forecasting skill contributes to creative problem-solving. In fact, studies conducted by Byrne, Shipman, and Mumford (2010) and Shipman, Byrne, and Mumford (2010) indicate that forecasting skill does contribute to creative problem-solving. In the Byrne et al. (2010) study, undergraduates were asked to formulate a marketing campaign for a new high-energy root beer, while in the Shipman et al. (2010) study, undergraduates were asked to formulate plans for leading a new experimental secondary school. Both leadership plans and marking campaigns were appraised for quality, originality, and elegance. Prior to preparing their problem solutions, as part of a low-fidelity simulation, participants received emails from a consulting firm "hired" to help them. One email asked them to provide a summary of their forecasted outcomes. These forecasts were appraised by judges with respect to 27 attributes, including forecasting positive outcomes, forecasting negative outcomes, forecasting obstacles, and forecasting restrictions. These ratings of forecasted attributes were factored with four dimensions emerging: (a) forecasting extensiveness, (b) forecasting time frame, (c) forecasting negative outcomes, and (d) forecasting constraints. When quality, originality, and elegance ratings of problem solutions were correlated with and regressed on these four dimensions, it was found that forecasting skill was strongly, positively, related ($r = 0.40$) to evaluations of solution quality, originality, and elegance. Moreover, forecasting skill was more strongly related to creative problem-solving performance than traditional ability measures such as intelligence and divergent thinking.

Error Analysis

Forecasts are of value in creative problem-solving because not only do they allow evaluation of process outputs, they also allow people to anticipate errors in execution of creative thinking processes. In creative thought, however, errors are not always just an issue to be fixed or avoided, errors may also provide a basis for learning in the course of creative work. Other scholars such as Cropley (2006) and Parnes and Noller (1972) have made similar observations. These observations, however, suggest that error analysis and/or error management skill may also contribute to the execution of a number of the processes held to be critical to creative thought.

The impact of errors on creative problem-solving has been examined in a study by Blair and Mumford (2007). They presented undergraduates with ideas, potential problem solutions, for a foundation. Ideas were appraised with respect to certain attributes: norm consistency, risk, ease of understanding, complexity, probability of success, benefits for many, and effort to execute. When asked to choose ideas, participants preferred ideas that were easy to understand, were norm consistent, and provided short-term benefits. These biases, errors, in evaluation of creative ideas, and creative process execution, are not new (Mumford & Gustafson, 1988). However, these errors may have a basis in cognition. Licuanan et al. (2007) asked 181 undergraduates to appraise the originality of marketing campaigns developed by six teams. Manipulations were induced to vary team complexity and encourage active processing. They found that when people processed actively, and in depth, they were more likely to identify truly original ideas. Thus, errors in creative problem-solving are, in part, a function of cognition. And, it therefore seems plausible to argue that error analysis skills might also contribute to creative problem-solving.

Some support for this argument has been provided in a study by Robledo et al. (2012). They asked 275 undergraduates to formulate a plan for leading a new experimental secondary school. Judges were asked to appraise the quality, originality, and elegance of these plans. Prior to preparing these plans, participants were asked to complete two sets of self-paced instructional modules. One set of training modules taught participants how to illustrate their mental models for understanding problems. The other set of training modules provided participants training in certain strategies that might prove useful in error analysis: (a) identify critical errors that might arise in problem-solving, (b) identify "chains" of errors, (c) identify errors under personal control, and (d) think about the impact of errors on different stakeholders. It was found that this error analysis training resulted in the production of higher-quality, more original, and more elegant solutions to this creative problem. Moreover, it was found that error analysis resulted in the acquisition of stronger mental models for understanding the problem. Thus, it appears that error analysis skill, like causal analysis skill and forecasting skill, may also contribute to the execution of multiple processes involved in creative thought and the knowledge needed for creative thought.

Constraint Analysis

Any creative problem solution is inherently constrained. People only have so many resources, so much time, and so much help when executing creative problem solutions. Similarly, execution of any creative process is inherently constrained. Traditionally, constraints have been viewed as a phenomena inhibiting creative problem-solving (Osborn, 1953). Constraints, however, may operate in a far more complex fashion than is typically assumed. For example, some, albeit not all, constraints are subject to manipulation, and qualitative studies (e.g., Morgan, 1992; Wentorf, 1992) indicate that creative people often spend substantial time and effort seeking to control critical, potentially manipulable, constraints. More centrally, work by Stokes (2001, 2005, 2008) suggests that active manipulation of identified constraints during process execution may, in fact, contribute to eminent achievement and creative problem-solving, as well as effective execution of key processes involved in creative thought.

As noted earlier, constraints appear especially important when people seek to define problems. By the same token, it is possible that constraints also influence the effective execution of multiple other creative thinking processes. Thus, Onarheim and Biskjaer (2015) have argued that different constraints may operate at different points in a cycle of creative problem-solving activities, sometimes contributing to and sometimes inhibiting process execution and creative problem-solving. Medeiros (2016) has examined this proposition. She asked 350 undergraduates to assume the role of a new product development manager for a restaurant chain where they were asked to provide a plan to be presented to the executive board to establish a new type of restaurant. The resulting plans were appraised by judges for quality, originality, and elegance. As participants worked on the plan, they received a series of emails from other members of the firm. These emails were intended to prompt the execution of four creative thinking processes: (a) problem definition, (b) conceptual combination, (c) idea generation, and (d) idea evaluation. Written responses to these emails were evaluated by judges to assess the effectiveness of process execution. Constraints were induced through an additional email, summarizing a national restaurant association report specifying three resource constraints, three goal constraints, or three goal and three resource constraints, as well as a no constraint control. It was found that induction of constraints prior to process execution influenced not only problem definition but also conceptual combination, idea generation, and idea evaluation. Although the strongest effects of constraint induction occurred during problem definition, it was found that constraint induction did contribute to production of higher-quality solutions.

These findings, of course, suggest that constraint analysis might represent a noteworthy cross-process creative thinking skill. Some support for this conclusion has been provided in another study by Peterson et al. (2013). In this study, some 200 undergraduates were asked to assume the role of principal of a new, experimental secondary school and prepare a plan for leading the school, with the plans being appraised for quality, originality, and elegance. Prior to starting work on this task, participants were asked to complete a series of self-paced instructional modules where participants were trained to think about (a) resource constraints, (b) system capability constraints, (c) user skill constraints, and (d) goal constraints in solving complex problems. It was found that training in these constraint analysis strategies, especially analysis of resource constraints, resulted in production of higher-quality, more original, and more elegant solutions to this creative problem-solving task.

Wisdom

In discussions of complex problem-solving, many scholars assume constraint analysis skills are subsumed under the rubric of wisdom. Zaccaro, Mumford, Connelly, Marks, and Gilbert (2000) attempted to appraise wisdom on social judgment skills in a sample of 1,818 Army officers ranging in ranks from second lieutenant to full colonel. Two scenarios were presented drawn from the business literature (Shorris, 1981), describing a managerial failure due to failure to attend to conflicting social cues. Officers were asked to provide answers to these questions: (a) Why did this situation occur? (b) What was the central mistake made? and (c) What would you do in this situation? Judges appraised responses to these questions with respect to self-objectivity, self-reflection, systems perception, awareness of solution fit, judgment under uncertainty, and systems commitment – all key attributes of wisdom. Officers were also asked to work through a creative problem-solving task where effective process execution was assessed through a modified think-aloud protocol. It was found that these attributes of wisdom were strongly, positively, related to execution of all of the creative thinking processes. Notably, however, solution fit, a variable implying effective analysis of constraints, produced the strongest predictive relationships.

Although it may seem surprising at first glance to argue creative problem-solving requires wisdom, it should be recognized that wisdom involves analysis of constraints. And, historical analysis of eminent individuals and analyses focusing on creative problem solutions also point to the importance of both wisdom and constraint analysis skills. Thus, Weisberg (2011) found, in his analysis of Frank Lloyd Wright's work in the design of Fallingwater, a careful analysis of relevant constraints. Similarly, Mumford and Van Doorn (2001) in their analysis of one "wise" person's social innovations, those of Benjamin Franklin, found that constraint analysis was critical to many key innovations such as establishment of volunteer fire departments and paper currency.

Discussion

The various studies examined in the present effort do lead to a number of noteworthy conclusions. We now know what people must do to generate creative problem solutions. Specifically, they must define the problem, gather information, select concept or cases, combine and reorganize concepts or cases, generate ideas, evaluate ideas, plan idea implementation, and additionally, monitor idea implementation. The effectiveness with which people execute each of these processes is strongly related to the production of higher-quality, original, and elegant solutions to the kind of novel, complex, ill-defined problems that call for creative thought (Mumford & Gustafson, 2007). Just as important, however, is the finding that effective execution of these processes contributes to creative problems drawn from a number of different domains (Baer, 1998, 2014). Thus, the model by Mumford et al. (1991) does appear to provide a general description of creative thinking processes. The key propositions derived from this model, for example, error flow-through, have been validated (Friedrich & Mumford, 2009). Moreover, effective execution of these processes appears to be a powerful predictor of real-world creative achievement (Connelly et al., 2000).

What should be recognized here, however, is that each and every one of these processes represents a complex mental operation in its own right. One implication of this observation is that there is great value in studies that explicitly define and study the requirements for execution of each particular process. Although some processes, for example, problem definition (Reiter-Palmon & Robinson, 2009) and conceptual combination and reorganization (Ward, Patterson, & Sifonis, 2004), have received some attention in this regard, other processes, for example, information gathering and idea evaluation, warrant more attention. More work, moreover, needs to be done defining what processes are particularly important to creative work in fields where people are presented with tasks of complex, novel, ill-defined problems that call for creative thought (Mumford et al., 2010).

Although work along these lines is valuable, the work examined in the present effort makes clear another point. Some strategies are far more useful than others for effective execution of these processes in incidents of creative problem-solving. For example, creative people do not define problems based on goals, but rather on procedures for problem-solving and constraints. Creative people, in conceptual combination, search for shared features of concepts and elaborate on emergent new features. Although we have begun to attain an understanding of the strategies contributing to effective execution of these creative thinking processes, clearly other strategies might exist that contribute to effective process execution. Moreover, some strategies used in executing some processes may prove more, or less, valuable for creative efforts in one field, or one type of task, than others. More research, far more research, along these lines is necessary if we are to obtain a complete, full understanding of how people go about solving creative problems.

Nonetheless, the findings available at this juncture point to a noteworthy conclusion. Creative problem-solving requires substantial procedural and declarative knowledge and thus real expertise (Ericsson, 1999; Weisberg, 2010). This point is of some importance because it brings to question the merits of studies of creativity where people do not possess the expertise needed for creative problem-solving. Traditionally, however, studies of expertise have not focused on procedural knowledge, or skills, but instead have focused on declarative, factual, knowledge as the key determinant of performance. In fact, in recent years, we have begun to see real progress in our understanding of how declarative knowledge is employed in creative thought. More specifically, it appears that creative problem-solving requires an array of critical concepts, as well as case-based experience in applying these concepts in solving "real-world" problems (Scott et al. 2005; Vessey et al. 2011). Moreover, these concepts and experiences must be organized into viable, well-developed mental models that may be applied to the problem at hand if people are to produce creative problem solutions (Mumford et al., 2012).

In this regard, however, it is important to bear in mind two ambiguities. First, we do not really know how people integrate concepts, case-based knowledge, and mental models in incidents of creative problem-solving. Second, it is clear the strategies people employ in process execution depend on the nature of the knowledge being applied. Aside from the Scott et al. (2005) study, no investigations have sought to establish how declarative and procedural knowledge systems interact in the production of creative problem solutions.

Despite these ambiguities, however, our observations indicate truly exceptional procedural and declarative knowledge, or truly exceptional expertise, is required to develop creative problem-solving skills. Although prior work indicates time, substantial amounts of time, is needed to acquire concepts, experiences, and mental models (the declarative knowledge needed for creative thought) (Ericcson, 2014), the available evidence indicates that procedural expertise (strategies for process execution) can be acquired far more quickly when requisite declarative knowledge is available (Clapham, 1996). Thus, Scott, Leritz, and Mumford (2004) found that creativity training programs, programs that focus on providing people with requisite procedural knowledge or skills, are often effective, reasonably highly effective, in improving peoples' creative problem-solving skills. In this regard, however, it is important to bear in mind a key point emerging from the Scott et al. (2004) meta-analytic study. Those creativity training programs that proved most effective were those that expressly sought to develop or encourage application of the various strategies held to induce effective execution of the eight key creative thinking processes (e.g., problem definition, conceptual combination, and reorganization).

Of course, other procedures than formal instruction might prove of value in enhancing peoples' potential for creative problem-solving. For example, the observations of Ericsson, Krampe, and Tesch-Romer (1993) suggest that deliberative practice might prove of value in the acquisition of the procedural and declarative knowledge needed for creative problem-solving. In fact, if deliberative practice focuses on key strategies and provides feedback bearing on strategy application, it may prove especially valuable. Some support for this proposition is provided in the Marcy and Mumford (2007, 2010) studies cited earlier. Another approach that might prove of value is to encourage self-reflection on the causes of success and failure in creative efforts. Still another approach that might prove of value is systematic attempts to develop the cross-functional skills that have been found to contribute to creative problem-solving – skills such as causal analysis, error analysis, forecasting, constraint analysis, and wisdom.

Our foregoing observations also point to another noteworthy implication of the present effort. More specifically, the findings emerging in the present study point to a number of new measures that might prove of value in assessing peoples' – perhaps job applicants' – creative potential. For example, one might give applicants prior cases where error emerged in problem-solving and ask them to identify critical errors in an attempt to assess error analysis skill. Alternatively, prior cases of creative problem-solving, where case outcomes are known, might be presented and people asked to forecast various outcomes, or obstacles encountered, in an attempt to assess forecasting skill. Another approach, an approach applying to occupations where conceptual combination is important, would be to present discrepant cases, or concepts, and ask people to define the few features of the problem they see emerging. Yet another approach might entail presenting a broad, vague problem statement and asking people to describe the key procedural steps they would take to solve this problem. These examples of potential measures point to a tangible, practical implication of studying creative problem-solving. Our understanding of creative problem-solving may allow the development of a new wave of measures for the assessment of creative potential.

Not only does the study of creative problem-solving processes have some real practical value, it also helps resolve many of the inconsistencies found in studies of creativity as a general phenomenon. For example, Antes and Mumford (2009) found, in contradiction to our stereotypes, that creative people in solving creative problems think about the past – not the future. Of course, thinking about past experience provides people with access to the case-based knowledge that might be used in creative problem-solving. In another illustration of this point, Mumford, Feldman, Hein, and Nagao (2001) found that training teams in creativity irrelevant knowledge, in fact, resulted in improved creative problem-solving. However, this finding may reflect the emergence of a shared mental model among team members – shared mental models that contribute to creative problem-solving. In still another illustration of this point, time pressure has been found, at times, to encourage rather than inhibit creative problem-solving (Baer & Oldham, 2006). In part, however, such effects may arise due to the tendency of people under time pressure to focus on critical causes. And, causal analysis skill has been found to contribute to creative problem-solving (Marcy & Mumford, 2007).

The fact that our understanding of creative problem-solving skills, skills that emerge with the acquisition of expertise, allows anomalous findings to be resolved points to the real value of studying creative problem-solving apart from other phenomena influencing creativity. Creative problem-solving is the fundamental phenomena we must understand when we study creativity and innovation. In recent years, we have made real progress in understanding creative problem-solving. We hope the present effort will provide a background, and impetus, for further research along these lines.

Acknowledgments

We would like to thank Roni Reiter-Palmon, Sam Hunter, Rick Marcy, Tristan McIntosh, and Tyler Mulhearn for their contributions to the present effort. Correspondence may be addressed to Dr. Michael D. Mumford, Department of Psychology, the University of Oklahoma, Norman, Oklahoma 73019 or mmumford@ou.edu.

References

Amabile, T. M. 1996. *Creativity in context: Update to "The Social Psychology of Creativity."* Boulder, CO: Westview Press.

Antes, A. L., & Mumford, M. D. 2009. Effects of time frame on creative thought: Process versus problem-solving effects. *Creativity Research Journal,* 21, 166–182.

Audretsch, D. B. 1995. Innovation, growth and survival. *International Journal of Industrial Organization*, 13, 441–457.

Baas, M., De Dreu, C. K., & Nijstad, B. A. 2008. A meta-analysis of 25 years of mood-creativity research: Hedonic tone, activation, or regulatory focus? *Psychological Bulletin*, 134, 779–806.

Baer, J. 1998. The case for domain specificity of creativity. *Creativity Research Journal*, 11, 173–177.

Baer, J. 2014. *Creativity and divergent thinking: A task-specific approach.* New York, NY: Psychology Press.

Baer, M., & Oldham, G. R. 2006. The curvilinear relation between experienced creative time pressure and creativity: Moderating effects of openness to experience and support for creativity. *Journal of Applied Psychology*, 91, 963–970.

Barrett, J. D., Peterson, D. R., Hester, K. S., Robledo, I. C., Day, E. A., Hougen, D. P., & Mumford, M. D. 2013. Thinking about applications: Effects on mental models and creative problem-solving. *Creativity Research Journal*, 25, 199–212.

Barrett, J. D., Vessey, W. B., & Mumford, M. D. 2011. Getting leaders to think: Effects of training, threat, and pressure on performance. *The Leadership Quarterly*, 22, 729–750.

Batey, M., & Furnham, A. 2006. Creativity, intelligence, and personality: A critical review of the scattered literature. *Genetic, Social, and General Psychology Monographs*, 132, 355–429.

Baughman, W. A., & Mumford, M. D. 1995. Process-analytic models of creative capacities: Operations influencing the combination-and-reorganization process. *Creativity Research Journal*, 8, 37–62.

Besemer, S. P., & O'Quin, K. 1999. Confirming the three-factor creative product analysis matrix model in an American sample. *Creativity Research Journal*, 12, 287–296.

Bink, M. L., & Marsh, R. L. 2000. Cognitive regularities in creative activity. *Review of General Psychology*, 4, 59–78.

Bird, K., & Sherwin, M. J. 2005. *American Prometheus: The triumph and tragedy of J. Robert Oppenheimer.* New York, NY: Vintage Books.

Blair, C. S., & Mumford, M. D. 2007. Errors in idea evaluation: Preference for the unoriginal? *The Journal of Creative Behavior*, 41, 197–222.

Byrne, C. L., Shipman, A. S., & Mumford, M. D. 2010. The effects of forecasting on creative problem-solving: An experimental study. *Creativity Research Journal*, 22, 119–138.

Carmeli, A., Reiter-Palmon, R., & Ziv, E. 2010. Inclusive leadership and employee involvement in creative tasks in the workplace: The mediating role of psychological safety. *Creativity Research Journal*, 22, 250–260.

Caughron, J. J., & Mumford, M. D. 2008. Project planning: The effects of using formal planning techniques on creative problem-solving. *Creativity and Innovation Management*, 17, 204–215.

Cefis, E., & Marsili, O. 2005. A matter of life and death: Innovation and firm survival. *Industrial and Corporate Change*, 14, 1167–1192.

Chandy, R. K., & Tellis, G. J. 1998. Organizing for radical product innovation: The overlooked role of willingness to cannibalize. *Journal of Marketing Research*, 35, 474–487.

Christiaans, H. H. 2002. Creativity as a design criterion. *Communication Research Journal*, 14, 41–54.

Clapham, M. M. 1996. The construct validity of divergent scores in the Structure-of-Intellect Learning Abilities Test. *Educational and Psychological Measurement*, 56, 287–292.

Connelly, M. S., Gilbert, J. A., Zaccaro, S. J., Threlfall, K. V., Marks, M. A., & Mumford, M. D. 2000. Exploring the relationship of leadership skills and knowledge to leader performance. *The Leadership Quarterly*, 11, 65–86.

Costanza, D. P., Fleishman, E. A., & Marshall-Mies, J. C. 1999. Knowledge. In N. G. Peterson, M. D. Mumford, E. C. Bormna, P. R. Jeanneret, & E. A. Fleishman (Eds.), *An occupational information system for the 21st century: The development of O*NET* (pp. 71–90). Washington, DC: American Psychological Association.

Cropley, A. 2006. In praise of convergent thinking. *Creativity Research Journal*, 18, 391–404.

Crouch, T. D. 1992. Why Wilbur and Orville? Some thoughts on the Wright brothers and the process of invention. In R. J. Weber & D. N. Perkins (Eds.), *Inventive minds*. London, England: Oxford University Press.

Dailey, L., & Mumford, M. D. 2006. Evaluative aspects of creative thought: Errors in appraising the implications of new ideas. *Creativity Research Journal*, 18, 385–390.

Dewey, J. 1910. Science as subject-matter and as method. *Science*, 31, 121–127.

Engel, D., & Keilbach, M. 2007. Firm-level implications of early stage venture capital investment—An empirical investigation. *Journal of Empirical Finance*, 14, 150–167.

Ericsson, K. A. 1999. Creative expertise as superior reproducible performance: Innovative and flexible aspects of expert performance. *Psychological Inquiry*, 10, 329–333.

Ericsson, K. A. 2002. Attaining excellence through deliberate practice: Insights form the study of expert performance. In M. Ferrari (Ed.), *The Pursuit of Excellence in Education* (pp. 21–55). Hillsdale, NJ: Erlbaum.

Ericsson, K. A. 2007. An expert-performance perspective of research on medical expertise: The study of clinical performance. *Medical Education*, 41, 1124–1130.

Ericsson, K. A. 2009. *Development of professional expertise: Toward measurement of expert performance and design of optimal learning environments.* Cambridge, England: Cambridge University Press.

Ericsson, K. A. 2014. *The road to excellence: The acquisition of expert performance in the arts and sciences, sports, and games.* New York, NY: Psychology Press.

Ericsson, K. A., Krampe, R. T., & Tesch-Römer, C. 1993. The role of deliberate practice in the acquisition of expert performance. *Psychological Review*, 100, 363–406.

Finke, R. A., Ward, T. B., & Smith, S. M. 1992. *Creative cognition: Theory, research, and applications.* Cambridge, MA: MIT Press.

Friedrich, T. L., & Mumford, M. D. 2009. The effects of conflicting information on creative thought: A source of performance improvements or decrements? *Creativity Research Journal*, 21, 265–281.

Gibson, C., & Mumford, M. D. 2013. Evaluation, criticism, and creativity: Criticism content and effects on creative problem solving. *Psychology of Aesthetics, Creativity, and the Arts*, 7, 314–331.

Giorgini, V., & Mumford, M. D. 2013. Backup plans and creative problem-solving: Effects of causal, error, and resource processing. *The International Journal of Creativity and Problem Solving*, 23, 121–147.

Goldvarg, Y., & Johnson-Laird, P. N. 2000. Illusions in modal reasoning. *Memory & Cognition*, 28, 282–294.

Gordon, R. J. 2016. *The rise and fall of American growth: The US standard of living since the Civil War.* Princeton, NJ: Princeton University Press.

Guilford, J. P. 1950. Creativity. *American Psychologist,* 5, 444–454.

Hammond, K. J. 1990. Case-based planning: A framework for planning from experience. *Cognitive Science,* 14, 385–443.

Hester, K. S., Robledo, I. C., Barrett, J. D., Peterson, D. R., Hougen, D. P., Day, E. A., & Mumford, M. D. 2012. Causal analysis to enhance creative problem-solving: Performance and effects on mental models. *Creativity Research Journal,* 24, 115–133.

Huber, J. C. 1998. Invention and inventivity is a random, Poisson process: A potential guide to analysis of general creativity. *Creativity Research Journal,* 11, 231–241.

Hunter, S. T., Bedell-Avers, K. E., Hunsicker, C. M., Mumford, M. D., & Ligon, G. S. 2008. Applying multiple knowledge structures in creative thought: Effects on idea generation and problem-solving. *Creativity Research Journal,* 20, 137–154.

Kanigel, R. 2005. *The one best way: Frederick Winslow Taylor and the enigma of efficiency.* Cambridge, MA: MIT Press.

Latham, G. P., & Arshoff, A. S. 2015. Planning: A mediator in goal setting theory. In M. Frese & M. D. Mumford (Eds.), *Organization planning: The psychology of performance.* New York, NY: Routledge.

Licuanan, B. F., Dailey, L. R., & Mumford, M. D. 2007. Idea evaluation: Error in evaluating highly original ideas. *The Journal of Creative Behavior,* 41, 1–27.

Lonergan, D. C., Scott, G. M., & Mumford, M. D. 2004. Evaluative aspects of creative thought: Effects of appraisal and revision standards. *Creativity Research Journal,* 16, 231–246.

Lord, R. G., & Shondrick, S. J. 2011. Leadership and knowledge: Symbolic, connectionist, and embodied perspectives. *The Leadership Quarterly,* 22, 207–222.

Majchrzak, A., More, P. H., & Faraj, S. 2012. Transcending knowledge differences in cross-functional teams. *Organization Science,* 23, 951–970.

Marcy, R. T., & Mumford, M. D. 2007. Social innovation: Enhancing creative performance through causal analysis. *Creativity Research Journal,* 19, 123–140.

Marcy, R. T., & Mumford, M. D. 2010. Leader cognition: Improving leader performance through causal analysis. *The Leadership Quarterly,* 21, 1–19.

Marta, S., Leritz, L. E., & Mumford, M. D. 2005. Leadership skills and the group performance: Situational demands, behavioral requirements, and planning. *The Leadership Quarterly,* 16, 97–120.

Medeiros, K. 2016. *Assembling the box: Investigating the role of constraints and creative problem solving,* ProQuest Dissertation and Theses.

Medeiros, K. E., Partlow, P. J., & Mumford, M. D. 2014. Not too much, not too little: The influence of constraints on creative problem solving. *Psychology of Aesthetics, Creativity, and the Arts,* 8, 198–210.

Mobley, M. I., Doares, L. M., & Mumford, M. D. 1992. Process analytic models of creative capacities: Evidence for the combination and reorganization process. *Creativity Research Journal,* 5, 125–155.

Morgan, T. E. 1992. Discovery and invention in polymer chemistry. In R. J. Weber & D. N. Perkins (Eds.), *Inventive minds: Creativity in technology.* Oxford, England: Oxford University Press.

Mumford, M. D., Antes, A. L., Caughron, J. J., Connelly, S., & Beeler, C. 2010. Cross-field differences in creative problem-solving skills: A comparison of health, biological, and social sciences. *Creativity Research Journal,* 22, 14–26.

Mumford, M. D., Baughman, W. A., Maher, M. A., Costanza, D. P., & Supinski, E. P. 1997a. Process-based measures of creative problem-solving skills: IV. Category combination. *Creativity Research Journal*, 10, 59–71.

Mumford, M. D., Baughman, W. A., Supinski, E. P., & Maher, M. A. 1996. Process-based measures of creative problem-solving skills: II. Information encoding. *Creativity Research Journal*, 9, 77–88.

Mumford, M. D., Baughman, W. A., Threlfall, K. V., Supinski, E. P., & Costanza, D. P. 1996. Process-based measures of creative problem-solving skills: I. Problem construction. *Creativity Research Journal*, 9, 63–76.

Mumford, M. D., Bedell-Avers, K. E., & Hunter, S. T. 2008. Planning for innovation: A multi-level perspective. In M. D. Mumford, S. T. Hunter, & K. E. Bedell-Avers (Eds.), *Research in multi-level issues: Vol. VII*. Oxford, England: Elsevier.

Mumford, M. D., Connelly, M. S., Scott, G. M., Espejo, J., Sohl, L. M., Hunter, S. T., & Bedell, K. E. 2005. Career experiences and scientific performance: A study of social, physical, life, and health sciences. *Creativity Research Journal*, 17, 105–129.

Mumford, M. D., Feldman, J. M., Hein, M. B., & Nagao, D. J. 2001. Tradeoffs between ideas and structure: Individuals versus group performance in creative problem solving. *Journal of Creative Behavior*, 35, 1–23.

Mumford, M. D., & Gustafson, S. B. 1988. Creativity syndrome: Integration, application, and innovation. *Psychological Bulletin*, 103, 27–43.

Mumford, M. D., & Gustafson, S. B. 2007. Creative thought: Cognition and problem solving in a dynamic system. *Creativity Research Handbook*, 2, 33–77.

Mumford, M. D., Hester, K. S., Robledo, I. C., Peterson, D. R., Day, E. A., Hougen, D. F., & Barrett, J. D. 2012a. Mental models and creative problem-solving: The relationship of objective and subjective model attributes. *Creativity Research Journal*, 24, 311–330.

Mumford, M. D., Marks, M. A., Connelly, M. S., Zaccaro, S. J., & Johnson, J. F. 1998. Domain-based scoring in divergent-thinking tests: Validation evidence in an occupational sample. *Creativity Research Journal*, 11, 151–163.

Mumford, M. D., Medeiros, K. E., & Partlow, P. J. 2012. Creative thinking: Processes, strategies, and knowledge. *The Journal of Creative Behavior*, 46, 30–47.

Mumford, M. D., Mobley, M. I., Reiter-Palmon, R., Uhlman, C. E., & Doares, L. M. 1991. Process analytic models of creative capacities. *Creativity Research Journal*, 4, 91–122.

Mumford, M. D., Supinski, E. P., Baughman, W. A., Costanza, D. P., & Threlfall, K. V. 1997. Process-based measures of creative problem-solving skills: I. Overall prediction. *Creativity Research Journal*, 10, 77–85.

Mumford, M. D., Supinski, E. P., Threlfall, K. V., & Baughman, W. A. 1996. Process-based measures of creative problem-solving skills: III. Category selection. *Creativity Research Journal*, 9, 395–406.

Mumford, M. D., Todd, E. M., Higgs, C., & Elliott, S. 2018. The skills needed to think creatively: Within-process and cross-process skills. In R. Reiter-Palmon & J. Kaufmann (Eds.), *Individual Creativity in the Workplace* (pp. 129–152). New York: Academic Press.

Mumford, M. D., Todd, E. M., Higgs, C., & McIntosh, T. 2017. Cognitive skills and leadership performance: The nine critical skills. *The Leadership Quarterly*, 28, 24–39.

Mumford, M. D., & Van Doorn, J. R. 2001. The leadership of pragmatism: Reconsidering Franklin in the age of charisma. *The Leadership Quarterly*, 12, 274–309.

Onarheim, B., & Biskjaer, M. M. 2015. Balancing constraints and the sweet spot as coming topics for creativity research. In L. J. Ball (Ed.), *Creativity in design: Understanding, capturing, supporting* (pp. 1–19). Copenhagen, Denmark: DTU.

Osborn, A. F. 1953. *Applied imagination.* New York, NY: Scribner's.

Osburn, H. K., & Mumford, M. D. 2006. Creativity and planning: Training interventions to develop creative problem-solving skills. *Creativity Research Journal*, 18, 173–190.

Osburn, W. J. 1954. Teaching spelling by teaching syllables and root words. *The Elementary School Journal*, 55, 32–41.

Pant, P. N., & Starbuck, W. H. 1990. Innocents in the forest: Forecasting and research methods. *Journal of Management*, 16, 433–460.

Parnes, S. J., & Noller, R. B. 1972. Applied creativity: The creative studies project. *The Journal of Creative Behavior*, 6, 164–186.

Peterson, D. R., Barrett, J. D., Hester, K. S., Robledo, I. C., Hougen, D. F., Day, E. A., & Mumford, M. D. 2013. Teaching people to manage constraints: Effects on creative problem-solving. *Creativity Research Journal*, 25, 335–347.

Redmond, M. R., Mumford, M. D., & Teach, R. 1993. Putting creativity to work: Effects of leader behavior on subordinate creativity. *Organizational Behavior and Human Decision Processes*, 55, 120–151.

Reiter-Palmon, R., & Robinson, E. J. 2009. Problem identification and construction: What do we know, what is the future? *Psychology of Aesthetics, Creativity, and the Arts*, 3, 43–47.

Robledo, I. C., Hester, K. S., Peterson, D. R., Barrett, J. D., Day, E. A., Hougen, D. P., & Mumford, M. D. 2012. Errors and understanding: The effects of error-management training on creative problem-solving. *Creativity Research Journal*, 24, 220–234.

Rouse, W. B., & Morris, N. M. 1986. On looking into the black box: Prospects and limits in the search for mental models. *Psychological Bulletin*, 100, 349–363.

Scott, G., Leritz, L. E., & Mumford, M. D. 2004. Types of creativity training: Approaches and their effectiveness. *The Journal of Creative Behavior*, 38, 149–179.

Scott, G. M., Lonergan, D. C., & Mumford, M. D. 2005. Conceptual combination: Alternative knowledge structures, alternative heuristics. *Creativity Research Journal*, 17, 79–98.

Shipman, A. S., Byrne, C. L., & Mumford, M. D. 2010. Leader vision formation and forecasting: The effects of forecasting extent, resources, and timeframe. *The Leadership Quarterly*, 21, 439–456.

Shorris, E. 1981. *The oppressed middle: Politics of middle management: Scenes from corporate life.* New York, NY: Anchor Press/Doubleday.

Simonton, D. K. 1997. Creative productivity: A predictive and explanatory model of career trajectories and landmarks. *Psychological Review*, 104, 66–89.

Sternberg, R. 2011. The purpose of college education: Producing a new generation of positive leaders. In S. E. Murphy & R. J. Reichard (Eds.), *Early development and leadership: Building the next generation of leaders* (pp. 293–308). New York, NY: Psychology Press/Routledge.

Sternberg, R. J., & O'Hara, L. A. 1999. Creativity and intelligence. In R. J. Sternberg (Ed.), *Handbook of creativity* (pp. 297–312). Cambridge, England: Cambridge University Press.

Stokes, P. D. 2001. Variability, constraints, and creativity: Shedding light on Claude Monet. *American Psychologist*, 56, 355–359.

Stokes, P. D. 2005. *Creativity from constraints: The psychology of breakthrough.* Berlin, Germany: Springer.

Stokes, P. D. 2008. Creativity from constraints: What can we learn from Motherwell? from Modrian? from Klee? *The Journal of Creative Behavior,* 42, 223–236.

Strange, J. M., & Mumford, M. D. 2005. The origins of vision: Effects of reflection, models, and analysis. *The Leadership Quarterly,* 16, 121–148.

Tierney, P., & Farmer, S. M. 2002. Creative self-efficacy: Its potential antecedents and relationship to creative performance. *Academy of Management Journal,* 45, 1137–1148.

Vessey, W. B., Barrett, J., & Mumford, M. D. 2011. Leader cognition under threat: "Just the Facts." *The Leadership Quarterly,* 22, 710–728.

Vincent, A. S., Decker, B. P., & Mumford, M. D. 2002. Divergent thinking, intelligence, and expertise: A test of alternative models. *Creativity Research Journal,* 14, 163–178.

Wallas, G. 1926. *The art of thought.* New York, NY: Harcourt Brace.

Ward, T. B., Patterson, M. J., & Sifonis, C. M. 2004. The role of specificity and abstraction in creative idea generation. *Creativity Research Journal,* 16, 1–9.

Weisberg, R. 2010. The study of creativity: From genius to cognitive science. *International Journal of Cultural Policy,* 16, 235–253.

Weisberg, R. W. 2011. Frank Lloyd Wright's Fallingwater: A case study in inside-the-box creativity. *Creativity Research Journal,* 23, 296–312.

Weisberg, R. W. 2015. Toward an integrated theory of insight in problem solving. *Thinking and Reasoning,* 21, 5–39.

Wentorf, R. H. 1992. The synthesis of diamonds. *Inventive minds: Creativity in Technology,* 154–165.

Zaccaro, S. J., Mumford, M. D., Connelly, M. S., Marks, M. A., & Gilbert, J. A. 2000. Assessment of leader problem-solving capabilities. *The Leadership Quarterly,* 11, 37–64.

4

ABILITIES THAT CONTRIBUTE TO CREATIVITY AND INNOVATION AT WORK

Mark A. Runco

Very likely, creative and innovative performances at work are both overdetermined. That simply means that there are various influences and determinants. This idea of overdetermination fits nicely with theories of creativity that emphasize creativity as a complex or syndrome (MacKinnon, 1965; Mumford & Gustafson, 1988). After all, if creativity is multifaceted, performances that depend on it (which include innovation) are probably also complicated. The creative complex is generally described as including several different abilities, creative attitudes, motivation (both intrinsic and extrinsic), personality traits, and metacognition. A realistic view also recognizes that context plays a role, in which case opportunity and reinforcement need to be included in a description of the creativity complex and in any plan to support innovation.

This chapter focuses on the abilities that contribute to creative and innovative performances at work. It uses the idea of a creativity complex and touches on various abilities and their relationships with motivation, metacognition, and context. The starting point is a brief discussion of how creativity and innovation are related to one another. There is also a need to offer a brief discussion of problem-solving, for much of the research defines creativity and innovation at work as a kind of problem-solving. As is the case of all chapters in this volume, the overarching concern throughout this chapter follows from the need to improve creative problem-solving in firms. Several theories, summarized in the next section, suggest that when creative problem-solving is improved, innovation will follow.

Creativity and Innovation

There are several views of how creativity and innovation are related to one another. One of them follows from *the standard definition of creativity* (Runco & Jaeger, 2012). The standard definition focuses on two attributes or requirements: originality and effectiveness. All creative things, be they ideas, patents, designs, services, or products of any sort, must, in this view, be both original and effective. Importantly, the labels may vary. Originality is often called novelty, for example, and is implicit in the notion that creative things are new or unconventional. Effectiveness is varied as well, sometimes being labeled fit, relevance, or appropriateness. When creativity is in fact a kind of problem-solving, effectiveness is apparent when the solution does in fact solve the problem. It is an effective solution but also a new and original one.

There are extensions and concerns about the standard definition. Indeed, a slew of fairly recent papers has suggested alternatives and limitations to the standard definition (Acar et al., 2017; Corazza, 2016; Kharkhurin, 2012; Simonton, 2012; Weisberg, 2015). Kharkhurin questioned the cross-cultural validity of the standard definition and suggested that adding *authenticity* and aesthetic *appeal* to the definition would improve its validity. These are good suggestions, but authenticity and aesthetic appeal are both notoriously difficult to operationalize, and thus it is more difficult to be objective about them and any definition that uses them. Simonton (2012) cited the procedures of the U.S. Patent and Trademark Office and suggested that *nonobvious* (or simply *surprise*) be considered. His logic was compelling, and apparently the U.S. Patent and Trademark Office is able to use nonobvious in a reliable fashion. As an aside, Bruner (1979) had previously tied surprise specifically to effectiveness in his view of creativity.

One description of the relationship of creativity and innovation relies on the two-part standard definition, originality and effectiveness. In this view, creative things are highly original, and in some way effective, while innovation is highly effective but must have some originality. The difference is in the ratio of originality (which must be high in creativity but just somehow present in innovation) to effectiveness (which must be high for innovation, and in some way present for creativity). Certainly, creativity and innovation both require some effectiveness. Without effectiveness, even crazy ideas that are outstandingly original but not in any way realistic or effective would be creative, and they are not. They are simply original or crazy. And without originality, ideas that are effective but not new would be creative, but they are not. They are obvious, old, cliche.

A related view of creativity and innovation takes these ideas a step further and describes innovation as an adaptation of something that already existed. In this view, the hybrid automobile is an innovation but not really creative because the (internal combustion) car and the electric battery both existed long before hybrid cars. The hybrid did not bring anything new into existence but instead adapted something (or two things) such that there was an effective product.

A third view of the relationship of creativity and innovation involves stages. There is in fact a very widely cited theory of creativity that relies on stages, namely that of Wallas (1926). This view is nearly 100 years old, yet newer theories of the creative process still draw heavily from it (see collection in Runco & Chand, 1994). Wallas' original conception of the creative process started with preparation, then moved to incubation, illumination, and verification. Newer conceptions of the creative process often use different labels, but these same four stages are still usually included (Basadur, 1994; Runco, 2003). Preparation, for example, is now usually viewed as a kind of problem finding, problem identification, or problem formulation. Most important for the present purposes is that the stage conception of the creative process has been extended so that it covers innovation. The extension involves a fifth stage, which is usually labeled *implementation*. In that light, a person can invest in the first four stages and have a creative idea, but to qualify as an innovation, the idea must somehow be implemented. This would seem to fit nicely with the assumption that innovation is always practical. This stage view of the relationship of creativity and innovation is actually not all that far from the first view, summarized earlier. After all, they both emphasize the practicality of innovation. Note also the implications of a stage view: time is a precious resource and must be provided so individuals and teams can move through all stages and eventually get to the implementation stage.

Problem-solving can also be used to distinguish creativity from innovation. Simplifying some, innovations may always solve a problem. That is how they are effective, or in what sense they are effective. Creativity, alternately, may not always require problem-solving. To see this last point, consider the concept previously mentioned, namely, problem *finding*. A great deal of research suggests that problem finding is distinct from problem-solving (Csikszentmihalyi, 2003; Mumford, 1998; Reiter-Palmon, Mumford, O'Connor Boes, & Runco, 1997; Runco, 1998). It seems that some of the time the former is actually more important than the latter for creativity. Getzels (1975) went as far as to suggest that a creative solution depends on a creative problem. Psychometric research confirms that some people are good at one but not necessarily good at the other (Okuda et al., 1991). This is all relevant in that it would probably not be very practical to simply identify a problem without solving it. It might be creative to do so, but it would not be very innovative, given the lack of practicality.

These last few paragraphs have been a bit theoretical, but they have provided some of the concepts that can be used later. This discussion does seem to indicate that creativity is necessary, but perhaps not sufficient, for innovation. Creativity and innovation are related but not one and the same. With that in mind, it is now possible to turn to abilities that contribute to creativity and innovation.

The first ability to be explored here involves the capacity to think divergently. That is the starting point, because so much research has been directed at *divergent thinking* – and for good reason. That is comprehensive theory to suggest that divergent thinking plays a role in creativity as well as a large body of empirical research testing the key features of the theory. Interestingly, a review of the research on divergent thinking will take us to the role of intelligence and expertise as related prerequisites for creativity and innovation.

Divergent Thinking Ability

Divergent thinking (DT) is the process by which ideation moves in varied and sometimes new directions. It can be contrasted with the *convergent thinking* (CT) that is involved when ideation moves toward conventional and rote ideas instead of new and varied ideas.

The idea of DT goes back nearly 100 years, though the label was coined by Guilford in the 1950s (see Guilford, 1968; Runco & Acar, 1991). Guilford (1950) devoted his 1949 Presidential Address to the American Psychological Association to creativity, even though the topic was at that time largely ignored in the sciences. Before Guilford – and too often still – creativity is either associated solely with the arts or thought to be too subjective for scientific study. Guilford's address elicited quite a bit of attention, especially because he described creativity as a natural resource, an idea that has been extended in more recent descriptions of creativity as a form of human capital (Rubenson & Runco, 1992, 1995; Sternberg & Lubart, 1995; Walberg & Stariha, 1992). Also, Guilford offered a cogent theory of thinking that included suggested methods for the objective measurement of creative potential. Much of his work was intended to describe all of cognition, which is why the final version of his *Structure of Intellect model* contained 180 different kinds of cognition (Guilford, 1984). What really caught on was the distinction between DT and CT. Guilford actually preferred the terms *divergent* and *convergent production*. These labels were used because they indicated where each fit into the Structure of Intellect (SOI) model. They do make sense in that both are forms of cognition that lead to the production of ideas, solutions, options, and so on, but for years now people have preferred the term *divergent thinking* over *divergent production*.

Although the idea of DT has been used and extended since Guilford, the SOI model, with all 180 cells, did not fare well. In particular, Guilford's statistical methods (e.g., subjective rotation in factor analysis) were justifiably criticized (e.g., Undheim & Horn, 1977). Guilford's lasting contribution is not the SOI but is the concept of DT. Many of the tests he developed (e.g., Consequences, Uses, Titles) are still used today. A number of these are described later, along with newer tests of DT. Special attention is given to assessments that work well in organizations.

Recent theoretical advances have been made with theories of DT. Acar and Runco (2014; 2015), for example, voiced a concern about measures of DT too often actually precluding DT. They described how individuals could find ideas and thus perform well on measures of DT using cognitive abilities that do not actually involve divergence (e.g., linear associative processes). They reported several investigations that attempted to operationalize *literal divergent thinking*, where divergence is involved. Interestingly, this line of thought led to the concept of *cognitive hyperspace*, the idea being that individuals may think divergently by first following one dimension of thought, and then shifting such that they follow a perpendicular dimension of thought. Human cognition is such that individuals can do this indefinitely, going into *n*-dimensions and thus cognitive hyperspace. It is quite likely that individuals who do indeed tap such varied dimensions will find original ideas.

The usual definitions of DT and CT imply that the two are opposites, but in actuality there may be a continuum of thought with DT and CT at the extremes (Eysenck, 2003). The even more practical idea, which is quite useful for organizations that want to hire or encourage creative and innovative thinking, is that DT and CT work together. Think back on the definition of creativity requiring originality and effectiveness. The former may result from DT, but very likely the latter involves some CT. For this reason, some of the important ways of defining and measuring CT are explored later in this chapter.

A huge amount of research has examined DT since Guilford (1968) developed the SOI model and developed his tests of DT. Some of this research uses different labels, and some has identified the ideal conditions for DT and the more reliable ways to assess it. The ideal conditions and the more reliable assessments are also briefly summarized later in this chapter, but first something more should be said about exactly what information is provided by tests of DT.

DT is an important kind of ideation and usually leads to a number of varied ideas. These ideas are taken to be indicative of several different things. Most of the research on DT suggests that there are three important characteristics. First is simply the number of ideas produced when thinking divergently. This is referred to as *ideational fluency*. If a practitioner offers a workshop to a business, for example, and uses the SWOT test of DT to practice problem-solving, he or she might ask those employees to "list as many threats to this business as you can think of." That, of course, is the "T" in SWOT. The other tasks (strengths, weaknesses, and opportunities) could also be used as exercises or even assessments (Ames & Runco, 2005), and it would be good to give all four tasks to any examinees. Occasionally only one task is given when testing people, but one task is not reliable. Tests are more reliable when there is more information and the sample of behaviors is larger, which is why four tasks is better than one. Note that "list as many threats as you can" is open ended; there is no one correct idea. If there was one correct or even highly conventional idea, it would be a CT task instead of a DT task. To be complete, an example of a CT task can be given: "What year was this company founded" or "who is the current president of this company" are examples. There is likely to be only one correct answer to those questions, so the thinking that is used to find the answer is convergent rather than divergent. Given that "threats" is open ended, employees can list quite a few ideas. Those are counted and, in order to provide feedback on the DT, this count is used as the fluency score.

Ideational fluency is quite important. In fact, when a person or group gives a large number of ideas, it is likely that some of the ideas will be original. This is why the well-known brainstorming methods emphasize "quantity over quality." That method assumes that when there is a large number of ideas, some of them will be high-quality ideas. It also assumes that if people focus on quantity and deemphasize the quality of the ideas, at least temporarily, they are more likely to explore diverse directions and options and thus find truly creative ideas. Brainstorming is explicit about this: groups are to give as many ideas as possible (quantity over quality), to postpone judgment, and to try to hitchhike ideas (use each other's ideas to stimulate one's own thinking, also known as piggybacking). There are concerns about the brainstorming method (see Rickards, 1999; Richards & DeCock, 2003), including the tendency of many people toward *social loafing* (not investing much effort when others are there to help) and *production loss* (being less fluent when in groups than when alone), and there are implications of this line of research for the creative problem-solving at work. Work settings are usually social settings; organizations generally have a number of employees, and some of the findings about brainstorming suggest that originality drops when one person is required to share ideas with others.

This is probably the most true when the idea is highly original, because then it would be especially difficult to predict if other people would appreciate the idea or not. There is always a bit of risk involved with creative thinking, given that it depends on originality, and by definition, *originality* means that other people may not see the value of new ideas and solutions. This is an example of how creative abilities, such as DT, depend on extra-cognitive influences, such as *risk tolerance*. It certainly should be possible for organizations to create expectations and settings that communicate the idea that new ideas are appreciated and, probably even more important, that risk-taking when solving problems is desirable.

In the context of DT, originality is operationalized in terms of the statistical infrequency of ideas. In other words, original ideas are those that few people find or produce when solving open-ended problems. If a large number of employees in the earlier situation gave "being bought out by a competitor" when asked to list threats, that would not be a highly original idea. It would be a common or popular idea. But if only one person thought of "sinkholes" or "sunspots" when asked about threats, those would be statistically infrequent (i.e., unique) and thus original ideas. These two ideas may sound impractical, but keep in mind that this index from DT tasks is about originality, not creativity. Creativity does require originality and effectiveness, but to be operational, DT methods look at originality and assume that, since it is a prerequisite for creativity, it is indicative of the potential for actual creative problem-solving. That is the best way to view DT, as an indication of the potential for creativity. Note also the wording used, "thought of sinkholes or sunspots." There is sometimes a difference between what a person thinks and what the individual shares with others or acts on.

There are ways to ensure that employees and other members of an organization do share what they think of, which is helpful if the interest is in fact in original problem-solving. Virtual brainstorming has potential in this regard, for example, for when people work together on computer but are not face to face, they may not inhibit each other's thinking, and sharing and intellectual risk-taking may be more likely (Nemiro, 2002). Managers may also ensure that employees know that they place a value on original ideas, for this signals that originality is a good thing and not something to hide. Managers can minimize perceived risks associated with creative problem-solving, and originality is likely to increase (Rubenson & Runco, 1995).

One last point about originality: It may seem that many ideas, like "sinkholes" and "sunspots," are not all that practical (and lacking in effectiveness and the potential for implementation), but there are methods that bring effectiveness back into the problem-solving process, after diverse ideas are produced. This is exactly why brainstorming merely postpones judgment. The theory is that judgment is important, especially for ensuring that ideas are effective and have the potential for practical implementation, but at first it may be best to throw a wide net and allow broad DT. Later, after original ideas have been pooled, the team can go back and evaluate and judge the ideas, selecting those that are both original and effective.

A third characteristic of DT is *ideational flexibility*. This is apparent in ideas that are varied and diverse. If an individual or group is asked to list strengths of a business and offers, "this organizations has good owners, good managers, good supervisors, good support staff, and good employees," there is very little variety. Each of those ideas represents one conceptual category (i.e., people in organizations). If that individual or group instead offered "this organizations has good owners, plenty of material resources, offices with plenty of space and good interior design, services and products that are timely and that can change with the times," there is more variety. That is because the thinking leading to those varied ideas is flexible and uses different conceptual categories. Flexibility is an important characteristic of DT, in part because it may lead to originality, but also because it is associated with adaptive thinking that can change as needed (when tasks or demands change).

The SWOT task has been cited in the examples so far in this chapter, but a large amount of research has compared different kinds of tasks. Another way of stating this is that there are many ways to tap and exercise DT, and significant differences among them. One concern with the SWOT was that it was too realistic; respondents could draw from their own experience and thus may not actually use their imaginations and capacity for original problem-solving. It they are merely pulling ideas from long-term memory, there is no real creativity. No new ideas are being created. Instead, old ones are remembered. It appears that the more realistic the DT task, the more likely people are to look to long-term memory and experience rather than creating anew. Some tasks are better than others for DT and especially for originality. Various DT tests are described in some detail in the Organizational Applications section of this chapter.

All DT tests allow various ideas to be explored. They vary in terms of exactly how much structure is imposed. Another way of describing the open nature of DT tasks is that they are *ill defined*. This term is often used in the research on problem-solving and is important because in the natural environment many problems are indeed ill defined. This similarity between (a) ideation as captured by DT research and (b) the problem-solving that is involved when solving ill-defined problems in the natural environment may explain why DT tests have respective predictive validity, as well as fairly good reliability. In one investigation, Runco (1986) found that a combination of the fluency, originality, and flexibility measures produced a predictive correlation coefficient of 0.55. Later, Runco, Millar, Acar, and Cramond (2011) used the Torrance Tests of Creative Thinking and data from Torrance's own longitudinal study, initiated in the late 1950s, and found significant predictive correlation coefficients (approximately 0.30) over a 50-year span. To interpret this impressive result, the criteria used must be recognized. They included measures of both personal and professional creative achievement. Interestingly, the former seemed to be more strongly related to DT than the latter. Plucker (1999) had also reported quite reasonable predictive validities with varied criteria, and most predictive validity studies include criteria that assume a kind of creativity that is socially recognized and not entirely personal. Plucker, Runco, and Lim (2006) reasoned that DT is a test of ideation, so they developed a self-report measure that focused on ideas produced in real-world settings, and when it was as a criterion measure, they found quite reasonable predictive validity coefficients.

In what is probably the predictive validity with the most relevance to organizations, Vincent, Decker, and Mumford (2002) examined DT, along with expertise and general intelligence as predictors of leadership. They chose the Consequences test of DT, which makes sense because leaders often need to think about the consequences of decisions and policies. Vincent et al. also used a method where DT scores are based on *ideational pools* rather than on single ideas. This is a cost-efficient method of scoring, because the rating of ideas is based on any single leader's total output of ideas – all ideas combined or listed so they can all be judged at once – so only one ideational product (the pool) is scored instead of scoring each single idea, one at a time. This method of ideational pools also makes sense because it provides raters with all available information. Recall the psychometric principle that was emphasized earlier: assessments tend to be the most accurate when a large sample of information is available. This is analogous to making a decision about, say, buying a car based either on what one person recommends (not much information) or on a large report or survey, where thousands of car owners have provided feedback. More information is better, which is part of the rationale for ideational pools. Vincent et al. estimated general intelligence from the verbal reasoning scale of the Employee Aptitudes Survey. They estimated expertise using a method that had proven to be useful in previous research on leadership, namely, from performance on classification and definition of 70 task statements reflecting leadership activities. Results indicated that the DT accurately predicted problem-solving performances of the leaders above and beyond that explained by expertise and intelligence. Expertise and intelligence were also related to leadership, but DT explained variance that they did not.

Thus, there is support for the predictive validity of DT tests, in various populations, including leaders. Recall also the research cited earlier that used the SWOT DT test with entrepreneurs (Ames & Runco, 2005). Before turning from DT and reviewing other relevant abilities, one last strength of the DT approach to creative problem-solving should be noted, namely, that DT is compatible with other views of the creative process. Wallach and Kogan (1965), for example, cited associative theory to justify the use of DT tests. They felt that examinees probably concatenated ideas together, one after another, as they were thinking divergently. There are, then, several theories of creativity that point to the value of DT, and research supporting the predictive validity of DT. But other abilities are relevant to organizational problem-solving and innovation.

Intelligence, Evaluative Skill, and Forecasting

The research just summarized by Vincent et al. (2002) is a reminder that DT and creative ability do not work alone. They work with other abilities when people solve problems and when leaders support innovation. There is research that specifically examines how DT and creativity are related to creative problem-solving, innovation, leadership, and other organizational concerns.

Guilford (1968) can again be cited, for he investigated how general intelligence was related to creativity. He referred to *triangular theory* and showed that when DT is graphed along with some measure of traditional intelligence such that the former is on the Y-axis and the latter is on the X-axis, a triangle of data is likely to appear (with the vertex on the left and the base of the triangle on the right). This is especially easy to picture if you think about the four quadrants of the same graph, with data points in the lower left quadrant representing anyone who has low scores on both some estimate of DT and some estimate of traditional intelligence; data points in the lower right representing anyone who had high score on traditional intelligence but low scores on creative problem-solving; data points in the upper right representing anyone with high scores on both intelligence and creativity; and data points in the upper left representing anyone with low scores on intelligence but high scores on creativity. But wait – there is no one in that last quadrant. It is empty. That is because it is very difficult to be highly creative with only a low level of traditional intelligence. The best explanation for such a triangle, which suggests that intelligence is necessary but not sufficient for creativity, is that intelligence is a kind of information processing efficiency, and without that, it is impossible to produce one's own (original) ideas. Sometimes this view is called the *threshold theory* with that in mind, the implication being that some minimum threshold of intelligence is necessary (but not sufficient) for creativity (Jauk et al., 2013; Runco & Albert, 1986).

The threshold view does not really do a good job at explaining exactly how creativity works with intelligence. It does not offer a mechanism that allows any sort of creativity-intelligence relationship. It was proposed some time ago, and like many theories of that period, those early perspectives on the creativity and intelligence relationship depended on the tests that existed at that time. As is the case in many areas, the relationship of the constructs depends a great deal on how they are defined and measured. In the 1980s, the possibility did arise that both creativity and intelligence both depend on information processing efficiency, so there was one process that was involved in both creativity and intelligence. That was, however, mere hypothesis, and newer research has attempted to develop a functional explanation, which describes a mechanism, for the interplay. It should also be noted that there is research that suggests that the threshold view does not always hold up. It depends on the measures used for both creativity and intelligence (Runco & Albert, 1986), and this is not a good sign for a valid theory.

There are theories that define creativity such that it does work along with intelligence. Gardner's (1983) theory of multiple intelligences goes well beyond the IQ, for example, and it allows creative work. It does not give any credibility to the concept of general intelligence but instead raises the possibility of exceptional performance within domains. The IQ may tap verbal and mathematical domains, but other expressions of intelligence, equally valid, may involve spatial, musical, bodily-kinesthetic, naturalistic, or inter- or intrapersonal abilities. A person can be creative in one but not the other domains, or in some combination of domains. In this view, creativity operates within domains and tested general intelligence (IQ) is actually misleading. Admittedly, that is not really using any creativity-intelligence interplay but instead, by replacing general intelligence with domain-specifics, it circumvents the need for such a mechanism.

Another perspective focuses on knowledge. True, IQ tests can be viewed as assessments of how much knowledge the person has, and indirectly of how well he or she selects and retains knowledge, but there are newer conceptions of knowledge that allow for realistic interactions with creative ability. One of these was outlined by Baughman and Mumford (1995). They described creative ability as requiring the combination and reorganization of knowledge structures. After careful empirical work, they concluded that "available evidence indicates that the combination and reorganization of extant knowledge structures plays an important role in the generation of new ideas" (p. 37). Another helpful take on knowledge distinguishes between procedural and conceptual (or declarative) knowledge (Runco & Chand, 1995). The latter is essentially factual. It can be declared; hence, it is "declarative" knowledge. The former is knowledge that informs about how to get something done. This is in turn related to strategies and tactics, which are certainly useful for creative problem-solving (Runco, in press).

The overarching message in this brief review of intelligence is that it may involve the depth as well as the organization of knowledge, but knowledge may be domain specific or involve facts and concepts, or procedures. There is a huge literature on intelligence – much larger than what was presented here, so far – but most of it is not relevant to creative problem-solving or to organizations. The interest here is in the theories that allow for an interplay with creative abilities and may have relevance to organizations. Newer conceptions of intelligence seem to allow for a more realistic interplay where creative ability does in fact benefit from intelligence. They often do not use the label "intelligence" but are in the same direction; namely, they involve information, knowledge, and CT. Two examples of this kind of work focus not on intelligence, per se, but on *evaluative abilities* and *forecasting*. Like tested intelligence, these tend to be more convergent than divergent, but unlike tested intelligence, they are easily tied, in a functional way, to many kinds of creative problem-solving, including that which occurs in organizations.

Most models that attempt to capture the entire creative process include an evaluative component (see Figure 2, from Runco & Chand, 1995, for example), and evaluative skills have been operationalized in a handful of investigations and have been found to relate to DT and idea generation. Runco (1989; Runco & Basadur, 1993; Runco & Vega, 1990) used a method that started by administering DT tasks to various groups. At first the concerns were educational, and one hypothesis was that evaluative abilities might be used indiscriminately or to excess, leading to overly critical judgments of ideas and solutions, the result being a loss of originality. These ideas were taken to explain the well-known fourth-grade slump in creativity (Charles & Runco, 2000; Torrance, 1968). To test this hypothesis, highly original and highly unoriginal (conventional) ideas were identified in the DT of schoolchildren and placed on a rating form. This was given to the children who had given the ideas, after some time had passed (so they would not recognize their own ideas), and to other students, parents, and teachers. These groups were asked to rate the originality of the ideas. Results indicated that all groups were poor at recognizing original ideas as original. The ideas that were statistically original (unique or at least highly unusual) were not rated as original. The highest accuracy level when this methodology was used was 50%, meaning that at most half of the truly original ideas were recognized as original. One conclusion was that people are not very good at evaluating the originality of ideas. That would be easy to believe because original ideas are new and untested. They may represent a new line of thought or a shift in perspective that is surprising and difficult to judge using previous knowledge.

Mumford and his colleagues took another approach to evaluative skills. Lonergan, Scott, and Mumford (2004), for example, broke evaluative ability down into subskills, including forecasting, appraisal, and revision. They felt that each of these was dependent on the standards used and that those standards would vary from subskill to subskill. To test this, Dailey and Mumford asked a group of undergraduates to first appraise and then revise the ideas involved in advertising campaigns. Manipulations varied the standards that were to be used in the evaluations. Analyses indicated that the higher-quality advertising campaigns were indeed related to certain experimental conditions and standards. Lonergan, Scott, and Mumford concluded that "evaluation may serve to remediate deficiencies in ideas but that the standards applied must vary with the nature of the idea and the context in which it is to be implemented" (p. 231).

Dailey and Mumford (2006) extended this line of work by examining how well individuals evaluate the consequences of and resources needed for the implementation of plans. This investigation used case studies that each contained specific ideas actually found in existing public policy or education histories. Results indicated that individuals were accurate when evaluating what resources would be needed and what outcomes were likely, but this varied with familiarity with the cases. When individuals were familiar with the actual cases, they tended to underestimate resources needed and overestimate outcomes. Like the previous investigation, the results have unknown generalizability, given the undergraduate samples, and additional research with actual employees or organizational members would be useful. That being said, this research on appraisals and evaluations of plans and campaigns would seem to fit with what is actually needed in the natural environment.

Yet another related ability involves *forecasting*. Forecasting is quite important for certain kinds of creative problem-solving within organizations. Byrne, Shipman, and Mumford (2010) reported an experimental study with a task with clear relevance to business. In particular, the forecasting task asked the participants of the research to formulate and explain advertising campaigns.

This was an open-ended task, though they were given a product to be advertised. The campaigns were rated for originality, quality, and elegance. Forecasting ability was assessed by asking the participants to identify the implications of the ideas in their campaigns. They were also asked to compose plans for implementing their campaigns and to forecast the implications of these plans. Analyses indicated that the "extensiveness of forecasting" of their implications was significantly associated with the originality, quality, and elegance of the plans themselves. This research relied on a sample of undergraduates, so the generalizations to actual organizations are again unknown, but this line of research does point to forecasting as an important and practical ability, with relevance to creative problem-solving in organizations. Further research on forecasting is needed.

Organizational Applications

This chapter touched on a variety of abilities that are of some relevance to organizations. DT, for example, is an important contribution to creative problem-solving, and one that should be appreciated by organizations when targeting innovation. DT was considered first in this chapter because the research on DT is plentiful, and it uses reliable measures that are justified by sound theory (Acar & Runco, 2015, 2017; Guilford, 1968; Mumford, 1998; Runco & Acar, 2019; Torrance, 1995). Several of these measures of DT were mentioned in this chapter, including the Consequences test, Alternative Uses, Similarities, Titles, and the SWOT. The former is an older test, but as noted by Vincent et al. (2002), it presents tasks that are certainly similar to the problems that arise in organizations. The SWOT was developed specifically for business assessments. Other DT tests include Similarities (e.g., "how is a small business like a large business?" or "how is a manager like a parent?"), Instances (e.g., "list as many resources as you can that are vital for innovation in an organization"), Many Uses (e.g., "list as many uses as you can for how a paper clip can be used"), or Product Improvements (e.g., "list ways that a computer pointer or mouse could be improved"). There are also more realistic tests (Okuda et al., 1991; Mumford, Reiter-Palmon, & Redmond., 1994) and several that rely on figural, visual, or nonverbal stimuli. The figural DT tests tend to elicit fewer ideas, so there are low fluency scores, but they also tend to elicit a large number of original ideas, which is a very good thing given that originality is a prerequisite for creativity (Runco & Jaeger, 2012). These tests can be used in various ways in organizations, including when selecting from applicants and in the hiring process (Runco, 2015).

DT is emphasized here because there is so much information available about it, including that summarized earlier supporting predictive validity, but organizations should consider more than DT, which is why intelligence, problem finding, forecasting, and idea and solution evaluations and appraisals were all covered herein. These two might be considered when hiring employees, or perhaps when teams are being formed.

Much of the research on abilities has implications for teams that are formed within organizations (also see Paulus et al., 2018; Rubenson & Runco, 1995). Recall here the dangers of social loafing and production loss. These concerns suggest that organizations allow some autonomous work and do not depend entirely on teams; when teams are formed, they should probably not be too large, for larger teams are more likely to suffer from loafing and loss. Another suggestion from the research is to compose teams that are heterogeneous in order to maximize creative results, and that heterogeneity might be in ability, as well as in style, expertise, or background. There is research showing that some people are better at DT than at evaluating ideas and solutions, and a heterogeneous team should probably ensure that each relevant ability is represented. Recall also what was said about familiarity influencing creative problem-solving. Teams should thus also be heterogeneous in that regard as well. Related to familiarity is expertise, and quite clearly diverse expertise should be built into teams. Experts contribute certain things (e.g., large knowledge bases), but novices contribute as well (e.g., in their openness to new options and their flexibility).

There are, then, implications of the research on creative abilities for composing teams in organizations and for hiring practices. The research reviewed in this chapter also suggests that organizations should recognize that originality plays a vital role in all creative work. Effectiveness is also important, as suggested by the standard definition of creativity, but all creativity – and thus all innovation – depends in part on originality. That, in turn, points to risk tolerance as an important part of the organizational climate. This brings us to the last section of the chapter. It further explores organizational climate and context as influences on creative abilities.

Qualifiers and Context Effects

This chapter samples the abilities that are involved in creative problem-solving. It is a sample in that other abilities are described in the research. Still, this chapter presents a representative sample of abilities, and those described herein were chosen because they have clear empirical support. They also have some practicality, and as the preceding section suggests, there are implications for the workplace. A few qualifications are in order. Something must be said, for example, about the context in which abilities are likely to be expressed. It would be remiss to point to various abilities as involved in creative problem-solving and innovation at work without recognizing that each of them is likely to be influenced by the setting in which the employee finds him- or herself.

This idea of a context effect was proposed decades ago in the educational research on creativity (e.g., Wallach & Kogan, 1965), but findings in education seem to be quite consistent with what has been uncovered in research on the impact of organizational settings. Consider in this regard findings from the educational research showing that examinees are the most original and creative when evaluation is eliminated and when there is a feeling of "psychological safety" (Wallach & Kogan, 1965). This same thing seems to apply to children in the home, when parents provide *psychological safety* (Harrington, Block, & Block, 1987). It is theoretically justified by Roger's (1959) theory of creativity as well. Very importantly for the present purposes is that Carmeli, Reiter-Palmon, and Ziv (2010) demonstrated that the same thing applies to employees in organizations. They too tend to be the most creative and original when the organizational environment communicates the feeling of psychological safety. Creative abilities are best expressed when there is psychological safety. This may be related to the risk tolerance mentioned previously.

Apparently, settings that have diverse cues (Reiter-Palmon et al., 1997) may stimulate one kind of creative problem-solving, namely, *problem construction*.

This ability is one of the newer ways of conceiving the problem finding mentioned earlier. This research is noteworthy in part because it pointed to the need for "active engagement" by the individual. That may seem like an obvious point, but it certainly is a critical one. Individuals may have an ability, but they may not use it unless engaged. Often in the creativity literature such engagement is aligned with intrinsic motivation, which means that the problem at hand is interesting to the individual without any contingency or outside guidance. The research on problem construction also demonstrated that open-ended problems – similar to but not identical with the DT tasks mentioned previously – could be scored for quality of solutions, as well as originality and even creativity per se. See also Reiter-Palmon, Mumford, and Threfall (1993).

Something should also be said about the need for further theoretical integration. Most research on creativity still relies on quite focused theory. This is apparent not only in the moderate connection between theories of creativity and theories of innovation but also in much of the empirical work on creativity. Consider the operational definitions of creativity used in that research. Some point to socially recognized creativity and some to personal creativity (Runco, 2019). The theory of personal creativity proposes that creative things are original and effective but perhaps just for the individual. There is no social recognition. Theories of personal creativity are quite useful for understanding individuals who are creative but do not produce things that others use. It also helps with everyday creativity (Richards, 1990). Social creativity is that which depends on social recognition, the premise being that things are creative only if some audience judges them to be creative (Kasof, 1995). One step toward an integration was recently offered (Runco & Beghetto, 2018), but it would be good to integrate personal and social creativity with methods for encouraging creative problem-solving at work. This is especially true because, according to the existing theory of personal creativity, all creativity starts with the individual and may eventually be shared and lead to social recognition. If this is true, personal creativity does occur in organizations but is probably recognized as the starting point for social creativity and innovation.

Integration may also produce new ways of tying creativity to innovation. Several were mentioned early in this chapter, including one that focused on stages of the creative process, with innovation requiring a fifth (implementation) stage, and another focused on the ratio of originality to effectiveness. There is a debate about originality, some questioning the possibility that humans can be truly original. Some theories suggest that humans are so good at thinking analogically that what seems to be an original idea is in fact somehow related to what was already conceived, in which case the originality could be questioned. Much the same is apparent in the neuroscientific research on creativity, for it usually looks at creative things as combinations and recombinations of ideas or mental elements that were already a part of the individual's cognitive system. Again, the originality of a recombination could be questioned.

There are, then, interesting questions to be explored in future theory and research. For now, it seems that there is a benefit to encouraging creativity in the workplace, for creativity provides some of the prerequisites for innovation. Research also points to the value of DT and, in particular, to ideational fluency, originality, and flexibility, as well as forecasting ability. It points to an approach that respects both DT and CT, or at least knowledge and evaluative skills that are involved when truly creative solutions and ideas are produced. Research supports the value of psychological safety and various other contextual influences on creative ability. More research is needed, but at this point there are some clear messages about key creative abilities for the workplace.

References

Acar, S., Burnett, C., & Cabra, J. F. 2017. Ingredients of creativity: Originality and more. *Creativity Research Journal*, 29, 133–144.

Acar, S., & Runco, M. A. 2014. Assessing associative distance among ideas elicited by tests of divergent thinking. *Creativity Research Journal*, 26, 229–238.

Acar, S., & Runco, M. A. 2015. Thinking in multiple directions: Hyperspace categories in divergent thinking. *Psychology of Art, Creativity, and Aesthetics*, 9, 41–53.

Acar, S., & Runco, M. A. 2017. Latency predicts category switch in divergent thinking. *Psychology of Aesthetics, Creativity, and the Arts*, 11, 43–51. http://dx.doi.org/10.1037/aca0000091

Ames, M., & Runco, M. A. 2005. Predicting entrepreneurship from ideation and divergent thinking. *Creativity and Innovation Management*, 14, 311–315.

Basadur, M. 1994. Managing the creative process in organizations. In M. A. Runco (Ed.). *Problem solving, problem finding, and creativity* (pp. 237–268). Norwood, NJ: Ablex.

Baughman, W. A., & Mumford, M. D. 1995. Process-analytic models of creative capacities: Operations influencing the combination-and-reorganization process. *Creativity Research Journal*, 8, 37–62.

Bruner, J. 1979. The conditions of creativity. In J. Bruner (Ed.), *On knowing: Essays for the left hand*. Cambridge, MA: Harvard University Press.

Byrne, C. L., Shipman, A. S., & Mumford, M. D. 2010. The effects of forecasting on creative problem-solving: An experimental study. *Creativity Research Journal*, 22, 119–138.

Carmeli, A., Reiter-Palmon, R., & Ziv, E. 2010. Inclusive leadership and employee involvement in creative tasks in the workplace: The mediating role of psychological safety. *Creativity Research Journal*, 22, 250–260.

Charles, R., & Runco, M. A. 2000. Developmental trends in the evaluative and divergent thinking of children. *Creativity Research Journal*, 13, 415–435.

Corazza, G. E. 2016. Potential originality and effectiveness: The dynamic definition of creativity. *Creativity Research Journal*, 28, 258–267.

Csikszentmihalyi, M. 2003. The domain of creativity. In M. A. Runco & R. S. Albert (Eds.), *Theories of creativity (rev. ed.)*. Cresskill, NJ: Hampton Press.

Dailey, L., & Mumford, M. D. 2006. Evaluative aspects of creative thought: Errors in appraising the implications of new ideas. *Creativity Research Journal*, 18, 385–390.

Eysenck, H. 2003. Creativity, personality, and the convergent-divergent continuum. In M. A. Runco (Ed.), *Critical creative processes* (pp. 95–114). Cresskill, NJ: Hampton Press.

Gardner, H. 1983. *Frames of mind: The theory of multiple intelligences*. New York: Basic Books.

Getzels, J. W. 1975. Problem finding and the inventiveness of solutions. *Journal of Creative Behavior*, 9, 12–18.

Guilford, J. P. 1950. Creativity. *American Psychologist*, 5, 444–454.

Guilford, J. P. 1968. *Creativity, intelligence, and their educational implications*. San Diego, CA: EDITS/ Robert Knapp.

Guilford, J. P. 1984. Varieties of divergent production. *Journal of Creative Behavior*, 1–10.

Harrington, D. M., Block, J. H., & Block, J. 1987. Testing aspects of Carl Rogers' theory of creative environments: Child-rearing antecedents of creative potential in young adolescents. *Journal of Personality and Social Psychology*, 52, 851–856.

Jauk, E., Benedek, M., Dunst, B., & Neubauer, A. C. 2013. The relationship between intelligence and creativity: New support for the threshold hypothesis by means of empirical breakpoint detection. *Intelligence*, 41, 212–221.

Kasof, J. 1995. Explaining creativity: The attributional perspective. *Creativity Research Journal*, 8, 311–366.

Kharkhurin, A. V. 2012. *Multilingualism and Creativity*. Bristol: Multilingual Materials.

Lonergan, D. C., Scott, G. M., & Mumford, M. D. 2004. Evaluative aspects of creative thought: Effects of appraisal and revision standards. *Creativity Research Journal*, 16, 231–246.

MacKinnon, D. W. 1965. Personality and the realization of creative potential. *American Psychologist*, 20, 273–281.

Mumford, M. D., & Gustafson, S. B. 1988. Creativity syndrome: Integration, application, and innovation. *Psychological Bulletin*, 103, 27–43.

Mumford, M. D., Reiter-Palmon, R., & Redmond, M. R. 1994. Problem construction and cognition: Applying problem representations in ill-defined domains. In M. A. Runco (Ed.), *Problem finding, problem solving, and creativity* (pp. 3–39). Norwood, NJ: Ablex.

Nemiro, J. 2002. The creative process in virtual teams. *Creativity Research Journal*, 14, 69–83.

Okuda, S. M., Runco, M. A., & Berger, D. E. 1991. Creativity and the finding and solving of real-world problems. *Journal of Psychoeducational Assessment*, 9, 45–53.

Paulus, P. B., Baruah, J., & Kenworthy, J. B. 2018. Enhancing collaborative ideation in organizations. *Frontiers in Psychology*, 9, 2024.

Plucker, J. A. 1999. Is the proof in the pudding? Reanalyses of Torrance's (1958 to Present) longitudinal data. *Creativity Research Journal*, 12, 103–114.

Plucker, J., Runco, M. A., & Lim, W. 2006. Predicting ideational behavior from divergent thinking and discretionary time on task. *Creativity Research Journal*, 18, 55–63.

Reiter-Palmon, R., Mumford, M. D., & Threlfall, K. V. 1993. Solving everyday problems creatively: The role of problem construction and personality type. *Creativity Research Journal*, 11, 187–197.

Reiter-Palmon, R., Mumford, M. D., O'Connor Boes, J., & Runco, M. A. 1997. Problem construction and creativity: The role of ability, cue consistency, and active processing. *Creativity Research Journal*, 10, 9–23.

Richards, R. 1990. Everyday creativity, eminent creativity, and health: "Afterview" for Creativity Research Journal issues on creativity and health. *Creativity Research Journal*, 3, 300–326.

Rickards, T. J. 1999. Brainstorming. In M. A. Runco & S. R. Pritzker (Eds.), *Encyclopedia of creativity* (Vol. 1, pp. 219–227). San Diego, CA: Academic Press.

Rickards, T., & DeCock, C. 2003. Understanding organizational creativity: Towards a multi-paradigmatic approach. In M. A. Runco (Ed.), *Creativity research handbook* (vol. 2). Cresskill, NJ: Hampton Press.

Rogers, C. R. 1959. Toward a theory of creativity. In H. H. Anderson (Ed.), *Creativity and its cultivation* (pp. 69–82). New York: Harper & Row.

Rubenson, D. L., & Runco, M. A. 1992. The psychoeconomic approach to creativity. *New Ideas in Psychology*, 10, 131–147.

Rubenson, D. L., & Runco, M. A. 1995. The psychoeconomic view of creative work in groups and organizations. *Creativity and Innovation Management*, 4, 232–241.

Runco, M. A. (in press). Tactics and strategies for creativity. In M. A. Runco & S. Pritzker (Eds.), *Encyclopaedia of creativity* (3rd ed.). San Diego, CA: Elsevier.

Runco, M. A. 1986. Divergent thinking and creative performance in gifted and nongifted children. *Educational and Psychological Measurement*, 46, 375–384.

Runco, M. A. 1989. Parents' and teachers' ratings of the creativity of children. *Journal of Social Behavior and Personality*, 4, 73–83.

Runco, M. A. 2003. Idea evaluation, divergent thinking, and creativity. In M. A. Runco (Ed.). *Critical creative processes* (pp. 69–94). Cresskill, NJ: Hampton Press.

Runco, M. A. 2015. Original ideas, ideational flexibility, and openness to new ideas: Thoughts about hiring creative staff. *TelevLZlon* (Spring, 28/2015/E), pp. 30–33.

Runco, M. A. 2019. Creativity as a dynamic, personal, parsimonious process. In R. Beghetto & G. Corazza (Eds.), *Dynamic perspectives on creativity: New directions for theory, research, and practice in education* (pp. 181–188). New York: Springer.

Runco, M. A., & Acar, S. 2019. Divergent thinking. In J. C. Kaufman & R. J. Sternberg (Eds.), *The Cambridge handbook of creativity* (pp. 224–253). New York: Cambridge University Press.

Runco, M. A., & Albert, R. S. 1986. The threshold hypothesis regarding creativity and intelligence: An empirical test with gifted and nongifted children. *Creative Child and Adult Quarterly*, 11, 212–218.

Runco, M. A. & Basadur, M. S. 1993. Assessing ideational and evaluative skills and creative styles and attitudes. *Creativity and Innovation Management*, 2, 166–173.

Runco, M. A., & Beghetto, R. 2018. Primary and secondary creativity. *Current Opinion in Behavior Science*, 27, 7–10.

Runco, M. A., & Chand, I. 1994. Problem finding, evaluative thinking and creativity. In M. A. Runco (Ed.), *Problem finding, problem solving, and creativity*, (pp. 40–76). Norwood, NJ: Ablex.

Runco, M. A., & Chand, I. 1995. Cognition and creativity. *Educational Psychology Review*, 7, 243–267.

Runco, M. A., & Jaeger, G. J. 2012. The standard definition of creativity. *Creativity Research Journal*, 24, 92–96.

Runco, M. A., Millar, G., Acar, S., & Cramond, B. 2011. Torrance tests of creative thinking as predictors of personal and public achievement: A 50 year follow-up. *Creativity Research Journal*, 22, 361–368.

Runco, M. A., & Vega, L. 1990. Evaluating the creativity of children's ideas. *Journal of Social Behavior and Personality*, 5, 439–452.

Simonton, D. K. 2012. Taking the US Patent Office criteria seriously: A quantitative three-criterion creativity definition and its implications. *Creativity Research Journal*, 24, 97–106.

Sternberg, R. J., & Lubart, T. I. 1995. *Defying the crowd: Cultivating creativity in a culture of conformity*. New York, NY: Free Press.

Torrance, E. P. 1968. A longitudinal examination of the fourth-grade slump in creativity. *Gifted Child Quarterly*, 12, 195–199.

Undheim, J. O., & Horn, J. L. 1977. Critical evaluation of Guilford's structure-of-intellect theory. *Intelligence*, 1, 65–81

Vincent, A. S., Decker, B. P., & Mumford, M. D. 2002 Divergent thinking, intelligence, and expertise: A test of alternative models. *Creativity Research Journal*, 14, 163–178. DOI: 10.1207/S15326934CRJ1402_4

Walberg, H. J. & Stariha, W. E. 1992. Productive human capital: Learning, creativity and eminence. *Creativity Research Journal*, 5, 23–340.

Wallach, M. A., & Kogan, N. 1965. *Modes of thinking in young children: A study of the creativity-intelligence distinction*. New York: Holt, Reinhart, & Winston.

Wallas, G. 1926. *The art of thought*. London, England: Watts & Co.

Weisberg, R. W. (2015). On the usefulness of "value" in the definition of creativity. *Creativity Research Journal*, 27, 111–124.

5

PERSONALITY AND CREATIVITY AT WORK

Adrian Furnham

Introduction

This chapter addresses four issues. First, it reviews and summarizes what we know of the relationship between personality traits, personality disorders, and creativity, particularly in the workplace. Second, it looks at what we know about business or work creativity as opposed to artistic and scientific creativity. Third, implications for practice are considered, such as encouraging a creative corporate culture and hiring creative people. Finally, an academic and a business agenda will be considered.

With regard to definitions, it is widely agreed that *creativity* is the production of novel/original and useful/elegant solutions to specific problems that are often ill defined and complex. Creativity is determined by many things, including a divergent thinking style, which appears to facilitate the capability for creative thinking. *Innovation* is different from creativity in that it is the application/introduction of new and creative ideas. The personality correlates of innovation are different from those associated with creativity, though there may be some overlap. This chapter is mainly concerned with personality correlates of creativity, though we argue that two key identifiable characteristics, namely, imaginativeness and obsessionality, appear to be related to *both* creativity and innovation. Both the bulk of the research literature and this chapter are mainly concerned with personality correlates of creativity rather than innovation.

A Skeptical Caveat

If you ask a group of senior executives if they would like to have more creative people in their organization, they nearly all agree, irrespective of the type of organization they are in. Next, if you ask whether they would like their organizational culture to foster more creativity, again they say "yes" with enthusiasm. Creativity seems a sort of talisman: the secret of success in business.

I usually respond to the first question by asking whether they have worked with, or for, really creative people and what that was like. I am trying to differentiate genuine from "self-confessed" creatives and also suggest that "real creatives" can be (very) difficult to manage. I then ask them to name some groups of people doing various tasks that may really not need much creativity. Do pilots or dentists or bus drivers need to be creative? Certainly, they may need to solve new problems, but is that ability more to do with intelligence rather than creativity?

Finally, I ask them about their understanding of the difference between creativity and innovation at work and which is more difficult. Most have experienced many failed attempts with regard to the innovation of changes to work practices and outcomes. Many confess the vast majority failed however "creative" the idea was.

I believe, and I think I can provide data to support the following ideas: (a) Creativity, like almost every other human characteristic, is normally distributed. This means that just as not everyone is tall, or intelligent and musical, not everyone is creative. (b) Creativity, like intelligence, cannot *easily* be trained or taught, though well-designed programs that teach cognitive skills and heuristics in specific situations have been demonstrated to be effective (Scott, Leritz, & Mumford, 2004). One can learn useful strategies that increase the likelihood of having more divergent ideas, as well as skills and concepts relevant to particular creative products, but both artistic and scientific creativity are relatively stable and dependent on various abilities. (c) There is a dark side to many creatives, more so in the arts than sciences. Personality correlates of creativity suggest that it may often be associated with pathology that has potential personal and behavioral problems. This is perhaps the most debatable of my assertions.

Personality Traits and Creativity

The early studies of creativity and personality were characterized by the diversity and dubiousness of the personality measures used. This makes the interpretation of the results particularly difficult. They were essentially correlational studies where measures of the one factor (personality) were correlated with measures of the other (creativity). However, whereas there remains considerable development in the definition and measurement of personality, there remains few widely used, psychometrically valid, and generally accepted measures of creativity.

Early researchers used personality measures now much less used. For instance, MacKinnon (1965) used expert ratings and the California Personality

Inventory (CPI) to investigate the creativity of architects. Domino (1974) also utilized the CPI, in addition to the Edwards Personal Preference Schedule, ACL scored for creativity (Domino, 1970), Barron-Welsh Art Scale, and the RAT to assess the creativity of cinematographers versus matched controls.

One interesting issue for this research remains, however, because even very well-known traits are defined and measured differently in different questionnaires. This can lead to opposite findings. For example, when extraversion is defined in terms of the Big Three or Big Five models (being associated with stimulus seeking), it has often been shown to be *positively* related to creativity, but if defined from a Jungian (Myers-Briggs) perspective (getting energy and stimulation externally), it is *negatively* associated with creativity. Measurement differences often account for ambiguous and unreplicable findings in this literature.

Big Three and Power of Psychoticism

A large number of early creativity studies used the various Eysenckian measures still recognized as robust and valid. For instance, Gotz and Gotz (1979a) studied professional artists and found them to have higher scores on psychoticism than a group of controls. In a follow-up study, Gotz and Gotz (1979b) compared the personality scores of highly successful and less successful professional artists. They found that successful artists scored significantly higher on the P (psychoticism) scale than less successful artists, but differences were found between the two groups on the E (introversion-extraversion), N (neuroticism), or L (lie) scales. Woody and Claridge (1977) demonstrated the link between P and trait creativity. Yet, Kline and Cooper (1986) cast doubt on the generality of the link between creativity and P.

Eysenck (1993, 1994, 1995), however, produced a model to explain how P and creativity were related. He suggested there are cognitive variables (intelligence, knowledge, technical skills, particular talents), environmental factors, and personality variables (internal motivation, confidence, nonconformity and trait creativity). For Eysenck, it is the process of *over inclusive* or *allusive thinking* that characterizes both psychotic and creative thinking.

Studies have examined the relationship between creativity and psychopathology (Carson, Peterson, & Higgins, 2003; Goertzel et al., 1978; Jamison, 1989, 1993; Peterson, Smith & Carson, 2002; Prentky, 2001; Sass, 2001), and many of them have found evidence to support Eysenck's hypothesis that there are similarities between creatives and schizophrenics or sufferers of bipolar disorder. Schizotypy is postulated to contribute toward a creative thinking style, while bipolar disorder is postulated to contribute toward creativity by predisposing sufferers to experience the extremes of affect.

Most of these studies concluded that there are signs of psychopathology (especially psychoses) among famous creators, and they pointed to a link between creativity and psychopathology. However, historiometric analyses of eminent individuals may reveal that they suffered from psychoses but do not indicate whether it is the thought disorder, the social anhedonia, or both that contribute to creativity (Batey & Furnham, 2007). There are also those who fundamentally challenge the notion of the relationship between various pathologies/forms of madness and creativity of any sort (Weisberg, 2011).

Eysenck (1993) pointed out that much of the debate about whether or not creative geniuses are psychotic could be resolved by disregarding the assumption that psychiatric abnormality is categorical rather than dimensional. He suggested that psychopathology can be conceptualized as an exaggeration/extension of underlying personality traits. Accordingly, psychosis lies at the extreme end of the distribution of "psychoticism," a hypothetical dispositional personality trait that is conceived of as a continuum "ranging from normal to psychotic." Psychoticism has been described as consisting of several characteristics, one of which is creativity. Other characteristics include aggressiveness, impersonal and antisocial behavior, coldness, egocentricity, impulsivity, unempathic behavior, and tough-mindedness.

The assumption of Eysenck (1993), therefore, is that creative people possess the personality characteristics of psychoticism at a higher level than the mean normal individual and that, if adequate controls are missing or if they experience stressful situations, then they may develop psychosis. Equally, the personality characteristics of the high P scorer make them predisposed toward creativity. The coexistence of both dominant/independent attitudes with a cognitive style that allows for greater flexibility would ensure that high P scorers could be creative, providing they also possess the necessary motivational traits, cognitive variables, and environment conducive to creative expression.

Researchers in the Eysenkian tradition therefore argue that common *information-processing patterns* can be found in both creative people and psychotics. Close examination of the theories developed in order to explain the cognitive deficits in psychotics (Hemsley, 1991) and those relating to the cognitive aspects of creativity (Martindale, 1999) reveals many similarities.

Martindale (1999) has shown that creative people have a high resting level of activation and that they are oversensitive to stimuli. However, they also have a low level of inhibition, so that the more they are stimulated, the more their level of arousal drops, favoring creative performance. Again, the notions of reduced inhibition and mood fluctuation (arousal levels rising and falling) are common notions in the literature on schizophrenia. Recent experimental research has indicated that those rated as superior in creative ability also demonstrate low levels of latent inhibition in comparison with people not rated as being creative (Carson et al., 2003; Peterson & Carson, 2000). This evidence is supportive of Eysenck's (1994) theory of creativity.

What this literature implies is that creative people may be very difficult to work with as they are cold, unreliable, and odd. Indeed, there are many reports from people working in "creative environments" to support this assertion. This is much more true of artistic, rather than scientific, creativity, which is relevant for business. Thus, people in advertising and fashion are more likely to have higher P scores than those in research and development (R&D) jobs in engineering, pharmaceutical, and manufacturing firms.

Research Using Big Five and the Opening up of Openness

During the 1980s and 1990s, popularity began to form around a new conceptualization of personality, namely, the Big Five. McCrae (1987) found that Divergent Thinking (often used as a reliable, necessary, but not sufficient measure of creativity) was consistently associated with self-reports and peer ratings of Openness to Experience, but not with Extraversion, Neuroticism, Agreeableness, or Conscientiousness. However, he noted:

"Creative ability does not inevitably lead to recognized creativity, and a variety of personality traits may be involved in being conceived as creative. Conscientious individuals may complete their creative projects more often; extraverts may exhibit them more readily; adjusted individuals may be less distracted from creative work by personal problems.... smart extraverts make intelligent conversation, smart introverts read difficult books; conscientious individuals use their intellectual gifts, lackadaisical individuals do not. Openness to experience and divergent thinking abilities may also interact as mutually necessary conditions for creativity, the former providing the inclination and the latter providing the aptitude for original thinking" (McCrae, 1987, p. 1264).

Researchers who have examined DT and the Big Five have always found evidence for the role of *Openness to Experience* (King, Walker, & Broyles, 1996; McCrae, 1987; Wuthrich & Bates, 2001). There is a potential explanation of why Openness may be implicated in rated products but not DT tests. The products of DT tests are rarely qualitatively judged. It is most common to take measures of fluency (number of responses) or originality (statistical infrequency). As there is no judgment of quality in these measures, then an individual high in Openness to new experiences will not be discernable from an individual who is not, rather the test will select an individual with high ideational fluency. When the quality or ingenuity of a product is rated, qualitative judgments are performed regarding the novelty or utility of the product. In this scenario, a preference for new and surprising behaviors (as measured by O) will be rated (Batey & Furnham, 2007).

Early studies suggested that indeed Openness was the best predictor of Creativity (King et al., 1996). Gelade (1997) gave the NEO-PI to a group of advertising and design creatives, and to a comparable group of professionals and managers in occupations that were not apparently creative. Compared to the "noncreatives," the "commercial creatives" were more Neurotic (particularly in terms of angry hostility, depression, self-consciousness, impulsivity, and vulnerability), more Extraverted (especially in terms of gregariousness and excitement seeking), more Open to experiences (particularly fantasy, aesthetics, and feelings), and less Conscientious (particularly in terms of overall competence, order, self-discipline, and deliberation).

George and Zhou (2001) demonstrated that the application of creative potential depends on several factors. They found that rated creative behavior was highest when individuals with high Openness were set tasks that had unclear demands or unclear means of achieving ends and were given positive feedback. Their analyses of the role of Conscientiousness also yielded clear findings. They found that if an individuals' supervisor monitored their work closely and their coworkers were unsupportive of creative endeavor, then high Conscientiousness inhibited creative behavior.

Batey and Furnham (2007) noted that if the findings of this study are generalized from the workplace to the laboratory, then it may explain why some studies have produced contradictory findings. It may be that participants in laboratory studies have been influenced by the environment (experimenter attitude, exam-like conditions, etc.) and that these unaccounted-for variables have influenced the expression of creative potential. It may be that Wallach and Kogan (1965) were indeed correct; the conditions of testing can affect creativity.

However, most studies have found that Open-to-Experience is the highest and most consistent correlate of various measures of creativity in different cultures.

Batey and Furnham (2007) argued that when the criterion of creativity employed is a DT test, the results tend to suggest that *Extraversion* is predictive (Aguilar-Alonso, 1996; King et al., 1996, Wuthrich & Bates, 2001). This finding holds true whether the instrument is from the Gigantic Three or the Big Five (Martindale & Dailey, 1996) but different from that of McCrae (1987) who found Extraversion did not reach significance. It may be that DT tests are often administered in group settings, which is a more conducive setting for an Extravert than an Introvert. Also, Extraverts may perform better at DT tests, because they seek stimulation (Eysenck & Eysenck, 1975), and the DT test environment provides the perfect opportunity to do just that. McCrae (1987) suggested that extraverts may be happier to exhibit their work. Some investigators have demonstrated relationships between DT and the P scale of the EPQ (Aguilar-Alonso, 1996; Merten & Fischer, 1999), but others have failed to note such a correlation (Kline & Cooper, 1986, Martindale & Dailey, 1996; Rawlings, 1985).

It seems, therefore, that there is no doubt that *certain* personality traits are important for explaining and predicting *certain* types of creativity. This may account for as much as one-quarter to one-third of the variance in explaining the causes of creative work and tests. However, most personality studies have assumed that underlying personality traits are domain-general (i.e., arts, science, business creativity). This approach has resulted in mixed evidence concerning which personality traits are important in what circumstances. As suggested, possessing certain traits, such as Openness or tough-mindedness (Psychoticism), is probably necessary but not sufficient for creativity as achievement.

To ensure that a person fulfills his or her potential, other requisite cognitive and situational variables will need to be present. That is, a person's setting needs to foster and encourage creativity, and where appropriate reward it. More recent attempts have been to review the biological foundations of the creative personality and investigate physiological processes that may explain it. However, these neuroscience attempts to understand creative processes are still in their infancy.

Mental Illness and Creativity: Darkness and Bright Lights

Since ancient times, people have held the belief that creativity and madness are intrinsically linked. In the last two decades, there have been numerous studies into the alleged relationship between creativity and mental illness. Many have argued that the mad genius idea is a myth. However, due to the debilitating state that occurs during mental illness, patients are difficult to study, and if they do participate, it is unclear whether what is being studied is due to medication, poor motivation, or the effects of the illness itself.

Studies using various different methodologies have examined the relationship between creativity and psychopathology (Carson et al., 2003; Jamison, 1989, 1993; Lloyd-Evans et al., 2007; Peterson et al., 2002; Sass, 2001).

Reviews have tended to show that when studies are chosen by strict criteria, there remains clear evidence of the relationship between creativity and mental disorder of many sorts. One study of over 300,000 people showed that bipolar and schizophrenic people were overrepresented in creative professors. Though a variety of mental illnesses have been implicated, like mania and attention deficit hyperactivity disorder (ADHD), the two illnesses that are nearly always associated with creativity are schizophrenia and bipolar disorder.

a. *Schizophrenia*: Batey and Furnham (2007) suggest that most of the theories relating to the cognitive deficit in schizophrenia seem to propose that there is a deficit in selective attention mechanisms, which results in schizophrenics being unable to inhibit irrelevant information from entering consciousness (Hemsley, 1991). This is also called the cognitive disinhibition thesis. However, the research interest is now with Schizotypy – a related disorder to schizophrenia – rather than schizophrenia per se (see next section).
b. *Bipolar disorder*: There is an equally rich and diverse literature on the creativity of many people with bipolar disorder. It has been shown that there is a strong relationship between the two. Jamison (1993) inspected autobiographical, biographical, and, where available, medical records of 36 major British poets born between 1705 and 1805. They were 30

times more likely to have suffered from bipolar disorder, 10 to 20 times more likely to be cyclothymic, more than 20 times as likely to have been admitted to a mental asylum, and at least 5 times as likely to have committed suicide, compared to the general population (Jamison, 1993). Jamison interpreted this as persuasive evidence for a relationship between mood disorders and artistic creativity. There have been critiques of this work, and a recent review has suggested that while there is evidence of a link, the understanding of the processes and mechanisms remains weak.

Indeed, there are now a number of scholars who are deeply skeptical about the whole "mad genius" hypothesis. Many argue that mental illness would act as a major handicap in ensuring a person is able to realize his or her creativity activity. This is particularly true in business, perhaps less so in the creative arts.

Creativity in the Arts, the Sciences, and Business

There has long been an interest in the different thinking styles of those in Arts from those in Science. This debate was structured by C. P. Snow in his 1959 lecture entitled *The Two Cultures*. He stressed the differences and poor communication between those in the sciences and those in the humanities. This debate has continued for 50 years.

It was the work of Hudson (1966) that arguably stimulated psychological research in this Art versus Science area. He suggested that those with a bias toward convergent thinking moved toward the physical sciences, while those with a divergent thinking bias moved toward the humanities. The book became a citation classic receiving 225 citations up to 1980 (Hudson, 1980) and many hundreds more since then.

The Hudson book and its conclusion attracted criticism but also replication and extensions (Hocevar, 1980). Hartley and Greggs (1997) gave four groups of students, pure arts, arts and social science, social science and science, and pure science, some divergent thinking tests. The hypothesis that divergent thinking would decline along the arts–science continuum found support in that arts students as a whole scored significantly higher than science students on four tests of divergent thinking.

Researchers have tested the idea that personality and thinking style differences between arts and science students account for differences in the creativity. However, one study of 116 British undergraduates found there were small learning styles differences and no problem-solving differences in arts and science students, leading the author to conclude that modern students have a more balanced educational profile than their more specialized predecessors (Williamson, 2011).

Furnham and Crump, (2013) compared students of arts and science on the Jackson's 16 Personality Factor (16PF) inventory and found half of the scales yielded significant differences. The biggest differences were on Sensitivity and Abstractness, both where Arts students scored higher than Science students.

There have been various, more recent, studies that have looked at individual difference predictors of creativity in the arts and sciences (Furnham, Batey, Booth, Patel, & Lozinskaya, 2011). There have also been studies that looked at creativity and vocational preference. Kaufman, Pumaccahua, and Holt, (2013) reported that Artistic and Investigative student majors, as predicted, scored higher on self-assessed creativity. Though studies differ on many dimensions, it is possible to summarize the findings of many studies in this area; thus, Artists are significantly higher on Neuroticism and Openness, but lower on Extraversion, Agreeableness, and Conscientiousness than nonartists. Artists are significantly higher on psychoticism than nonartists. But Scientists are significantly higher on Intelligence and Conscientiousness than nonscientists. Everyday creatives are significantly higher on Extraversion than artists or scientists. Everyday creatives are significantly higher on Agreeableness than artists or scientists.

Furnham (2008) summarized this as follows, where + and − signs indicate the strength of relationships. See Table 5.1, which is reprinted with the permission of the author.

Thus, we have the picture of the artist and scientific creative. Both tend to be ambitious, driven, introverted individuals. The creative artist (at worst) can be seen as aloof, cold, independent, and nonconforming. Similarly, the creative scientist could be seen as arrogant, autonomous, dominant, and self-confidant. But what about creativity in business? Certainly, business people employ both artistic and scientific creativity to do what they are good at. But are there other characteristics associated with business creativity?

TABLE 5.1 Relationships between intelligence, personality, and three types of creativity

Trait	Artistic Creativity	Scientific Creativity	Everyday Creativity
Intelligence			
Fluid	+	+++	+
Crystallized	++	+++	++
Personality			
Neuroticism	+++	− −	−
Extraversion	− −	−	++
Openness	+++	+++	++
Agreeableness	− −	−	+
Conscientiousness	− −	+++	+
Psychoticism	+++	++	+

Furnham (2017) argued that the search for creativity was about Game Changers in Business. The question is how to define that relatively small group of identifiable people whose motivation and talent lead them to become and stay "game changers." Game Changers tend to be both entrepreneurs and intrapreneurs. However, they often have a reputation for being difficult, as they keep challenging how things are done. Some leave organizations out of pure frustration at the resistance to their ideas.

Their biography often offers some clues as to what drives them. What is often the case is their history of "differentness" or "discontinuity." They often do not fit in very well, but when the corporate culture is right they thrive, and so does the company.

So how do you spot a Game Changer? They seem to have lots of characteristics: creative and quirky, ambitious and a go-getter, focused and also resilient, and bright and have vision. Colleagues of Furnham (John Mervyn-Smith) interviewed over 20 people who were working with or worked with creative people in business. At the heart of the interview was the Repertory Grid, a technique used to reveal the underlying dimensions of a person's perceptions. He found two factors or dimensions that others believed characterized these people. What is interesting from a psychological perspective is that they do not often seem to "go together."

The dimensions are discussed in the following sections.

Imaginativeness

This is associated with creativity thinking but in very applied settings. It is associated with the desire to "do things differently," invent products and systems that are more efficient, and show an interest in how technology can be used to solve current problems. It is at the heart of innovation and divergent thinking. But this is "scientific" not "artistic" creativity that is often problem oriented.

Productive Obsessionality

This is associated with an ability to become highly focused on work-related issues. It is not associated with compulsivity and related disorders (obsessive-compulsive disorder [OCD]) but with very clear focus and dedication to solving problems, a trait often observed in inventors. It is about getting "in the flow" and having a healthy, all-absorbing passion. But it is about "getting it right," making it more efficient, cheaper, and user friendly.

Imaginativeness and creativity are often associated with being difficult and unreliable. Equally, Obsessionality is often associated with self-defeating compulsive behaviors. To be both original and dedicated to a practical outcome in business is indeed rare. At a glance, the key behaviors of a Game Changer may seem quite common, but it is the combination of these characteristics and their "Obsessive Imagination" that makes them so difficult to spot and unleash within the corporate world. On the basis of this work, I devised a measure of the two dimensions that can be used to categorize people. The idea is that those in business with great imagination are good at articulating a vision or big picture. If they also have productive obsession, they can turn the idea into reality, and through their intensity and vigor, they can become creative. According to the model, Game Changers are high on both dimensions. Those high on imagination but low on obsession are good strategists, while those with the opposite pattern are "polishers" of good ideas.

This questionnaire and model have been developed into a successful commercial product used for identifying those with potential and managing creative teams (https://www.thegcindex.com).

Creative Environments

Social and organizational psychologists have always attacked personality theorists for their attribution errors: that is, they attribute (most if not all) the creative outcome to the individual ignoring contextual, physical, and social factors that also contribute to the creativity process and outcomes. They argue that situational factors are more important in explaining behavior, though it is not always clear what they are.

There seem to be at least four types of environmental factors that have been argued, though not always demonstrated, to be related to creativity. First, there is the *physical environment*, where architects and designers have tried to create spaces that encourage creativity. These may include spaces designed to either facilitate or reduce interpersonal interaction and stimulation. It may include the use of lighting, music, or other factors to induce moods associated with creativity. Various organizations make many claims for how a product they produce (particular music, furnishings) stimulate creativity, but there remain few good empirical studies to evidence these claims.

Second, there is *corporate culture* defined quite simply as "the way we do things around here." It has been that some cultures encourage and others effectively punish creativity by the implicit messages that are sent. This often has to do with how competitive or cooperative these environments are. While there is a rich literature in management science on the conceptualization, measurement, and consequences of corporate culture, there appears to be little to no empirical evidence showing that certain corporate cultures inhibit or facilitate creativity.

Third, and related to culture, is *group dynamics*. While artistic creativity is nearly always portrayed as the result of individual (artists, writers) working alone, a great deal of business and scientific creativity is associated with groups or teams working together on a project. The team dynamic, often a function of the leaders' beliefs and behaviors, can very easily impact on the whole creativity enterprise. There is a growing literature on team makeup (i.e., homo- versus heterogeneity), size and structure, but few studies have looked at how team processes, measured over time, affect creativity.

Fourth, there is the *reward system*. To be intrinsically motivated means to do something for the love of the activity. The word *amateur* derives from the Latin word for "love." Amateurs take part for the joy of the activity, while professionals do it also for the money, status, or some other specific reward. Intrinsic and extrinsic motivation are opposite ends of a scale. Most people are part intrinsically and part extrinsically motivated at work. All jobs have a mixture of the two factors – for some people, a job choice, a trade-off between choosing a job that they love versus choosing a less desirable job with very good rewards like salary, pension, perks, or holidays. However, there does appear to be replicated evidence that intrinsic rewards are more successful than extrinsic rewards in sustaining creativity at work.

Doing good research in this area is difficult. Ideally, this involves longitudinal, experimental studies with robust measures of creativity.

Implications for Practice

Assuming that it is desirable to foster creativity in organizations, the question is how that is best done. It seems that researchers have adopted essentially one of four approaches to the problem:

The creative person: Differential psychologists have attempted to delineate the particular and peculiar set of abilities, motives, and traits that together describe the creative individual. Thus, organizations that value creativity and innovation need to attract, select, and nurture those "special" individuals.

The creative process: This is an attempt to understand the thought (cognitive) processes that go on in the process of creativity. It is not so much an attempt at the *who*, but the *how* question. Once the process is understood, it is more likely that it can be harnessed for business success.

The creative situation: Social and business psychologists are particularly interested in cultural, environmental, and organizational factors that inhibit or facilitate creativity. The idea is that one can therefore construct situations that induce creativity even in the not particularly creative. This includes the physical environment as well as the social environment best understood in terms of the corporate culture.

The creative product: This approach attempts to study all aspects of creativity by looking at those products that are clearly defined as creative. For businesses, however, producing creative products is not enough: People must want to purchase them.

For people in business, the question is how to select, motivate, and nurture those who are likely to be creative, as well as develop a corporate culture that encourages creativity. Certainly, there is considerably more agreement on the former than the latter.

Two other issues are important. The first is that most people work with others: We are not independent or dependent but interdependent on others. We work in teams. But are "creative teams" different from "less-creative teams"? What is the optimal mix of people working in a creative team in terms of ability, personality, and motivation? Is it best to maximize homogeneity or heterogeneity? Do they require a different environment or "reward package" to be both happy and successful? These are important questions that require careful empirical analysis. While there are many consultant-led recommendations with respect to these questions, there remains a dearth of good studies which address them.

Conclusion

There is no doubt that *certain* personality traits are important for explaining and predicting *certain* types of creativity. This may account for as much as one-quarter to one-third of the variance in explaining the origins of creative processes and products. However, most personality studies have assumed that underlying personality traits are domain-general with respect to creativity (i.e., arts, science, business creativity). This approach has resulted in mixed evidence concerning which personality traits are important and in what circumstances. As suggested, possessing certain traits, such as Openness or Tough-mindedness (Psychoticism), is probably necessary but not sufficient for creativity production.

Perhaps the most important gap in this literature is a theoretical account of how the process works: namely, the interaction of individual (personality, intelligence, motivation), team/group, and situational/environmental (physical features, corporate culture) variables in stimulating creativity inside (and outside) the workplace.

More recent attempts have been to review the biological foundations of the creative personality and investigate physiological processes that may explain it (Chavez-Eakle et al., 2012). However, these neuroscience attempts to understand creative processes are still in their infancy.

To ensure that a person fulfills his or her potential, other requisite cognitive and situational variables will need to be present. This includes sufficient cognitive ability, an "ideal" personality profile, and the motivation/desire to create ideas, products, and processes. Moreover, it requires the individual to really want to produce novel and useful products. Organizations therefore not only need to select and sensitively manage creative people, but they need to find ways on intrinsic and extrinsic rewards, which is far from straightforward.

Innovation may be defined as the application of creative ideas. It may well be that the skills and talents of innovative individuals and organizations are quite different from creative individuals and organizations. The former takes a quite different mind-set and skill base than the latter. Innovative people have to *apply creative ideas*: they tend to be more "business-like" and extrinsically motivated, as well as skilled in organizational change and development. Many "artistically creative" people tend to have a very different profile from successful businesspeople, whose survival often depends on being innovative (Furnham, 2008).

The fact that so many of these important theoretical and practical questions remain unanswered should stimulate potential research in this important area to attempt to research them.

References

Aguilar-Alonso, A. 1996. Personality and creativity. *Personality and Individual Differences*, 21, 959–969.
Batey, M. & Furnham, A. 2007. Creativity, intelligence and personality. Unpublished paper.
Carson, S. H., Peterson, J. B., & Higgins, D. M. 2003: Decreased latent inhibition is associated with increased creative achievement in high-functioning individuals. *Journal of Personality and Social Psychology*, 85, 499–506.
Furnham, A. 2008. *Personality and Intelligence at Work*. London: Routledge.
Furnham, A. 2017. Individual differences in intelligence, personality and creativity. In J. Baer, & J. Kaufman (Eds.), *The Cambridge companion to creativity and reasoning in cognitive development* (2nd ed.). Cambridge, UK: Cambridge University Press.
Furnham, A. & Crump, J. 2013. The sensitive, imaginative, articulate art student and conservative, cool, numerate science student: Individual differences in art and sciences students. *Learning and Individual Differences*, 25, 150–155.
Furnham, A., Batey, M., Booth, T. W., Patel, V., & Lozinskaya, D. 2011. Individual difference predictors of creativity in Art and Science students. *Thinking Skills and Creativity*, 6(2), 114–121.
Gelade, G. 1997. Creativity in conflict: The personality of the commercial creative. *Journal of Genetic Psychology*, 165, 67–78.
George, J. M. & Zhou, J. 2001. When openness to experience and conscientiousness are related to creative behavior: An interactional approach. *Journal of Applied Psychology*, 86, 513–524.
Goertzel, M. G., Goertzel, V., & Goertzel, T. G. 1978. *Eminent personalities*. San Francisco, CA: Jossey-Bass.
Gotz, K. O. & Gotz, K. 1979a. Personality characteristics of professional artists. *Perceptual and Motor Skills*, 49, 327–334.
Gotz, K. O. & Gotz, K. 1979b. Personality characteristics of successful artists. *Perceptual and Motor Skills*, 49, 919–924.
Hartley, J. & Greggs, M. A. 1997. Divergent thinking in Arts and Science students: Contrary Imaginations at Keele revisited. *Studies in Higher Education*, 22, 93–97.
Hemsley, D. 1991. An experimental psychological model of schizophrenia. In A. Hafner, W. Gattaz, & F. Janzarik (Eds.), *Search for causes of schizophrenia*. Hiedelberg, Germany: Springer-Verlag.
Hudson, L. 1966. *Contrary imaginations*. London, UK: Methuen.

Hudson, L. 1980. The question of creativity. In P.E. Vernon (Ed.), *Creativity: Selected readings*. Harmondsworth, UK: Penguin.

Jamison, K. R. 1989. Mood disorders and patterns of creativity in British writers and artists. *Psychiatry*, 52, 125–134.

Jamison, K. R. 1993. *Touched with fire: Manic depressive illness and the artistic temperament*. New York, NY: Free Press.

Kaufman, J. C., Pumaccahua, T. T., & Holt, R. E. 2013. Personality and creativity in realistic, investigative, artistic, social, and enterprising college majors. *Personality and Individual Differences*, 54(8), 913–917.

King, L., Walker, L., & Broyles, S. 1996. Creativity and the five factor model. *Journal of Research in Personality*, 30, 189–203.

MacKinnon, D. W. 1965. Personality and the realization of creative potential. *American Psychologist*, 20(4), 273–281.

Martindale, C. 1999. Biological bases of creativity. In R. J. Sternberg (Ed.), *Creativity research handbook*. Cambridge, UK: Cambridge University Press.

Martindale, C. & Dailey, A. 1996. Creativity. Primary process cognition and personality. *Personality and Individual Differences*, 20, 409–414.

McCrae, R. 1987. Creativity, divergent thinking and openness to experience. *Journal of Personality and Social Psychology*, 52, 1258–1265.

Merten, T. & Fischer, I. 1999. Creativity, personality and word association responses: Associative behaviour in forty supposedly creative persons. *Personality and Individual Differences*, 27, 933–942.

Peterson, J. B. & Carson, S. 2000. Latent inhibition and openness to experience in a high-achieving student population. *Personality and Individual Differences*, 28, 323–332.

Peterson, J. B., Smith, K. W., & Carson, S. H. 2002. Openness and extraversion are associated with reduced latent inhibition: Replication and commentary. *Personality and Individual Differences*, 33, 1137–1147.

Prentky, R. A. 2001. Mental illness and roots of genius. *Creativity Research Journal*, 13, 95–104.

Rawlings, D. 1985. Psychoticism, creativity and dichotic shadowing. *Personality and Individual Differences*, 6, 737–742.

Sass, L. A. 2001. Schizophrenia, modernism, and the "creative imagination": On creativity and psychopathology. *Creativity Research Journal*, 13, 55–74.

Scott, G., Leritz, L., & Mumford, M. 2004. The effectiveness of creativity training. *Creativity Research Journal*, 16, 361–388.

Wallach, M. A. & Kogan, N. 1965. *Modes of thinking in young children*. New York, NY: Holt, Rinehart & Winston.

Weisberg, R. 2011. Frank Lloyd Wright's Fallingwater. *Creativity Research Journal*, 23, 296–312.

Woody, E. & Claridge, G. 1977. Psychoticism and thinking. *British Journal of Social and Clinical Psychology*, 16, 241–248.

Wuthrich, V. & Bates, T. C. 2001. Schizotypy and latent inhibition: Non-linear linkage between psychometric and cognitive markers. *Personality and Individual Differences*, 30, 783–798.

6
TEMPORAL DYNAMICS OF CREATIVITY AND MOTIVATION
What We Know, What We Do Not, and a Few Suggestions for Filling the Gap

Logan M. Steele

As good ideas become harder to find (Bloom, Jones, Van Reenen, & Webb, 2018) and the nature of work rapidly changes (Burtch, Carnahan, & Greenwood, 2018), having a creative workforce becomes increasingly important for the viability and profitability of organizations. Popular press headlines are littered with evidence of this, from *Fast Company*'s "Lessons in fearless creativity" (Ifeanyi, 2018) to *Harvard Business Review*'s "How to use mindfulness to increase your team's creativity" (Byrne & Thatchenkery, 2018) and *Inc.*'s "3 ways you might accidentally be making yourself less creative, according to science" (Venkatraman, 2018). As the final article title implies, the scientific study of creativity has indeed generated a substantial body of knowledge giving insights into *who* is most likely to produce creative work (Hunter, Cushenbery, & Friedrich, 2012), *when* they are most likely to do so (e.g., Shalley, Zhou, & Oldham, 2004), and *why* (Liu, Jiang, Shalley, Keem, & Zhou, 2016). This chapter focuses on the topic of *why*. Specifically, this chapter presents what we know about the relationship between motivation and creativity (i.e., the generation of new and useful ideas; Amabile, 1996; Runco & Jaeger, 2012) *as it unfolds over time*. Presented in the pages that follow is an explanation of why a longitudinal, within-person perspective is essential to an accurate and precise understanding of the motivation-creativity link. Next, the studies published in the past 15 years that examine motivation and creativity over time are reviewed. Finally, the boundaries of our current state of knowledge are discussed, and some suggestions for pushing beyond them are given.

Within-Person Perspective on Creativity and Motivation

Motivation refers to the psychological processes that determine the direction, intensity, and persistence of one's effort and the individual and environmental factors that influence these processes (Kanfer, 1990). It is the force that enables people to interact with their environment. For much of the history of studying motivation, motivational variables have been studied using a cross-sectional design. That is, participants respond to a measure of motivation, such as intrinsic motivation (i.e., a motivational state characterized by performing an activity for its own sake; Deci, 1971; see also Kruglanski et al., 2018) at a given point in time, and then these scores are correlated with a criterion measure, such as a manager's ratings of creative behavior. In this case, a significant, positive relationship between intrinsic motivation and the manager's creative behavior ratings indicates that they covary more than would be expected by chance, and that as one variable increases, the other increases as well. In other words, people with higher intrinsic motivation scores tend to also have higher scores on the creative behavior scale, while people with lower motivation scores tend to have lower scores on the creative behavior scale. Note that this is a between-person comparison. What is known is that there is a positive association between intrinsic motivation and creative behaviors at a given point in time. Just as importantly is what is unknown – such as, what is the directionality of this relationship (intrinsic motivation → creative behaviors, intrinsic motivation ← creative behaviors, intrinsic motivation ↔ creative behaviors), and can this relationship be explained by a third variable? Furthermore, does this between-person comparison actually answer the question in which we are interested? Do we want to know if intrinsic motivation covaries with creative behaviors at a particular point in time, or do we want to know if intrinsic motivation *causes* people to engage in creative behaviors over time, such as gathering information and generating new ideas?

To investigate questions concerning how motivation is related over time with creativity – whether it is operationalized as a more proximal variable, such as information-gathering behaviors, or as a more distal variable, such as the novelty and usefulness of a new product design (Batey, 2012; Montag, Maertz, & Baer, 2012) – different types of research designs are required. The reason is due to the nature of the phenomena being explored. A highly creative product, of course, is not created instantaneously. It often requires working hours upon hours to generate and evaluate ideas, seek feedback, happen across insights, test prototypes, combine old and new approaches, and start and restart many times over until a final product emerges. A person takes many hundreds or thousands of actions during this process, and it is easy to imagine how a person's motivation varies wildly throughout. This variability is not captured in designs that take single "snapshots." The fluctuations in a person's motivation over time reflect a *within-person* level of analysis.

Understanding how this variation in motivation relates to creativity is critical for this domain of knowledge to advance. Dalal and Hulin (2008), speaking of motivation research generally, noted, "The distinction between within-person and between-person structures of behaviors is ignored at the researcher's peril" (p. 69). An example of this can be seen in the recent debate over the nature of the relationship between self-efficacy and performance (Bandura, 2012; Vancouver, 2012). Self-efficacy refers to the belief that one has to achieve a certain level of performance in a given task (Bandura, 1997). Self-efficacy was long held to have a positive, *causal* effect on performance (Stajkovic & Luthans, 1998). However, the majority of research on self-efficacy up until the late 1990s took place at the between-person level of analysis. When operationalized at the within-person level, a new picture emerged – self-efficacy had a negative effect on performance (Vancouver, More, & Yoder, 2008; Vancouver, Thompson, & Williams, 2001). In a recent meta-analysis, Sitzmann and Yeo (2013) demonstrated that under most conditions, self-efficacy has a weak positive or null effect on future performance, while past performance has a strong positive effect on self-efficacy. In 1998, it was thought that self-efficacy "represents a 28% gain in performance" (Stajkovic & Luthans, 1998, p. 252). Fifteen years later, Sitzmann and Yeo (2013) concluded, "[T]he reason there are differences between people with high and low self-efficacy is because those with high self-efficacy have been successful in the past" (p. 556). The stark contrast in these statements underscores the importance of understanding the within-person perspective. Presented later in this chapter is a discussion of the relevance of the self-efficacy–performance relationship in creativity research.

The key point is this: where a motivation construct is expected to vary, not only between persons but also within, this variation should be modeled. It is not the case that between-person analyses in this domain ought to be disregarded; rather, they should be complemented by within-person analyses where it is appropriate to do so. The decision to measure a variable at the within-person level depends on the research question being asked and the rate at which the target variable is expected to change. Regarding the first point, let's return to an earlier example on intrinsic motivation and information gathering behaviors. A research question at the between-person level might be as follows: are people higher in intrinsic motivation at a given point in time more likely to be engaging in information gathering behaviors? If one were interested in going beyond establishing covariance and wanted to also investigate temporal precedence, she could measure intrinsic motivation first, allow for a time lag, then measure information gathering later. At the within-person level, research questions concerning these two variables can look quite different from the between-person level. For instance, does a person seek out new information when he or she is more intrinsically motivated than usual, or when new information is discovered, does a person become more intrinsically motivated, or both? Another example: to what extent does a person's intrinsic motivation vary across tasks, and to the extent that it does vary, does it have a reliable relationship between information gathering behaviors? If the intrinsic motivation–information gathering relationship varies across tasks, one might be interested in exploring moderators that explain this variation (e.g., task complexity, level of mastery).

In addition to considering the research question, when deciding whether to measure a construct at the within-person level, one must also consider the extent to which the construct is expected to change over time. Motivation constructs range on a continuum (Kanfer, 1992) from being very proximal to action (e.g., self-efficacy, metacognition) to being very distal to action (e.g., personality, achievement motivation). The extent to which a variable is more proximal to action, the more dynamic it is – that is, the more rapidly it changes values (Johnson, Chang, & Lord, 2006). Because motivation variables change at different rates, a within-person analysis will not always be appropriate for answering questions concerning the relationship between motivation and creativity. For example, because personality is relatively stable over time (McCrae & Costa, 2003; cf. Mischel, 1973; Tasselli, Kilduff, & Landis, 2018), there is no significant within-person variability. In other words, people will respond very similarly from one measurement occasion to the next (unless the measurement takes place over decades; Roberts, Walton, & Viechtbauer, 2006). Thus, if one is interested in the relationship between personality and creativity, a within-person approach will not yield insights beyond what is observed at the between-person level. Alternatively, a variable more proximal to action, such as metacognition (i.e., cognitive processes that regulate self-knowledge and self-control during the learning process; Flavell, 1979), varies significantly minute to minute (Hardy, Day, & Steele, in press), which makes it amenable to a within-person analysis.

The two criteria just highlighted for deciding whether a motivation construct should be examined at the within-person level reflect the importance of aligning theory with methodology. If a research question concerns within-person processes, then the type of evidence gathered to answer those questions should reflect that. To date, very few studies of this kind exist in the published literature. A recent meta-analytic review of the motivation and creativity literature concluded, "Due to the lack of longitudinal studies ... how motivational variables impact creativity over an extended period of time is not clear" (Liu et al., 2016, p. 249). In addition, a review of creativity and intrinsic motivation studies published between 1990 and 2010 did not find a single study that utilized a within-person approach (de Jesus, Rus, Lens, & Imaginário, 2013). Given the scope of previous reviews of the motivation and creativity literature, none has provided a thorough examination of research that includes a within-person approach. That is the topic we turn to now.

State-of-the-Science Review

To identify relevant studies for this review, a search was conducted of the databases PsycINFO and Business Source Premier using the terms "creativity

AND motivation" and "innovation AND motivation." The search was constrained to the past 15 years (i.e., 2003–2018). This was originally done to ensure that the review could be completed in a timely manner, but it would also turn out to be the case that the vast majority (86%) of relevant studies were published after 2009. Thus, one can be reasonably confident of the comprehensiveness of this review. Using the first and second sets of search terms, 466 and 825 studies were identified, respectively. Studies with quantitative data ($k = 28$) were included in this review if there were at least two time points at which a motivation and creativity variable were measured. Previous research has defined a longitudinal study as consisting of *three* or more repeated measures (Ployhart & Vandenberg, 2010). Due to the limited number of studies identified in the review that met this criterion, studies with two time points were included as well. For a discussion on the important differences in the implications that can be drawn from designs with three or more repeated measures, rather than two, see Singer and Willett (2003, pp. 9–10). Three qualitative studies that examined creativity and motivation across time were also included. See Table 6.1 for a final list of independent samples.

Following Kanfer, Chen, and Pritchard (2008), studies included in this review are organized into three groups, based on the motivation variable used in a given study: content-based, context-based, or process-based. *Content-based* theories of motivation aim to answer the question, what needs or wants elicit action? *Context-based* theories focus on the role of environmental factors in motivation. And *processed-based* theories examine the psychological processes through which individual and environmental factors affect the direction, intensity, and persistence of one's effort.

Process-Based Approaches

Of the three approaches, process-based theories were the most frequently examined, accounting for nearly 80% of the identified studies ($k = 22$). This is not surprising given that constructs in these theories are expected to be dynamic and, thus, are more likely to be studied longitudinally. Within this category, the effects of affect on creativity were investigated most often, followed by effort, inspiration, and self-efficacy.

Affect

Affect is a general term that encompasses both long-lasting mood states and temporary emotional responses to a specific event (Frijda, 1993). In other words, there is both a more stable element of affect and a more dynamic one. Although this fact is intuitive, the first study to examine the association between natural fluctuations of affect (rather than experimentally induced) and creativity did not take place until 2005. Amabile, Barsade, Mueller, and

TABLE 6.1 Repeated-measures studies on creativity and motivation between 2003 and 2018.

Study	Time points	Motivation variables	Motivation category	Criterion variables
Thrash & Elliot (2003, Study 4)	14	Inspiration	Process	Self-reported creative experience
Amabile et al. (2005)	52[a]	Positive affect	Process	Creative thought and peer-rated creativity
Dineen & Niu (2008)	2	Confidence in experimentation, effort, enjoyment	Process	Creativity, originality, and quality of artwork
Binnewies et al. (2009a,b)	2	Positive work reflection, negative work reflection	Context	Self-reported idea generation at work
Thrash et al. (2010, Study 1)	4	Inspiration	Process	Self-reported, day-to-day creative ideation
Thrash et al. (2010, Study 2)	4.6[a]	Inspiration and effort	Process	Other-rated creativity of writing
Van Dijk & Kluger (2011, Study 2)	2	Intended effort	Process	Alternative uses for an object
Binnewies & Wörnlein (2011)	10	Positive and negative affect	Process	Self-reported creative behaviors at work
Tierney & Farmer (2011)	2	Creative self-efficacy	Process	Creativity at work
Stanko-Kaczmarek (2012)	4	Positive affect	Process	Satisfaction with progress on creative art project
To et al. (2012)	30	Positive and negative affect	Process	Creative process engagement
Huber et al. (2012)	–	Effort	Process	Creativity of a scale model of a lounge chair
Watson et al. (2012)	–	Inspiration, intrinsic motivation, self-efficacy	Process	Dance creativity
Liang et al. (2012)	2	Felt obligation for constructive change, organization-based self-esteem	Content	Promotive voice (idea suggestion)
Groenendijk et al. (2013)	2	Intrinsic motivation	Content	Visual and verbal product creativity

(*Continued*)

TABLE 6.1 (Continued) Repeated-measures studies on creativity and motivation between 2003 and 2018

Study	Time Points	Motivation Variables	Motivation Category	Criterion Variables
Bledow et al. (2013)	5	Positive and negative affect	Process	Self-reported creativity at work
Silvia et al. (2014)	38.1[a]	Positive and negative affect	Process	Doing something creative
Conner and Silvia (2015); Conner et al. (2018)[b]	13	Positive and negative affect	Process	Time spent doing creative activities
Strauss et al. (2015)	2	Job satisfaction	Context	Proactivity (idea suggestion)
Dong et al. (2015)	10	State promotion focus	Content	Customer-rated creativity
Reznickova & Zepeda (2016)	–	Basic psychological needs satisfaction, intrinsic motivation	Content	Idea suggestion
Unsworth & Mason (2016)	2	Effort	Process	Self-reported creativity at work
Beuk & Basadur (2016)	2	Task engagement/enjoyment[c]	Process	Fluency and flexibility of ideas
Ng & Lucianetti (2016)	3	Creative self-efficacy	Process	Idea generation
Karwowski et al. (2017, Study 1)	6	Emotion	Process	Doing something creative
Karwowski et al. (2017, Study 2)	14	Emotion	Process	Time devoted to creative activities and everyday creativity
Benedek et al. (2017)	14	Positive emotion, negative emotion, anxiety, stress, flow, etc.	Process	Self-reported progress on artwork
Steele (2018)	10	Creative self-efficacy	Process	Other-rated creativity of products

Note: Time Points, the number of times the variables in a study were measured; –, number of time points not available because these were qualitative studies.

[a] Average number of observations per participant was reported, rather than maximum.

[b] These two studies are reported together because they used the same sample.

[c] Beuk and Basadur (2016) use the term *task engagement* instead of *intrinsic motivation*; however, in the text of this chapter, I chose to use the latter because the measure they used was adapted from two measures of intrinsic motivation.

Staw (2005) used an experience sampling methodology (Csikszentmihalyi & Larson, 1987) to assess knowledge workers across multiple organizations and industries. Daily measures (on average, 52 per participant) of self-reported creative thought and positive affect were taken, as well as monthly measures of peer-rated creativity. The results of this study showed there was a positive linear relationship between positive affect and creativity, both self- and peer-reported. Furthermore, Amabile et al. found that there were four distinct temporal patterns to this relationship: (a) positive affect occurred simultaneously with creative thought; (b) positive affect predicted next-day creative thought; (c) creative thought produced brief, positive affect 86% of the time; and (d) 20% of the time, sharing one's creative ideas led with others led to a negative reaction, which in turn produced negative emotions in the participant.

Along similar lines, in a week-long study of college students (on average, 38 observations per participant), Silvia and colleagues (2014) also found that happiness and feeling active were significantly, positively related with doing a creative activity. These results are consistent with the experimental literature (Baas, De Dreu, & Nijstad, 2008). No negative moods or other positive moods were significantly related. Importantly, Silvia et al. centered the within-person predictors (i.e., moods) at each person's own means (Hox, 2010), which changes the interpretation slightly from the results of Amabile et al.'s (2005) analyses. Specifically, while Silvia et al. (2014) show that a person is feeling happier *than he usually is*, he is more likely to be doing something creative, Amabile et al. (2005) show that when a person is happier *than the average of the sample*, she is more likely engaging in creative thought. Ignore for a moment the difference in the criterion. What should be noted here is the difference in the reference point of the predictor. Within-person centering in Silvia et al.'s study affords the reader a different conclusion by making each individual's own average the reference point, rather than the collective average of the sample. For an approachable introduction to centering and multilevel modeling generally, see Silvia (2007).

Several other studies have observed significant relationships between mood valence (i.e., positive and negative) and creativity. For example, Binnewies and Wörnlein (2011) asked a sample of 90 interior architects to fill out two daily measures over the course of one week. Measures of affect were completed in the morning, and a measure of creative behaviors was completed before finishing work in the afternoon. This study found that feeling positive affect in the morning was a significant predictor of daily creative behaviors ($r = 0.30$), while negative affect was a significant negative predictor ($r = -0.10$). At the between-person level, comparable correlations were observed for both positive affect ($r = 0.48$) and negative affect ($r = -0.18$). In another study, a sample of 36 undergraduate art students were asked to create a collage in approximately 15 minutes (Stanko-Kaczmarek, 2012). At the end of three 5-minute intervals, participants stopped working on their collages to fill out measures of positive affect and satisfaction with the progress of their creative project. The results of this study showed that every measure of positive affect during the task was significantly correlated with nearly every measure of satisfaction with progress ($r = 0.37$ to 0.64). A third study used pre–post measures of motivation and creativity to test the effects of a teaching intervention in a sample of 54 undergraduate graphic design students (Dineen & Niu, 2008). Over the seven-week period, the treatment group reported enjoying the workshop significantly more than the control group. Participants in the treatment group also produced artwork that was rated by expert judges as significantly more original (Cohen's $d = 1.93$). Finally, in a 14-day study of 38 professional visual artists, participants responded to a daily questionnaire as they worked on a project that would be submitted for an international art competition at the end of the two-week period (Benedek, Jauk, Kerschenbauer, Anderwald, & Grond, 2017). At the end of each workday, participants responded to items concerning their process (e.g., "I have changed the material I plan to work with."), experience (e.g., "When I am working, I forget myself."), mood (e.g., "I have anxieties regarding my work."), and sense of progress (e.g., "How far advanced is the realization of your work?"). After controlling for a linear trend in their model (a necessity in longitudinal research; Singer & Willett, 2003), Benedek et al. (2017) observed that progress on one's artwork was significantly, positively related to enjoying one's work and significantly, negatively related to being anxious about it.

In addition to examining the valence of moods, previous longitudinal studies have looked at the impact of a mood's activating or deactivating quality (Russell, 1980). Activation refers to experiencing "a sense of mobilization or energy" (Barrett & Russell, 1999, p. 10) and is present at high or low levels in positive and negative moods. That is, there are positive moods with high activation (e.g., excited, enthusiastic) and low activation (e.g., calm, content), just as there are negative moods with high activation (e.g., tense, anxious) and low activation (e.g., discouraged, sad). Whether positive or negative in valence, it is the activating moods that have been theorized to foster creativity and, conversely, the deactivating moods to reduce creativity (De Dreu, Baas, & Nijstad, 2008). De Dreu et al. (2008) found initial support for these proposed links in a series of four experimental studies, and a few years later, their findings were corroborated in a study that examined activating and deactivating moods over time (To, Fisher, Ashkanasy, & Rowe, 2012).

To and colleagues (2012) conducted their study using a sample of 30 doctoral and postgraduate honors students. These participants reported their creative behaviors (e.g., problem identification, information gathering) and mood three times a day for 10 working days. The results of this study showed that creative behaviors were positively associated with activating moods, whether positive ($r = 0.35$) or negative ($r = 0.10$). Conversely, creative behaviors were unrelated to deactivating positive moods ($r = 0.00$) and significantly negatively related to deactivating negative moods ($r = -0.13$). Interestingly, although negative activating moods had a much smaller relationship with concurrent creative behaviors, they were significantly related to creative behaviors at the following time point, whereas positive activating moods were not. Congruent with De Dreu et al. (2008), To and colleagues (2012) explained that this effect is due to how activating negative moods motivate people to exert effort for longer, promoting perseverance and time spent on creative tasks. Three other studies have examined the effect of activating negative moods on creativity. Silvia et al. (2014) observed nonsignificant, negative relationships for two activating negative moods (i.e., angry, annoyed). A similar effect was observed in Karwowski, Lebuda, Szumski, and Firkowska-Makiewicz's (2017) Study 2, where, in a sample of 433 adults, anger was nonsignificantly, negatively related to engaging in a creative activity. However, Karwowski et al. (2017) also found that anger had a positive, significant relationship with *time spent* doing a creative activity. Likewise, in Conner and colleagues' (Conner, DeYoung, & Silvia, 2018; Conner & Silvia, 2015) two-week study of 658 college students, high-activation negative mood was positively related ($r = 0.12$) to how much time was spent doing creative activities in a day. These studies provide a fair amount of evidence supporting the perseverance mechanism through which negative activating moods are related to creativity.

Nevertheless, the majority of evidence concerning the link between mood and creativity over time points to positive moods, especially *activating* positive moods, having the strongest relationship, relative to deactivating moods and activating negative moods (Amabile et al., 2005; Binnewies & Wörnlein, 2011; Conner & Silvia, 2015; Karwowski et al., 2017; Silvia et al., 2014; To et al., 2012). The lagged effects between positive mood and creativity are less clear. When engaging in creative behaviors is the criterion, To et al. (2012) and Conner et al. (2018) observed a nonsignificant relationship, while Amabile et al. (2005) observed a statistically significant one. (The magnitude of the relationships could not be directly compared because Amabile et al. did not provide effect size estimates.) Similarly, when the criterion is positive mood and creativity is the predictor, one study found that engaging in creative activities on one day is positively related to positive affect the following day (Conner et al., 2018), while another study found that this effect is shorter lived than that – the positive mood that follows creativity lasted minutes or hours, not to the next day (Amabile et al., 2005).

All of the studies discussed so far have examined the effects of (or effects on) positive and negative affect independently. Only one study has examined their interactive relationship with creativity over time (Bledow, Rosing, & Frese, 2013). Specifically, Bledow and colleagues (2013) hypothesized that when an increase in positive affect was paired with a *decrease* in negative affect, people would be more creative than if the increase in positive affect was paired with *unchanged* negative affect. This hypothesis was tested using a sample of 116 full-time workers, who filled out measures of affect in the morning before starting work and measures of affect and creativity in the afternoon before the end of the workday. Bledow and colleagues (2013) found support for their hypothesis. They then conducted a follow-up experiment where shifts in affect were induced by asking participants (in this case, 80 psychology master's students) to write essays that reflected the target mood. Participants who first wrote a story inducing negative affect (rather than neutral affect) then wrote a story inducing positive affect were able to generate more original and flexible ideas in a subsequent divergent thinking task.

Inspiration

The concept of inspiration has a rich and complex history in creativity research with roots that can be traced back to Plato (Weiner, 2000). In developing one of the earliest models of creative thought, Wallas quotes physicist and physiologist Hermann von Helmholtz as saying, "Happy ideas came unexpectedly without effort, like an inspiration" (Wallas, 1926, p. 80). Wallas argued that after a phase of trying to solve a problem without success, it can be useful to walk away from the problem and allow the information one has gathered to incubate. Following this time of putting a problem aside, a solution may begin to emerge at a semiconscious level (or in *fringe consciousness*; Sadler-Smith, 2015), until the final "'flash' or 'click'" of illumination occurs (Wallas, 1926, pp. 93–94). The idea of inspiration as being necessary for creative production persists today in lay theories of creativity (Sawyer, 2012). A few studies conducted in the last decade and a half have shed new light on this relationship. Thrash and Elliot (2003, 2004) developed a conceptualization of inspiration that integrated an interdisciplinary literature (e.g., psychology, theology, music). They concluded it is a state defined by transcendence (i.e., awareness of new, extraordinary possibilities), evocation (i.e., prompted by a particular stimulus, such as idea, person, or action), and approach motivation (i.e., striving to express or actualize the idea or vision). In Study 4, Thrash and Elliot (2003) emailed daily questionnaires over 14 consecutive days to 150 undergraduate students. In the daily questionnaire, inspiration was measured by asking the extent to which a participant had "a feeling of inspiration" that day. Creativity was measured by asking participants the extent to which they experienced creativity that day. Time-lagged analyses were used, where the dependent variable at time *t* was predicted by the independent variable at time $t-1$. The results showed that, although positively correlated ($r = 0.34$) when measured on the same day, inspiration and creativity were nonsignificantly related in the next-day analyses, whether creativity was the dependent variable or inspiration was. However, when averaged over the course of a week, someone who felt more inspired during Week 1 was likely to experience more creativity during Week 2. The reverse (i.e., average Week 1 Creativity → average Week 2 Inspiration) was also positive and statistically significant.

A subsequent set of studies by Thrash, Maruskin, Cassidy, Fryer, and Ryan (2010) built on Thrash and Elliot's (2003) studies by using richer measures of creativity. In Study 1, Thrash et al. (2010) surveyed 157 undergraduate students once a week for 4 weeks. They were asked how frequently they thought of creative ideas or solutions to problems and how frequently they felt inspired. Using cross-lagged models, the results showed that creative ideation positively predicted next-week inspiration, but the effects of inspiration on creative ideation were not statistically significant. In Study 2, Thrash et al. (2010) used a sample of 148 undergraduate psychology students who were writing a paper for a course assignment. On each page of their papers, participants responded to a questionnaire regarding their inspiration. After the papers were submitted, judges rated them for creativity and technical merit. At the within- and between-person levels, self-reported inspiration was positively related to ratings of creativity. Interestingly, self-reported inspiration at the within-person level was *negatively* related to technical merit. The different effects of inspiration on these two criteria highlight the importance of measuring creativity as a multidimensional construct (Montag et al., 2012; Sullivan & Ford, 2010).

In a final study on inspiration, Watson, Nordin-Bates, and Chappell (2012) utilized a qualitative approach to investigate intrapersonal and environmental factors that facilitate creativity in preprofessional dancers. Over the course of three months, Watson and colleagues observed and interviewed three dancers (ages 14–15), five instructors, and three visiting choreographers. The themes from these interviews suggested that participants believed that inspiration was indeed an important facilitator of their own creativity. Furthermore, they described finding inspiration in two ways. First, they exposed themselves to works of art (e.g., visual art, music) and created art outside of the domain of dance (e.g., writing, drawing). Second, they reflected on previous movements they had learned or on earlier life experiences. The latter topic of reflection was more common for older dancers. Watson et al.'s study offers useful insights for future investigations into the antecedents of inspiration, which Thrash and colleagues observed to have significant, positive effects on creativity (Thrash & Elliot, 2003; Thrash et al., 2010).

Self-Efficacy

As discussed earlier, the long-standing view that self-efficacy causes better performance has faced significant scrutiny in the past 15 years (Sitzmann & Yeo, 2013; Vancouver, 2012). Nevertheless, this debate has been slow to enter discussions of *creative* self-efficacy, a construct introduced by Tierney and Farmer (2002) around the same time the negative effects of self-efficacy were first published (Vancouver et al., 2001). Tierney and Farmer (2002) defined creative self-efficacy as "the belief one has the ability to produce creative outcomes" (p. 1138). Since this time, at least 68 studies have examined the relationship between creative self-efficacy and creativity (Liu et al., 2016), only two of which statistically examined this relationship over time. Tierney and Farmer's (2011) study used a sample of 145 employees at an organization that provided social services. Participants self-reported their creative self-efficacy at two timepoints, six months apart. Their supervisors provided ratings of creative behavior. The results of this study showed that an increase in creative self-efficacy from Time 1 to Time 2 was significantly, positively related to increases in creative behaviors.

Building on these results, Ng and Lucianetti (2016) argued that creative self-efficacy may be more strongly associated with generating new ideas, while persuasion and change self-efficacy may be more strongly associated with disseminating and implementing ideas, respectively. These hypotheses were tested in a sample of 267 employees across 60 organizations. At three timepoints, participants self-reported their self-efficacy beliefs and behaviors with respect to idea generation, dissemination, and implementation. Because the focus of the present review is motivation and creativity, not innovation, the focus here is just on the relationship between creative self-efficacy and idea generation (Anderson, Potočnik, & Zhou, 2014; Hughes, Lee, Tian, Newman, & Legood, 2018). The results of Ng and Lucianetti's (2016) study showed that, similar to Tierney and Farmer (2011), increases in creative self-efficacy were significantly, positively related to idea generation behaviors. Importantly, Ng and Lucianetti also demonstrated that this covariation is significantly higher than what would be expected to occur by chance between two variables that share a linear trend (Singer & Willett, 2003).

There are two other studies worth mentioning here, despite lacking direct evidence on the self-efficacy–creativity relationship. The first is Dineen and Niu's (2008) study, which examined the effects of a teaching intervention in a sample of undergraduate graphic design students. Their preintervention scores on a single-item measure of confidence in one's capacity to experiment were nonsignificantly different (Cohen's $d = 0.31$); however, the postinterventions scores showed that the treatment and control groups diverged sharply. Although the confidence of both groups increased, the treatment group had an average confidence score that was 4.59 standard deviations higher than the control group. This was accompanied by a sharper increase in creativity, relative to the control group. This pattern is comparable to the one observed in Tierney and Farmer (2011).

The second study that indirectly speaks to the self-efficacy–performance relationship is Watson et al.'s (2012) qualitative study of preprofessional dancers. The three dancers talked about confidence as being integral to their creativity. In fact, one dancer said, "I would put confidence as number 1"

(p. 159). The instructors and choreographers, however, felt very differently. Three instructors said that confidence was not a requirement for creativity, and one choreographer went as far as saying the link between confidence and creativity "is the biggest lie" (p. 159). Confidence in one's capacity for generating new ideas may not only be unrelated to creativity, but it could be an obstacle, according to one instructor. This instructor reported that the most confident dancer must be challenged the most to move out of her comfort zone and try something new. It should be noted that this study differentiated between types of self-efficacy beliefs, such as those that are more trait-like rather than state-like (Chen, Gully, & Eden, 2001). Thus, where the dancers may have been referring to how confident they were to perform a dance creatively, the instructors may have had in mind a more general confidence in the self.

Taken together, at this stage, the within-person research on the link between creative self-efficacy and creativity does not offer many insights. What it does tell us is that creative self-efficacy is dynamic, but the rate at which it fluctuates is not precisely known – time lags as short as 7 weeks (Dineen & Niu, 2008) and as long as 6 months (Tierney & Farmer, 2011) were utilized. Self-efficacy beliefs have been conceptualized at both general levels (e.g., Chen et al., 2001) and task-specific levels (e.g., Beck & Schmidt, 2012). They have also been conceptualized somewhere in between, at the domain-specific level (e.g., teacher self-efficacy; Tschannen-Moran & Hoy, 2001), which is where creative self-efficacy may exist. A key implication of the presumed level at which creative self-efficacy is conceptualized is its expected rate of change (Grether, Sowislo, & Wiese, 2018). To the extent that creative self-efficacy might be more task specific, it should be expected to meaningfully change over seconds, minutes, and days (Gist & Mitchell, 1992), let alone weeks and months. To capture this variability – if it exists – future research ought to consider utilizing much shorter time spans (Beghetto & Karwowski, 2017).

For example, I conducted a study where a sample of 119 undergraduate students were asked to build creative structures out of craft materials (Steele, 2018). Conforming to the traditional, two-dimensional definition of creativity (Amabile, 1996; Runco & Jaeger, 2012), participants were asked to build structures that were both high in quality (i.e., tall and stable) and originality (i.e., novel designs and uses of materials). Participants were given nine minutes to build a structure that could stand independently. The structure was then photographed by the study proctor, so judges could later rate the quality and originality of each structure. Meanwhile, participants completed measures of self-efficacy that reflected the two dimensions of the criterion. That is, for the quality of the structure, participants were asked to indicate on a scale from 0 to 100 how certain they were that they could build an independently standing structure that reached a given height. Participants then rated their level of certainty across ten items that demarcated different levels of performance (i.e., 6, 12, 18, ... 60 inches). Similarly, for the originality of the structure, participants were asked to rate on a 0–100 scale how certain they were that they could build a structure representing different levels of originality. The five items were written descriptions of various levels of originality, rather than objective markers. The first item, representing the lowest level of originality, read, "Commonplace, routine, or ordinary," while the fifth item read, "Rare, having mostly original, unique, or completely new features." After responding to these items, participants were given nine minutes to build a new structure. This process was repeated five times total.

The results of this study revealed a different pattern across the two dimensions of creativity. With respect to the quality of the structure, between-person self-efficacy had a significant positive relationship, while within-person self-efficacy had a significant negative relationship. (The linear trend was also significant and positive.) This pattern has been observed repeatedly in previous research (e.g., Hardy et al., in press; Sitzmann & Yeo, 2013; Vancouver & Kendall, 2006). It suggests that while someone who has a higher average self-efficacy will generally perform better than someone with lower average self-efficacy, an increase in one's self-efficacy relative to one's typical level is associated with lower performance. With respect to the originality of the structure, self-efficacy was nonsignificant at the within- and between-person levels. As important as the results, what this study illustrates is a different approach to conceptualizing creative self-efficacy. Rather than asking people about how confident they are that they can generate new ideas in general, this approach operationalizes creative self-efficacy as a task-specific measure – how confident are you that you can build something new and functional right now? This approach affords greater precision in hypothesis generation and testing, which ultimately provides a better understanding of the constructs themselves and the thoughts and behaviors they are meant to represent.

Effort

The final group of studies within the domain of process-based approaches are those that looked at effort. Effort refers to "the intentional exertion of forces ... to produce some desired outcome" (Massin, 2017, p. 243). It is the final link in the chain connecting motivation with action (Johnson et al., 2006; Kanfer, 1992). Kanfer (1990) describes three dimensions along which effort can be described – intensity, persistence, and direction. I organize my review of the six studies examining effort and creativity into these three dimensions.

Intensity

The most frequently examined dimension of effort is intensity. It is assessed with items that ask participants how hard they are working or how much effort they are exerting. In Thrash et al. (2010, Study 2), where undergraduate students were writing papers for a course assignment, participants reported their level of effort on each page. The results of this study showed that a participant's average level of effort was significantly, positively related to ratings of technical quality. However, effort was nonsignificantly related to technical quality at the within-person level (i.e., page by page). Furthermore, it was not significantly related to the creativity of the paper, neither at the between- nor within-person level. In Dineen and Niu's (2008) study of undergraduate graphic design students, they found that a teaching intervention where experimentation was encouraged significantly increased self-reported effort levels and expert-rated artwork creativity, relative to a control group.

A similar finding was observed in Unsworth and Mason's (2016, Study 2) field experiment, where 131 employees drawn from five organizations completed a five-week training module. Over these five weeks, participants were trained to use self-management strategies (e.g., using to-do lists, setting goals for oneself) and self-concordant strategies (e.g., seeking out work one enjoys, surrounding oneself with people who bring out one's best; Houghton & Neck, 2002). Participants who reported high use of both self-management and self-concordant strategies exhibited the highest self-reported creativity and effort expenditure. Interestingly, however, effort and creativity were nonsignificantly correlated ($r = 0.02$ to 0.16). One possible explanation for this is that participants were asked how much effort they were devoting to their jobs in general, not to doing creative work specifically. Unless creativity was a requirement for their job, we should not expect more job-related effort to be related to higher levels of creativity (Unsworth, 2001). Related to this point is a study by Van Dijk and Kluger (2011, Study 2). In their study, 112 undergraduate students completed two divergent thinking tasks for ten minutes each. Between the first and second tasks, fabricated feedback (either positive or negative) was delivered regarding their performance. Unlike Unsworth and Mason's (2016, Study 2) study, Van Dijk and Kluger (2011, Study 2) observed significant, positive correlations between effort and creativity ($r = 0.23$ to 0.27). It should be noted that significance (including marginal significance, $p < 0.10$) was only observed when measures were taken at the same time point. That is, effort at Time 1 was unrelated to idea generation at Time 2.

Persistence

Only one study examined the relationship between persistence of effort and creativity across multiple time points. Beuk and Basadur (2016) asked a nonstudent sample of 341 people to complete two divergent thinking tasks. Responses were rated by two independent judges for the fluency (i.e., number of ideas generated), flexibility (i.e., number of idea categories represented), and originality (i.e., novelty or uncommonness of an idea) of ideas generated during the second task. Persistence of effort was measured in terms of how many seconds were spent working on a task. The results of this study showed that persistence of effort during Task 1 was significantly correlated with fluency, flexibility, and originality in Task 2 ($r = 0.41$ to 0.42). Effort persistence was also fairly highly correlated across tasks ($r = 0.63$), suggesting that there may be significant between-person differences in the willingness to sustain effort when working on divergent thinking tasks.

Direction

The direction of effort refers to decisions regarding which goal (or set of goals) a person allocates her effort toward, given the goals that are available to pursue (Neal, Ballard, & Vancouver, 2017). These choices can involve concrete decisions, such as choosing between an apple and a chocolate chip cookie, and more abstract prioritizations, such as choosing between one's health and immediate gratification. Longitudinal studies of effort directionality (or goal choice) are increasingly common in applied psychology research (e.g., Ballard, Yeo, Loft, Vancouver, & Neal, 2016; Northcraft, Schmidt, & Ashford, 2011; Schmidt & Dolis, 2009), but only one such study relevant to creativity is identified. A qualitative study by Huber, Leigh, and Tremblay (2012) followed the work of 20 undergraduate students over two weeks, during which time they each created a scale model of a lounge chair. Participants wrote about their process in four journal entries, which were subsequently analyzed by the researchers. The creativity of the final product was evaluated by two expert judges. The results of this study showed that participants who explored varied and disparate sources (e.g., end-user research, trade periodicals) before generating ideas were more likely to produce a creative model. Furthermore, reporting specific information that they learned from these sources was positively related to creativity.

Content-Based Approaches

Whereas process-based approaches generally examine the *how* of motivation, content-based approaches examine the *what* (Kanfer et al., 2008). That is, what traits, dispositions, and orientations give rise to particular behaviors? Trait-based motives (e.g., personality) were the focus of much of the early research on creativity (Feist, 1998; Nicholls, 1972). With the introduction of intrinsic motivation as an integral element in the creative process (Amabile, 1983), need-based motives became prominent (Deci, 1975; Gagné & Deci, 2005). Because content-based approaches specify constructs that are expected to change over years and decades, it is not surprising that this review identified only eight studies that met the inclusion criteria. It is argued shortly why it need not be the case, however, that traits and motives are excluded from longitudinal research. First, let us examine the present state of research in this area, beginning with four studies on intrinsic motivation.

Intrinsic Motivation

One of the most interesting insights comes from Beuk and Basadur's (2016) study in which participants completed two divergent thinking tasks. They found that people who were intrinsically motivated working on one divergent thinking task also tended to be intrinsically motivated working on a second divergent thinking task ($r = 0.58$). Furthermore, intrinsic motivation during the first task was positively related to how much time was spent on the second task ($r = 0.18$). Finally, intrinsic motivation during the first task was positively related to the fluency (i.e., number of ideas generated), flexibility (i.e., number of idea categories represented), and originality (i.e., novelty or uncommonness of an idea) of ideas generated during the second task; however, performance on the first task was unrelated to intrinsic motivation during the second task. Taken together, the results of this study have the following two implications: intrinsic motivation varies across a short time frame (the two tasks were performed back-to-back), and, congruent with prevailing theory (Amabile, 1996), intrinsic motivation appears to be more of an antecedent to, rather than a consequence of, novel idea generation.

In a qualitative study, Reznickova and Zepeda (2016) interviewed 19 volunteer members of an organization that provides healthy, sustainably sourced meals to the local community. The results of their inductive analysis mapped closely onto self-determination theory (Gagné & Deci, 2005), which argues that people will feel intrinsically motivated (i.e., completing a task for its own sake, rather than to earn a reward) to the extent that their needs for competence, relatedness, and autonomy are met. Furthermore, the authors found that different psychological needs held more or less importance to different people. For some participants, it was the feeling of autonomy to which they attributed their intrinsic motivation: "[T]he responsibility of being our own bosses ... was something that, at least for me, made it so motivating" (p. 12). For others, it was relatedness: "[T]he only way people are going to put that much time into it is if they're enjoying it and feel like they're part of the community" (p. 12). Reznickova and Zepeda went on to conclude that it was because of this intrinsic motivation that people continually suggested new ideas for making their organization better. Along similar lines, Watson et al. (2012) concluded from their interviews with preprofessional dancers that intrinsic motivation was a "key factor in developing creativity" (p. 160).

In the final study incorporating intrinsic motivation (Groenendijk, Janssen, Rijlaarsdam, & van den Bergh, 2013), 131 high school students were assigned to groups where either they watched videos of someone demonstrating how to creatively make a collage and write a poem then began the two tasks themselves, or they began the tasks immediately without watching any videos. In the observational learning conditions, half the participants watched someone who was skillful at the two tasks, while the other half watched someone who was less competent. The results of a pre–post analysis showed that the participants in the observational learning conditions created significantly more creative collages, according to a panel of judges with domain-relevant expertise, and they reported higher levels of intrinsic motivation. Comparable, albeit weaker, effects were observed in the second task (i.e., writing poems).

Taken together, what these studies show is that intrinsic motivation is multifaceted, consisting of both stable between-person differences as well as dynamic within-person variation. Although intrinsic motivation is rarely studied longitudinally (Van den Broeck, Ferris, Chang, & Rosen, 2016), Amabile (1983) herself noted that "intrinsic motivation can be viewed as both a state and a trait (although this trait should not be thought of as general and pervasive but as specific to particular class of activities)" (p. 365). Thus, this area is ripe for future research. This can begin with the basic question, to what extent does the satisfaction of basic psychological needs vary over time? If a sample completed brief surveys at multiple points throughout the day over the course of a week or two, would we see more variability within persons or between persons? If it is the former, this might suggest that one's context or current activity was more important for determining the person's need fulfillment. If it is the latter (i.e., more variability at the between-person level), this might suggest that need satisfaction is more dispositional. That is, there could be differences between people in how earnestly they seek out satisfying their basic psychological needs or in their sensitivity to varying degrees to which their needs are satisfied. Greater between-person variability could indicate a constancy of circumstances across multiple domains in life (e.g., work, home, social gatherings) that either fulfill or leave unfulfilled one's basic psychological needs. Another question one might ask is, to what extent are varying levels of need satisfaction related to variation in intrinsic motivation? A recent meta-analysis (Van den Broeck et al., 2016) showed that autonomy had a significantly higher correlation with intrinsic motivation ($\rho = 0.64$) than either competence ($\rho = 0.32$) or relatedness ($\rho = 0.44$). This might suggest that in circumstances where one's need for competence and relatedness are not met but one's need for autonomy is, she may still be intrinsically motivated. However, it could also indicate that people who are interested in a task for its own sake also tend to seek out contexts in which they are free to direct their own work. Cross-sectional relationships are not well suited for answering these questions, but longitudinal models could advance our knowledge here.

Regulatory Focus

Just as intrinsic motivation exhibits stable and dynamic elements, regulatory focus strategies consist of both as well (Brockner & Higgins, 2001; Wallace & Chen, 2006). Regulatory focus refers to two coexisting self-regulatory systems (i.e., promotion or prevention) that prioritize different needs during goal pursuit (Scholer & Higgins, 2010). In a study of 380 hairstylists, state-level promotion focus was examined as an antecedent to customer-rated creativity (Dong, Liao, Chuang, Zhou, & Campbell, 2015). There was an average of 9.3 customer interactions recorded per employee. The results of this study showed that higher state promotion focus was significantly, positively related to employee creativity.

Affiliation motives

An affiliation motive refers to a preference for building and maintaining positive relationships with others (McClelland, 1965). In a two-wave panel design (six weeks between waves), Liang, Farh, and Farh (2012) collected data from 231 employees in a retail company. They measured two affiliation motives – organization-based self-esteem (OBSE) and felt obligation for constructive change (FOCC). OBSE refers to one's beliefs about his social worth in the workplace (Pierce, Gardner, Cummings, & Dunham, 1989), and FOCC refers to a personal norm one has for reciprocating rewards received from her organization (Fuller, Marler, & Hester, 2006). In Liang et al.'s (2012) study, OBSE at Time 1 was significantly, positively related to suggesting new ideas (referred to as *promotive voice* in this study) at Time 2. Interestingly, the reverse was also positively and statistically significant – suggesting new ideas at Time 1 and OBSE and Time 2. After accounting for other variables in the model, only the latter relationship was statistically significant, indicating that offering new ideas may increase one's sense of belonging and value in an organization, but not the other way around. In contrast, FOCC at Time 1 was significantly related to suggesting new ideas at Time 2, while the reverse relationship was not statistically significant.

Context-Based Approaches

The final set of studies falls under the category of context-based approaches. These studies examined environmental influences on motivation, including the effects of how the environment is perceived. In one study, Binnewies and Wörnlein (2011) examined the relationship between daily fluctuations in job demands with creativity in a sample of interior architects. The results of the study showed that at the within-person level, daily time pressure had a curvilinear relationship with creativity, such that moderate levels of time pressure were related to the highest level of creativity. Furthermore, for people with high (rather than low) levels of job control, daily situational constraints were significantly, negatively related to creativity. The remaining three studies focused on people's attitudes about their context, rather than the effects of different contexts. In a study of 358 employees who worked with people with special needs, Binnewies, Sonnentag, and Mojza (2009a,b) collected data on how participants thought about their work experiences during their leisure time and self-reported idea generation behaviors. Reflecting positively about one's work at Time 1 was significantly, positively related to idea generation behaviors at Time 2 ($r = 0.22$). However, although the relationships were quite small, it was also observed that idea generation behaviors at Time 1 were negatively related to feeling recovered ($r = -0.09$) and positively related to reflecting negatively about work ($r = 0.12$). This finding bears some similarity to Amabile et al.'s (2005) observation that sharing new ideas with others sometimes led to negative reactions from others.

Examining the relationship between job satisfaction and idea generation (referred to as *proactivity* in this study) over time, Strauss, Griffin, Parker, and Mason (2015) sampled 75 public-sector employees at two timepoints separated by two years. They found that job satisfaction at Time 1 was only positively related to suggesting new ideas at Time 2 if they were already suggesting new ideas at Time 1. Finally, in To and colleagues' (2012) study of doctoral and postgraduate students, in addition to measuring mood and creative behavior, they examined momentary psychological empowerment (i.e., a set of four cognitions that reflect an active orientation toward one's work role; Spreitzer, 1995). The results of their study showed that empowerment exhibited the second-strongest relationship (after activating positive mood) with creative behaviors ($r = 0.31$). It was also positively related to activating and deactivating positive moods ($r = 0.39$ and 0.14, respectively), while being negatively related to deactivating negative moods ($r = -0.13$).

Discussion and Future Research

What We Know

In this review, the findings from 28 studies were discussed. Yet, the varied constructs examined in these studies make it challenging to draw conclusions in which one can be reasonably confident. Consequently, just two statements about this literature are offered, both of which are supported by multiple studies. First, positive activating moods play an important role in the creative process. Multiple studies observed that when people were engaging in creative behaviors, they also reported being excited, happy, and enthusiastic (e.g., Amabile et al., 2005; Benedek et al., 2017; Karwowski et al., 2017; Silvia et al., 2014; To et al., 2012). Furthermore, positive moods were sometimes *antecedents* to creative behaviors (Amabile et al., 2005; Bledow et al., 2013); however, this relationship was not always statistically significant (Conner et al., 2018; To et al., 2012). The inconsistency may be due to differences in the time intervals between measurements, but the intervals were varied within the two pairs of studies. Another possible explanation is that Amabile et al. and Bledow et al. ignored the activating–deactivating dimension of affect, while Conner et al. and To et al. incorporated it in their studies. Future research is needed to determine what types of positive moods are antecedents to creative behaviors and for what duration a positive mood exhibits a significant relationship with creative behaviors. A practical implication from this body of research is that managers can encourage creativity by fostering positive, activating moods among their employees. As shown in Amabile et al.'s study, positive, activating moods can emerge from the work itself when people have an opportunity to do something creative. In other words, rather than orchestrating a positive emotional experience, managers can simply provide the opportunity for these experiences to emerge.

Second, intrinsic motivation is dynamic. While this was suggested over 35 years ago (Amabile, 1983), I could not identify a single study that investigated this directly. In an earlier review of intrinsic motivation and creativity studies conducted between 1990 and 2010 (de Jesus et al., 2013), no within-person studies were found then either. That intrinsic motivation varies over time is an inference based on three empirical studies (Beuk & Basadur, 2016; Groenendijk et al., 2013; Reznickova & Zepeda, 2016), which provided indirect evidence of its dynamism, and on self-determination theory itself (Gagné & Deci, 2005), which suggests that intrinsic motivation should vary according to the degree to which one's basic psychological needs are satisfied. Given that intrinsic motivation varies over time, managers may wonder how they can best promote it in their employees. According to self-determination theory (Gagné & Deci, 2005), managers can foster intrinsic motivation in their followers by helping them to satisfy their needs for autonomy, competence, and relatedness. A recent meta-analysis showed that satisfaction of one's need for autonomy is most strongly related to intrinsic motivation (Van den Broeck et al., 2016). Managers can help to satisfy employees' needs for autonomy through various strategies, including giving discretion about how tasks are accomplished, allowing them to influence how tasks are prioritized, and providing room for failure (Gilbert & Kelloway, 2014).

What We Do Not Know and Suggestions for Future Research

This review has highlighted a number of gaps in our knowledge of how motivation is related to creativity over time. Although one could find the dearth of information disheartening, I feel encouraged about the recent uptick in this line of research with 82% of within-person studies having been published since 2010. This is commensurate with a broader trend in the organization sciences literatures (e.g., Industrial–Organizational Psychology, Management, Organizational Behavior, Human Resources), where 80% of within-person research has been published since 2005 (McCormick, Reeves, Downes, Li, & Ilies, in press). I am also excited about the prospects that this line of research opens up to creativity scholars. The potential research questions presented throughout this chapter will hopefully foster excitement in others as well.

Going forward, I offer the following two suggestions for future research. First, motivational variables that have an established relationship with creativity at the between-person level should be investigated at the within-person level. A recent meta-analysis on motivation and creativity provides a list of variables from which to start (Liu et al., 2016) – for example, job autonomy, job complexity, intrinsic motivation, extrinsic motivation, and creativity self-efficacy. Investigating these relationships at the within-person level is important for aligning motivational theories, most of which discuss intraindividual processes, with an appropriate methodology (Dalal & Hulin, 2008). Furthermore, although between- and within-person relationships differ in magnitude only about 25% of the time (McCormick et al., in press), the nature of the processes underlying these relationships may very well be different. For example, consider the positive relationship between intrinsic motivation and creativity. Intrinsic motivation is related to the exploration of new ideas (Amabile, 1996). Thus, *at the between-person level*, the link between intrinsic motivation and creativity may be mediated by knowledge from distal domains (Acar & van den Ende, 2016), while *at the within-person level*, this link is mediated by experimentation in the moment. It could also be the case that the intrinsic motivation–creativity link shares a common mediator, such as persistence of effort. If intrinsic motivation is reliably related to the amount of time a person spends on a task (e.g., Beuk & Basadur, 2016), and if the amount of time one spends on a task is reliably related to creativity (Simonton, 2014), we would expect both of the following: (a) someone who spends more time on a task on average than another person is more likely to produce something creative, and (b) someone who devotes more effort than she usually does toward coming up with a new idea is more likely to do so. Taken together, it could be the case that across the between- and within-person levels, the relationship between a motivation construct and creativity could look quite different or very similar. Even in the case of the latter, the mechanisms through which this occurs, whether they are the same or different across levels, should be considered.

Second, we should continue to strive for precision in the criterion measurement. This suggestion applies to both the description of the measurement tool and the tool itself. Of course, the problem of poor criterion measurement is not unique to creativity research (Austin & Villanova, 1992), but measuring creativity does provide a unique set of challenges. To the extent that we can move away from treating creativity as a unitary construct, our field will be better served. An important starting place is avoiding the conflation of processes and outcomes (Montag et al., 2012). In this review, special care has been taken in describing the various criterion measures – whether they were behaviors (e.g., generating new ideas, engaging in creative thought) or outcomes (e.g., works of art, originality of an idea set) – but in the studies themselves, these measures often fell under the same label of *creativity*. Doing within-person research presents an opportunity to disambiguate interrelated processes (e.g., problem definition, idea generation, information gathering) and evaluate directionality among them (e.g., Hardy et al., in press). Intuitively, we know these processes to be distinct, but without discrete assessments of each of them, our understanding of how creative ideas develop over time is obfuscated. This may require fairly narrow intervals between measurements – seconds or minutes, rather than hours, days, or weeks. To et al.'s (2012) study is an example of how highly correlated creative processes can be (in this case, problem identification, information processing, and idea generation; Zhang & Bartol, 2010), even when their assessment is just hours apart (average Cronbach's $\alpha = 0.92$). To capture variability at such a narrow temporal level, self-assessment measures may be problematic if they quickly induce fatigue in participants or distract participants from the task at hand and thereby diminish the data quality. When this is a concern, an alternative is to execute a think-aloud protocol (Ericsson & Simon, 1984), where participants say what they are thinking out loud while working on a task (e.g., Khandwalla, 1993; Ruscio, Whitney, & Amabile, 1998). The transcripts are then coded by judges. A similar process can be utilized at the team level as well (Lehmann-Willenbrock & Allen, 2018). Ultimately, to better understand the dynamic relationships between motivation, creative processes, and creative outcomes, we should aim to gather data through the use of more precise instruments and use more precise language to describe these instruments.

Conclusion

What motivates people to come up with new ideas is an important and pressing economic and social question. The scholarly literature on creativity has done much to advance our understanding in this area. Now, as our knowledge, methods, and analytic capabilities continue to develop, new opportunities are available to learn about how and when motivation fosters creativity over time. The present review showed that the past few years have seen a significant uptick in within-person research in this domain. I hope that this chapter encourages this trend to continue.

References

Acar, O. A., & van den Ende, J. (2016). Knowledge distance, cognitive-search processes, and creativity: The making of winning solutions in science contests. *Psychological Science*, 27, 692–699.

Amabile, T. M. (1983). The social psychology of creativity: A componential conceptualization. *Journal of Personality and Social Psychology*, 45, 357–376.

Amabile, T. M. (1996). *Creativity in context*. New York: Westview Press.

Amabile, T. M., Barsade, S. G., Mueller, J. S., & Staw, B. M. (2005). Affect and creativity at work. *Administrative Science Quarterly*, 50, 367–403.

Anderson, N., Potočnik, K., & Zhou, J. (2014). Innovation and creativity in organizations: A state-of-the-science review, prospective commentary, and guiding framework. *Journal of Management*, 40, 1297–1333.

Austin, J. T., & Villanova, P. (1992). The criterion problem: 1917–1992. *Journal of Applied Psychology*, 77, 836–874.

Baas, M., De Dreu, C. K., & Nijstad, B. A. (2008). A meta-analysis of 25 years of mood-creativity research: Hedonic tone, activation, or regulatory focus? *Psychological Bulletin*, 134, 779–806.

Ballard, T., Yeo, G., Loft, S., Vancouver, J. B., & Neal, A. (2016). An integrative formal model of motivation and decision making: The MGPM. *Journal of Applied Psychology*, 101, 1240–1265.

Bandura, A. (1997). *Self-efficacy: The exercise of control*. New York, NY: W. H. Freeman.

Bandura, A. (2012). On the functional properties of perceived self-efficacy revisited. *Journal of Management*, 38, 9–44.

Barrett, L. F., & Russell, J. A. (1999). The structure of current affect: Controversies and emerging consensus. *Current Directions in Psychological Science*, 8, 10–14.

Batey, M. (2012). The measurement of creativity: From definitional consensus to the introduction of a new heuristic framework. *Creativity Research Journal*, 24, 55–65.

Beck, J. W., & Schmidt, A. M. (2012). Taken out of context? Cross-level effects of between-person self-efficacy and difficulty on the within-person relationship of self-efficacy with resource allocation and performance. *Organizational Behavior and Human Decision Processes*, 119, 195–208.

Beghetto, R. A., & Karwowski, M. (2017). Toward untangling creative self-beliefs. In M. Karwowski & J. C. Kaufman (Eds.), *Creative self: Effects of beliefs, self-efficacy, mindset, and identity* (pp. 4–24). San Diego, CA: Academic Press.

Benedek, M., Jauk, E., Kerschenbauer, K., Anderwald, R., & Grond, L. (2017). Creating art: An experience sampling study in the domain of moving image art. *Psychology of Aesthetics, Creativity, and the Arts*, 11, 325–334.

Beuk, F., & Basadur, T. (2016). Regulatory focus, task engagement and divergent thinking. *Creativity and Innovation Management*, 25, 199–210.

Binnewies, C., Sonnentag, S., & Mojza, E. J. (2009a). Feeling recovered and thinking about the good sides of one's work. *Journal of Occupational Health Psychology*, 14, 243–256.

Binnewies, C., Sonnentag, S., & Mojza, E. J. (2009b). Daily performance at work: Feeling recovered in the morning as a predictor of day-level job performance. *Journal of Organizational Behavior*, 30, 67–93.

Binnewies, C., & Wörnlein, S. C. (2011). What makes a creative day? A diary study on the interplay between affect, job stressors, and job control. *Journal of Organizational Behavior*, 32(4), 589–607.

Bledow, R., Rosing, K., & Frese, M. (2013). A dynamic perspective on affect and creativity. *Academy of Management Journal*, 56, 432–450.

Bloom, N., Jones, C. I., Van Reenen, J., & Webb, M. (2018). Are ideas getting harder to find? NBER Working Paper No. 23782. Cambridge, MA: National Bureau of Economic Research.

Brockner, J., & Higgins, E. T. (2001). Regulatory focus theory: Implications for the study of emotions at work. *Organizational Behavior and Human Decision Processes*, 86, 35–66.

Burtch, G., Carnahan, S., & Greenwood, B. N. (2018). Can you gig it? An empirical examination of the gig economy and entrepreneurial activity. *Management Science*, 64(12), 5497–5520.

Byrne, E. K., & Thatchenkery, T. (2018, July). How to use mindfulness to increase your team's creativity. *Harvard Business Review*. Retrieved from https://hbr.org/2018/07/how-to-use-mindfulness-to-increase-your-teams-creativity.

Chen, G., Gully, S. M., & Eden, D. (2001). Validation of a new general self-efficacy scale. *Organizational Research Methods*, 4, 62–83.

Conner, T. S., DeYoung, C. G., & Silvia, P. J. (2018). Everyday creative activity as a path to flourishing. *The Journal of Positive Psychology*, 13, 181–189.

Conner, T. S., & Silvia, P. J. (2015). Creative days: A daily diary study of emotion, personality, and everyday creativity. *Psychology of Aesthetics, Creativity, and the Arts*, 9(4), 463–470.

Csikszentmihalyi, M., & Larson, R. (1987). Validity and reliability of the experience-sampling method. *The Journal of Nervous and Mental Disease*, 175, 526–536.

Dalal, R. S., & Hulin, C. L. (2008). Motivation for what? A multivariate dynamic perspective of the criterion. In R. Kanfer, G. Chen, & R. Pritchard (Eds.), *Work motivation: Past, present, and future* (pp. 63–100). New York, NY: Taylor & Francis.

Deci, E. L. (1971). Effects of externally mediated rewards on intrinsic motivation. *Journal of Personality and Social Psychology*, 18(1), 105–115.

Deci, E. L. (1975). *Intrinsic motivation*. New York, NY: Plenum.

De Dreu, C. K., Baas, M., & Nijstad, B. A. (2008). Hedonic tone and activation level in the mood-creativity link: Toward a dual pathway to creativity model. *Journal of Personality and Social Psychology*, 94, 739–756.

de Jesus, S. N., Rus, C. L., Lens, W., & Imaginário, S. (2013). Intrinsic motivation and creativity related to product: A meta-analysis of the studies published between 1990-2010. *Creativity Research Journal*, 25, 80–84.

Dineen, R., & Niu, W. (2008). The effectiveness of western creative teaching methods in China: An action research project. *Psychology of Aesthetics, Creativity, and the Arts*, 2, 42–52.

Dong, Y., Liao, H., Chuang, A., Zhou, J., & Campbell, E. M. (2015). Fostering employee service creativity: Joint effects of customer empowering behaviors and supervisory empowering leadership. *Journal of Applied Psychology*, 100, 1364–1380.

Ericsson, K. A., & Simon, H. A. (1984). *Protocol analysis: Verbal reports as data*. Cambridge, MA: MIT Press.

Flavell, J. H. (1979). Metacognition and cognitive monitoring: A new area of cognitive–developmental inquiry. *American Psychologist*, 34, 906–911.

Feist, G. J. (1998). A meta-analysis of personality in scientific and artistic creativity. *Personality and Social Psychology Review*, 2, 290–309.

Frijda, N. H. (1993). Moods, emotion episodes, and emotions. In M. Lewis & J. M. Haviland (Eds.), *Handbook of emotions* (pp. 381–403). New York, NY: Guilford Press.

Fuller, J. B., Marler, L. E., & Hester, K. (2006). Promoting felt responsibility for constructive change and proactive behavior: Exploring aspects of an elaborated model of work design. *Journal of Organizational Behavior*, 27, 1089–1120.

Gagné, M., & Deci, E. L. (2005). Self-determination theory and work motivation. *Journal of Organizational Behavior*, 26, 331–362.

Gilbert, S. L., & Kelloway, E. K. (2014). Leadership. In M. Gagné (Ed.), *The Oxford handbook of work engagement, motivation, and self-determination* (pp. 181–198). New York, NY: Oxford Unviersity Press.

Gist, M. E., & Mitchell, T. R. (1992). Self-efficacy: A theoretical analysis of its determinants and malleability. *Academy of Management Review*, 17, 183–211.

Grether, T., Sowislo, J. F., & Wiese, B. S. (2018). Top-down or bottom-up? Prospective relations between general and domain-specific self-efficacy beliefs during a work-family transition. *Personality and Individual Differences*, 121, 131–139.

Groenendijk, T., Janssen, T., Rijlaarsdam, G., & van den Bergh, H. (2013). The effect of observational learning on students' performance, processes, and motivation in two creative domains. *British Journal of Educational Psychology*, 83, 3–28.

Hardy III, J. H., Day, E. A., & Steele, L. M. (In press). Interrelationships among self-regulatory processes: Toward a dynamic process-based model of self-regulated learning. *Journal of Management*. Retrieved from https://doi.org/10.1177/0149206318780440.

Houghton, J. D., & Neck, C. P. (2002). The revised self-leadership questionnaire: Testing a hierarchical factor structure for self-leadership. *Journal of Managerial Psychology*, 17, 672–691.

Hox, J. J. (2010). *Multilevel analysis: Techniques and applications* (2nd ed.). New York, NY: Routledge.

Huber, A., Leigh, K., & Tremblay, K. (2012). Creativity processes of students in the design studio. *College Student Journal*, 46, 903–913.

Hughes, D. J., Lee, A., Tian, A. W., Newman, A., & Legood, A. (2018). Leadership, creativity, and innovation: A critical review and practical recommendations. *The Leadership Quarterly*, 29, 549–569.

Hunter, S. T., Cushenbery, L., & Friedrich, T. (2012). Hiring an innovative workforce: A necessary yet uniquely challenging endeavor. *Human Resource Management Review*, 22, 303–322.

Ifeanyi, K. C. (2018, July). Lessons in fearless creativity. *Fast Company*. Retrieved from https://www.fastcompany.com/90203681/lessons-in-fearless-creativity-from-composer-max-richter.

Johnson, R. E., Chang, C. H., & Lord, R. G. (2006). Moving from cognition to behavior: What the research says. *Psychological Bulletin*, 132, 381–415.

Kanfer, R. (1990). Motivation and individual differences in learning: An integration of developmental, differential and cognitive perspectives. *Learning and Individual Differences*, 2, 221–239.

Kanfer, R. (1992). Work motivation: New directions in theory and research. In C. L. Cooper & I. T. Robertson (Eds.), *International review of industrial and organizational psychology* (Vol. 7, pp. 1–54). Chichester, UK: Wiley.

Kanfer, R., Chen, G., & Pritchard, R. D. (2008). The three C's of work motivation: Content, context, and change. In R. Kanfer, G. Chen, & R. D. Pritchard (Eds.), *Motivation: Past, present, and future* (pp. 1–16). New York, NY: Taylor and Francis Group.

Karwowski, M., Lebuda, I., Szumski, G., & Firkowska-Mankiewicz, A. (2017). From moment-to-moment to day-to-day: Experience sampling and diary investigations in adults' everyday creativity. *Psychology of Aesthetics, Creativity, and the Arts*, 11, 309–324.

Khandwalla, P. N. (1993). An exploratory investigation of divergent thinking through protocol analysis. *Creativity Research Journal*, 6, 241–259.

Kruglanski, A. W., Fishbach, A., Woolley, K., Bélanger, J. J., Chernikova, M., Molinario, E., & Pierro, A. (2018). A structural model of intrinsic motivation: On the psychology of means-ends fusion. *Psychological Review*, 125, 165–182.

Lehmann-Willenbrock, N., & Allen, J. A. (2018). Modeling temporal interaction dynamics in organizational settings. *Journal of Business and Psychology*, 33, 325–344.

Liang, J., Farh, C. I., & Farh, J. L. (2012). Psychological antecedents of promotive and prohibitive voice: A two-wave examination. *Academy of Management Journal*, 55, 71–92.

Liu, D., Jiang, K., Shalley, C. E., Keem, S., & Zhou, J. (2016). Motivational mechanisms of employee creativity: A meta-analytic examination and theoretical extension of the creativity literature. *Organizational Behavior and Human Decision Processes*, 137, 236–263.

Massin, O. (2017). Towards a definition of efforts. *Motivation Science*, 3, 230–259.

McClelland, D. C. (1965). Toward a theory of motive acquisition. *American Psychologist*, 20, 321–333.

McCormick, B. W., Reeves, C. J., Downes, P. E., Li, N., & Ilies, R. (In press). Scientific contributions of within-person research in management: Making the juice worth the squeeze. *Journal of Management*. Retrieved from https://doi.org/10.1177/0149206318788435.

McCrae, R. R., & Costa, P. T., Jr. (2003). *Personality in Adulthood: A Five-Factor Theory Perspective* (2nd ed.). New York, NY: Guilford Press.

Mischel, W. (1973). Toward a cognitive social learning reconceptualization of personality. *Psychological Review*, 80(4), 252–283.

Montag, T., Maertz, C. P., Jr. & Baer, M. (2012). A critical analysis of the workplace creativity criterion space. *Journal of Management*, 38, 1362–1386.

Neal, A., Ballard, T., & Vancouver, J. B. (2017). Dynamic self-regulation and multiple-goal pursuit. *Annual Review of Organizational Psychology and Organizational Behavior*, 4, 401–423.

Ng, T. W., & Lucianetti, L. (2016). Within-individual increases in innovative behavior and creative, persuasion, and change self-efficacy over time: A social–cognitive theory perspective. *Journal of Applied Psychology*, 101, 14–34.

Nicholls, J. G. (1972). Creativity in the person who will never produce anything original and useful: The concept of creativity as a normally distributed trait. *American Psychologist*, 27, 717–727.

Northcraft, G. B., Schmidt, A. M., & Ashford, S. J. (2011). Feedback and the rationing of time and effort among competing tasks. *Journal of Applied Psychology*, 96, 1076–1086.

Pierce, J. L., Gardner, D. G., Cummings, L. L., & Dunham, R. B. (1989). Organization-based self-esteem: Construct definition, measurement, and validation. *Academy of Management Journal*, 32, 622–648.

Ployhart, R. E., & Vandenberg, R. J. (2010). Longitudinal research: The theory, design, and analysis of change. *Journal of Management*, 36, 94–120.

Reznickova, A., & Zepeda, L. (2016). Can self-determination theory explain the self-perpetuation of social innovations? A case study of slow food at the University of Wisconsin–Madison. *Journal of Community and Applied Social Psychology*, 26, 3–17.

Roberts, B. W., Walton, K. E., & Viechtbauer, W. (2006). Patterns of mean-level change in personality traits across the life course: A meta-analysis of longitudinal studies. *Psychological Bulletin*, 132, 1–25.

Runco, M. A., & Jaeger, G. J. (2012). The standard definition of creativity. *Creativity Research Journal*, 24, 92–96.

Ruscio, J., Whitney, D. M., & Amabile, T. M. (1998). Looking inside the fishbowl of creativity: Verbal and behavioral predictors of creative performance. *Creativity Research Journal*, 11, 243–263.

Russell, J. A. (1980). A circumplex model of affect. *Journal of Personality and Social Psychology*, 39, 1161–1178.

Sadler-Smith, E. (2015). Wallas' four-stage model of the creative process: More than meets the eye? *Creativity Research Journal*, 27, 342–352.

Sawyer, R. K. (2012). *The science of human innovation: Explaining creativity.* New York, NY: Oxford University Press.

Schmidt, A. M., & Dolis, C. M. (2009). Something's got to give: The effects of dual-goal difficulty, goal progress, and expectancies on resource allocation. *Journal of Applied Psychology*, 94, 678–691.

Scholer, A. A., & Higgins, E. T. (2010). Regulatory focus in a demanding world. In R. H. Hoyle (Ed.), *Handbook of personality and self-regulation* (pp. 291–314). Malden, MA: Blackwell.

Shalley, C. E., Zhou, J., & Oldham, G. R. (2004). The effects of personal and contextual characteristics on creativity: Where should we go from here? *Journal of Management*, 30, 933–958.

Silvia, P. J. 2007. An introduction to multilevel modeling for research on the psychology of art and creativity. *Empirical Studies of the Arts*, 25, 1–20.

Silvia, P. J., Beaty, R. E., Nusbaum, E. C., Eddington, K. M., Levin-Aspenson, H., & Kwapil, T. R. (2014). Everyday creativity in daily life: An experience-sampling study of "little c" creativity. *Psychology of Aesthetics, Creativity, and the Arts*, 8, 183–188.

Simonton, D. K. (2014). Creative performance, expertise acquisition, individual differences, and developmental antecedents: An integrative research agenda. *Intelligence*, 45, 66–73.

Singer, J. D., & Willett, J. B. (2003). *Applied longitudinal data analysis.* New York, NY: Oxford University Press.

Sitzmann, T., & Yeo, G. (2013). A meta-analytic investigation of the within-person self-efficacy domain: Is self-efficacy a product of past performance or a driver of future performance? *Personnel Psychology*, 66, 531–568.

Spreitzer, G. M. (1995). Psychological empowerment in the workplace: Dimensions, measurement, and validation. *Academy of Management Journal*, 38, 1442–1465.

Stajkovic, A. D., & Luthans, F. (1998). Self-efficacy and work-related performance: A meta-analysis. *Psychological Bulletin*, 124, 240–261.

Stanko-Kaczmarek, M. (2012). The effect of intrinsic motivation on the affect and evaluation of the creative process among fine arts students. *Creativity Research Journal*, 24, 304–310.

Steele, L. M. (2018). *When creative self-efficacy is positively related to creativity and when it isn't.* Manuscript in preparation.

Strauss, K., Griffin, M. A., Parker, S. K., & Mason, C. M. (2015). Building and sustaining proactive behaviors: The role of adaptivity and job satisfaction. *Journal of Business and Psychology*, 30, 63–72.

Sullivan, D. M., & Ford, C. M. (2010). The alignment of measures and constructs in organizational research: The case of testing measurement models of creativity. *Journal of Business and Psychology*, 25, 505–521.

Tasselli, S., Kilduff, M., & Landis, B. (2018). Personality change: Implications for organization behavior. *Academy of Management Annals*, 12, 467–493.

Thrash, T. M., & Elliot, A. J. (2003). Inspiration as a psychological construct. *Journal of Personality and Social Psychology*, 84, 871–889.

Thrash, T. M., & Elliot, A. J. (2004). Inspiration: Core characteristics, component processes, antecedents, and function. *Journal of Personality and Social Psychology*, 87, 957–973.

Thrash, T. M., Maruskin, L. A., Cassidy, S. E., Fryer, J. W., & Ryan, R. M. (2010). Mediating between the muse and the masses: Inspiration and the actualization of creative ideas. *Journal of Personality and Social Psychology*, 98, 469–487.

Tierney, P., & Farmer, S. M. (2002). Creative self-efficacy: Its potential antecedents and relationship to creative performance. *Academy of Management Journal*, 45, 1137–1148.

Tierney, P., & Farmer, S. M. (2011). Creative self-efficacy development and creative performance over time. *Journal of Applied Psychology*, 96, 277–293.

To, M. L., Fisher, C. D., Ashkanasy, N. M., & Rowe, P. A. (2012). Within-person relationships between mood and creativity. *Journal of Applied Psychology*, 97, 599–612.

Tschannen-Moran, M., & Hoy, A. W. (2001). Teacher efficacy: Capturing an elusive construct. *Teaching and Teacher Education*, 17, 783–805.

Unsworth, K. (2001). Unpacking creativity. *Academy of Management Review*, 26, 289–297.

Unsworth, K. L., & Mason, C. M. (2016). Self-concordance strategies as a necessary condition for self-management. *Journal of Occupational and Organizational Psychology*, 89, 711–733.

Van den Broeck, A., Ferris, D. L., Chang, C. H., & Rosen, C. C. (2016). A review of self-determination theory's basic psychological needs at work. *Journal of Management*, 42, 1195–1229.

Van Dijk, D., & Kluger, A. N. (2011). Task type as a moderator of positive/negative feedback effects on motivation and performance: A regulatory focus perspective. *Journal of Organizational Behavior*, 32, 1084–1105.

Vancouver, J. B. (2012). Rhetorical reckoning: A response to Bandura. *Journal of Management*, 38, 465–474.

Vancouver, J. B., & Kendall, L. N. (2006). When self-efficacy negatively relates to motivation and performance in a learning context. *Journal of Applied Psychology*, 91, 1146–1153.

Vancouver, J. B., More, K. M., & Yoder, R. J. (2008). Self-efficacy and resource allocation: Support for a nonmonotonic, discontinuous model. *Journal of Applied Psychology*, 93, 35–47.

Vancouver, J. B., Thompson, C. M., & Williams, A. A. (2001). The changing signs in the relationships among self-efficacy, personal goals, and performance. *Journal of Applied Psychology*, 86, 605–620.

Venkatraman, R. (2018, January). 3 ways you might accidentally be making yourself less creative, according to science. *Inc.* Retrieved from https://www.inc.com/rohini-venkatraman/3-simple-methods-to-make-2018-your-most-creative-year-yet.html.

Wallace, C., & Chen, G. (2006). A multilevel integration of personality, climate, self-regulation, and performance. *Personnel Psychology, 59*, 529–557.

Wallas, G. (1926). *The art of thought.* New York: Harcourt Brace.

Watson, D. E., Nordin-Bates, S. M., & Chappell, K. A. (2012). Facilitating and nurturing creativity in pre-vocational dancers: Findings from the UK Centres for Advanced Training. *Research in Dance Education, 13*, 153–173.

Weiner, R. P. (2000). *Creativity and beyond: Cultures, values, and change.* Albany, NY: State University of New York Press.

Zhang, X., & Bartol, K. M. (2010). Linking empowering leadership and employee creativity: The influence of psychological empowerment, intrinsic motivation, and creative process engagement. *Academy of Management Journal, 53*, 107–128.

7

INTEGRATING CREATIVE CLIMATE AND CREATIVE PROBLEM-SOLVING

Samuel T. Hunter, James L. Farr, Rachel L. Heinen, and Julian B. Allen

A characteristic distinguishing highly creative organizations from their less inventive peers is a general sense that novel approaches to problem-solving are of value. These companies make a strong, concerted effort to cultivate environments that tell employees who might operate a bit differently that such an approach is respected, accepted, and more pointedly, desired. Organizations such as Pixar, Amazon, Google, and Facebook take a number of steps to send a message that creativity is possible – in fact that it *should* occur – within their walls, be they virtual or physical. Within the academic community, perceptions about how an organization approaches creative problem-solving, often collectively so, have been labeled *climate* and in the specific case of supporting novel and useful idea production, *creative climate*.

Creative climate has been shown to be a key factor driving innovative performance in a number of organizations and across a number of studies (Tesluk, Farr, & Klein, 1997). In a study of 608 employees in Chinese firms, for example, Hon, Bloom, and Crant (2014) found that an environment encouraging open discussion was helpful in overcoming resistance to change and was positively related to creative performance. Similarly, in a study of firm product performance, Dul and Ceylan (2014) revealed that organizations with more creative climates introduced larger numbers of new products to market. Moreover, creative climates were also linked to overall performance operationalized through product sales. Considering the consistency and volume of these findings, there is consensus that climate is a nontrivial, if not essential, component of creative success and performance.

In a summary of these trends, a meta-analysis of 42 studies and more than 5,000 employees revealed climate to be a consistently positive and strong predictor of performance across 14 different dimensions (Hunter, Bedell, &

Mumford, 2007). Although all of the dimensions demonstrated sizable cross-criteria effect sizes, there were dimensions that exerted particularly large effects in the prediction of creative performance. The dimensions of positive interpersonal exchange ($\Delta = 0.91$, $SE = 0.39$), intellectual stimulation ($\Delta = 0.88$, $SE = 0.18$), and challenge ($\Delta = 0.85$, $SE = 0.14$) produced the largest effect sizes across the dimensions (Hunter, Bedell, & Mumford, 2007). Further, the authors found that creative climate wielded particularly strong effects on creative performance when innovation was essential for performance and in the context of turbulent and highly competitive environments.

Although general findings on the utility of creative climate are notable, the recent growth in interest of process views (Mumford, Medeiros, & Partlow 2012; Perry-Smith & Mannucci, 2017) in the study of creativity and innovation as well as the emerging issues around the dimensionality of creative climate (James et al., 2008; Neely, Lovelace, Kundro, & Hunter, 2016) have resulted in a number of pressing, unanswered queries. The first is in acknowledging that creative problem-solving is most accurately represented by a series of interrelated and dynamic processes, the question emerges as to whether climate has a consistent effect on *all* aspects of the creative process. Relatedly, a second key question emerges in light of dimensionality issues surrounding creative climate as a construct. Specifically, it is unclear how each of the various subdimensions of creative climate relates to the range of often distinctively demanding processes comprising creative problem-solving. In light of such emerging issues, the aim of the present effort is to explore these two core questions and ultimately shed light on the increasingly critical role of creative climate in creative problem-solving.

Creative Problem-Solving and the Creative Process

Researchers define creativity as the generation of ideas that are both novel and useful, with innovation defined as the implementation of those creative ideas (Mumford & Gustafson, 1988). Such ideas and their implementation are typically spurred by the need to solve a complex and ill-defined problem or series of problems. This general approach to viewing creativity as a form of complex problem-solving has helped drive growth and interest in the creativity field and has served as a strong foundation for investigating the phenomenon. As such, we utilize the problem-solving perspective on creativity as a framework for this chapter (see Mumford et al., 2012).

Inherent in such core definitions and perspectives on the phenomenon of creativity is an acknowledgement that creativity and innovation are best viewed as pieces of a larger, interconnected puzzle (Perry-Smith & Mannucci, 2017). That is, generating ideas is a necessary component of ultimately implementing an idea with generation serving as a precursor to implementation. More directly stated, creativity is a complex and often-messy *process* and should not be viewed as a singular activity or black box phenomenon (Bunge, 1963). Process models of creativity have been discussed in the creativity literature for more than 100 years (Dewey, 1910; Wallas, 1926). Despite the existence of such models, however, the bulk of researchers have been seemingly fixated on only a few processes, with one in particular receiving the most attention: idea generation. In an exception to this trend, Mumford and colleagues conducted a series of studies expanding the view of creativity beyond idea generation to include seven additional processes. These eight processes (see Mumford, Mobley, Reiter-Palmon, Uhlman, & Doares, 1991) are as follows: problem definition, information gathering, information organization, conceptual combination, idea generation, idea evaluation, implementation planning, and solution monitoring. These processes have been utilized and examined in a range of studies focused on creative phenomena (see Mumford et al., 2012, for a summary).

Three additional issues emerge that operate in conjunction with the process perspective. The first is that the creative process is nonlinear and must be depicted as a dynamic rather than static, phenomenon (Finke, Ward, & Smith, 1992). That is, as individuals and groups move through the creative process, they will necessarily oscillate backward and forward to various other processes. During a planning phase, for example, unforeseen problems might arise that require new ideas to be generated. Moreover, to fully evaluate an idea, a team may turn to an information gathering process to do a better job at making that assessment. Again, the key point here is that the creative process is dynamic, iterative, and at times somewhat unpredictable in how it proceeds.

The second key trend emerging directly from a process perspective is the need to consider differing antecedents for varying processes. In a discussion of creative processes, Perry-Smith and Mannucci (2017), for example, considered the social context in relation to four creative processes: idea generation, elaboration, championing, and implementation. What is particularly notable about Perry-Smith and Manucci's work is their finding that "relational and structural elements that are beneficial for one phase ... are detrimental for another" (p. 53). This observation is consistent with our work on personality and creative performance (Hunter & Cushenbery, 2013). In this study, Hunter and Cushenberry (2013) found that some qualities (e.g., agreeableness) were not related to idea generation but were related, negatively, to idea implementation in a group setting. Although other illustrations exist (e.g., Axtell et al., 2000; Mumford & Hunter, 2005), this should suffice to demonstrate a key point. Namely, by acknowledging that creativity is best depicted as a series of related processes, researchers must also recognize that these processes may have unique antecedents and drivers. Further, at times, these drivers may even conflict with one another.

Third, a final trend that is closely linked to the earlier discussion is the observation that as ideas move through the creative process, activities become more formalized, structured, and resource intensive (Hunter, Cassidy, & Ligon, 2012; Hunter & Cushenbery, 2013). Early activities, for example, may be driven by a single individual, while later processes will often require greater resources and commitment. In perhaps overly simplistic and colloquial terms, it costs relatively little to sketch something on a napkin, but it takes substantially more to see that sketch realized in a showroom or store shelf. A key concession here is that the dynamic and iterative nature of the creative process means individuals, teams, and organizations will necessarily oscillate between formalized and unstructured activities as different phases of the creative process are engaged in. However, with this caveat being noted, in general the progression from conception to implementation coincides with a nontrivial level of increased formalization, resource requirements, and structure (Hunter, Gutworth, Crayne, & Jayne, 2015).

Facilitators of Creative Problem-Solving

Following the work of Mumford and colleagues (2012), as well as the previous discussion, the framing of key processes comprising creative problem-solving must be trailed by consideration of what actions help support and drive success in each of these processes. Mumford and colleagues propose that there are several drivers and facilitators of creative problem-solving, including strategies applied (e.g., Scott, Lonergan, & Mumford, 2005) and knowledge (Hunter, Bedell-Avers, Hunsicker, Mumford, & Ligon, 2008) as key foundational elements. We extend this line of thinking and suggest that a broader environment (Woodman & Schoenfeldt, 1990) that fosters these key foundational elements is central to understanding the means and mechanisms of driving each of the processes of creativity outlined by Mumford and colleagues (1991). Thus, we turn to a key aspect of the environment and how it is perceived: creative climate.

Creative Climate

Defining Climate

Although climate has been defined in a number of ways (James, James, & Ashe, 1990; Rousseau, 1988; Schneider, Ehrhart, & Macey, 2013; Schneider & Reichers, 1983), we follow previous efforts and offer that climate is "reflected in peoples' perceptions of, or beliefs about, environmental attributes shaping expectations about outcomes, contingencies, requirements, and interactions in the work environment" (Hunter et al., 2007, p. 70). Moreover, climate has been discussed in broad terms (i.e., molar climate), and more recent approaches have broken climate into various types and subtypes, also known as focused climate (Schneider et al., 2013). Examples include safety climate (e.g., Zohar &

Polachek, 2014), service climate (e.g., Bowen & Schneider, 2014), and error management climate (Frese & Keith, 2015). Of central interest to this chapter is creative climate.

Creative Climate

In what appears to be one of the first direct discussions of a creative work climate, Ekvall and Tångeberg-Anderson (1986) identified a Swedish newspaper that was engaging in novel approaches to covering news as illustrated by their decision to forgo scandalous and sensationalized reports for more in-depth and rigorous interviews with knowledgeable individuals. This approach stood in stark contrast to competitor approaches and resulted in notable growth among new subscribers and readers. The authors investigated the newspaper outlet by utilizing a number of tools including a climate measure (Ekvall, Arvonen, & Waldenström-Lindblad, 1983). The researchers observed a number of key climate features in the organization. They noted, for example, that employees in the innovative organization "perceived challenge and meaning in their work" (p. 223). The employees also had a strong sense of teamwork and commitment to both individual and group performance, and while there was some level of conflict, it was not destructive. Leadership, similarly, helped define the creative climate – the supervisor, described by subordinates as encouraging of risk-taking, often engaged in role modeling behavior of the phenomenon itself.

Similar efforts have been undertaken by other scholars to illustrate the nature and complexity of creative climate. Amabile, Conti, Coon, Lazenby, and Herron (1996), for example, developed the KEYS measure of creative climate, characterized by five broad categories (encouragement, autonomy, resources, pressures, impediments), with a number of subscales within each. In a data set composed of 306 projects across a variety of organizations, these dimensions all aided in discriminating creative projects from noncreative projects. Notably, however, some dimensions were stronger discriminators than others. Challenging work, a subscale of pressures, for example, was more discriminating than the perception of resources and resource availability.

Along related lines, Tesluk and colleagues (1997) integrated culture and climate literature in a comprehensive review of creative environments. The researchers suggested that an organization's culture is established by key decision-makers in the organization (e.g., founders) and is inherently bound to the values of those individuals. These values dictate organizational actions (e.g., human resource practices) that, in turn, shape the climate for creativity. In their review, the authors suggested that creative climate was composed of five dimensions: goal emphasis, means emphasis, reward orientation, task support, and socioemotional support.

As a final illustration, work by Ekvall defined climate as "a conglomerate of attitudes, feelings, and behaviors that characterizes life in the organization" (1996, p. 105). In early work, climate was conceptualized as having four broad categories: mutual trust and confidence, challenge and motivation, freedom, and pluralism in views, knowledge, and experience. However, when developing their measure, the creative climate questionnaire (CCQ), these broader categories gave way to ten proposed dimensions (see Ekvall, 1996). In a study comparing ten innovative and five less innovative or stagnant organizations, Ekvall and Arvonen (1991) reported that the innovative organizations scored higher on all ten dimensions comprising creative climate.

Dimensionality and Creative Climate

As may be surmised, one of the most pressing issues surrounding an accurate and precise definition of climate is reaching a consensus on climate dimensionality. In a review of 45 differing climate taxonomies, Hunter, Bedell, and Mumford (2005) found the number ranged from a single dimension (Holahan, Aronson, Jurkat, & Schoorman, 2004) to 13 (Damanpour, 1991). In an attempt to synthesize this literature and permit a subsequent meta-analysis, Hunter and colleagues (2005) followed procedures outlined by Fleishman et al. (1991) to develop a taxonomic framework of climate, unfolding 14 differing dimensions of creative climate. The dimensions were comprehensive in that all previous studies could be mapped onto at least a subset of the dimensions comprising the taxonomy. What was not discussed in the paper by Hunter and colleagues (2005) or in their meta-analysis (Hunter et al., 2007) subsequently following this work, however, was that the 14-dimension framework was never intended to be representative of an underlying factor structure. Rather, the goal of these early efforts was to offer a framework that permitted synthesis among a rather complex landscape of climate conceptualizations. Thus, the question has persisted across conceptualization efforts – if not 14, how many dimensions actually comprise creative climate?

In an attempt to answer this question, Hunter and colleagues engaged in a series of follow-up studies over, approximately, the past ten years. This began with the development of a scale by following procedures outlined by Hinkin (1995) and writing several items based on each of the 14 dimensions described in the previous efforts. After engaging in a number of sorting tasks and culling down through established procedures, the first scale Hunter and colleagues gathered data on was made up of 56 items composed of 4 items per dimension. In the first sample, data were gathered on 423 engineering students at a large northeastern university. Exploratory factor analyses revealed a five-factor model as best fitting (Neely et al., 2016), with those five dimensions being (a) work autonomy and stimulation, (b) positive peer exchange, (c) leader direction and encouragement, (d) organizational capacity and support, and (e) organizational

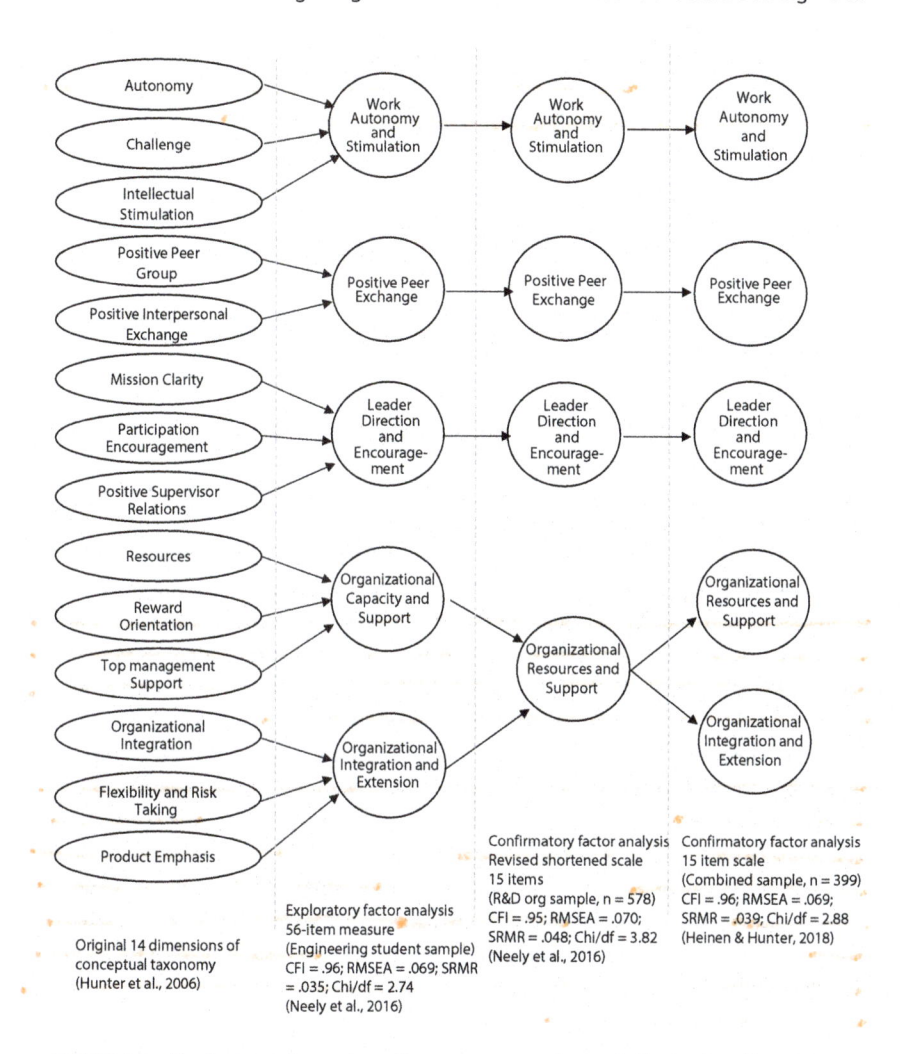

FIGURE 7.1 Evolution of creative climate taxonomies and dimensionality.

integration and extension. The evolution of these dimensions and the iterations following may be seen in Figure 7.1.

Hunter and colleagues followed up this exploratory effort by examining scale items that most accurately fit these five dimensions and adjusted others to more closely align with the potential emergence of underlying constructs. The number of items was ultimately reduced to 15, having three items per dimension. In a follow-up sample of 578 adults working in a research and development laboratory in the United States, Hunter and colleagues found that both three- and four-factor models fit the data well. Through exploratory investigation, Hunter and colleagues settled on a four-factor model as best fitting, with two of the factors being represented by an overarching social environment factor. The two factors driven by this latent construct were positive peer relations and leader direction and encouragement. The remaining two factors were challenging work and organizational integration and extension. Although there were some differences across these early efforts, Hunter and colleagues viewed the consistency in the general factor structures across the two studies as an indicator that there was a stable underlying structure.

In the most recent work as a follow-up to these two studies, Heinen and Hunter (2018) examined three sets of data from three different organizations. These data sets were combined into a larger sample to substantiate generalizability. The first sample consisted of 200 employees in a UK company. The second sample consisted of 61 employees from a gaming company in the southern region of the United States. The third sample consisted of 138 employees of a primarily student-run news organization in the northeast region of the United States. Using confirmatory factor analyses and comparatively testing one-, two-, three-, four-, and five-factor models, the strongest support for the correlated five-factor solution was once again found, composed of (a) work autonomy and stimulation, (b) positive peer exchange, (c) leader direction and encouragement, (d) organizational capacity and support, and (e) organizational integration and extension.

Thus, through a series of iterative investigations across multiple samples, creative climate has been most accurately conceptualized as comprising five related dimensions. Namely, individuals in a creative climate perceive their work as challenging and stimulating, where they are exposed to novel and interesting problems to solve. Individuals also view their peers and supervisors as supportive, allowing for candid dialogue and sharing of potentially risky ideas. Finally, individuals in a creative climate also see their organization and those at upper levels of management as having the resources and flexibility to fully realize creative solutions.

Notably, this five-factor solution is rather consistent with the work by James and James (1990) who suggested that psychological climate, broadly defined, was similarly composed of four general factors. This work is further based on the efforts of Locke (1976) who utilized a valuation-based perspective of work life. The first factor was termed job challenge and autonomy; the second was work-group cooperation, friendliness, and warmth; the third was leadership facilitation and support; and the fourth was role stress and lack of harmony, which included elements tied to top management and organizational support. Thus, there appear to be unique elements when referencing creativity specifically in the form of employees needing to go out of their immediate circle to integrate ideas from others to form novel solutions, but the linkage to more general models of psychological climate provides some degree of support for the emerging framework of creative climate.

Levels of Analysis and Climate

One final topic that warrants discussion in a definition of climate is levels of analysis and, by proxy, issues of aggregation. Issues surrounding levels of analysis and appropriate levels of theoretical conceptualization have been discussed by a number of scholars for more than 70 years (Argyris, 1957; Lewin, Lippitt, & White, 1939; Paruchuri, Perry-Smith, Chattopadhyay, & Shaw, 2018; Schneider, Ehrhart, & Macey, 2013). Following the work of James and colleagues (2008), we view creative climate as most appropriately considered at the psychological or individual level of analysis with a few notable exceptions discussed later in this section.

The argument to focus on the individual or psychological level of analysis is threefold. First, aforementioned work on the dimensionality of the construct reveals that individual perceptions about the work environment are central to defining the construct. The first dimension, perceptions of autonomy and stimulating work, particularly stands out as a dimension that would make less theoretical or conceptual sense to aggregate to a higher unit of analysis given that in many organizations, individual jobs and tasks vary heavily across employees. Moreover, as originally discussed by James and James (1990) and expanded on by James and colleagues (2008), some elements of climate include "perceptions that assess the significance and meaning of work environments to individuals—as partial functions of personal value systems" (p. 2008). Whether stimulating work is of value would factor into assessments of this dimension and, thus, is appropriately viewed at the individual level.

Second, there is substantial value in being able to assess *disagreement* among employees on their individual views of the work environment. As some scholars have argued, focusing on a higher unit of analysis, such as the organization level, may mean that individual employees will have less opportunity to interact and ultimately develop shared meaning (Payne, 1990). Thus, employees may be less likely to see things in a similar manner and sharedness, and by extension, agreement would not be expected. Extending this line of thinking further, rather than asking if agreement among perceivers exists as a precursor to aggregation before ultimately performing analyses, potentially greater value exists in having the capacity to explore and model the variance when disagreement exists. This requires, in turn, considering investigations at the individual level unit of analysis to allow for capturing this variance.

Finally, with advances in quantitative methods comes a collection of emerging scholars that have the ability and savvy to model multiple units of analysis. The ubiquity of multilevel modeling, in particular, means that researchers have the ability to test how much variance is occurring at several levels of investigation (e.g., teams, departments, organizations) (Preacher, Curran, & Bauer, 2006). Such testing, however, is dependent on having both criterion and predictor data at a lower unit of analysis. Moreover, assessment at the individual level does not preclude aggregation should a high level of agreement be observed. It must be conceded that such aggregation is somewhat crude in that the construct itself is framed as an individual level construct, and it may be argued that aggregation is inappropriate. However, when viewed appropriately as an individual perception that is consistently regarded by members of a group or organization, such aggregation has appropriate conceptual value. Thus, on the whole, we see greater value and utility in viewing climate as a psychological construct; that is, an individual's perception about a work environment.

Tied to the preceding paragraph, there is a notable caveat to the argument for viewing climate as a psychological construct; however, that occurs when the construct itself is specified conceptually and with regard to measurement at a unit of analysis that is not at the individual level. The most prominent illustration of this is the work linked to the team climate inventory (TCI) developed by Anderson and West (1996). This view of climate is conceptually and theoretically framed at the team unit of analysis. Moreover, the items comprising the scale itself are reflective of this theoretical framing and ask questions with a broader group in mind. An item provided by the authors, for example, is, "We share information generally in the team rather than keeping it to ourselves" (p. 246). Thus, in the instances where a specific level of creative climate is of interest to a researcher and a measure is utilized that is framed in such a way as to be congruent with that construct (LeBreton & Senter, 2008), researchers should consider steps for aggregation to the appropriate unit of analysis.

Integrating Climate and Process Views of Creative Problem-Solving

Having established the problem-solving processes and dimensions of climate, the question emerges as to how climate shapes and impacts the creative process. There are two key issues surrounding an understanding of this linkage, discussed next.

Climate as a Mediator

As James and colleagues (2008) noted, "Psychological climate appears to mediate the relationship between the work environment and affective reactions to that environment" (p. 15). Thus, in understanding how climate impacts creative outcomes and creative processes in particular, it is necessary to view climate as one of the factors that connects or bridges action in an organization to outcomes of interest. As an extension, the question emerges as to what types of organizational actions shape creative outcomes – as such actions or aspects of the work environment are precursors to shaping climate. A review of these actions reveals that drivers of creativity are multilevel in nature (Mumford &

Hunter, 2005). That is, drivers of creativity include aspects of individuals, groups, leaders, organizations, and the broader context or environment beyond the organization. Further, we offer that mediators of the link between antecedents of creativity and creative outcomes will also contain some multilevel aspects, as well. More specifically, we expect creative climate to have multilevel aspects that are consistent with the antecedents of creative performance. Upon inspection of the dimensions emerging from the efforts outlined earlier and in Figure 7.1, this indeed appears to be the case.

The implications of viewing climate as a mediator are twofold. First, as noted previously, the various dimensions of creative climate will likely have unique antecedents that are driven by differing aspects of an organization. In particular, these drivers are likely to range from individual aspects of work (e.g., is the task itself interesting) to group (e.g., do my peers support me) to leader (is my leader providing direction) to organization (e.g., are resources available to pursue ideas). Perhaps more importantly, the second implication of having unique, multilevel drivers is that it is likely that various dimensions of climate will differentially shape creative outcomes. We discuss this implication next.

Conflicting Drivers of Creative Performance

A growing observation in the creativity literature is the phenomenon of differential and, at times, conflicting antecedents of creative problem-solving. In a review of multilevel antecedents of creative performance, for example, Mumford and Hunter (2005) found that what predicted performance at the individual level was in conflict with those elements that predicted creative performance at the group level. In a study of a type of grassroots, bottom-up creativity, Axtell and colleagues (2000) examined both individual and group-level performance in an investigation of 148 machine operators. The researchers found that variables such as role breadth impacted creative idea generation but were not related to idea implementation. Similarly, leadership support, team role breadth, and top management support were predictive of idea implementation but not idea generation. In a review of the social influences of creativity and innovation processes, Perry-Smith and Mannucci (2017) propose that more intimate social ties will drive processes such as idea generation while more external, organizationally driven ties will play a larger role in idea implementation. Finally, there has been ample evidence that what helps facilitate creativity during early stages of the creative process can vary substantially from what helps in later stages of the process (Hunter & Cushenbery, 2011; Jayne & Hunter, 2016). The consistent and emerging theme is as follows: drivers of creative problem-solving are complex, residing at multiple levels of analysis. Moreover, the differing demands of the creative process dictate that what is needed at a given stage of the process may vary from what is needed at a later stage of the process. As such, given the nature and dimensionality of creative climate, we contend that the dimensions of climate will also differentially predict varying stages of the creative process. Specific propositions of the five dimensions of climate and creative problem-solving are discussed in the following sections, as well as illustrated in Figure 7.2.

Climate Dimension 1: Work Autonomy and Stimulation

The early stages of the creative process involve constructing and defining the problem itself, acquiring information to understand that problem more fully,

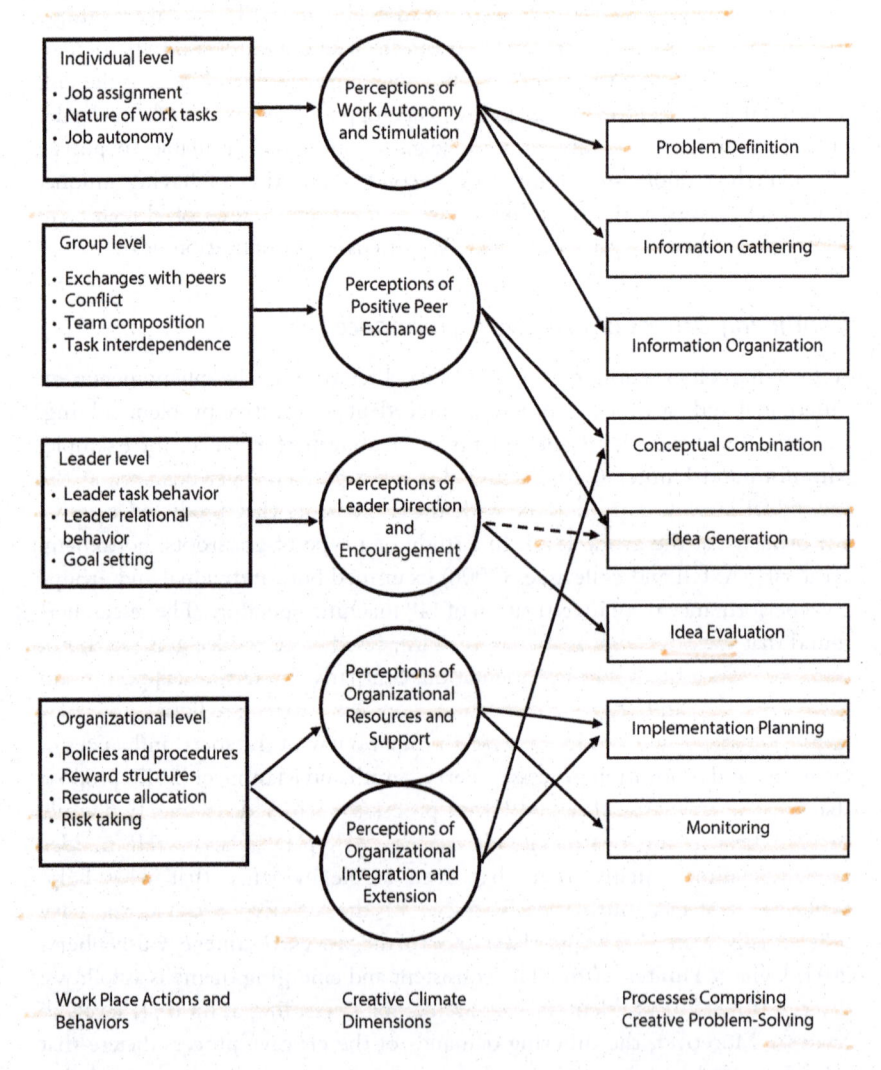

FIGURE 7.2 Heuristic model of strongest climate and problem-solving process relationships.

and organizing that information in a meaningful manner. As evidenced by the meta-analysis on climate (Hunter et al., 2007), it is likely that *all* aspects of climate will positively shape performance in these early stages as well as later stages. Leaders, for example, help to establish what goals are set and, by extension, how problems may be framed (Mumford & Hemlin, 2017; Mumford et al., 2017). However, we propose that these early stages are most strongly shaped by the work autonomy and stimulation dimension of climate.

The proposition is based on the notion that how a problem is framed sets the stage for how that problem is ultimately solved. Problems with clearly outlined parameters that do not embrace the ill-defined nature of complex problems are less likely to produce novel solutions (Schraw, Dunkle, & Bendixen, 1995). In contrast, problems that are framed dynamically and acknowledge the nuance and complexity that are precursors to creative idea generation are key conditions to support creative problem-solving (Reiter-Palmon, Mumford, O'Connor Boes, & Runco, 1997). Thus, climate conditions that allow for autonomy and exploration are essential to defining problems in open and nuanced ways. Moreover, work that is challenging and stimulating ensures the types of problems arising are similarly engaging and dynamic. Thus, our first proposition is as follows:

> Proposition 1: *The climate dimension of work autonomy and stimulation will be positively related to all phases of the creative process but will be most strongly related to the early stages of the problem-solving processes of problem construction, information gathering, and information organization.*

Climate Dimension 2: Positive Peer Exchange

Once a problem has been framed, work can begin on generating solutions to that problem. Although initial ideas are often generated by individuals, more intensive and substantive creative work is increasingly done in groups (Binyamin & Carmeli, 2017). In particular, the processes of selecting core ideas to focus on (i.e., information organization), choosing which concepts to combine, and formal idea generation processes are rarely done in isolation by individuals operating alone. Instead, individual group members must put forth and share ideas, allowing those ideas to be shaped by other work group members. Thus, having a social environment defined by positive peer exchange will be particularly critical to these middle-stage processes of creative problem-solving. The second proposition is as follows:

> Proposition 2: *The climate dimension of positive peer exchange will be positively related to all phases of the creative process but will be most strongly related to the middle-stage processes of information organization, conceptual combination, and idea generation.*

Climate Dimension 3: Leadership Direction and Encouragement

As ideas emerge and crystalize, they must be evaluated for utility. That is, before an idea is fully implemented at significant cost to the organization, that idea must be seen as being of high enough quality to be deemed worth the risk of further pursuit. As leaders are often the key decision-makers on resource allocation, they play a fundamental role in evaluating the utility of an idea as well as making initial planning steps toward seeing those ideas realized (Mumford, Steele, Mulhearn, McIntosh, & Watts, 2017; Watts, Mulhearn, Todd, & Mumford, 2017). As noted by Watts and colleagues (2017), "creative thinking by leaders often begins with idea evaluation immediately after some follower's presentation of an idea" (p. 85).

Although the premise that effective idea evaluation on the part of the leader has been shown to positively shape creative performance (e.g., Mumford, Schultz, & Osburn, 2002), the focus here is not on a given leader's skills, capabilities, or ability to successfully evaluate an idea (see Mumford et al., 2017 for a review of leader cognitions). Rather, the focus of this chapter is on perceptions of work climate with a primary focus on individual employee performance. As such, the role of climate, particularly when reflecting on the nature of the dimension itself, is more nuanced than might appear on the surface. Namely, it is necessary to consider that the dimension in question is composed of having a supportive leader who provides direction and encourages participation.

In light of the nature of the dimension, we argue that climate will shape evaluation and implementation processes in such a way that ideas may be successfully iterated upon completion of feedback received during idea evaluation. Mumford and colleagues (2002, 2003) have noted that a key aspect of idea evaluation is allowing for idea refinement as an outcome of idea evaluation. Recall the dynamic and iterative nature of the creative process, and in doing so, idea evaluation becomes more than merely a gate that ideas must pass through to be ultimately implemented. Instead, idea evaluation is more appropriately viewed as the first step of refining an idea, utilizing aspects of idea generation in engagement of such activities. As an extension, leaders who encourage participation, create an environment of support, and provide clear goals for such activities will ensure that as subordinates go back to the drawing board and revise their initial ideas, they will be willing to return with refined, yet still original, concepts. As such, our third proposition is as follows:

> Proposition 3a: *The climate dimension of leader direction and encouragement will be positively related to all phases of the creative process but will be most strongly related to the later-stage process of idea evaluation.*

> Proposition 3b: *In addition to idea evaluation, how a leader approaches idea evaluation will subsequently shape subordinate idea refinement and revision.*

Thus, the climate dimension of leader direction and encouragement will have both direct and indirect influences on idea generation with the indirect path operating through how leaders manage idea evaluation as a process.

Climate Dimension 4: Organizational Capacity and Support

Once ideas have been evaluated and refined, decision-makers in the organization will determine how to most effectively implement those ideas. Upon implementation, moreover, those ideas that have been implemented can be tracked and assessed over time to determine if more refinement is needed (i.e., solution monitoring process). These processes, relative to earlier stage processes, are more formalized, structured, and resource intensive than activities in earlier stages (Hunter et al., 2015). As an extension, these processes are performed by individuals at higher ranks within the organization and are driven by organizational, rather than individual, factors. As such, we propose that the climate dimension that maps onto more formalized and organizationally oriented elements will be most predictive of later-stage processes. Specifically, the dimension of organizational capacity and support will have its strongest relationship with the processes of implementation planning and solution monitoring. The mechanism linking climate and performance is that employees are most likely to pursue efforts they believe will be supported and allowed to be fully realized. An organization with the resources to ensure their ideas will have a chance to be implemented will find a collection of subordinates more engaged with such processes and likely those that come before it. Formally, our fourth proposition is as follows:

> Proposition 4: *The climate dimension organizational resources and support will be positively related to all phases of the creative process but will be most strongly related to implementation planning and solution monitoring processes.*

Climate Dimension 5: Organizational Integration and Extension

A unique aspect of creativity is that it often benefits from multiple perspectives and ideas to form a novel and useful solution to a creative problem. This requires the organizations to support cross-functional cooperation and to give employees the capability to obtain additional resources and support from individuals outside of their immediate peer groups or supervisor (Hunter et al., 2007). Further, a climate of support and cooperation will relate to several stages of the creative process, in both earlier and later stages. For example, employees may seek out others' expertise outside of their immediate department or peers who may have similar backgrounds. This would aid in conceptual combination, where concepts and ideas can be combined to form one or a few novel solutions. Similarly, employees may seek out cross-functional help in the implementation of ideas to acquire resources that outside departments or organizations may have. As such, our fifth and final proposition is as follows:

> Proposition 5: *The climate dimension organizational integration and extension will be positively related to all phases of the creative process but will most strongly be related to conceptual combination and implementation planning phases.*

Implications, Limitations, and Future Directions

To summarize, in this chapter we explored the intersection between creative problem-solving and creative climate. Although climate has been discussed and examined as a key predictor of creative performance (e.g., Hunter et al., 2007), no effort to date has considered relationships between discrete climate dimensions and the various processes comprising creative problem-solving. To do so, we utilized findings from a range of studies including early taxonomic and meta-analytic efforts, to more recent investigations that explored the dimensionality of climate directly. What emerged was a five-dimensional framework that is consistent with proposed climate frameworks (e.g., James et al., 2008). More centrally, the dimensional framework permitted a discussion on how climate may relate to the various stages of creative problem-solving.

Upon consideration of these specific relationships, we observed that there was a trend in antecedents, climate dimensions, and aspects of creative problem-solving whereby all aspects had components that increase in formalization, resource intensity, and structure as creative ideas moved through the problem-solving process (Hunter et al., 2015; Hunter & Cushenbery, 2011). This trend allowed for propositions to be made about what aspects of the creative process each dimension of climate was most strongly related to. The implications of these propositions are discussed next.

Implications

Practical Implications

There are two primary practical implications emerging from the present effort. The first requires acknowledgement that the nature of the creative problem-solving process is such that individuals involved in idea framing may not be the same group of individuals involved in implementation or solution monitoring. The creative process is both challenging and quite lengthy. Moreover, the skills needed to successfully engage in all aspects of the creative process vary, indicating that differing individuals will be tasked with completing differing phases of the process. Consider, for example, the concept team that hands their car design off to the manufacturing group or the storyboard designers who hand their concepts off to artists in animated films. Perhaps even consider the architectural firm who transitions their designs to a general contractor to build a home. In these aforementioned cases, the baton is passed from one group of individuals to the other between stages of the creative process.

In acknowledging the differing demands of each phase of the creative process, a key implication for climate emerges. Namely, the nature of the process an individual or team is engaging in may dictate the nature of the climate to most strongly encourage. Again, this is not to say that an organization should not aspire to elicit all phases of a positive creative climate – all dimensions are useful and predictive of creative success. Rather, when prioritizing what dimensions of climate to most strongly enhance, it is worth considering what aspects of the creative process a given unit most often engages in.

The second practical implication is tied to the perceptual nature of climate. That is, we have utilized a definition of climate that is grounded in an individual's perception of the work context. Although organizational actions (e.g., providing resources) have the potential to shape such perceptions, there is a key issue tied to that linkage: visibility and awareness. To shape an employee's view of how an organization is operating, that employee must be aware of the organizational actions. Thus, to increase the effectiveness of climate, decision-makers in organizations may find time well spent on making their efforts on supporting creativity well known. Such efforts will increase the linkage between organizational actions and climate and, by extension, linkages between organizational actions and performance in creative problem-solving.

Theoretical Implications

Although the focus of the chapter was not on developing a new theory for climate, there are theoretical implications emerging from the present effort. The first is tied to the general support observed for the taxonomic framework of James and colleagues (James & James, 1989; James et al., 2008). By proxy, support for this five-dimensional taxonomy also lends support to James and colleagues' suggestion that psychological climate (i.e., individual level of analysis) may be the most appropriate level with which to view climate or at least a taxonomy of climate that is consistent with the framework put forward. Moreover, the similarity of the dimensions we have observed in work by Hunter and colleagues on creative climate and the broader climate taxonomy put forth by James and James (1990) suggests that there is utility in a framework that embraces a valuation-based view of climate. That is, an employee's perception of the work environment is derived both from the actions in the environment as well as the individual's unique values (Locke, 1976). These unique, employee-centric values, moreover, suggest that perceptions will vary by individual, further indicating support for focusing on climate perceptions at the psychological level of analysis.

Limitations

Although we believe the chapter makes a number of key contributions to the creative climate and problem-solving literatures, it is necessary to acknowledge several limitations. The first is that we chose to focus on the strongest proposed relationships among climate dimensions and creative problem-solving processes. In reality, all dimensions of climate will have positive and unique relationships with each of the creative processes. We felt that a discussion of each would have resulted in an unwieldy chapter with less practical utility for the reader. In truncating our discussion, however, a number of interesting relationships were omitted (e.g., the role of leadership in shaping problem construction) and stand as a limitation of the chapter.

The second limitation is that in Mumford and colleagues' (2012) discussion of creative problem-solving, the authors discuss two factors that shape successful engagement of the creative processes: strategies (Baughman & Mumford, 1995) and knowledge (Ericsson & Moxley, 2012). In particular, aspects of strategy development such as causal analysis (Marcy & Mumford, 2007) may prove quite valuable in understanding the linkages between climate and problem-solving success. Additionally, Mumford, Antes, Caughron, Connelly, and Beeler (2010) also note that the importance of any given creative process varies as a function of field or discipline, and this may subsequently impact the relationships between climate dimensions and creative thinking processes. However, space constraints limited our ability to discuss how these factors may be integrated into the climate and problem-solving processes. As such, our framework is limited to a discussion on creative problem-solving that is focused on a subset of elements outlined by Mumford and colleagues (2012) and on industry more broadly, and should be viewed as a limitation.

Finally, we presented evidence for a five-dimensional taxonomy derived from a broader framework designed to capture the range of possible creative climate conceptualizations. Although we have witnessed reasonable consistency across several studies on the nature of this dimensionality, it is important to note that this perspective is one among many (see Mathisen & Einarsen, 2004). As noted earlier in the chapter, the nature and range of dimensions have varied substantially across researchers and samples. It is possible that a more stable variation of this taxonomy will emerge and serve as the foundation for understanding creative climate. Thus, it must be acknowledged that the framework offered in this chapter was reasonably justified but nonetheless is one possible perspective among many.

Future Directions

In light of the discussion in this chapter, we recommend several broad future directions. The first is further testing and refinement of the differential relationships outlined via the five propositions in the chapter. As a growing amount of research is suggesting (e.g., Axtell et al., 2000; Perry-Smith & Mannucci, 2017), those elements predictive of one creative process may not predict performance in another process. Researchers can observe these relationships by measuring climate in an organization and observing the creative process in its true dynamism, such as by using creative process report diaries (Botella, Nelson, & Zenasni, 2017). Should such differential prediction be observed, and there is some indication of this (e.g., Hunter et al., 2007), implications for practice are substantial.

The second area of future research that appears warranted is the investigation of climate influence over time. In particular, given the perceptual nature of climate, it would appear worthy to investigate the stability of climate and whether it fluctuates based on recent or salient events or is more stable and based on a more global perception. Along related lines, more work is needed linking culture and climate literatures (Schneider et al., 2013; Tesluk, Farr, & Klein, 1997), as this link may provide the key to understanding the stability of climate.

Tied to this, it is critical that future work further establish the link between organizational antecedents and the emerging dimensions of climate. Undoubtedly, actions on the part of the organization and its members will shape views of climate, but the perception-based nature of creative climate suggests that additional factors will play a role. This may be the values of the perceiver, as noted by James and colleagues (2008) and Locke (1976), but may also be aspects of how organizational policies are shared and expressed to individuals in the organization. Rewarding creativity, for example, while not clearly indicating that such rewards are available, will not likely result in as strong of a perception of organizational support for creativity than would exist if clarity about the availability of rewards was equally advertised. Using the framework proposed in this chapter will aid future endeavors to investigate additional interactive effects of creative climate. Scholars have already begun to investigate factors such as play cues (West, Hoff, & Carlsson, 2016), hindrance stressors (Ren & Zhang, 2015), and authentic leadership (Edú-Valsania, Moriano, & Molero, 2016).

Further, Friedrich and Mumford (2009) found that antecedents to creative processes are not bound by time, where hindrances to one creative process may carry over to impact later creative processes. This means that the expected relationships discussed previously in this chapter could be masked or subdued by carryover effects among processes (Friedrich & Mumford, 2009). Future research should examine the carryover effects across creative processes, as well as how this impacts creative processes' relationships with creative climate.

This chapter also focuses on a new line of propositions linking creative climate's impact on the execution of creative processes, rather than the more traditionally examined link between creative climate and motivation. Evidence supporting the link between creative climate and creative process execution or performance is currently not available, which provides a fruitful avenue for future research to explore. However, the motivation-based models should be compared with the models depicting the impact of creative climate directly on creative performance. Therefore, explicit tests of these competing models provide yet another avenue for future research.

Finally, as alluded to in our discussion on levels of analysis, we see substantial value in shifting views on climate as an inherently shared construct to a phenomenon where differences are likely. Just as individuals have different and unique relationships with their supervisors (e.g., Dansereau, Graen, & Haga, 1975), individual employees will have differential views on their work environment based on these experiences, as well as a range of individual differences. It is these differences – asking why there is a lack of sharedness or agreement – that may be the most fruitful and interesting avenue for future research.

Concluding Comments

To close, the aim of this chapter was to explore the dimensionality of the creative climate and integrate these dimensions with the creative problem-solving perspective. In doing so, we proposed that some dimensions of climate will play a larger role in the various processes comprising creative problem-solving. Such a prediction has implications for how to shape and influence climate as a means to enhance creative problem-solving. Although we view the discussion in this chapter as a necessary first step in integrating these literature bases, we believe it is only the foundation for a fruitful area of investigation in the years to come.

References

Amabile, T. M., Conti, R., Coon, H., Lazenby, J., & Herron, M. 1996. Assessing the work environment for creativity. *Academy of Management Journal*, 39, 1154–1184.

Anderson, N., & West, M. A. 1996. The team climate inventory: Development of the TCI and its applications in teambuilding for innovativeness. *European Journal of Work and Organizational Psychology*, 5, 53–66.

Argyris, C. 1957. The individual and organization: Some problems of mutual adjustment. *Administrative Science Quarterly*, 2, 1–24.

Axtell, C. M., Holman, D. J., Unsworth, K. L., Wall, T. D., Waterson, P. E., & Harrington, E. 2000. Shopfloor innovation: Facilitating the suggestion and implementation of ideas. *Journal of Occupational and Organizational Psychology*, 73, 265–285.

Baughman, W. A., & Mumford, M. D. 1995. Process-analytic models of creative capacities: Operations influencing the combination-and-reorganization process. *Creativity Research Journal*, 8, 37–62.

Binyamin, G., & Carmeli, A. 2017. Fostering members' creativity in teams: The role of structuring of human resource management processes. *Psychology of Aesthetics, Creativity, and the Arts*, 11, 18.

Botella, M., Nelson, J., & Zenasni, F. 2017. It is time to observe the creative process: How to use a creative process report diary (CRD). *The Journal of Creative Behavior*, 53. https://doi.org/10.1002/jocb.172

Bowen, D. E., & Schneider, B. 2014. A service climate synthesis and future research agenda. *Journal of Service Research*, 17, 5–22.

Bunge, M. 1963. A general black box theory. *Philosophy of Science*, 30, 346–358.

Damanpour, F. 1991. Organizational innovation: A meta-analysis of effects of determinants and moderators. *Academy of Management Journal*, 34, 555–590.

Dansereau, F., Graen, G., & Haga, W. J. 1975. A vertical dyad linkage approach to leadership within formal organizations: A longitudinal investigation of the role making process. *Organizational Behavior and Human Performance*, 13, 46–78.

Dewey, J. 1910. *How we think*. Boston, MA: DC Heath.

Dul, J., & Ceylan, C. 2014. The impact of a creativity-supporting work environment on a firm's product innovation performance. *Journal of Product Innovation Management*, 31, 1254–1267.

Edú-Valsania, S., Moriano, J. A., & Molero, F. 2016. Authentic leadership and employee knowledge sharing behavior: Mediation of the innovation climate and workgroup identification. *Leadership and Organization Development Journal*, 37, 487–506.

Ekvall, G. 1996. Organizational climate for creativity and innovation. *European Journal of Work and Organizational Psychology*, 5, 105–123.

Ekvall, G., & Arvonen, J. 1991. Change centered leadership: An addition to the two-dimensional model. *Scand J Manag*, 7, 17–26.

Ekvall, G., & Tångeberg-Andersson, Y. L. V. A. 1986. Working climate and creativity: A study of an innovative newspaper office. *The Journal of Creative Behavior*, 20, 215–225.

Ekvall, G., Arvonen, J., & Waldenström-Lindblad, I. 1983. Creative organizational climate: Construction and validation of a measuring instrument. *Swedish Council for Management and Organizational Behaviour*.

Ericsson, K. A., & Moxley, J. H. 2012. The expert performance approach and deliberate practice: Some potential implications for studying creative performance in organizations. In M. D. Mumford (Ed.), *The handbook of organizational creativity* (pp. 141–167). New York, NY: Academic Press.

Finke, R. A., Ward, T. B., & Smith, S. M. 1992. *Creative cognition: Theory, research, and applications*. Cambridge, MA: MIT Press.

Fleishman, E. A., Mumford, M. D., Zaccaro, S. J., Levin, K. Y., Korotkin, A. L., & Hein, M. B. 1991. Taxonomic efforts in the description of leader behavior: A synthesis and functional interpretation. *The Leadership Quarterly*, 2, 245–287.

Friedrich, T. L., & Mumford, M. D. 2009. The effects of conflicting information on creative thought: A source of performance improvements or decrements? *Creativity Research Journal*, 21, 265–281.

Frese, M., & Keith, N. 2015. Action errors, error management, and learning in organizations. *Annual Review of Psychology*, 66, 661–687.

Heinen, R. L., & Hunter, S. T. 2018. *An extension of the work on the dimensionality of creative climate* (Master's thesis). The Pennsylvania State University, University Park.

Hinkin, T. R. 1995. A review of scale development practices in the study of organizations. *Journal of Management*, 21, 967–988.

Holahan, P. J., Aronson, Z. H., Jurkat, M. P., & Schoorman, F. D. 2004. Implementing computer technology: A multiorganizational test of Klein and Sorra's model. *Journal of Engineering and Technology Management*, 21, 31–50.

Hon, A. H., Bloom, M., & Crant, J. M. 2014. Overcoming resistance to change and enhancing creative performance. *Journal of Management*, 40, 919–941.

Hunter, S. T., & Cushenbery, L. 2011. Leading for innovation: Direct and indirect influences. *Advances in Developing Human Resources*, 13, 248–265.

Hunter, S. T., Bedell, K. E., & Mumford, M. D. 2005. Dimensions of creative climate. *The International Journal of Creativity and Problem Solving*, 15, 97–116.

Hunter, S. T., Bedell, K. E., & Mumford, M. D. 2007. Climate for creativity: A quantitative review. *Creativity Research Journal*, 19, 69–90.

Hunter, S. T., Bedell-Avers, K. E., Hunsicker, C. M., Mumford, M. D., & Ligon, G. S. 2008. Applying multiple knowledge structures in creative thought: Effects on idea generation and problem-solving. *Creativity Research Journal*, 20, 137–154.

Hunter, S. T., Cassidy, S. E., & Ligon, G. S. 2012. Planning for innovation: A process oriented perspective. In M. D. Mumford (Ed.), *Handbook of organizational creativity* (pp. 515–545). New York, NY: Elsevier.

Hunter, S. T., Cushenbery, L., Ginther, N., & Fairchild, J. 2013. Chapter 4: Leadership, Innovation, and Technology. In: S. Hemlin et al. (Eds.), *Creativity and Leadership in Science, Technology, and Innovation*, pp. 81–110.

Hunter, S. T., Gutworth, M., Crayne, M., & Jayne, B. 2015. Planning for innovation: The critical role of agility. In M. D. Mumford & M. Frese (Eds.), *The psychology of planning in organizations* (pp. 146–165). New York, NY: Routledge.

James, L. R., James, L. A., & Ashe, D. K. 1990. The meaning of organizations: The role of cognition and values. *Organizational Climate and Culture*, 40, 84.

James, L. R., Choi, C. C., Ko, C. H. E., McNeil, P. K., Minton, M. K., Wright, M. A., & Kim, K. I. 2008. Organizational and psychological climate: A review of theory and research. *European Journal of Work and Organizational Psychology*, 17, 5–32.

Jayne, B., & Hunter, S. T. 2016, April. *Examining the impact of dual leadership on team innovation*. Poster presented at the Society for Industrial and Organizational Psychology annual conference.

LeBreton, J. M., & Senter, J. L. 2008. Answers to 20 questions about interrater reliability and interrater agreement. *Organizational Research Methods*, 11, 815–852.

Lewin, K., Lippitt, R., & White, R. K. 1939. Patterns of aggressive behavior in experimentally created "social climates." *The Journal of Social Psychology*, 10, 269–299.

Locke, E. A. 1976. The nature and causes of job satisfaction. *Handbook of Industrial and Organizational Psychology*, 1, 1297–1343.

Marcy, R. T., & Mumford, M. D. 2007. Social innovation: Enhancing creative performance through causal analysis. *Creativity Research Journal*, 19, 123–140.

Mathisen, G. E., & Einarsen, S. 2004. A review of instruments assessing creative and innovative environments within organizations. *Creativity Research Journal*, 16, 119–140.

Mumford, M. D., & Gustafson, S. B. 1988. Creativity syndrome: Integration, application, and innovation. *Psychological Bulletin*, 103, 27.

Mumford, M. D., & Hunter, S. T. 2005. Innovation in organizations: A multi-level perspective on creativity. In F. Dansereau & F. J. Yammarino (Eds.), *Multi-level issues in strategy and methods* (pp. 9–73). Bingley, UK: Emerald Group Publishing.

Mumford, M. D., & Hemlin, S. (Eds.). 2017. *Handbook of research on leadership and creativity*. Cheltenham, UK: Edward Elgar Publishing.

Mumford, M. D., Connelly, S., & Gaddis, B. 2003. How creative leaders think: Experimental findings and cases. *The Leadership Quarterly*, 14, 411–432.

Mumford, M. D., Antes, A. L., Caughron, J. J., Connelly, S., & Beeler, C. 2010. Cross-field differences in creative problem-solving skills: A comparison of health, biological, and social sciences. *Creativity Research Journal*, 22, 14–26.

Mumford, M. D., Medeiros, K. E., & Partlow, P. J. 2012. Creative thinking: Processes, strategies, and knowledge. *The Journal of Creative Behavior*, 46, 30–47.

Mumford, M. D., Mobley, M. I., Reiter-Palmon, R., Uhlman, C. E., & Doares, L. M. 1991. Process analytic models of creative capacities. *Creativity Research Journal*, 4, 91–122.

Mumford, M. D., Schultz, R. A., & Osburn, H. K. 2002. Planning in organizations: Performance as a multi-level phenomenon. In F. J. Yammarino & F. Dansereau (Eds.), *The many faces of multi-level issues* (pp. 3–65). Bingley, UK: Emerald Group Publishing.

Mumford, M. D., Steele, L. M., Mulhearn, T. J., McIntosh, T., & Watts, L. L. 2017. Leader planning skills and creative performance: Integration of past, present, and future. In M. D. Mumford & S. Hemlin (Eds.), *Handbook of research on leadership and creativity* (pp. 17–39). Cheltenham, UK: Edward Elgar Publishing.

Neely, B., Lovelace, J., Kundro, T., & Hunter, S. T. 2016, April. *Creative climate measurement: A multilevel scaling approach*. Poster presented at the Society for Industrial and Organizational Psychology annual conference.

Paruchuri, S., Perry-Smith, J. E., Chattopadhyay, P., & Shaw, J. D. 2018. New ways of seeing: Pitfalls and opportunities in multilevel research. *Academy of Management Journal*, 61, 797–801.

Payne, R. L. 1990. Madness in our method: A comment on Jackofsky and Slocum's paper "A longitudinal study of climates." *Journal of Organizational Behavior*, 11, 77–80.

Perry-Smith, J. E., & Mannucci, P. V. 2017. From creativity to innovation: The social network drivers of the four phases of the idea journey. *Academy of Management Review*, 42, 53–79.

Preacher, K. J., Curran, P. J., & Bauer, D. J. 2006. Computational tools for probing interactions in multiple linear regression, multilevel modeling, and latent curve analysis. *Journal of Educational and Behavioral Statistics*, 31, 437–448.

Reiter-Palmon, R., Mumford, M. D., O'Connor Boes, J., & Runco, M. A. 1997. Problem construction and creativity: The role of ability, cue consistency, and active processing. *Creativity Research Journal*, 10, 9–23.

Ren, F., & Zhang, J. 2015. Job stressors, organizational innovation climate, and employees' innovative behavior. *Creativity Research Journal*, 27, 16–23.

Rousseau, D. M. 1988. The construction of climate in organizational research. In C. L. Cooper & I. T. Robertson (Eds.), *International review of industrial and organizational psychology* (pp. 139–158). New York, NY: John Wiley and Sons.

Schneider, B., & Reichers, A. E. 1983. On the etiology of climates. *Personnel Psychology*, 36, 19–39.

Schneider, B., Ehrhart, M. G., & Macey, W. H. 2013. Organizational climate and culture. *Annual Review of Psychology*, 64, 361–388.

Schraw, G., Dunkle, M. E., & Bendixen, L. D. 1995. Cognitive processes in well-defined and ill-defined problem solving. *Applied Cognitive Psychology*, 9, 523–538.

Scott, G. M., Lonergan, D. C., & Mumford, M. D. 2005. Conceptual combination: Alternative knowledge structures, alternative heuristics. *Creativity Research Journal*, 17, 79–98.

Tesluk, P. E., Farr, J. L., & Klein, S. R. 1997. Influences of organizational culture and climate on individual creativity. *The Journal of Creative Behavior*, 31, 27–41.

Wallas, G. 1926. *The art of thought*. New York, NY: Harcourt Brace.

Watts, L. L., Mulhearn, T. J., Todd, E. M., & Mumford, M. D. 2017. Leader idea evaluation and follower creativity: Challenges, constraints, and capabilities. In M. D. Mumford & S. Hemlin (Eds.), *Handbook of research on leadership and creativity* (pp. 82–99). Cheltenham, UK: Edward Elgar Publishing.

West, S. E., Hoff, E., & Carlsson, I. 2016. Play and productivity: Enhancing the creative climate at workplace meetings with play cues. *American Journal of Play*, 9, 71.

Woodman, R. W., & Schoenfeldt, L. F. 1990. An interactionist model of creative behavior. *The Journal of Creative Behavior*, 24, 279–290.

Zohar, D., & Polachek, T. 2014. Discourse-based intervention for modifying supervisory communication as leverage for safety climate and performance improvement: A randomized field study. *Journal of Applied Psychology*, 99, 113.

8

COGNITIVE AND SOCIAL PROCESSES IN TEAM CREATIVITY

Roni Reiter-Palmon and Paul B. Paulus

Research on the topic of creativity and innovation in organizations has increased steadily over the last few decades. The interest in creativity and innovation and the factors that facilitate or hinder these has developed due to the importance of these issues for organizational survival and growth (Shalley, Zhou, & Oldham, 2004). Factors such as rapid changes in the marketplace due to technology and globalization have increased the need of organizations to develop creative ideas, solutions, processes, and products (Shalley et al., 2004; West, Hirst, Richter, & Shipton, 2004).

As problems facing organizations have become more complex, in part due to technology and globalization, and as work has become more interdependent, it has become clear that solutions to these problems cannot be developed by a single individual (Kozlowski & Bell, 2008; Paulus & Nijstad, 2003). The use of teams in the workplace to address these complex problems has increased, and with it, the interest in team creativity (Reiter-Palmon, Wigert, & de Vreede, 2011). The use of teams to address complex problems also indicates that it is critical to understand how teams solve problems creatively. While there are multiple models that focus on creative problem-solving at the individual level (Mumford, Mobley, Uhlman, Reiter-Palmon, & Doares, 1991; Sternberg, 1988; Ward, Smith & Finke, 1999), work on the cognitive processes associated with creative problem-solving in teams, with the exception of idea generation, has been lagging (Reiter-Palmon, Herman, & Yammarino, 2008; Reiter-Palmon et al., 2011). Using the individual creative problem-solving models as a starting point, we suggest that work on creative problem-solving in teams has focused on three main processes: problem identification and construction, idea generation, and idea evaluation and choice. While other processes mentioned in the individual models are of importance, they have been researched even less than these three processes.

One important issue to acknowledge when studying cognitive processes of teams in relation to team creativity is that the only way for these processes to occur at the team level is through social processes and interactions (Cooke, 2015; Reiter-Palmon, Wigert, & de Vreede, 2011). Team social processes and interaction can therefore not only influence the effectiveness of the application of these cognitive processes, they may also be direct signals for the effectiveness of the application of cognition. Using these three core processes of problem identification and construction, idea generation, and idea evaluation as a starting point, we provide a summary of empirical findings of these processes. We then discuss how social processes, which are critical to teamwork, may influence the application and effectiveness of these cognitive processes in teams. We then evaluate the role of design thinking within this framework. Finally, we conclude by identifying gaps in our knowledge and suggesting avenues for future research.

Problem Identification and Construction

The increasing uncertainty facing organizations means that employees are confronted with problems that are ill defined and ambiguous. Ill-defined problems are characterized by multiple possible goals, multiple ways of solving the problems, and multiple possible and acceptable solutions. It is this ambiguity, complexity, and novelty that allows for creative solutions to arise (Mumford et al., 1991; Schraw, Dunkle, & Bendixen, 1995). Given that many problems facing organizations and teams are not only complex and ambiguous but also novel, the creative problem-solver must first construct and define the problem to be solved. During the problem construction process, the problem-solver must recognize that there is a problem to be solved, define the problem parameters, and construct the problem (Reiter-Palmon & Robinson, 2009). This structuring is viewed as the first step in creative problem-solving; therefore, it provides the context for the application of later processes (Mumford, Reiter-Palmon, & Redmond, 1994). As a result, it has been suggested that problem identification and construction will have a marked impact on creative problem-solving through its effect on later processes (Arreola & Reiter-Palmon, 2016; Ma, 2009; Scott, Leritz, & Mumford, 2004).

Research on problem identification and construction has been mainly conducted at the individual level (Reiter-Palmon, 2018a). At the individual level, a few key findings have important implications for team problem construction and identification. First, the way in which individuals structure and construct problems is based on past experiences solving similar problems (Holyoak, 1984; Mumford et al., 1994). At the team level, this means that diverse experiences may translate to diverse problem constructions. Second, problem construction and identification appear to occur in an automatic fashion, and individuals who are more creative, or those who have expertise, tend to engage in the process more deliberately (Getzels & Csikszentmihályi, 1975; Reiter-Palmon, Mumford, O'Connor Boes, & Runco, 1997; Rostan, 1994; Voss, Wolfe, Lawrence, & Engle, 1991). When individuals are asked to actively engage in problem identification and construction, or must engage in the process due to information inconsistency, they are more likely to be creative (Miron-Spektor, Gino, & Argote, 2011; Paletz & Peng, 2009; Redmond, Mumford, & Teach, 1993). It is expected that this automaticity will carry over into a team context. Further, because of this, individuals may not discuss potential discrepancies and differences in how the problems are constructed leading to potential differences in solutions generated and evaluations of these solutions (Reiter-Palmon et al., 2008).

Research has provided support for both of these assertions. Cronin and Weingart (2007) coined the term *representational gap* or *rGaps* to indicate a situation when team members have different ways of conceptualizing the problem. Teams with larger rGaps tend to have difficulty during problem construction, leading to poor cognitive integration as a team and lower creativity (Weingart, Cronin, Houser, Cagan, & Vogel, 2005). However, other research has suggested that larger rGaps may increase team creativity when teams identify the discrepancies early and use them to communicate about alternative pathways to solving the problem (Weingart, Todorova, & Cronin, 2008).

Support for the automaticity of the problem construction processes in teams has also been found. Research by Leonardi (2011) using qualitative methods found that people from different departments had differences in the goals identified, key problems, strategies to solve the problem, knowledge required, and criteria that a solution should meet, all elements of problem representations that guide problem construction (Holyoak, 1984). Team members were largely unaware that other departments were constructing the problem differently, and these different constructions negatively influenced the creativity of the solutions. Leonardi further found that when leaders encouraged teams to discuss problem features, they were able to develop a shared framework, a common problem representation that in turn guided the innovation process. A study by Gish and Clausen (2013) further supports these findings and suggests that preexisting knowledge influenced how problems were constructed in teams. Team members were unaware of these differences, and as a result, there was conflict and disagreement during idea generation. This conflict, in turn, resulted in lowered creativity. However, when additional information was introduced that facilitated divergence in problem construction to identify multiple problem definitions, diverse teams were more effective at generating an innovative solution.

Another concept related to problem construction is that of mental models about causal relationships and relationships among concepts that group members bring to the problem-solving task. Mumford and colleagues have found that various features of such mental models influence different features of the outcome of the problem-solving process, such as novelty and quality (Barrett et al., 2013; Mumford et al., 2012). In a team context, an important factor is whether such models are shared (Cannon-Bowers, Salas, & Converse, 1993). Shared mental models (SMMs) are a representation of knowledge shared by team members regarding task, team interaction, and teammates (Cannon-Bowers et al., 1993; Smith-Jentsch, Mathieu, & Kraiger, 2005). Cannon-Bowers et al. (1993) suggested that there are four distinct types of mental models, regarding task, technology and equipment, team interactions, and team members. Of these four types of mental models, the task knowledge one is the most similar to the problem representations. Cannon-Bowers et al. (1993) hypothesized that when tasks are unpredictable, task SMMs become more important as these improve team effectiveness. Unpredictable tasks share similar features with ill-defined problems in the sense that these tasks also may not have known or even correct solutions. Empirical studies have supported this hypothesis, finding that SMMs foster team adaptation and team creativity (Mumford, Feldman, Hein, & Nagao, 2001; Santos, Uitdewilligen, & Passos, 2015; Uitdewilligen, Rico, & Waller, 2018). While SMMs may facilitate creativity through understanding of task requirements and team interactions, SMMs can lead to reduced creativity through too much similarity and conformity (Cannon-Bowers et al., 1993). Reiter-Palmon, Herman, and Yammarino (2008) suggested that automatic application of problem representations at the individual as well as the team level, due to SMMs, may result in lowered creativity.

The research previously described leads to a number of conclusions. First, it is clear that team members indeed can have different conceptualizations and constructions of the problem and that these different constructions can lead to differences in the ideas generated and what ideas are viewed as beneficial. Further, the research indicates that conflict and disagreements can result from lack of a common problem construction among team members. Finally, the research suggests that social processes can influence the effectiveness in which the problem identification and construction process is applied in teams, and as a result influence creative performance. It is therefore important to discuss how and what type of social processes can influence problem construction.

Social Processes and Problem Construction

Research to date has suggested that conflict can arise when individuals within the team construct the problem in very different ways based on their previous experience, and in turn, this conflict can hurt the problem construction process (Gish & Clausen, 2013; Santos et al., 2015; Weingart et al., 2005). However, research also suggests that differences in the way problems are constructed can lead to creativity if these differences are discussed effectively

(Leonardi, 2011; Weingart et al., 2008). These findings indicate a number of ways in which social processes influence problem identification and construction. First, differences in problem construction must be acknowledged and discussed. That is, communication regarding problem constructions must take place. This requires that team members are cognizant of the problem identification and construction process, which is typically automatic (Reiter-Palmon & Robinson, 2009). As a result, team members may completely forego this step and move directly into discussing solutions to the problem. At this point, differences in problem constructions may manifest as differences in idea generation (Gish & Clausen, 2013; Leonardi, 2011).

However, even when team members are cognizant of the problem construction process, they must be willing to discuss the way in which the problem is constructed. This may be more difficult and contentious when constructions are diverse, which is more likely to occur when teams are diverse. Previous research indicates that identifying and discussing these divergent problem constructions will likely result in increased creativity (Leonardi, 2011; Weingart et al., 2008). Reiter-Palmon and Murugavel (2018) found that when teams were instructed to be engaged in problem construction prior to solving the problem, they were more likely to generate original ideas and reported less conflict and increased satisfaction. These findings suggest that when teams discuss the different problem constructions, and do so early in the process, the result is not only improved creativity but potentially also improved overall communication.

While the effect of conflict on creativity, as measured by the final product or supervisory evaluation, is well documented (de Witt de, Greer, & Jehn, 2011), the role of conflict in problem construction is less understood. When problem constructions are diverse, conflict may arise, which can lead to poor team problem construction and reduced creativity (Weingart et al., 2005). This may include both task conflict and relationship conflict (Santos et al., 2015). It is also possible that conflict will only shift in timing and occur early, during the problem construction stage, as opposed to later during the idea generation phase. What is clear, is that when conflict is managed effectively, it can be resolved and may facilitate creativity (Carmeli, Reiter-Palmon, & Ziv, 2010; Fairchild and Hunter, 2014).

In a related vein, issues of trust and psychological safety will likely also play a role in the degree to which team members are willing to discuss problem constructions. When trust and psychological safety are low, and team members are aware that their problem constructions may differ, they likely will be more hesitant to discuss the differences, potentially to avoid conflict. Additionally, when trust and psychological safety are low, minor disagreements and ambiguous information tend to be interpreted in a negative way (Nicholson & West, 1988; Salas, Sims, & Burke, 2005; West & Richter, 2008). Since situations and problems that allow for creativity are ill defined and ambiguous, and problem construction allows for a reduction of this ambiguity, the problem construction process may be particularly vulnerable to the negative effects of low trust and psychological safety, which then impact the rest of the creative process.

Collaborative Idea Generation

Although creative problem-solving can take many forms (Ward, 2012), much of the research at the collaborative level has focused on the idea generation process in which groups or teams generate ideas related to a specific problem or issue. This is, of course, a common occurrence in the everyday life of organizations and can happen in formal meetings, informal "hallway interactions," or structured "brainstorming sessions." The research on team innovation suggests that the process of exchanging ideas in teams is an important factor in innovation (Hülsheger, Anderson, & Salgado, 2009; Hunter, Bedell, & Mumford. 2007; Klijn & Tomic, 2010; Oldham & Baer, 2012). However, much of the theoretical grounding for the idea exchange process comes from controlled laboratory studies on group creativity (Paulus & Nijstad, 2003, 2019).

Idea generation in groups or teams involves tapping one's knowledge base, sharing ideas, building on shared ideas, and refinement and integration of shared ideas. Several models have outlined some of the basic elements of the cognitive and social processes involved (De Dreu, Nijstad, Bechtold, & Baas, 2011; Nijstad & Stroebe, 2006; Paulus & Brown, 2003, 2007). The search of one's knowledge base for relevant information is an individualistic process and may be hindered by the team interaction processes and the pressure to come up with relevant and novel ideas in a group context. Furthermore, in face-to-face settings, only one person can share his or her ideas at one time, and the sharing process can have both distracting and stimulating effects. Thus, it is not surprising that individual ideation can be more productive than verbal group ideation in terms of number of ideas. Sharing ideas by electronic methods or writing can avoid the types of problems noted and allow for a more efficient and productive of exchange of ideas (Dennis, Minas, & Williams, 2019; Paulus & Yang, 2000). However, it is likely that most organized collaborative innovation meetings and sessions involve the face-to-face context. Thus, we outline the basic principles that underlie effective collaborative ideation regardless of context.

Once team members are presented with the problem, it is helpful to first discuss the various components or categories of the problem (Deuja, Kohn, Paulus, & Korde, 2014). This can help guide the cognitive search process in that it will ensure that each of those elements will receive consideration and, in a potentially deeper search process in each of these categories, yield a greater number of novel ideas (Rietzschel, Nijstad, & Stroebe, 2014). In formal brainstorming sessions, team members are also instructed to follow the rules or guidelines suggested by Osborn (1963): say whatever comes to mind, focus on quantity of ideas, do not evaluate or criticize ideas as they are shared, and build on the shared ideas. Each of these guidelines can be theoretically justified. To generate a flow of ideas, it is important not to censor ideas as to quality as one is generating them. Concerns about quality of ideas and the potential negative reactions of others to unconventional or half-baked ideas may limit the spontaneity and potential novelty of the exchange process. There is an extensive literature on the inhibiting effects of evaluation apprehension (Camacho & Paulus, 1995; Diehl & Stroebe, 1987) and the benefits of psychological safety (contexts that allow for failure; Edmondson & Lei, 2014; Stollberger, West, & Sacramento, 2019). Thus, it is important to ensure that the team members feel free to express novel ideas in the idea generation phase.

Collaborative ideation is often promoted because it is presumed that sharing different perspectives will increase the potential of creative outcomes or solutions. The fact that teams do indeed produce many creative products supports this perspective (Reiter-Palmon, 2018b; Uzzi & Spiro, 2005) and provides support for the use of multidisciplinary teams for research and innovation (Tebes & Thai, 2018). However, collaborative ideation is a complex process that requires careful attention to the shared ideas, the comprehension of those ideas, the linking of those ideas to one's own knowledge or expertise, and the subsequent development of ideas that build on or integrate the shared perspectives. Considering the conceptual gaps that may exist among team members (Cronin & Weingart, 2007), it is not surprising that cognitively diverse groups face considerable challenges in effectively tapping their potential (Mello & Rentsch, 2015). Thus, it is important to have frequent meetings and experience in collaborative projects for such teams to function at a high level (Cummings & Kiesler, 2008). In general, it appears that differences in knowledge or expertise among team members (functional diversity) have positive effects on innovation, but demographic diversity does not have as clear an effect (Bell, Villado, Lukasik, Belau, & Briggs, 2011; van Dijk, van Engen, & van Knippenberg, 2012). The lack of effects of demographic diversity may be related to some degree of intergroup bias or discomfort in such groups in initial interactions or the fact that such groups may not have much cognitive diversity related to the task (Paulus, van der Zee, & Kenworthy, 2019). When demographic diversity is related to differences in knowledge or experience related to the task, positive effects of diversity can be observed (Nakui, Paulus, & van der Zee, 2011; Paulus & van der Zee, 2015), especially when groups have a positive attitude to diversity (Homan, van Knippenberg, van Kleef, & De Dreu, 2007; Nakui et al., 2011).

The information processing capacity of groups can also be enhanced by using procedures that are well suited for the efficient sharing and processing of ideas. Although this can be challenging in verbal ideation groups, when groups use electronic or writing methods of exchanging ideas, ideas can be shared without team members having to wait turns, and ideas can be attended to or processed when group members feel the need or desire to tap the shared ideas (for reviews, see Dennis et al., 2019; Paulus & Kenworthy, 2019). Thus, these procedures allow group members to tap their own knowledge base with minimal unwanted interference and also enable them to tap the cognitive resources of the group. Studies have shown that groups using electronic or writing methods can exceed the creative performance of similar size collections of individual idea generators (De Rosa, Smith, & Hantula, 2007; Paulus, Korde, Dickson, Carmeli, & Cohen-Meitar, 2015). Furthermore, when groups are exposed to the ideas of others, they are able to generate more ideas in a subsequent individual ideation session (Paulus & Korde, 2017; Paulus & Yang, 2000). This most likely reflects a carryover of the cognitive stimulation derived from the prior group sharing session.

Social Processes and Idea Generation

Collaborative ideation involves a variety of cognitive processes, but it is also influenced by various social factors (Paulus, Dugosh, Dzindolet, Coskun, & Putman, 2002). When ideas are being generated, group members can compare their performance with those of others. When there is a competitive atmosphere or some internal or external incentive to perform at a high level, group members may compare themselves to the high-performing members (upward comparison, Paulus & Dzindolet, 2008; Wood, 1989). When there is no strong incentive for high levels of performance, group members may move their performance in the direction of low performers (Paulus & Dzindolet, 1993). When group members are not identifiable or accountable for their performance, they may reduce their motivation level, especially in larger groups (social loafing, Karau & Williams, 1993). The importance of motivational factors is also emphasized by the Motivated Information Processing in Groups (MIP-G) model. De Dreu et al. (2011) have also highlighted the importance of individual motivation to perform well (epistemic) and social motivation that may be focused on individual outcomes (pro-self) or group outcomes (pro-social). Epistemic motivation may be influenced by personal characteristics such as conscientiousness or openness to experience or external factors such as task incentives or pressures. Social motivation may also be influenced by personal characteristics or the social context. In general, it is expected that a pro-social motivation will lead to higher levels of performance, but it can also lead to a tendency to be "too agreeable," and therefore, group members may not challenge the group consensus when they have a different perspective. (For review, see Nijstad, Bechtoldt, & Choi, 2019.)

One of the key social factors is the extent to which groups effectively deal with conflict. When group members have very disparate perspectives, the cognitive conflict could stimulate deeper information processing and lead to higher levels of creativity (Nemeth & O'Conner, 2019). However, such conflicts can also lead to negative interpersonal feelings that may inhibit team performance (De Dreu & Weingart, 2003; de Wit et al., 2011). De Dreu (2006) has suggested that moderate levels of conflict may be optimal for group performance. Thus, it is important for group leaders to effectively manage the group dynamics to ensure that group members do not take intellectual conflicts personally but as an important means of increasing depth of processing about an issue (Fairchild & Hunter, in press). Conflict is also more likely to have a positive effect on the novelty of products generated by a team if the team members report feelings of psychological safety (Fairchild & Hunter, 2014).

Idea Evaluation and Selection

Once ideas have been generated, it is important to spend some time evaluating them to determine which ideas are most worthy of further consideration and development. Mumford, Lonergan, and Scott (2002) proposed that idea evaluation and selection include three major activities: forecasting possible consequences and outcomes of selecting and implementing an idea; judging how well the characteristics of an idea fit with specific standards and criteria; and choosing, revising, or rejecting the idea as a solution. The idea evaluation and selection process is typically viewed as more convergent; however, it also includes divergent elements (Runco & Chand, 1995), such as the need to forecast, for example, which requires thinking about various options and their impact. Idea evaluation and selection are critical for creative problem-solving; in organizational settings many ideas can be generated but only a few of the ideas reach the implementation phase (Sharma, 1999). There is considerable research on the evaluation process by individuals (cf., Rietzschel & Ritter, 2018), but only a few studies have examined this process in groups.

At the individual level, research suggests that individuals are able to accurately evaluate ideas of originality and novelty (Basadur, Runco, & Vega, 2000; Runco & Basadur, 1993; Runco & Chand, 1995; Runco & Smith, 1992; Runco & Vega, 1990) and that this accuracy improves when individuals are creative themselves (Basadur et al., 2000; Berg, 2016; Blair & Mumford, 2007; Kaufman & Beghetto, 2013; Kaufman, Beghetto, & Watson, 2016). Research on individuals has found that participants tend to favor feasible ideas over novel ones (Blair & Mumford, 2007; Mueller, Melwani, & Goncalco, 2011; Rietzschel, Nijstad, & Stroebe, 2019). Although this bias makes sense, it is also important for novel ideas to get full consideration for potential development. When groups and individuals are asked to select the best ideas, they do not typically exceed the average novelty of all of the ideas generated and do not usually select the most creative or original idea (Putman & Paulus, 2009; Reiter-Palmon, Illies Young, Kobe, Buboltz, & Nimps, 2009; Rietzschel,

Nijstad, & Stroebe, 2006). Groups tend to pick an idea that occurred early in the idea generation session as their best idea (Johnson & D'Lauro, 2018). This idea tended to be above average in feasibility and not particularly novel. The novel ideas tended to come later in the session. Thus, groups may have a bias for the first "good ideas" they encounter in the exchange process.

Early work on team idea evaluation and selection has focused on comparing nominal groups with interactive groups and found that there were no differences between groups and individuals in terms of the creativity of the ideas selected (Faure, 2004; Girotra, Terwiesch, & Ulrich, 2010; Kramer, Kuo, & Dailey, 1997; Putman & Paulus, 2009; Rietzschel et al., 2006). Interestingly, the more ideas groups generate, the less likely they are to pick the more novel ideas (Mumford, Feldman, Hein, & Nagao, 2001). Putman and Paulus (2009) found that groups tended to select ideas that were relatively more frequent, and groups whose members had generated ideas individually before group discussion selected more novel ideas than those who both generated and selected as a group. Thus, there seems to be bias to selecting more feasible ideas and more common ideas in groups. Presumably, it is easier to gain group consensus on those ideas. However, when individuals have generated their own individual ideas, it is possible that when they share their choices for the best ideas, novelty has more impact. Alternatively, since ideas were generated individually, possibly there was less group cohesion and more willingness to advocate for novel ideas.

The group decision literature suggests that there may be considerable pressure for premature consensus in groups (Stasser & Abele, 2019) and avoidance of cognitive and social conflict (e.g., De Dreu & Van Vianen, 2001). Although it may be beneficial for work teams to avoid social conflicts (De Dreu & Van Vianen, 2001), research suggests that it is beneficial to constructively deal with task conflicts (Vollmer & Seyr, 2013). Research by Hunter and colleagues (Fairchild & Hunter, 2014; Hunter & Cushenbery, 2015) provides some support for this notion with their finding that disagreeable individuals were more likely to have their ideas, especially creative ideas, used by the group, indicating that indeed that when teams avoid task conflict, creativity may suffer.

Other research has focused on determining the processes that underlie idea evaluation and idea selection, with the goal of identifying ways in which these can be improved. Similar to the research at the individual level, research findings suggest that teams are not always effective in evaluating ideas accurately and that idea evaluation accuracy determines which ideas are then further selected for implementation. Not surprisingly, teams do not select ideas that team members believe are not effective. Rather, issues in idea selection and choice may stem from lack of accuracy in the idea evaluation process (Basadur, 1995; Faure, 2004; Reiter-Palmon, 2018a). However, only limited research has evaluated both processes in the same study allowing for this determination. Kennel and Reiter-Palmon (2012) found that teams consistently selected ideas that team members believed and evaluated as effective. Solution evaluation accuracy (relative to expert evaluations) was related to idea selection. When teams evaluated quality of ideas accurately, they tended to select solutions that were of high quality and were effective. When solutions were accurately evaluated for originality, the teams tended to select ideas that were creative. However, overall, teams selected either a creative idea or an effective idea 55% of the time, with 45% of the teams choosing ideas that were less than optimal as evaluated by experts. Reiter-Palmon, Kennel, de Vreede and de Vreede (2019) studied whether providing more guidance at the idea evaluation phase and idea selection phase would facilitate effective idea evaluation and idea selection. Their results suggest that when teams are provided a structure and guidance for idea evaluation and idea selection, more original ideas will be selected for implementation.

Social Processes and Idea Evaluation and Selection

Idea evaluation is the most convergent process of the three described earlier. As such, one would expect that team members will feel comfortable during this process and would carry it out effectively. As noted in the previous section, idea evaluation efforts often are not effective, as individuals and teams fail to identify or select creative (highly original and effective) ideas. As with the other two processes, idea evaluation and selection are also influenced by social processes. However, empirical literature on this is sparse. It is likely that the bias toward safe, less risky, and therefore less novel and original ideas is a result of evaluation apprehension and social comparison. That is, due to social norms that focus on appropriateness and effectiveness of solutions, and risk avoidance, team members may be reluctant to support more risky and novel ideas (Blair & Mumford, 2007). Organizations that are more innovative have been found to have cultures and climates that are supportive of risk and novelty, and allow for failure (Hunter, Bedell, & Mumford, 2007). These organizational norms, in turn, may come into play during the evaluation and selection phase of the problem-solving, allowing team members to voice support for more unusual and risky ideas, as they know these ideas may be more accepted.

As with the other two processes, conflict may arise during the idea evaluation phase. Conflict during idea evaluation and selection may be the outcome of previous processes. First, conflict can be a result of differences in understanding the problem and problem construction (Cronin & Weingart, 2007; Reiter-Palmon, Herman, & Yammarino, 2008). In addition, during the idea generation processes, team members may become committed to specific ideas and will not be willing to evaluate the merits of other ideas (Harvey & Kou, 2013). This entrenchment may be particularly pronounced in teams that are composed of two or more distinct subgroups (Harvey & Kou, 2013). The

MIP-G theory (De Dreu et al., 2011) indicates that individuals with a pro-social motivation may be particularly effective here. Pro-social motivation may allow those team members to reach across subgroups and to be willing to listen to others regarding the merit of additional ideas. Therefore, they may change their minds regarding the effectiveness or creativity of new ideas.

The idea evaluation process is inherently a process where ideas are being reviewed critically. Research on conflict suggests that moderate levels of task conflict can be beneficial for creativity (De Dreu, 2006); however, other work has suggested that criticism may be detrimental to psychological safety and creativity (Osborn, 1963; De Dreu & Weingart, 2003). Just as with conflict, the relationship between criticism and creativity is more nuanced. Criticism of ideas may be necessary to improve ideas and build on those ideas (Harvey & Kou, 2013). However, not all criticism will be beneficial. Gibson and Mumford (2013) found that when participants provided effective and deep criticism, they developed solutions that were more creative. But when participants provided a large number of criticisms, solutions were less creative (see also Puccio et al., 2018).

Information and Knowledge Sharing

One important issue regarding team creativity and cognition is that individual cognitions must be shared in some way in order to create a group outcome, such as a solution or product. In order to do that, information about how team members construct the problem, knowledge about different aspects of the problem and alternative solutions, and different frames of reference, must be shared by the team members. Therefore, it is not surprising that all of the previously mentioned processes, problem identification and construction, idea generation, and idea evaluation and selection, are dependent on information and knowledge sharing. Information and knowledge sharing have been found to be significant predictors of team creativity and innovation (Carmeli, Gelbard, & Reiter-Palmon, 2013; Damanpour, 1991; Howell & Shae, 2006; Hulsherger et al., 2009).

Research on the cognitive aspect of information sharing typically uses the hidden profile paradigm, which identifies the conditions under which team members will be more likely to share information. These studies suggest that shared information, information that is available to all team members prior to team discussion, is more likely to be discussed, while information that is not available to all or most team members is less likely to be discussed (Mesmer-Magnus & DeChurch, 2009). Teams that are specifically asked to discuss information prior to reaching a decision are more likely to discuss unshared information (Stewart & Stasser, 1995). In addition, having some degree of overlap between team members in terms of their knowledge, experience, and function facilitated information sharing within a team (Bunderson & Sutcliffe,

2002). This is potentially a result of the availability of shared mental models that allow for easier communication (Bunderson & Sutcliffe, 2002; Mumford et al., 2001; Salas, Cooke, & Rosen, 2008). In addition, teams that are specifically asked to share information are more likely to do so (Stewart & Stasser, 1995), and group members who were designated as experts tended to discuss more information, including previously unshared information, especially when the group was aware of their expert status (Franz & Larson, 2002; Stasser & Stewart, 1992).

However, the nature of the knowledge and information sharing is critical (Lovelace, Shapiro, & Weingart, 2001). The results of Lovelace et al.'s study indicated that collaborative communication – that is, communication that is positive and intended to find mutually beneficial solutions – was related to higher creativity and innovation. Contentious communication – that is communication that is less positive and focuses on win-lose situations – was related to lower creativity and innovation. Further, the effect of contentious communication was found to be particularly detrimental when frequency of information exchange is high. Supporting these results, Kratzer, Leenders, and van Engelen (2004) found that frequent information exchange resulted in reduced creativity and innovation as it led to cognitive overload and production blocking. Similarly, work on psychological safety suggests that when team members feel psychologically safe, they are more likely to share information, and in turn, this results in greater team creativity (Carmeli, Sheaffer, Binyamin, Reiter-Palmon, & Sihmoni, 2014; Hu, Erdogan, Jiang, Bauer, & Liu, 2018; Moser, Dawson, & West, 2018).

Leading Teams for Effective Creative Problem-Solving in Work Settings

We described three important phases of the collaborative creative process. Effective team innovation requires that each of these processes be done in as optimal a fashion as possible. This involves some degree of divergent and convergent thinking in all phases and effective team leadership (cf., Mumford, Higgs, Todd, & Martin, 2019). Leaders can facilitate the effective application of these cognitive processes (Reiter-Palmon & Royston, 2017). One critical decision to make at the beginning of the process is the size of teams. Although larger teams may have more intellectual resources, they also limit the information exchange processes and the opportunity for each team member to make a significant contribution (Moser et al., 2018; Vreede, Briggs, & Reiter-Palmon, 2010). Thus, it may be best to divide the participants into relatively small teams that still represent a diversity of areas of expertise and interest (Cummings, Kiesler, Zadeh, & Balakrishnan, 2013). Although some research suggests that pairs may be optimal (at least for idea generation, Mullen, Johnson, & Salas, 1991), in practice somewhat larger groups may work better for teams that are going through the entire process of problem construction, ideation, and evaluation because of increased diversity of perspectives (Cummings et al., 2013). After going through each phase, the teams can compare their output or decisions with that of the other teams. The leader also has to decide the interaction format. It is typically most convenient to use face-to-face discussion groups. However, in the ideation sessions, electronic or writing approaches may facilitate generation of more ideas. These different modes of collaborating have not been assessed in relation to the problem construction and the evaluation phases. Research on electronic methods of decision-making suggests that face-to-face settings may work better than electronic ones for the group decision-making aspects of the problem construction and evaluation phases (Kerr & Murthy, 2004).

Problem Construction

In the problem construction phase, team members need to discuss a wide variety of ways in which the problem can be framed and the different elements of the problem. However, at some point, they need to converge on a specific problem focus or a limited set of options. This will require both a determination of how much time should be spent on this type of preliminary process and how the team will come to a consensus. The amount of time spent would depend on many factors, such as the complexity of the problem and the importance of the issue for an organization. Although there is some popular writing about the efficacy of making quick intuitive decisions, in teams it will be important not to rush to consensus before a full discussion of all of the alternatives (Turner & Pratkanis, 2014). The team leader should encourage a full exchange of information and positive exchange of different opinions. In addition, team leaders should facilitate the engagement in this process, as it tends to occur automatically (Redmond, Mumford, & Teach, 1993; Reiter-Palmon & Illies, 2004; Reiter-Palmon & Royston, 2017). Then the team should phase into the more convergent task of selecting a specific approach or set of alternatives. This could involve combining different perspectives. Consensus in the group could be attained naturally if one alternative stands out above the rest and gains enthusiastic support from the team. In addition, during this process, team members can integrate divergent problem constructions, which likely will facilitate a better understanding of the problem from multiple perspectives, and more creative solutions (Leonardi, 2011; Weingart et al., 2008). The team can then move to the idea generation stage. Leaders can also facilitate such integration by encouraging team members to take different perspectives, which has been found to facilitate creativity (Hoever, van Knippenberg, van Ginkel, & Barkema, 2012).

Idea Generation

In the idea generation phase, the leader has to decide which modality to utilize for the idea exchange process. Most leaders will not have experience with the writing and electronic methods and thus default to the verbal exchange process. The electronic approach would require some expert assistance, but the writing approach can be done by simply following the guidance provided in the literature (Heslin, 2009; Paulus, Baruah, & Kenworthy, 2018). If done effectively and with a little practice, the writing approach can lead to the generation of many more ideas.

The brainstorming literature suggests that following certain rules enhances the number of ideas generated. Thus, instructions on those rules and enforcing them may increase the overall production of ideas. However, there is little precise evidence for the individual rules except for the benefit of the quantity rule. So it may not be necessary to follow a formal brainstorming protocol. By emphasizing quantity of ideas rather than quality initially, teams should be comfortable in sharing novel ideas and not focus much on premature evaluation. It is also important to emphasize that ideas should be presented precisely without much elaboration to facilitate the exchange of a wide variety of ideas in a relatively short time (Paulus, Nakui, Putman, & Brown, 2006).

We have found that ad hoc groups tend to start off with a fairly high rate of idea generation but then steadily decrease their rate over a short period of time. This, of course, depends on the breadth and complexity of the problem. However, it is important for teams to persist longer in the ideation process than they might prefer since the most novel ideas tend to come later in the process (Baruah & Paulus, 2016). So the leader should encourage teams to persist if there is a "lull" in the ideation process. This can also be accomplished by providing brief breaks, since teams often show continued high levels of performance after short breaks (Paulus et al., 2006).

Idea Evaluation and Selection

Although each of the phases of the problem-solving process can be quite intellectually challenging, the evaluation process may be the most difficult, especially if a large number of good ideas have been generated (Mumford et al., 2001). The leader needs to decide how to best accomplish the task of coming with those ideas that have the most promise for implementation in the organization. First, team members need to be instructed as to the criteria to be used in evaluating ideas, such as novelty, feasibility, utility, and breadth of impact (Mumford, Lonergan, & Scott, 2002). Each of these criteria should be clearly described. Although there may be individual and organizational biases for feasible ideas, the leader should emphasize that novel ideas should be given full consideration, especially if they have the potential for modification in the direction of greater feasibility, utility, and impact. One problem with verbal ideation sessions is that team members may not remember all of the ideas unless the ideas are also transcribed in some fashion. Often someone may be assigned to write the ideas as they are generated or individual team members may write their own. The former may be preferable since this will provide a summary not linked to a specific person and may thus help overcome a bias in favor on one's own ideas. If the writing process is used, the written papers provide a convenient summary.

One unresolved issue is whether the evaluation process should be interspersed at different times during the ideation process. The most common approach is probably to have a full ideation phase followed by the evaluation phase. Osborn (1963) suggested that idea generation and evaluation should be separated, since evaluation would inhibit idea generation. Several studies suggest that this may not be the case (Harvey & Kou, 2013; Rietzschel et al., 2006). Furthermore, shorter ideation sessions interspersed with evaluation sessions would allow for easier evaluation processes, since there will be fewer ideas to process in each session, avoiding the problem of cognitive overload (de Vreede, Briggs & Reiter-Palmon, 2010; Girotra et al., 2010). These sessions may also work as breaks for rejuvenating the motivation for ideation. Furthermore, evaluation sessions should also allow for the building or elaboration of ideas that come to the fore as the most promising. In a collaborative evaluation session, it is possible for the team to come up with a totally new idea or combination that is better than ideas already generated (Putman & Paulus, 2009).

As in the case of the problem construction process, if only a limited number of alternatives can be considered for possible further development, the team will need to have some means of coming to consensus. This could be done in various ways. It may be best if each team evaluates its own ideas (Faure, 2004). Thus, each team could be charged with coming up with a small number of "best ideas" by consensus. These could then be shared with the entire population involved in the process for voting. This could be done by the classic posted note process of putting pasting colored dots on posted notes or having group members rate ideas summarized on a sheet or projected slide.

Application to Design Thinking

One creativity approach that has gained popularity both in management and industry is design thinking. One major stimulus for this approach were the experiences at the product design firm, IDEO (cf. Brown & Wyatt, 2010). It is based on observations of what designers do and have found useful in the innovation process. Although there are many variations of this approach, Liedtka (2014) has suggested that the core processes involved are exploration, idea generation, and experimentation. Exploration typically involves evaluating criteria for design and obtaining input from user studies. Experimentation may include prototyping ideas and testing them on potential users. Others have used the terms of need finding, brainstorming, and prototyping to describe the different phases (cf., Seidel & Fixson, 2013). The design thinking approach has found a receptive audience in the design community, education, and management (Glen, Suciu, & Baughn, 2014; Henriksen, Richardson, & Mehta, 2017). However, the exact conceptualization of design thinking and its application is quite varied, it does not have a strong theoretical base, there is very little research on its effectiveness, and organizations appear to have difficulty with its implementation (Carlgren, Elmquist, & Rauth, 2016; Johansson-Sköldberg, Woodilla, & Çetinkaya, 2013).

Even though the design thinking area has significant limitations, there may be some benefit to linking it to the theory and literature discussed in this chapter. The three phases outlined by Liedtka (2014) are similar to some of the major phases of the innovative process that we emphasized. Furthermore, much design thinking occurs in teams. Thus, the principles and applications outlined in this chapter may also be relevant for the design thinking field. They may facilitate implementation of design thinking by giving it more structure and theoretical grounding.

The literature on design thinking also meshes nicely with some of the issues discussed in this chapter. Ho (2001) found that expert designers are more likely to decompose problems into subproblems than nonexperts, suggesting the potential importance of expertise in the problem construction process. A number of studies have addressed the different phases of the creativity process. For example, Seidel and Fixson (2013) evaluated the use of various innovation methods including design thinking in case studies using novice interdisciplinary teams of students over the course of a semester. Both design methods and brainstorming were found to be useful for the high-performing teams for both the initial generation of conceptual ideas and then the subsequent refinement/prototyping process and selection. However, they noted that there needs to be an appropriate balance of brainstorming and other aspects of design thinking. Too much time spent on brainstorming rather than on evaluation processes may be counterproductive. Thus, this study highlights the importance of determining the appropriate balance among the various creative problem-solving phases. Similarly, Stempfle and Badke-Schaub (2002) also evaluated the phases of the design processes in student project teams. They noted the importance of balancing the different phases in terms of timing. In particular, they suggested the potential benefit of early questions or evaluation activities so that ideas can be eliminated early in the process. Otherwise, the group might waste more time than needed on less promising ideas. This study highlights the importance of understanding the appropriate balancing of time across the different phases.

Although the design thinking literature is focused on the different phases of the innovative process, there is very little recognition of the relevant literature on problem construction, idea generation, and evaluation. Alternatively, the collaborative creativity literature has focused on the ideation and evaluation phases but has not focused much on the preliminary problem or need finding phase or the later prototyping or refinement and development stages. Thus, there is likely a significant benefit in integrating the insights of the two different literatures.

Future Directions

This chapter has provided a review of the current literature focusing on the interrelationship between cognitive and social processes that facilitate team creativity. We noted a number of gaps in the literature that need to be addressed in further research. There is a need for more research on collaborative or team problem construction and evaluation to determine the most optimal process. Both processes have some research conducted at the individual level (but more limited than that on idea generation); however, research focusing on team outcomes is noticeably lacking for problem construction and is fairly minimal for idea evaluation and selection. Additional research is necessary to understand how these processes operate at the team level, how they are similar or different than individual level processes, and the factors that influence these processes.

For idea generation, additional work is needed on how written exchanges of ideas in teams help in the generation of large number of ideas. Further, studies that examine its efficacy, the factors that influence it and its utility, and comparisons with other types of approaches are needed. It is also important to note that much of the research on idea generation in teams focuses on fluency, or the number of ideas. The factors that influence the quality or originality of ideas generated may be different and have not received sufficient attention.

Research on all three cognitive processes tends to focus on each process in isolation, rarely evaluating the interrelationships among them. The extent to which the different phases of the creative problem-solving process need to be distinct or can be effectively interspersed with one another needs further exploration. Both experimental studies that evaluate the role of these processes in combination and field studies that evaluate the naturally occurring transitions and changes are necessary. In addition, the focus of the chapter was on the interrelationship between cognitive and social processes, but only a limited number of studies explicitly evaluate both, and most of those focus on social processes and their effect on idea generation. Work by Reiter-Palmon and Murugavel (2018) suggests that engagement in a cognitive process such as problem construction can influence social processes such as conflict. Additional research evaluating the role of cognitive processes on social processes needs to be conducted.

The issue of time and timing has also received very little attention. Some research at the individual level suggests that timing of processes or interventions may be important and can significantly influence the creative outcome (cf., Baruah & Paulus, 2016). However, there has been little research of the time factors related to the different phases. What happens over time in these sessions? Do longer sessions lead to better outcomes, or should longer sessions be broken up into shorter ones? This is also a call for more observational methodologies that allow for evaluation of how the processes unfold over time (as opposed to surveys at specific points in time).

This chapter focused on three core processes that are common to many of the cognitive models of creativity (Mumford et al., 1991). It is important to note that additional processes have received even less attention at the team level and should be studied in the future. For example, conceptual combination has been found to be important to creativity (Kohn, Paulus, & Korde, 2011; Malycha & Maier, 2017; Mobley, Doares, & Mumford, 1992; Scott, Lonergan, & Mumford, 2005). However, to the best of our knowledge, there is no research evaluating this process at the team level. Harvey (2014) discussed the concept of creative synthesis, which is similar to the conceptual combination process in teams, where ideas generated by team members are synthesized and combined to create a breakthrough idea. What is still unclear is how teams reach this creative synthesis. Are these insights offered by individual members and then adopted by the team or is this truly accomplished as a team interaction? What are the factors that facilitate this conceptual combination and lead to more creative ideas as opposed to combining routine ideas?

Another process that has not been fully evaluated at the team level is that of information gathering or fact finding (Mumford et al., 1991). While information sharing, which was discussed earlier, provides a review of research on information gathering within the team, a focus on information gathering outside of the team is more limited. Previous research suggests that communication with entities external to the team will facilitate creativity (Ancona & Caldwell, 1992; Howell & Shea, 2006; Hülsherger et al., 2009). Work on the strength of weak ties (Baer, 2010; Perry-Smith & Shalley, 2003, 2014) provides some insight to this matter. They found that network ties with members outside the group are related to increased creativity and innovation among the team members. However, additional research should focus on additional ways that team members may gather information as well as the specific mechanisms by which weak ties may facilitate creativity. Information about the type and content of the information that is being used and whether that influences the effectiveness of the application of the processes is also needed.

Finally, later processes of creativity such as planning for implementation and monitoring have not been reviewed. Work on planning focused on the sequencing of actions to attain a goal and monitoring of the plan's success, and the mental simulation of the action sequences and consequences should be explored (Hayes-Roth & Hayes-Roth, 1979; Mumford, Schultz, & Osburn, 2002). Research on team innovation implementation focuses on issues of coordination, persuasion, organizational climate that supports innovation, and other social phenomenon and not the role of the team in implementation planning and monitoring (Klein & Knight, 2005; Scott & Bruce, 1994; Shalley et al., 2004). One reason that innovation implementation is viewed as so important at the team level is because of the need to coordinate different parties and address their concerns, which has unique implications on the interaction between cognition and social processes in teams. West (2002) suggests that external demands are an important issue that facilitates innovation and innovation planning. External demands can be viewed in this context as contributing to task complexity. In a series of studies, West and his colleagues found that innovation implementation and implementation planning were a direct response to external demands such as workload, consumer demands, and interpersonal and procedural difficulties (Bunce & West, 1995; West et al., 2004). This provides an example of the interdependence between the cognitive processes of planning and monitoring and interpersonal processes such as relationships and external consumer demands. However, it is still unclear how specific interpersonal factors may inhibit or facilitate implementation planning. While interpersonal difficulties may lead teams to need more planning, these may in fact inhibit the planning process by making discussions more difficult.

Team size is an important factor in group dynamics. The study of group size is quite challenging from a logistical point of view, but since some research suggests that there is wisdom in larger crowds (Le Mens, Kovacs, Avrahami, & Kareev, 2018), this issue deserves further examination. Research on team size has typically focused on brainstorming or idea generation. It is unclear what effect team size might have on other relevant cognitive and social processes.

This chapter also evaluated the role of leadership in facilitating the cognitive and social processes that provide support. The research reviewed suggests that leadership matters; however, there is only limited research, and mostly it focuses on the role of leaders in social processes (Reiter-Palmon & Royston, 2017). Research that evaluates the role of leadership on team cognitive processes and the interaction between cognition and social processes is needed.

Finally, in this chapter we tried to address the question of design thinking. Design thinking has become a popular tool in recent years; however, process based and theoretical research on design thinking is limited. It would be particularly fruitful to evaluate and research design thinking based on the cognitive and social principles and findings already available in the team creativity and innovation literature and systematically evaluate the unique insights of the design thinking field in team contexts.

References

Ancona, D., & Caldwell, D. (1992). Demography and design: Predictors of new product team performance. *Organization Science*, 3, 321–341.

Arreola, N., & Reiter-Palmon, R. (2016). The effect of problem construction creativity on solution creativity across multiple real-world problems. *Psychology of Aesthetics, Creativity, and the Arts*, 10, 287–295.

Baer, M. (2010). The strength-of-weak-ties perspective on creativity: A comprehensive examination and extension. *Journal of Applied Psychology*, 95, 592–601.

Barrett, J. D., Peterson, D. R., Hester, K. S., Robledo, I. C., Day, E. A., Hougen, D. P., & Mumford, M. D. (2013). Thinking about applications: Effects on mental models and creative problem-solving. *Creativity Research Journal*, 25, 199–212.

Baruah, J., & Paulus, P. B. (2016). The role of time and category relatedness in electronic brainstorming. *Small Group Research*, 47, 333–342

Basadur, M. (1995). Optimal ideation-evaluation ratios. *Creativity Research Journal*, 8, 63–75.

Basadur, M., Runco, M. A., & Vega, L. A. (2000). Understanding how creative thinking skills, attitudes and behaviors work together: A causal process model. *The Journal of Creative Behavior*, 34, 77–100.

Bell, S. T., Villado, A. J., Lukasik, M. A., Belau, L., & Briggs, A. (2011). Getting specific about demographic diversity variable and team performance relationships: A meta-analysis. *Journal of Management*, 37, 709–743.

Berg, J. M. (2016). Balancing on the creative highwire: Forecasting the success of novel ideas in organizations. *Administrative Science Quarterly*, 61, 433–468.

Blair, C. S., & Mumford, M. D. (2007). Errors in idea evaluation: Preference for the unoriginal? *The Journal of Creative Behavior*, 41, 197–222.

Brown, T., & Wyatt, J. (2010). Design thinking for social innovation. *Development Outreach*, 12, 29–43.

Bunce, D., & West, M. A. (1995). Self perceptions and perceptions of group climate as predictors of individual innovation at work. *Applied Psychology: An International Review*, 44, 199–215.

Bunderson, J. S., & Sutcliffe, K. M. (2002). Comparing alternative conceptualizations of functional diversity in management teams: Process and performance effects. *Academy of Management Journal*, 45, 875–893.

Camacho, L. M., & Paulus, P. B. (1995). The role of social anxiousness in group brainstorming. *Journal of Personality and Social Psychology*, 68, 1071–1080.

Cannon-Bowers, J., Salas, E., & Converse, S. (1993). Shared mental models in expert team decision making. In N. J. Castellan, Jr. (Ed.), *Individual and group decision making: Current issues* (pp. 221–246). Hillsdale, NJ: Lawrence Erlbaum Associates.

Carlgren, L., Elmquist, M., & Rauth, I. (2016). The challenges of using design thinking in industry – Experiences from five large firms. *Creativity and Innovation Management*, 25, 344–362.

Carmeli, A., Gelbard, R., & Reiter-Palmon, R. (2013). Leadership, creative problem solving capacity, and creative performance: The importance of knowledge sharing. *Human Resource Management*, 52, 95–122.

Carmeli, A., Reiter-Palmon, R., & Ziv, E. (2010). Inclusive leadership and employee involvement in creative tasks in the workplace: The mediating role of psychological safety. *Creativity Research Journal*, 22, 250–260.

Carmeli, A., Sheaffer, Z., Binyamin, G., Reiter-Palmon, R., & Sihmoni, T. (2014). Transformational leadership and creative problem solving: The mediating role of psychological safety and reflexivity. *Journal of Creative Behavior*, 48, 115–135.

Cooke, N. J. (2015). Team cognition as interaction. *Current Directions in Psychological Science*, 24, 415–419.

Cronin, M. A., & Weingart, L. R. (2007). Representational gaps, information processing, and conflict in functionally diverse teams. *Academy of Management Review*, 32, 761–773.

Cummings, J. N., & Kiesler, S. (2008, November). Who collaborates successfully? Prior experience reduces collaboration barriers in distributed interdisciplinary research. In *Proceedings of the 2008 ACM conference on computer supported cooperative work* (pp. 437–446).

Cummings, J. N., Kiesler, S., Zadeh, R. B., & Balakrishnan, A. D. (2013). Group heterogeneity increases the risks of large group size: A longitudinal study of productivity in research groups. *Psychological Science*, 24, 880–890.

Damanpour, F. (1991). Organizational innovation: A meta-analysis of effects of determinants and moderators. *Academy of Management Journal*, 34, 555–590.

De Dreu, C. K. (2006). When too little or too much hurts: Evidence for a curvilinear relationship between task conflict and innovation in teams. *Journal of Management*, 32, 83–107.

De Dreu, C. K., Nijstad, B. A., Bechtoldt, M. N., & Baas, M. (2011). Group creativity and innovation: A motivated information processing perspective. *Psychology of Aesthetics, Creativity, and the Arts*, 5, 81–89.

De Dreu, C. K. W., & Van Vianen, A. E. M. (2001). Managing relationship conflict and the effectiveness of organizational teams. *Journal of Organizational Behavior*, 22, 309–328.

De Dreu, C. K. W., & Weingart, L. R. (2003). Task versus relationship conflict, team performance, and team member satisfaction: A meta-analysis. *Journal of Applied Psychology*, 88, 741–749.

De Rosa, D. M., Smith, C. L., & Hantula, D. A. (2007). The medium matters: Mining the long-promised merit of group interaction in creative idea generation tasks in a meta-analysis of the electronic group brainstorming literature. *Computers in Human Behavior*, 23, 1549–1581.

de Vreede, G.-J., Briggs, R. O., & Reiter-Palmon, R. (2010). Exploring asynchronous brainstorming in large groups: A field comparison of serial and parallel subgroups. *Human Factors*, 52, 189–202.

de Wit, F. R. C., Greer, L. L., & Jehn, K. A. (2011). The paradox of intragroup conflict: A meta-analysis. *Journal of Applied Psychology*, 97, 360–390.

Dennis, A. R., Minas, R. K., & Williams, M. I. (2019). Creativity in computer-mediated virtual groups. In P. B. Paulus & B. A. Nijstad (Eds.), *The Oxford handbook of group creativity and innovation* (pp. 253–270). New York, NY: Oxford.

Deuja, A., Kohn, N. W., Paulus, P. B., & Korde, R. (2014). Taking a broad perspective before brainstorming. *Group Dynamics; Theory, Research, and Practice*, 18, 222–236.

Diehl, M., & Stroebe, W. (1987). Productivity loss in brainstorming groups: Toward the solution of a riddle. *Journal of Personality and Social Psychology*, 53, 497–509.

Edmondson, A. C., & Lei, Z. (2014). Psychological safety: The history, renaissance, and future of an interpersonal construct. *Annual Reviews Organizational Psychology Organizational Behavior*, 1, 23–43.

Fairchild, J., & Hunter, S. T. (2014). "We've got creative differences": The effects of task conflict and participative safety on team creative performance. *The Journal of Creative Behavior*, 48, 64–87.

Fairchild, J., & Hunter, S. T. (In press). "Everyone's a critic": The effects of expertise and design complexity on assessments of creative performance. *Psychology of Aesthetics, Creativity, and the Arts*.

Faure, C. (2004). Beyond brainstorming: Effects of different group procedures on selection of ideas and satisfaction with the process. *The Journal of Creative Behavior*, 38, 13–34.

Franz, T. M., & Larson, J. R. (2002). The impact of experts on information sharing during group discussion. *Small Group Research*, 33, 383–411.

Getzels J. W., & Csikszentmihalyi, M. (1975). From problem-solving to problem finding. In A. Taylor & J.W. Getzels (Eds.), *Perspectives in creativity* (pp. 90–116). Chicago, IL: Aldine.

Gibson, C., & Mumford, M. D. (2013). Evaluation, criticism, and creativity: Criticism content and effects of creative problem solving. *The Psychology of Aesthetics, Creativity, and the Arts*, 7, 314–331.

Girotra, K., Terwiesch, C., & Ulrich, K. T. (2010). Idea generation and the quality of the best idea. *Management Science*, 56, 591–605.

Gish, L., & Clausen, C. (2013). The framing of product ideas in the making: A case study of the development of an energy saving pump. *Technology Analysis and Strategic Management*, 25, 1085–1101.

Glen, R., Suciu, C., & Baughn, C. (2014). The need for design thinking in business schools. *Academy of Management Learning and Education*, 13, 653–667.

Harvey, S. (2014). Creative synthesis: Exploring the process of extraordinary group creativity. *Academy of Management Review*, 39, 324–343.

Harvey, S., & Kou, C. Y. (2013). Collective engagement in creative tasks: The role of evaluation in the creative process in groups. *Administrative Science Quarterly*, 58, 346–386.

Hayes-Roth, B., & Hayes-Roth, F. (1979). A cognitive model of planning. *Cognitive Science*, 3, 275–310.

Henriksen, D., Richardson, C., & Mehta, R. (2017). Design thinking: A creative approach to educational problems of practice. *Thinking Skills and Creativity*, 26, 140–153.

Heslin, P. A. (2009). Better than brainstorming? Potential boundary conditions to brainwriting for idea generation in organizations. *Journal of Occupational and Organizational Psychology*, 82, 129–145.

Ho, C. -H. (2001). Some phenomena of problem decomposition strategy for design thinking: Differences between novices and experts. *Design Studies*, 22, 27–45.

Hoever, I. J., van Knippenberg, D., van Ginkel, W. P., & Barkema, H. G. (2012). Fostering team creativity: Perspective taking as key to unlocking diversity's potential. *Journal of Applied Psychology*, 97(5), 982–996.

Holyoak, K. J. (1984). Mental models in problem solving. In J. R. Anderson & S. M. Kosslyn (Eds.), *Tutorials in Learning and memory: Essays in honor of Gordon Bower* (pp. 193–218). San Francisco, CA: W.H. Freeman.

Homan, A. C., van Knippenberg, D., van Kleef, G. A., & De Dreu, C. K. (2007). Bridging faultlines by valuing diversity: Diversity beliefs, information elaboration, and performance in diverse work groups. *Journal of Applied Psychology*, 92, 1189–1199.

Howell, J., & Shea, C. (2006). Effects of champion behavior, team potency, and external communication activities on predicting team performance. *Group and Organization Management*, 31, 180–211.

Hu, J., Erdogan, B., Jiang, K., Bauer, T. N., & Liu, S. (2018). Leader humility and team creativity: The role of team information sharing, psychological safety, and power distance. *Journal of Applied Psychology*, 103, 313–323.

Hülsheger, U. R., Anderson, N., & Salgado, J. F. (2009). Team-level predictors of innovation at work: A comprehensive meta-analysis spanning three decades of research. *Journal of Applied Psychology*, 94, 1128–1145.

Hunter, S. T., Bedell, K. E., & Mumford, M. D. (2007). Climate for creativity: A quantitative review. *Creativity Research Journal*, 19, 69–90.

Hunter, S. T., & Cushenbery, L. (2015). Is being a jerk necessary for originality? Examining the role of disagreeableness in the sharing and utilization of original ideas. *Journal of Business and Psychology*, 30, 621–639.

Johansson-Sköldberg, U., Woodilla, J., & Çetinkaya, M. (2013). Design thinking: Past, present and possible futures. *Creativity and Innovation Management*, 22, 121–146.

Johnson, B. R., & D'Lauro, C. J. (2018). After brainstorming, groups select an early generated idea as their best idea. *Small Group Research*, 49, 177–149.

Karau, S. J., & Williams, K. D. (1993). Social loafing: A meta-analytic review and theoretical integration. *Journal of Personality and Social Psychology*, 65, 681–706.

Kaufman, J. C., & Beghetto, R. A. (2013). In praise of Clark Kent: Creative metacognition and the importance of teaching kids when (not) to be creative. *Roeper Review*, 35, 155–165.

Kaufman, J. C., Beghetto, R. A., & Watson, C. (2016). Creative metacognition and self-ratings of creative performance: A 4-C perspective. *Learning and Individual Differences*, 51, 394–399.

Kennel, V., & Reiter-Palmon, R. (2012, August). *Teams and creativity: Accuracy in idea evaluation and selection.* Paper presented at the 120th American Psychological Association Conference in Orlando, FL.

Kerr, D. S., & Murthy, U. S. (2004). Divergent and convergent idea generation in teams: A comparison of computer-mediated and face-to-face communication. *Group Decision and Negotiation*, 13, 381–399.

Klein, C. G., & Knight, A. P. (2005). Innovation Implementation. *Current Directions in Psychological Science*, 14, 243–246.

Klijn, M., & Tomic, W. (2010). A review of creativity within organizations from a psychological perspective. *Journal of Management Development*, 29, 322–343.

Kohn, N. W., Paulus, P. B., & Korde, R. M. (2011). Conceptual combinations and subsequent creativity. *Creativity Research Journal*, 23, 203–210.

Kozlowski, S. J., & Bell, B. S. (2008). Team learning, development, and adaptation. In V. I. Sessa, M. London, V. I. Sessa, & M. London (Eds.), *Work group learning: Understanding, improving and assessing how groups learn in organizations* (pp. 15–44). New York, NY: Taylor and Francis Group/Lawrence Erlbaum Associates.

Kramer, M. W., Kuo, C. L., & Dailey, J. C. (1997). The impact of brainstorming techniques on subsequent group processes beyond generating ideas. *Small Group Research*, 28, 218–242.

Kratzer, J., Leenders, R. T. A. J., & van Englen, J. M. L. (2004). Stimulating the potential: Creative performance and communication innovation teams. *Creativity and Innovation Management*, 13, 63–71.

Le Mens, G., Kovacs, B., Avrahami, J., & Kareev, Y. (2018). How endogenous crowd formation undermines the wisdom of the crowd in online ratings. *Psychological Science*, 29, 1–16.

Leonardi, P. M. (2011). Innovation blindness: Culture, frames, and cross-boundary problem construction in the development of new technology concepts. *Organization Science*, 22, 347–369.

Liedtka, J. (2014). Perspective: Linking design thinking with innovation outcomes through cognitive bias reduction. *Journal of Product Innovation Management*, 32, 925–936.

Lovelace, K., Shapiro, D. L., & Wiengart, L. R. (2001). Maximizing cross-functional new product teams' innovativeness and constraint adherence: A conflict communications perspective. *Academy of Management Journal*, 44, 779–793.

Ma, H. H. (2009). The effect size of variables associated with creativity: A meta-analysis. *Creativity Research Journal*, 21, 30–42.

Malycha, C. P., & Maier, G. W. (2017). The random-map technique: Enhancing mind-mapping with a conceptual combination technique to foster creative potential. *Creativity Research Journal*, 29, 114–124.

Mello, A. L., & Rentsch, J. R. (2015). Cognitive diversity in teams: A multidisciplinary review. *Small Group Research*, 46, 623–658.

Mesmer-Magnus, J., & DeChurch, L. (2009). Information sharing and team performance: A meta-analysis. *Journal of Applied Psychology*, 94, 535–546.

Miron-Spektor, E., Gino, F., & Argote, L. (2011). Paradoxical frames and creative sparks: Enhancing individual creative through conflict and integration. *Organizational Behavior and Human Decision Processes*, 116, 229–240.

Mobley, M. I., Doares, L. M., & Mumford, M. D. (1992). Process analytic models of creative capacities: Evidence for the combination and reorganization process. *Creativity Research Journal*, 5, 125–155.

Moser, K. S., Dawson, J. F., & West, M. (2018). Antecedents of team innovation in health care teams. *Creativity and Innovation Management*, 28, 72–81.

Mullen, B., Johnson, C., & Salas, E. (1991). Productivity loss in brainstorming groups: A meta-analytic integration. *Basic and Applied Social Psychology*, 12, 3–23.

Muller, J. S., Melwani, S., & Goncalo, J. A. (2011). The bias against creativity: Why people desire but reject creative ideas. *Psychological Science*, 23, 13–17.

Mumford, M. D., Feldman, J. M., Hein, M. B., & Nagao, D. J. (2001). Tradeoffs between ideas and structure: Individuals versus group performance in creative problem solving. *Journal of Creative Behavior*, 35, 1–23.

Mumford, M. D., Hester, K. S., Robledo, I. C., Peterson, D. R., Day, E. A., Hougen, D. F., & Barrett, J. D. (2012). Mental models and creative problem-solving: The relationship of objective and subjective model attributes. *Creativity Research Journal*, 24, 311–330.

Mumford, M. D., Higgs, C., Todd, E. M., & Martin, R. (2019). Leading creative groups: What must leaders think about? In P. B. Paulus & B. A. Nijstad (Eds.), *Handbook of group creativity and innovation* (pp. 353–370). New York, NY: Oxford University Press.

Mumford, M. D., Lonergan, D. C., & Scott, G. (2002). Evaluating creative ideas: Processes, standards, and context. *Inquiry: Critical Thinking Across the Disciplines*, 22, 21–30.

Mumford, M. D., Mobley, M., Uhlman, C., Reiter-Palmon, R., & Doares, L. (1991). Process analytic models of creative capacities. *Creativity Research Journal*, 4, 91–122.

Mumford, M. D., Reiter-Palmon, R., & Redmond, M. R. (1994). Problem construction and cognition: Applying problem representations in ill-defined domains. In M.A. Runco (Ed.), *Problem finding, problem solving, and creativity*. New York, NY: Ablex Publishing.

Mumford, M. D., Schultz, R. A., & Osburn, H. K. (2002). Planning in organizations: Performance as a multi-level phenomenon. In F.J. Yammarino & F. Dansereau (Eds.), *The many faces of multi-level issues* (pp. 3–65). New York, NY: Elsevier Science.

Nakui, T., Paulus, P. B., & van der Zee, K. I. (2011). The role of attitudes in reactions toward diversity in workgroups. *Journal of Applied Social Psychology*, 41, 2327–2351.

Nemeth, C. J., & O'Conner, A. (2019). Better than individuals? Dissent and creativity. In P. B. Paulus & B. A. Nijstad (Eds.), *Handbook of group creativity and innovation* (pp. 73–85). New York, NY: Oxford University Press.

Nicholson, N., & West, M. (1988). *Managerial job change: Men and women in transition*. New York, NY: Cambridge University Press.

Nijstad, B. A., Bechtoldt, M., & Choi, H. -S. (2019). Information processing, motivation, and group creativity. In P. B. Paulus & B. A. Nijstad (Eds.) *The Oxford handbook of group creativity and innovation* (pp. 87–102). New York, NY: Oxford University Press.

Nijstad, B. A., & Stroebe, W. (2006). How the group affects the mind: A cognitive model of idea generation in groups. *Personality and Social Psychology Review*, 10, 186–213.

Oldham, G. R., & Baer, M. (2012). Creativity and the work context. In M. Mumford (Ed.), *Handbook of organizational creativity* (pp. 387–420). New York, NY: Elsevier.

Osborn, A. F. (1963). *Applied imagination* (2nd ed.). New York, NY: Scribner.

Paletz, S. B., & Peng, K. (2009). Problem finding and contradiction: Examining the relationship between naive dialectical thinking, ethnicity, and creativity. *Creativity Research Journal*, 21, 139–151.

Paulus, P. B., Baruah, J., & Kenworthy, J. (2018). Enhancing collaborative ideation in organizations. *Frontiers in Organizational Psychology*, 9, 1–12.

Paulus, P. B., & Brown, V. (2003). Enhancing ideational creativity in groups: Lessons from research on brainstorming. In P. B. Paulus & B. A. Nijstad (Eds.), *Group creativity: Innovation through collaboration* (pp. 110–136). New York, NY: Oxford University Press.

Paulus, P. B., & Brown, V. R. (2007). Toward more creative and innovative group idea generation: A cognitive-social-motivational perspective of group brainstorming. *Social and Personality Psychology Compass*, 1, 248–265.

Paulus, P. B., Dugosh, K. L., Dzindolet, M. T., Coskun, H., & Putman, V. L. (2002). Social and cognitive influences in group brainstorming. Predicting production gains and losses. *European Review of Social Psychology*, 12, 299–325.

Paulus, P. B., & Dzindolet, M. (1993). Social influence processes in group brainstorming. *Journal of Personality and Social Psychology*, 64, 5, 575–586.

Paulus, P. B., & Dzindolet, M. T. (2008). Social influence, creativity and innovation. *Social Influence*, 3, 228–247.

Paulus, P. B., & Kenworthy, J. (2019). Effective brainstorming. In P. B. Paulus & B. A. Nijstad (Eds.), *The Oxford handbook of group creativity and innovation* (pp. 287–306). New York, NY: Oxford University Press.

Paulus, P. B., & Korde, R. M. (2017). Alternating individual and group idea generation: Finding the elusive synergy. *Journal of Experimental Social Psychology*, 70, 177–190.

Paulus, P. B., Korde, R. M., Dickson, J. J., Carmeli, A., Cohen-Meitar, R. (2015). Asynchronous brainstorming in an industrial setting: Exploratory studies. *Human Factors*, 57, 1076–1094.

Paulus, P. B., Nakui, T., Putman, V. L., & Brown, V. R. (2006). Effects of task instructions and brief breaks on brainstorming. *Group Dynamics: Theory, Research, and Practice*, 10, 206–219.

Paulus, P. B., & Nijstad, B. A. (2003). *Group creativity: Innovation through collaboration*. New York, NY: Oxford University Press.

Paulus, P. B., & Nijstad, B. A. (Eds.). (2019). *Handbook of group creativity and innovation*. New York, NY: Oxford University Press.

Paulus, P. B., & van der Zee, K. I. (2015). Creative processes in culturally diverse teams. In S. Otten, K. I. van der Zee, & M. Brewer (Eds.), *Towards inclusive organizations: Determinants of successful diversity management at work* (pp. 108–131). New York, NY: Psychology Press.

Paulus, P. B., van der Zee, K. I., & Kenworthy, J. (2019). Diversity and group creativity. In P. B. Paulus & B. A. Nijstad (Eds.), *The Oxford handbook of group creativity and innovation* (pp. 33–50). New York, NY: Oxford University Press.

Paulus, P. B., & Yang, H. C. (2000). Idea generation in groups: A basis for creativity in organizations. *Organizational Behavior and Human Decision Processes*, 82, 76–87.

Perry-Smith, J., & Shalley, C. (2003). The social side of creativity: A static and dynamic social network perspective. *Academy of Management Review*, 28, 89–106.

Perry-Smith, J., & Shalley, C. (2014). A social comparison view of team creativity: The role of member nationality-heterogeneous ties outside of the team. *Organization Science*, 25, 1287–1571.

Puccio, G. J., Burnett, C., Acar, S., & Yudess, J. A., Hollinger, M., & Cabra, J. F. (2018). Creative problem solving in small groups: The effects of creativity training on idea generation, solution creativity, and leadership effectiveness. *Journal of Creative Behavior* 0, 1–19. doi: 10.1002/jocb.381

Putman, V. L., & Paulus, P. B. (2009). Brainstorming, brainstorming rules and decision making. *The Journal of Creative Behavior*, 43, 29–40.

Redmond, M. R., Mumford, M. D., & Teach, R. (1993). Putting creativity to work: Effects of leader behavior on subordinate creativity. *Organizational Behavior and Human Decision Processes*, 55, 120–151.

Reiter-Palmon, R. (2018a). Creative cognition at the individual and team level: What happens before and after idea generation. In R. Sternberg & J. Kaufman (Eds.), *The Nature of Human Creativity* (pp.184–208). New York, NY: Cambridge Press.

Reiter-Palmon, R. (Ed.). (2018b). *Team Creativity and Innovation*. New York, NY: Oxford University Press.

Reiter-Palmon, R., & Illies, J. J. (2004). Leadership and creativity: Understanding leadership from a creative problem-solving perspective. *Leadership Quarterly*, 15, 55–77.

Reiter-Palmon, R., & Murugavel, V. (2018). The effect of problem construction on team process and creativity. *Frontiers Psychology*, 9, 2098.

Reiter-Palmon, R., & Robinson, E. J. (2009). Problem identification and construction: What do we know, what is the future? *The Psychology of Aesthetics, Creativity, and the Arts*, 3, 43–47.

Reiter-Palmon, R., & Royston, R. (2017). Leading for creativity: How leaders manage creative teams. In M. D. Mumford & S. Hemlin (Eds.), *Handbook of research on leadership and creativity* (pp. 159–184). Northampton, MA: Edward Elgar.

Reiter-Palmon, R., Herman, A. E., & Yammarino, F. (2008). Creativity and cognitive processes: A multi-level linkage between individual and team cognition. In M. D. Mumford, S. T. Hunter, & K. E. Bedell-Avers (Eds.), *Multi-level issues in creativity and innovation* (Vol. 7, pp. 203–267). Bingley, UK: JAI Press.

Reiter-Palmon, R., Illies Young, M., Kobe, L., Buboltz, C., & Nimps, T. (2009). Creativity and domain specificity: The effect of task type of multiple indices on creative problem solving. *The Psychology of Aesthetics, Creativity, and the Arts,* 3, 73–80.

Reiter-Palmon, R., Kennel, V., de Vreede, T., & de Vreede, G. J. (2019). Structuring team idea evaluation and selection of solution: Does it influence creativity? In I. Lebuda & V. Glavenou (Eds.), *Palgrave handbook of social creativity research.* Basingstoke, UK: Palgrave Press.

Reiter-Palmon, R., Mumford, M. D., O'Connor Boes, J., & Runco, M. A. (1997). Problem construction and creativity: The role of ability, cue consistency, and active processing. *Creativity Research Journal,* 10, 9–23.

Reiter-Palmon, R., Wigert, B., & de Vreede, T. (2011). Team creativity and innovation: The effect of team composition, social processes and cognition. In M. D. Mumford (Ed.), *Handbook of organizational creativity* (pp. 295–326). New York, NY: Academic Press.

Rietzschel, E. F., Nijstad, B. A., & Stroebe, W. (2006). Productivity is not enough: A comparison of interactive and nominal brainstorming on idea generation and selection. *Journal of Experimental Social Psychology,* 42, 244–251.

Rietzschel, E. F., Nijstad, B. A., & Stroebe, W. (2014). Effects of problem scope and creativity instructions on idea generation and selection. *Creativity Research Journal,* 26(2), 185–191.

Rietzschel, E. F., Nijstad, B. A., & Stroebe, W. (2019). Why great ideas are often overlooked: A review and theoretical analysis of research on idea evaluation and selection. In P. B. Paulus & B. A. Nijstad (Eds.), *Handbook of group creativity and innovation* (pp. 179–198). New York, NY: Oxford University Press.

Rietzschel E. F., & Ritter, S. (2018). Moving from creativity to innovation. In R. Reiter-Palmon, V. L. Kennel, & J. C. Kaufman (Eds.), *Individual creativity in the workplace* (pp. 3–34). New York, NY: Academic Press.

Rostan, S. M. (1994). Problem finding, problem solving, and cognitive controls: An empirical investigation of critically acclaimed productivity. *Creativity Research Journal,* 7, 97–110.

Runco, M. A., & Basadur, M. (1993). Assessing ideational and evaluative skills and creative styles and attitudes. *Creativity and Innovation Management,* 2(3), 166–173.

Runco, M. A., & Chand, I. (1995). Cognition and creativity. *Educational Psychology Review,* 7, 243–267.

Runco, M. A., & Smith, W. R. (1992). Interpersonal and intrapersonal evaluations of creative ideas. *Personality and Individual Differences,* 13, 295–302.

Runco, M. A., & Vega, L. (1990). Evaluating the creativity of children's ideas. *Journal of Social Behavior and Personality,* 5, 439–452.

Salas, E., Cooke, N., & Rosen, M. (2008). On teams, teamwork, and team performance: Discoveries and developments. *Human Factors,* 50, 540–547.

Salas, E., Sims, D. E., & Burke, C. S. (2005). Is there a "Big Five" in teamwork? *Small Group Research,* 36, 555–599.

Santos, C. M., Uitdewilligen, S., & Passos, A. M. (2015). Why is your team more creative than mine? The influence of shared mental models on intra-group conflict, team creativity and effectiveness. *Creativity and Innovation Management,* 24, 645–658.

Schraw, G., Dunkle, M. E., & Bendixen, L. D. (1995). Cognitive processes in well-defined and ill-defined problem-solving. *Applied Cognitive Psychology*, 9, 523–538.

Scott, G., Leritz, L. E., & Mumford, M. D. (2004). The effectiveness of creativity training: A quantitative review. *Creativity Research Journal*, 16, 361–388.

Scott, G. M., Lonergan, D. C., & Mumford, M. D. (2005). Conceptual combination: Alternative knowledge structures, alternative heuristics. *Creativity Research Journal*, 17, 79–98.

Scott, S. G., & Bruce, R. A. (1994). Determinants of innovative behavior: A path model of individual innovation in the workplace. *Academy of Management Journal*, 37, 580–607.

Seidel, V. P., & Fixson, S. K. (2013). Adopting "design thinking" in novice multidisciplinary teams: The application and limits of design methods and reflexive practices. *Journal of Product Innovation Management*, 30, 19–33.

Shalley, C., Zhou, J., & Oldham, G. (2004). The effects of personal and contextual characteristics on creativity: Where should we go from here? *Journal of Management*, 30, 933–958.

Sharma, A. (1999). Central dilemmas of managing innovation in large firms. *California Management Review*, 41, 146–164.

Smith-Jentsch, K. A., Mathieu, J. E., & Kraiger, K. (2005). Investigating linear and interactive effects of shared mental models on safety and efficiency in a field setting. *Journal of Applied Psychology*, 90, 523–535.

Stasser, G., & Abele, S. (2019). Group creativity and collective choice. In P. B. Paulus & B. A. Nijstad (Eds.), *The Oxford handbook of group creativity and innovation* (pp. 199–215). New York, NY: Oxford University Press.

Stasser, G., & Stewart, D. (1992). Discovery of hidden profiles by decision-making groups: Solving a problem versus making a judgment. *Journal of Personality and Social Psychology*, 63, 426–434.

Stempfle, J, & Badke-Schaub, P. (2002). Thinking in design teams – An analysis of team communication. *Design Studies*, 23, 473–496.

Sternberg, R. J. (1988). A three-facet model of creativity. In R.J. Sternberg (Ed.), *The nature of creativity: contemporary psychological perspectives* (pp. 125–147). New York, NY: Cambridge University Press.

Stewart, D., & Stasser, G. (1995). Expert role assignment and information sampling during collective recall and decision making. *Journal of Personality and Social Psychology*, 69, 619–628.

Stollberger, J., West, M. A., & Sacramento, C. A. (2019). Innovation in work teams. In P. B. Paulus & B. A. Nijstad (Eds.), *Handbook of group creativity and innovation*. (pp. 231–252) New York, NY: Oxford University Press.

Tebes, J. K., & Thai, N. D. (2018). Interdisciplinary team science and the public: Steps toward a participatory team science. *American Psychologist*, 73, 549–562.

Turner, M. E., & Pratkanis, A. R. (2014). Preventing groupthink risk through deliberative discussion: Further experimental evidence for a social identity maintenance model. *International Journal of Risk and Contingency Management*, 3, 12–24.

Uitdewilligen, S., Rico, R., & Waller, M. J. (2018). Fluid and stable: Dynamics of team action patterns and adaptive outcomes. *Journal of Organizational Behavior*, 39(9), 1–16.

Uzzi, B., & Spiro, J. (2005). Collaboration and creativity: The small world problem. *American Journal of Sociology*, 111, 447–504.

van Dijk, H., van Engen, M. L., & van Knippenberg, D. (2012). Defying conventional wisdom: A meta-analytical examination of the differences between demographic and job-related diversity relationships with performance. *Organizational Behavior and Human Decision Processes*, 119, 38–53.

Vollmer, A., & Seyr, S. (2013). Constructive controversy research in the business organizational context: A literature review. *International Journal of Conflict Management*, 24, 399–420.

Voss, J. F., Wolfe, C. R., Lawrence, J. A., & Engle, R. A. (1991). From representation to decision: An analysis of problem solving in international relations. In R.J. Sternberg & P.A. Frensch (Eds.), *Complex problem solving: Principles and mechanisms*, (pp. 119–158). Mahwah, NJ: Lawrence Erlbaum Associates.

Vreede, de G. J., Briggs, R., & Reiter-Palmon, R. (2010). Exploring asynchronous brainstorming in large groups: A field comparison of serial and parallel subgroups. *Human Factors*, 52, 189–202.

Ward, T. B. (2012). Problem solving. In M. D. Mumford (Ed.), *Handbook of organizational creativity* (pp. 169–187). New York, NY: Elsevier.

Ward, T. B., Smith, S. M., & Finke, R. A. (1999). Creative cognition. In R.J. Sternberg (Ed.), *Handbook of creativity* (pp. 189–212). New York, NY: Cambridge University Press.

Weingart, L. R., Cronin, M. A., Houser, C. J. S., Cagan, J., & Vogel, C. M. (2005). Functional diversity and conflict in cross-functional product development teams: Considering representational gaps and task characteristics. In L. L. Neider & C. A. Schriesheim (Eds.), *Understanding teams* (pp. 89–110). Greenwich, CT: IAP.

Weingart, L. R., Todorova, G., & Cronin, M. A. (2008, March). *Representational gaps, team integration and team creativity: The mediating roles of conflict and coordination.* Paper presented at the meeting of Carnegie Melon University Research Showcase, Pittsburgh, PA.

West, M., Hirst, G., Richter, A., & Shipton, H. (2004). Twelve steps to heaven: Successfully managing change through developing innovative teams. *European Journal of Work and Organizational Psychology*, 13, 269–299.

West, M., & Richter, A. (2008). Climates and cultures for innovation and creativity at work. In J. Zhou & C. E. Shalley (Eds.), *Handbook of organizational creativity* (pp. 211–237). Mahwah, NJ: Lawrence Erlbaum Associates.

West, M. A. (2002). Sparkling fountains or stagnant ponds: An integrative model of creativity and innovation implementation in work groups. *Applied Psychology: An International Review*, 51, 355–387.

Wood, J. V. (1989). Theory and research concerning social comparisons of personal attributes. *Psychological Bulletin*, 106, 231–248.

9
THE LEADERSHIP ROLE IN CREATIVE PROBLEM-SOLVING AND INNOVATION

Miriam Erez, Alon Lisak, and Raveh Harush

Introduction

The global competitive work context, with its dynamically changing environment, has accelerated the need for creative problem-solving and innovative solutions (Amabile 1996; Anderson, Potočnik, & Zhou, 2014). Improved life longevity and education levels, alongside the growth of human population and technological, environmental, and geopolitical changes, have created new needs and opened up new opportunities for creative problem-solving and innovation (Herman & Reiter-Palmon, 2011). The creative solutions and innovative outcomes are just the tip of the iceberg, which covers the long and complex process of innovation, and organizations today struggle with the challenge of successfully managing the process of creative problem-solving toward innovative outcomes (Miron-Spektor, Erez, & Naveh, 2011). Interestingly, the research literature on creative problem-solving (Osborn, 1953) and on the innovation management process (Tushman, 1977) have developed in parallel, but separate from, one another. Creative problem-solving takes an in-depth look into the ideation phase, starting from problem definition, continuing through search for information and idea generation, up to evaluation and selection of the idea (Reiter-Palmon & Illies, 2004). The innovation process complements creative problem-solving by also focusing on the implementation phases, including stages from ideation to idea mobilization to the implementatin phase and ending the process when the innovation product enters the market (Klein & Sorra, 1996). Creative problem-solving concentrates on identifying solutions to ill-defined problems (Medeiros, Steele, Watts, & Mumford, 2018), whereas the innovation process aims to bring to market the generated creative ideas (Klein & Knight, 2005). We suggest that the creative problem-solving process and the innovation process research complement each other. Furthermore, the constructs of creativity and innovation add to the complexity of the process because each embodies two competitive components. Creativity comprises the generation of novel ideas, though they must also converge on usefulness and relevance (Amabile, 1996). Similarly, innovation consists of creative ideas and their implementation toward one best outcome (Bledow, Frese, Anderson, Erez, & Farr, 2009; Miron-Spektor & Erez, 2017; O'Reilly & Tushman, 2008; Smith & Lewis, 2011). Hence, leaders today face the challenge of integrating the complex but complementary process of creative idea generation and implementation (Miron-Spektor & Erez, 2017; Rosing, Frese, & Bausch, 2011; Smith, Erez, Jarvenpaa, Lewis, & Tracey, 2017).

A plethora of studies in the last decades have explored the relationship between leadership behaviors and creative and innovative outcomes, looking at potential mediators and moderators of these relationships (e.g., Amundsen & Martinsen 2015; Eisenbeiss, Van-Knippenberg, & Boerner, 2008; Hirst, Van-Knippenberg, & Zhou, 2009; Nijstad, Berger-Selman, & De Dreu, 2014; Shin & Zhou, 2007). However, a meta-analysis by Rosing et al. (2011) revealed that there is inconsistency in the correlations between leadership behaviors (e.g., transformational leadership) and creative or innovative outcomes. We propose that the inconsistent findings may be further understood by studying the process leading to these outcomes and by identifying how leaders cope with managing the complex processes of creative problem-solving and innovation. These processes consist of multiple phases, which differ from each other in their divergent versus convergent focus, but also complement one another in regard to the final innovative outcome. It is reasonable to expect that certain leadership characteristics, which positively impact some of the phases in the process of creative problem-solving and innovation, may not fit with other phases. Recognizing the duality embedded in the creative idea generation and the implementation phases, research has recently proposed that leaders for innovation should be ambidextrous; namely, they should be able to open their followers up to explore new ways but should also be able to close their followers' behavior and exploit existing ways of doing things in the organization (Zacher & Rosing, 2015). Paradoxical leadership is a similar construct to convey the competitive nature of today's leaders who struggle with the duality embedded in the creative problem-solving and innovation processes (Zhang, Waldman, Han, & Li, 2015).

Given the limited empirical research on the effects of leadership on the processes of creativity and innovation, the objective of this chapter is threefold. First, we aim to develop a comprehensive model, which integrates the in-depth nature of the phases of the creative problem-solving model together with the complementary phases of the innovation process, including initiating and mobilizing the idea to the implementation phase of the new product development and production, followed by getting it to market. Second, we set out to identify the leadership behaviors that best fit in with each one of the phases in the integrative model of creative problem-solving and innovation processes. Third, we examine the behaviors of the ambidextrous leaders, as they should best adapt to the complementary nature of creative problem-solving and innovation.

Complementary Processes of Creative Problem-Solving and Innovation

Creative problem-solving involves producing high-quality and original solutions to new, ill-defined problems (Medeiros et al., 2018; Runco & Jaeger, 2012).

The process of creative problem-solving consists of four main stages: (a) problem identification and construction, (b) identification of relevant information, (c) generation of new ideas, and (d) evaluation and selection of these ideas (Reiter-Palmon & Illies, 2004). The first three stages compose the idea generation phase and require the use of divergent thinking (Guilford, 1950). The fourth phase, idea evaluation and selection, requires convergent thinking to select and offer the best solution for implementation (Guilford, 1950). Mumford, Medeiros, and Partlow (2012) proposed a higher resolution to understand the creative problem-solving process, with seven phases in the process: problem definition, information gathering, information organization, conceptual combination, idea generation, idea evaluation, and solution monitoring. Evidently, creative problem-solving models put great emphasis on the different phases in the idea generation process, rather than on the implementation phase (Reiter-Palmon & Illies, 2004). The creative problem-solving process thus corresponds to the ideation phase in the innovation process, defined as the implementation of creative ideas (Amabile, 1996) that bring value to customers.

Whereas most models of innovation consisted mostly of the two phases of ideation and implementation (Clark & Wheelwright, 1992), a model proposed by Erez (Erez, Arbel, & Hadassa-Blank, 2015) consists of a six-stage model, with an equal emphasis on both the ideation and the implementation phases. The ideation phase consists of three steps: (a) identification of the challenge, the need, or the opportunity; (b) idea generation; and (c) idea evaluation and selection. The implementation phase consists of the following three steps: (a) idea mobilization in the organization, which includes "selling" the idea, preferably with visual presentation, and getting others to accept it; (b) implementation, which conveys the execution, consisting of the new product design and production; and (c) market penetration, reaching out to the customers, whether they are individuals, communities, or private or public organizations. This model is nonlinear and iterative. Throughout the process of innovation management, there are feedback loops that often require returning to an earlier phase and making adaptations. This means that organizations should monitor the innovation process and reexamine its fit to the dynamic and changing business environment, as well as identify new technologies, new competitors, and changes in customers' needs and expectations.

The creative problem-solving model zooms into the ideation phase more closely than the innovation management process. But the innovation process expands the journey of the idea throughout the transition phase of mobilizing the idea to the implementation, implementing the new product design and its production, and bringing it to the market. We propose to get a more comprehensive view of the process of creative problem-solving and innovation by integrating the two models, as can be seen in Figure 9.1, which provides a visual representation of the integrated model of creative problem-solving and the innovation process.

How does this process get initiated, and how is it developed and sustained until it brings the innovative solution to the market? The next section examines the role of leaders as the initiators of the problem-solving and innovation process, and as the change agents that enable transformation of the idea into an innovative product that gets to the market and responds to customers' needs and expectations. We develop the chapter along the different stages of the integrated creative problem-solving and innovation process and articulate on the leadership role at each one of these stages.

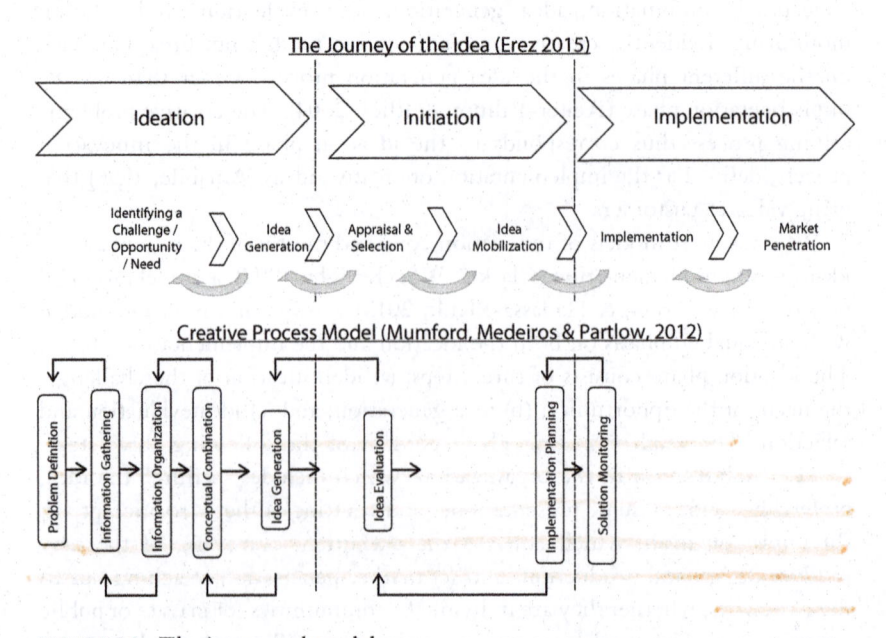

FIGURE 9.1 The integrated model.

Effective Leadership Behaviors in Different Stages of the Integrative Model of the Journey of the Idea

Leadership and the Idea Generation Phase

Stage One: Identifying the Challenge, Problem, Need, or Opportunity, and Structuring It

The objective of this stage is to identify the challenges facing leaders as they strive to maintain their organization's sustainable competitive advantage. To meet this objective, leaders should continuously search for new knowledge and information external to the organization, identifying new opportunities, technologies, competitors, trends, and changes in the market and in customers' needs and expectations. They should also continuously search for new knowledge and information internal to the organization, identifying changes in organizational resources that raise opportunities from within the organization for better adaptation to external changes. The creative problem-solving literature proposes that at this stage, leaders are engaged in identifying challenges and opportunities by scanning, forecasting, and generating a clear vision for organizational innovation.

Scanning the environment for innovation means identifying new trends, new technologies, and market changes to make sense of the environment and generate ideas for future organizational directions (Mumford, Bedell-Avers, & Hunter, 2008; Robledo, Peterson, & Mumford, 2012; Stenmark, Shipman, & Mumford, 2011). The focus is on general trends, as they are typically less volatile and more predictable than specific information. Scanning and analyzing the environment is the first step toward a clear definition of the new challenge (or problem) for which the organization will search a solution (Byrne, Mumford, Berrett, & Vessey, 2009; Koberg, Uhlenbruck, & Sarason, 1996; Mumford, Eubanks, & Murphy, 2007a; Verhaeghe & Kfir, 2002). When scanning, leaders actively seek out information regarding significant events in the environment, as well as emergent technologies that can be exploited. Therefore, the leader must actively monitor both the internal and external environments with a variety of sources, including customer feedback, supplier feedback, market research, technology monitoring, competitors, joint ventures, and international alliances (Byrne et al., 2009; Mumford et al., 2007a). During this process, the leader analyzes the accumulated information, looking for abnormalities in the environment and identifying new trends vis-à-vis the organization's strategy, resources, and capabilities (Stenmark et al., 2011). This activity involves high exploration and high uncertainty. Therefore, potential missions should be defined broadly, keeping the structure of the mission open to allow sufficient time and resources for continuous effective scanning (Stenmark et al., 2011).

Forecasting allows leaders to predict potential outcomes that arise from whatever they may identify as a new opportunity, new technology, or new trend in the market or in customer needs and expectations (Rouse & Morris, 1986). Forecasting is a complex form of prediction where neither predictors nor outcomes are fixed (Shipman, Byrne, & Mumford, 2010). To forecast effectively, the leader needs to consider a wide range of situations, identify a variety of problems and potential solutions, plan accordingly, and suggest alternatives (Mumford, Schultz, & Osburn, 2002; Osburn & Mumford, 2006). Mumford, Steele, McIntosh, and Mulhearn (2015) suggested a model that portrays the relationship between leaders' forecasting and their performance. According to this model, effective leaders need to forecast reactions, behaviors, processes, and problems within their organization and units, while considering other relevant organizations or institutions in their environment (see also Mumford, Peterson, & Robledo, 2013). Forecasting future trends enables leaders to prepare for future changes and developments, to select optimal solutions, and to reduce uncertainty and risks.

Effective forecasting relates to the leader's cumulative experiences and knowledge that enable them to better understand their leadership roles, their organization, and their environment. Activation of relevant mental models based on past experience and analyses of causal relationships are essential for the accurate forecasting of future directions (Mumford et al., 2015).

Visionary leadership There is a positive relationship between leaders' forecasting ability and the quality, originality, elegance, perceived utility, and emotional impact of their vision statements (Shipman et al., 2010). Vision is defined as ideal, future-oriented images that focus on values and norms (Berson, Shamir, Avolio, & Popper, 2001). It represents the leader's idealized image of the future of the organization (Conger, 1999). In that sense, a vision differs from forecasting because rather than just predict the future, it aims to shape the future, based on the leader's values and norms (Berson et al., 2001). Furthermore, forecasting involves specific and challenging goals that are time constrained, whereas a vision is formulated in relatively abstract, far-reaching, and timeless terms (Berson, Halevy, Shamir, & Erez, 2015). In that sense, vision becomes a powerful compass that navigates the innovative organization in its dynamic, competitive, and fast-changing environment (Caridi-Zahavi, Carmeli, & Arazy, 2016).

Although research has shown how leaders inspire innovation in their organizations (e.g., Elenkov & Manev, 2005; Jung, Chow, & Wu, 2003), only a limited number of studies have specifically explored how leaders' vision activates this process. One of these studies (Caridi-Zahavi et al., 2016) revealed that a chief executive officer's (CEO) vision for innovation in high-tech ventures is related to connectedness and to knowledge integration, and leads to higher levels of innovative products. Taken together, the vision of the leader sets the direction and defines the challenge (or problem) on which future stages of the innovation process will focus.

Stage Two: Creative Idea Generation

Following the scanning, the forecasting, and the developing of a vision for future directions, is the next stage of generating creative ideas for problem-solving and satisfying certain customers' needs and expectations (e.g., Clark & Wheelwright, 1992; Erez et al., 2015; Mumford, et al., 2008, 2015; Nijstad & Stroebe, 2006; Paulus & Yang, 2000). The contribution of idea generation to creative outcomes has been well recognized since the early days of creativity research, when scholars explored the nature of divergent thinking as the cognitive process responsible for creative idea generation (Guilford, 1950, 1967; Torrance, 1980). In parallel, researchers developed methods and tools for activating creative idea generation, such as the techniques of brainstorming (Osborn, 1953; Taylor, Berry, & Block, 1958), brainwriting, Triz (Altshuller, 1990), and more. Generally, more than 170 idea-generation techniques have appeared in the research literature at the individual and team levels (Smith, 1998). Leaders serve as facilitators of the idea generation process because of their ability to use diverse techniques and behaviors to impact their followers in three major ways: (a) leadership behaviors that stimulate creative idea generation, (b) leaders' task engagement approach to creative idea generation, and (c) leaders as designers of the climate for creative idea generation.

Leadership Behaviors that Stimulate Idea Generation

Transformational leadership behaviors have been found to motivate followers to generate creative ideas. Transformational leaders intellectually stimulate their followers to think creatively by questioning assumptions, reframing problems, and taking a novel approach to thinking about problems. Leaders' individualized consideration, exhibited by the consideration and recognition of each group member's viewpoint and ideas, motivates followers to express their unique ideas. Inspirational motivation inspires followers to gain intrinsic interest and enjoyment from getting involved in the process of creative idea generation (Sosik, Kahai, & Avolio, 1998). Furthermore, employees become engaged in creative idea generation when their leaders empower them to be autonomous and take responsibility and ownership for generating new ideas (Kirkman & Rosen, 1997, 1999; Zhang & Bartol, 2010).

More recent research has demonstrated that employees exhibit exploration behaviors that lead to innovation under leaders with "opening," rather than "closing," behaviors (Rosing et al., 2011; Zacher, Robinson, & Rosing, 2016). Opening leadership behaviors are defined as "a set of leader behaviors that includes encouraging doing things differently, and experimenting, giving room for independent thinking and acting, and supporting attempts to challenge established approaches" (Rosing et al., 2011, p. 967). Therefore, leadership behaviors that allow for different ways of accomplishing a task and for tolerance of errors enhance creative idea generation (Carmeli & Paulus, 2015; Kark & Carmeli, 2009).

Leaders' Task Engagement Approach to Creative Idea Generation

Leaders can facilitate followers' idea generation through specific instructions. These instructions can be in one of two forms: focusing on a specific technique to facilitate idea generation (Reiter-Palmon & Illies, 2004) or supporting adequate knowledge structures that will allow followers to produce higher-quality ideas (Hunter, Bedell-Avers, Hunsicker, Mumford, & Ligon, 2008; Mumford, Marks, Connelly, Zaccaro, & Reiter-Palmon, 2000). Leaders who themselves possess idea generation skills were more effective in facilitating creative idea generation among their followers (Gist, 1989; Puccio et al., 2018; Shalley & Gilson, 2004). Research has also shown that leaders influenced creativity and innovation by specifically instructing their followers to get engaged in the creative process, including engagement in problem identification, information search, and idea generation phases (Zhang & Bartol, 2010).

Leaders as Designers of the Climate for Creative Idea Generation

Leaders influence idea generation, not just by direct stimulation and inspiration, but also by shaping the work climate that facilitates creativity or innovation (e.g., Amabile, Schatzel, Moneta, & Kramer, 2004; Eisenbeiss et al., 2008; Isaksen & Akkermans, 2011). These leaders enhanced creative idea generation by setting the structure and developing the organizational culture that enable employees to express their creative thinking by encouraging their followers to explore and consider a variety of factual information that bears on the problem, and then to integrate them toward a proposed solution (Hunter, Bedell, & Mumford, 2007; Mumford, Scott, Gaddis, & Strange, 2002). This climate of intellectual stimulation also means a climate that facilitates employee autonomy, rather than controlling and limiting followers' freedom to express their unique ideas and giving them sufficient time for the idea generation process and recognizing and rewarding creative ideas (Byrne et al., 2009; Hunter, Bedell & Mumford, 2005, 2007; Mumford et al., 2008).

To sum, leaders have a significant role in inspiring and motivating their followers to be creative, in directing them toward engaging in the creative process, and in laying out the organizational climate that facilitates their followers' involvement in creative idea generation. Leaders can themselves be highly creative, serving as role models (Reiter-Palmon & Illies, 2004) and integrating their own creative ideas with those of their followers to reach the highest levels of creative idea generation. But even noncreative leaders can motivate and direct their followers to express their creative ideas (Mainemelis, Kark, & Epitropaki, 2015).

Stage Three: Evaluating and Selecting the Idea for Implementation

Idea generation provides leaders with multiple potential ideas for innovation. Leaders are responsible for the evaluation and selection of ideas for implementation, based on their added value to the market and to the organization and given the dynamic capabilities of the organization to harness the resources needed for the implementation (Blair & Mumford, 2007; Runco, 2003). Leaders' ability to evaluate and select ideas is a critical cognitive skill that contributes to leaders' innovative performance outcomes (Mumford, Todd, Higgs, & McIntosh, 2017; Watts, Mulhearn, & Todd, 2016). Evaluating and selecting creative ideas for implementation involve ambiguity and risk-taking. Hence, even at this convergent stage toward one solution, leaders need to keep the evaluation open and consider multiple criteria before making the final "yes/no" decision (Mumford, Lonergan, & Scott, 2002). Market consideration serves as a major evaluation criterion for the decision whether to continue processing the idea toward implementation or stop it. Furthermore, market competition and the availability of reliable suppliers serve as additional criteria for evaluation and selection (Lokiec & Erez, 2010; Mumford, Hunter, Eubanks, Bedell, & Murphy, 2007). This requires a broad range and a deep level of information search, including market research and familiarity with customers' needs and behaviors as well as with potential partners and suppliers, whose presence will attenuate the risk (Gruber & Tal, 2018; Mumford et al., 2007). Second, leaders also consider the fit of the creative idea to the organizational strategy, mission, and future directions, as well as its potential synergistic fit and contribution to other existing projects in the organization (Stenmark et al., 2011). Third, resource availability, including technology, human resources, and financial resources, plays a crucial role in deciding whether to select an idea for implementation (Mumford et al., 2002). Fourth, other factors that increase the uncertainty and risk involved in the selection decision relate to potential pitfalls and difficulties that may arise during the execution process (Mumford, Mobley, Reiter-Palmon, Uhlman, & Doares, 1991; Mumford et al., 2007). Taken together, the diverse knowledge base needed for making a decision reflects the ill-defined nature of the evaluation and selection stage, which has a crucial short- and long-term impact on the decision as to whether to implement a particular course of action in the organization (Byrne et al., 2009).

The complexity of the evaluation and selection process raises the need to identify the leadership characteristics that enable tolerating the risk involved in this ambiguous situation, making sense of multiple sources of information and evaluating them in light of relevant criteria for making the one correct choice. Research has shown that at this convergence stage, leaders who elaborate on the idea from competing considerations were more successful than others in selecting the right idea for implementation. An experiment conducted by Mumford et al. (2002) showed that leaders who used a compensatory strategy of appraising highly original ideas for their quality or high-quality ideas for their originality achieved a higher success rate in their idea evaluation and selection than others.

Expert (rather than nonexpert) leaders and high-level officers, compared with mid-level officers, had higher levels of cognitive skills and demonstrated a better understanding of the ideas to be selected for implementation (Lord & Brown, 2004; Lord & Hall, 2005; Mumford et al., 2000). During the idea evaluation process, leaders actively seek to improve the workability of ideas, building upon their personal experiences and actively generating new ideas during the evaluation process (Basadur, Runco, & Vega, 2000; Licuanan, Dailey, & Mumford, 2007; Lonergan, Scott, & Mumford, 2004; Mumford, Connelly, & Gaddis, 2003).

Last, Reiter-Palmon and Illies (2004) proposed that building the organizational culture that facilitates open exchange of opinions, feedback, and trust between leaders and their followers will provide the leader with different points of view regarding the criteria for evaluation, and with additional input concerning potential consequences of implementing certain ideas. The exchange of opinions and feedback provides an additional important input to the evaluation and selection process, improving its effectiveness.

Taken all together, the evaluation and selection of the creative ideas for implementation is an active, creative process that despite receiving less attention than the problem identification and idea generation stages, serves as a milestone for the effective completion of the ideation phase (Erez et al., 2015; Mumford et al., 2012). The success of the evaluation and selection stage is crucial for mobilizing the idea toward its successful implementation, from the execution and implementation stage up through the successful market penetration stage. Once again, we notice that the convergence and divergence cognitive processes are intertwined, complementing each other along the ideation process and the idea selection and implementation.

Stage Four: Idea Mobilization: Leading the Transition Phase from Ideation to Implementation

Leaders may act as innovation champions and manage the process of transition from the ideation to the implementation stage themselves, or they may take the role of "champions breeders," providing individual and organizational support to innovation champions (Howell, 2005; Škerlavaj, Černe, & Dysvik, 2014). Drawing from issue selling, change, and innovation management literatures (e.g., Dutton, Ashford, O'Neill, & Lawrence, 2001; Hughes, Lee, Tian, Newman, & Legood, 2018; Todnem By, 2005), we first describe the set of effective implementation behaviors necessary for leaders in their role of innovation champions, and then describe effective behaviors in their role of supporting others who manage the transition to the implementation stage.

Implementing creative ideas also means leading an organization through change (Todnem By, 2005). Therefore, it is crucial to build support and harness acceptance from key stakeholders for the innovation and its implementation (Howell & Boies, 2004). To manage the idea mobilization successfully and secure resources, innovation leaders engage in promotional activities to persuade others that the innovation is worth pursuing (Howell, Shea, & Higgins, 2005). Such issue-selling efforts can be conceptually divided into two categories: packaging that relates to issue content and the process of promoting the issue in the organization (Dutton et al., 2001). Effective leaders' packaging behaviors include demonstrating enthusiastic support for the idea, presenting it using business plan logic, framing the change positively, and linking it to valued goals like profitability, market share, or organizational image (Dutton et al., 2001; Howell, 2005; Howell & Boies, 2004). These kinds of behaviors resonate with the stage of creating a common vision, direction, and strategy described in emergent change management models (Kanter, Stein, & Jick, 1992; Kotter, 2007; Luecke, 2003). In terms of process, effective behaviors of innovation leadership include getting the right people involved (Howell, Shea, & Higgins, 2005), aiming to create a coalition, and lining up political support by communicating the vision for the proposed change (Kanter, Stein, & Jick, 1992; Kotter, 2007). Such efforts are effective when they communicate the idea through both informal and formal channels (Howell, 2005; Howell & Boies, 2004) and involve individuals at different levels in the organizational hierarchy (Dutton et al., 2001). Additionally, the prospect of leading such idea mobilization efforts depends on leaders' contextual knowledge. Leaders who are knowledgeable about the relational aspect of stakeholders (e.g., who will be affected, who care, who can promote or hinder, etc.), the normative aspects of the organization (e.g., protocols, processes, decision forums, etc.), and organizational strategic goals, are more likely to be effective in their idea mobilization efforts (Dutton et al., 2001; Howell, 2005; Howell & Boies, 2004). In particular, successful leaders consider the need to get the acceptance of others at the stage of idea evaluation and selection, shaping the selected idea to fit in with significant others in the organization and getting them to support the transition to the implementation stage (Lauche & Erez, 2015).

Leaders are often not the champions of innovation but take the role of "champions breeders," providing individual and organizational support to the innovation champions (Howell, 2005; Škerlavaj et al., 2014). Supervisor support and a pro-innovation attitude can provide employees with access to the resources necessary for them to mobilize the idea from the ideation phase to implementation (Damanpour & Schneider, 2008; Škerlavaj et al., 2014). Such support may take the form of generating short-term wins (Kotter, 2007) or recognizing innovation achievements (Howell, 2005). More broadly, in terms of leadership style, support may take the form of empowering, authentic, or servant leadership, all of which are found to highly correlate with innovation (Hughes et al., 2018). As change management facilitators, leaders' behaviors can positively shape the reaction to change by followers. Such behaviors can be broadly divided to three key functions: (a) effective communication (e.g., providing a shared vision), (b) providing support and attention to followers' concerns, and (c) involving followers in the change process (Oreg & Berson, 2019). Furthermore, Kotter (1995, 2007) proposed that employees are more likely to accept the change when there is a sense of urgency, which emphasizes the need for immediate change to avoid negative consequences of keeping the status quo. Finally, to sustain the change, Kotter (1995) proposes building an organizational culture of innovation to support the sustainability of the change overtime.

Stage Five: Implementation Stage: Transforming Creative Ideas into Products, Services, or Processes

The fifth stage in the journey of the idea aims at implementing the creative idea, transforming it into the final product, service, or process. At this stage, the innovation process continues to narrow toward the exploitation and implementation stage (Clark & Wheelwright, 1992).

New product design and production differ from the production of standard products, which exploits existing capabilities and follows existing work plans, standards, and procedures. Designing new innovative products is an ill-defined problem (Simon, 1991), requiring exploration and experimentation during the development and the production process. Therefore, while the goal is to converge and execute, the process is still exploratory in nature. Furthermore, new product development is a complex process. Managers at this stage face two major challenges: (a) minimize time to market and penetrate the market before others and (b) develop and produce a product that best fits in with customers' expectations (Schilling & Hill, 1998). These two challenges compete with each other for management's attention, time, and resources, making it difficult for management to respond to both of them concurrently. However, these challenges also depend on each other, because time to market is meaningless if the product does not fit with customers' needs and expectations. Similarly, satisfying customers' needs is not sufficient if a competitor has already attracted customer attention toward another product.

The need to respond to these two challenges together adds to the complexity of the new product development and implementation. The question is how leaders respond to these two challenges interdependently.

Minimize Time to Market

A short cycle of time to market conveys the execution of a highly complex work plan within a relatively short time. For this purpose, leaders for innovation began using the agile method, which had originally been implemented in software development due to the high degree of change and uncertainty (Coram & Bohner, 2005). Agile methodology consists of three basic elements, including *scrum*, reflecting creative and adaptive teamwork in solving complex problems; *lean development*, expressed in eliminating waste; and *kanban*, which aims to reduce work time (Rigby, Sutherlands, & Takeuchi, 2016). The agile methodology enables the team learning process that is needed to cope with ill-defined problems and ambiguous situations (Julian, 2008; Leifer, O'Connor, & Rice, 2001). The process is transparent to all team members, who meet on a daily basis to identify obstacles, resolve disagreement, and test pieces of their work. To shorten the process, agile teams invite feedback from potential customers during the new product development, rather than postpone feedback seeking until after the new product gets to the market (Julian, 2008; Leifer et al., 2001). Leaders who use the agile method act as facilitators, encourage transparent information communication, and seek teamwork and feedback from customers during the new product development (Coram & Bohner, 2005). The agile method enables teams to reduce potential errors by getting them to meet daily to resolve errors and increase collaboration. Empirical support of this approach demonstrated that unit teams who held weekly meetings to reflect on their team feedback on product defects, to generate solutions for reducing defects, and to set specific improvement goals significantly reduced the percentage of defects from 25% to 2%. This process introduces a culture of innovation, which further supports the continuous process of team learning and product improvement (Naveh & Erez, 2004). Furthermore, teams whose members come from multidisciplinary backgrounds and multifunctional organizational units require a high level of coordination and collaboration among multiple organizational functions and disciplines. This suggests that leaders should have the power to influence their followers to change their routines and learn to collaborate and coordinate across multiple organizational functions and fields of expertise. One methodology that enables multifunctional and multidisciplinary teams to systematically learn how to collaborate and coordinate their behaviors under a highly complex task is briefing-debriefing (Tannenbaum, Smith-Jentsch, & Behson, 1998). Briefing refers to a scheduled team meeting prior to the performance of a team activity, in which team members plan their coordinated roles and actions and set the criteria for performance outcomes. Debriefing is the postaction review of evaluating the outcomes in comparison to the criteria set during the briefing meeting and sharing team members' learning and take-aways from the event. The briefing-debriefing learning cycle serves as an input for the next set of coordinated actions. The indirect outcome of this learning process is the emergence of a learning culture, which supports the continuous learning and improvement process (Vashdi, Bamberger, Erez, & Weiss-Meilik, 2007). A learning culture encourages employees to document difficulties in the production process and the actions taken to resolve them. The cumulative learning episodes shape the knowledge base and the pool of coordinated behaviors, which can then be implemented in the next event that requires the cooperation and coordination of the actions of multiple domains of expertise (Vashdi, Bamberger, & Erez, 2013). Building followers' expectations for adopting specific practices and displaying consistent supportive behaviors facilitates the coordination and integration among employees, whose role is to transform ideas into products (Carmeli & Waldman, 2010). Research has also shown that in particular, transformational leaders positively influence collaboration and coordination of diverse teams by fostering in-depth processing of task-relevant information and building the collective team identity, which is needed for collaboration and coordination of the team members' actions (Kearney & Gebert, 2009).

Develop and Produce a Product that Best Fits in with Customers' Expectations

Meeting the challenge of time to market is a necessary but not sufficient condition to successfully designing the new product at the implementation phase. The other necessary condition is that customers embrace the product and get excited about it (Kano et al., 1984). Brown and Katz (2011) introduced the design thinking methodology, which aims to provide a deep understanding of customers' needs, as well as their overt and covert expectations by observing customers' actual experiences and behaviors by attempting "to seek them out where they live, work and play" (Brown & Katz, 2011, p. 382). Furthermore, this approach encourages observing the experiences and behaviors of not only normative customers but also customers whose behavioral response deviates from the norm. Successful leaders at this phase go beyond simply documenting observations and can develop empathy with the customers and understand their close emotional attachment to the new product. Microsoft CEO Satya Nadella, in his book, *Hit Refresh* (2018), views empathy as an important characteristic of the innovation leader, enabling him or her to have a deep understanding of customers, employees, external companies' stakeholders and alliances, as well as humanity at large. Furthermore, effective leaders do not wait until their product gets to market to receive customer responses. Rather, they invite customer input during the development and implementation phase, before it officially gets to the market (Hoyer, Chandy, Dorotic, Krafft, & Singh, 2010). Leaders who endorse open innovation encourage potential consumers to cocreate the new product. Leaders get consumers excited to have the opportunity to influence the new product development, provide a psychologically shared climate, and build consumer trust in the final product. Involving customers in cocreation not only shortens time to market but also increases the customers' understanding of the development and production processes, the attractiveness of the product, and the likelihood of having them become first movers to adopt the new product (Hoyer et al., 2010). For example, threadless.com gets their customers involved in new T-shirt design, and LEGO invites customers to develop new kits of LEGO pieces that later get to the market as new products (Lüscher & Lewis, 2008). Involving customers at the new product development stage and getting their feedback before the product gets to the market attests to the high interdependence between the fifth stage of the implementation and the sixth stage of market penetration, which closes the complete cycle of the innovation process.

Stage Six: Market Penetration, Reaching the Customers

Intensive marketing efforts begin as early as the evaluation and selection stage and continue through the implementation and product development stage, though they are given full attention during the market penetration stage, which closes the process of innovation. Considerations such as market size and potential market growth begin at the evaluation and selection stage. In their book, *Where to Play*, Gruber and Tal (2018) propose the Market Opportunity Navigator, which enables leaders to consider the potential of different markets and the expected challenges by searching broadly, assessing deeply, and strategizing smartly. Once ideas get to the implementation stage, developers of new products need to consider more than just technology-related issues; they must also have an in-depth understanding of and familiarity with customers' needs and, as mentioned, get them involved in the development and production process (Hoyer et al., 2010). Feedback from first movers and early adopters serves to help finalize the product design, packaging, branding distribution channels, advertisement design, and more (Gruber & Tal, 2018). At this phase, leaders are more likely to succeed in bringing the innovation product to its target market if they demonstrate perspective taking and empathy, empathize with customers, and consider the expectations for customer experience, beyond the technology and functional properties of the innovative product (Brown & Katz, 2011; Kano et al., 1984; Nadella, 2018).

Successful marketing of new products is crucial for sustaining the competitive advantage of the organization. Yet, the failure rate of marketing new products is relatively high (Srinivasan, Pauwels, Silva-Risso, & Hanssens,

2004). Some failures stem from overlooking the different consumer segments and the time it takes them to adopt new products. Market penetration theories describe the process of the diffusion of innovation and the product life cycle (Levitt, 1965; Moore, 1991; Rogers, 2003). Understanding the different phases of market evolution has important implications for leaders who aim to compete for market share (Tao, Probert, & Phaal, 2010). Rogers' (2003) diffusion of the innovation model portrays the pattern of adopting a new product as a sequence of adopter's segments: Innovators (2.5%) are the first movers, followed by Early Adopters (13.5%), Early Majority (34%), Late Majority (34%), and last, Laggards (16%). Moore's (1991) Technology Adoption Life Cycle describes the propensity of the generic segment to adopt new technology, typifying the specific traits for each segment, communication and information seeking patterns, and various risk orientations toward technological innovation. The model also describes the challenges of progress from one category to the next, identifying the biggest challenge, "crossing the chasm" (Moore, 1991), or "riding the saddle" (Goldenberg, Libai, & Muller, 2002), as the gap between early adopters to early majority segments.

The first consumer segment to try the new products is the innovators (Rogers, 2003), characterized as technophiles or technology enthusiasts, who are willing to try new products, ignore missing elements, seek information in professional sources, and enjoy taking part in the process (Moore, 1991). Innovators are most likely to be engaged in the cocreation of new product development (Hoyer et al., 2010). Thus, as described in stage five, innovation leaders should approach innovators and invite them to take part in the development process.

The next consumer segment that innovation marketers need to reach are the early adopters, characterized as visionaries, who look for the "vision" of the application and not only its technological innovation (Giglierano, Vitale, & McClatchy, 2011; Moore, 1991). Effective leaders at this stage should emphasize their vision about the product and communicate the fit of that vision to the early adopters' identity, expectations, values, and lifestyle. However, the success of the market effort depends very much on "crossing the chasm" (Moore, 1991) to get acceptance by the early majority, who are typically pragmatists. Goldenberg et al. (2002) found that 30%–50% of new product market diffusion involves a pattern of sales decrease that can last for up to two years. This happens due to a lack of communication between the early market and main market, and because the marketing efforts directed to the early market consumers do not affect the main market. The main market users, in general, want to get reliable services, such that the adoption of the new technology will be pain free. To progress to the main market, an innovative product usually requires the industry to agree on a dominant design standard (Anderson & Tushman, 1990), after which a phase of rapid growth can commence (Golder & Tellis, 1997; Levitt, 1965). Here, there is usually more competition in the market, and price gradually becomes more important to consumers. Leaders of innovation should be familiar with the different consumers' segments, understand when a product is ready for the transition from early to main market, and shift the marketing communication to fit the main market and its pragmatic consumers. Moreover, leaders should foresee and prepare the company internally for the takeoff in sales, and the increased competition in the market.

Each innovation cycle reaches its last point by the diffusion of the innovation product from the early majority to the late majority and then to the laggards (Rogers, 2003). Standardization and price are more important for the maturation and decline in the product life cycle (Levitt, 1965).

A relevant question is, therefore, how leaders can facilitate market penetration of innovative products, considering the complexity of the process as described earlier. The strategic leadership literature articulates a line between *entrepreneurial leadership* behaviors and market penetration (Moriano, Molero, Topa, & Mangin, 2014). Entrepreneurial leaders take the initiative to identify new market opportunities. They familiarize themselves with the market characteristics (Chen, 2007; Kuratko, 2007) and develop a campaign that presents the new product as the ultimate solution to consumers' needs and expectations (Greenberg, McKone-Sweet, & Wilson, 2011; Leitch, McMullan, & Harrison, 2012). A successful case that exemplifies the leader's entrepreneurial approach to market penetration is the case of SodaStream. From an old traditional industry, SodaStream (https://sodastream.com/) has since become the number one sparkling water brand in volume in the world and the leading manufacturer and distributor of sparkling water makers. In August 2018, PepsiCo acquired SodaStream for $3.2 billion. How did Daniel Birnbaum, who was nominated CEO in 2010, transform an old, traditional company, founded in 1998, into the leading sparkling water brand? Birnbaum paid attention to two new trends in the market – sustainability and health. Under his leadership, SodaStream has rebranded itself as a fizzy water company, providing a healthier alternative that enables consumers to control the sugar level – and thus reduce it – compared to all other soft drinks in the market; at the same time, the drink, despite this reduction in sugar, maintains its good flavor and is "fun and exciting" to drink. The company also rebranded itself as one that saves the environment, because it makes machines, while easily transforming ordinary tap water into a carbonated beverage, take advantage of reusable bottles, in contrast to SodaStream competitors who use planet-killing plastic bottles. SodaStream has numerous distribution channels that allow customers easy access to its products across 45 countries. Furthermore, SodaStream positioned itself among the biggest beverage companies in the world, including Coca-Cola and PepsiCo, by using known personalities like Scarlett Johansson, Paris Hilton, Mayim Bialik, and "Game of Thrones" personalities in its campaigns, most visibly during the World Cup.

PepsiCo viewed SodaStream as a disruptive company with all the features that align with market trends, for which reason it decided to acquire SodaStream for over $3.2 billion. The case of SodaStream exemplifies the CEO's leadership role in transforming a traditional beverage company into an innovative market disruptor that is threatening the biggest players in the beverage market.

Discussion and Integration

The journey of the idea from its inception to its maturation is a journey of discovery of the complex nature of the creative problem-solving and innovation processes, as well as their interrelationships. The two fields of research, creative problem-solving and innovation, have long been studied independent of each other. Creative problem-solving has mostly focused on the ideation phase and deepening the understanding of the different cognitive and behavioral processes that compose it (Mumford et al., 2012), whereas the innovation management process has focused on the ideation and implementation, without zooming into each one of them in search of more fine-tuned processes (Clark & Wheelwright, 1992). Erez's model (see Erez et al., 2015) extends the implementation phase to include the transition phase, mobilizing the idea from the ideation to the implementation phase, and the market penetration phase. This follows the actual implementation and completes the innovation process, as it is when the innovative product gets to the marketplace.

This chapter has taken an integrative approach and developed an integrative model, which displays the complementary nature of the creative problem-solving and the innovation management processes into one model, as captured in Figure 9.1. By integrating the two lines of research, this chapter contributes to the research in a number of ways: *First*, it enriches the knowledge of creative problem-solving by expanding it to include the transition phase of mobilizing the idea toward the implementation phase, and by further elaborating on the implementation phase and on the process of market penetration. *Second*, the proposed integrative model enriches the research on the innovation process by introducing an in-depth view of the components of the ideation phase, as proposed by the creative problem-solving approach; this includes scanning, information gathering, and information organization as the basis for structuring the problem and defining it. *Third*, the integrative model underscores the transition stage from ideation to implementation, for such a transition does not occur by itself. Leaders should take the initiative to transfer the idea to the implementation phase because innovation requires change and change involves uncertainty and risk. Because of this, change often encounters resistance, and it is the responsibility of leaders at this stage to reduce ambiguity and increase trust by communicating their vision effectively and introducing an implementable work plan to reduce the level of ambiguity. *Fourth*, this chapter contributes to the understanding of the duality involved in creativity and innovation between phases and within phases. The transition from ideation to implementation reflects the duality of divergent and convergent thinking: exploration and exploitation. Within the ideation phase, the transition from opening up to gathering information from multiple sources and then closing toward identifying the problem or challenge to focus on represents the duality within the ideation phase. Generating novel ideas that should also be useful and relevant represents this duality at the idea generation phase. Implementing the idea – all the while struggling with the ill-defined nature of the product to be developed and the need to observe and communicate with customers – requires an opening approach during the implementation phase. Finally, getting into the market is another ill-defined problem because there is a gap between customers' expectations of the final product and the final product as it will be in reality. Sometimes, customers cannot consciously articulate why they like or do not like the new product because the attractiveness of a new product depends on multiple reasons, including but not limited to the emotions it elicits, its association with other products, the values that it represents, and the responses of others to the product. Therefore, getting to know the market and the customers is another complex challenge for the leader, one that requires openness to customer feedback even before the product gets to market or learning how to market the product. *Fifth*, the complementary nature of creative problem-solving and of the innovation process suggests that leaders for innovation should endorse the duality of the process and adjust to it by having the flexibility to shift between opening and closing, and between divergent and convergent cognitive processes. Rosing et al. (2011) call this leadership type *ambidextrous* to characterize a leader who can switch between opening and closing behavioral types to deal with the changing requirements of the innovation process. Zacher and Rosing (2015) assess the opening and closing leadership behaviors as two independent variables. They found that teams who evaluated their leaders to be high on both opening and closing behaviors reached the highest levels of innovation.

A similar approach to the ambidextrous leaders is the paradoxical leader, who endorses competing behaviors such as maintaining decision control while allowing autonomy or enforcing job requirements while allowing flexibility (Zhang et al., 2015). It is interesting to note that while ambidextrous leadership and paradoxical leadership capture the duality embedded in the leadership behaviors, they differ in the way they perceive the duality. Zacher and Rosing (2015) conceptualize the duality as the coexistence of two independent behaviors that do not correlate with one another, yet both correlate with transformational leadership. Zhang et al. (2015), who represented the Far East philosophy of the Yin and Yang and conducted their research in China, conceptualize the duality as being embedded in the same dimension, such as controlling followers' behaviors while allowing for autonomy, or maintaining both distance and closure. Overall, the complexity of the work requirements, and specifically of innovation, calls for a new leadership type that has the flexibility to manage both aspects of opening and closing behavior in line with the work demands. *Sixth,* the review of the two lines of research – the creative problem-solving and the innovation process – suggests that the problems and needs that require innovative solutions are ill-defined involving ambiguity and risk. Leaders who manage under such conditions should be open to learn and adapt, and to encourage their followers to continuously learn and adapt. The learning process reflects opening to new knowledge acquisition and assimilation, which further reduces the ambiguity and risk, while also allowing for convergence on the innovative solution.

We close this chapter by calling for future research that empirically studies the integrated multistage process of creative problem-solving in innovation, and the shifts from opening to closing behaviors as the leader adapts to the dynamic and changing nature of the process of innovation.

References

Altshuller, G. S. 1990. On the theory of solving inventive problems. *Design Methods and Theories,* 24, 1216–1222.

Amabile, T. M. 1996. *Creativity in context: Update to the social psychology of creativity.* Boulder, CO: Westview.

Amabile, T. M., Schatzel, E. A., Moneta, G. B., & Kramer, S. J. 2004. Leader behaviors and the work environment for creativity: Perceived leader support. *The Leadership Quarterly,* 15, 5–32.

Amundsen, S., & Martinsen, Ø. L. 2015. Linking empowering leadership to job satisfaction, work effort, and creativity: The role of self-leadership and psychological empowerment. *Journal of Leadership and Organizational Studies,* 22, 304–323.

Anderson, N., Potočnik, K., & Zhou, J. 2014. Innovation and creativity in organizations: A state-of-the-science review, prospective commentary, and guiding framework. *Journal of Management,* 40, 1297–1333.

Anderson, P., & Tushman, M. L. 1990. Technological discontinuities and dominant designs: A cyclical model of technological change. *Administrative Science Quarterly,* 35, 604–633.

Basadur, M., Runco, M. A., & Vega, L. A. 2000. Understanding how creative thinking skills, attitudes, and behaviors work together: A causal process model. *Journal of Creative Behavior,* 34, 77–100.

Berson, Y., Halevy, N., Shamir, B., & Erez, M. 2015. Leading from different psychological distances: A construal-level perspective on vision communication, goal setting, and follower motivation. *The Leadership Quarterly,* 26, 143–155.

Berson, Y., Shamir, B., Avolio, B. J., & Popper, M. 2001. The relationship between vision strength, leadership style, and context. *The Leadership Quarterly,* 12, 53–73.

Blair, C. S., & Mumford, M. D. 2007. Errors in idea evaluation: Preference for the unoriginal? *The Journal of Creative Behavior,* 41, 197–222.

Bledow, R., Frese, M., Anderson, N., Erez, M., & Farr, J. 2009. A dialectic perspective on innovation: Conflicting demands, multiple pathways, and ambidexterity. *Industrial and Organizational Psychology,* 2, 305–337.

Brown, T., & Katz, B. 2011. Change by design. *Journal of Product Innovation Management*, 28, 381–383.

Byrne, C. L., Mumford, M. D., Barrett, J. D., & Vessey, W. B. 2009. Examining the leaders of creative efforts: What do they do, and what do they think about? *Creativity and Innovation Management*, 18, 256–268.

Caridi-Zahavi, O., Carmeli, A., & Arazy, O. 2016. The influence of CEOs' visionary innovation leadership on the performance of high-technology ventures: The mediating roles of connectivity and knowledge integration. *Journal of Product Innovation Management*, 33, 356–376.

Carmeli, A., & Paulus, P. B. 2015. CEO ideational facilitation leadership and team creativity: The mediating role of knowledge sharing. *The Journal of Creative Behavior*, 49, 53–75.

Carmeli, A., & Waldman, D. A. 2010. Leadership, behavioral context, and the performance of work groups in a knowledge-intensive setting. *The Journal of Technology Transfer*, 35, 384–400.

Chen, M. H. 2007. Entrepreneurial leadership and new ventures: Creativity in entrepreneurial teams. *Creativity and Innovation Management*, 16, 239–249.

Clark, K. B., & Wheelwright, S. C. 1992. Organizing and leading "heavyweight" development teams. *California Management Review*, 34, 9–28.

Conger, J. A. 1999. Charismatic and transformational leadership in organizations: An insider's perspective on developing streams of research. *The Leadership Quarterly*, 10, 145–179.

Coram, M., & Bohner, S. 2005, April. The impact of agile methods on software project management. In *ECBS'05. 12th IEEE International Conference and Workshops on the Engineering of Computer-Based Systems* (pp. 363–370). New York, NY: IEEE.

Damanpour, F., & Schneider, M. 2008. Characteristics of innovation and innovation adoption in public organizations: Assessing the role of managers. *Journal of Public Administration Research and Theory*, 19, 495–522.

Dutton, J. E., Ashford, S. J., O'Neill, R. M., & Lawrence, K. A. 2001. Moves that matter: Issue selling and organizational change. *Academy of Management Journal*, 44, 716–736.

Eisenbeiss, S. A., van Knippenberg, D., & Boerner, S. 2008 Transformational leadership and team innovation: Integrating team climate principles. *Journal of Applied Psychology*, 93, 1438–1446.

Elenkov, D. S., & Manev, I. M. 2005. Top management leadership and influence on innovation: The role of socio-cultural context. *Journal of Management*, 31, 381–402.

Erez, M., Arbel, I., & Hadassa-Blank, T. 2015. *Organizational innovation management guidelines*. Tel Aviv, Israel: The Standards Institute of Israel.

Giglierano, J., Vitale, R., & McClatchy, J. J. 2011. Business development in the early stages of commercializing disruptive innovation: Considering the implications of Moore's life cycle model and Christensen's model of disruptive innovation. *Innovative Marketing*, 7, 29–39.

Gist, M. E. 1989. The influence of training method on self-efficacy and idea generation among managers. *Personnel Psychology*, 42, 787–805.

Goldenberg, J., Libai, B., & Muller, E. 2002. Riding the saddle: How cross-market communications can create a major slump in sales. *Journal of Marketing*, 66, 1–16.

Golder, P. N., & Tellis, G. J. 1997. Will it ever fly? Modeling the takeoff of really new consumer durables. *Marketing Science*, 16, 256–270.

Greenberg, D., McKone-Sweet, K., & Wilson, H. J. 2011. *The new entrepreneurial leaders: Developing leaders who shape social and economic opportunity.* San Francisco, CA: Berrett-Koehler.

Gruber, M., & Tal, S. 2018. *Where to play: 3 Steps for discovering your most valuable market opportunity.* London, UK: Financial Times Publications.

Guilford, J. P. 1950. Creativity. *American Psychologist,* 5, 444–454.

Guilford, J. P. 1967. *The nature of human intelligence.* New York, NY: McGraw-Hill.

Herman, A., & Reiter-Palmon, R. 2011. The effect of regulatory focus on idea generation and idea evaluation. *Psychology of Aesthetics, Creativity, and the Arts,* 5, 1–13.

Hirst, G., Van Knippenberg, D., & Zhou, J. 2009. A cross-level perspective on employee creativity: Goal orientation, team learning behavior, and individual creativity. *Academy of Management Journal,* 52, 280–293.

Howell, J. M. 2005. The right stuff: Identifying and developing effective champions of innovation. *Academy of Management Perspectives,* 19, 108–119.

Howell, J. M., & Boies, K. 2004. Champions of technological innovation: The influence of contextual knowledge, role orientation, idea generation, and idea promotion on champion emergence. *The Leadership Quarterly,* 15, 123–143.

Howell, J. M., Shea, C. M., & Higgins, C. A. 2005. Champions of product innovations: Defining, developing, and validating a measure of champion behavior. *Journal of Business Venturing,* 20, 641–661.

Hoyer, W. D., Chandy, R., Dorotic, M., Krafft, M., & Singh, S. S. 2010. Consumer cocreation in new product development. *Journal of Service Research,* 13, 283–296.

Hughes, D. J., Lee, A., Tian, A. W., Newman, A., & Legood, A. 2018. Leadership, creativity, and innovation: A critical review and practical recommendations. *The Leadership Quarterly,* 29, 549–569.

Hunter, S. T., Bedell, K. E., & Mumford, M. D. 2005. Dimensions of creative climate. *The International Journal of Creativity and Problem Solving,* 15, 97–116.

Hunter, S. T., Bedell, K. E., & Mumford, M. D. 2007. Climate for creativity: A quantitative review. *Creativity Research Journal,* 19, 69–90.

Hunter, S. T., Bedell-Avers, K. E., Hunsicker, C. M., Mumford, M. D., & Ligon, G. S. 2008. Applying multiple knowledge structures in creative thought: Effects on idea generation and problem-solving. *Creativity Research Journal,* 20, 137–154.

Isaksen, S. G., & Akkermans, H. J. 2011. Creative climate: A leadership lever for innovation. *The Journal of Creative Behavior,* 45, 161–187.

Julian, J. L. 2008. *An exploratory study of project management office leaders and their role in facilitating cross-project learning.* New York, NY: Teachers College, Columbia University.

Jung, D. I., Chow, C., & Wu, A. 2003. The role of transformational leadership in enhancing organizational innovation: Hypotheses and some preliminary findings. *The Leadership Quarterly,* 14, 525–544.

Kano, N., Nobuhiku, S., Fumio, T., & Shinichi, T. 1984. Attractive quality and must-be quality. *Journal of the Japanese Society for Quality Control (in Japanese),* 14, 39–48.

Kanter, R. M., Stein, B. A., & Jick, T. D. 1992. *The challenge of organizational change.* New York, NY: Free Press.

Kark, R., & Carmeli, A. 2009. Alive and creating: The mediating role of vitality and aliveness in the relationship between psychological safety and creative work involvement. *Journal of Organizational Behavior,* 30, 785–804.

Kearney, E., & Gebert, D. 2009. Managing diversity and enhancing team outcomes: The promise of transformational leadership. *Journal of Applied Psychology*, 94, 77–89.

Kirkman, B. L., & Rosen, B. 1997. A model of work team empowerment. In R. W. Woodman & W. A. Pasmore (Eds.), *Research in organizational change and development* (Vol. 10, pp. 131–167). Greenwich, CT: JAI Press.

Kirkman, B. L., & Rosen, B. 1999. Beyond self-management: Antecedents and consequences of team empowerment. *Academy of Management Journal*, 42, 58–74.

Klein, K. J., & Knight, A. P. 2005. Innovation implementation: Overcoming the challenge. *Current Directions in Psychological Science*, 14, 243–246.

Klein, K. J., & Sorra, J. S. 1996. The challenge of innovation implementation. *Academy of Management Review*, 21, 1055–1080.

Koberg, C. S., Uhlenbruck, N., & Sarason, Y. 1996. Facilitators of organizational innovation: The role of life-cycle stage. *Journal of Business Venturing*, 11, 133–149.

Kotter, J. P. 1995. Leading change: Why transformation efforts fail. *Harvard Business Review*, 73, 59–67.

Kotter, J. P. 2007. Leading change. Why transformation efforts fail. *Harvard Business Review*, 85, 96–103.

Kuratko, D. F. 2007. Entrepreneurial leadership in the 21st century: Guest editor's perspective. *Journal of Leadership and Organizational Studies*, 13, 1–11.

Lauche, K. & Erez, M.. August, 2015. Emotional Dynamics of Issue Selling and Collective Moaning. How innovators negotiate resources. *Academy of Management Meeting, Vancouver*, Canada.

Leifer, R., O'Connor, G. C., & Rice, M. 2001. Implementing radical innovation in mature firms: The role of hubs. *Academy of Management Perspectives*, 15, 102–113.

Leitch, C. M., McMullan, C., & Harrison, R. T. 2012. The development of entrepreneurial leadership: The role of human, social and institutional capital. *British Journal of Management*, 24, 347–366.

Levitt, T. 1965. *Exploit the product life cycle* (Vol. 43). Graduate School of Business Administration, Harvard University.

Licuanan, B. F., Dailey, L. R., & Mumford, M. D. 2007. Idea evaluation: Error in evaluating highly original ideas. *The Journal of Creative Behavior*, 41, 1–27.

Lokiec, M., & Erez, M. 2010. The chronicle of an idea. *Academy of Management Annual Conference*, August 6–10, Montreal, Canada.

Lonergan, D. C., Scott, G. M., & Mumford, M. D. 2004. Evaluative aspects of creative thought: Effects of appraisal and revision standards. *Creativity Research Journal*, 16, 231–246.

Lord, R. G., & Brown, D. J. 2004. *Leadership processes and follower self-identity*. Mahwah, NJ: Lawrence Erlbaum.

Lord, R. G., & Hall, R. J. 2005. Identity, deep structure and the development of leadership skill. *The Leadership Quarterly*, 16, 591–615.

Luecke, R. 2003. *Managing change and transition* (Vol. 3). Boston, MA: Harvard Business Press.

Lüscher, L. S., & Lewis, M. W. (2008). Organizational change and managerial sensemaking: Working through paradox. *Academy of Management Journal*, 51(2), 221–240.

Mainemelis, C., Kark, R., & Epitropaki, O. 2015. Creative leadership: A multi-context conceptualization. *The Academy of Management Annals*, 9, 393–482.

Medeiros, K. E., Steele, L. M., Watts, L. L., & Mumford, M. D. 2018. Timing is everything: Examining the role of constraints throughout the creative process. *Psychology of Aesthetics, Creativity, and the Arts*, 12, 471–488.

Miron-Spektor, E., & Erez, M. 2017. Looking at creativity through a paradox lens. In W. K. Smith, M. W. Lewis, P. Jarzabkowski, & A. Langley (Eds.), *The Oxford Handbook of Organizational Paradox* (pp. 434–451). New York, NY: Oxford University Press.

Miron-Spektor, E., Erez, M., & Naveh, E. 2011. The effect of conformist and attentive-to-detail members on team innovation: Reconciling the innovation paradox. *Academy of Management Journal*, 54, 740–760.

Moore, G. A. 1991. *Crossing the chasm: Marketing and selling high-tech products to mainstream customers (Collins Business Essentials)*. New York, NY: Harper Business.

Moriano, J. A., Molero, F., Topa, G., & Mangin, J. P. L. 2014. The influence of transformational leadership and organizational identification on intrapreneurship. *International Entrepreneurship and Management Journal*, 10, 103–119.

Mumford, M. D., Bedell-Avers, K. E., & Hunter, S. T. 2008. Planning for innovation: A multi-level perspective. In F. J. Yammarino, & F. Dansereau (series eds.) and M. D. Mumford, S. T. Hunter, & K. E. Bedell-Avers (vol. eds.), *Research in multi-level issues: Vol. 7. Multi-level issues in creativity and innovation* (pp. 107–154). Oxford, UK: Elsevier.

Mumford, M. D., Connelly, S., & Gaddis, B. 2003. How creative leaders think: Experimental findings and cases. *The Leadership Quarterly*, 14, 411–432.

Mumford, M. D., Eubanks, D. L., & Murphy, S. T. 2007a. Creating the conditions for success: Best practices in leading for innovation. In J. A. Conger & R. E. Riggio (Eds.), *The practice of leadership* (pp. 107–197). San Francisco, CA: Jossey-Bass.

Mumford, M. D., Hunter, S. T., Eubanks, D. L., Bedell, K. E., & Murphy, S. T. 2007. Developing leaders for creative efforts: A domain-based approach to leadership development. *Human Resource Management Review*, 17, 402–417.

Mumford, M. D., Lonergan, D. C., & Scott, G. 2002. Evaluating creative ideas: Processes, standards, and context. *Inquiry: Critical Thinking Across the Disciplines*, 22, 21–30.

Mumford, M. D., Marks, M. A., Connelly, M. S., Zaccaro, S. J., & Reiter-Palmon, R. 2000. Development of leadership skills: Experience and timing. *The Leadership Quarterly*, 11, 87–114.

Mumford, M. D., Medeiros, K. E., & Partlow, P. J. 2012. Creative thinking: Processes, strategies, and knowledge. *The Journal of Creative Behavior*, 46, 30–47.

Mumford, M. D., Mobley, M. I., Reiter-Palmon, R., Uhlman, C. E., & Doares, L. M. 1991. Process analytic models of creative capacities. *Creativity Research Journal*, 4, 91–122.

Mumford, M. D., Peterson, D., & Robledo, I. 2013. Leading scientists and engineers: Cognition in a socio-technical context. In S. Hemlin, C. M. Allwood, B. Martin, & M. D. Mumford (Eds.), *Leadership in science, technology, and innovation*. London, England: Routledge.

Mumford, M. D., Schultz, R. A., & Osburn, H. K. 2002. Planning in organizations: Performance as a multi-level phenomenon. In F. J. Yammarino & F. Dansereau (Eds.), *Research in multi-level issues (vol. 1): The many faces of multi-level issues* (pp. 3–36). Oxford, England: Elsevier.

Mumford, M. D., Scott, G. M., Gaddis, B., & Strange, J. M. 2002. Leading creative people: Orchestrating expertise and relationships. *The Leadership Quarterly*, 13, 705–750.

Mumford, M. D., Steele, L., McIntosh, T., & Mulhearn, T. 2015. Forecasting and leader performance: Objective cognition in a socio-organizational context. *The Leadership Quarterly*, 26, 359–369.

Mumford, M. D., Todd, E. M., Higgs, C., & McIntosh, T. 2017. Cognitive skills and leadership performance: The nine critical skills. *The Leadership Quarterly*, 28, 24–39.

Nadella, S. 2018. *Hit Refresh*. Bentang Pustaka.

Naveh, E., & Erez, M. 2004. Innovation and attention to detail in the quality improvement paradigm. *Management Science*, 50, 1576–1586.

Nijstad, B. A., Berger-Selman, F., & De Dreu, C. K. 2014. Innovation in top management teams: Minority dissent, transformational leadership, and radical innovations. *European Journal of Work and Organizational Psychology*, 23, 310–322.

Nijstad, B. A., & Stroebe, W. 2006. How the group affects the mind: A cognitive model of idea generation in groups. *Personality and Social Psychology Review*, 10, 186–213.

O'Reilly III, C. A., & Tushman, M. L. 2008. Ambidexterity as a dynamic capability: Resolving the innovator's dilemma. *Research in Organizational Behavior*, 28, 185–206.

Oreg, S. & Berson Y. 2019. Leaders' impact on organizational change: Bridging theoretical and methodical chasms. *Academy of Management Annals*, 23, 272–307.

Osborn, A. F. 1953. *Applied imagination: Principles and procedures of creative problem-solving*. New York, NY: Scribner.

Osburn, H. K., & Mumford, M. D. 2006. Creativity and planning: Training interventions to develop creative problem solving skills. *Creative Research Journal*, 18, 173–190.

Paulus, P. B., & Yang, H. C. 2000. Idea generation in groups: A basis for creativity in organizations. *Organizational Behavior and Human Decision Processes*, 82, 76–87.

Puccio, G. J., Burnett, C., Acar, S., Yudess, J. A., Holinger, M., & Cabra, J. F. (2018). Creative problem solving in small groups: The effects of creativity training on idea generation, solution creativity, and leadership effectiveness. *The Journal of Creative Behavior*, 0, 1–19.

Reiter-Palmon, R., & Illies, J. J. 2004. Leadership and creativity: Understanding leadership from a creative problem-solving perspective. *The Leadership Quarterly*, 15, 55–77.

Rigby, D. K., Sutherland, J., & Takeuchi, H. 2016. Embracing agile. *Harvard Business Review*, 94, 40–50.

Robledo, I. C., Peterson, D. R., & Mumford, M. D. 2012. Leadership of scientists and engineers: A three-vector model. *Journal of Organizational Behavior*, 33, 140–147.

Rogers, E. M. 2003. *Diffusion of innovations* (5th ed.). New York, NY: Free Press.

Rosing, K., Frese, M., & Bausch, A. 2011. Explaining the heterogeneity of the leadership-innovation relationship: Ambidextrous leadership. *The Leadership Quarterly*, 22, 956–974.

Rouse, W. B., & Morris, N. M. 1986. On looking into the black box: Prospects and limits in the search for mental models. *Psychological Bulletin*, 100, 349–363.

Runco, M. A. 2003. Idea evaluation, divergent thinking, and creativity. In M. A. Runco (Ed.), *Perspectives on creativity research. Critical creative processes* (pp. 69–94). Cresskill, NJ: Hampton Press.

Runco, M. A., & Jaeger, G. J. 2012. The standard definition of creativity. *Creativity Research Journal*, 24, 92–96.

Schilling, M. A., & Hill, C. W. 1998. Managing the new product development process: Strategic imperatives. *Academy of Management Perspectives*, 12, 67–81.

Shalley, C. E., & Gilson, L. L. 2004. What leaders need to know: A review of social and contextual factors that can foster or hinder creativity. *The Leadership Quarterly*, 15, 33–53.

Shin, S. J., & Zhou, J. 2007. When is educational specialization heterogeneity related to creativity in research and development teams? Transformational leadership as a moderator. *Journal of Applied Psychology*, 92, 1709–1721.

Shipman, A. S., Byrne, C. L., & Mumford, M. D. 2010. Leader vision formation and forecasting: The effects of forecasting extent, resources, and timeframe. *The Leadership Quarterly*, 21, 439–456.

Simon, H. A. 1991. Bounded rationality and organizational learning. *Organization Science*, 2, 125–134.

Škerlavaj, M., Černe, M., & Dysvik, A. 2014. I get by with a little help from my supervisor: Creative-idea generation, idea implementation, and perceived supervisor support. *The Leadership Quarterly*, 25, 987–1000.

Smith, G. J. 1998. Idea-generation techniques: A formulary of active ingredients. *Journal of Creative Behavior*, 32, 107–133.

Smith, W. K., & Lewis, M. W. 2011. Toward a theory of paradox: A dynamic equilibrium model of organizing. *Academy of Management Review*, 36, 381–403.

Smith, W. K., Erez, M., Jarvenpaa, S., Lewis, M. W., & Tracey, P. 2017. Adding complexity to theories of paradox, tensions, and dualities of innovation and change: Introduction to organization studies special issue on paradox, tensions, and dualities of innovation and change. *Organization Studies*, 38, 303–317.

Sosik, J. J., Kahai, S. S., & Avolio, B. J. 1998. Transformational leadership and dimensions of creativity: Motivating idea generation in computer-mediated groups. *Creativity Research Journal*, 11, 111–122.

Srinivasan, S., Pauwels, K., Silva-Risso, J. M., & Hanssens, D. M. 2004. Product innovations, promotions, and long-term firm value. *Journal of Marketing*, 68, 142–156.

Stenmark, C. K., Shipman, A. S., & Mumford, M. D. 2011. Managing the innovative process: The dynamic role of leaders. *Psychology of Aesthetics, Creativity, and the Arts*, 5, 67–80.

Tannenbaum, S. C., Smith-Jentsch, K. A., & Behson, S. J. 1998. Training team leaders to facilitate team learning and performance. In J. A. Cannon-Bowers & E. Salas (Eds.), *Making decisions under stress: Implications for individual and team training*. Washington, DC: APA.

Tao, L., Probert, D., & Phaal, R. 2010. Towards an integrated framework for managing the process of innovation. *R&D Management*, 40, 19–30.

Taylor, D. W., Berry, P. C., & Block, C. H. 1958. Does group participation when using brainstorming facilitate or inhibit creative thinking? *Administrative Science Quarterly*, 3, 23–47.

Todnem By, R. 2005. Organisational change management: A critical review. *Journal of Change Management*, 5, 369–380.

Torrance, E. P. 1980. Creativity and style of learning and thinking characteristics of adaptors and innovators. *Creative Child and Adult Quarterly*, 5, 80–85.

Tushman, M. L. 1977. Special boundary roles in the innovation process. *Administrative Science Quarterly*, 22, 587–605.

Vashdi, D. R., Bamberger, P. A., & Erez, M. 2013. Can surgical teams ever learn? The role of coordination, complexity, and transitivity in action team learning. *Academy of Management Journal*, 56, 945–971.

Vashdi, D. R., Bamberger, P. A., Erez, M., & Weiss-Meilik, A. 2007. Briefing-debriefing: Using a reflexive organizational learning model from the military to enhance the performance of surgical teams. *Human Resource Management*, 46, 115–142.

Verhaeghe, A., & Kfir, R. 2002. Managing innovation in a knowledge intensive technology organization (KITO). *R&D Management*, 32, 409–417.

Watts, L. L., Mulhearn, T. J., & Todd, E. M. 2016. Leader idea evaluation and follower creativity: Challenges, constraints, and capabilities. In M. D. Mumford & M. D. Mumford (Eds.), *Handbook of research on creativity and leadership*. Cheltenham, UK: Edward Elgar.

Zacher, H., & Rosing, K. 2015. Ambidextrous leadership and team innovation. *Leadership and Organization Development Journal*, 36, 54–68.

Zacher, H., Robinson, A., & Rosing, K. 2016. Ambidextrous leadership and employees' self-reported innovative performance: The role of exploration and exploitation behaviors. *The Journal of Creative Behavior*, 50, 24–46.

Zhang, X., & Bartol, K. M. 2010. Linking empowering leadership and employee creativity: The influence of psychological empowerment, intrinsic motivation, and creative process engagement. *Academy of Management Journal*, 53, 107–128.

Zhang, Y., Waldman, D. A., Han, Y. L., & Li, X. B. 2015. Paradoxical leader behaviors in people management: Antecedents and consequences. *Academy of Management Journal*, 58, 538–566.

10
FIRM STRATEGY FOR INNOVATION AND CREATIVITY

Danielle D. Dunne and Kimberly S. Jaussi

Innovation is one important way that firms adapt to changing environments, become and remain competitive, and outperform their competitors. Due in part to its practical importance, research on innovation has been a central theme for organizational strategy and theory scholars for decades. This focus has produced a large body of academic research on innovation and related areas such as knowledge creation and learning. However, in spite of its importance and the significant amount of attention paid to innovation, how to accomplish innovation in today's complex work environments remains elusive to many practitioners and scholars (Dougherty, 2018; Leonard-Barton, 1995). While innovation is central to almost all firms' ability to survive and thus intricately linked to firms' strategy, the misalignment of strategy, structure, and culture for innovation and its associated and necessary activities result in less than optimal innovation processes and outcomes. As the competitive environment across all industries becomes increasingly complex and dynamic (Dunne & Dougherty, 2016), organizations will be faced with needing new innovative capabilities and business models. The typical approach for innovation of building on fundamental technologies that has worked for decades – such as DuPont building numerous innovations around polymer chain technology – will no longer suffice as cross-industry fusions will become the norm that can address the complexity and merging of markets (Chesbrough, 2012; Dougherty & Dunne, 2011). Cross-industry fusion is needed, in part, because many fruitful areas of innovation within traditional industry boundaries have already been developed (Dunne & Dougherty, 2012) and new avenues for ideas, elaboration, and bringing products to market are necessary. Tomorrow's innovations will increasingly span traditional industry boundaries and involve entirely new ways of thinking about products, processes, and business models.

In an effort to address these issues, this chapter explores the interrelationship between firm innovation and firm strategy. We theorize how expertise is a common component of both, and we highlight differences as well. We then consider how three key innovation activities (searching for avenues to leverage expertise through abductive reasoning, connecting across multiple entities to deepen and complement expertise, and adapting to help expertise meet existing or emerging markets) serve as core capabilities for the firm to build on in formulating and executing its strategy. Then, we focus on how strategy, structure, and culture support these activities and align for innovation and overall organizational strategy. Finally, we offer suggestions for future research and practice. In doing so, our goal is to clearly outline how and why firms should integrate a firm-level innovation strategy into their overall strategy, structure, and culture – something that organizations typically struggle with doing in a comprehensive way.

Definitions and Strategy Foundations

In efforts to remain competitive in an increasingly complex and rapidly changing environment, firms must innovate. How they do that varies from industry to industry and firm to firm, but the integral role of developing and using new ideas remains central to performance in most environments. Innovation is defined as the commercialization of something new, often in the form of a product, process, business model, or service (Rothaermel, 2019; Schilling, 2016). The process of innovation has been studied extensively and is typically described as involving invention, development, and implementation (Garud, Tuertscher, & Van de Ven, 2013). Innovation is a collective process and involves the use of organization-wide resources and capabilities. Most innovative work in organizations relies heavily on the use of teams, often multifunctional teams. As innovative work becomes more complex, many teams must work together across organizations (Glynn, Kazanjian, & Drazin, 2010). For example, Glynn and colleagues (2010) explored how team member identification and interteam interdependence affected an individual's propensity to innovate in the setting of a large, diversified manufacturing firm developing a technologically intense new product for the world market. While many tools and processes have been developed to manage the innovation process, people in organizations still struggle to integrate knowledge and coordinate across organizations in ways that are required for the development of continuous streams of innovation. Many firms struggle to make these capabilities a regular part of their organizational strategy. This chapter aims to consider firm innovation strategy and the structures and culture that align with it, considering it against the backdrop of the organization's strategy overall. In order to do so, we first turn to a discussion of the basics of traditional firm strategy and strategic decision-making.

Basics of Strategy

Traditional strategy views suggest that there are only two or three business-level strategies that firms can pursue: cost leadership, differentiation, and a combination of cost leadership and differentiation (Porter, 1980; Rothaermel, 2019). Cost-leadership strategies emphasize the need for process innovation. Organizations such as Walmart have built their cost leadership advantages by developing process innovations that leverage information technology. Differentiation strategies emphasize the need for uniqueness and/or high-quality products or services, often emphasizing the need for product innovation. Organizations using differentiation strategies may put more resources into new product development and marketing. The combination of cost leadership and differentiation strategies requires what has been referred to as "value innovation," or something that simultaneously addresses the demand of lower cost and higher quality (Kim & Mauborgne, 2005; Rothaermel, 2019). The typical example of a company using this combined strategy is Toyota in the car manufacturing process, in which innovation enabled them to produce higher-quality cars at a lower cost. Although innovation may not be discussed at length in basic considerations of strategy, many firms rely on new product or process development to implement these basic strategies.

Resources and Capabilities

A firm's strategy must be supported by resources and capabilities that are aligned with its focus on cost leadership, differentiation, or a combination of the two business-level strategies. A popular view of the firm in the field of strategy is that the firm is a collection of resources and capabilities (sometimes referred to as competencies). Resources are tangible and intangible assets that firms draw on, and capabilities are the organizational or managerial skills to orchestrate and deploy those resources (Rothaermel, 2019).

Organizational and strategic management scholars have studied a variety of capabilities (e.g., manufacturing, marketing, etc.) in different contexts (e.g., Fortune & Mitchel, 2012; Mäkelä, Sumelius, Hoglund, & Ahlvik, 2012; Orlikowski, 2002; Parmigiani & Howard-Grenville, 2011). Many capabilities that researchers study are concerned with operational activities of firms, such as manufacturing or marketing (Fortune & Mitchell, 2012). Other types of capabilities involve more complex activities such as learning and new product development (Fortune & Mitchell, 2012; Orlikowski, 2002). Dynamic capabilities have been examined as a particularly useful way to explore innovation in organizations because they emphasize knowledge creation and learning that are integral to innovation (Dougherty, Barnard, & Dunne,

2005). Innovation is often characterized as a capability that is integral to firm performance.

Innovation and Capabilities

More specifically, scholarship in the area of innovation has focused on the capability to innovate (Dougherty, 2017) or to be continuously innovative. In order for innovative work to contribute to firm performance, the organization must have the capabilities to support the development (manufacturing, marketing, etc.) of the innovation (Danneels, 2002; Dougherty, 1992; Dougherty 2017). Further, those capabilities must either fit or potentially fit into the firm's collection of resources and other capabilities (Danneels, 2002; Dougherty, 1992; Dougherty, 2017). New products, processes, and services must be developed in and supported by existing or new firm structures and must simultaneously meet market demands or needs. For example, new product innovation must be linked to market or customer needs and to production or manufacturing (Dougherty, 1992). Market knowledge is focused on understanding customer needs (e.g., how the product might be used), market size, and how customer needs might change (Dougherty, 1992). Further, new product innovation must be linked to the firm's capabilities available to develop and produce the product (e.g., manufacturing). Importantly, Rothaermel and Hess (2007) explain that "the antecedents to innovation capabilities clearly lie *across* different levels of analysis" (p. 916). The capabilities that support innovative activities are an integral element of how firms compete and must be consistently integrated into overall firm strategy.

However, firms will not utilize capabilities that support innovative activities unless those making the strategic decisions for the organization identify the need for those to be utilized and make them strategic priorities. As Eggers and Kaplan (2013) explain, "the mere possession of capabilities does not affect performance – outcomes are contingent on what managers decide to do with their organizations' capabilities" (p. 300). Therefore, we next address how strategic decision-making occurs in organizations and how that decision-making process results in top management teams pursuing either an exploration or an exploitation strategy.

Strategic Decision-Making

In the strategy literature, scholars consider how the decisions about which type of strategy the firm should pursue occur at the "upper-echelon" level of the organization, or the top management team. Garg and Eisenhardt (2017) "define strategy making as the process of setting the overall business direction of the firm (Eisenhardt & Bourgeois, 1988; Kaplan, 2008)" (p. 1830). Typically taking place in the "C"-level suites of the organization, the strategic decision-making of the firm focuses on which resources and core capabilities to leverage in the face of market conditions. Essentially, the strategic decision-making of these top management teams involves setting the organization's course given the organization's expertise and capabilities for building on that expertise.

Research looking at how strategic decisions are made by the upper echelon of organizations has discovered a number of influential factors in the process. For example, Garg and Eisenhardt (2017) examined how the relationship between venture chief executive officers (CEOs) and their boards affects the strategy-making process. Their study highlights that CEOs who are successful in the strategy-making process seek out expertise from their board members (focus on expertise-oriented dyadic interactions from their board members) and use group brainstorming outside of formal meetings (Garg & Eisenhardt, 2017). Kaplan (2008) develops a model of the strategy-making process as a framing contest bridging cognitive and political perspectives on the process. She uses ethnographic techniques to explore how often contested cognitive frames of managers shape strategic choices in a time of high uncertainty at a firm (Kaplan, 2008).

Smith and Tushman (2005) also examine cognitive frames, but they focus on how the strategic decision-making of top management teams must balance the tension between exploration and exploitation. They identify the top management team as a "point of integration" between exploration and exploration – two activities that are important for short- and long-term performance and develop a model for managing strategic contradictions (Smith & Tushman, 2005, p. 524). Studies in the area of organizational strategy and theory have largely focused on this two-pronged framework of exploration and exploitation (March, 1991). The concept of balancing these two activities has been central to much work on innovation and strategy.

Exploration and exploitation relate to and involve a perspective on innovation for the execution of the strategy. For example, exploration is characterized as distant search, or the search for new knowledge and ways to complement existing expertise in a more radical fashion. Exploitation, characterized by more local search, involves the use or refinement of existing knowledge and expertise for incremental innovation (Greve 2007; Katila & Ahuja 2002; March, 1991). Thus, when a top management team chooses either strategic decision, they are essentially choosing a requirement for one type of innovation over the other. For example, Andriopoulos and Lewis (2009) describe how the two relate to innovation, and citing Atuahene-Gima (2005), they explain:

> [E]xploitation hones and extends current knowledge, seeking greater efficiency and improvements to enable incremental innovation. Exploration, on the other hand, entrails the development of new knowledge experimenting to foster the variation and novelty need for more radial innovation. (p. 696)

However, it is often not an either/or strategic decision that must be made between exploration (and radical innovation) and exploitation (and incremental innovation). Rather, the tensions between exploration and exploitation are ones that can be felt, and even purposefully balanced and effectively managed. Organizations that manage this tension well are considered to be ambidextrous organizations (Andriopoulos & Lewis, 2009).

Andriopoulos and Lewis (2009) outline the different perspectives on how to balance these two strategies and in turn the related range of innovation-oriented activities or tension. In line with previous research, they describe this balancing as organizational ambidexterity. They note that balancing through dual structures (architectural ambidexterity) and through behavioral and social means of integrating exploitation and exploration (contextual ambidexterity) (Andriopoulos & Lewis, 2009) is necessary in order for firms to be most effective. However, balancing incremental and radical innovation trajectories has always been challenging for organizations. The architectural ambidexterity that results in dual structures – with one specifically being tasked for innovation – is well known and practiced in many organizations. Many organizations developed *skunkworks* programs in which more radical ideas were developed separately. Yet, other researchers (c.f. Gibson & Birkinshaw, 2004) have noted that these ideas are better leveraged when they are integrated through contextual ambidexterity and become key parts of the entire organization, its strategy, structure, and culture. Andriopoulos and Lewis (2009) theorize about virtuous cycles of ambidexterity and propose that three factors enable organizational ambidexterity: developing a multilevel approach, using integration and differentiation as complementary tactics, and leveraging learning synergies of exploitation and exploration. Their theory highlights that while exploitation and exploration and ambidexterity are a common focus of innovation research in general, there is still more research to be done in order to better understand how these things are enacted. We suggest that looking deeper into the firm's innovation strategy and specific activities that enable that strategy to be effective sheds new light on how exploitation, exploration, and ambidexterity help organizations innovate.

Having addressed organizational strategy, strategic decision-making, and how they relate to balancing the tensions of innovation in general, we now turn to a firm's innovation strategy and consider how it is similar but different from the firm's overall strategy. After considering those with respect to expertise, we then turn to three key innovation activities. Then we explore the structures and culture that are needed to support them.

Expertise, Firm Innovation, and Overall Strategy

A commonality between a firm's innovation strategy and the firm's overall strategy centers on the development of and leveraging of expertise. In order for innovation to occur and for a firm's overall strategy to be successful, firms must focus on leveraging the deep expertise of the firm. In traditional strategy, this will involve exploiting core competencies, or things the firm has deep expertise in. This can involve simply leveraging core competencies as part of geographic expansion, increasing the number of product lines, or diversifying into new markets. Expansion may rely on innovation in limited ways in terms of exploiting existing products in new geographic markets, which might involve incremental changes, or it may rely more heavily on the innovative core or fundamental technologies of the organization. For example, expertise within the firm may involve a specific knowledge base that can be harnessed as fundamental for further exploration and innovation.

Expertise also leads to one difference between a firm's innovation strategy and the firm's overall strategy. That difference involves the strategic decision-making process as it relates to innovation. While innovation may play an integral role in the success of a firm, typically innovation strategy is set by different players in the organization than is the overall firm strategy. Because of the need for innovation to be centered on existing expertise, scientists, being the core of the expert knowledge base from which to generate ideas related to the development of innovative capabilities, are often the key members of the organization setting the innovation strategy. Additional members of the innovation strategy formulation process may be individuals from marketing and sales, who can articulate market needs. They have senses from the environmental scanning they engage in as part of their functions. This bifurcation of strategic decision-making, whereby innovation is handled by a subgroup of the organization while the overall business strategy is addressed by the upper echelon of the organization, is potentially disastrous and often results in big challenges of bringing ideas to market in a seamless and timely way. As we continue to argue throughout this chapter, alignment among the innovation strategy-making process and the overall firm strategy-making process is vital to effective leveraging of the organizational expertise and capabilities for innovation and overall firm performance.

Having established the relationship, similarity, and difference between firm strategy and firm innovation strategy, we next turn to a discussion of how to facilitate innovation through the firm's structure and culture before introducing three specific activities that facilitate innovation and the execution of an innovation strategy. Before turning to that discussion, however, we would first like to note a clarification regarding the relationship between creativity in a firm and firm innovation. Strategy scholars suggest that the root of innovation is the generation of new ideas (Rothaermel, 2019; Schilling, 2016), and that generation of new ideas is creativity (Schilling, 2016). In innovation research, the role of creativity is often emphasized in the stage of idea generation but is not depicted as remaining solely there. Creativity is important through the entire innovation process as it may be integral not only to idea generation but also to the intricacies of producing and commercializing a product or process (Dougherty, 1992). Creativity plays a fundamental role in innovation, and this chapter focuses on exploring concepts that are important to both innovation and creativity.

Strategy, Structure, Culture, and Innovation Activities

At least since Alfred Chandler's (1962) exploration of the connection between organizational strategy and structure in the transformation of General Motors, these two concepts have been thought of as inseparable. In the context of innovative and creative work, a close link between strategy and structure is vital. This section focuses on three specific innovation facilitating activities: abductive searching to leverage expertise, building connections across multiple entities to deepen and complement expertise, and adaptation to help expertise meet existing or emerging markets. We provide a brief overview of the basics and definitions of structure and culture, then we explain the three activities. Finally, we provide specific examples of how structure and culture can support these three activities.

Organizational Structure

Organizational structure is vital to innovation and creativity. Innovation and creativity require many different activities (e.g., market sensing, idea sharing, and intensive teaming to note just a few). Innovation and creativity require teamwork, in particular, multifunctional teaming, in order to combine knowledge from all parts of the organization (manufacturing, marketing, research and development) that is necessary for innovative work such as new product development. In Burns and Stalker's (1961) traditional framing, more organic organizational structures enable these types of relationships. More organic structures emphasize flexibility, decentralization, and less hierarchy. The other end of the continuum away from organic structures is more mechanistic structures, characterized by centralization and more levels of management. More mechanistic structures can make innovative work challenging to accomplish. However, as noted in our discussion of exploration and exploitation, approaches that focus on structural separation such as different units may create problems with coordination and isolation (Andriopoulos & Lewis, 2009).

While the Chandler perspective on strategy and structure being inextricably intertwined holds for both firm-level strategy and firm innovation strategy as briefly discussed, the two diverge in terms of specific organizational structures to execute a firm-level innovation strategy. Specifically, structures that facilitate a firm-level innovation strategy allow and foster three important activities: abductive searching to leverage expertise, building connections across multiple entities to deepen and complement expertise, and adapting to help expertise meet existing or emerging markets. If these three activities are enabled by the structure, harnessing and further exploration and exploitation of the firm's expertise will be possible. We consider these three activities not only in light of the structures that support them but also in terms of the organizational cultural elements that are necessary for them to exist and flourish throughout the organization.

Organizational Culture

Organizational culture is generally thought of as a shared set of basic assumptions within an organization (Schein, 1992). Harrison and Corley (2011) offer a more detailed perspective and frame culture as follows:

> [T]raditional managerial views on organizational culture tend to favor it as an objective reality bound within organizations (Sewell, 2005), made up of consistent sets of attitudes and values and collections of shared meanings (Van Maanen & Barley, 1984), or patterns of shared basic assumptions (Schein, 1992) that signify structural stability and directly influence thinking and behavior within an organization (Ashkanasy, Wilderom, & Peterson, 2000; Trice & Beyer, 1984, 1993) (p. 392)

These shared sets of basic assumptions are very powerful in shaping behaviors and driving creativity and innovation. Organizational cultures can be strong, and felt by all in a similar fashion, or weak, with every member having a different understanding of what the norms and rituals are. Research suggests that a strong culture can substitute for formal rules and structures because it can guide behavior so strongly. In terms of creativity and innovation, this has also been shown. For example, research suggests that a strong organizational culture can facilitate creativity in employees and innovation.

As noted earlier, organizational strategy, firm innovation strategy, structures, and culture must all be in alignment with the activities that support innovation if optimal innovation and performance are to result. Therefore, next we consider the three organizational activities for innovation of searching, connecting, and adapting. Then we discuss specific examples of how structure and culture may facilitate the application of expertise that occurs within and as a result of these activities.

Activities that Facilitate Innovation

Searching for Avenues to Leverage Expertise through Abductive Reasoning

As organizations innovate, the process by which they search for applications and new combinations of their expertise are integral to creativity and innovation. From an organizational perspective, the process of innovation has been depicted as a problem-solving process (Dougherty & Hardy, 1996). For example, Katila and Ahuja (2002) explore "how firms *search*, or solve problems (Nelson & Winter, 1982), to create new products" (p. 1183; italics in original) as part of a firm's innovative capabilities.

Search can be challenging in the case of complex innovation and creativity process. However, the development of structures that support this type of activity are central to innovation and creativity, particularly in the cases of complex product innovation. Dunne and Dougherty (2016) explain that complexity presents significant challenges for innovations because it "involves searching for solutions to problems that are poorly defined" (p. 132). Dunne and Dougherty (2016) adopt Denrell, Fang, and Levinthal's (2004) metaphor of navigating in the labyrinth to explain how scientists deal with complex problems in which feedback is protracted, interdependencies among components are not anticipated, and the process is nonlinear and uncertain. They study scientists who are innovators and suggest that they use abductive reasoning, reasoning that "suggests something *may be*" as opposed to deductive reasoning that "that something *must* be" and inductive reasoning that shows "something *actually is* operative" (all italics in original) to navigate in this challenging context (Locke, Golden-Biddle, & Feldman, 2008, p. 907).

Dunne and Dougherty (2016) explain several characteristics of complex search landscapes in the context of biopharmaceuticals that create challenges for innovators. In these landscapes, there are high levels of uncertainty, there is a huge amount of noisy information that must be processed, and there are significant dangers of getting stuck in local optima (Afuah & Tucci, 2012; Nightingale, 1998). These challenges are in line with some of the challenges that Katila and Ahuja (2002) discuss, such as the idea that when exploring more distant solutions innovators are less familiar with consequences of these solutions. Further, in complex problem-solving, it may not be possible to break the problem or solution down into manageable parts. Dunne and Dougherty (2016) explore abductive reasoning as a potential way to address these challenges of complexity.

Dunne and Dougherty (2016) allude to the importance of expertise as they explain Denrell et al.'s (2004) suggestion that mental models of the problem help to constrain the search process. Moreover, Weick (2005) also implies the importance of expertise in a firm's innovation strategy and suggests that in formulating a hypothesis, innovators "starts with a clue and then discovers or invents a world in which that clue is meaningful" (p. 433). Weick's "clues" are only recognizable once expertise exists; without the expertise as a foundation, a "clue" will not be recognizable as a "clue," and it will be missed.

Connecting across Multiple Entities to Deepen and Complement Expertise

By connecting across boundaries, we mean people connecting formally and informally within and across organizations. These connections are central to the innovation process because innovation requires different types of basic science expertise as well as knowledge about customer needs. Within an organization, this might mean that early stage researchers need to connect with people in the organization who have a better understanding of customer needs. Across organizations, this might mean alliances that bring in important scientific knowledge or important distribution channels for products. The emphasis on connections has traditionally been an important emphasis in the development of innovation. For example, close relationships (often oriented around a project or publication) between scientists within an organization and at universities have been fruitful for innovation processes in many industries.

The communities of practice literature add to our understanding of how people make connections across organizations to deepen and complement expertise. Communities of practice bring people together on the basis of their participation in similar work activities – people who are potentially solving similar problems (Brown & Duguid, 1991; Lave & Wenger, 1991). Brown and Duguid (1991) focus on working, learning, and innovating as they discuss communities of practice. Central to their discussion is the idea that knowledge is intricately intertwined with practice (Brown & Duguid, 1991; Lave & Wenger, 1991). As they explain, drawing on Lave and Wenger's (1990) concept of legitimate peripheral participation:

> Workplace learning is best understood, then, in terms of communities being formed or joined and personal identities being changed. The central issue in learning is *becoming* a practitioner not learning *about* practice. (Brown & Duguid, 1991, p. 48)

Brown and Duguid (1991) explain the benefits of communities of practice as including the potential to be more capable of change than large organizations. Embracing communities of practice within organizations can be particularly useful in large organizations (Brown & Duguid, 1991). As they explain:

> Large, *atypical*, enacting organizations have the potential to be highly innovative and adaptive. Within an organization perceived as a collective of communities, not simply of individuals, in which enacting experiments are legitimate, separate community perspectives can be amplified by interchanges among communities. Out of this friction of competing ideas can come the sort of improvisational sparks necessary for igniting organizational innovation. Thus large organizations, *reflectively structured*, are perhaps particularly well positioned to be highly innovative and deal with discontinuities. (Brown & Duguid, 1991, p. 54)

Communities of practice are about learning, specifically emergent learning that may deepen and complement expertise. In their recent article, Pyrko, Dorfler, and Eden (2017) discuss the emergent nature of communities of practice: they "refer to groups of people who genuinely care about the same real-life problem or hot topics, and who on that basis interact regularly to learn together and from each other (Wenger et al., 2002)" (p. 390). A "thinking together" process is necessary for a community of practice to be successful, which "calls for a view of knowledge sharing where knowledge is not transferred in a literal sense like an object, but it is re-created by knowers during those acts of knowledge (Bechky, 2003; Velencei et al., 2009; Von Krogh, 2011)" (Pyrko et al., 2017, p. 395). This perspective enables deep connections between people and their expertise.

Boundary objects, such as sketches or drawings that show how a product might come together, can be integral to working within and across organizations for new product innovation. For example, Bechky (2003) and Carlile (2002) emphasize the role of boundary objects in the work within organizations' boundaries. Carlile's (2004) study explains that three progressively complex processes of transfer, translation, and transformation may be used to manage knowledge at three different types of knowledge boundaries (syntactic, semantic, and pragmatic). As this work suggests, working within and across boundaries is not necessarily a straightforward process and may involve significant knowledge transformation to support innovation and creativity.

Adapting to Help Expertise Meet Existing or Emerging Markets

Adapting is closely related to the concept of learning but emphasizes the need for flexibility. More specifically, by adapting, we mean learning that involves change for organizations and the ability to let go of previous ways of thinking and doing. As the strategic environment is constantly changing, the source of new market needs and the flow of new information that could provide clues for addressing those needs also changes rapidly. Therefore, organizations must facilitate the activity of adapting to help expertise meet these needs. This is particularly important because change is often assumed to be part of innovation, but yet many organizations emphasize the importance of innovation without paying enough attention to the activity of adapting.

Organizational routines are often fundamental building blocks for the activities that facilitate innovation. The activity of adapting is no different, in that it too can benefit from routines. At first glance, routines may seem like things that would enforce inertia and promote the status quo. Some research frames routines as the antithesis of innovation and creativity, in part because routines do not enable adaptability. Sonenshein (2016) begins his paper on routines and creativity by noting that routines and creativity are often seen as contradictory, citing work by Ford and Gioia (2000) and Amabile and Conti (1999), among others. This body of work suggests that because routines create predictability, they stifle creativity and solidify the status quo. Put simply, routines are believed by many to control and maintain behaviors and processes, not to bring about change. And, routines that are centered on an organization's expertise will likely yield efficiency, economies of scale, and cost effectiveness – not necessarily innovation.

However, other scholars push back on the assumption that routines stifle creativity and innovation. Sonenshein (2016) then expands on the "hinted at" idea that routine dynamics might lead to creative outcomes. He describes how the very routine of pushing back on assumptions and patterns underlying existing routines can result in adaptation and creative outcomes. Sonenshein (2016) explains:

> According to a routine dynamics approach, routines necessarily involve creativity because actors regularly exercise agency in moving between revising abstract patterns of routines and devising ways to engage in situationally relevant performances of routines (Feldman & Pentland, 2003). (p. 739)

In the routine dynamic approach, routines are innovative and creative and may play a central role in these processes. While the purpose of the routine may be the same, the way in which the routine is enacted can be different. Additionally, organizations can have routines that prompt and invite information that requires adaptability. Similarly, learning organizations are known for having routines that help them learn effectively. Thus, these scholars and this theoretical approach help shed light on how routines can facilitate, rather than stifle, adaptation, which will help promote creativity and innovation.

Structures: Specific Examples

Structures that Support Searching, Connecting, and Adapting

Structures that support these three activities, such as organic structures, are important as a potential way to address the challenges of complexity in the environment, particularly in the complex innovation contexts. As noted in the introduction of this chapter, complexity may be a common characteristic of many or most innovative work in the future.

Dunne and Dougherty (2016) provide insight regarding the kinds of structures and systems that might facilitate these activities for creativity and innovation. They describe three social mechanisms and the structures that support them to enable innovators to use abductive reasoning in the complex system of drug discovery. First, as noted earlier, innovators use clues to imagine a configuration of interactions. The configuration of interactions serves as an intermediary model or abductive hypothesis that innovators use to move the process forward in the face of the huge amount of uncertainty that is inherent in the drug discovery process (Denrell et al., 2004; Dunne & Dougherty, 2016). Structures that support the processes, such as "using clues to imagine" the configuration of interactions, will allow for the examination of alternatives and subsequent building on intermediary models. These structures would first recognize the important role of clues in the process and highlight the use of abductive reasoning. For example, encouraging scientists to use the emergent process and providing them with tools to search for and test out their ideas with their colleagues at their firm and through potential external collaborations. This may help them to imagine important connections that could lead to the building of useful intermediary models. We might even imagine a "think room" where scientists are pushed to articulate ideas and build on each other's thoughts. Even if specific projects did not progress through this type of activity (though they might), the value of doing it would be in signaling the importance of the searching for clues process throughout the organization. This type of structure would also support connecting among scientists as it emphasizes scientists interacting together. Further, the focus on ideas would help scientists to become comfortable with small changes or adjustments to their ways of thinking that could become the foundation for adapting on a daily basis.

Organizational investment in technological structures also can aid and enable innovators as they reframe their ideas in efforts to leverage their expertise for innovation. For example, the second mechanism for abductive reasoning is elaborating and narrowing around the "configuration of interactions," which enables scientists to build on their intermediary models. As scientists enact this mechanism, they anchor on one part of their configuration and then reach out to other scientists to explore more information. This mechanism enables scientists to narrow in on the details without closing off potentially important future directions. The more an organization can enable its scientists to reach out in a low-risk way, the more they will be able to elaborate and narrow in on ideas without closing off potential future avenues for search.

Participating in the activities of searching, connecting, and adapting requires scientists to work with people across the organization. According to Dunne and Dougherty (2016), as scientists are iteratively integrating, they cross disciplinary boundaries to reframe the configuration. This reframing of the configuration allows for the accumulation of further insights. Structures that support this crossing of disciplinary boundaries inside the organization will make it easy for scientists to see and interact with others from different disciplines. For example, formal mechanisms for daily connection with other scientists, such as open lab space design configurations where cross-functional interactions can occur, or a company cafeteria with seating that fosters interactions among scientists from different specialties, will be among the type of structural elements that facilitate configurations of interactions.

Organizational structures that enable internal boundary crossing, such as things that allow the crossing of silos, have been shown to be integral to innovation and creativity because they support the activities of searching, connecting, and adapting. Bechky (2003) looks at knowledge sharing across internal organizational boundaries (between engineers, technicians, and assemblers). Bechky's work emphasizes that knowledge needs to be transformed as people work across different internal communities. She explains that when communication issues come up, members should "provide solutions that invoke the differences in the work contexts and create common ground between the communities" (Bechky, 2003, p. 314). This enables them to transform what they know and move the process forward (Bechky, 2003). Bechky (2003) studies this at a high-tech manufacturing firm where handoffs of a project between different parts of the organization provided an opportunity for transformation. In one example, she notes how an engineer and assembler worked together by using a physical demonstration of the problem (Bechky, 2003).

Further, formal alliances with external firms support searching, connecting, and adapting. Due to the increasing complexity and distributed nature of the knowledge that is necessary for innovation, interorganizational collaborations are integral for the development of innovation (Powell Koput & Smith-Doerr, 1996). Research suggests that firms that participate in alliance networks grow faster and are more innovative than other firms in their industries (Ahuja, 2000; Powell, et al., 1996; Shan, Walker, & Kogut, 1994).

A linked body of research also looks at networks that are external to the organization and the effects of star scientists. Murray (2004) explores the importance of a firm's embeddedness in a scientific network. Zucker, Darby, and Brewster (1998) link performance of entrepreneurial firms to relationships with star scientists. However, intraorganizational networks are also important for innovation and creativity. Rothaermel and Hess (2007) take a multilevel approach and find that it is not only star scientists but also the other scientists at the firm that matter for innovative outcomes, suggesting that star scientists may only be valuable when combined with teams of other scientists.

Further, it is critical for an organization to have a structure that allows for the emergent nature, rather than a forced nature. According to Pyrko and colleagues (2017), communities of practice cannot be set up, for example, as formal teams. They come together as people think together. Further, Pyrko and colleagues (2017, p. 392) conceptualize "thinking together" – through "lived practice."

Structures that support external scanning and experimentation will also enable searching, connecting, and adapting. These might include structures that support external scanning and working with customers. If innovators are better able to know what is happening outside the organization, and to sense trends, then they will be better able to adapt. Organic structures, noted earlier, may support this type of flexibility. Further, by using cross-functional teams to enable information sharing across the organization in combination with external scanning, they will be better able to proactively adapt.

Culture: Specific Examples

Types of Cultures that Support Searching, Connecting, and Adapting

Strong cultures that are committed to emphasizing change and emergence are likely to support these three activities. For example, cultures that value time for experimentation would support this type of culture (Randel & Jaussi, 2019). Building this type of culture might involve an emphasis on the imperative to constantly look for reasons to change; this would contrast with strong cultures that seem to emphasize constantly looking for reasons to stay the same. These cultures might commonly ask questions such as: "What are we doing differently?" and "What can we do differently?" They then may push their people to come up with implementable answers to these questions. They could focus on the importance of small wins and quick prototyping to support these ideas.

A culture that recognizes and enables the emergence inherent in the activities of searching, connecting, and adapting is vital to supporting creativity and innovation in organizations. By emergence, we mean that as people participate in these activities the next steps unfold. For organizations, this means that these innovators may not benefit from deadlines imposed by other parts of the organization, especially if the deadlines do not account for the nature of the work. While scientists are often criticized for never wanting to give up on a project or not working quickly enough, they need the resources to let the search process unfold. This means that they need useful goalposts and progress markers that connect to the quality of the work. A culture that recognizes that in order to be successful at innovation the entire process must be conceived as a whole. Many organizations separate product innovation into different parts, but they need to conceptualize not only their organization, but also the innovation process, as a *whole* to see what the clues might indicate.

At some organizations, there are limitations on what scientists can do and discuss outside of the organization, but these limitations can stunt the process of abductive reasoning. Encouraging more discussions and connections inside and outside of organizations (described in greater detail later) based on science and the abductive reasoning process might help create a culture where abductive reasoning is recognized and valued. Additionally, developing a culture where the abductive reasoning process and the expertise that lies behind it are valued is integral to supporting this process. This means that decisions about which projects to resource or fund and which to bring to the next step of the innovation process must be made with attention paid to science. Obviously, market and commercialization considerations need to be made, but keeping scientific expertise central to the process will motivate scientists to value their own expertise that drives this process.

A culture that emphasizes open innovation is also important in supporting these innovation activities. Chesbrough and Appleyard (2007) present the idea of open innovation and strategy, inspired by open source software and other "open" concepts that have become commonplace in the past decade. Recently, scholars have revisited and reemphasized the importance of open innovation for scholarship, practice, and policy development (Bogers, Chesbrough, & Moedas, 2018). A practice-oriented article suggests that open innovation is important even in manufacturing processes. Companies can move to a more open culture by opening up internally (sharing success stories on inside and across facilities), focusing on the pace of process innovation, using technology/ leveraging data systems, focusing on bringing in external ideas, looking outside the organization, and using unconventional sources of knowledge (von Krogh, Netland, & Worter, 2018).

Strong cultures that emphasize how innovators and other people working throughout the organization can make decisions based on their expertise may facilitate this type of culture. This may happen through the use of the routines noted earlier. In particular, some scholars have emphasized the role that routines play in developing an adaptive culture. They suggest that routines and culture or organizational schemata are co-constituted – developed together (Rerup & Feldman, 2011). Connections between people through understandings of routines in context enable them to adapt as they work.

As we discussed earlier, organizational structures and cultures that facilitate the application of firm expertise through various activities will help an organization execute its innovation strategy. However, the old saying "culture eats structure and strategy for breakfast" rings true with respect to innovation. Without the organizational culture in alignment with the innovation strategy and the structures to support it and build on the firm's expertise, innovation and creativity will suffer and fail.

Strategies, Structure, and Culture for Innovation Failure

Previously, we theorized at length a wide range of things that will help organizations succeed in their innovation strategy. However, we would be remiss if we only focused on those things that help innovation and did not mention known pitfalls for innovation. While a detailed discussion of these things is beyond the scope of this chapter, we would like to briefly discuss three things. First, if organizational strategy is not aligned with innovative capabilities, it is a recipe for disaster. An organization pursuing a strategy of being a second mover, for example, will be consistently in a hurry to go to market a short period after the first mover has hit and imitate rather than innovate. If the innovation strategy has built into it the processes for abductive search, for example, the two strategies and the decision-makers associated with them will have misaligned temporal perspectives. Structurally, a number of organizations often create separate "silos" that handle the exploitation or production and efficiency on one hand, with a different one that focuses on the exploration, or innovation. However, such bifurcation results in turf wars, misunderstandings, and frustrations. It also makes it difficult to provide field-based feedback on firm cross-functional teams. Finally, an organizational culture that fosters interoffice politics, disrespect, a lack of diversity and homogenous thinking, and a fear of failure, will also make the perfect storm for innovation to fail.

Discussion and Future Research Agenda

As we described previously, a firm's strategy and a firm's innovation strategy have similarities and differences in the way in which they are conceptualized by scholars as well as operationalized in practice. However, both involve leveraging expertise and ensuring that the structures and culture are in alignment for the most effective execution of that strategy. We described in detail three activities or processes that a firm's innovation strategy should include, and outlined the structural and cultural elements necessary to support and encourage those.

The literature on firm innovation strategy is quite diffuse, with some looking specifically at particular parts of the process, the overall processes as a whole, and how it works in different industries. Our hope is that through considering the three processes of searching, connecting, and adapting in conjunction with organizational structure and culture, future research can focus on providing connections across the literature that allow for a more interlocking picture of how firm innovation strategy is formulated. We still know very little about things such as how do firms select which fundamentals and expertise to build on? When should firms drop creative products because they are inconsistent with firm fundamentals? The case of Xerox and graphical interfaces is a salient example of this question in action. The first graphical interfaces, now ubiquitously used in computers and mobile devices, were created by Xerox's Palo Alto Research Center (PARC) team (Chesbrough, 2006) for their Alto, and then their Star, computers. However, they soon sold the Alto to Apple in exchange for stock options. After trying to bring the Star to market too late to capture any market share, they abandoned the computer market space. The Xerox example begs the question of whether companies should have innovation strategies that stray from their fundamental technologies, as the rest of the structure and culture are unlikely to be able to understand and harness the innovations that are sparked in a separate, siloed innovation "skunkworks" organization if it is not integrated and aligned with the entire organization. Said differently, how should ideas be appraised and invested in given a fundamentals perspective that builds on core expertise?

The issues outlined here suggest important opportunities for scholars who are able to work across different research streams. While this may be a semantic question of translation (Carlile, 2004), it may also be a more complex question of knowledge transformation (Bechky, 2003; Carlile, 2004). As many scholars have suggested, objects and images have the potential to play a central role in this process (Bechky, 2003; Carlile, 2002, 2004). In our own community of practice, as scholars working to bridge these gaps, we need to form our own community of practice focused on first simply bridging definitions.

Additionally, this work calls for advances in how we combine our research methods. For example, new combinations of qualitative methods, computational modeling, and traditional quantitative methods could overcome the challenge of generalizability that many practice studies face. The combinations may also be able to take into account the effect of time in new ways in studies of innovation and creativity. This would enable a discussion across research streams leveraging new combinations of methods.

Our work set out to address how a firm's strategy relates to a firm's innovation strategy, and how a firm may best execute its innovation strategy. In doing so, we framed the discussion around the fundamental building block of firm expertise. Expertise has long been hailed as a core component of creativity and innovation, and here we show how it is also importantly aligned with innovation strategy.

References

Afuah, A., & Tucci, C. (2012). Crowdsourcing as a solution to distant search. *Academy of Management Review*, 37, 355–375.

Ahuja, G. (2000). Collaboration networks, structural holes, and innovation: A longitudinal study. *Administrative Science Quarterly*, 45, 425–456.

Amabile, T. M., & Conti, R. (1999). Changes in the work environment for creativity during downsizing. *Academy of Management Journal*, 42, 630–640.

Andriopoulous C., & Lewis, M. W. (2009). Exploitation-exploration tensions and organizational ambidexterity: Managing paradoxes of innovation. *Organization Science*, 20, 696–717.

Ashkanasy, N. M., Wilderom, C. P. M., & Peterson, M. F. (Eds.). (2000). *Handbook of organizational culture and climate*. Thousand Oaks, CA: Sage.

Atuahene-Gima, K. (2005). Resolving the capability-rigidity paradox in new product innovation. *Journal of Marketing*, 69, 61–83.

Bechky, B. (2003). Sharing meaning across organizational communities: The transformation of understanding on a production floor. *Organization Science*, 14, 312–330.

Bogers, M., Chesbrough, H., & Moedas, C. (2018). Open innovation: Research, practices, and policies. *California Management Review*, 60, 5–16.

Brown, J. S., & Duguid, P. (1991). Organizational learning and communities-of-practice: Toward a unified view of working, learning and innovation. *Organization Science*, 2, 40–57.

Burns, T., & Stalker, G. M. (1961). *The Management of Innovation*. New York: Oxford University Press.

Carlile, P. R. (2002). A pragmatic view of knowledge and boundaries: Boundary objects in new product development. *Organization Science*, 13, 442–455.

Carlile, P. R. (2004). Transferring, translating, and transforming: An integrative framework for managing knowledge across boundaries. *Organization Science*, 15, 555–568.

Chandler, A. (1962). *Strategy and structure*. Cambridge, MA: MIT Press.

Chesbrough, H. W. (2006). *Open innovation. The new imperative for creating and profiting from technology*. Boston, MA: Harvard Business Press.

Chesbrough, H. W. (2012). Open innovation. Where we've been and where we're going. *Research-Technology Management*, 55, 20–27.

Chesbrough, H. W., & Appleyard, M. M. (2007). Open innovation and strategy. *California Management Review*, 50, 57–76.

Danneels, E. (2002). The dynamics of product innovation and firm competences. *Strategic Management Journal*, 23, 1095–1121.

Denrell, J., Fang, C., & Levinthal, D. (2004). From t-mazes to labyrinths: Learning from model-based feedback. *Management Science*, 50, 1366–1378.

Dougherty, D., & Dunne, D. D. (2011). Ecologies of complex innovation. *Organization Science*, 22, 1214–1223.

Dougherty, D. (1992). A practice-centered model of organizational renewal through product innovation. *Strategic Management Journal*, 13, 77–92.

Dougherty, D. (2017). Innovation in the practice perspective. In H. Bathelt, P. Cohendet, S. Henn, & L. Simon (Eds.), *The Elgar companion to innovation and knowledge creation* (pp. 138–151). Cheltenham, UK: Edward Elgar Publishing.

Dougherty, D. (2018). Managers fail to innovate and academics fail to explain how. *Management and Organizational Review*, 14, 229–239.

Dougherty, D., & Hardy, C. (1996). Sustained product innovation in large, mature organizations: Overcoming innovation-to-organization problems. *Academy of Management Journal*, 39, 1120–1153.

Dougherty, D., Barnard, H., & Dunne, D. (2005). The rules and resources that generate the dynamic capability for sustained product innovation. In K. Elsbach (Ed.), *Qualitative organizational research* (pp. 37–74). Greenwich, CT: Information Age Publishing.

Dunne, D. D., & Dougherty, D. (2016). Abductive reasoning: How innovators navigate in the labyrinth of complex product innovation. *Organization Studies*, 37, 131–159.

Dunne, D. D., & Dougherty, D. (2012). Organizing for change, innovation, and creativity. In M. Mumford (Ed.), *Handbook of organizational creativity* (pp. 569–583). New York, NY: Elsevier.

Eggers, J. P., & Kaplan, S. (2013). Cognition and capabilities: A multi-level perspective. *The Academy of Management Annals*, 7, 295–340.

Eisenhardt, K. M., & Bourgeios, L. J. (1988). Politics of strategic decision making in high-velocity environments: Toward a midrange theory. *Academy of Management Journal*, 31, 737–770.

Feldman, M. S., & Pentland, B. T. (2003). Reconceptualizing organizational routines as a source of flexibility and change. *Administrative Science Quarterly*, 481, 94–118.

Ford, C. M., & Gioia, D. A. (2000). Factors influencing creativity in the domain of managerial decision making. *Journal of Management*, 26, 705–732.

Fortune, A., & Mitchell, W. (2012). Unpacking firm exit at the firm and industry levels: The adaptation and selection of firm capabilities. *Strategic Management Journal*, 33, 794–819.

Garg, S., & Eisenhardt, K. M. (2017). Unpacking the CEO-board relationship: How strategy making happens in entrepreneurial firms. *Academy of Management Journal*, 60, 1828–1858.

Garud, R., Tuertscher, P., & Van de Ven, A. H. (2013). Perspectives on innovation processes. *The Academy of Management Annals*, 7, 775–819.

Gibson, C. B., & Birkinshaw, J. (2004). The antecedents, consequences, and mediating role of organizational ambidexterity. *Academy of Management Journal*, 47, 209–226.

Glynn, M. A., Kazanjian, R., & Drazin, R. (2010). Fostering innovation in complex product development settings: The role of team member identity and interteam interdependence. *Journal of Product Innovation Management*, 27, 1082–1095.

Greve, H. (2007). Exploration and exploitation in product innovation. *Industrial and Corporate Change*, 16, 945–975.

Harrison, S. H., & Corley, K. G. (2011). Clean climbing, carabiners, and cultural cultivation: Developing an open-systems perspective of culture. *Organization Science*, 22, 391–412.

Kaplan, S. (2008). Framing contests: Strategy making under uncertainty. *Organization Science*, 19, 729–752.

Katila, R., & Ahuja, G. (2002). Something old, something new: A longitudinal study of search behavior and new product introduction. *Academy of Management Journal*, 45, 1183–1194.

Kim, C. W., & Mauborgne, R.. (2005). *Blue ocean strategy: How to create uncontested market space and make competition irrelevant*. Boston, MA: Harvard Business School Publishing.

Lave, J., & Wenger, E. (1991). *Situated learning: Legitimate peripheral participation*. Beverly Hills, CA: Sage.

Leonard-Barton, D. (1995). *Well-springs of knowledge: Building and sustain the sources of innovation*. Boston, MA: Harvard Business School Press.

Locke, K., Golden-Biddle, K., & Feldman, M. (2008). Making doubt generative: Rethinking the role of doubt in the research Process. *Organization Science*, 19, 907–918.

March, J. G. (1991). Exploration and exploitation in organizational learning. *Organization Science*, 2, 71–87.

Mäkelä, K., Sumelius, J., Höglund, M., & Ahlvik, C. (2012). Determinants of strategic HR capabilities in MNC subsidiaries. *Journal of Management Studies*, 49, 1459–1483.

Murray, F. (2004). The role of academic inventors in entrepreneurial firms: Sharing the laboratory life. *Research Policy*, 33, 643–659.

Nelson, R. R., & Winter, S. (1982). *An evolutionary theory of economic change*. Cambridge, MA: Belknap Press/Harvard University Press.

Nightingale, P. (1998). A cognitive theory of innovation. *Research Policy*, 27, 689–709.

Orlikowski, W. J. (2002). Knowing in practice: Enacting a collective capability in distributed organizing. *Organization Science*, 13, 249–273.

Parmigiani, J. A., & Howard-Grenville, J. (2011). Routines revisited: Exploring the capabilities and practice perspectives. *The Academy of Management Annals*, 5, 413–453.

Porter, M. E. (1980). *Competitive strategy: Techniques for analyzing industries and competitors.* New York, NY: Free Press.

Powell, W. W., Koput, K. W., & Smith-Doerr, L. (1996). Interorganizational collaboration and the locus of innovation: Networks of learning in biotechnology. *Administrative Science Quarterly*, 41, 116–145.

Pyrko, I., Dorfler, V., & Eden, C. (2017). Thinking together: What makes communities of practice work. *Human Relations*, 70, 389–409.

Randel, A. E., & Jaussi, K.S. (2019). Giving rise to creative leadership: Contextual enablers and redundancies. *Group and Organization Management*, 44, 288–319.

Rerup, C., & Feldman, M. S. (2011). Routines as a source of change in organizational schemata: The role of trial-and-error learning. *Academy of Management Journal*, 54, 577–610.

Rothaermel, F. T. (2019). *Strategic management concepts* (4th ed.). New York, NY: McGraw-Hill Education.

Rothaermel, F. T., & Hess, A. H. (2007). Building dynamic capabilities: Innovation driven by individual-, firm-, and network-level effects, *Organizational Science*, 18, 898–921.

Schein, E. H. (1992). *Organizational culture and leadership* (2nd ed.). San Francisco, CA: Jossey-Bass.

Schilling, M. (2016). *Strategic management of technological innovation* (5th ed.). New York, NY: McGraw-Hill Education.

Sewell, W. H. (2005). The concept(s) of culture. In G. M. Spiegel (Ed.), *Practicing history: New directions in historical writing after the linguistic turn* (pp. 76–95). New York, NY: Routledge.

Shan, W., Walker, G., & Kogut, B. (1994). Interfirm cooperation and startup innovation in the biotechnology industry. *Strategic Management Journal*, 5, 387–394.

Kogut, B., Walker, G., Shan, W., & Kim, D. J. (1994). Platform technologies and national industrial networks. In J. Hagedoorn (Ed.), *Technical change and the world economy, (pp. 58–82)*. London: Edward Elgar.

Smith, W. K., & Tushman, M. L. (2005). Managing strategic contradictions: A top management model for managing innovation streams. *Organization Science*, 16, 522–536.

Sonenshein, S. (2016). Routines and creativity: From dualism to duality. *Organization Science*, 27, 739–758.

Trice, H. M., & Beyer, J. M. (1984). Studying organizational cultures through rites and ceremonials. *Academy of Management Review*, 9, 653–669.

Trice, H., & Beyer, J. 1993. *The cultures of work organizations*. Englewood Cliffs, NJ: Prentice-Hall.

Van Maanen, J., & Barley, S. R. (1984). Occupational communities: Culture and control in organizations. *Research in Organizational Behavior*, 6, 287–365.

Velencei, J., Baracskai, Z., & Dorfler, V. (2009). Knowledge sharing in knowledge restaurants. In E. Noszkay (Ed.), *The capital of intelligence – The intelligence of capital* (pp. 203–220). Budapest: Infota.

Von Krogh, G. (2011). Knowledge sharing in organizations: The role of communities. In M. A. Lyles & M. Easterby-Smith (Eds.), *Handbook of organizational learning and knowledge management* (pp. 403–422). Chichester, UK: John Wiley and Sons.

Von Krogh, G., Netland, T., & Worter, M. (2018). Winning with open process innovation. *MIT Sloan Management Review*, 59, 53–56.

Weick, K. E. (2005). Organizing and failures of imagination. *International Public Management Journal*, 8, 425–438.

Wenger, E., McDermott, R., & Snyder, W. M. (2002) *Cultivating Communities of practice*. Boston, MA: Harvard Business School Press.

Zucker, L., Darby, M., & Brewster, M. (1998). Intellectual human capital and the birth of U.S. biotechnology enterprises. *American Economic Review*, 88, 290–306.

11
HOW DO LEADERS PLAN FOR FIRM INNOVATION? STRATEGIC PLANNING PROCESSES AND CONSTRAINTS

Logan L. Watts, Kajal R. Patel, Ethan G. Rothstein, and Alessa N. Natale

Innovation is by nature a complex and risky enterprise. Investments in research and development (R&D) do not always pay off, and sometimes highly innovative firms fail. Such a case may be observed in the rise and fall of Polaroid, once a multibillion-dollar firm that has been described as "the Apple of its day" (Feeney, 2017). The story of Polaroid now serves as a cautionary tale. What was the cause of the firm's decline? Of course, any complex event such as a large firm's failure is caused by a number of factors. Former Polaroid executives, however, have primarily attributed the firm's decline to faulty assumptions held by managers. That is, managers fundamentally believed that customers would always want a hard-copy print of photographs (Smith, 2009). While this assumption proved useful for driving investment in instant picture technology that created robust consumer demand and large profit margins in the mid-20th century, this same assumption proved fatal to the firm's competitiveness in the late 20th century. The digital revolution turned out to be far more revolutionary than leaders at Polaroid predicted.

It is now well established that leaders have a critical influence on firm innovation (Aragón-Correa, García-Morales, & Cordón-Pozo, 2007; Steele, Watts, & Den Hartog, 2018), as well as the extent to which innovation occurs in areas that enhance firm competitiveness. Much has been written, for example, about how senior leaders might support firm innovation by inspiring organizational members with an innovative, change-oriented vision of the future (Amabile, 1988; Baum, Locke, & Kirkpatrick, 1998; Gumusluoglu & Ilsev, 2009), investing in R&D efforts (Cohen & Levinthal, 2000; Freeman, 1982; Shefer & Frenkel, 2005), and establishing a climate that supports creativity and innovation (Ekvall, 1996; Hunter, Bedell-Avers, & Mumford, 2007; Sarros, Cooper, & Santora, 2008). While senior leaders certainly play a strategic role in helping to create an organizational environment in which innovations are more likely to emerge, we know that mid-level leaders – such as R&D managers, creative directors, and project supervisors – can produce even more direct impacts on innovation processes given their proximity to the creative work (Floyd & Wooldridge, 1997; Pirola-Merlo, Härtel, Mann, & Hirst, 2002; Thamhain, 2003). Nevertheless, little attention has been given to the processes by which leaders at different levels draw on information stemming from internal and external constraints to identify strategic objectives and develop formal plans for capitalizing on novel market opportunities – what we call strategic planning for firm innovation.

Innovation is not enough to ensure firm competitiveness. Polaroid continued investing heavily in R&D and introducing new products right up until declaring bankruptcy. This example serves to make our basic point: Innovation must be strategic to be useful to firms. By improving our understanding of the mechanisms by which leaders strategically plan for innovation, including the factors internal and external to the organization that shape strategic planning, firms might improve their ability to survive and thrive in an increasingly competitive and globalized marketplace. Thus, the objectives of this chapter are to examine (a) the relationships between strategic planning, firm innovation, and firm performance; (b) the processes involved in strategic planning for firm innovation; and (c) internal and external constraints that influence, and are influenced by, the execution of strategic planning processes.

Strategic Planning, Innovation, and Performance

Firm innovation refers to the dynamic set of processes by which organizations generate, acquire, and implement viable solutions to novel, complex, and ill-defined problems (Mumford & Gustafson, 1988). Although radical innovations often draw the most attention (e.g., Apple's introduction of the first iPhone in 2007), firm innovation more frequently occurs incrementally through improvements in products and processes. Early models of firm innovation focused on technological advancements (e.g., Utterback, 1971). More recently, Damanpour (1991) argued that "an innovation can be a new product or service, a new production process technology, a new structure or administrative system, or a new plan or program pertaining to organizational members," and that innovations may be "internally generated or purchased" (p. 556). In other words, innovation comes in many forms, and firms may choose to invest in internal or external strategies, or a blend of the two, in order to facilitate innovation that enhances firm performance. Internal investment strategies include actions by which innovations emerge from within the firm (e.g., level of R&D intensity), whereas external investment strategies involve acquiring innovations (e.g., patents, technology) from other firms (Rhéaume & Gardoni, 2016).

A robust and growing pool of studies have provided support for the link between firm innovation and performance (e.g., Bowen, Rostami, & Steel, 2010; Calantone, Cavusgil, & Zhao, 2002; Camisón & Villar-López, 2014; Damanpour & Evan, 1984; Damanpour, Szabat, & Evan, 1989; Rosenbusch, Brinckmann, & Bausch, 2011; Rousseau, Mathias, Madden, & Crook, 2016; Rubera & Kirca, 2012; Wang & Wang, 2012). This link is not surprising when one considers the many ways that innovation can directly and indirectly facilitate firm growth. When a technology company, for example, markets a new product, the additional revenue produced contributes directly to the firm's bottom line. When a manufacturing company makes improvements to procedures or equipment that boosts operating efficiency, this can increase firm performance by lowering manufacturing costs and increasing product quality. When a management consulting firm adopts new software that improves the efficiency of internal communication and knowledge sharing, this can result in improved client satisfaction and retention. Of course, we might continue listing examples such as these. But the central point is that while innovation might look different depending on the company, it is difficult to imagine a firm whose performance would not benefit to some extent from innovation – assuming that the innovation is strategic.

This line of reasoning brings to the fore another key fact: Not all firm innovation is strategic. To be strategic, innovation must involve developing or acquiring viable solutions to complex problems *that enhance the competitiveness of the firm*. Although firms may occasionally "get lucky," such that their innovative efforts enhance firm competitiveness by chance, the complexity and risk inherent in innovation suggest that investing in innovation willy-nilly is an unsustainable business model. In other words, firms must plan. However, not any type of planning will do. For example, formal planning systems that require leaders at all levels to write down a plan for the next quarter too often become viewed as nothing more than another repetitive piece of paperwork (Van de Ven, 1986). To facilitate firm innovation that enhances performance, leaders must plan strategically. Put differently, we argue that strategic planning is one of the primary mechanisms by which leaders facilitate sustainable, performance-enhancing innovation within firms.

The facilitative effects of strategic planning on firm performance have been recognized for some time (although not without debate; see Greenley [1986]; Leontiades & Tezel [1980]; Mintzberg [1994]; and Pearce, Freeman, & Robinson [1987]). For example, using a sample of 93 American manufacturing firms, Ansoff, Avner, Brandenburg, Portner, and Radosevich (1970) found that firms led by strategic planners – that is, top management teams who formally defined their objectives and a comprehensive implementation strategy for executing these objectives – exhibited higher performance (e.g., earnings growth rates) following an acquisition, compared with firms led by nonstrategic planners. The economic performance of firms led by strategic planners was not only more positive, it was also found to be more stable during the years immediately following acquisitions. More robust evidence for the generalizability of the relationship between strategic planning and firm performance can be observed in a meta-analysis by Miller and Cardinal (1994). Aggregating data across 26 studies, Miller and Cardinal found an overall small but positive relationship ($\bar{r} = 0.10$s) between strategic planning and firm performance (i.e., growth and profitability). It is noteworthy that the relationship between strategic planning and firm performance was amplified under certain conditions (e.g., turbulent markets) – a point we return to later when discussing the influence of external constraints.

While the positive relationship between strategic planning and firm performance is now well established, the relationship between strategic planning and firm innovation has received less attention, in spite of the fact that early models of firm innovation processes presented planning as a critical first step (e.g., Amabile, 1988; King, 1973). Mumford, Bedell-Avers, and Hunter (2008) proposed that strategic planning facilitates firm innovation and performance in at least four key ways. First, strategic planning results in the identification of objectives – objectives that can serve to propel and direct the innovative activities of the firm along pathways that strengthen its competitive advantage. Second, strategic planning results in the generation of new ideas, or strategies, that support innovation. Strategy generation is stimulated by the identification of threats and opportunities emerging within the firm and from the external environment (Bryson & Roering, 1987). Third, strategic planning supports innovation by encouraging the evaluation of competing strategies for goal attainment – evaluation that enhances strategy selection and refinement. Fourth, strategic planning improves the firm's execution of innovation strategies by explicitly mapping out implementation sequences and contingencies (e.g., backup plans), coordinating collective action, and monitoring performance over time (Rothstein, Patel, Giorgini, Steele, & Watts, 2018).

Two studies have provided empirical evidence of the positive relationship between strategic planning and firm innovation. In a study of 227 high-technology firms, Song, Im, van der Bij, and Song (2011) found that strategic planning was positively related to the number of new product development (NPD) projects, but this was only the case in larger firms and in firms that invested heavily in R&D. Thus, strategic planning does appear to enhance firm innovation, but sufficient resources must be provided in order to realize the innovation-enhancing benefits of strategic planning. In another study of 448 firms across multiple industries, Dibrell, Craig, and Neubaum (2014) found that the use of formal strategic planning processes by senior leaders was positively related to firm engagement in innovative activities (e.g., developing and upgrading products, improving processes, investing in new R&D facilities). Further, it was found that engaging in innovative firm activities fully mediated the relationship between strategic planning processes and objective metrics of firm performance. Thus, the available empirical evidence suggests a positive relationship between strategic planning and firm innovation, particularly when firms are capable of investing significant resources toward innovation strategies.

Strategic Planning Processes

Whereas planning has commonly been defined as the conscious mental simulation of future, goal-oriented action sequences (Hayes-Roth & Hayes-Roth, 1979; Mumford, Schultz, & Van Doorn, 2001), strategic planning may be defined as the conscious mental simulation of future action sequences that results in a formal plan that supports the firm's objectives. Several models of strategic planning have been proposed over the years (e.g., Armstrong, 1982; Bryson & Roering, 1987; Mintzberg, 1973; Mintzberg, Raisinghani, & Theoret, 1976; Mumford, Mecca, & Watts, 2015; Steiner, 2010). Some models have emphasized the role of strategic planning as a critical, early stage function carried out by leaders across organizational levels in order to support firm innovation (e.g., Amabile, 1988; Cummings & O'Connell, 1978; Hunter, Cassidy, & Ligon, 2012; Mumford et al., 2008; Woodman, Sawyer, & Griffin, 1993).

While these models differ to some extent in terms of number of strategic planning processes, labels for these processes, the level of leadership examined, and the particular constraints emphasized, these models converge around a set of four general processes that appear fundamental to strategic planning for firm innovation, including (a) goal specification, (b) generation of strategies, (c) evaluation of strategies, and (d) strategy implementation. Empirical support for each of these processes as key elements of strategic planning and as facilitators of innovation has been provided in a number of studies (e.g., Boyd & Reuning-Elliott, 1998; Grover & Segars, 2005; Shrivastava & Grant, 1985). As illustrated in Figure 11.1, these four general processes are held to unfold sequentially over time in order to facilitate the execution of activities that enhance strategic innovation. Next, we describe each of these processes in detail and examine their relationships with firm innovation and performance.

Goal Specification

The effectiveness of any strategic planning effort is likely to hinge on the goals, or objectives, specified at the beginning of the process. Indeed, it is the extra attention paid to firm objectives that makes planning *strategic*. Of course, the importance of identifying the right goals – or those that direct the firm

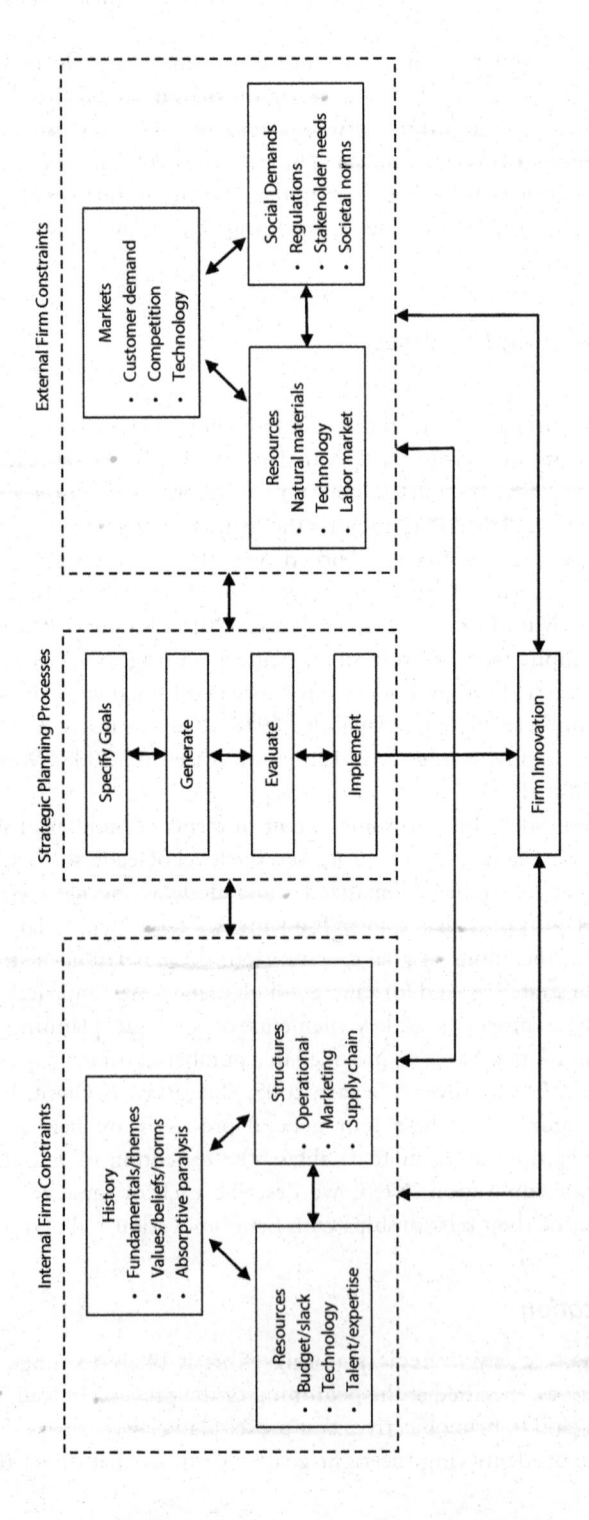

FIGURE 11.1 Model of strategic planning for firm innovation.

toward strategies that enhance its competitive advantage – cannot be overstated. As a result, it is not uncommon for leaders to spend long periods of time discussing, and reflecting upon, goals prior to engaging in strategic decisions (Strange & Mumford, 2005).

Goal specification appears to enhance strategic planning for innovation in a number of ways. Specifically, goal specification leads to the identification of viable threats and opportunities (Albright, 2004; Simons, 1990); stimulates the creative generation, evaluation, and monitoring of strategies for responding to threats and opportunities (Latham & Locke, 1991; Rothwell & Robertson, 1973); and motivates collective implementation (Ellemers, De Gilder, & Haslam, 2004). In other words, goal specification provides the foundation for all subsequent strategic planning processes that facilitate firm innovation.

The process of specifying the firm's objectives involves a number of demanding activities on the part of leaders. First, leaders must scan the internal and external environment to identify potential threats and opportunities – a mental operation that provides the basis for opportunity recognition (O'Connor & Rice, 2001). However, opportunity recognition consists of more than generating a list of potential threats and opportunities. Leaders must also evaluate these potential threats and opportunities, of which there are many, to assess their viability (Baron & Ensley, 2006). Threats and opportunities are considered more viable when they are judged to have a high likelihood of occurring and the potential magnitude of their consequences is great (Atuahene-Gima, 2005). Of course, threats and opportunities that are judged to have a low likelihood of occurring should not necessarily be ignored, particularly when the potential magnitude of consequences or benefits is great.

It is also noteworthy that the threats and opportunities emerging from the internal and external environment are in many cases industry specific (Weihrich, 1982). For example, if there is a shortage of software development experts in the labor market, firms specializing in software development are likely to perceive this talent shortage as a critical threat to the viability of their business. Advances in technology in the external environment can also pose significant threats to the competitiveness of firms and, in some cases, entire industries. With the rise of ride-sharing services such as Uber and Lyft, the traditional taxi service industry is quickly becoming obsolete. Of course, environmental changes that some firms or industries see as a threat, others are uniquely positioned to capitalize on as a golden opportunity (Aram & Cowen, 1990; Miller & Friesen, 1982). These examples point to an important conclusion: Goal specification is a highly complex and challenging process that demands substantial expertise. At any moment, leaders are faced with appraising dozens of potential threats and opportunities, emerging from within and outside the firm, with limited time and incomplete information (Eisenhardt, 1989). Thus, not only must leaders possess considerable skill in identifying, gathering information about, and evaluating potential threats and opportunities, they must also possess ample amounts of knowledge, particularly experiential knowledge, in their industry or domain (Mumford, Scott, Gaddis, & Strange, 2002). As a result of these knowledge requirements, leaders must routinely depend on the expertise possessed by others during goal specification (Ren & Guo, 2011), as well as subsequent processes involved in strategic planning for firm innovation.

Strategy Generation

Once viable threats and opportunities have been identified, and goals have been specified for managing or exploiting these elements along lines that enhance the competitiveness of the firm, leaders must engage in strategy generation – that is, the process of developing creative ideas that facilitate the achievement of firm objectives (Mumford, 2000). A variety of strategies may be pursued depending on several internal and external constraints operating in the firm's environment. Some example strategies for innovation include conceptual combination, imitation, acquisition, experimentation, and marketing.

Conceptual combination involves integrating the value components of multiple ideas, products, processes, or services to introduce a novel concept (Scott, Lonergan, & Mumford, 2005). For example, the introduction of the first smartphone may be viewed as the result of a conceptual combination strategy that integrated the personal computer concept with the cell phone concept. The imitation strategy involves imitating (or stealing) a competitor's concept because there is additional room for market growth. One famous example of innovation inspired by imitation may be observed in the story of how Steve Jobs capitalized on ideas for graphical user interface technology that he observed during tours at Xerox (Isaacson, 2014). The acquisitions strategy involves licensing or purchasing the concepts of other firms or acquiring firms that own valuable concepts (Ahuja & Katila, 2001). The experimentation strategy is perhaps what most people think of when they think of firm innovation. That is, the experimentation strategy often involves investing in the firm's R&D department as well as R&D alliances with the goal of organically growing innovations in products and processes (Hall & Bagchi-Sen, 2002). Finally, a marketing-based strategy might involve identifying untapped or underserved markets into which the firm's current product lines might be expanded (Schmidt & Watts, 2017).

Of course, these are not all of the strategies for firm innovation that might be pursued, and firms are not limited to the use of a single strategy. For example, manufacturing firms may pursue an operational efficiency strategy focused on innovating processes that improve firm competitiveness by improving quality and reducing waste (Benner & Tushman, 2002). The most competitive firms pursue a portfolio of innovation strategies that facilitate both short-term and long-term innovation in the context of the firm's unique constraints (e.g., resources, history, market dynamics) and tolerance for risk. Thus, firms that wish to pursue an experimentation strategy must be prepared to invest heavily in R&D and tolerate the many projects that are likely to fail. In sum, generating many potential strategies for innovation is a critical process, but generation is not enough. Leaders must evaluate a range of potential solutions in order to select a viable portfolio of innovation strategies that align with firm objectives – the third process involved in strategic planning for firm innovation.

Strategy Evaluation

Mumford, Lonergan, and Scott (2002) proposed that the process of evaluating creative ideas involves three cognitive operations: idea appraisal, forecasting, and refinement. We suggest these operations also apply to the evaluation of strategies for firm innovation. The first of these cognitive operations, idea appraisal, involves judging each potential strategy with respect to relevant standards. Specifically, the goals defined in earlier strategic planning processes serve as critical standards by which the viability of strategies may be judged (Licuanan, Dailey, & Mumford, 2007). Put simply, if a strategy is unlikely to facilitate goal execution, this strategy is unlikely to be pursued. However, some flexibility is needed at this stage. Strategies judged to have great potential, even if they otherwise fail to align with extant goals, may stimulate a return to earlier processes in order to refine these goals.

Forecasting is the second cognitive operation involved in the evaluation of strategies for firm innovation. Forecasting involves mentally simulating the downstream consequences, both positive and negative, that might result if a strategy is pursued (Mumford, Medeiros, & Partlow, 2012). A number of internal and external constraints come into play during forecasting (Watts, Mulhearn, Todd, & Mumford, 2017). For example, strategies that require significant changes to the firm's operational structures (e.g., supply chains) may be passed on due to the difficulty and cost of manipulating entrenched operational structures. Further, strategies that are likely to "draw heat" from stakeholders (e.g., customers, policymakers, media) due to a perceived violation of social expectations may be passed on even if the strategy is expected to enhance the bottom line. Moreover, leaders responsible for several creative teams or projects (e.g., R&D directors) must forecast how the simultaneous pursuit of multiple strategies for innovation might interact to influence goal execution – including the possibility of facilitating and conflicting interactions among strategies (Benner & Tushman, 2002). Thus, forecasting involves a careful calculation of the full range of consequences that are likely to emerge from strategy implementation.

Refinement is the final cognitive operation involved in the evaluation of innovative strategies. Drawing on information gathered during strategy appraisal and forecasting, the goal of refinement is to tweak strategies judged to have "good bones," or potential, in order to improve their viability. Refinement may involve combining strategies, elaborating on or tweaking particular aspects of strategies, or reorienting strategies to improve the likelihood of effective implementation in novel contexts (Watts, Steele, Medeiros, & Mumford, 2018). In other words, through idea appraisal, forecasting, and refinement, leaders reduce the number of solutions considered to a small number of viable strategies. One of the key functions served by strategic planning for innovation is narrowing the range of strategies considered – through idea evaluation – in order to invest firm resources where they count the most (Song et al., 2011).

Strategy Implementation

The final process involved in strategic planning for firm innovation is strategy implementation. The planning literature has historically focused on early stages of planning, such as identifying strategies, as opposed to later stages, such as managing the implementation of strategic plans (Poister, 2010). Nevertheless, the importance of implementation to the viability of any innovation strategy cannot be overstated. Three key operations involved in strategy implementation include the generation of action sequences, the generation of contingencies (i.e. back-up plans), and execution. Generating action sequences involves identifying key stakeholders along all critical aspects of the supply chain (e.g., R&D, manufacturing, marketing), identifying major activities that support implementation, and plotting out the general time frames and stages in which these activities must be executed (Bourgeois & Brodwin, 1984).

Of course, implementation plans are never perfect. Leaders have limited control over future events. Key creative talent may leave the firm. A downturn in the market can trigger a tighter R&D budget. New technology may emerge that renders the current strategic plan obsolete. In other words, leaders must create backup plans (Honig, 2004). Backup plans enhance the flexibility of innovation efforts, allowing firms to quickly adapt to changes in internal and external constraints. The formulation of viable backup plans also appears to depend on forecasting (Giorgini & Mumford, 2013). Forecasting downstream consequences allows leaders to identify key situational contingencies that are fundamental to the development of backup plans in order to support adaptive goal execution.

Finally, leaders must not only plan for innovation; they must execute. Execution involves a number of demanding activities, including communicating, selling, investing, boundary-spanning, and monitoring. First, execution involves clearly communicating strategic plans to key stakeholders, particularly the individuals and groups whose involvement is fundamental to goal attainment. Second, leaders must sell their strategy and plan to these stakeholders in order to motivate commitment (Mumford, Mulhearn, Watts, Steele, & McIntosh, 2017). The goal of selling is to develop a shared mental model about key actors, goals, resources, constraints, and contingencies in order to remove resistance and build support for innovative projects (Rhéaume & Gardoni, 2016). Third, leaders must invest in innovation. That is, they must be prepared to risk resources in support of the strategy they are selling. Fourth, leaders support plan execution through internal and external boundary-spanning activities (Tushman, 1977). Boundary-spanning involves developing informational bridges between key individuals and groups within and outside the firm in order to create collaborative networks that support strategy execution (Rosenkopf & Nerkar, 2001). Fifth, plan execution involves carefully monitoring strategy implementation activities and their results over time (Amabile, 1988).

Constraints and Strategic Planning Processes

Constraints refer to internal and external factors that limit the number and nature of strategies for innovation that might be pursued by the firm (Garriga, Von Krogh, & Spaeth, 2013). Constraints can directly impact the viability of a firm's innovation efforts (Teece, 1994), and they provide critical information that influences strategic planning processes (Vincent, Bharadwaj, & Challagalla, 2004). Figure 11.1 shows six categories of constraints – three internal and three external – that are discussed with respect to their influences on strategic planning for innovation.

Internal Constraints

Internal constraints are factors emerging from within the firm that place limitations on the range of innovation strategies that might be exploited. As shown in Figure 11.1, the following are the three categories of internal constraints examined here: (a) history, (b) resources, and (c) structures. Unlike external constraints that emerge from outside the firm, leaders tend to have greater control over internal constraints (Medeiros, Watts, & Mumford, 2017). However, some internal constraints (e.g., fundamentals) are more fixed than others (e.g., resources), suggesting that some constraints operate as relatively inflexible boundaries that must be worked around during strategic planning, whereas other constraints serve as more flexible levers that might be acted on to pursue an alternative strategy for innovation (Onarheim, 2012).

History

First and foremost, strategic planning for innovation in firms takes place in the context of the firm's history. Elements of a firm's history include memories of past failures and successes, core beliefs and assumptions about these events that form the basis of its culture and mission (Bart, 1997; Boyd & Reuning-Elliott, 1998), and the underlying fundamentals and product themes that provide the foundation for its core market strategy (Teece, 2010). For example, service firms operate with a different set of fundamentals compared with manufacturing firms, resulting in the pursuit of different strategies for innovation (Ettlie & Rosenthal, 2011). History characteristics tend to operate as highly stable constraints over time and have a strong influence on strategic planning for innovation. Leaders, for instance, tend to ignore innovation strategies that fail to align with their firm's fundamentals (Elkins & Keller, 2003).

A firm's history of innovation and innovation-related norms, or the lack thereof, also appear to constrain absorptive capacity, or the firm's ability to acquire and exploit new information that is needed to innovate in the future (Cohen & Levinthal, 1990; Zahra & George, 2002). Empirical support for this conclusion has been provided in Fosfuri and Tribo's (2008) study of 2,464 companies. Fosfuri and Tribo found that a firm's history of absorptive capacity behaviors was positively related to objective indices of innovation and firm performance. In other words, leaders operating in firms that do not possess a history of innovation-friendly norms – those characterized by absorptive paralysis – will find planning for innovation more challenging. This type of history constraint may be found more commonly in particular types of firms, including publicly funded bureaucracies where stability and tradition, as opposed to innovation and change, are the status quo.

This is not to suggest that firms without strong histories of innovation cannot change or strengthen their absorptive capacity over time. In fact, one mechanism by which leaders might strategically plan for innovation is by investing in their future capacity to acquire and exploit new knowledge (Gray, 2006). Another strategy for "breaking free" from the constraints of firm history is sensebreaking. Sensebreaking involves reframing mental models – or the cognitive structures used to interpret complex events – in order to motivate a collective shift toward some alternative model (Marcy, 2015). For sensebreaking to facilitate strategic planning for innovation, old narratives of events and traditional organizational identities must give way to new narratives that support alternative interpretations and organizational change (Landau, Drori, & Terjesen, 2014).

Resources

The availability of firm resources has long been recognized as an important constraint on strategic planning processes and firm innovation (Barney, 1991). While access to funding and size of R&D budgets are often the first things that come to mind when considering resource constraints (Ayyagari, Demirgüç-Kunt, & Maksimovic, 2011) – and financial resources are certainly important to a firm's strategic decision-making (Fazzari, Hubbard, & Petersen,

1987) – it is also critical to consider a firm's technological and human resources. Technological resources may include intellectual property (e.g., patents, trademarks), products, processes, and equipment (Bharadwaj, 2000; Srivastava & Gnyawali, 2011), whereas human resources refers to employees' creative thinking skills and professional expertise in the domains required to pursue certain innovation strategies (Damanpour, 1991; Mumford, McIntosh, Mulhearn, Steele, & Watts, 2015; Zhou & Li, 2012). Of course, technological and human resources can be developed or acquired, but these activities depend on the availability of financial resources, among other factors. In addition to requiring financial resources, it takes time to realize the innovation-enhancing capabilities of new technology and talent (Ahuja & Katila, 2001).

Resource constraints may inhibit strategic planning for innovation by reducing the number and quality of innovation strategies that might be pursued by the firm. In a study of 57 companies in the pharmaceutical industry, Cardinal (2001) found that firm size – a proxy for resources – was strongly related ($r = 0.30$s to 0.50s) to the number of incremental and radical innovations introduced by these firms (i.e., drug enhancements and new drugs). Leaders with limited resources at their disposal must be extra cautious about where these precious resources are allocated. As a result, smaller firms are more likely to avoid investing in innovation strategies that are perceived as too risky, such as radical innovation projects, even though radical innovations are critical for supporting transformative organizational growth (Chandy & Tellis, 2000). Put differently, in small firms, one false move, such as pursuing the wrong strategic direction, can sink the ship. In contrast, large firms can afford to weather many storms. Given the high stakes of strategic decision-making in small firms, some scholars have argued that the execution of strategic planning processes may be even more critical in smaller firms (Robinson & Pearce, 1984; Watts & Ormsby, 1990). Nevertheless, larger firms tend to realize greater returns from strategic planning (Song et al., 2011).

Although resource constraints have traditionally been cast in a negative light in the organizational innovation and planning literatures, in some instances, resource constraints may serve to stimulate creative thinking on the part of leaders (Medeiros et al., 2017). We are all familiar with tales of highly successful entrepreneurial ventures – radical innovations – that began as low-budget experiments in basements or garages. On the flip side, there are many stories of large firms spending vast amounts of money on innovation strategies that failed (e.g., Google Glass). Thus, small budgets do not preclude firms from being highly innovative, and large budgets do not guarantee firm innovation will occur or be strategic. Observations such as these led Nohria and Gulati (1996) to propose that a moderate degree of resource constraints may be optimal for stimulating creative thinking that supports innovation – a conclusion supported by experimental and field research (Medeiros, Partlow, & Mumford, 2014; Nohria & Gulati, 1997). Just as placing one's thumb at the end of a garden hose can amplify water pressure, some degree of resource constraints may amplify organizational innovation. Additional work is needed, however, to identify the optimum degree of resource constraints, as well as how resource constraints might interact with other types of constraints to influence planning and innovation processes.

Structures

The final category of internal constraints discussed here includes the operational structures of the firm. Operational structures refer to the firm's current infrastructure used to develop, sell, and distribute its products and services, such as manufacturing processes, marketing channels, and supply chains. Some structures in the supply chain are more flexible than others. For example, in discussing the four P's of marketing (i.e., product, price, place, and promotion) as constraints on firm innovation, Schmidt and Watts (2017) demonstrated that price constraints are typically far more flexible than product constraints. Whereas pricing may be manipulated overnight, changing a firm's product offerings may take years of strategic planning. Thus, some internal constraints must be worked around when planning for innovation, while others may be more feasibly acted on directly to facilitate firm innovation.

Flexibility in manufacturing operations is also a major concern, particularly for product-based firms. Traditionally, changes to manufacturing processes were extremely costly (Gerwin, 1987). However, advancements in technology (e.g., computer processing speed, three-dimensional printing) have led to the development of dynamic manufacturing processes that update automatically or with the push of a few buttons (Rayna & Striukova, 2016). Flexibility in manufacturing processes has become a key competitive advantage, allowing leaders to rapidly shift their product development strategy in response to changes in market dynamics (Camisón & Villar López, 2010; Mehrabi, Ulsoy, & Koren, 2000). In other words, one potential strategy for firm innovation involves acting on internal constraints in order to ensure the firm's competitiveness in the face of shifting external constraints (Lee, 2002) – our next topic of discussion.

External Firm Constraints

External constraints refer to factors emerging in a firm's external environment that limit the range of innovation strategies that might be feasibly pursued. Unlike some internal constraints (e.g., resources) that are somewhat flexible and amenable to change, leaders tend to have less control over external constraints, suggesting external constraints in most cases must be worked around. As illustrated in Figure 11.1, the three categories of external constraints discussed here include (a) markets, (b) resources, and (c) social demands.

Markets

Markets have received the most attention of all the external constraints discussed in the strategic planning and innovation literature. Market factors refer to changes in demand, competition, and technology. Together, these factors contribute to market uncertainty (Haveman, 1992). For some time, it has been recognized that strategic planning appears to be even more critical for firms operating in rapidly changing, uncertain markets (Kukalis, 1989; Miller & Cardinal, 1994; Powell, 1992; Thune & House, 1970). Further, market uncertainty appears to act as a catalyst that stimulates firm planning for innovation (Ettlie, 1983; Özsomer, Calantone, & Di Benedetto, 1997), perhaps by causing leaders to invest more resources toward the recognition of emerging threats and opportunities. Of course, a failure to plan contributes to a failure to adapt, and a failure to adapt in turbulent environments is simply unsustainable (e.g., Polaroid).

Changes in demand can result from shifts in customer characteristics (e.g., demographics, income, preferences) as well as broader market forces such as market maturity and saturation. Once a market matures to the point of near total saturation, such as the case of the iPhone in the United States, firms must identify and expand to new markets to continue growing (Tidd, Bessant, & Pavitt, 2005). In addition, firms must carefully monitor the characteristics of their customers to adapt marketing strategies as needed (Rust, Lemon, & Zeithaml, 2004).

Changes in competition represent another noteworthy market constraint. When competitors introduce new products and processes, or acquire firms with valuable natural, technological, and human resources, these events provide critical information for strategic planning processes (Zajac & Bazerman, 1991). Changes in competition may stimulate strategic planning throughout all points in the planning cycle. For example, changes in competition may be perceived as threats that stimulate opportunity recognition – a fundamental activity involved in market scanning that facilitates goal specification and strategy generation. In addition, changes in competition may serve as cues that signal the need to adapt innovation strategies during later stages of execution.

Changes in technology, sometimes referred to as technological turbulence, represent a third major source of market uncertainty. The introduction of some novel technology has the potential to completely disrupt a firm's portfolio of innovation strategies, and in some cases, the very fundamentals of the firm. Polaroid's decline, for example, may be attributed to its inability to adapt to the rise of digital camera technology, as well as the shifts in customer demand spurred by change in technology. Thus, changes in markets, competition, and technology are not independent, but they influence one another. Each must be carefully monitored to increase the probability that the innovation strategies pursued contribute to the competitiveness of the firm.

Resources

The availability of resources in a firm's environment represents another set of external constraints that impact strategic planning for innovation. External resource constraints include limitations in the market with respect to natural resources, talent, and technology, among others. One example of the power of natural resources as a constraint may be observed in recent news reports of a predicted global shortage in cobalt – a key material used in the production of lithium-ion batteries for electric vehicles, smartphones, and other electronics (Holmes, 2018). Concerns over a shortage of this resource, which is critical to the manufacturing of its products, led Apple to pursue a major new partnership with the cobalt mining industry (Reisinger, 2018). While one strategy may involve obtaining greater control over access to limited natural resources, another strategy may involve restructuring the firm's supply chain to rely on an alternative natural resource that might serve as a substitute in product manufacturing. In fact, firms may simultaneously pursue both strategies, with the former acting as a short-term solution that buys the firm time to identify a viable resource substitute that serves as a long-term solution.

Access to human resources, such as professionals with specialized expertise, also represents a critical constraint in the external environment of many firms (Florida, 2006). To circumvent the negative influence of labor market shortages, firms might pursue a number of strategies, such as retraining workers, opening offices in trendy locations to attract creative professionals, developing local partnerships with educational institutions, and engaging in cross-cultural alliances to tap into professional labor markets in other countries (Frank, Finnegan, & Taylor, 2004). The goal of long-term resource acquisition strategies such as these is to develop talent pipelines that support the firm's capacity to pursue strategic innovations in the future. Of course, none of these solutions are "quick fixes," suggesting the importance of long-term human resources planning for firms operating in markets with limited access to technical and professional expertise.

Technology appears to influence strategic planning for firm innovation not only as a market constraint, such as when the introduction of a radical new product fundamentally shifts customer demand, but also as a resource constraint. For some time, it has been recognized that the current state of technical knowledge in a firm's environment has a direct impact on its ability to develop innovative, related technologies (Gruber & Marquis, 1969). The invention of satellite communication technology at Bell Labs, for example, depended on technical knowledge stemming from over a dozen former inventions (Gertner, 2013). Clearly, the current state of technology in the external environment acts as a pervasive constraint on firm innovation, perhaps by limiting opportunity recognition and strategy generation. Put simply, it is difficult to imagine what does not yet exist. However, firms are not helpless in the face of technology constraints. Highly innovative firms may, in fact, act directly on technology constraints by investing in organic innovation strategies such as conceptual combination and experimentation.

Social Demands

Social demands refer to the legal and corporate social responsibility expectations of external stakeholders, including policymakers, customers, social/environmental groups, and the media. Of course, policies and regulations at the national, state, and local levels act as one obvious set of constraints on the range of innovation strategies that might be legally pursued by firms (Sapat, 2004). It is also noteworthy that the number of legal expectations that constrain a firm's decision-making is greatly impacted by its market, or industry (Ring & Perry, 1985). Mature industries in which the safety of customers is a chief concern (e.g., pharmaceuticals, transportation) tend to face far more constraints than younger industries with products that pose few health risks (e.g., information technology, entertainment).

Beyond legal constraints, leaders are increasingly recognizing the importance of fostering a socially responsible corporate reputation to running a profitable business (Judge & Douglass, 1998). No doubt much of the increasing pressure on firms to foster a socially responsible reputation stems from advancements in information technology, such as the rise of social media. Due to social media, it is now possible for a significant portion of the population to learn about a firm's actions within moments of an event occurring. In other words, it is no longer enough that firms follow the law. They must also forecast how potential actions will be perceived by various external stakeholder groups and actively manage stakeholder perceptions throughout all strategic planning processes.

Conclusion

A number of limitations must be considered with respect to the present discussion. First, while there is some empirical research establishing the positive relationships between strategic planning, firm innovation, and performance, there is less research investigating the underlying processes involved in strategic planning for innovation. Second, a body of empirical research has begun to emerge examining how leaders of innovative firms analyze, manipulate, and manage constraints (Medeiros et al., 2017), as well as the knowledge and cognitive skills that facilitate the leadership of creative efforts (Mumford, Steele, Mulhearn, McIntosh, & Watts, 2017; Mumford, Watts, & Partlow, 2015; Watts, Steele, & Song, 2017). However, this body of empirical work is still relatively small, and not all possible constraints were discussed here (e.g., social dynamics, field norms, alliances, multinational factors). In other words, more work is needed to test and expand on these ideas in order to develop a comprehensive model of constraints involved in strategic planning for firm innovation. Third, in this effort, we define innovation broadly as a set of processes by which firms develop, acquire, and implement novel solutions to complex problems. In future work, differentiating predictions among innovation types (e.g., incremental versus radical, product versus process) and stages (e.g., early, middle, late) may yield additional insights about the situations in which firms benefit from executing strategic planning processes the most (Friedrich, Mumford, Vessey, Beeler, & Eubanks, 2010; Medeiros, Steele, Watts, & Mumford, 2018; Song & Montoya-Weiss, 1998), as well as the internal and external constraints playing the most active roles in different innovation activities.

Bearing these limitations in mind, a number of conclusions may be drawn based on the relationships illustrated in Figure 11.1. First, internal and external constraints have a pronounced range of influences on strategic planning processes. These constraints may stimulate creative thinking on the part of leaders, such as when perceiving a change in the external environment leads to opportunity recognition (Gibbons & O'Connor, 2005). In addition, these constraints serve as a source of critical information that must be accounted for throughout the strategic planning processes (Tushman, 1997). Constraints have been identified as having an important impact on firm innovation for some time (Woodman et al., 1993), but more work is needed to specify the constraints that are most important for innovation as well as how specific processes executed by different levels of leaders are influenced by these constraints.

Second, as shown in Figure 11.1, internal and external constraints may, in some cases, be altered through the execution of strategic planning processes, or by the act of innovation itself. This suggests that constraint management skills – the capacity to recognize and exploit information bearing on constraints in the internal and external environment – may be critical to the leadership of firm innovation. Constraint management may also involve acting on, manipulating, or removing constraints as a pathway to firm innovation (Onarheim, 2012). This line of reasoning suggests a number of practical implications for the selection and development of those charged with leading for innovation. For example, leaders might be trained in constraint management (Medeiros et al., 2017; Peterson et al., 2013), strategic thinking (Liedtka, 1998), or both. Further, firms might consider incorporating assessment exercises involving constraint analysis and strategy formulation in selection programs designed to evaluate leadership potential.

Although the present effort discussed constraints in mostly a one-at-a-time fashion for the sake of clarity, a third conclusion that can be drawn from Figure 11.1 is that constraints interact with one another to influence strategic planning and firm innovation. For example, Andersen (2004) demonstrated that in a more dynamic market environment, firms with decentralized decision structures tended to outperform firms with more hierarchical decision structures. Further, it was found that the execution of strategic planning processes was critical for managing the complexity emerging from exposure to a dynamic market. Given the complexity involved in accounting for multiple, interacting constraints during the goal specification, generation, evaluation, and implementation processes, flexibility in strategic planning appears to be critical (Bouncken, Koch, & Teichert, 2007; Damanpour, Walker, & Avellaneda, 2009). Thus, these strategic processes should not necessarily be executed in a rigid sequence but with a fluid approach that allows for improvisation in response to dynamic environments (Mintzberg, 2000).

A final conclusion emerging from the present effort may be observed in the form of a caveat. While this chapter presented a parsimonious model of strategic planning from the leader's perspective, strategic planning for firm innovation is rarely a one-leader activity. Given the complex demands of executing these strategic planning processes, as well as the challenges involved in monitoring and acting on internal and external constraints, no leader can be expected to effectively execute all of these processes alone. Rather, strategic planning for innovation is a team effort (Mumford et al., 2008). Not only must leaders of innovation possess ample domain-specific, technical expertise, they must also heavily rely on the technical expertise of those they are leading. This dependence on followers, as well as alliances with external experts, becomes even more important as leaders ascend the organizational hierarchy. Thus, top management teams who are most distant from the innovation process must depend on project supervisors and middle managers (e.g., R&D directors) to identify emerging threats and opportunities relevant to the firm and to take calculated risks based on these insights (Floyd & Wooldridge, 1994). To gain support for innovation strategies identified in a bottom-up fashion, project supervisors and middle managers must also possess the requisite expertise to vertically and horizontally champion these strategies to key stakeholders (Howell & Sheab, 2001). In sum, strategic planning for firm innovation is not just an activity for senior leaders; it takes a village.

To survive and thrive in an increasingly complex, fast-paced, and global marketplace, it is not enough that firms be innovative. The objectives achieved through innovation must be strategic. Further, innovative efforts must be strategically executed to increase the probability that their benefits outweigh their risks. Leaders at all levels of the firm play a critical role in facilitating innovation through specifying goals, generating and evaluating action strategies and contingencies, and executing implementation plans. For strategic planning efforts to result in viable innovation plans, however, leaders must effectively manage the dynamic interplay of constraints situated in the firm's internal and external environment. Clearly, strategic planning for firm innovation is a highly complex endeavor. Nevertheless, it is a critical skillset for leaders – one that supports the growth and competitiveness of firms.

Acknowledgments

We would like to thank Logan Steele, Kelsey Medeiros, and Michael Mumford for providing helpful feedback on earlier drafts of this work. Please address all correspondence to Dr. Logan Watts, Department of Psychology, Baruch College, CUNY, New York, NY, 10010, Logan.Watts@baruch.cuny.edu.

References

Ahuja, G., & Katila, R. (2001). Technological acquisitions and the innovation performance of acquiring firms: A longitudinal study. *Strategic Management Journal*, 22, 197–220.

Albright, K. S. (2004). Environmental scanning: Radar for organizational success. *Information Management Journal*, 38, 38–45.

Amabile, T. M. (1988). A model of creativity and innovation in organizations. In B. S. Cummings (Ed.), *Research in organizational behavior* (pp. 123–167). Greenwich, CT: JAI Press.

Andersen, T. J. (2004). Integrating decentralized strategy making and strategic planning processes in dynamic environments. *Journal of Management Studies*, 41, 1271–1299.

Ansoff, H. I., Avner, J., Brandenburg, R. G., Portner, F. E., & Radosevich, R. (1970). Does planning pay? The effect of planning on success of acquisitions in American firms. *Long Range Planning*, 3, 2–7.

Aragón-Correa, J. A., García-Morales, V., & Cordón-Pozo, E. (2007). Leadership and organizational learning's role on innovation and performance: Lessons from Spain. *Industrial Marketing Management*, 36, 349–359.

Aram, J. D., & Cowen, S. S. (1990). Strategic planning for increased profit in the small business. *Long Range Planning*, 23, 63–70.

Armstrong, J. S. (1982). The value of formal planning for strategic decisions: Review of empirical research. *Strategic Management Journal*, 3, 197–211.

Atuahene-Gima, K. (2005). Resolving the capability-rigidity paradox in new product innovation. *Journal of Marketing*, 69, 61–83.

Ayyagari, M., Demirgüç-Kunt, A., & Maksimovic, V. (2011). Firm innovation in emerging markets: The role of finance, governance, and competition. *Journal of Financial and Quantitative Analysis*, 46, 1545–1580.

Barney, J. B. (1991). Firm resources and sustained competitive advantage. *Journal of Management*, 17, 99–120.

Baron, R., & Ensley, M. (2006). Opportunity recognition as the detection of meaningful patterns: Evidence from comparisons of novice and experienced entrepreneurs. *Management Science*, 52, 1331–1344.

Bart, C. K. (1997). Industrial firms and the power of mission. *Industrial Marketing Management*, 26, 371–383.

Baum, J. R., Locke, E. A., & Kirkpatrick, S. A. (1998). A longitudinal study of the relation of vision and vision communication to venture growth in entrepreneurial firms. *Journal of Applied Psychology*, 83, 43–54.

Benner, M. J., & Tushman, M. (2002). Process management and technological innovation: A longitudinal study of the photography and paint industries. *Administrative Science Quarterly*, 47, 676–707.

Bharadwaj, A. S. (2000). A resource-based perspective on information technology capability and firm performance: An empirical investigation. *MIS Quarterly*, 24, 169–196.

Bouncken, R. B., Koch, M., & Teichert, T. (2007). Innovation strategy explored: Innovation orientation's strategy preconditions and market performance outcomes. *Zeitschrift für Betriebswirtschaft*, 77, 19–43.

Bourgeois, L. J., & Brodwin, D. R. (1984). Strategic implementation: Five approaches to an elusive phenomenon. *Strategic Management Journal*, 5, 241–264.

Bowen, F. E., Rostami, M., & Steel, P. (2010). Timing is everything: A meta-analysis of the relationships between organizational performance and innovation. *Journal of Business Research*, 63, 1179–1185.

Boyd, B. K., & Reuning-Elliott, E. (1998). A measurement model of strategic planning. *Strategic Management Journal*, 19, 181–192.

Bryson, J., & Roering, W. D. (1987). Applying private-sector strategic planning in the public sector. *Journal of the American Planning Association*, 53, 9–22.

Calantone, R. J., Cavusgil, S. T., & Zhao, Y. (2002). Learning orientation, firm innovation capability, and firm performance. *Industrial Marketing Management*, 31, 515–524.

Camisón, C., & Villar López, A. (2010). Effect of SMEs' international experience on foreign intensity and economic performance: The mediating role of internationally exploitable assets and competitive strategy. *Journal of Small Business Management*, 48, 116–151.

Camisón, C., & Villar López, A. (2014). Organizational innovation as an enabler of technological innovation capabilities and firm performance. *Journal of Business Research*, 67, 2891–2902.

Cardinal, L. B. (2001). Technological innovation in the pharmaceutical industry: The use of organizational control in managing research and development. *Organization Science*, 12, 19–36.

Chandy, R. K., & Tellis, G. J. (2000). The incumbent's curse? Incumbency, size, and radical product innovation. *Journal of Marketing*, 64, 1–17.

Cohen, W. M., & Levinthal, D. A. (1990). Absorptive capacity: A new perspective on learning and innovation. *Administrative Science Quarterly*, 35, 128–152.

Cohen, W. M., & Levinthal, D. A. (2000). Absorptive capacity: A new perspective on learning and innovation. In R. Cross & S. Israelit (Eds.), *Strategic learning in a knowledge economy: Individual, collective and organizational learning process* (pp. 39–67). Woburn, MA: Butterworth-Heinemann.

Cummings, L. L., & O'Connell, M. J. (1978). Organizational innovation: A model and needed research. *Journal of Business Research*, 6, 33–50.

Damanpour, F. (1991). Organizational innovation: A meta-analysis of effects of determinants and moderators. *Academy of Management Journal*, 34, 555–590.

Damanpour, F., & Evan, W. M. (1984). Organizational innovation and performance: The problem of "organizational lag." *Administrative Science Quarterly*, 29, 392–409.

Damanpour, F., Szabat, K. A., & Evan, W. M. (1989). The relationship between types of innovation and organizational performance. *Journal of Management Studies*, 26, 587–602.

Damanpour, F., Walker, R. M., & Avellaneda, C. N. (2009). Combinative effects of innovation types and organizational performance: A longitudinal study of service organizations. *Journal of Management Studies*, 46, 650–675.

Dibrell, C., Craig, J. B., & Neubaum, D. O. (2014). Linking the formal strategic planning process, planning flexibility, and innovativeness to firm performance. *Journal of Business Research*, 67, 2000–2007.

Eisenhardt, K. M. (1989). Agency theory: An assessment and review. *Academy of Management Review*, 14, 57–74.

Ekvall, G. (1996). Organizational climate for creativity and innovation. *European Work and Organizational Psychology*, 5, 105–123.

Elkins, T., & Keller, R. T. (2003). Leadership in research and development organizations: A literature review and conceptual framework. *The Leadership Quarterly*, 14, 587–606.

Ellemers, N., De Gilder, D., & Haslam, S. A. (2004). Motivating individuals and groups at work: A social identity perspective on leadership and group performance. *Academy of Management Review*, 29, 459–478.

Ettlie, J. E. (1983). Organizational policy and innovation among suppliers to the food processing sector. *Academy of Management Journal*, 26, 27–44.

Ettlie, J. E., & Rosenthal, S. R. (2011). Service versus manufacturing innovation. *Journal of Product Innovation Management*, 28, 285–299.

Fazzari, S. M., Hubbard, R. G., & Petersen, B. C. (1987). Financing constraints and corporate investment. *Brookings Papers on Economic Activity*, 1, 141–195.

Feeney, M. (2017, November 2). When the future was named Polaroid. The Boston Globe. Retrieved from https://www.bostonglobe.com/arts/art/2017/11/02/when-future-was-named-polaroid/OhGPvHpulJ4dK0p8hTOWYM/story.html

Florida, R. (2006). The flight of the creative class: The new global competition for talent. *Liberal Education*, 92, 22–29.

Floyd, S. W., & Wooldridge, B. (1994). Dinosaurs or dynamos? Recognizing middle management's strategic role. *Academy of Management Perspectives*, 8, 47–57.

Floyd, S. W., & Wooldridge, B. (1997). Middle management's strategic influence and organizational performance. *Journal of Management Studies*, 34, 465–485.

Fosfuri, A., & Tribó, J. A. (2008). Exploring the antecedents of potential absorptive capacity and its impact on innovation performance. *Omega*, 36, 173–187.

Frank, F. D., Finnegan, R. P., & Taylor, C. R. (2004). The race for talent: Retaining and engaging workers in the 21st century. *Human Resource Planning*, 27, 12–25.

Freeman, C. (1982). *The economics of industrial innovation* (2nd ed.). Cambridge, MA: MIT Press.

Friedrich, T. L., Mumford, M. D., Vessey, B., Beeler, C. K., & Eubanks, D. L. (2010). Leading for innovation: Reevaluating leader influences on innovation with regard to innovation type and complexity. *International Studies of Management and Organization*, 40, 6–29.

Garriga, H., Von Krogh, G., & Spaeth, S. (2013). How constraints and knowledge impact open innovation. *Strategic Management Journal*, 34, 1134–1144.

Gertner, J. (2013). *The idea factory: Bell Labs and the great age of American innovation*. New York, NY: Penguin Press.

Gerwin, D. (1987). An agenda for research on the flexibility of manufacturing processes. *International Journal of Operations and Production Management*, 7, 38–49.

Gibbons, P. T., & O' Connor, T. (2005). Influences on strategic planning processes among Irish SMEs. *Journal of Small Business Management*, 43, 170–186.

Giorgini, V., & Mumford, M. D. (2013). Backup plans and creative problem-solving: Effects of causal, error, and resource processing. *The International Journal of Creativity and Problem Solving*, 23, 121–126.

Gray, C. (2006). Absorptive capacity, knowledge management and innovation in entrepreneurial small firms. *International Journal of Entrepreneurial Behavior and Research*, 12, 345–360.

Greenley, G. E. (1986). Does strategic planning improve company performance? *Long Range Planning*, 19, 101–109.

Grover, V., & Segars, A. H. (2005). An empirical evaluation of stages of strategic information systems planning: Patterns of process design and effectiveness. *Information and Management*, 42, 761–779.

Gruber, W. H., & Marquis, D. G. (Eds.). (1969). *Factors in the transfer of technology*. Cambridge, MA: MIT Press.

Gumusluoglu, L., & Ilsev, A. (2009). Transformational leadership, creativity, and organizational innovation. *Journal of Business Research*, 62, 461–473.

Hall, L. A., & Bagchi-Sen, S. (2002). A study of R&D, innovation, and business performance in the Canadian biotechnology industry. *Technovation*, 22, 231–244.

Haveman, H. A. (1992). Between a rock and a hard place: Organizational change and performance under conditions of fundamental environmental transformation. *Administrative Science Quarterly*, 37, 48–75.

Hayes-Roth, B., & Hayes-Roth, F. (1979). A cognitive model of planning. *Cognitive Science*, 3, 275–310.

Holmes, F. (2018, February 27). The world's cobalt supply is in jeopardy. *Forbes*. Retrieved from https://www.forbes.com/sites/greatspeculations/2018/02/27/the-worlds-cobalt-supply-is-in-jeopardy/#4640f2c01be5

Honig, B. (2004). Entrepreneurship education: Toward a model of contingency based business planning. *The Academy of Management Learning and Education*, 3, 258–273.

Howell, J. M., & Sheab, C. M. (2001). Individual differences, environmental scanning, innovation framing, and champion behavior: Key predictors of project performance. *Journal of Product Innovation Management*, 18, 15–27.

Hunter, S. T., Bedell-Avers, K. E., & Mumford, M. D. (2007). The typical leadership study: Assumptions, implications, and potential remedies. *The Leadership Quarterly*, 18, 435–446.

Hunter, S. T., Cassidy, S. E., & Ligon, G. S. (2012). Planning for innovation: A process oriented perspective. In M. D. Mumford (Ed.), *Handbook of organizational creativity* (pp. 515–545). Chicago, IL: Elsevier.

Isaacson, W. (2014). *The innovators: How a group of hackers, geniuses, and geeks created the digital revolution*. New York, NY: Simon and Schuster.

Judge, W. Q., & Douglas, T. J. (1998). Performance implications of incorporating natural environmental issues into the strategic planning process: An empirical assessment. *Journal of Management Studies*, 35, 241–262.

King, S. (1973). *Developing new brands*. New York, NY: Pitman.

Kukalis, S. (1989). The relationship among firm characteristics and design of strategic planning systems in large organizations. *Journal of Management*, 15, 565–579.

Landau, D., Drori, I., & Terjesen, S. (2014). Multiple legitimacy narratives and planned organizational change. *Human Relations*, 67, 1321–1345.

Latham, G. P., & Locke, E. A. (1991). Self-regulation through goal setting. *Organizational Behavior and Human Decision Processes*, 50, 212–247.

Lee, H. (2002). Aligning supply chain strategies with product uncertainties. *California Management Review*, 44, 105–119.

Leontiades, M., & Tezel, A. (1980). Planning perceptions and planning results. *Strategic Management Journal*, 1, 65–75.

Licuanan, B. F., Dailey, L. R., & Mumford, M. D. (2007). Idea evaluation: Error in evaluating highly original ideas. *Journal of Creative Behavior*, 41, 1–27.

Liedtka, J. M. (1998). Strategic thinking: Can it be taught? *Long Range Planning*, 31, 120–129.

Marcy, R. T. (2015). Breaking mental models as a form of creative destruction: The role of leader cognition in radical social innovations. *The Leadership Quarterly*, 26, 370–385.

Medeiros, K. E., Partlow, P. J., & Mumford, M. D. (2014). Not too much, not too little: The influence of constraints on creative problem solving. *Psychology of Aesthetics, Creativity, and the Arts*, 8, 198–210.

Medeiros, K. E., Steele, L. M., Watts, L. L., & Mumford, M. D. (2018). Timing is everything: Examining the role of constraints throughout the creative process. *Psychology of Aesthetics, Creativity, and the Arts*, 12, 471–488.

Medeiros, K. E., Watts, L. L., & Mumford, M. D. (2017). Thinking inside the box: Educating leaders to manage constraints. In C. Zhou (Ed.), *Handbook of research on creative problem-solving skill development in higher education* (pp. 25–50). Hershey, PA: IGI Global.

Mehrabi, M. G., Ulsoy, A. G., & Koren, Y. (2000). Reconfigurable manufacturing systems: Key to future manufacturing. *Journal of Intelligent Manufacturing*, 11, 403–419.

Miller, C. C., & Cardinal, L. B. (1994). Strategic planning and firm performance: A synthesis of more than two decades of research. *Academy of Management Journal*, 37, 1649–1665.

Miller, D., & Friesen, P. H. (1982). Innovation in conservative and entrepreneurial firms: Two models of strategic momentum. *Strategic Management Journal*, 3, 1–25.

Mintzberg, H. (1973). Strategy-making in three modes. *California Management Review*, 16, 44–53.

Mintzberg, H. (1994). *The rise and fall of strategic planning: Reconceiving roles for planning, plans, planners*. New York, NY: Toronto, Canada: Free Press, Maxwell Macmillian Canada.

Mintzberg, H. (2000). *The rise and fall of strategic planning*. Edinburgh, UK: Pearson Education.

Mintzberg, H., Raisinghani, D., & Théoret, A. (1976). The structure of "unstructured" decision processes. *Administrative Science Quarterly*, 21, 246–274.

Mumford, M. D. (2000). Managing creative people: Strategies and tactics for innovation. *Human Resource Management Review*, 10, 313–351.

Mumford, M. D., Bedell-Avers, K. E., & Hunter, S. T. (2008). Planning for innovation: A multi-level perspective. In M. D. Mumford, S. T. Hunter, & K. E. Bedell-Avers (Eds.), *Multi-level issues in creativity and innovation* (pp. 107–154). Oxford, UK: JAI Press.

Mumford, M. D., & Gustafson, S. (1988). Creativity syndrome: Integration, application, and innovation. *Psychological Bulletin*, 103, 27–43.

Mumford, M. D., Lonergan, D. C., & Scott, G. (2002). Evaluating creative ideas: Processes, standards, and context. *Inquiry: Critical Thinking Across the Disciplines*, 22, 21–30.

Mumford, M. D., McIntosh, T., Mulhearn, T., Steele, L., & Watts, L. L. (2015). Processes, strategies, and knowledge in creative thought: Multiple interacting systems. In J. Kaufman (Ed.), *Creativity and reason in cognitive development* (2nd ed., pp. 164–186). Cambridge, UK: Cambridge University Press.

Mumford, M. D., Mecca, J. T., & Watts, L. L. (2015). Planning processes: Relevant cognitive operations. In M. D. Mumford & M. R. Frese (Eds.), *The psychology of planning in organizations: Research and applications* (pp. 9–30). New York, NY: Routledge.

Mumford, M. D., Medeiros, K. E., & Partlow, P. J. (2012). Creative thinking: Processes, strategies, and knowledge. *Journal of Creative Behavior*, 46, 30–47.

Mumford, M. D., Mulhearn, T., Watts, L. L., Steele, L., & McIntosh, T. J. (2017). Leader impacts on creative teams: Direction, engagement, and sales. In R. Reiter-Palmon (Ed.), *Handbook of team creativity* (pp. 131–155). Oxford, UK: Oxford University Press.

Mumford, M. D., Schultz, R. A., & Van Doorn, J. R. (2001). Performance in planning: Processes, requirements, and errors. *Review of General Psychology*, 5, 213–240.

Mumford, M. D., Scott, G. M., Gaddis, B., & Strange, J. M. (2002). Leading creative people: Orchestrating expertise and relationships. *The Leadership Quarterly*, 13, 705–750.

Mumford, M. D., Steele, L., Mulhearn, T. J., McIntosh, T. J., & Watts, L. L. (2017). Leader planning skills and creative performance: Integrating past, present, and future. In M. D. Mumford & S. Hemlin (Eds.), *Handbook of research on leadership and creativity* (pp. 17–39). Cheltenham, UK: Elgar.

Mumford, M. D., Watts, L. L., & Partlow, P. P. (2015). Leader cognition: Approaches and findings. *The Leadership Quarterly*, 26, 301–306.

Nohria, N., & Gulati, R. (1996). Is slack good or bad for innovation? *Academy of Management Journal*, 39, 1245–1264.

Nohria, N., & Gulati, R. (1997). What is the optimum amount of organizational slack? A study of the relationship between slack and innovation in multinational firms. *European Management Journal*, 15, 603–611.

O'Connor, G. C., & Rice, M. P. (2001). Opportunity recognition and breakthrough innovation in large established firms. *California Management Review*, 43, 95–116.

Onarheim, B. (2012). Creativity from constraints in engineering design: Lessons learned from Coloplast. *Journal of Engineering Design*, 23, 323–336.

Özsomer, A., Calantone, R. J., & Di Bonetto, A. (1997). What makes firms more innovative? A look at organizational and environmental factors. *Journal of Business and Industrial Marketing*, 12, 400–416.

Pearce, J. A., Freeman, E. B., & Robinson, R. B. Jr. (1987). The tenuous link between formal strategic planning and financial performance. *Academy of Management Review*, 12, 658–675.

Peterson, D. R., Barrett, J. D., Hester, K. S., Robledo, I. C., Hougen, D. F., Day, E. A., & Mumford, M. D. (2013). Teaching people to manage constraints: Effects on creative problem-solving. *Creativity Research Journal*, 25, 335–347.

Pirola-Merlo, A., Härtel, C., Mann, L., & Hirst, G. (2002). How leaders influence the impact of affective events on team climate and performance in R&D teams. *The Leadership Quarterly*, 13, 561–581.

Poister, T. H. (2010). The future of strategic planning in the public sector: Linking strategic management and performance. *Public Administration Review*, 70, 246–254.

Powell, T. C. (1992). Strategic planning as competitive advantage. *Strategic Management Journal*, 13, 551–558.

Rayna, T., & Striukova, L. (2016). From rapid prototyping to home fabrication: How 3D printing is changing business model innovation. *Technological Forecasting and Social Change*, 102, 214–224.

Reisinger, D. (2018, February 21). Here's why Apple wants to buy cobalt directly from miners. *Fortune*. Retrieved from http://fortune.com/2018/02/21/apple-buy-cobalt-miners/

Ren, C. R., & Guo, C. (2011). Middle managers' strategic role in the corporate entrepreneurial process: Attention-based effects. *Journal of Management*, 37, 1586–1610.

Rhéaume, L., & Gardoni, M. (2016). Strategy-making for innovation management and the development of corporate universities. *International Journal on Interactive Design and Manufacturing (IJIDeM)*, 10, 73–84.

Ring, P. S., & Perry, J. L. (1985). Strategic management in public and private organizations: Implications of distinctive contexts and constraints. *Academy of Management Review*, 10, 276–286.

Robinson, R. B. Jr., & Pearce, J. A. (1984). Research thrusts in small firm strategic planning. *Academy of Management Review*, 9, 128–137.

Rosenbusch, N., Brinckmann, J., & Bausch, A. (2011). Is innovation always beneficial? A meta-analysis of the relationship between innovation and performance in SMEs. *Journal of Business Venturing*, 26, 441–457.

Rosenkopf, L., & Nerkar, A. (2001). Beyond local search: Boundary-spanning, exploration, and impact in the optical disk industry. *Strategic Management Journal*, 22, 287–306.

Rothstein, E., Patel, K. R., Giorgini, V. D., Steele, L. M., & Watts, L. L. (2018, April). *The facilitative effects of competition, workload, and timeframe on planning.* Poster presented at the 33rd annual conference of the Society for Industrial and Organizational Psychology, Chicago, IL.

Rothwell, R., & Robertson, A. B. (1973). The role of communications in technological innovation. *Research Policy*, 2, 204–225.

Rousseau, M. B., Mathias, B. D., Madden, L. T., & Crook, T. R. (2016). Innovation, firm performance, and appropriation: A meta-analysis. *International Journal of Innovation Management*, 20, 1–29.

Rubera, G., & Kirca, A. H. (2012). Firm innovativeness and its performance outcomes: A meta-analytic review and theoretical integration. *Journal of Marketing*, 76, 130–147.

Rust, R. T., Lemon, K. N., & Zeithaml, V. A. (2004). Return on marketing: Using customer equity to focus marketing strategy. *Journal of Marketing*, 68, 109–127.

Sapat, A. (2004). Devolution and innovation: The adoption of state environmental policy innovations by administrative agencies. *Public Administration Review*, 64, 141–151.

Sarros, J. C., Cooper, B. K., & Santora, J. C. (2008). Building a climate for innovation through transformational leadership and organizational culture. *Journal of Leadership and Organizational Studies*, 15, 145–158.

Schmidt, J. B., & Watts, L. L. (2017). Creative leadership in the marketing arena. In M. D. Mumford & S. Hemlin (Eds.), *Handbook of research on leadership and creativity* (pp. 435–444). Cheltenham, UK: Elgar.

Scott, G. A., Lonergan, D. C., & Mumford, M. D. (2005). Conceptual combination: Alternative knowledge structures, alternative heuristics. *Creativity Research Journal*, 17, 79–98.

Shefer, D., & Frenkel, A. (2005). R&D, firm size and innovation: An empirical analysis. *Technovation*, 25, 25–32.

Shrivastava, P., & Grant, J. H. (1985). Empirically derived models of strategic decision-making processes. *Strategic Management Journal*, 6, 97–113.

Simons, R. (1990). The role of management control systems in creating competitive advantage: New perspectives. *Accounting, Organizations and Society*, 15, 127–143.

Smith, A. N. (2009, November 4). What was Polaroid thinking? *Yale Insights*. Retrieved from https://insights.som.yale.edu/insights/what-was-polaroid-thinking

Song, M., Im, S., Bij, H. V. D., & Song, L. Z. (2011). Does strategic planning enhance or impede innovation and firm performance? *Journal of Product Innovation Management*, 28, 503–520.

Song, X. M., & Montoya-Weiss, M. M. (1998). Critical development activities for really new versus incremental products. *Journal of Product Innovation Management*, 15, 124–135.

Srivastava, M. K., & Gnyawali, D. R. (2011). When do relational resources matter? Leveraging portfolio technological resources for breakthrough innovation. *Academy of Management Journal*, 54, 797–810.

Steele, L. M., Watts, L. L., & den Hartog, D. N. (2018, April). *Transformational leadership and innovation across cultures: A meta-analysis*. Poster presented at the 33rd annual conference of the Society for Industrial and Organizational Psychology, Chicago, IL.

Steiner, G. A. (2010). *Strategic planning*. New York, NY: Simon and Schuster.

Strange, J. M., & Mumford, M. D. (2005). The origins of vision: Effects of reflection, models, and analysis. *The Leadership Quarterly*, 16, 121–148.

Teece, D. J. (1994). Firm organization, industrial structure, and technological innovation. *Journal of Economic Behavior and Organization*, 31, 193–224.

Teece, D. J. (2010). Business models, business strategy and innovation. *Long Range Planning*, 43, 172–194.

Thamhain, H. J. (2003). Managing innovative R&D teams. *R&D Management*, 33, 297–311.

Thune, S. S., & House, R. J. (1970). Where long-range planning pays off: Findings of a survey of formal, informal planners. *Business Horizons*, 13, 81–87.

Tidd, J., Bessant, J. R., & Pavitt, K. (2005). *Managing innovation integrating technology, market and organizational change* (3rd ed.). Hoboken, NJ: Wiley.

Tushman, M. L. (1977). Special boundary roles in the innovation process. *Administrative Science Quarterly*, 22, 587–605.

Tushman, M. L. (1997). Winning through innovation. *Strategy and Leadership*, 25, 14–19.

Utterback, J. M. (1971). The process of technological innovation within the firm. *Academy of Management Journal*, 14, 75–88.

Van de Ven, A. H. (1986). Central problems in the management of innovation. *Management Science*, 32, 590–607.

Vincent, L. H., Bharadwaj, S. G., & Challagalla, G. N. (2004). *Does innovation mediate firm performance? A meta-analysis of determinants and consequences of organizational innovation*. Working paper, Georgia Institute of Technology, Atlanta, GA.

Wang, Z., & Wang, N. (2012). Knowledge sharing, innovation and firm performance. *Expert Systems with Applications*, 39, 8899–8908.

Watts, L. L., Mulhearn, T. J., Todd, E. M., & Mumford, M. D. (2017a). Leader idea evaluation and follower creativity: Challenges, constraints, and capabilities. In M. D. Mumford & S. Hemlin (Eds.), *Handbook of research on leadership and creativity* (pp. 82–99). Cheltenham, UK: Elgar.

Watts, L. R., & Ormsby, J. G. (1990). The effect of operational and strategic planning on small firm performance. *Journal of Small Business Strategy*, 1, 27–35.

Watts, L. L., Steele, L. M., Medeiros, K. E., & Mumford, M. D. (2018). Minding the gap between generation and implementation: Effects of idea source, goals, and climate on selecting and refining creative ideas. *Psychology of Aesthetics, Creativity, and the Arts*, 13, 2–14.

Watts, L. L., Steele, L. M., & Song, H. (2017). Re-examining the relationship between need for cognition and creativity: Predicting creative problem solving across multiple domains. *Creativity Research Journal*, 29, 21–28.

Weihrich, H. (1982). Strategic career management: A missing link in management by objectives. *Human Resources Management*, 21, 58–66.

Woodman, R. W., Sawyer, J. E., & Griffing, R. W. (1993). Toward a theory of organizational creativity. *The Academy of Management Review*, 18, 293–321.

Zahra, S. A., & George, G. (2002). Absorptive capacity: A review, reconceptualization, and extension. *The Academy of Management Review*, 27, 185–203.

Zajac, E. J., & Bazerman, M. H. (1991). Blind spots in industry and competitor analysis: Implications of interfirm (mis)perceptions for strategic decisions. *The Academy of Management Review*, 16, 37–56.

Zhou, K. Z., & Li, C. B. (2012). How knowledge affects radical innovation: Knowledge base, market knowledge acquisition, and internal knowledge sharing. *Strategic Management Journal*, 33, 1090–1102.

12
CREATIVITY AND INNOVATION IN THE CONTEXT OF FIRMS

Kyriaki Hadjikosta and Tamara Friedrich

Introduction

As creativity and innovation are becoming increasingly important to organizational survival (Cox, 2005; European Union, 2009; Florida & Goodnight, 2005; Hennessey & Amabile, 2010; Ligon, Graham, Edwards, Osburn, & Hunter, 2012; Madden, 2017; Puccio & Cabra, 2010), organizations need to identify and implement strategies and practices that are conducive to creativity and innovation in order to remain competitive. Typically, organizations limit their investment or support for innovation to specific areas of the organization, such as research and development (R&D). However, as we discuss in this chapter, embedding support for innovation across the organization is important for legitimizing an organization's innovation strategy.

Thus, it is important to consider how the strategies and practices of each department and the strategies and practices of top management teams can contribute to organizational creativity and innovation. In addressing this question, many scholars have focused on one function or a small group of functions at a time, omitting the inspection of the organization as a whole. As this chapter highlights, however, it is important to take a better look at the greater picture. The discussion that follows reveals that when organizational functions collaborate (cross-functional integrations) and align their unique strategies, organizational innovation is further supported, suggesting there is a value in implementing strategic alignment and collaboration across an organization.

For example, the alignment of the human resources (HR) innovation strategy with the corporate strategy can guide the development of human resources management (HRM) practices that help achieve strategic objectives (Jiménez-Jiménez & Sanz-Valle, 2005), the alignment of corporate and purchasing innovation strategies can lead to successful new product development (NPD) (Luzzini & Ronchi, 2011), and the alignment of corporate and marketing innovation strategies can increase the perceived need for integration with other departments (e.g., a marketing-R&D integration, Gupta et al., 1986), which can lead to the enhancement of marketing's capabilities to capture customer needs (Weerawardena, 2003).

Note that the terms *creativity* and *innovation* are often used interchangeably in the literature (McLean, 2005). We refer to creativity as the process of generating novel and useful ideas (Amabile, 1988; Plucker, Beghetto, & Dow, 2004; Rhodes, 1961; Sawyer, 2012). Unlike other works that refer to innovation as something new (Damanpour, 1991) or the process of implementing new or imported ideas (Amabile, 1988; Ayyagari, Demirgüç-Kunt, & Maksimovic, 2011; Damanpour & Schneider, 2006; Shipton, Lin, Sanders, & Yang, 2017a), we refer to innovation as the combined process of generating and implementing ideas (Kanter, 1983; Thompson, 1965; Van de Ven, 1986; Van de Ven, Angle, & Poole, 2000).

The need for strategic alignment and collaboration between organizational functions is revealed through a review of how the unique strategies and practices of departments, top management teams, departmental management teams, individually and in coordination, contribute to innovation. In the remainder of the chapter, we dedicate one section to the unique contributions of each function – top management teams, human resources, finance, purchasing, marketing and sales, legal, as well as departmental management teams – and discuss the benefits of their cooperation and alignment with other functions. In each section, we consider management implications and offer guidance for future research. We conclude the chapter with a call for further examination of the contributions of global strategic alignment and cross-functional collaboration for legitimizing innovation in the firm.

Top Management Teams

Vision

One important practice exercised by top management teams that can promote organizational innovation is the articulation and communication of a corporate vision (Martins & Martins, 2002; Martins & Terblanche, 2003; Thamhain, 2003; Tidd & Bessant, 2013a): "a transcended goal that represents shared values, has moral overtones, and provides meaning; it reflects what the organisation's future could and should be" (Andriopoulos, 2001, p. 834). It is theorized that to be effective, a corporate vision needs to define objectives, clarify pathways toward achieving those objectives, act as a basis for decision-making (Mumford, Scott, Gaddis, & Strange, 2002), and be accompanied by inspirational communication that motivates, encourages, and instills pride in employees (Rafferty & Griffin, 2004). This is because such mission-oriented visions can direct the organization, concentrate its attention to innovations that support its vision, and create an organizational climate favorable to innovation (McDonald, 2007). Furthermore, it can act as the framework that guides idea generation by employees and idea oversight by leaders (Perkins, Lean, & Newbery, 2017), promote the belief that the organization is supportive of innovation, and create a culture that also promotes this belief (Sarros, Cooper, & Santora, 2011).

Leadership

The literature also suggests that top management teams can directly and indirectly influence innovation through their leadership styles or leadership characteristics (Elenkov & Manev, 2005; Hughes, Lee, Tian, Newman, & Legood, 2018). Several forms of leadership, including transformational leadership, high-quality leader-member exchange (LMX), transactional leadership, empowering leadership, authentic leadership, and servant leadership have exhibited correlations ranging from small to medium with creativity and innovation. While a lot of attention has been given to the positive effects of transformational leadership and high-quality LMX on creativity and innovation (Amabile, Conti, Coon, Lazenby, & Herron, 1996; Amabile, Schatzel, Moneta, & Kramer, 2004; Elkins & Keller, 2003; Gumusluoglu & Ilsev, 2009; Jaiswal & Dhar, 2015; Jung, Chow, & Wu, 2003; Jung, Wu, & Chow, 2008; Scott & Bruce, 1994; Shin & Zhou, 2003), a more nuanced examination of the effects of leadership style subfactors (for example, intellectual stimulation and individual attention) is necessary before firm conclusions about the relationship between leadership and the innovation process are made (Friedrich, Mumford, Vessey, Beeler, & Eubanks, 2010; Hughes et al., 2018).

With findings suggesting that different leadership styles or leadership characteristics might be more effective at different stages of the innovation process (Elenkov & Manev, 2005; Hughes et al., 2018), it is argued that leaders might have to adjust their leadership styles depending on the stage of the innovation process (Anderson, Potočnik, & Zhou, 2014), or, alternatively, multiple leaders may serve varying roles throughout the innovation process. For instance, senior leadership teams may adopt collective leadership in order to utilize varying skills necessary to initiate and manage innovative work (Friedrich & Zhong, 2017; Mumford, Mulhearn, Watts, Steele, & McIntosh, 2018b). More research is needed to clarify which are the most appropriate approaches, under what conditions, and for which types of innovation (e.g., product, process, administrative, incremental, radical, exploitative, and explorative) (Friedrich et al., 2010).

In addition, more attention needs to be given to the effects of top management teams' leadership on innovation. Though discussed indirectly as firm-level or organizational-level leadership in the most recent comprehensive review (Hughes et al., 2018), only a small fraction of studies focus on the effects of top management teams on innovation (e.g., Nijstad, Berger-Selman, & De Dreu, 2014). As innovation should be embedded across the organization, it is important to understand how the team at the top, which includes leaders of key aspects of the organization, can be composed or what collection of leadership styles would be important to have on the team. This would be an important area for future innovation and leadership research to further understand how senior leaders can give legitimacy and support to innovation efforts.

Culture and Climate

In addition to their contributions through vision and leadership, top management teams can affect the innovation process by shaping the organizational climate and culture. One argument is that senior leadership can essentially shape the organizational culture, practices, and procedures that will allow for innovation to thrive by giving priority to innovation and installing innovation-oriented practices and procedures (Ahmed, 1998).

Focusing on culture, which can be defined as "all the institutionalized ways and the implicit beliefs, norms, values and premises which underline and govern behavior" (Ahmed, 1998, p. 32), the literature suggests that organizational cultures supportive of innovation emphasize learning and development, divergence, participation in decision-making, empowerment, communication, idea generation, debate, caring, freedom, and autonomy (Ahmed, 1998; Andriopoulos, 2001; Hurley & Hult, 1998; Martins & Terblanche, 2003; Naranjo-Valencia, Jiménez-Jiménez, & Sanz-Valle, 2016; Woodman, Sawyer, & Griffin, 1993). It is also proposed that innovative organizations engage in risk-taking and risk management (Ahmed, 1998; Martins & Terblanche, 2003; Woodman et al., 1993), embrace mistakes and failure as learning experiences (Martins & Terblanche, 2003), and maintain a focus on their relations with external actors, such as suppliers and customers, rather than internal affairs (Ahmed, 1998; Cameron & Quinn, 2011; Naranjo-Valencia et al., 2016).

Similar characteristics to organizational culture are also reflected in the organizational climate for creativity, which can be defined as the "perceptions of environmental conditions that shape individuals' beliefs about the work environment" (Friedrich, Stenmark, & Mumford, 2011, p. 208). Early research on organizational innovation identified that environmental conditions as well as individuals' perceptions about those conditions promote or hinder innovation by increasing or decreasing individuals' intrinsic motivation to engage in innovative work (Amabile, 1988, 1998; Amabile et al., 1996; Perkins et al., 2017; Woodman et al., 1993). The list of perceptions about work conditions that are instrumental to innovation includes believing that you have positive and supportive peer and supervisory relationships; thinking that you work on challenging and interesting projects with a clear mission, autonomy, and freedom; feeling that you receive support, encouragement, and recognition from supervisors and top management; and maintaining that you work for a well-connected organization that is committed to quality and originality, is eager to provide the necessary resources, is willing to take risks and manage uncertainty and ambiguity, is encouraging of participation and debate over ideas, and is rewarding of innovation (Hunter, Bedell, & Mumford, 2007; Soriano de Alencar, 2012). Top management teams that want to ensure that their efforts to support innovation are truly embedded should consider the perceptions of those in the organization. It may be beneficial to assess current perceptions of these climate factors and look for strengths and weaknesses across the organization (Amabile et al., 1996). Identifying areas of strength, for instance, strong perceptions of autonomy or challenging, engaging work, may be points to capitalize on, while identifying areas of weakness will provide an indication for where key barriers to innovation may be. Efforts to legitimize innovation in the firm through policies and procedures across different departments may well be undermined if the climate is not supportive.

Structure

Beyond culture and climate, leaders can shape another component of the organization that influences innovation: the organizational structure (Schein, 2010). Leaders might organize their businesses from rigid, mechanistic structures with centralized decision-making to organic structures with decentralized decision-making (Schein, 2010, p. 251). In addition to decision-making, these organizational structures determine the organization's communication channels, with mechanistic structures often characterized by a vertical flow of information and more organic structures typically characterized by lateral flow of information (McLean, 2005). With innovation flourishing under conditions of employee participation in decision-making and smooth and cross-functional exchange of knowledge and ideas, it is expected that structures with less centralized decision-making and more lateral communication channels will encourage innovation (Ahmed, 1998; Martins & Terblanche, 2003; Woodman et al., 1993).

The optimal degree of centralization of decision-making is still debated, with studies reporting different results depending on the type of innovation under investigation (Damanpour & Aravind, 2012; Jansen, Van Den Bosch, & Volberda, 2006) and contemporary reviews recommending the adoption of the most appropriate, flexible, and adaptable structures under the given circumstances (Mitra, 2017a; Tidd & Bessant, 2013a). Despite the debate on the centralization of decision-making, there is consensus on the need for integrative organizational structures that allow for cross-functional collaboration and smooth, cross-functional flow of information, knowledge, and ideas (Ateş, van Raaij, & Wynstra, 2018; Ellegaard & Koch, 2012; Troy, Hirunyawipada, & Paswan, 2008). This agreement suggests that, regardless of the organization's level of decision-making centralization, senior management needs to work toward implementing more integrative organizational structures to promote innovation. This may include formal systems like knowledge management or idea sharing tools, or it may be less formal, like holding cross-departmental gatherings or town halls where information can be shared.

Strategy

Finally, top management teams can influence innovation through the innovation strategies they formulate and communicate across the organization. An innovation strategy, defined as "a set of coherent, mutually reinforcing policies or behaviors aimed at achieving a specific competitive goal" (Pisano, 2015, p. 46), can promote alignment across the organization, clarify objectives and priorities, concentrate efforts around these objectives and priorities (Pisano, 2015), guide the selection of innovations that align with the organization's objectives (Dodgson, Salter, & Gann, 2008; Pisano, 2015), guide decision-making, attract creative talent (Dodgson et al., 2008), improve innovative capabilities (Yu, Dong, Shen, Khalifa, & Hao, 2013), improve business performance (Ezzi & Jarboui, 2016; Li, Zhang, & Chan, 2005; Rauch, Wiklund, Lumpkin, & Frese, 2009), and promote firm growth (Soininen, Martikainen, Puumalainen, & Kyläheiko, 2012). Evidence to support the positive relationship of strategy on innovative outcomes has been observed in a variety of contexts, such as small and medium UK manufacturing companies (Laforet, 2008), medium and large Chinese high-tech manufacturing companies (Guan, Yam, Tang, & Lau, 2009), small and medium Greek manufacturing companies (Avlonitis & Salavou, 2007), small Finnish companies across a range of sectors (Soininen et al., 2012), Chinese companies implementing information technology portfolios (Yu et al., 2013), and Tunisian companies in R&D-intensive sectors (Ezzi & Jarboui, 2016).

The formulation of an innovation strategy involves the analysis of the organization's innovation processes, innovative capabilities, resources, strengths, weaknesses, challenges, and opportunities; the identification of innovations that will create the greatest value for the organization; and the development of resources, innovative capabilities, and innovation processes that will facilitate the organization's innovative efforts (Dodgson et al., 2008; Pisano, 2015; Tidd & Bessant, 2013c). The innovation strategy should be aligned with the organization's overall business strategy, while accommodating for the uncertainty entailed in innovation (Dodgson et al., 2008; Pisano, 2015), and must be adjusted in light of new information (Dodgson et al., 2008; Pisano, 2015; Tidd & Bessant, 2013c).

Summary

What can be learned from the preceding review is that, to promote organizational innovation, top management teams could formulate and communicate mission-oriented organizational visions that can guide innovative work and create a climate favorable to innovation. They could install organizational practices and procedures that will generate cultures and climates favorable to innovation, as well as implement organizational structures that allow for smooth cross-functional collaboration and flow of information, knowledge, and ideas. Finally, they could articulate and communicate specific corporate innovation strategies, as these can promote alignment and focus for innovative work across the organization, help set objectives and priorities, guide decision-making, and attract creative talent.

Regarding leadership, practitioners should be aware that a number of leadership styles and leadership characteristics appear to be related to creativity and innovation (Elenkov & Manev, 2005; Hughes et al., 2018), suggesting that not one leadership style or characteristic is best at managing the innovation process from start to finish. To assist top management teams in adopting the appropriate leadership approaches under their organization's individual characteristics and innovation aims, the research community could focus on investigating the effects of top management team leadership on innovation, as the number of studies investigating the effects of leadership on innovation at the top level is limited. Finally, innovation scholars could continue investigating and debating the optimal degree of decision-making centralization under a range of environmental conditions, organizational characteristics, and innovation aims in order to assist top management teams in installing the most beneficial degrees of decision-making centralization across their organizations.

Human Resources Department

Human Resource Management Practices

The HR department undertakes a range of responsibilities, including the hiring of personnel with the desired knowledge and expertise, the further training of employees with skills necessary for the organization's success, the appraising and rewarding of personnel performance, and the management of personnel career paths (Belker, McCormick, & Topchik, 2012). The HRM practices the department follows in fulfilling these duties have a central role in creating and cultivating organizational cultures, capabilities, and knowledge reserves that support innovation. Having a corporate innovation strategy can guide the development and implementation of HRM practices that will help the organization achieve its innovation objectives (Jiménez-Jiménez & Sanz-Valle, 2005).

A number of positive relationships between innovation-oriented HRM practices and innovation have been reported in the literature (Cano & Cano,

2006; Chang, Gong, & Shum, 2011; Gupta & Singhal, 1993; Gutierrez-Gutierrez, Barrales-Molina, & Kaynak, 2018; Michie & Sheehan, 1999; Shipton, West Michael, Dawson, Birdi, & Patterson, 2006; Zhou, Hong, & Liu, 2013), with some authors concluding that HRM practices play a critical role in "creating and sustaining a culture that supports creativity and innovation" (McLean, 2005, p. 228). It is also accepted that the benefits become significantly greater when complementary HRM practices, an HRM system, are adopted together than when individual practices are adopted in isolation (Haneda & Ito, 2018; Jiménez-Jiménez & Sanz-Valle, 2005; Laursen & Foss, 2003; c.f. Cano & Cano, 2006). For example, permitting employees to participate in problem-solving will bear more fruit if the appropriate training is provided to them (Laursen & Foss, 2003). Conversely, employees will likely invest in their training if they are permitted to participate in problem-solving, especially if they are offered desirable intrinsic and extrinsic rewards to do so (Laursen & Foss, 2003).

Despite the overwhelmingly positive results, however, some findings call for caution in the implementation of HRM practices. First, there are some negative relationships between some HRM practices and innovation (e.g., contingent pay and product innovation and technical innovation capabilities under conditions of low exploratory learning) (Beugelsdijk, 2008; Chang et al., 2011; Shipton et al., 2006; Zhou et al., 2013). In addition, not all practices are positively associated with all different forms of innovation (Haneda & Ito, 2018; Tan & Nasurdin, 2011). What is more, it might be easier to promote incremental innovation by adopting innovation-oriented HRM practices than it is to promote radical innovation, as incremental innovation is positively associated with a greater number of HRM practices compared to radical innovation (Beugelsdijk, 2008). In light of such conflicting findings, more research is needed on the configurations of HRM systems that enable the desirable forms of innovation (Shipton, Sparrow, Budhwar, & Brown, 2017b).

Culture

There appears to be a mediating relationship between HRM systems, culture, and innovation performance. An HRM system that expands employees' knowledge and skills, enhances knowledge transfer and learning, rewards personnel for their performance, and emphasizes team development helps build a developmental culture that contributes to the improvement of new product and service creation, as has been shown in medium and large companies in Hong Kong (Lau & Ngo, 2004). HRM systems are also instrumental in creating a culture of knowledge sharing within organizations with a functional organizational structure (Currie & Kerrin, 2003) – an organizational structure that tends to create vertical communication channels rather than innovation-conducive lateral communication channels (Haneda & Ito, 2018). The relationship between HRM practices and innovation is summarized in Figure 12.1.

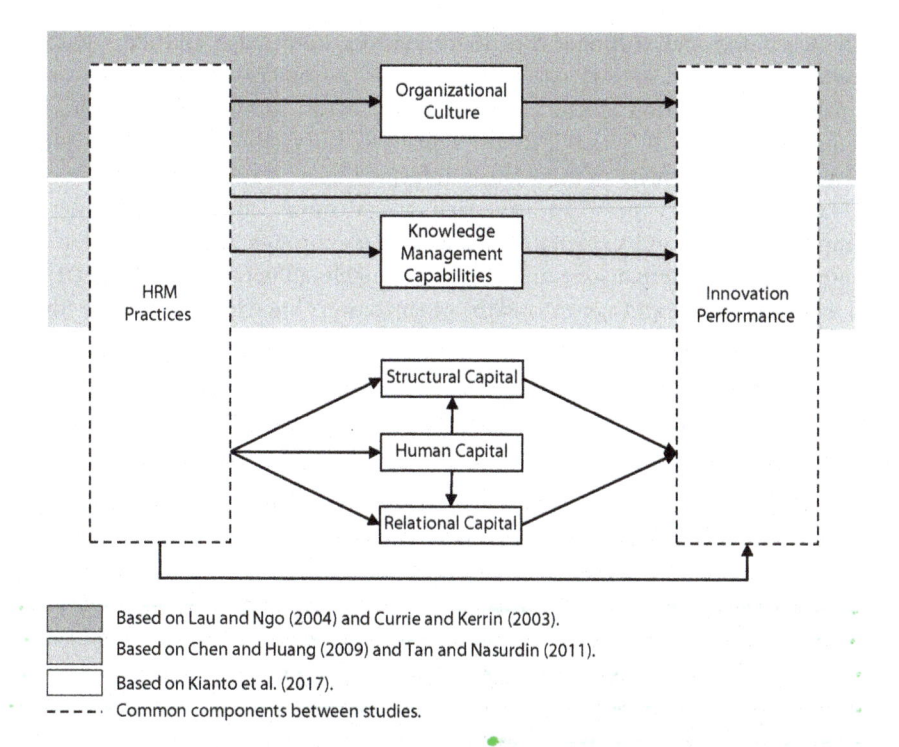

Creativity and Innovation in the Context of Firms **279**

FIGURE 12.1 The relationship between HRM practices and innovation performance.

Knowledge Management Capabilities

In addition to culture, innovation-oriented HRM practices can contribute to the creation and cultivation of knowledge management capabilities (KMCs) that promote innovation, including knowledge acquisition, sharing, and application. It is argued that innovation-oriented HRM practices focused on hiring, compensating, and promoting the careers of employees can enhance innovation performance by promoting knowledge acquisition and knowledge sharing (Scarbrough, 2003). Supporting this early argument, studies on top Taiwanese companies and large Malaysian manufacturing companies have shown that innovation-oriented HRM practices can enhance KMCs, which, in turn, can promote administrative innovation, new product and service development, and process development (Chen & Huang, 2009; Tan & Nasurdin, 2011).

Knowledge sharing in particular, which is theorized to be mediated by affective commitment (Camelo-Ordaz, García-Cruz, Sousa-Ginel, & Valle-Cabrera, 2011) (that is, "identification with, involvement in, and emotional attachment to the organization" (Allen & Meyer, 1996, p. 253), is considered vital in both idea generation and idea implementation. This is because having the capability and willingness to share existing knowledge and ideas with coworkers as well as external agents, such as customers and suppliers, can enable the cocreation of knowledge and ideas with external agents, such as suppliers (Hadaya & Cassivi, 2009; Veugelers, Bury, & Viaene, 2010); can drive the improvement of innovations informed by new knowledge and ideas (Handfield, 2006, p. 179); can facilitate a more efficient evaluation, implementation, and exploitation of new ideas through the organization's internal and external communication channels (Shipton et al., 2017b; Thamhain, 2003); and can expand the organization's knowledge reserves with knowledge and ideas that can be pursued or combined to generate new ideas within the firm (see also section on Purchasing Department).

Knowledge Base

HRM practices can also help in the development and expansion of the organization's knowledge base with new knowledge and ideas and, thus, can have another indirect influence on organizational innovation. Specifically, innovation-oriented HRM practices can positively influence individuals' knowledge and skills (human capital), the collective knowledge embedded in the relationships among employees and among employees and external agents (relational capital), and the organization's nonhuman reserves of knowledge (structural capital), which, in turn, can promote new product development and product improvements, and improve manufacturing and market processes, production methods and processes, and marketing and administrative innovation, as shown in recent studies on technological and industrial companies in Spain (Donate, Peña, & Sánchez de Pablo, 2016; Kianto et al., 2017).

The composition of the organization's knowledge base can also influence innovative activity in two ways: organizations appear to engage in the innovation process differently depending on their knowledge base (Zhou & Wu, 2010) and organizations should, indeed, evaluate their knowledge base and engage in the innovation process differently depending on their knowledge (Tsai, Tsai, & Wang, 2012; Zhou & Li, 2012). Regarding the influences of knowledge base on innovation engagement, the existing research reveals that as organizations accumulate knowledge, they participate in exploitative innovation (that is, they exploit the accumulated knowledge) for NPD at an accelerating rate (Zhou & Wu, 2010). At the same time, they partake in explorative innovation (that is, they explore new knowledge and skills) but only to a certain point; any further increase of accumulated knowledge decreases the organization's engagement in explorative innovation (Zhou & Wu, 2010).

In regard to how organizations should engage in innovation depending on their knowledge base composition, it is argued that organizations possessing a diverse knowledge base will need to share knowledge internally to produce radical innovations, that organizations possessing specialized knowledge will need to acquire market intelligence in order to deliver radical innovations (Zhou & Li, 2012), and that organizations with a lot of accumulated knowledge can perform better in NPD by establishing firm-supplier collaborations (Tsai et al., 2012). Taken together, the findings on the overall impact of an organization's knowledge base on innovation highlight the need for organizations to evaluate their knowledge base and select and pursue the innovative activities that will move them toward their innovation aims.

Summary

In summary, the HR department can promote organizational innovation through its innovation-oriented HRM practices and HRM systems. It is, therefore, important for executives and HR managers to carefully develop and implement HRM practices and systems that are aligned with the organization's innovation strategy, as these can improve innovation capabilities and innovation performance by creating a culture conducive to innovation, contributing to the development of the knowledge management capabilities of knowledge acquisition, sharing, and application, and developing and expanding the organization's knowledge base.

Care should be taken in the development of the appropriate HRM practices and systems, however, as not all practices and systems are positively related to all forms of innovation and under all conditions. To support professionals in developing and implementing the most suitable HRM practices, innovation scholars could aim to identify which HRM practices and systems are most appropriate for each type of innovation (Shipton et al., 2017b) and under what conditions.

Finally, practical advice for HR professionals would be to begin by evaluating the composition of their existing knowledge base in order to steer innovative teams toward the organization's innovation aspirations, as organizations tend to engage in exploitative or explorative innovation differently and should, indeed, engage in knowledge acquisition and sharing in different ways in order to achieve their innovation objectives. After examining their internal knowledge capabilities and establishing how to manage them effectively, efforts should be made to recruit, select, and effectively manage the performance of individuals with the appropriate knowledge and skills necessary for supporting innovative efforts (Hunter, Cushenbery, & Friedrich, 2012).

Finance Department

Being provided with the necessary resources was an "obvious," yet neglected, factor promoting innovation performance (Amabile, 1988, p. 154). Today, those who study innovation recognize that not only the availability of resources but also individuals' perceptions about the availability of resources affect their innovation performance (Amabile et al., 1996; Hunter et al., 2007; Soriano de Alencar, 2012). For that reason, an organization interested in facilitating innovative activity needs to provide the necessary resources, such as time, finance, and space, to employees expected to engage in it.

For resources to be available, the organization needs to secure and invest funds for innovation and acquire and allocate resources where needed. This highlights the importance of strategies and practices followed by the Finance department in acquiring funds and financing innovative initiatives and the significance of strategies and practices implemented by the purchasing department in acquiring and allocating resources. The following two sections focus on finance and purchasing.

External and Internal Finance Availability

Innovation is affected by both external and internal finance availability. At the most macro level, the development of a region's financial system can improve innovative activity by evaluating innovative projects and financing the most auspicious ones, diversifying the risks involved in innovative projects for investors, revealing the financial rewards of successful innovative projects (King & Levine, 1993b), producing information on investments, monitoring and influencing capital expenditure by firms, mobilizing savings, and easing barter exchange (Levine, 2005). Innovative activity, in turn, fosters economic growth (King & Levine, 1993a, 1993b; Schumpeter, 1911). Whether the financial system is predominately bank or market based as well as its exact composition seem to be of little importance (Levine, 2005), with the availability of internal and external finance playing the most important role in encouraging innovation (Brown, Fazzari, & Petersen, 2009).

A higher quality of institutions, including a well-developed legal system, as well as government support programs and policies, can boost firm and economic growth by contributing to the development of a region's financial system (Beck & Levine, 2002; Bekaert, Harvey, & Lundblad, 2005; Brown, Martinsson, & Petersen, 2013, 2017; Demirgüç-Kunt & Maksimovic, 2002). Particularly, higher-quality institutions can contribute to the development of a financial system in two ways: by improving conditions for investors (Beck, Demirgüç-Kunt, & Maksimovic, 2008b; Bekaert et al., 2005; Kerr & Nanda, 2015) and by improving conditions for banks and innovative firms (Amore, Schneider, & Žaldokas, 2013; Chava, Oettl, Subramanian, & Subramanian, 2013; Cornaggia, Mao, Tian, & Wolfe, 2015). By improving and enforcing laws that protect domestic and international investors (e.g., insider trading laws, property rights laws), institutions make investments to innovative firms more attractive. As a result, the supply of external finance from investors to organizations increases. By deregulating banking using measures that increase the local market power of banks (e.g., geographical diversification of risks, competition among banks), institutions make banks more likely to offer, and innovative firms more likely to apply for, loans. As a result, the supply of external finance from banks to organizations increases. In both cases, the availability of external finance promotes innovation (Brown et al. 2009), leading to firm and economic growth.

A higher quality of institutions can also influence innovative activity by affecting the availability of internal finance through government programs and policies, such as tax incentives and subsidies. Such an availability of internal finance is considered critical for R&D investment, as the cost of credit or equity financing of R&D activity tends to be high (Hall & Lerner, 2010). For that reason, tax incentives and other government programs and policies that increase internal finance can facilitate firm innovation and growth in both developed and developing countries (Bronzini & Piselli, 2016; Czarnitzki, Hanel, & Rosa, 2011; Guo, Guo, & Jiang, 2016; Hall & Lerner, 2010; Kasahara, Shimotsu, & Suzuki, 2014; Minniti & Venturini, 2017a; Szczygielski, Grabowski, Pamukcu, & Tandogan, 2017; Wonglimpiyarat, 2011; Yang, Huang, & Hou, 2012), particularly in small and young firms (Hall & Lerner, 2010). It should be noted, however, that the effectiveness of certain government programs and policies is debatable, and further investigation is needed (Chen & Gupta, 2017; Crespi, Giuliodori, Giuliodori, & Rodriguez, 2016; Hall & Lerner, 2010; Howell, 2016; Huergo & Moreno, 2017; Rao, 2016).

Taken together, the two systems – institutions and financial systems – facilitate the availability of internal and external finance that can fuel innovation and, consequently, promote firm and economic growth, which is summarized in Figure 12.2. Overall, the positive effects of finance availability appear to be greater for small, young, and growing innovative firms (Beck, Demirgüç-Kunt, Laeven, & Levine, 2008a; Beck et al., 2008b; Benfratello, Schiantarelli, & Sembenelli, 2008; Brown et al., 2013; OECD, 2015) and firms in particular industries, such as the high-tech sector, the services sector, and the manufacturing sector (Benfratello et al., 2008; Castellacci & Lie, 2015; Minniti & Venturini, 2017b). While it may be difficult for firms to manage these forces in the external environment, they can organize themselves with other organizations in the region to advocate for advantageous policies or choose regions to operate in that provide these advantages.

Firm Finance Differences

Firms differ in their access to, source of, and cost of finance, depending on their age, size, and industry characteristics. For example, small and medium

```
┌──────────────┐   ┌──────────────┐   ┌──────────────┐   ┌──────────────┐
│     High     │   │  Developed   │   │   Improved   │   │   Firm and   │
│   Quality    │──▶│  Financial   │──▶│  Innovative  │──▶│   Economic   │
│ Institutions │   │    System    │   │   Activity   │   │    Growth    │
└──────────────┘   └──────────────┘   └──────────────┘   └──────────────┘
```

- Protect investors by improving and enforcing laws.
- Promote financing through loans by deregulating banks.
- Reduce cost of R&D activity financing through policy and government programmes.

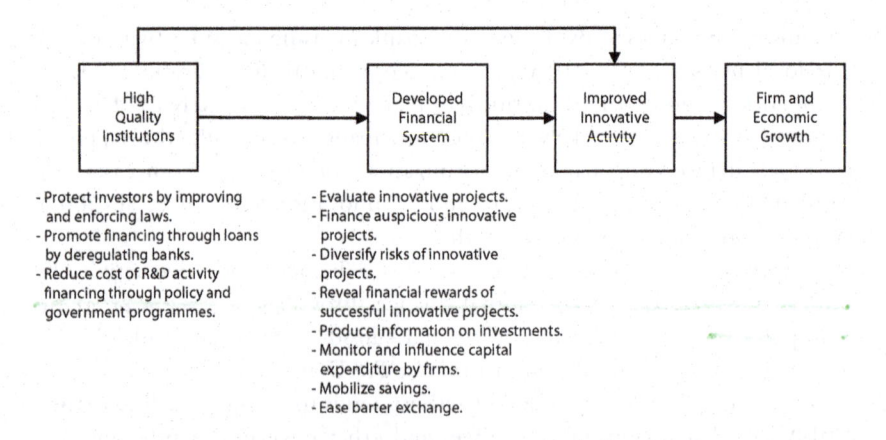

- Evaluate innovative projects.
- Finance auspicious innovative projects.
- Diversify risks of innovative projects.
- Reveal financial rewards of successful innovative projects.
- Produce information on investments.
- Monitor and influence capital expenditure by firms.
- Mobilize savings.
- Ease barter exchange.

FIGURE 12.2 The role of institutions and financial systems in innovation and firm and economic growth.

firms in the high-tech industry, an R&D-intensive industry, can face difficulties acquiring external finance and, therefore, resort to personal finances and short-term bank loans, as shown in a study on Italian companies (Giudici & Paleari, 2000), while young and small firms in R&D-intensive industries can face higher costs of capital than larger competitors and firms in other industries (Hall & Lerner, 2010).

What is more, a study on small and medium Canadian companies showed that more-innovative and less-innovative firms appear to evaluate and use their available finances in different ways depending on their individual characteristics. For instance, small and medium innovative firms appear to consider access to capital and cost of capital as more important contributors to their past growth and to rely more heavily on venture capital, public equity, and government subsidies as sources of finance than less innovative firms (Baldwin & Johnson, 1995), while large firms tend to finance their investments using internal finance (Hall & Lerner, 2010).

In terms of finance spending and government support, small and medium innovative firms tend to engage in investment expenditures, spend a greater proportion of their capital for product and process innovation by R&D, and believe they spend more on R&D than their competitors compared to less innovative firms (Baldwin & Johnson, 1995). In addition, more innovative firms appraise and utilize government programs, such as R&D tax incentives, to a greater degree than less innovative firms (Baldwin & Johnson, 1995). Supporting some of these early findings on the importance of government support for innovative firms, it has been found that R&D-intensive industries have a higher tendency to apply for R&D tax incentives (Bodas Freitas, Castellacci, Fontana, Malerba, & Vezzulli, 2017).

Finance Integration

In addition to the selection of finance sources and the investment in innovation, the finance department can influence organizational innovation through its integration with other departments. Unfortunately, the effects of finance integrations on innovation performance remain largely unexplored (Hempelmann & Engelen, 2015). The single study on the effects of finance integrations on innovation focuses on the success of new products developed by small, medium, and large companies across a range of sectors in developed countries (Hempelmann & Engelen, 2015). The findings are encouraging and highlight the need for further research on the effects of finance integrations. Specifically, the findings suggest that a finance-R&D integration is particularly critical in the early stages (conceptualization and evaluation) of projects, as the finance department can perform "business and profitability assessment[s]" and make and communicate go/no-go decisions on innovative projects based on their assessments (Hempelmann & Engelen, 2015, p. 640). Therefore, a finance-R&D integration, characterized by the sharing of assessment conclusions in the early stages of NPD, can reduce the uncertainty surrounding the financial attractiveness and profitability of projects and ensure that only the most promising projects progress to later stages (Hempelmann & Engelen, 2015).

Furthermore, the study shows that a finance-marketing integration is important in the late stages (production and commercialization) of less innovative projects, as the finance department can perform and communicate a launch financial analysis that helps the marketing department through a costly and critical product launch (Hempelmann & Engelen, 2015). Thus, a finance-marketing integration characterized by the sharing of a launch financial analysis can increase the effectiveness of a product launch and increase the likelihood of the launch's success (Hempelmann & Engelen, 2015).

Summary

To summarize, firms interested in improving their innovation performance could begin by reevaluating and assigning higher importance to internal and external finance availability, access to finance, and cost of finance in achieving higher performance. Furthermore, with cost of finance in mind, these firms could reevaluate their sources of internal and external finance (e.g., investors and government programs) and select the most advantageous source combinations. Last, for innovation performance improvements to be observed, these firms could also reconsider and increase their investment in organizational innovation and look at facilitating connections between the finance department and other areas of the organization working on innovative efforts.

As not all institutional programs and policies are equally effective in increasing internal and external finance availability (Chen & Gupta, 2017; Crespi et al., 2016; Hall & Lerner, 2010; Howell, 2016; Huergo & Moreno, 2017; Rao, 2016), the research community could examine the effectiveness of existing programs and policies that are frequently implemented and make recommendations to organizations on which programs and policies tend to be more beneficial based on their individual characteristics. This line of research will also allow scholars to provide guidance on the improvement of existing programs and the implementation of new programs and policies by institutions.

Finally, the integration of finance with other functional units can be beneficial to NPD (e.g., finance-R&D and finance-marketing integrations in Hempelmann and Engelen [2015]). Arguably, such integrations, encouraged and facilitated by senior management, can also support innovative efforts across the organization. Considering the potential benefits and the lack of adequate investigation, more research needs to be conducted on the effects of finance integrations on organizational innovation so that the particular effects of each integration under a range of conditions are revealed and so that organizational leaders receive sufficient guidance on how to implement and facilitate these integrations effectively.

Purchasing Department

In cooperation with the finance department, the purchasing department is tasked with strategically managing the firm's supply base in such a way that all the resources necessary to the firm's operations, including knowledge, are obtained "under the most favourable conditions" (van Weele, 2010, p. 3). Innovation involves the unique reconfiguration and recombination of existing knowledge (Sawyer, 2012), and often, valuable knowledge resides outside the firm. In addition, the need to improve NPD performance by reducing errors and time-to-market speed has led many firms to embrace open innovation (that is, innovation through the exploitation of knowledge existing within and outside the firm [Chesbrough, 2003]) using their supply base as one source of external knowledge (van Weele, 2010).

The purchasing department holds a unique position as the gatekeeper of knowledge between the organization itself and its supply base. Because of its unique position, the department has the potential to make great contributions to organizational innovation. For that reason, its role appears to be shifting toward a more strategic, value-adding role; a role that boosts innovation by facilitating knowledge sharing and knowledge creation within the organization itself and between the organization and its supply base (Pierangelini, 2017).

Structure and Responsibilities

Recognition of the potential contributions has ignited more research around the effects of the department's structure, responsibilities, and strategic activities on innovation. Research reveals that in organizations successful in NPD, the purchasing department reports to the organizations' chief executive officers (CEOs) or chief operating officers (COOs) (Luzzini & Ronchi, 2011), confirming the evidence for an upward shift of purchasing report levels (Johnson & Leenders, 2006) and indicating that the department plays an important role in achieving organizational objectives (Monczka, Handfield, Giunipero, & Patterson, 2015). In addition, in these organizations, the department's strategy is highly aligned with corporate strategy and other departments' strategies (Luzzini & Ronchi, 2011). The department is also adequately, or at least similarly, integrated with other departments (Luzzini & Ronchi, 2011), echoing the importance of strategic alignment and internal integration in business and supplier performance emphasized in other studies (Ateş et al., 2018; Baier, Hartmann, & Moser, 2008; Cousins, 2005; Ellegaard & Koch, 2012; González-Benito, 2007; Jansen et al., 2006). In addition, the department's personnel are part of hybrid groups, rather than exclusive groups (e.g., groups based on geography) depending on the needs of the organization. Finally, the organization's decision-making centralization is hybrid, with some decisions being made locally by the purchasing department and others being made at a corporate level (Luzzini & Ronchi, 2011).

As mentioned in the section on Top Management Teams, however, further research on the effects of decision-making centralization is needed as the effects of high centralization are not always negative (Damanpour & Aravind, 2012) and can influence the various types of innovation differently (e.g., exploitative and explorative innovation) (Jansen et al., 2006).

Supplier Market Intelligence

One strategic activity supporting purchasing in fulfilling its responsibilities and strengthening its position as an influencer on strategic decision-making at the corporate level is the development and sharing of supplier market intelligence (SMI) (Handfield, 2006). This involves the development of knowledge (intelligence) about the organization's supply market and supply base characteristics and the use of that intelligence during decision-making (Handfield, 2010; Handfield, Petersen, Cousins, & Lawson, 2009; McGonagle & Vella, 2012). Such external intelligence can also be communicated throughout the organization, facilitating innovation in four ways. First, it allows the organization to establish appropriate firm-supplier collaborations (Veugelers et al., 2010) that enable knowledge cocreation and sharing that can lead to innovation (Hadaya & Cassivi, 2009). Second, having communication networks with external agents, such as suppliers, enables the organization to evaluate, implement, and exploit new ideas and products more effectively through these networks (Shipton et al., 2017b; Thamhain, 2003). Third, it drives the improvement of innovations within the organization using intelligence on new innovations developed outside the organization (Handfield, 2006), including innovations developed by the organization's supply market and supply base. And fourth, it arguably enriches the organization's knowledge reserves with knowledge and ideas that can be used to generate new knowledge and ideas in the future.

Once SMI is collected and added to the organization's knowledge base, the organization's capacity to appraise it as useful, assimilate it, and exploit it in value-adding activities, also known as absorptive capacity, will determine whether the added intelligence will be exploited in the organization's innovation initiatives (Cohen & Levinthal, 1990). This underscores the importance of absorptive capacity in utilizing any collected SMI (Tsai, 2001; Zhou & Wu, 2010) and highlights that, in addition to developing SMI, organizations will benefit by improving their absorptive capacity (Tsai, Hsieh, & Hultink, 2011) so that SMI contributes to organizational innovation. This becomes an important point of collaboration with the HR department in building the appropriate body of expertise within the organization.

Finally, as discussed in the Human Resources Department section, organizations need to evaluate their knowledge base and engage in the most advantageous innovative activities based on that evaluation. The responsibilities of expanding the organization's knowledge base through the development of SMI, facilitating internal knowledge sharing, and establishing appropriate firm-supplier collaborations are often left to the purchasing department. This means that the purchasing department needs to not only be able to fulfill these responsibilities, but also to be able to evaluate the organization's existing knowledge reserves in order to complete these responsibilities effectively.

The requirement to understand the organization's knowledge base composition has not received much attention in the purchasing literature. Future research could focus on how the department can contribute to the development, maintenance, sharing, and evaluation of the organization's knowledge base through a cooperation with a central unit undertaking these responsibilities, such as the knowledge management unit (Dalkir, 2011, p. 13), or through a cooperation with other functional units that contribute to the organization's knowledge reserves, such as HR, marketing, and sales (see the Marketing Department and Sales Department section).

Strategic Sourcing

SMI collected by the purchasing department can also indirectly promote innovation performance by informing the organization's strategic sourcing

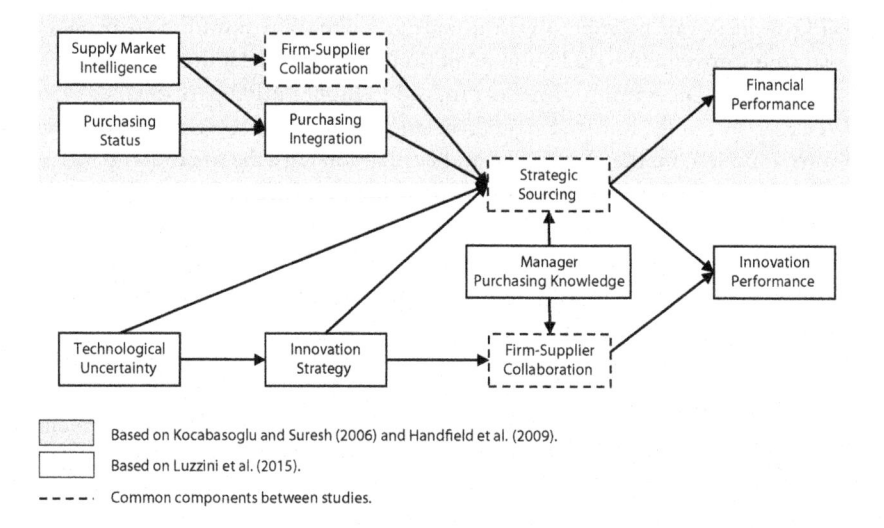

FIGURE 12.3 The role of strategic sourcing in financial and innovation performance.

(i.e., a strategic approach toward lowering supply total costs through strategic purchasing and firm-supplier collaborations [Parniangtong, 2016]). Research shows that SMI is regarded as the basis for purchasing integrations and firm-supplier collaborations (Handfield et al., 2009; Handfield, 2006), both of which contribute to more rigorous strategic sourcing (Handfield et al., 2009; Kocabasoglu & Suresh, 2006). In turn, strategic sourcing positively influences financial performance and NPD, as demonstrated in studies examining UK manufacturing and services companies and European and North American manufacturing companies (Handfield et al., 2009; Luzzini, Amann, Caniato, Essig, & Ronchi, 2015).

Note that in addition to cross-functional and firm-supplier collaborations, the status of purchasing within the organization (Handfield et al., 2009; Kocabasoglu & Suresh, 2006) and the purchasing manager's knowledge are also believed to positively contribute to strategic sourcing, underscoring the important role of purchasing in this strategic activity. See Figure 12.3 for a more detailed model of purchasing's contributions to strategic sourcing and organizational innovation.

New Product Development

In addition to SMI development, the early involvement of purchasing in NPD can improve NPD performance through appropriate supplier selection, early supplier involvement, and appropriate firm-supplier collaboration facilitation. In particular, purchasing involvement in the early stages of the

NPD process can improve supplier sourcing decisions resulting in product quality improvements, lead-time reductions, and cost reductions (Handfield, 2006, p. 47). These improvements can lead to higher NPD performance (van Weele, 2010) and improved overall business performance (growth in sales, return on assets, market share gain, and satisfaction with the firm's competitive position), as shown in studies on U.S. manufacturing companies (Tracey, 2004). The early involvement of purchasing in NPD also makes an early involvement of suppliers in NPD more likely (Hillebrand & Biemans, 2004; Tracey, 2004), which, in turn, promotes higher business performance (Tracey, 2004) and improves NPD performance (Laursen & Andersen, 2016). Finally, with firm-supplier collaborations requiring different facilitation by the purchasing department depending on the ambiguity surrounding a project in the early stages of NPD (Laursen & Andersen, 2016), the early involvement of purchasing in NPD could allow the department to offer the appropriate facilitation.

Summary

The purchasing department, with its unique position as the gatekeeper of knowledge flow between the organization itself and its supply base, can make a contribution to organizational innovation through the responsibilities and strategic activities it undertakes. Based on the preceding literature review, organizations interested in improving supplier-dependent innovation, such as new product and service development, could make sure that the department is strategically aligned to the corporate innovation strategy and other department's strategies, is adequately integrated with other departments, has a high report level, engages in SMI development, performs knowledge base evaluations, and participates in the early stages of NPD. Through these strategic activities, purchasing can directly and indirectly influence innovation by developing and providing supply market and supply base intelligence that expands the organization's knowledge base; informs the establishment of firm-supplier collaborations; enables the evaluation, implementation, and exploitation of new ideas and products through firm-supplier collaborations; drives the improvement of innovations in light of new knowledge; and influences critical activities at the departmental and corporate levels, including strategic sourcing, supplier selection, supplier involvement in NPD, and firm-supplier collaboration facilitation.

Organizations interested in enhancing innovation could also invest in improving their capacity to appraise, assimilate, and exploit new knowledge, so that new knowledge, including new knowledge collected by the purchasing department, can be utilized to benefit organizational innovation. Top management teams could also strive to assist purchasing in assuming its new strategic role as a facilitator of knowledge sharing and knowledge creation and undertaking greater responsibility in the development, maintenance, sharing, and evaluation of the organization's knowledge base. To contribute to this effort, the research community could investigate how the purchasing department can effectively assume its new value-adding roles. Innovation scholars could also examine the benefits of assuming these new roles and responsibilities in order to improve our currently limited understanding in these two unexplored areas.

Marketing Department and Sales Department

The marketing department has long been recognized as a critical link between customers and the organization itself. Its integration with other departments for market intelligence sharing became of particular interest in the 1970s (Ruekert & Walker, 1987). The department is responsible for understanding "the target market's needs, wants, and demands" (Kotler, 2000, p. 6) and influencing "the level, timing and composition of demand to meet the organisation's objectives" (Kotler, 2016, p. 10). These responsibilities can be met through market research and forecasting, the development of marketing strategies for the complete life cycle of products and services, the development of marketing programs that detail marketing budget allocation and expenditure, and the management of marketing resources required for the organization, implementation, and control of marketing programs (Kotler, 2000, 2016).

The sales department, often with different characteristics and separated from marketing (Homburg, Jensen, & Krohmer, 2008), is primarily in charge of successfully closing product and service sales (Jobber & Lancaster, 2012). To accomplish this, front-line personnel engage in a process of identifying the customers' needs, presenting and demonstrating the products or services that meet those needs, managing concerns and questions raised by customers, and negotiating the terms of the transaction before closing the sale (Jobber & Lancaster, 2012). Strategic responsibilities of sales include the management of the ongoing relationships with customers and the development of sales strategies and programs that will allow the department to reach business objectives (Parravicini, 2015).

Marketing and Sales Integrations

The two departments, marketing and sales, can support innovative work and directly and indirectly promote business and innovation performance in two ways: by aligning their departmental strategies to the organization's innovation strategy and by sharing their collected market intelligence through integrations with each other and other departments (Griffin & Hauser, 1996; Gupta et al., 1986). With both marketing and sales acting as the interface between the organization and its clients, their good cooperation is positively related to the organization's market and financial performance (Homburg & Jensen, 2007; Homburg et al., 2008).

With cross-departmental team integrations expected to have a greater positive influence on new product success than integrations of entire departments (Troy et al., 2008), marketing collaborations with other functional units can deliver a range of improvements. For example, a finance-marketing integration, which is highly valued by top management teams (Verhoef & Leeflang, 2009), can lead to the improvement of new product success when implemented at the later stages of NPD, as has been observed in companies across a range of sectors (Hempelmann & Engelen, 2015). A marketing-R&D integration can lead to the improvement of new product success and cost and time efficiency as indicated in studies across a range of sectors and countries (Brettel, Heinemann, Engelen, & Neubauer, 2011; Gupta et al., 1986; Hempelmann & Engelen, 2015; Lu & Yang, 2004; O'Cass & Ngo, 2011; Shim, Kim, & Altmann, 2016; Song & Thieme, 2006). A marketing-manufacturing integration during commercialization has been shown, in German companies in knowledge-intensive sectors, to promote new product market performance of incremental innovations (Brettel et al., 2011). Finally, a marketing integration with manufacturing, R&D, and design can improve employee satisfaction, new product quality, time-to-market, and product market performance (Olson, Walker, & Ruekert, 1995).

Focusing on marketing and R&D, the two departments share responsibilities involving the development of new, and the improvement of existing, products and services (Griffin & Hauser, 1996). Their integration, especially under high technological and market uncertainty (Gemser & Leenders, 2011), can have positive effects on NPD and product improvement, as marketing can share valuable information on customer needs that R&D can use during product development, and R&D can share technological and product information that marketing can use in the development of marketing programs (Shim et al., 2016, p. 310).

The perception that there is a need for a marketing-R&D integration is expected to increase as the level of focus on innovation in the organization's corporate strategy increases (Gupta et al., 1986). The level of focus on innovation in corporate strategy can also lead to the enhancement of marketing's capabilities to capture customer needs (Weerawardena, 2003), which when appropriately shared with a well-equipped R&D unit can reinforce R&D innovative activity (Gupta et al., 1986; O'Cass & Ngo, 2011; Weerawardena, 2003). This enhanced activity can, in turn, lead to higher new product success (Gupta et al., 1986; Lu & Yang, 2004; O'Cass & Ngo, 2011; Shim et al., 2016; Song & Thieme, 2006) and a sustained competitive advantage (Weerawardena, 2003). These known effects of marketing-R&D integrations on innovation are summarized in Figure 12.4.

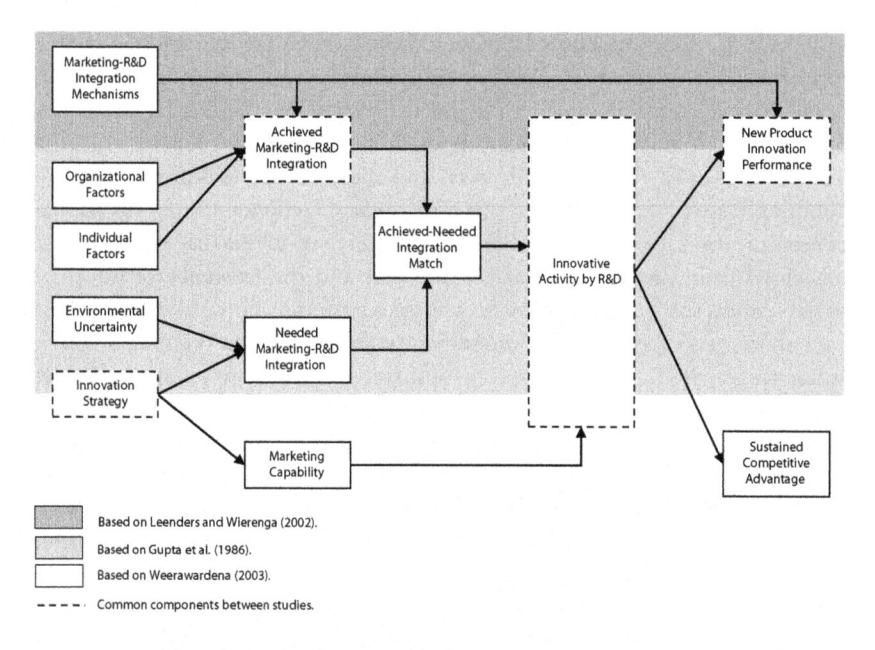

FIGURE 12.4 The relationship between marketing-R&D integrations and innovation.

In addition to knowledge sharing through marketing-R&D integrations, the sharing of market and product knowledge through sales-marketing and sales-R&D integrations can also improve new product success (Ernst, Hoyer, & Rübsaamen, 2010; Homburg, Alavi, Rajab, & Wieseke, 2017; Kuester, Homburg, & Hildesheim, 2017), with both integrations being more effective under specific organizational and environmental conditions (e.g., technological undcertainty and power dynamics) (Kuester et al., 2017). What is more, a recent study on the top 10% of Hungarian companies (by sales revenue) found that sales-marketing encroachment during NPD (i.e., the undertaking of strategic marketing activities by sales during NPD) can directly and indirectly, through customer involvement, promote new product financial and market performance (Keszey & Biemans, 2016). Encroachment has been found to be higher when there are high levels of trust and low levels of rivalry between the two departments, when their interactions are formalized, and when sales offers valuable and actionable information to marketing (Keszey & Biemans, 2016).

To overcome marketing integration barriers (Griffin & Hauser, 1996; Gupta, Raj, & Wilemon, 1985), organizations can employ a set of mechanisms that differ in their degree of influence on each collaboration (Gonzalez-Zapatero, Gonzalez-Benito, & Lannelongue, 2016; Leenders & Wierenga, 2002). In a marketing-R&D integration for instance, relocating marketing and R&D closer to each other and establishing formal decision-coordination systems (e.g., cross-functional phase review boards) are the most effective mechanisms in overcoming collaboration hinderance as shown in a study on large pharmaceutical companies (Leenders & Wierenga, 2002). The existence of equal reward systems and career opportunities for the two departments, the existence of cross-functional projects, and the presence of information and communication technologies (ICTs) that facilitate cross-functional communication appear to be slightly less effective, while the movement of personnel from one department to the other and the existence of informal social systems that facilitate cross-functional communication make the smallest contributions to the quality of the integration (Leenders & Wierenga, 2002). Interestingly, ICTs can also have a positive, direct effect on new product success, whereas cross-functional phase review boards can have a negative, direct effect due to their degree of formalization and complexity (Leenders & Wierenga, 2002).

In a marketing-purchasing integration, building cross-functional teams between the two departments and installing ICTs can promote information sharing and understanding in both functional units as evidenced in a recent study on medium and large Spanish companies in patent-intensive sectors (Gonzalez-Zapatero et al., 2016). Ensuring physical proximity can only marginally increase information sharing and understanding, while establishing equal reward systems can only promote information sharing and understanding in marketing (Gonzalez-Zapatero et al., 2016). Finally, establishing formal decision-coordination systems appears to have no effect on information sharing and understanding in either functional unit (Gonzalez-Zapatero et al., 2016).

Taken together, the findings on integration mechanisms suggest that installing ICTs that facilitate cross-functional communication and establishing cross-functional teams are effective in overcoming marketing integration barriers. Furthermore, ensuring physical proximity and equal reward systems appear to be promising mechanisms that deserve further exploration. As personnel movement between departments and informal social systems make the smallest contributions to integrations, and formal decision-coordination systems produce mixed results and potentially negative consequences, future research examining their effectiveness under certain conditions could add more insight. More insight could also be provided by the investigation of mechanisms that ease other cross-functional collaborations across the organization.

Summary

Marketing and sales are the interface between the clients and the organization itself. Through their market research and their interactions with customers, the two departments collect valuable market intelligence. To utilize this collected intelligence for the benefit of new product and service developments, organizations need to ensure that the two departments align their departmental strategies to the organization's innovation strategy, as this can increase the perceived need for integrations with other departments. It can also lead to the enhancement of marketing's capabilities to capture customer needs, which when shared with R&D can reinforce R&D innovative activity, leading to enhanced new product success and sustained competitive advantage.

Organizations could also strive to facilitate cross-functional integrations between marketing and sales and other functional units, as the sharing of market intelligence through such collaborations can lead to the improvement of the organization's market and financial performance, new product success, cost and time efficiency, employee satisfaction, new product quality, and time-to-market performance.

Finally, organizations could install ICTs that facilitate cross-functional communication and establish cross-functional teams, as these mechanisms appear to be effective in overcoming marketing integration difficulties. To assist management teams in overcoming collaboration hinderance, researchers could further explore the effects of known mechanisms (such as ICTs, cross-functional teams, physical proximity, equal reward systems, personnel movement, informal social systems, and formal decision-coordination systems) across all potential integrations within an organization in order to advance our understanding and aid practitioners in selecting and implementing the most appropriate ones.

Legal Department

Often directed by a general counsel, the legal department ensures the organization's legal compliance to all law regimes related to the business (Chayes & Chayes, 1985; DeMott, 2005). As the head of the department, the general counsel typically provides legal advice to senior management and the board of directors; identifies and communicates the anticipated impact of present law and trends in the law; participates in the formulation of corporate and departmental strategies; takes part in the development and implementation of corporate compliance programs; monitors, reports, and corrects compliance violations; defines the organization's bylaws; manages the legal department's budget and policies; recruits and supervises the legal team; and acts as the agent of the organization in interactions with external parties, such as outside counsel and the government (Chayes & Chayes, 1985; DeMott, 2005).

Legal Integrations

The legal team, which itself has to be innovative in order to be effective (Moppett, 2013), can support the firm's innovative work through cross-functional collaborations at different stages of the process. As mentioned in the Finance Department section, access to external and internal finance is critical for innovation, and the legal systems in regions in which the organization operates influence the availability and accessibility of funds. To maximize the available funding for innovation, a continuous collaboration between legal, finance, and top management teams can assist the finance department in navigating the legal system, evaluating the available options for finance, and selecting the most appropriate combinations. For example, a general counsel that is a member of the senior team can help reduce the firm's explicit tax liabilities (Abernathy, Kubick, & Masli, 2016), thus increasing the firm's internal finances. In addition, the general counsel, acting as the agent of the organization in interactions with external parties, can participate in the drafting and enforcement of legal contracts of firm-client collaborations formed by the sales department (Vashisht, 2006, p. 104) and firm-supplier collaborations formed by the purchasing department.

Furthermore, having the strongest legal expertise within the organization, the team can help the organization identify and exploit innovation opportunities arising from the introduction of new, or the alteration of existing, regulations and legislations. For instance, the need for compliance to the Clean Air Act, a legislation introduced in the United Kingdom in 1956 to restrict smoke emissions (The National Archives, 2018), fueled innovation in materials, processes, and product designs (Tidd & Bessant, 2013d). As these changes can encourage but also inhibit future innovation (Mitra, 2017b; Tidd & Bessant, 2013d), the legal team can utilize its knowledge to help the organization make adjustments to existing projects and pursue new projects that are aligned with its innovation aims.

Finally, the legal office can assist R&D, and the organization in general, on issues relating to intellectual property (IP) laws. IP laws emerged as a system of laws specifically designed to restrict the unauthorized exploitation of aesthetic or functional intellectual products for a limited period (Christie, 2011; Dreyfuss & Pila, 2017), for instance, through copyrights (Christie, 2011; IPO Information Centre, 2018a; Long, 2008), patents (Christie, 2011; Dreyfuss & Pila, 2017; Epstein, 2017, p. 36), trademarks (Dreyfuss & Pila, 2017; IPO Information Centre, 2018c; USPTO, 2018), and designs (Christie, 2011; IPO Information Centre, 2018b).

By protecting novel and original work from being used by others without authorization by the creators, IP laws can promote competition between creators and, through that, increase productivity and diversity of intellectual products, ensure transparency in the marketplace that enables consumers to make informed decisions, and secure the creators' ability to benefit from their creations (Christie, 2011; Dreyfuss & Pila, 2017; Kultti, Takalo, & Toikka, 2007; Leiponen, 2013; Long, 2008; Mandel, 2011).

The legal department could especially help the R&D department navigate IP laws and negotiate licensing of others' creations when selecting which protected innovations the department would like to build on or work around. The legal team could also participate in the development and implementation of the most beneficial protection strategies for intellectual products created by R&D and the organization more broadly. Usually, an organization can choose to register those creations and protect them with IP laws or to keep them secret from the public (Arundel, 2001; Dass, Nanda, & Xiao, 2015; Kultti et al., 2007; Tidd & Bessant, 2013b), with the latter strategy entailing the danger of those creations being independently developed elsewhere or being copied (Dass et al., 2015, p. 1). Whether one strategy is preferred over the other will depend on the extent to which IP laws and trade secrecy laws are enforced as well as the costs and benefits involved in each strategy for each innovation independently (Arundel, 2001; Dass et al., 2015; Leiponen, 2013).

Some organizations implement strategic patenting that emphasizes future licensing negotiations and lawsuit avoidance, with some industries relying more heavily than others on patenting for a return on innovation investment (Leiponen, 2013). Patent data can indicate an organization's capacity to innovate, and it has been found that companies with above average patent portfolio quality and higher linkage of their patents to scientific research tend to be highly valued by investors and generate higher stock-market returns (Tidd & Bessant, 2013b).

To ensure that IP laws effectively support innovation, the imposed boundaries need to be balanced with the benefits delivered to innovators. It is argued that the delays in progress caused by patents, the lack of reward for small innovations, the excessively high license fees posed by patent owners (Sawyer, 2008), and the restriction of large collaborations (Mandel, 2011) can sometimes prevent the sharing of ideas and, therefore, can hold innovative work back. For example, it was found that Celera's move to protect the human genes sequenced by Celera for the period 2001–2003 reduced subsequent scientific research and innovation by 20%–30% (Williams, 2013). In addition, the rules restraining large-scale collaborations can hinder modern scientific and artistic endeavors, which involve the collaboration of vast networks of individuals with diverse knowledge (Mandel, 2011). But it is also argued that, since innovation flourishes under moderate regulation, some constraints created by IP law can spur innovation, leading to an increase in the number and variety of problem solutions and artistic expressions for the benefit of the general public (Fishman, 2014).

Taken together, these two opposing arguments suggest that an equilibrium needs to be reached so that organizational innovation is inspired by a certain degree of limitations, while at the same time it is not hindered by them. To help promote organizational innovation, the research community could identify such an equilibrium and guide legislators through the implementation of new, and the adjustment of existing, IP laws.

Summary

Being the legal experts of the organization, the legal department can support innovative work by contributing to the decision-making of top management teams and other functional units. To utilize this expertise in supporting innovation, organizations could include a representative of the legal team in top management teams and strive to facilitate legal integrations with other departments, as these collaborations can improve the selection of financing options for innovation, can assist in drafting and enforcing legal firm-supplier and firm-client contracts, can aid the organization in capitalizing on innovation opportunities arising from changes in the law, can help navigate IP laws and negotiate licensing contracts for external creations, and can contribute in the development and implementation of the most appropriate protection strategies for intellectual products developed by the organization.

The literature generally lacks a discussion of the benefits of legal integrations with other departments. As a result, the importance of integrating legal with other functions of the organization is not pronounced enough, despite the potential benefits. To help highlight the importance of legal integrations and assist organizations in implementing beneficial integrations based on their individual characteristics (e.g., size, age, sector, innovation aims), organizational innovation scholars could engage in a more rigorous investigation of the benefits of legal integrations, the obstacles of implementing such collaboration, and the mechanisms that can help overcome those obstacles. Last, the research community could also participate in the identification and implementation of balanced IP laws that will allow organizational innovation to flourish by imposing restrictions that spur but do not impede innovation.

Departmental Management Teams

We have already addressed how leaders at the top of the organization can influence innovation. Here, we discuss how department-level leaders requesting innovative work from their employees can take additional measures to support engagement with such work. Arguably, each department is a microcosm of the organization. Thus, innovative work occurring at the departmental level is affected by departmental vision (Anderson et al., 2014; Pearce & Ensley, 2004), leadership, practices and procedures, structure, and strategy. Innovation at this level can also be influenced by how line managers choose to develop their supervisees' expertise and creative-thinking skills through training, increase their supervisees' intrinsic motivation through challenge, instill a sense of freedom, ensure resource availability, make appropriate team selections in terms of supportiveness and diversity, and demonstrate supervisory and organizational support and encouragement (Amabile, 1998). Note that perceptions about all these elements are part of the overall climate for creativity (see the Top Management Teams section).

Moreover, team leaders who are experts in the field of the innovative work can support their teams by defining and communicating a mission that will direct the innovative effort, planning and structuring the project, and assisting in defining the problem to be solved. Once the work is underway, they can support the team by evaluating any work completed against the mission, forecasting the consequences of their teams' actions, wisely assessing their teams' options and acting accordingly, and selling the innovative project to management and key stakeholders (Mumford & Barrett, 2011; Mumford, Durban, Gujar, Buck, & Todd, 2018a; Mumford et al., 2018b).

Team leaders can also contribute to innovative efforts by supporting innovative teams through the cognitive and social processes they must engage in. With more work organized around teams rather than individuals in today's organizations (Edmondson & Roloff, 2008; Kozlowski & Bell, 2008; Reiter-Palmon, Wigert, & Vreede, 2012; Royston & Reiter-Palmon, 2017), leaders will need to ensure that teams working on innovative projects have a rich repertoire of strategies to help them overcome additional obstacles inherent in teamwork. Focusing on the cognitive process of idea generation, teamwork involves both individual ideation and group idea exchange (Paulus, 2008). Though, theoretically, interactive groups (i.e., groups that generate ideas together) are expected to be as productive, if not more, in ideation as nominal groups (i.e., groups of people generating ideas independently and subsequently combining them) (Brown & Paulus, 2002; Oxley, Dzindolet, & Paulus, 1996; Valacich, Dennis, & Connolly, 1994), the notion has not received sufficient empirical support (Paulus, 2000; Paulus, Dzindolet, & Kohn, 2012; Paulus & Nijstad, 2003).

It is argued that for team ideation to become more effective, team leaders can introduce additional strategies, such as exchanging ideas in writing (Brown & Paulus, 2002), note taking and reading others' ideas before contributing (Paulus & Yang, 2000), alternating between intervals of individual and group ideation that will allow for reflection on exchanged ideas and generation of new ones (Baruah & Paulus, 2008; Brown & Paulus, 2002; Paulus & Yang, 2000), training on ideation (Baruah & Paulus, 2008), adding further instructions for ideation (e.g., generate creative ideas), adding ideation facilitators to enforce instructions (Reiter-Palmon & Royston, 2017), reducing distractions and irrelevant discussions, introducing ideas during brainstorming to facilitate further ideation, breaking ideation into subtasks, and taking breaks (Paulus et al., 2012).

To combat the effects of social and group influences involved in social processes, team leaders can introduce individual accountability for individual contributions to minimize motivation loss, encourage asynchronous idea exchange (e.g., in writing or using computers) to reduce production blocking caused by the fact that only one member can contribute at any given time in concurrent exchanges, build team cohesion and goal commitment to decrease performance comparison between group members, and endorse the sharing and accepting of unique information and ideas to lessen the tendency to focus on common information and ideas (Paulus, 2008; Paulus et al., 2012). Team leaders can also boost teams' innovation performance by shaping the environmental conditions in such a way that team members feel psychologically safe to take interpersonal risks; trust that they will not be harmed and that the team will accomplish its objectives; engage in open communication, collaboration, and participation; have enough time to dedicate to coordination and discussion of information and ideas; have the necessary resources and external collaboration; and feel that their leaders support innovation (Reiter-Palmon et al., 2012; Royston & Reiter-Palmon, 2017).

Summary

In summary, departmental leadership interested in facilitating innovation could, in addition to focusing on visions, leadership, practices and procedures, structures, and strategies that are conducive to innovation, apply their expertise in the field at every stage of the innovative project to assist and guide innovative teams. They could also implement additional strategies that will support innovative teams in engaging with the cognitive and social processes entailed in innovative teamwork.

Conclusion

In this chapter, we looked at how Top Management Teams, Departmental Management Teams, and the functional units of the organization – human resources, finance, purchasing, marketing, sales, and legal – can influence organizational innovation. In addition to highlighting how each individual function can support and facilitate innovation, our review reveals the important role of strategic alignment and cross-functional collaboration in meeting innovation objectives as shown in Figure 12.5. The significance of organizational-level strategic alignment and cross-functional collaboration remains largely unexplored, as the majority of scholars focus on the strategic alignment and cross-functional collaboration between a limited number of organizational functions and not the organization as a whole. Looking at each individual function, we found that these organizational characteristics often foster innovation in a number of ways. Based on these findings, we could argue that implementing strategic alignments and cross-functional collaborations across the organization will greatly benefit organizational innovation, with each strategic alignment and cross-functional collaboration making its own contributions to innovation performance.

To identify the role of strategic alignment and cross-functional collaboration in organizational innovation and assist management teams in implementing

Organizational Functions	Functional Characteristics Influencing Innovation	Elements Important to Innovation Influenced by Functional Characteristics
Top Management Teams	Vision Leadership Practices & Procedures Structure Strategy	Direction Focus Culture Climate
Human Resources (HR)	Departmental Strategic Alignment HRM Practices	Culture Knowledge Management Capabilities Knowledge Base
Finance Purchasing Marketing Sales Legal Departmental Management Teams	Departmental Strategic Alignment Cross-Functional Collaboration Collaboration with External Agents Vision Mission Leadership Support Strategies	Knowledge Base Knowledge Management Capabilities (sharing) External Networks for Evaluation, Implementation, Exploitation Direction Focus Climate

FIGURE 12.5 Function influence on legitimacy and support for innovation.

them, innovation scholars could begin investigating their effects on organizational innovation and the barriers preventing such alignments and collaborations to materialize. These two lines of research can reveal the most valuable strategic alignments and cross-functional collaborations and guide management teams through their implementation.

References

Abernathy, J. L., Kubick, T. R., & Masli, A. (2016). General counsel prominence and corporate tax policy. *Journal of the American Taxation Association*, 38, 39–56.

Ahmed, P. K. (1998). Culture and climate for innovation. *European Journal of Innovation Management*, 1, 30–43.

Allen, N. J., & Meyer, J. P. (1996). Affective, continuance, and normative commitment to the organization: An examination of construct validity. *Journal of Vocational Behavior*, 49, 252–276.

Amabile, T. M. (1988). A model of creativity and innovation in organizations. *Research in Organizational Behavior*, 10, 123–167.

Amabile, T. M. (1998). How to kill creativity. *Harvard Business Review*, 76, 77–87.

Amabile, T. M., Conti, R., Coon, H., Lazenby, J., & Herron, M. (1996). Assessing the work environment for creativity. *Academy of Management Journal*, 39, 1154–1184.

Amabile, T. M., Schatzel, E. A., Moneta, G. B., & Kramer, S. J. (2004). Leader behaviors and the work environment for creativity: Perceived leader support. *The Leadership Quarterly*, 15, 5–32.

Amore, M. D., Schneider, C., & Žaldokas, A. (2013). Credit supply and corporate innovation. *Journal of Financial Economics*, 109, 835–855.

Anderson, N., Potočnik, K., & Zhou, J. (2014). Innovation and creativity in organizations: A state-of-the-science review, prospective commentary, and guiding framework. *Journal of Management*, 40, 1297–1333.

Andriopoulos, C. (2001). Determinants of organisational creativity: A literature review. *Management Decision*, 39, 834–841.

Arundel, A. (2001). The relative effectiveness of patents and secrecy for appropriation. *Research Policy*, 30, 611–624.

Ateş, A. M., van Raaij, E. M., & Wynstra, F. (2018). The impact of purchasing strategy-structure (mis)fit on purchasing cost and innovation performance. *Journal of Purchasing and Supply Management*, 24, 68–82.

Avlonitis, G. J., & Salavou, H. E. (2007). Entrepreneurial orientation of SMEs, product innovativeness, and performance. *Journal of Business Research*, 60, 566–575.

Ayyagari, M., Demirgüç-Kunt, A., & Maksimovic, V. (2011). Firm innovation in emerging markets: The role of finance, governance, and competition. *Journal of Financial and Quantitative Analysis*, 46, 1545–1580.

Baier, C., Hartmann, E. V. I., & Moser, R. (2008). Strategic alignment and purchasing efficacy: An exploratory analysis of their impact on financial performance. *Journal of Supply Chain Management*, 44, 36–52.

Baldwin, J., & Johnson, J. (1995). Business strategies in innovative and non-innovative firms in Canada. *Micro-Economic Studies and Analysis Division, Statistics Canada*, 73, 1–37.

Baruah, J., & Paulus, P. B. (2008). Effects of training on idea generation in groups. *Small Group Research*, 39, 523–541.

Beck, T., Demirgüç-Kunt, A., Laeven, L. U. C., & Levine, R. (2008a). Finance, firm size, and growth. *Journal of Money, Credit and Banking*, 40, 1379–1405.

Beck, T., Demirgüç-Kunt, A., & Maksimovic, V. (2008b). Financing patterns around the world: Are small firms different? *Journal of Financial Economics*, 89, 467–487.

Beck, T., & Levine, R. (2002). Industry growth and capital allocation: Does having a market- or bank-based system matter? *Journal of Financial Economics*, 64, 147–180.

Bekaert, G., Harvey, C. R., & Lundblad, C. (2005). Does financial liberalization spur growth? *Journal of Financial Economics*, 77, 3–55.

Belker, L. B., McCormick, J., & Topchik, G. S. (2012). *The first-time manager*. New York, NY: AMACOM.

Benfratello, L., Schiantarelli, F., & Sembenelli, A. (2008). Banks and innovation: Microeconometric evidence on Italian firms. *Journal of Financial Economics*, 90, 197–217.

Beugelsdijk, S. (2008). Strategic human resource practices and product innovation. *Organization Studies*, 29, 821–847.

Bodas Freitas, I., Castellacci, F., Fontana, R., Malerba, F., & Vezzulli, A. (2017). Sectors and the additionality effects of R&D tax credits: A cross-country microeconometric analysis. *Research Policy*, 46, 57–72.

Brettel, M., Heinemann, F., Engelen, A., & Neubauer, S. (2011). Cross-functional integration of R&D, marketing, and manufacturing in radical and incremental product innovations and its effects on project effectiveness and efficiency. *Journal of Product Innovation Management*, 28, 251–269.

Bronzini, R., & Piselli, P. (2016). The impact of R&D subsidies on firm innovation. *Research Policy*, 45, 442–457.

Brown, J. R., Fazzari, S. M., & Petersen, B. C. (2009). Financing innovation and growth: Cash flow, external equity, and the 1990s R&D boom. *The Journal of Finance*, 64, 151–185.

Brown, J. R., Martinsson, G., & Petersen, B. C. (2013). Law, stock markets, and innovation. *The Journal of Finance*, 68, 1517–1549.

Brown, J. R., Martinsson, G., & Petersen, B. C. (2017). What promotes R&D? Comparative evidence from around the world. *Research Policy*, 46, 447–462.

Brown, V. R., & Paulus, P. B. (2002). Making group brainstorming more effective: Recommendations from an associative memory perspective. *Current Directions in Psychological Science*, 11, 208–212.

Camelo-Ordaz, C., García-Cruz, J., Sousa-Ginel, E., & Valle-Cabrera, R. (2011). The influence of human resource management on knowledge sharing and innovation in Spain: The mediating role of affective commitment. *The International Journal of Human Resource Management*, 22, 1442–1463.

Cameron, K. S., & Quinn, R. E. (2011). *Diagnosing and changing organizational culture: Based on the Competing Values Framework* (3rd ed.). Hoboken, NJ: Jossey-Bass/John Wiley and Sons.

Cano, C. P., & Cano, P. Q. (2006). Human resources management and its impact on innovation performance in companies. *International Journal of Technology Management*, 35, 11–28.

Castellacci, F., & Lie, C. M. (2015). Do the effects of R&D tax credits vary across industries? A meta-regression analysis. *Research Policy*, 44, 819–832.

Chang, S., Gong, Y., & Shum, C. (2011). Promoting innovation in hospitality companies through human resource management practices. *International Journal of Hospitality Management*, 30, 812–818.

Chava, S., Oettl, A., Subramanian, A., & Subramanian, K. V. (2013). Banking deregulation and innovation. *Journal of Financial Economics*, 109, 759–774.

Chayes, A., & Chayes, A. H. (1985). Corporate counsel and the elite law firm. *Stanford Law Review*, 37, 277–300.

Chen, C. J., & Huang, J. W. (2009). Strategic human resource practices and innovation performance – The mediating role of knowledge management capacity. *Journal of Business Research*, 62, 104–114.

Chen, M. -C., & Gupta, S. (2017). The incentive effects of R&D tax credits: An empirical examination in an emerging economy. *Journal of Contemporary Accounting & Economics*, 13, 52–68.

Chesbrough, H. W. (2003). *Open innovation: The new imperative for creating and profiting from technology*. Boston, MA: Harvard Business School Press.

Christie, A. F. (2011). Creativity and innovation: A legal perspective. In L. Mann & J. Chan (Eds.), *Creativity and innovation in business and beyond: Social science perspectives and policy implications* (pp. 103–116). New York, NY: Routledge/Taylor and Francis Group.

Cohen, W. M., & Levinthal, D. A. (1990). Absorptive capacity: A new perspective on learning and innovation. *Administrative Science Quarterly*, 35, 128–152.

Cornaggia, J., Mao, Y., Tian, X., & Wolfe, B. (2015). Does banking competition affect innovation? *Journal of Financial Economics*, 115, 189–209.

Cousins, P. D. (2005). The alignment of appropriate firm and supply strategies for competitive advantage. *International Journal of Operations and Production Management*, 25, 403–428.

Cox, G. (2005). *Cox review of creativity in business: Building on the UK's strengths*. London, UK: HM Treasury.

Crespi, G., Giuliodori, D., Giuliodori, R., & Rodriguez, A. (2016). The effectiveness of tax incentives for R&D+i in developing countries: The case of Argentina. *Research Policy*, 45, 2023–2035.

Currie, G., & Kerrin, M. (2003). Human resource management and knowledge management: Enhancing knowledge sharing in a pharmaceutical company. *The International Journal of Human Resource Management*, 14, 1027–1045.

Czarnitzki, D., Hanel, P., & Rosa, J. M. (2011). Evaluating the impact of R&D tax credits on innovation: A microeconometric study on Canadian firms. *Research Policy*, 40, 217–229.

Dalkir, K. (2011). *Knowledge management in theory and practice* (2nd ed.). Cambridge, MA: MIT Press.

Damanpour, F. (1991). Organizational innovation: A meta-analysis of effects of determinants and moderators. *Academy of Management Journal*, 34, 555–590.

Damanpour, F., & Aravind, D. (2012). Organizational structure and innovation revisited: From organic to ambidextrous structure. In M. D. Mumford (Ed.), *Handbook of organizational creativity* (pp. 483–513; E-book). New York, NY: Academic Press.

Damanpour, F., & Schneider, M. (2006). Phases of the adoption of innovation in organizations: Effects of environment, organization and top managers. *British Journal of Management*, 17, 215–236.

Dass, N., Nanda, V., & Xiao, S. C. (2015). Intellectual property protection and financial markets: Patenting vs. Secrecy. *Social Science Research Network (SSRN)*, 2018, 1–49.

Demirgüç-Kunt, A., & Maksimovic, V. (2002). Law, finance, and firm growth. *The Journal of Finance*, 53, 2107–2137.

DeMott, D. A. (2005). The discrete roles of general counsel. *Fordham Law Review*, 74, 955–981.

Dodgson, M., Salter, A. J., & Gann, D. (2008). *The management of technological innovation: Strategy and practice*. New York, NY: Oxford University Press.

Donate, M. J., Peña, I., & Sánchez de Pablo, J. D. (2016). HRM practices for human and social capital development: Effects on innovation capabilities. *The International Journal of Human Resource Management*, 27, 928–953.

Dreyfuss, R., & Pila, J. (2017). Intellectual property law: An anatomical overview. In R. Dreyfuss & J. Pila (Eds.), *The Oxford handbook of intellectual property law* (pp. 3–22; E-book). New York, NY: Oxford University Press.

Edmondson, A. C., & Roloff, K. S. (2008). Overcoming barriers to collaboration: Psychological safety and learning in diverse teams. In E. Salas, G. F. Goodwin, & S. C. Burke (Eds.), *Team effectiveness in complex organizations: Cross-disciplinary perspectives and approaches* (pp. 183–208). New York, NY: Routledge/Taylor and Francis Group.

Elenkov, D. S., & Manev, I. M. (2005). Top management leadership and influence on innovation: The role of sociocultural context. *Journal of Management*, 31, 381–402.

Elkins, T., & Keller, R. T. (2003). Leadership in research and development organizations: A literature review and conceptual framework. *The Leadership Quarterly*, 14, 587–606.

Ellegaard, C., & Koch, C. (2012). The effects of low internal integration between purchasing and operations on suppliers' resource mobilization. *Journal of Purchasing and Supply Management*, 18, 148–158.

Epstein, R. A. (2017). The basic structure of intellectual property law. In R. Dreyfuss & J. Pila (Eds.), *The Oxford handbook of intellectual property law* (pp. 25–56; E-book). New York, NY: Oxford University Press.

Ernst, H., Hoyer, W. D., & Rübsaamen, C. (2010). Sales, marketing, and research-and-development cooperation across new product development stages: Implications for success. *Journal of Marketing*, 74, 80–92.

European Union. (2009). *Manifesto – European Year of Creativity and Innovation 2009*. Brussels, Belgium: European Ambassadors for Creativity and Innovation. Retrieved from http://www.create2009.europa.eu/about_the_year/manifesto.html

Ezzi, F., & Jarboui, A. (2016). Does innovation strategy affect financial, social and environmental performance? *Journal of Economics, Finance, and Administrative Science*, 21, 14–24.

Fishman, J. P. (2014). Creating around copyright. *Harvard Law Review*, 128, 1333–1404.

Florida, R., & Goodnight, J. (2005). Managing for creativity. *Harvard Business Review*, 83, 124–131.

Friedrich, T. L., Mumford, M. D., Vessey, B., Beeler, C. K., & Eubanks, D. L. (2010). Leading for innovation: Re-evaluating leader influences on innovation with regard to innovation type and complexity. *International Studies of Management and Organization*, 40, 6–29.

Friedrich, T. L., Stenmark, C. K., & Mumford, M. D. (2011). Climate for creativity. In M. A. Runco & S. R. Pritzker (Eds.), *Encyclopedia of creativity* (2nd ed.). (Vol. 1, pp. 208–213; E-book). New York, NY: Academic Press.

Friedrich, T. L., & Zhong, M. P. (2017). Collective leadership as a facilitator of innovation. In M. D. Mumford & S. Hemlin (Eds.), *Handbook of research on leadership and creativity* (pp. 297–315; E-book). Cheltenham, UK: Edward Elgar.

Gemser, G., & Leenders, M. A. A. M. (2011). Managing cross-functional cooperation for new product development success. *Long Range Planning*, 44, 26–41.

Giudici, G., & Paleari, S. (2000). The provision of finance to innovation: A survey conducted among Italian technology-based small firms. *Small Business Economics*, 14, 37–53.

González-Benito, J. (2007). A theory of purchasing's contribution to business performance. *Journal of Operations Management*, 25, 901–917.

Gonzalez-Zapatero, C., Gonzalez-Benito, J., & Lannelongue, G. (2016). Antecedents of functional integration during new product development: The purchasing–marketing link. *Industrial Marketing Management*, 52, 47–59.

Griffin, A., & Hauser, J. R. (1996). Integrating R&D and marketing: A review and analysis of the literature. *Journal of Product Innovation Management*, 13, 191–215.

Guan, J. C., Yam, R. C. M., Tang, E. P. Y., & Lau, A. K. W. (2009). Innovation strategy and performance during economic transition: Evidences in Beijing, China. *Research Policy*, 38, 802–812.

Gumusluoglu, L., & Ilsev, A. (2009). Transformational leadership, creativity, and organizational innovation. *Journal of Business Research*, 62, 461–473.

Guo, D., Guo, Y., & Jiang, K. (2016). Government-subsidized R&D and firm innovation: Evidence from China. *Research Policy*, 45, 1129–1144.

Gupta, A. K., Raj, S. P., & Wilemon, D. (1985). The R&D-marketing interface in high-technology firms. *Journal of Product Innovation Management*, 2, 12–24.

Gupta, A. K., Raj, S. P., & Wilemon, D. (1986). A model for studying R&D-marketing interface in the product innovation process. *Journal of Marketing*, 50, 7–17.

Gupta, A. K., & Singhal, A. (1993). Managing human resources for innovation and creativity. *Research-Technology Management*, 36, 41–48.

Gutierrez-Gutierrez, L. J., Barrales-Molina, V., & Kaynak, H. (2018). The role of human resource-related quality management practices in new product development: A dynamic capability perspective. *International Journal of Operations and Production Management*, 38, 43–66.

Hadaya, P., & Cassivi, L. (2009). The role of knowledge sharing in a supply chain. In A. Dwivedi & T. Butcher (Eds.), *Supply chain management and knowledge management: Integrating critical perspectives in theory and practice* (pp. 19–39). Hampshire, UK: Palgrave Macmillan.

Hall, B. H., & Lerner, J. (2010). The financing of R&D and innovation. In B. H. Hall & N. Rosenberg (Eds.), *Handbook of the economics of innovation* (Vol. 1, pp. 609–639). Amsterdam, Netherlands: Elsevier-North-Holland.

Handfield, R. B. (2006). *Supply market intelligence: A managerial handbook for building sourcing strategies*. Boca Raton, FL: Auerbach/Taylor and Francis Group.

Handfield, R. B. (2010). Supply market intelligence: Think differently, gain an edge. *Supply Chain Management Review*, 14, 42–49.

Handfield, R. B., Petersen, K., Cousins, P., & Lawson, B. (2009). An organizational entrepreneurship model of supply management integration and performance outcomes. *International Journal of Operations and Production Management*, 29, 100–126.

Haneda, S., & Ito, K. (2018). Organizational and human resource management and innovation: Which management practices are linked to product and/or process innovation? *Research Policy*, 47, 194–208.

Hempelmann, F., & Engelen, A. (2015). Integration of finance with marketing and R&D in new product development: The role of project stage. *Journal of Product Innovation Management*, 32, 636–654.

Hennessey, B. A., & Amabile, T. M. (2010). Creativity. *Annual Review of Psychology*, 61, 569–598.

Hillebrand, B., & Biemans, W. G. (2004). Links between internal and external cooperation in product development: An exploratory study. *Journal of Product Innovation Management*, 21, 110–122.

Homburg, C., Alavi, S., Rajab, T., & Wieseke, J. (2017). The contingent roles of R&D–sales versus R&D–marketing cooperation in new-product development of business-to-business firms. *International Journal of Research in Marketing*, 34, 212–230.

Homburg, C., & Jensen, O. (2007). The thought worlds of marketing and sales: Which differences make a difference? *Journal of Marketing*, 71, 124–142.

Homburg, C., Jensen, O., & Krohmer, H. (2008). Configurations of marketing and sales: A taxonomy. *Journal of Marketing*, 72, 133–154.

Howell, A. (2016). Firm R&D, innovation and easing financial constraints in China: Does corporate tax reform matter? *Research Policy*, 45, 1996–2007.

Huergo, E., & Moreno, L. (2017). Subsidies or loans? Evaluating the impact of R&D support programmes. *Research Policy*, 46, 1198–1214.

Hughes, D. J., Lee, A., Tian, A. W., Newman, A., & Legood, A. (2018). Leadership, creativity, and innovation: A critical review and practical recommendations. *The Leadership Quarterly*, 29, 549–569.

Hunter, S. T., Bedell, K. E., & Mumford, M. D. (2007). Climate for creativity: A quantitative review. *Creativity Research Journal*, 19, 69–90.

Hunter, S. T., Cushenbery, L., & Friedrich, T. L. (2012). Hiring an innovative workforce: A necessary yet uniquely challenging endeavor. *Human Resource Management Review*, 22, 303–322.

Hurley, R. F., & Hult, G. T. M. (1998). Innovation, market orientation, and organizational learning: An integration and empirical examination. *Journal of Marketing*, 62, 42–54.

IPO Information Centre. (2018a). How copyright protects your work. Retrieved from https:// www.gov.uk/copyright.

IPO Information Centre. (2018b). Register a design. Retrieved from https://www.gov.uk/register-a-design.

IPO Information Centre. (2018c). Renew your trade mark. Retrieved from https://www.gov.uk/renew-your-trade-mark.

Jaiswal, N. K., & Dhar, R. L. (2015). Transformational leadership, innovation climate, creative self-efficacy and employee creativity: A multilevel study. *International Journal of Hospitality Management*, 51, 30–41.

Jansen, J. J. P., Van Den Bosch, F. A. J., & Volberda, H. W. (2006). Exploratory innovation, exploitative innovation, and performance: Effects of organizational antecedents and environmental moderators. *Management Science*, 52, 1661–1674.

Jiménez-Jiménez, D., & Sanz-Valle, R. (2005). Innovation and human resource management fit: An empirical study. *International Journal of Manpower*, 26, 364–381.

Jobber, D., & Lancaster, G. (2012). *Selling and sales management*. Harlow, UK: Pearson Education.

Johnson, P. F., & Leenders, M. R. (2006). A longitudinal study of supply organizational change. *Journal of Purchasing and Supply Management*, 12, 332–342.

Jung, D., Wu, A., & Chow, C. W. (2008). Towards understanding the direct and indirect effects of CEOs' transformational leadership on firm innovation. *The Leadership Quarterly*, 19, 582–594.

Jung, D. I., Chow, C., & Wu, A. (2003). The role of transformational leadership in enhancing organizational innovation: Hypotheses and some preliminary findings. *The Leadership Quarterly*, 14, 525–544.

Kanter, R. M. (1983). *The change masters: Innovation and entrepreneurship in the American corporation*. New York, NY: Simon and Schuster.

Kasahara, H., Shimotsu, K., & Suzuki, M. (2014). Does an R&D tax credit affect R&D expenditure? The Japanese R&D tax credit reform in 2003. *Journal of the Japanese and International Economies*, 31, 72–97.

Kerr, W. R., & Nanda, R. (2015). Financing innovation. *Annual Review of Financial Economics*, 7, 445–462.

Keszey, T., & Biemans, W. (2016). Sales–marketing encroachment effects on innovation. *Journal of Business Research*, 69, 3698–3706.

Kianto, A., Sáenz, J., & Aramburu, N. (2017). Knowledge-based human resource management practices, intellectual capital and innovation. *Journal of Business Research*, 81, 11–20.

King, R. G., & Levine, R. (1993a). Finance and growth: Schumpeter might be right. *The Quarterly Journal of Economics*, 108, 717–737.

King, R. G., & Levine, R. (1993b). Finance, entrepreneurship and growth: Theory and evidence. *Journal of Monetary Economics*, 32, 513–542.

Kocabasoglu, C., & Suresh, N. C. (2006). Strategic sourcing: An empirical investigation of the concept and its practices in U.S. manufacturing firms. *Journal of Supply Chain Management*, 42, 4–16.

Kotler, P. (2000). *Marketing management: Millennium edition* (Vol. 23, 10th ed.). Upper Saddle River, NJ: Prentice Hall.

Kotler, P. (2016). *Marketing management* (3rd ed.). Harlow, UK: Pearson Education.

Kozlowski, S., & Bell, B. (2008). Team learning, development, and adaptation. In V. I. Sessa & M. London (Eds.), *Work group learning: Understanding, improving and assessing how groups learn in organizations* (pp. 15–44). New York, NY: Lawrence Erlbaum Associates/Taylor and Francis Group.

Kuester, S., Homburg, C., & Hildesheim, A. (2017). The catbird seat of the sales force: How sales force integration leads to new product success. *International Journal of Research in Marketing, 34*, 462–479.

Kultti, K., Takalo, T., & Toikka, J. (2007). Secrecy versus patenting. *The RAND Journal of Economics, 38*, 22–42.

Laforet, S. (2008). Size, strategic, and market orientation effects on innovation. *Journal of Business Research, 61*, 753–764.

Lau, C. M., & Ngo, H. Y. (2004). The HR system, organizational culture, and product innovation. *International Business Review, 13*, 685–703.

Laursen, K., & Foss, N. J. (2003). New human resource management practices, complementarities and the impact on innovation performance. *Cambridge Journal of Economics, 27*, 243–263.

Laursen, L. N., & Andersen, P. H. (2016). Supplier involvement in NPD: A quasi-experiment at Unilever. *Industrial Marketing Management, 58*, 162–171.

Leenders, M. A. A. M., & Wierenga, B. (2002). The effectiveness of different mechanisms for integrating marketing and R&D. *Journal of Product Innovation Management, 19*, 305–317.

Leiponen, A. (2013). Intellectual property rights, standards, and the management of innovation. In M. Dodgson, D. M. Gann, & N. Phillips (Eds.), *The Oxford handbook of innovation management* (pp. 559–578; E-Book). New York, NY: Oxford University Press.

Levine, R. (2005). Finance and growth: Theory and evidence. In P. Aghion & S. N. Durlauf (Eds.), *Handbook of economic growth* (Vol. 1, pp. 865–934; E-book). New York, NY: Elsevier.

Li, H., Zhang, Y., & Chan, T. -S. (2005). Entrepreneurial strategy making and performance in China's new technology ventures – The contingency effect of environments and firm competences. *The Journal of High Technology Management Research, 16*, 37–57.

Ligon, G. S., Graham, K. A., Edwards, A., Osburn, H. K., & Hunter, S. T. (2012). Performance management: Appraising performance, providing feedback, and developing for creativity. In M. D. Mumford (Ed.), *Handbook of organizational creativity*. (pp. 633–666; E-book). New York, NY: Academic Press.

Long, D. E. (2008). When worlds collide: The uneasy convergence of creativity and innovation. *The John Marshall Journal of Information Technology and Privacy Law, 25*, 653–672.

Lu, L. Y. Y., & Yang, C. (2004). The R&D and marketing cooperation across new product development stages: An empirical study of Taiwan's IT industry. *Industrial Marketing Management, 33*, 593–605.

Luzzini, D., Amann, M., Caniato, F., Essig, M., & Ronchi, S. (2015). The path of innovation: Purchasing and supplier involvement into new product development. *Industrial Marketing Management, 47*, 109–120.

Luzzini, D., & Ronchi, S. (2011). Organizing the purchasing department for innovation. *Operations Management Research*, 4, 14–27.

Madden, R. (2017). Creativity in business. In J. A. Plucker (Ed.), *Creativity and innovation: Theory, research, and practice* (pp. 235–246). Waco, TX: Prufrock Press.

Mandel, G. N. (2011). To promote the creative process: Intellectual property law and the psychology of creativity. *Notre Dame Law Review*, 86, 1999–2026.

Martins, E., & Martins, N. (2002). An organisational culture model to promote creativity and innovation. *SA Journal of Industrial Psychology*, 28, 58–65.

Martins, E. C., & Terblanche, F. (2003). Building organisational culture that stimulates creativity and innovation. *European Journal of Innovation Management*, 6, 64–74.

McDonald, R. E. (2007). An investigation of innovation in nonprofit organizations: The role of organizational mission. *Nonprofit and Voluntary Sector Quarterly*, 36, 256–281.

McGonagle, J. J., & Vella, C. M. (2012). What is competitive intelligence and why should you care about it? In J. J. McGonagle & C. M. Vella (Eds.), *Proactive intelligence: The successful executive's guide to intelligence* (pp. 9–19; E-book). New York, NY: Springer.

McLean, L. D. (2005). Organizational culture's influence on creativity and innovation: A review of the literature and implications for human resource development. *Advances in Developing Human Resources*, 7, 226–246.

Michie, J., & Sheehan, M. (1999). HRM practices, R&D expenditure and innovative investment: Evidence from the UK's 1990 workplace industrial relations survey (WIRS). *Industrial and Corporate Change*, 8, 211–234.

Minniti, A., & Venturini, F. (2017a). The long-run growth effects of R&D policy. *Research Policy*, 46, 316–326.

Minniti, A., & Venturini, F. (2017b). R&D policy, productivity growth and distance to frontier. *Economics Letters*, 156, 92–94.

Mitra, J. (2017a). The characteristics and features of innovative organisations. In J. Mitra (Ed.), *The business of innovation* (pp. 126–146). London, UK: Sage.

Mitra, J. (2017b). Measuring innovation. In J. Mitra (Ed.), *The business of innovation* (pp. 279–314). London, UK: Sage.

Monczka, R. M., Handfield, R. B., Giunipero, L. C., & Patterson, J. L. (2015). *Purchasing and supply chain management (6th ed.)*. Boston, MA: Cengage Learning.

Moppett, S. A. (2013). Lawyering outside the box: Confronting the creativity crisis. *Southern Illinois University Law Journal*, 37, 253–303.

Mumford, M. D., & Barrett, J. D. (2011). Leadership. In M. A. Runco & S. R. Pritzker (Eds.), *Encyclopedia of creativity* (Vol. 2, 2nd ed., pp. 41–46; E-book). New York, NY: Academic Press.

Mumford, M. D., Durban, C., Gujar, Y., Buck, J., & Todd, E. M. (2018a). Leading creative efforts: Common functions and common skills. In C. Mainemelis, O. Epitropaki, & R. Kark (Eds.), *Creative leadership: Contexts and prospects* (pp. 59–78). New York, NY: Routledge.

Mumford, M. D., Mulhearn, T. J., Watts, L. L., Steele, L. M., & McIntosh, T. (2018b). Leader impacts on creative teams: Direction, engagement, and sales. In R. Reiter-Palmon (Ed.), *Team creativity and innovation* (pp. 131–166). New York, NY: Oxford University Press.

Mumford, M. D., Scott, G. M., Gaddis, B., & Strange, J. M. (2002). Leading creative people: Orchestrating expertise and relationships. *The Leadership Quarterly*, 13, 705–750.

Naranjo-Valencia, J. C., Jiménez-Jiménez, D., & Sanz-Valle, R. (2016). Studying the links between organizational culture, innovation, and performance in Spanish companies. *Revista Latinoamericana de Psicología*, 48, 30–41.

Nijstad, B. A., Berger-Selman, F., & De Dreu, C. K. W. (2014). Innovation in top management teams: Minority dissent, transformational leadership, and radical innovations. *European Journal of Work and Organizational Psychology*, 23, 310–322.

O'Cass, A., & Ngo, L. V. (2011). Winning through innovation and marketing: Lessons from Australia and Vietnam. *Industrial Marketing Management*, 40, 1319–1329.

OECD. (2015). *Meeting of the OECD Council at ministerial level: OECD Innovation Strategy 2015 – An agenda for policy action*. Paris, France: OECD Publishing.

Olson, E. M., Walker, O. C., & Ruekert, R. W. (1995). Organizing for effective new product development: The moderating role of product innovativeness. *Journal of Marketing*, 59, 48–62.

Oxley, N. L., Dzindolet, M. T., & Paulus, P. B. (1996). The effects of facilitators on the performance of brainstorming groups. *Journal of Social Behavior and Personality*, 11, 633–643.

Parniangtong, S. (2016). *Supply management: Strategic sourcing* (E-book). New York, NY: Springer.

Parravicini, M. (2015). *A guide to sales management: A practitioner's view of trade sales organizations* (E-book). New York, NY: Business Expert Press.

Paulus, P. B. (2000). Groups, teams, and creativity: The creative potential of idea-generating groups. *Applied Psychology*, 49, 237–262.

Paulus, P. B. (2008). Fostering creativity in groups and teams. In J. Zhou & C. E. Shalley (Eds.), *Handbook of organizational creativity* (pp. 165–188). New York, NY: Lawrence Erlbaum Associates/Taylor and Francis Group.

Paulus, P. B., Dzindolet, M., & Kohn, N. W. (2012). Collaborative creativity – Group creativity and team innovation. In M. D. Mumford (Ed.), *Handbook of organizational creativity*. (pp. 327–357; E-book). New York, NY: Academic Press.

Paulus, P. B., & Nijstad, B. A. (2003). Group creativity: An introduction. In P. B. Paulus & B. A. Nijstad (Eds.), *Group creativity: Innovation through collaboration* (pp. 3–11). New York, NY: Oxford University Press.

Paulus, P. B., & Yang, H. C. (2000). Idea generation in groups: A basis for creativity in organizations. *Organizational Behavior and Human Decision Processes*, 82, 76–87.

Pearce, C. L., & Ensley, M. D. (2004). A reciprocal and longitudinal investigation of the innovation process: The central role of shared vision in product and process innovation teams (PPITs). *Journal of Organizational Behavior*, 25, 259–278.

Perkins, G., Lean, J., & Newbery, R. (2017). The role of organizational vision in guiding idea generation within SME contexts. *Creativity and Innovation Management*, 26, 75–90.

Pierangelini, G. (2017). The role of purchasing as innovation "booster" in a multinational company. *Excellence HA – The Bridge Between Research and Field Application in Purchasing*, 9, 29–38.

Pisano, G. P. (2015). You need an innovation strategy. *Harvard Business Review*, 93, 44–54.

Plucker, J. A., Beghetto, R. A., & Dow, G. T. (2004). Why isn't creativity more important to educational psychologists? Potentials, pitfalls, and future directions in creativity research. *Educational Psychologist*, 39, 83–96.

Puccio, G. J., & Cabra, J. F. (2010). Organizational creativity: A systems approach. In J. C. Kaufman & R. J. Sternberg (Eds.), *The Cambridge handbook of creativity* (pp. 145–173). New York, NY: Cambridge University Press.

Rafferty, A. E., & Griffin, M. A. (2004). Dimensions of transformational leadership: Conceptual and empirical extensions. *The Leadership Quarterly*, 15, 329–354.

Rao, N. (2016). Do tax credits stimulate R&D spending? The effect of the R&D tax credit in its first decade. *Journal of Public Economics*, 140, 1–12.

Rauch, A., Wiklund, J., Lumpkin, G. T., & Frese, M. (2009). Entrepreneurial orientation and business performance: An assessment of past research and suggestions for the future. *Entrepreneurship Theory and Practice*, 33, 761–787.

Reiter-Palmon, R., & Royston, R. P. (2017). Leading for creativity: How leaders manage creative teams. In M. D. Mumford & S. Hemlin (Eds.), *Handbook of research on leadership and creativity* (pp. 159–184; E-book). Cheltenham, UK: Edward Elgar.

Reiter-Palmon, R., Wigert, B., & Vreede, T. D. (2012). Team creativity and innovation: The effect of group composition, social processes, and cognition. In M. D. Mumford (Ed.), *Handbook of organizational creativity* (pp. 295–326; E-book). New York, NY: Academic Press.

Rhodes, M. (1961). An analysis of creativity. *The Phi Delta Kappan*, 42, 305–310.

Royston, R. P., & Reiter-Palmon, R. (2017). Leadership and creativity: What leaders can do to facilitate creativity in organizations. In J. A. Plucker (Ed.), *Creativity and innovation: Theory, research, and practice* (pp. 247–266). Waco, TX: Prufrock Press.

Ruekert, R. W., & Walker, O. C. (1987). Marketing's interaction with other functional units: A conceptual framework and empirical evidence. *Journal of Marketing*, 51, 1–19.

Sarros, J. C., Cooper, B. K., & Santora, J. C. (2011). Leadership vision, organizational culture, and support for innovation in not-for-profit and for-profit organizations. *Leadership and Organization Development Journal*, 32, 291–309.

Sawyer, R. K. (2008). The shape of things to come: Creativity, innovation and obviousness. *Lewis and Clark Law Review*, 12, 461–486.

Sawyer, R. K. (2012). *Explaining creativity: The science of human innovation* (2nd ed.). New York, NY: Oxford University Press.

Scarbrough, H. (2003). Knowledge management, HRM and the innovation process. *International Journal of Manpower*, 24, 501–516.

Schein, E. H. (2010). *Organizational culture and leadership* (Vol. 2, 4th ed.). San Francisco, CA: Jossey-Bass.

Schumpeter, J. A. (1911). *The theory of economic development*. Cambridge, MA: Harvard University Press.

Scott, S. G., & Bruce, R. A. (1994). Determinants of innovative behavior: A path model of individual innovation in the workplace. *Academy of Management Journal*, 37, 580–607.

Shim, D., Kim, J. G., & Altmann, J. (2016). Strategic management of R&D and marketing integration for multi-dimensional success of new product developments: An empirical investigation in the Korean ICT industry. *Asian Journal of Technology Innovation*, 24, 293–316.

Shin, S. J., & Zhou, J. (2003). Transformational leadership, conservation, and creativity: Evidence from Korea. *Academy of Management Journal*, 46, 703–714.

Shipton, H., Lin, V., Sanders, K., & Yang, H. (2017a). We are not creative here! Creativity and innovation for non-creatives through HRM. In P. Sparrow & C. L. Cooper (Eds.), *A research agenda for human resource management* (pp. 184–200). Cheltenham, UK: Edward Elgar.

Shipton, H., Sparrow, P., Budhwar, P., & Brown, A. (2017b). HRM and innovation: Looking across levels. *Human Resource Management Journal*, 27, 246–263.

Shipton, H., West Michael, A., Dawson, J., Birdi, K., & Patterson, M. (2006). HRM as a predictor of innovation. *Human Resource Management Journal*, 16, 3–27.

Soininen, J., Martikainen, M., Puumalainen, K., & Kyläheiko, K. (2012). Entrepreneurial orientation: Growth and profitability of Finnish small- and medium-sized enterprises. *International Journal of Production Economics*, 140, 614–621.

Song, M., & Thieme, R. J. (2006). A cross-national investigation of the R&D–marketing interface in the product innovation process. *Industrial Marketing Management*, 35, 308–322.

Soriano de Alencar, E. M. L. (2012). Creativity in organizations: Facilitators and inhibitors. In M. D. Mumford (Ed.), *Handbook of organizational creativity* (pp. 87–111; E-book). New York, NY: Academic Press.

Szczygielski, K., Grabowski, W., Pamukcu, M. T., & Tandogan, V. S. (2017). Does government support for private innovation matter? Firm-level evidence from two catching-up countries. *Research Policy*, 46, 219–237.

Tan, C. L., & Nasurdin, A. M. (2011). Human resource management practices and organizational innovation: Assessing the mediating role of knowledge management effectiveness. *Electronic Journal of Knowledge Management*, 9, 155–167.

Thamhain, H. J. (2003). Managing innovative R&D teams. *R&D Management*, 33, 297–311.

The National Archives. (2018). Clean Air Act 1956. Retrieved from http://www.legislation.gov.uk/ukpga/Eliz2/4-5/52/enacted.

Thompson, V. A. (1965). Bureaucracy and innovation. *Administrative Science Quarterly*, 10, 1–20.

Tidd, J., & Bessant, J. (2013a). Building the innovative organisation. In J. Tidd & J. Bessant (Eds.), *Managing innovation: Integrating technological, market and organizational change* (5th ed., pp. 105–167). Chichester, UK: John Wiley and Sons.

Tidd, J., & Bessant, J. (2013b). Capturing the benefits of innovation. In J. Tidd & J. Bessant (Eds.), *Managing innovation: Integrating technological, market and organizational change* (5th ed., pp. 565–622). Chichester, UK: John Wiley and Sons.

Tidd, J., & Bessant, J. (2013c). Developing an innovative strategy. In J. Tidd & J. Bessant (Eds.), *Managing innovation: Integrating technological, market and organizational change* (5th ed., pp. 169–230). Chichester, UK: John Wiley and Sons.

Tidd, J., & Bessant, J. (2013d). Sources of innovation. In J. Tidd & J. Bessant (Eds.), *Managing innovation: Integrating technological, market and organizational change* (5th ed., pp. 233–297). Chichester, UK: John Wiley and Sons.

Tracey, M. (2004). A holistic approach to new product development: New Insights. *Journal of Supply Chain Management*, 40, 37–55.

Troy, L. C., Hirunyawipada, T., & Paswan, A. K. (2008). Cross-functional integration and new product success: An empirical investigation of the findings. *Journal of Marketing*, 72, 132–146.

Tsai, K. -H., Hsieh, M. -H., & Hultink, E. J. (2011). External technology acquisition and product innovativeness: The moderating roles of R&D investment and configurational context. *Journal of Engineering and Technology Management*, 28, 184–200.

Tsai, K. -H., Tsai, M. -L., & Wang, J. -C. (2012). Supplier collaboration and new product performance: A contingency model. *Industrial Management and Data Systems*, 112, 268–289.

Tsai, W. (2001). Knowledge transfer in intraorganizational networks: Effects of network position and absorptive capacity on business unit innovation and performance. *Academy of Management Journal*, 44, 996–1004.

USPTO. (2018). Keeping your registration alive. Retrieved from https://www.uspto.gov/trademarks-maintaining-trademark-registration/keeping-your-registration-alive
Valacich, J. S., Dennis, A. R., & Connolly, T. (1994). Idea generation in computer-based groups: A new ending to an old story. *Organizational Behavior and Human Decision Processes*, 57, 448–467.
Van de Ven, A. H. (1986). Central problems in the management of innovation. *Management Science*, 32, 590–607.
Van de Ven, A. H., Angle, H. L., & Poole, M. S. (2000). *Research on the management of innovation: The Minnesota studies*. New York, NY: Oxford University Press.
van Weele, A. J. (2010). *Purchasing and supply chain management: Analysis, strategy, planning and practice* (5th ed.). Hampshire, UK: Cengage Learning.
Vashisht, K. (2006). *A practical approach to sales management*. Delhi, India: Atlantic Publishers and Distributors.
Verhoef, P. C., & Leeflang, P. S. H. (2009). Understanding the marketing department's influence within the firm. *Journal of Marketing*, 73, 14–37.
Veugelers, M., Bury, J., & Viaene, S. (2010). Linking technology intelligence to open innovation. *Technological Forecasting and Social Change*, 77, 335–343.
Weerawardena, J. (2003). The role of marketing capability in innovation-based competitive strategy. *Journal of Strategic Marketing*, 11, 15–35.
Williams, H. L. (2013). Intellectual property rights and innovation: Evidence from the human genome. *Journal of Political Economy*, 121, 1–27.
Wonglimpiyarat, J. (2011). Government programmes in financing innovations: Comparative innovation system cases of Malaysia and Thailand. *Technology in Society*, 33, 156–164.
Woodman, R. W., Sawyer, J. E., & Griffin, R. W. (1993). Toward a theory of organizational creativity. *Academy of Management Review*, 18, 293–321.
Yang, C. -H., Huang, C. -H., & Hou, T. C. -T. (2012). Tax incentives and R&D activity: Firm-level evidence from Taiwan. *Research Policy*, 41, 1578–1588.
Yu, Y., Dong, X. -Y., Shen, K. N., Khalifa, M., & Hao, J.-X. (2013). Strategies, technologies, and organizational learning for developing organizational innovativeness in emerging economies. *Journal of Business Research*, 66, 2507–2514.
Zhou, K. Z., & Li, C. B. (2012). How knowledge affects radical innovation: Knowledge base, market knowledge acquisition, and internal knowledge sharing. *Strategic Management Journal*, 33, 1090–1102.
Zhou, K. Z., & Wu, F. (2010). Technological capability, strategic flexibility, and product innovation. *Strategic Management Journal*, 31, 547–561.
Zhou, Y., Hong, Y., & Liu, J. (2013). Internal commitment or external collaboration? The impact of human resource management systems on firm innovation and performance. *Human Resource Management*, 52, 263–288.

13
INSTITUTIONAL SUPPORTS FOR INNOVATION

Leif Denti and Sven Hemlin

Innovation, the successful implementation of novel and useful ideas, is viewed as a critical tool for businesses that are competing in the marketplace. Successful innovation brings about a "temporary monopoly" – a timed respite where the company enjoys a temporary competitive advantage that allows the firm to earn back the expenditures involved in researching, developing, and marketing the innovation (Schumpeter, 1942). Successful innovation positions a firm for future competitive advantages, for example, by expanding the firms' knowledge base (Kazanijan & Drazin, 2012) and creating technological platforms to aid in further exploration.

However, innovation is merely one of several goals within an organization. While innovation is future oriented, businesses must also generate value for stakeholders at the present. Thus, innovation activities within a firm will often conflict with other activities (Lavie, Stettner, & Tushman, 2010). This notion is not new. Forty years ago, Abernathy (1978) suggested that a firm's ability to compete over time was dependent on the simultaneous integration of two largely opposing organizational goals: increasing efficiency as well as increasing innovation. The conflict entails several key strategic questions, such as how to maximize utility from limited resources and how to manage risk (Sharma, 1999).

In this chapter, we focus on the organizational level of innovation research. It deals with central concepts such as organizational structure, processes, and resources. Much research on creativity – the forerunner of innovation – has focused on individual and team levels. At the individual level, research has been done on cognitive ability and style (e.g., expertise, divergent-convergent thinking styles), motivation (e.g., the roles of intrinsic and extrinsic motivation, creative self-efficacy), and personality (e.g., openness to experience, autonomy, proactivity, need for achievement). On the team level, research has been done on aspects such as structure (e.g., team heterogeneity, cohesion, size, interdependence), climate (e.g., internal/external communication, participative safety, conflict, task orientation), and leadership (e.g., leader support, expertise, problem-solving, visioning, and goal setting). However, individuals and teams are ultimately embedded in an organizational context. A firm's strategy, structure, processes, and system of task interdependencies across organizational units or across complex organizational systems create the milieu that surrounds and affects its members (Hemlin, Allwood, & Martin, 2008).

Scholars from different academic fields – economists, organizational and contextual technologists, variance and process sociologists, as well as industrial/organizational psychologists – have approached innovation at the organizational level from numerous perspectives. In his review of five generations of innovation models developed from the 1950s to the 1990s, Hobday (2005) concluded that the theoretical base of innovation from an organizational perspective is mostly incoherent and that even the latest models struggle to predict innovation across and within sectors. Hobday considered five types of models in his review: technology push models (technology advances in research and development [R&D] efforts drive innovation), marketing pull models (market needs drive innovation), coupling models (R&D and market needs interact more closely in pull-push configurations), integrated models (R&D, marketing, and manufacturing are closely integrated, and the organization may collaborate externally by joint ventures and partnerships), and networking models (innovation as a distributed networking process: fully integrated parallel development within the organization, strong linkages with customers, suppliers, and other codeveloping partners including joint ventures and collaborative research groupings). As an overall trend, the complexity of innovation models has increased. Innovation models have also shifted in their focus as an effect of changing markets, for example, increasing global markets. They have gone from viewing innovation as a phenomenon that originates from within the organization through R&D efforts, to viewing innovation as a mostly collaborative venture that requires joint decision-making and extensive information flows within and between actors. These actors are not only firms but may also include global and governmental bodies, local and regional authorities, and nongovernmental organizations (NGOs). One popular model, the Triple Helix model, proposes that innovations are best viewed as collaborative efforts that takes place between units (organizations, divisions, individuals, etc.) of university, government, and industry (Leydesdorff & Etzkowitz, 1996, 1998). In the same vein, an influential book from the 1990s analyzed the trends in society toward a new knowledge production where scientists and industry sought more collaboration in mutually beneficial projects to establish "robust" knowledge (Gibbons et al., 1994). This perspective on how new knowledge was produced certainly influenced innovation researchers. At the same period, the system perspective of innovation was introduced and adopted in a bulk of innovation studies. The system perspective (Edquist, 1997) views innovations as a result of connections and collaborations between the private (e.g., industries) and the public spheres (e.g., academic institutions).

Another attempt at reviewing interdisciplinary research on factors that determine an organization's innovation capabilities was conducted by Crossan and Apaydin (2010). They identified two sets of factors residing at the organizational level and the process domain. At the organizational level, Crossan and Apaydin counted five overarching factors: strategy, structure, resource allocation, knowledge management and organizational learning, and culture. Management influences each of these factors; therefore, the authors suggest that one can view these factors as "managerial levers." First, an *innovation strategy* is needed to ensure that the organization's innovation efforts are aligned with other strategic objectives. Second, innovation needs funding; thus, management can choose to *allocate resources* to absolute or relative R&D intensity, differentiated funding and decide the availability of slack resources. Third, *structural elements* play a role in innovation. Factors such as organizational complexity, decision-making locus, and formalization are important. (We take a deep dive into organizational structure later in this chapter.) Fourth, innovation is based on *knowledge and learning*. Organizations need systems for knowledge management: tools for idea generation, information sharing, and learning; processes for information gathering, such as external customer contact; as well as knowledge development relations with external knowledge producers such as universities. Leaders influence learning climates by supporting experimentation and the development of expertise. Fifth, leaders are key persons in creating the psychological culture that promotes new ideas and initiatives. Components of such cultures are experimentation and calculated risk-taking, autonomy and motivation, and a shared vision.

The second area of organizational innovation is the process domain. Here, the organization needs processes for recognizing the need for and initiating innovation, conducting information gathering and feeding (e.g., via market research), deciding whether to generate or adopt an innovation, implementing and producing the innovation, and executing commercialization (which entails market testing and marketing). As these processes take place, management needs to balance project portfolios, using process and project selection tools, calculating return on investment (ROI), and balancing risk. Further processes are needed for project management and efficiency (e.g., project costs and speed), as well as internal and external communication and collaboration.

Organizational Structure

Burns and Stalker (1961) laid the theoretical groundwork for research on organizational characteristics of innovation with their distinction between mechanistic and organic organizational structures. Mechanistic organizations (cf. Mintzberg's "machine bureaucracy" [1980]) function optimally in stable environments. As the rate of change is low in such environments, tasks can be standardized to minimize operational disturbances. Tasks are distributed among organizational units that have little reason to communicate. Instead, communication is vertical, along the organizational hierarchy, where managers act as information gates and sources of decision power. Organic organizations are rather more suitable for changing environments. A high rate of change places demands on flexibility, problem-solving, and continuous decision-making. Members of the organization in this environment need to communicate and share information across organizational boundaries.

A meta-analysis on the relationship between organizational structure and innovation was conducted by Damanpour (1991). The meta-analysis resulted in a number of structural factors that associated positively with innovation. As the 1991 analysis concerned studies up to that point in time, Damanpour and Aravind (2012) set out to scrutinize those findings in a new review of studies published between 1990 and 2012. The original findings were mainly corroborated. Four structural factors were put forward as salient antecedents to innovation: specialization, functional differentiation, technical knowledge resources, and external communication. In addition, three factors exhibited positive relationships with innovation across a majority of the post-1990 studies, as well as having positive effects in the pre-1990 studies: professionalism, internal communication, and managerial attitudes toward change.

Specialization, Professionalism, and Access to Knowledge Resources

Three of the seven structural factors pertain to management of knowledge and expertise. Innovative organizations have a high degree of *specialization* – that is, employees with different types of expert skills. Innovative organizations also tend to have employees with high levels of *professional knowledge* – an attribute that entails both higher education and experience in their field. High expertise and professionalism mean also that these organizations possess a larger knowledge base and a broader range of skills than others. The work often requires access to specialized knowledge. Therefore, innovative organizations help their employees to access knowledge that may otherwise be difficult to access. The knowledge resources of an organization have been estimated by investigating whether the organization has specialized knowledge acquisition and dissemination functions, but they can also be estimated as a more general measure of employee level of expertise. Organizations with high knowledge resources are also actively striving to increase employee expertise according to Damanpour and Aravind (2012).

Intensive Internal and External Communication

Innovative organizations communicate intensely with the outside world but also have a lively internal communication. A high level of internal communication allows knowledge and ideas to spread more easily throughout the organization. It also offers contact areas between people with different skills. The degree of internal communication has been estimated by measuring the amount of contact between employees on the same or different units (which can be visualized with sociograms) or the amount of new projects that contain cross-functional members. Innovative organizations are also more in contact with the outside world – external communication. This outward focus allows for faster opportunity scanning, knowledge absorption, and opportunities to form partnerships and alliances with other organizations. Researchers have estimated the degree of external communication by investigating how much of their employees' working hours are spent on contacts and cooperation with the outside world (e.g., Aiken, Bacharach, & French, 1980).

Positive Attitude to Change

Leaders in innovative organizations are more positive toward change. Their attitude is crucial for creating a permissive climate for new ideas and to challenge the status quo (Rosing, Frese, & Bausch, 2011). Particularly important is that the senior management level is positively oriented toward and rewards innovation initiatives, especially when new ideas are suggested as innovation projects (Elenkov, Judge, & Wright, 2005). These projects need to be resourced and coordinated. Often, different units may be involved, each with their own business logic, agenda, and idea of what the organization needs. Therefore, top management also needs to resolve any conflicts between subentities or individuals.

Functional Differentiation

Damanpour and Aravind (2012) concluded that innovative organizations allocate responsibilities for their organizational functions to separate entities (hence, the word *differentiation*). Examples of such devices may be units for development, finance, marketing, manufacturing, quality, communication, and human resources. With a high decision latitude, units have a considerable influence over how they best achieve their goals. This also means that they have the opportunity to accumulate expert knowledge and recruit specialists.

Structural Factors and Innovation Type

Are the influences of these structural factors contingent on different types of innovations, an innovation's degree of novelty, and whether the innovation was generated or adopted? One of the most used typologies of innovation is product versus process innovation. Product innovations (new or improved goods or services) are externally focused, often toward a market. Process innovations are internally focused as new elements are introduced to an organization's processes or systems (Damanpour & Aravind, 2006). Furthermore, an important innovation attribute is its degree of novelty. Incremental innovations build on the organization's existing knowledge and capabilities, leading to small changes to product offerings (or processes). In contrast, radical innovations require larger shifts in knowledge and technological expertise as they set off fundamental changes in an organization's product offerings (or processes). Last, an innovation can be generated or adopted, respectively. Innovation generation is a process in which the organization combines knowledge and ideas in a creative process to produce something novel and useful. Innovation adoption, alternatively, is a problem-solving process in which an existing innovation (often from the outside) is implemented to address identified needs or problems.

Damanpour (1991) tested the three typologies (product versus process, radical versus incremental, generation versus adaption) as moderators between structural factors and innovation. None of the typologies showed clear interaction effects with regard to the seven factors previously mentioned. This finding was corroborated by Damanpour and Aravind (2012) in their review of post-1990 studies. Rather, it seems that structural factors associated differently with innovation depending on the type of organization that was studied. In a manufacturing context, formalization was positively related to innovation, whereas direct supervision was negatively related. These relationships are reversed when examining organizations that are service based (Damanpour, 1991). These findings still lack sufficient explanation and call into question aspects of extant theory. For example, Tushman and Smith (2002) argue that radical and incremental innovations thrive in vastly different organizational environments: entrepreneurial versus efficiency cultures, decentralized versus centralized decision-making, and flexible versus coordinated work processes, respectively. Whether or not different innovation types and novelties require different organizational structures is a question that future research will have to scrutinize. More work is thus needed on variables that moderate structural factors' influence on innovation. As a starting point, we should taxonomize (a) moderator types, that is, whether or not a variable plays a role as a moderator, and (b) moderator specifics, that is, relationship strength at different levels of the moderator, as well as the moderator's mechanisms of action.

Cross-Level Effects of Structure on Innovation

A discussion with relevance to institutional supports of innovation is that of the cross-level effects of such supports. Let's examine the case of formalization and centralization. Both are major structural factors in theories of organizational innovation. Strongly formalized organizations rely on formal rules and procedures. They lean heavily on processes as governance instruments. Weakly formalized organizations allow employees to determine which decisions and directions are to be taken, leaning less on formal processes. Strongly centralized organizations concentrate decision-making to the top management level rather than distributing it among the organization's functions. They are typically hierarchically organized. The decision-making mandate is distributed to managers at each hierarchical level. Weakly centralized organizations distribute the decision-making mandate to functional units that are relatively more autonomous. In the literature, formalization and centralization have generally been thought to influence innovation negatively. For example, high formalization and centralization mean a loss of autonomy at the individual and team levels (Mumford et al., 2002). Increased managerial control and process reliance have also been tied to reduced exploration scope for individuals and groups who are expected to experiment with new ideas (Denti, 2013). Less autonomy has also been related to diminished feelings of responsibility, commitment, and involvement – strong motivational factors that underlie employees' willingness to innovate (Denti & Hemlin, 2016). As another example, strong hierarchical structures have been thought to hinder cross-functional collaboration (Burns & Stalker, 1961).

However, research shows mixed findings for these two factors (Damanpour & Aravind, 2012). That is, research has not been able to converge on whether they contribute positively or negatively to firms' innovation performance. Mumford and Hunter (2005) suggested that centralization and formalization may have positive and negative effects at the same time in an organization. Even though strong formalization may be undesirable for the motivation and practical capabilities of innovative individuals and groups, reliance on formal innovation processes may ensure that ideas are evaluated fairly and in line with the organization's strategy. In addition, formalized innovation processes ensure that the appropriate organizational functions are involved in time, and that resources are made available for new innovation projects. Likewise, while strong centralization reduces autonomy for individuals and groups, lowering their intrinsic motivation and commitment, centralized organizations are easier to manage according to strategic objectives. From a management point of view, it is necessary to ensure that innovation projects are in line with the market situation, identified consumer needs, competitors' offers, stakeholder expectations, or other strategic considerations. Thus, management wants control over what projects are started, how these are to be resourced, and expected timeline for deliverables. This requires a certain amount of centralization and formalization.

Taken together, the negative effect of centralization and formalization at the individual and team levels may be offset by a positive effect at the organization level as the organization as a whole gains coordination and strategic focus. A dilemma for organizations is to engage employees in business goals without simultaneously dousing their own passions (Cardinal, 2001). We agree with other scholars in our conclusion that more research is needed about cross-level effects (Mumford & Hunter, 2005; O'Reilly & Tushman, 2013; Stetler, 2015). Cross-level effects are also an important issue in theory development, especially on the process management side of innovation. Process control is a necessary element in successful innovation (Crossan & Apaydin, 2010), but the way processes are designed may affect perceptions of justice, creativity requirements, and autonomy at individual and team levels (Denti, 2013). Perhaps cross-level conflicts like these are unavoidable, but we still need more research on why and when they occur in order to inform process design decisions.

Processes in Innovation

The innovation process has been described by many scholars (e.g., Edquist, 1997; Tidd & Bessant, 2013). Although there is a logical progression where each stage of the process impacts subsequent ones, the innovation process is not inevitably linear (Hunter, Cassidy, & Scott Ligon, 2012). Insights or information gathered in one particular stage may influence other stages in the process, or spawn a new innovation process altogether. It should be noted that, from a process management perspective, an employee might be involved in any number of early phase or late-phase projects (Bledow, Frese, Anderson, Erez, & Farr, 2009).

In the initiation phase, the organization becomes aware of new opportunities that may come from the outside (such as new market opportunities, customer needs, new legislation) or from within (such as advances in technology). An innovation can be either generated within the firm or adopted from another firm (Gopalakrishnan & Damanpour, 1997). Planning is central to innovation generation (Hunter et al., 2012). Product developmental resources (such as R&D) and project hand-offs to subsequent development (or production, marketing) should be planned, directed, and executed in a timely manner. Planning further ensures that the organization's development efforts are in line with a broader innovation strategy and that knowledge is transferred between units. For example, technology that is being researched and applied in one early development project could be used to solve problems in more mature projects geared toward implementation (Corso, 2002). However, plans need not be rigid. Rather, they should be composed of contingencies in order to tackle emergent situations (Hunter et al., 2012). Innovations can also be adopted from the outside (Wolfe, 1994). Adoption decision-making can be broken down into three stages in the initiation phase: (a) preadoption, when the organization becomes aware of the innovation to adopt; (b) periadoption, when the organization learns more about and better understands the innovation; and (c) established adoption, when a decision is made to adopt and planning begins for its implementation (Wisdom, Chor, Hoagwood, & Horwitz, 2014).

After an innovation generation or adoption decision, development and implementation of the innovation follow. Subunits of the organization (e.g., R&D, design, engineering) are tasked with developing, designing, adapting, and testing prototypes and required technology (Crossan & Apaydin, 2010). Project management and problem-solving are central processes to this developmental stage. Adams, Bessant, and Phelps (2006) reviewed processes in innovation project management in R&D and found three factors for project success: (a) project efficiency, that is, project duration and speed in relation to the planned schedule; (b) internal and external communication; and (c) collaboration, not only within the project team, but also with teams farther down the hand-off chain (e.g., further development or production), as well as collaboration with customers and suppliers. Project management is an area where many tools and systems have been developed. Examples are the stage-gate process, phased development, product and cycle-time excellence, and total design (Adams et al., 2006). These management systems help the organization separate development efforts into discrete stages that can be subject to quality control and stop/go decisions. Formal management systems (such as stage-gate) have been shown to be valuable in assessing the quality of project ideas (Ettlie & Elsenbach, 2007). However, there is a catch. Sethi and Iqbal (2008) followed the formation and progression of 120 projects and reached the conclusion that firms systematically discarded project directions that were too novel and untested in favor of feasibility.

Specialized tools aimed at improving team decision-making and problem-solving can be used by project teams when encountering novel problems (Adams et al., 2006). The creative problem-solving process is fairly well understood. It has lately been updated and developed by Mumford and his colleagues (e.g., Baughman & Mumford, 1995; Mumford et al., 1991, 1996, 1997) as an eight-stage process: problem definition, information gathering, concept selection and conceptual combination, idea generation and evaluation, implementation planning, and monitoring. Formal tools for creative problem-solving can help teams stay focused on important aspects of the process (Puccio, Mance, & Murdock, 2010), especially at the important early stages of problem construction (Scott, Leritz, & Mumford, 2004).

Typically, an organization has several ongoing innovation projects in an innovation portfolio. Because innovation exhausts limited resources, how effectively an organization manages its innovation portfolio is a competitive advantage (Bard, Balachandra, & Kaufmann, 1988). Portfolio management entails models and processes that prompt project selection, prioritization, and resourcing (Cooper, Edgett, & Kleinschmidt, 1999), and post hoc evaluation (Lee, Son, & Lee, 1996). Examples are risk-return calculation (ROI) models, constrained optimization models (Schmidt & Freeland, 1992), and economic and benefit models (Hall & Nauda, 1990).

The successful innovation process ends up in marketing and commercialization (Corso, 2002; Crossan & Apaydin, 2010). The processes of commercialization involves a shift away from an organization's technical and developmental functions toward its management and administrative functions. Activities at this stage are market analysis and monitoring, market testing, marketing, and promotion (Verhaeghe & Kfir, 2002). Although marketing and commercialization are important for the success of an innovation in the marketplace, this area is less studied by innovation scholars (Adams et al., 2006). Adams and his colleagues note that activities tied to product launch as well as evaluations of launch success have traditionally been considered the domain of other research areas and specialists, such as marketers.

Organizational Ambidexterity

In recent years, there has been a surge in the number of studies employing the framework of organizational ambidexterity. Two concepts are central to ambidexterity: exploration and exploitation. Ambidexterity is to successfully manage exploration and exploitation simultaneously. Even though ambidexterity studies seem to lack consensus on how exploration and exploitation should be defined, operationalized, and measured (Birkinshaw & Gupta, 2013), many publications in the field refer to the definitions given by March (1991). Exploration, according to March, is concerned with innovation, risk-taking, discovery, and flexibility. Exploitation is concerned with efficiency, refinement, implementation, and execution. In relation to the innovation process, exploration activities are most concentrated in early stages (initiation and decision-making) and less in later stages (development, implementation, and commercialization) (Stetler, 2015). Organizational ambidexterity can be placed into the framework of dynamic capabilities (O'Reilly & Tushman, 2008) – "the firm's ability to integrate, build, and reconfigure internal and external competences to address rapidly changing environments" (Teece, Pisano, & Schuen, 1997, p. 516). Organizations must simultaneously pursue both emerging and mature strategies as a key prerequisite for long-term success. However, as O'Reilly and Tushman (2008, p. 196) point out, "ambidexterity as a dynamic capability is not itself a source of competitive advantage but facilitates new resource configurations that can offer a competitive advantage."

Reaching Ambidexterity

After reviewing the ambidexterity literature, Lavie, Stettner, and Tushman (2010) proposed four main strategies for achieving ambidexterity. Organizational separation entails purposing and separating organizational components; temporal separation entails separating exploration and exploitation in time; contextual ambidexterity involves the simultaneous merging of exploration and exploitation; and domain separation suggests using partnerships and alliances in exploration/exploitation management.

Organizational Separation

One of the most common approaches to achieve ambidexterity is Tushman and O'Reilly's (1996) proposal of organizational separation, also called structural ambidexterity. In this approach, different organizational units are purposed to either exploration or exploitation and are separated geographically as well as culturally. Exploitative units should be more centralized and formalized, maximizing efficiency. Conversely, explorative units should be more decentralized and flexible, maximizing learning and experimentation (Benner & Tushman, 2003). As a prominent example, the firm IKEA has successfully implemented this type of ambidexterity (Vahlne & Jonsson, 2017). Their external innovation lab Space10 experiments with concepts and prototypes, which are then fed into more exploitative units at the firm (i.e., production, logistics, and marketing). New product concepts are market tested in small scale, minimizing risk and resource needs for product launches. A key prerequisite for Space10 is a tight coupling between senior management at explorative and exploitative units, which ensures legitimacy, access to resources, as well as interfunctional coordination (O'Reilly & Tushman, 2004). However, a challenge for structurally ambidextrous organizations is to integrate organizational units with different cultures and work methods as projects inevitably move from exploration to exploitation (Stetler, 2015).

Temporal Separation

In this view, ambidexterity is achieved by cyclically shifting between exploration and exploitation. Temporal ambidexterity stems from the idea of the punctuated equilibrium, where long periods of stability are disrupted by shorter transition periods (punctuations) in which the organization adapts to new circumstances (Gersick, 1991). Although an organization may avoid conflicts related to simultaneous exploration and exploitation, temporal ambidexterity introduces another set of challenges. Management must promptly and successfully identify a pending transition period and mobilize resources toward exploratory innovation. As employees have enjoyed stable conditions for a long period of time, built up inertia may cause lower preparedness for change (Levinthal & March, 1993). A large simultaneous shift to exploration may also introduce path dependence (Lavie & Rosenkopf, 2006). Brunner, Staats, Tushman, and Upton (2010) have suggested that organizations may counter this inertia by introducing artificial transition periods, which they call deliberate perturbations. These are internally generated challenges that force the organization to dislodge from set routines, increasing readiness for externally induced punctuations.

Contextual Ambidexterity

Contextual ambidexterity proposes a balancing act in which exploration and exploitation are managed simultaneously in the organization. Typically, this balancing act is achieved on the individual or group level. This is the model chosen by Google. Their engineers split their time between today's core activities (70%), things that are emerging but related to the company's general vision (20%), and totally new areas that might have a high risk of failure but also be of major future importance (10%) (Steiber & Alänge, 2016). Akin to other types of ambidexterity, this configuration comes with its own set of trade-offs. Employees may be involved in several projects simultaneously, each somewhere along the exploration-exploitation continuum, which requires them to constantly shift between divergent and convergent frames of thinking (Stetler, 2015). It may be difficult to communicate and manage organizational goals and allocate resources effectively as explorative and exploitative goals may conflict (Gibson & Birkinshaw, 2004). However, Bledow et al. (2009) maintain that contextual ambidexterity is associated with lower costs compared to integrating something that once has been separated, for example, organizational units that are separated as per the structural approach to ambidexterity, or separations into cyclical shifts between exploration and exploitation as per the temporal approach.

Domain Separation

The most recent approach to ambidexterity (Stetler, 2015) is by domain separation. The organization may create a patchwork of alliances with external actors (e.g., research partnerships, joint ventures) to serve explorative and exploitative agendas. Thus, an organization does not need to purpose separate organizational units to either exploration or exploitation (as per the structural approach to ambidexterity), or reconcile exploration and exploitation within units (as per the contextual approach), as long as an overall balance is maintained across functional domains (Lavie et al., 2010). Lavie and Rosenkopf (2006) put forward three domains. The function domain refers to generating or exploiting knowledge within an alliance, the structure domain refers to building or maintaining alliances, and the attribute domain refers to building a portfolio of alliances with varying attributes (such as size and industry). Proponents of the domain separation approach to organizational ambidexterity maintain that it resolves some dilemmas that emerge in those approaches that seek to separate exploration and exploitation (either across organizational units or over time). A balance among domains is easier to maintain, meaning more efficient resource allocation and less conflicting organizational goals and processes (Lavie et al., 2010). However, the hand-off dilemma still occurs when exploration moves to exploitation. Research on the domain separation approach is, however, scarce. More research is needed that focuses on how to permeate organizational boundaries other than by creating alliances with external actors (Stetler, 2015).

Theoretical Issues in Ambidexterity

The four presented strategies for achieving ambidexterity can be viewed as theoretical archetypes. Each archetype is a proposition on how to handle the dilemma of exploring and exploiting simultaneously, and they come with their sets of advantages and disadvantages. Buried within the archetypes are also theoretical issues on which scholars disagree – that is, issues concerning how and when exploration and exploitation activities can be combined (Stetler, 2015). For example, proponents of the contextual approach to ambidexterity maintain that knowledge can be created and exploited within a given organizational unit or function (e.g., Birkinshaw & Gibson, 2004), and proponents of the domain separation approach argue that knowledge creation and exploitation cannot be combined within the same function domain, as they suggest that these activities are fundamentally dissimilar (e.g., Lavie & Rosenkopf, 2006). In practice, organizations mix several strategies when they strive toward ambidexterity. For example, Vahlne and Jonsson (2017) showed that AB Volvo and IKEA employ strategies for both contextual and structural ambidexterity. Some studies have demonstrated that companies' temporal transition between exploration and exploitation is not sudden, as suggested by the punctuated equilibrium model, but rather slow and gradual (O'Reilly & Tushman, 2013). There are also definitional issues. The field lacks consensus on how the terms *exploration* and *exploitation* should be defined and operationalized (Birkinshaw & Gupta, 2013). It is also unclear where innovation should be placed within the ambidexterity framework. While March (1991) places innovation squarely as an exploration activity, other scholars have suggested that certain types of innovation should be placed across the exploration-exploitation continuum: innovation as opposed to efficiency (Sarkees & Hulland, 2009), disruptive innovation as opposed to sustaining innovation (Danneels, 2006), and discontinuous innovation as opposed to incremental innovation (Tushman & O'Reilly, 1996). Another large issue for theory is that the definition of the term itself – *organizational ambidexterity* – has deviated from its original meaning of characterizing the tensions associated with exploration and exploitation. Some scholars have called for more theoretical work to integrate the definitions and create congruence of the concepts involved (e.g., Nosella et al., 2012), otherwise "our insights into how firms actually explore and exploit are likely to become less and less useful" (O'Reilly & Tushman, 2013, p. 331). A future theoretical challenge for the ambidexterity field is (a) to clearly delineate exploration and exploitation (e.g., define structure, processes, and output) and (b) decide where and in what form innovation should be placed within this continuum.

Resources and Creativity

The category of organizational resources is broad and can, according to Shalley, Litchfield, and Gilson (2017), entail time, rewards, physical resources, task characteristics, as well as team members' backgrounds (which is another broad category), knowledge, and personalities. A traditional view is that the size of firms and their bigger resources determined how successful they were in producing radical innovations. However, this view was challenged by Chandy and Tellis (1998), who showed that the willingness to cannibalize a firm's own resources was important, rather than size. By increasing resources to radical product innovation, these firms get an advantage.

Perhaps the least amount of research of the resources for creativity is conducted on knowledge management. Knowledge management is about the organizing, storing, and retrieving of knowledge and has been traced to concepts like knowledge economy and knowledge society, and that businesses possess intellectual capital (Stehr, 1994). Knowledge management literature uses the concept of codified and tacit knowledge (Fuller, 2002). Codified knowledge is seen as stored knowledge for common use by employees. It is typically knowledge that is factual and found in places such as books, manuals, or software. Tacit knowledge is not explicit and codified but is inherent and tied to a person's skills. Nonaka and Takeuchi (1995) are known for their theory of knowledge creation within firms, which at face value seems to denote a creativity process. However, their main thesis is that knowledge creation springs from transforming tacit knowledge into explicit and codified knowledge that can be shared among employees. This is certainly an important process in companies as well as in other organizations in order to make knowledge explicit and more easily spread. However, the tacit dimension of knowledge creation leaves aside humans' cognitive capacities. Human cognition relies to a great extent on codified knowledge rather than tacit knowledge in problem-solving, which leads to new knowledge. So, rather than seeing knowledge creation as transformations of tacit knowledge, we argue that new (and useful) knowledge is very much dependent on codified knowledge. Hence, creativity and creative problem-solving rely on codified knowledge. The tacit dimension of knowledge may be useful in innovation processes in manufacturing. Manufacturing skills that employees have and may be tacit are likely to be important for innovations. Particularly, we believe that incremental innovations in the manufacturing industry may benefit from the tacit dimension of skills.

More recent literature connects knowledge management or a knowledge-based view with organizational learning. For example, Kazanjian and Drazin (2012) analyze knowledge management as part of an organization's innovation efforts. These authors apply a business view on creativity and innovation, which implies that knowledge is seen as a resource for competitive advantage. A business organization depends, as they say, on a number of knowledge bases to be able to produce, for example, new engines or pharmaceuticals. It is suggested that new products are based on existing organizational knowledge (in-house) or on new knowledge that may be based on creative problem-solving and import of knowledge external from the organization. A crucial and strategic issue for top management, they suggest, is the choice between the knowledge exploring and exploiting alternatives (see ambidexterity earlier), which may be dependent on the market. It is clear that a business company is strongly dependent on its engineers, economists, and marketing managers in cross-functional teams to perform well here.

But why is expertise or expert knowledge considered a driver of creativity and innovation? Expertise is tied to a knowledge domain (Amabile, 1996; Csikszentmihalyi, 1999), for example, automotive engineering, organic chemistry, economics, or psychology. Inevitably, knowledge is a key resource in creative thinking (Amabile, 1996; Mumford et al., 2002; Mumford, Hemlin, & Mulhearn, 2017; Sternberg, 1999). To be creative in a domain, it is a fundamental asset to have vast and deep knowledge in this domain. Knowledge or expertise in a field is, so to speak, the material that creative thinking processes work with. Such thinking processes in science involve reasoning, problem-solving, and analogical thinking and are often conducted in a team context as distributed reasoning (Dunbar, 1995). Creativity is, in other words, completely dependent on expert knowledge. Therefore, expert resources are sought after and found in innovative organizations and particularly in research and development teams, where innovation is a key target. The achievement of expertise or expert performance is a process of practice and extended training of individual capabilities and skills in a domain (Ericsson & Charness, 1994). This period of training is approximately 10 years of extensive practice across domains. For example, a violinist must learn and exercise violin for a very long and intensive period of time to reach the elite of violinists. The same goes for professional expertise in an organization, such as in banking or chemistry (Ericsson & Moxley, 2012). Finally, it should be noted that it takes time for an organization to build up a package of expertise needed for advanced projects, for exploitation of projects and learning from projects.

Teams need domain-specific knowledge as well as technical expertise for activities such as planning, forecasting, building on experience, and learning (Mumford et al., 2017). Members of innovative teams are also aware of each member's expertise. They attend to and use each member's contribution. For these cognitive team processes to work efficiently, it is essential that communication is lively and that conflicts are resolved (Paulus & Kenworthy, 2018). Technical expertise is further important for leaders of innovative endeavors, enabling them to communicate effectively with their followers or teams. Expertise allows leaders to clarify knowledge requirements, integrate their follower's creative contributions, and facilitate creative problem-solving (Mainemelis, Kark, & Epitropaki, 2015).

A few recent empirical studies that connect knowledge management with creative teamwork have been conducted. In a study of 84 R&D groups in biotechnology, Hemlin (2009) found that knowledge management was critical for team creativity. Group leaders were concerned about how best to organize knowledge flows and to generate ideas. Moreover, they emphasized knowledge production, for example, by organizing science schools in specific domains, the specific nature of knowledge needed and the individual knowledge components. Moreover, Hemlin and Olsson (2011) conducted a critical incident technique study of 34 R&D teams in bioscience. They asked three questions: (a) In what situations are research group and team leaders stimulating creativity? (b) How is this done? (c) Why are these events important? The 42 university and 33 industry employees were doctoral students, postdocs, and engineers. Results showed that about half of the answers on the first question concerned research meetings and expert advice, where leaders used their expertise to guide and support team members to enhance their creativity. This expert advice comprised project planning, individual and group futures, scientific communication, methods, and idea generation. Even more convincing results about the importance of expertise were found in the analysis of the question about leader behaviors that increase follower creativity. The top category of behaviors (34%) was "provision of expertise." For example, leaders provided ideas and perspectives, evaluated research processes, provided required support, and introduced new knowledge to team members. But why did participants believe that the incidents were creativity stimulating? The main explanations (greater than 50% of reported incidents) concerned advancement of research and scientific exchange. For example, reports included improvements, possibilities to proceed, research communication, reaching closure, and securing future plans as parts of research advancements. In another study, Krause (2004) found that 399 German middle managers granting freedom and expert knowledge were the most influential factors in a regression on innovative behaviors. Knowledge utilization as part of managing knowledge was found by Sung and Choi (2012) to strengthen team creativity. We draw the conclusion that there is sound support to the claim that expertise is needed for research and innovation and a fundamental resource for creative efforts to be achieved.

Concluding Remarks and Future Research

Before turning to the broader conclusions of this chapter and implications for managers, we must note a few limitations. This chapter has taken a broad cross-domain perspective on organizational-level factors that influence innovation. This is a limitation as domains (e.g., manufacturing, service industries, etc.) seem to play a role as moderators of the associations of structural factors to innovation outcomes (Damanpour & Aravind, 2012). Another potential limitation regards the fact that there are more factors on the organizational level than we have reviewed, for example, organizational culture. Space did not permit an exploration of these factors, as we narrowed our scope to structure, processes, and resources. Last, the processes and models that are described in this chapter are discussed in a general sense. In practice, there are many methods and models in domains such as portfolio management, ROI calculation, or stage-gate models (Hunter et al., 2012).

This chapter has reviewed institutional supports for innovation at the organizational level. Organizational structures that support the attainment and application of expertise strengthen the innovation capacity of an organization. This is not surprising since all forms of creativity and innovation are essentially based on combinations of various knowledge domains, skills, and expertise (Hunter, Bedell-Avers, Hunsicker, Mumford, & Ligon, 2008). Knowledge is the raw material for new ideas. Skills and experience transform these ideas to realized innovations. Organizations with highly educated employees (professionals) with different types of expert competence (specialization), who are allowed autonomy within their own expert areas (functional differentiation), and where knowledge is readily attainable (knowledge resources), are better equipped to develop innovations. We have also shown the importance of communication and cross-functional cooperation. Innovative organizations communicate intensively within the organization, and they maintain a contact surface for communicating and collaborating with the outside world. This is made possible by their knowledge-intensive base (Damanpour & Aravind, 2012). Management and leaders, who influence their organization's culture, need to be open to new ideas and critical discussion about how things should be done – that is, they need to have a positive attitude toward change. Combining deep expertise with active communication in the organization is therefore strongly linked to organizational innovation. Perhaps there was nothing wrong with Steve Jobs' controversial design choice when he designed Pixar's campus in Emeryville, California, in 2000. Jobs placed all common spaces in a large atrium in the middle of the campus. All employees – new recruits as well as seniors – were forced to converse on their long trek to meeting rooms, toilets, and the cafeteria (Catmull & Wallace, 2014).

However, organizational knowledge must be directed and formed into an innovation. Through planning and using formal innovation management systems and innovation portfolios, the organization can ensure that its innovation processes (and projects) are serving its long-term strategy (Corso, 2002; Hunter et al., 2012). Each innovation process needs coordination to ensure that projects are linked to and handed off in the product development chain. On the project level, important processes and tools are project management processes (Adams et al., 2006) as well as creative problem-solving on individual (Mumford, Medeiros, & Partlow, 2012; Puccio et al., 2010) and team levels (Harms, Kennel, & Reiter-Palmon, 2018).

Finally, there is much we still do not know. We have mentioned two important areas for further research that both are concerned with how factors interact with the end goal of enhancing innovation performance. First, we need more research on when and how structural factors influence innovation – that is, knowledge on variables that moderate structural factors' relationships to innovation. Second, we need more knowledge on how organizational-level factors and processes affect individual- and team-level factors and processes, "cross-level" interactions.

Implications for Management

Management is often viewed by research and development teams as an obstacle to research and innovation. It circumscribes research, creativity, and innovation by hindering free thinking, hindering new ideas to be pursued, reducing risk-taking, and slowing down the research and development process by imposing management rules and administrative instruments on researchers and engineers. One classic tension in research organizations is therefore freedom and control (Pelz & Andrews, 1966) – that is, how much freedom may be allowed for researchers and engineers and how much of their activities should be controlled. This is what research management is about. Hemlin (2006) discussed how research management may become a resource rather than a hindrance for research and creativity. The analysis ends with a proposal of six methods to reconcile research management and creativity. His analysis focuses on university organizations but may be applied more broadly, for example, in knowledge-intensive organizations. First, it is suggested that an organization can manage the recruitment of appropriate people to creative research and innovation. Therefore, selection criteria include a track record of creative research and innovation (not only a high research production), abilities and skills that promote creativity and innovation, and strong motivation. In research groups and innovation teams, composition is also essential to make groups functionally heterogeneous. This means that people should have different field expertise and experience. Groups having such a composition have been found to be more creative than others. Second, and related to the first point, is that employees get training in generic creativity skills (rather than only information about creativity) and support for motivation. Rewards and incentives related to creativity are important also for researchers and engineers but should be handled with care. Creativity is mostly dependent on intrinsic motivation, but recent research findings show that rewards may be important and strengthen creativity if provided in a clever way that does not interfere with a person's knowledge interests (Steele, McIntosh, & Higgs, 2017). Third, management should provide support for the following basic activities related to creative performance: (a) freedom and time to develop ideas; (b) broad communication and collaboration with colleagues in the unit as well as with external sources of creativity; (c) creative decision-making, that is, making possible more than a few decision alternatives; (d) time sharing and priority of research and development tasks to administrative burdens, with the latter being subject to efficient routines handled by a slim administrative staff organization; and (e) a self-reflecting attitude by researchers and engineers toward their own doings – that is, self-evaluations that provide learning about improvement of research and innovation skills in a creative direction. Fourth, management work designs should be changed and adapted to make researchers and engineers able to create challenging and novel ideas to be pursued. Simple routine tasks and administration could often be done by other people than the researchers – that is, by support staff. This demands that management listen closely to researchers and developers and reallocate resources from management to direct support. For example, in Swedish universities, this is sometimes a neglected management area, since management itself has developed into large units decoupled from research in modern large universities. Fifth, psychological and social processes that stimulate creativity in research and development need to be supported by management. These processes entail psychological safety, open communication and transparent decision-making, coping with challenges, risk, hard work, effective teamwork, and good leadership skills. Management should provide training resources for researchers and engineers for these processes to come to work. Since most research and development is done as project teamwork, the psychological and social team processes are vital for creativity to occur (Reiter-Palmon & Harms, 2018). Finally, at the top level of organizations, senior managers who make decisions regarding organizational frames and rules should allow a degree of freedom for the self-organizing of teams aligned with the organization's innovation strategy, rather than impose new management on research and development units.

References

Abernathy, W. J. (1978). *The productivity dilemma*. Baltimore, MD: Johns Hopkins University Press.

Adams, R., Bessant, J., & Phelps, R. (2006). Innovation management measurement: A review. *International Journal of Management Reviews*, 8, 21–47.

Aiken, M., Bacharach, S. B., & French, J. L. (1980). Organizational structure, work process, and proposal making in administrative bureaucracies. *Academy of Management Journal*, 23, 631–652.

Amabile, T. M. (1996). *Creativity in context*. Boulder, CO: Westview Press.

Bard, J. F., Balachandra, R., & Kaufmann, P. E. (1988). An interactive approach to R&D project selection and termination. *IEEE Transactions on Engineering Management*, 35, 139–146.

Baughman, W. A., & Mumford, M. D. (1995). Process analytic models of creative capacities: Operations involved in the combination and reorganization process. *Creativity Research Journal*, 8, 37–62.

Benner, M. J., & Tushman, M. L. (2003). Exploitation, exploration, and process management: The productivity dilemma revisited. *Academy of Management Review*, 28, 238–256.

Birkinshaw, J., & Gibson, C. (2004). Building ambidexterity into an organization. *MIT Sloan Management Review*, 45, 47–55.

Birkinshaw, J., & Gupta, K. (2013). Clarifying the distinctive contribution of ambidexterity to the field of organization studies. *The Academy of Management Perspectives*, 27, 287–298.

Bledow, R., Frese, M., Anderson, N., Erez, M., & Farr, J. (2009). A dialectic perspective on innovation: Conflicting demands, multiple pathways, and ambidexterity. *Industrial and Organizational Psychology*, 2, 305–337.

Brunner, D., Staats, B., Tushman, M., & Upton, D. (2010). Wellsprings of creation: How perturbation sustains exploration in mature organizations. *Harvard Business School Organizational Behavior Unit Working Paper 09-011*.

Burns, T., & Stalker, G. (1961). *The management of innovation*. London, UK: Tavistock.

Cardinal, L. B. (2001). Technological innovation in the pharmaceutical industry: The use of organizational control in managing research and development. *Organization Science*, 12, 19–37.

Catmull E., & Wallace, A. (2014). *Creativity, Inc.: Overcoming the unseen forces that stand in the way of true inspiration*. New York, NY: Random House.

Chandy, R. J., & Tellis, G. J. (1998). Organizing for radical product innovation: The overlooked role of willingness to cannibalize. *Journal of Marketing Research*, 35, 474–487.

Cooper, R. G., Edgett, S. J., & Kleinschmidt, E. J. (1999). New product portfolio management: Practices and performance. *Journal of Product Innovation Management*, 16, 333–351.

Corso, M. (2002). From product development to continuous product innovation: Mapping the routes of corporate knowledge. *International Journal of Technology Management*, 23, 322–340.

Crossan, M. M., & Apaydin, M. (2010). A multi-dimensional framework of organizational innovation: A systematic review of the literature. *Journal of Management Studies*, 47, 1154–1191.

Csikszentmihalyi, M. (1999). Implications of a systems perspective for the study of creativity. In R. J. Sternberg (Ed.), *Handbook of creativity*. New York, NY: Cambridge University Press.

Damanpour, F. (1991). Organizational innovation: A meta-analysis of effects of determinants and moderators. *Academy of Management Journal*, 34, 555–590.

Damanpour, F., & Aravind, D. (2006). Product and process innovations: A review of organizational and environmental determinants. In J. Hage & M. Meeus (Eds.), *Innovation, science, and institutional change*. Oxford, UK: Oxford University Press.

Damanpour, F., & Aravind, D. (2012). Organizational structure and innovation revisited: From organic to ambidextrous structure. In M. D. Mumford (Ed.), *Handbook of organizational creativity*. London, UK: Elsevier.

Danneels, E. (2006). Dialogue on the effects of disruptive technology on firms and industries. *Journal of Product Innovation Management*, 23, 2–4.

Denti, L. (2013). *Leadership and innovation in R&D teams*. (Doctoral dissertation, University of Gothenburg, Gothenburg, Sweden).

Denti, L., & Hemlin, S. (2016). Modelling the link between leader-member exchange and individual innovation in R&D. *International Journal of Innovation Management*, 20, 1–23.

Dunbar, K. (1995). How do scientists really reason: Scientific reasoning in real-world laboratories. In R. J. Sternberg & J. E. Davidson (Eds.), *The nature of insight* (pp. 365–396). Cambridge, MA: MIT Press.

Edquist, C. (1997). Systems of innovation approaches—Their emergence and characteristics. In C. Edquist (Ed.), *Systems of innovation: Technologies, institutions and organizations*. London, UK: Pinter Publishers.

Elenkov, D. S., Judge, W., & Wright, P. (2005). Strategic leadership and executive innovation influence: An international multi-cluster comparative study. *Strategic Management Journal*, 26, 665–682.

Ericsson, K. A., & Charness, N. (1994). Expert performance. Its structure and acquisition. *American Psychologist*, 49, 725–747.

Ericsson, K. A., & Moxley, J. H. (2012). A critique of Howard's argument for innate limits of chess performance or why we need an account based on acquired skill and deliberate practice. *Applied Cognitive Psychology*, 26, 649–653.

Ettlie, J. E., & Eisenbach, J. M. (2007). Modified stage-gate regimes in new product development. *Journal of Product Innovation Management*, 24, 20–33.

Fuller, S. (2002). *Knowledge management foundations*. Boston, MA: Butterworth-Heinemann.

Gersick, C. J. (1991). Revolutionary change theories: A multilevel exploration of the punctuated equilibrium paradigm. *Academy of Management Review*, 16, 10–36.

Gibbons, M., Limoges, C., Nowotny, H., Schwartzman, S., Scott, P., & Trow, M. (1994). *The new production of knowledge: The dynamics of science and research in contemporary societies*. Thousand Oaks, CA: Sage.

Gibson, C. B., & Birkinshaw, J. (2004). The antecedents, consequences, and mediating role of organizational ambidexterity. *Academy of Management Journal*, 47, 209–226.

Gopalakrishnan, S., & Damanpour, F. (1997). A review of innovation research in economics, sociology and technology management. *Omega – International Journal of Management Science*, 25, 15–28.

Hall, D. L., & Nauda, A. (1990). An interactive approach for selecting IR&D projects. *IEEE Transactions on Engineering Management*, 37, 126–133.

Harms, M., Kennel, V., & Reiter-Palmon, R. (2018). Team creativity. Cognitive processes underlying problem solving. In R. Reiter-Palmon (Ed.), *Team creativity and innovation* (pp. 61–86). New York, NY: Oxford University Press.

Hemlin, S. (2006). Managing creativity in academic research. Could creative action and management be reconciled in research? *Science Studies*, 19(1), 83–92.

Hemlin, S. (2009). Creative knowledge environments: An interview study with group members and group leaders of university and industry R&D groups in biotechnology. *Creativity and Innovation Management*, 18, 178–185.

Hemlin, S., Allwood, C. M., & Martin, B. R. (2008). Creative knowledge environments. *Creativity Research Journal*, 20(2), 196–210.

Hemlin, S., & Olsson, L. (2011). Creativity stimulating leadership: A critical incident study of leaders' influence on creativity in R&D groups. *Creativity and Innovation Management*, 20, 49–58.

Hobday, M. (2005). Firm-level innovation models: Perspectives on research in developed and developing countries. *Technology Analysis and Strategic Management*, 17, 121–146.

Hunter, S. T., Bedell-Avers, K. E., Hunsicker, C. E., Mumford, M. D., & Ligon, G. S. (2008). Applying multiple knowledge structures in creative thought: Effects on idea generation and problem-solving. *Creativity Research Journal*, 20, 137–154.

Hunter, S. T., Cassidy, S. E., & Scott Ligon, G. (2012). Planning for innovation: A process oriented perspective. In M. D. Mumford (Ed.), *Handbook of organizational creativity* (pp. 515–545). London, UK: Academic Press.

Kazanijan, R. K., & Drazin, R. (2012). Organizational learning: Knowledge management and creativity. In M. Mumford (Ed.), *Handbook of organizational creativity*. London, UK: Elsevier.

Krause, D. E. (2004). Influence-based leadership as a determinant of the inclination to innovate and of innovation-related behaviors. An empirical investigation. *The Leadership Quarterly*, 15, 79–102.

Lavie, D., & Rosenkopf, L. (2006). Balancing exploration and exploitation in alliance formation. *Academy of Management Journal*, 49, 797–818.

Lavie, D., Stettner, U., & Tushman, M. L. (2010). Exploration and exploitation within and across organizations. *The Academy of Management Annals*, 4, 109–155.

Lee, M., Son, B., & Lee, H. (1996). Measuring R&D effectiveness in Korean companies. *Research-Technology Management*, 39, 28–31.

Levinthal, D. A., & March, J. G. (1993). The myopia of learning. *Strategic Management Journal*, 14, 95–112.

Leydesdorff, L., & Etzkowitz, H. (1996). Emergence of a triple helix of university-industry-government relations. *Science and Public Policy*, 23, 279–286.

Leydesdorff, L., & Etzkowitz, H. (1998). The triple helix as a model for innovation studies. *Science and Public Policy* 25, 195–203.

Mainemelis, C., Kark, R., & Epitropaki, O. (2015). Creative leadership: A multi-context conceptualization. *The Academy of Management Annals*, 9, 393–482.

March, J. G. (1991). Exploration and exploitation in organizational learning. *Organization Science*, 2, 71–87.

Mintzberg, H. (1980). Structure in 5's: A synthesis of the research on organizational design. *Management Science*, 26, 322–341.

Mumford, M. D., Hemlin, S., & Mulhearn, T. (2017). Leading for creativity: Functions, models, and domains. In M. D. Mumford & S. Hemlin (Eds.), *Handbook of research on leadership and creativity* (pp. 1–13). Cheltenham, UK: Edward Elgar.

Mumford, M. D., & Hunter S. T. (2005). Innovation in organizations: A multi-level perspective on creativity. *Research in Multi-Level Issues*, 4, 11–73.

Mumford, M. D., Baughman, W. A., Supinski, E. P., & Maher, M. A. (1996). Process-based measures of creative problem-solving skills: II. Information encoding. *Creativity Research Journal*, 9, 77–88.

Mumford, M. D., Mobley, M. I., Uhlman, C. E., Reiter-Palmon, R., & Doares, L. (1991). Process analytic models of creative capacities. *Creativity Research Journal*, 4, 91–122.

Mumford, M. D., Scott, G. M., Gaddis, B., & Strange, J. M. (2002). Leading creative people: Orchestrating expertise and relationships. *The Leadership Quarterly*, 13, 705–730.

Mumford, M. D., Supinski, E. P., Baughman, W. A., Costanza, D. P., & Threlfall, K. V. (1997). Process-based measures of creative problem-solving skills: I. Overall prediction. *Creativity Research Journal*, 10, 77–85.

Mumford, M. D., Medeiros, K. E., & Partlow, P. J. (2012). Creative thinking: Processes, strategies and knowledge. *The Journal of Creative Behavior*, 46(1), 30–47.

Nonaka, I., & Takeuchi, H. (1995). *The knowledge-creating company*. New York, NY: Oxford University Press.

Nosella, A., Gantarello, S., & Filippini, R. (2012). The intellectual structure of organizational ambidexterity: A bibliometric investigation into the state of the art. *Strategic Organization*, 10, 450–465.

O'Reilly, C. A., & Tushman, M. L. (2013). Organizational ambidexterity: Past, present, and future. *Academy of Management Perspectives*, 27, 324–338.

O'Reilly, C. A., & Tushman, M. L. (2008). Ambidexterity as a dynamic capability: Resolving the innovator's dilemma. *Research in Organizational Behavior*, 28, 185–206.

O'Reilly, C. A., & Tushman, M. L. (2004). The ambidextrous organization. *Harvard Business Review*, 82, 74–83.

Paulus, P. B., & Kenworthy, J. B. (2018). Overview of team creativity and innovation. In R. Reiter-Palmon (Ed.), *Team Creativity and Innovation* (pp. 11–38). New York, NY: Oxford University Press.

Pelz, D. C., & Andrews, F. M. (Eds.). (1966; revised edition 1976). *Scientists in organizations: productive climates for research and development*. Ann Arbor, MI: Institute for Social Research, University of Michigan.

Puccio, G. J., Mance, M., & Murdock, M. C. (2010). *Creative leadership: Skills that drive change* (2nd ed.). Thousand Oaks, CA: Sage.

Reiter-Palmon, R., & Harms, M. (2018). Team creativity and innovation. Importance and directions. In R. Reiter-Palmon (Ed.), *Team creativity and innovation* (pp. 3–10). New York, NY: Oxford University Press.

Rosing, K., Frese, M., & Bausch, A. (2011). Explaining the heterogeneity between the leadership-innovation relationship: Ambidextrous leadership. *The Leadership Quarterly*, 22, 956–974.

Sarkees, M. E., & Hulland, J. (2009). Efficiency and innovation: It is possible to have it all. *Business Horizons*, 52, 45–55.

Schmidt, R. L., & Freeland, J. R. (1992). Recent progress in modelling R&D project-selection processes. *IEEE Transactions on Engineering Management*, 39, 189–201.

Schumpeter, J. A. (1942). *Capitalism, socialism, and democracy*. New York, NY: Harper and Brothers.

Scott, G., Leritz, L. E., & Mumford, M. D. (2004). The effectiveness of creativity training: A quantitative review. *Creativity Research Journal*, 4, 361–388.

Sethi, R., & Iqbal, Z. (2008). Stage-gate controls, learning failure, and adverse effect on novel new products. *Journal of Marketing*, 72, 118–134.

Sharma, A. (1999). Central dilemmas of managing innovation in large firms. *California Management Review*, 41, 146–164.

Shalley, C. E., Litchfield, R. C., & Gilson, L. L. (2017). 20 years later. Organizational context for creativity. In R. Reiter-Palmon (Ed.), *Team creativity and innovation* (pp. 165–194). New York, NY: Oxford University Press.

Steele, L. M., McIntosh, T., & Higgs, C. (2017). Intrinsic motivation and creativity: Opening up a black box. In M. D. Mumford & S. Hemlin (Eds.), *Handbook of research on leadership and creativity* (pp. 100–130). New York, NY: Edward Elgar.

Stehr, N. (1994). *Knowledge societies*. London, UK: Sage.

Steiber, A., & Alänge, S. (2016). *The Silicon Valley Model: Management for entrepreneurship*. Schweiz: Springer.

Sternberg, R. J. (Ed.). (1999). *Handbook of creativity*. Cambridge, UK: Cambridge University Press.

Stetler, K. (2015). *Innovation under pressure. Reclaiming the micro-level exploration space*. (Doctoral dissertation, KTH Royal Institute of Technology, Stockholm, Sweden).

Sung, S. Y., & Choi, J. N. (2012). Effects of team knowledge management on the creativity and financial performance of organizational teams. *Organizational Behavior and Human Decision Processes*, 118, 4–13.

Teece, D. J., Pisano, G., & Schuen, A. (1997). Dynamic capabilities and strategic management. *Strategic Management Journal*, 18, 509–533.

Tidd, J., & Bessant, J. (2013). *Managing innovation: Integrating technological, market and organizational change* (5th ed.). London, UK: John Wiley and Sons.

Tushman, M., & O'Reilly, P. (1996). Ambidextrous organizations: Managing evolutionary and revolutionary change. *California Management Review*, 38, 8–30.

Tushman, M., & Smith, W. (2002). Technological change, ambidextrous organizations and organizational evolution. In J. Baum (Ed.), *The Blackwell companion to organizations* (pp. 386–414). Boston, MA: Blackwell Publishers.

Vahlne, J-E., & Jonsson, A. (2017). Ambidexterity as a dynamic capability in the globalization of the multinational business enterprise (MBE): Case studies of AB Volvo and IKEA. *International Business Review*, 26, 57–70.

Verhaeghe, A., & Kfir, R. (2002). Managing innovation in a knowledge intensive technology organization (KITO). *R&D Management*, 32, 409–417.

Wisdom, J. P., Chor, K. H. B., Hoagwood, K. E., & Horwitz, S. M. (2014). Innovation adoption: A review of theories and constructs. *Administration and Policy in Mental Health*, 41, 480–502.

Wolfe, R. A. (1994). Organizational innovation – Review, critique and suggested research directions. *Journal of Management Studies*, 31, 405–431.

14
UNLEASHING CREATIVE TALENT IN ORGANIZATIONS – LINKING LEARNING AND CREATIVITY THROUGH CREATIVE PROBLEM-SOLVING

Scott G. Isaksen

Introduction

We live in an increasingly volatile, uncertain, complex, and ambiguous (VUCA) world (Bennett & Lemoine, 2014). More than ever, we need to understand and nurture the creative talent of those who can help meet the innovation challenges that organizations face. The VUCA world also has changed the nature of work (Barley, Bechky, & Milliken, 2017; Noe, Clarke, & Klein, 2014), resulting in the concomitant demand for employees and managers to understand, develop, and apply creative talent.

Learning and creativity are complex, multifaceted, and multilevel constructs, and when we examine the conceptual and practical linkages between them, many implications emerge. This is not the first general effort to build conceptual bridges between learning and creativity (for examples, see Beghetto & Kaufman, 2009; Kazanjian & Drazin, 2012; Lubart, 2008; Pagano, 1979). Within the educational arena, there has been long-term interest in linking creativity and learning (Kagan, 1967). In fact, there are many resources that promote creative learning within our educational system (Sefton-Green, Thomson, Jones, & Bresler, 2011; Torrance & Myers, 1970; Treffinger, Schoonover, & Selby, 2013).

The purpose of this chapter is to examine these linkages with a focus on the organization. First, we review the conceptual and theoretical foundations of learning and creativity at the individual, group or team, and organizational levels. Once this foundation is laid, we identify a few key elements of integration. One of these will be the method of creative problem-solving (CPS) as a deliberate and practical way to unleash creative talent in organizations. This chapter provides a current description of CPS, discusses research supporting the approach, and identifies some productive pathways for future research.

Conceptual and Theoretical Foundations

Learning

Learning is one of those concepts that everyone uses, yet no universally agreed definition exists. It has been a core concept in psychology since the very origins of the discipline, but researchers are rarely explicit about what they mean by the term (De Houwer, Barnes-Holmes, & Moors, 2013). Arguments regarding the supremacy of taking a functional, structural, or operational approach to defining learning were prevalent in the first half of the 20th century (Kellogg & Britt, 1939; Washburne, 1936) and continue today. Illeris (2009) provided one comprehensive definition of learning: "any process that in living organisms leads to permanent capacity for change and which is not solely due to maturation or ageing" (p. 3).

Within the broad conceptual space associated with learning, we find constructs like perception, memory acquisition and retrieval, mental processing, reasoning, problem-solving, and others. Most researchers would agree that learning is a process that results in a change in knowledge, skill, or behavior based on experience derived from the learner's environment.

For the purposes of this chapter, learning is defined as a process in which people discover a problem, invent a solution to the problem, produce the solution, and evaluate the outcome, leading to the discovery of new problems – resulting in an increase, through experience, of problem-solving ability (Argyris, 1983; Washburne, 1936). Although learning is often seen as occurring at an individual level, it applies to teams or groups (Dayaram & Fung, 2012), as well as organizations (Kim, 1993).

Individual Level

Learning at the individual level is based on numerous theories that are supportive of this definitional approach (McLeod, 2003). For example, Piaget's theory of cognitive development was based on the fundamental notion that intellectual growth was the result of adaptation to the environment (Supratman, 2013). Piaget differentiated assimilation, using existing schemas to deal with newness, from accommodation – for situations in which the existing schemas do not work. The force that drives the learning is equilibration, which promotes integration of the existing with the new (Ayman-Nolley, 1988).

Dewey's theory of reflective thinking was based on the notion that learning is based on the experience of life adjustment to the environment (Archambault, 1966). The process of reflective thinking linked learning to sensing problems or gaps, thinking through suggestions or hypotheses, testing these, ultimately resulting in a postreflective stage in which the gap or problem situation is resolved (Dewey, 1933).

A more recent theoretical approach to learning is metacognition (Flavell, 1979). On an individual level, the degree to which people are able to provide explanations for how a problem may be solved and become more conscious of the problem-solving process is referred to as metacognition (Coutinho, Wiemer-Hastings, Skowronski, & Britt, 2005). Metacognition refers to higher-order learning processes such as making plans for learning, monitoring and predicting performance, and strategizing on approaches to solving problems – learning how to learn. The emerging theory of metacognition illustrates the importance of conscious awareness of cognitive activity within the individual and self-regulation of learning (Salonen, Vauras, & Efklides, 2005).

Group or Team Level

Even though it is most often considered an individual phenomenon, learning at the group or team level also has strong theoretical foundations (Levine & Resnick, 1993; Levine & Smith, 2013). Social learning theory is one of the most relevant here, in that learning is placed within continuous reciprocal interaction among cognitive, behavioral, and environmental influences (Bandura, 1977). In short, people learn from one another through observation and modeling.

Vygotsky's social development theory offers support for learning occurring within a group context (Frawley, 1997; Moran & John-Steiner, 2003). For Vygotsky, learning is more than the acquisition of thinking ability, it is the acquisition of a variety of specialized abilities and at particular developmental levels. The process of development does not coincide with learning – rather, it follows learning. He proposed the concept of the zone of proximal development as a way of explaining how people at different developmental levels can affect each other's learning through collaboration with peers or interaction with adults (Cole, John-Steiner, Scribner, & Souberman, 1978). For Vygotsky, human learning is a social construct, and it influences problem-solving and creativity (Lindqvist, 2003).

Social metacognition is an extension of individual metacognition and includes group members' monitoring and control of each other's knowledge, emotions, and actions (Chiu & Kuo, 2009). What we think about our own thinking is inextricably linked to experiences with others, ongoing social interactions, and cultural backgrounds (Jost, Kruglanski, & Nelson, 1998; Salonen, Vauras, & Efklides, 2005).

Organizational Level

Learning also occurs at the organizational level (Argyris, 1999; Argyris & Schon, 1995). Organizational learning can be conceived as a principal way for organizations to achieve strategic renewal by balancing the demands for both exploitation and exploration (Crossan, Lane, & White, 1999). Popova-Nowak and Cseh (2015) defined organizational learning as "a social process of individuals participating in collective situated practices and discourses that reproduce and simultaneously expand organizational knowledge" (p. 316).

The sensemaking perspective provides further support for learning occurring at the individual, team, and organizational levels (Weick, 1969, 1995). Maitlis and Christianson (2014) defined sensemaking as a process that is initiated through violated expectations stemming from the environment that yield intersubjective meaning. This meaning is derived from cycles of interpretation and action.

Since the environment is chaotic and uncertain, sensemaking is more about plausibility, rather than certainty when it comes to learning (Weick, Sutcliffe, & Obstfeld, 2005). It is also about dynamic and continuous learning. Given the volatile and ambiguous nature of life in organizations, sensemaking has also been related to ethical decision-making on the part of leaders (Thiel, Bagdasarov, Harkrider, Johnson, & Mumford, 2012). Since sensemaking takes a process-oriented approach to explain how people deal with complexity, novelty, and opacity, it has also been linked directly to organizational creativity (Drazin, Glynn, & Kazanjian, 1999).

The theory of situated cognition provides additional support for learning occurring at the organizational level (Elsbach, Barr, & Hargadon, 2005; Robbins & Ayded, 2009; Smith & Semin, 2004). Situated cognition focuses on the interaction between mental representations or schemas and the context. Rather than being stable, these schemas are extremely malleable and sensitive to details of current social situations (Smith & Semin, 2007). Schemas are derived from activities like environmental scanning and interpretation that construct perceptual frameworks to enable comprehension, understanding, and the taking of effective action. Lave (2009) described situated cognition as a dynamic system that centers on diverse people who improvise solutions stemming from the context, and seek to collaboratively define the situation.

Creativity

It would take volumes to adequately review and summarize the variety of definitions of creativity. The best single book I know that provides a rather comprehensive explanation is 555 pages (Sawyer, 2012). There is, however, emerging consensus that creativity can be defined as the production of new (original, novel) and useful (high-quality, elegant) ideas and solutions by individuals and groups (Amabile & Pratt, 2016; Mumford, Medeiros, & Partlow, 2012).

Creativity, defined this way, can occur at different levels of impact. At the highest level of impact is the rare realm of the eminent genius that is recognized historically as transformational, often referred to as "Big C" creativity

(Simonton, 2014, 2017). The next level is referred to as "Pro-C" and includes solid creative contributions by professionals who have obtained high levels of expertise but are not recognized historically as eminent (Kaufman & Beghetto, 2009). A third category is called "little c" and includes everyday creativity – outcomes that are acknowledged by others as new and useful but in which the average person can participate (Richards, 2007).

A final category is called "mini-c" and resides at the individual level. It includes a personal creative process involving the development of new understanding and knowledge creation (Beghetto & Kaufman, 2007). Mini-c creativity represents early stage creativity and can be most closely related to learning as it focuses on the interpretive and transformative aspects of information processing that occur at the individual level (Moran & John-Steiner, 2003).

Many of the theories outlined for learning have also been identified to support creativity. An early review of creativity theory (Roweton, 1970, p. 15) asserted that "no fully matured and comprehensive theoretical statement is available." It is well beyond the scope of this chapter to provide a comprehensive review of creativity theory, as there are plenty of other resources that do so (Beghetto & Kaufman, 2017; Kozbelt, Beghetto, & Runco, 2010; Paletz & Peng, 2008; Plucker, 2017; Runco, 2014; Runco & Albert, 1990; Treffinger, Isaksen, & Firestien, 1983). These reviews vary in the way they categorize creativity theories and their focus on people, process, product, or place, yet there are a few major similarities.

One example is the theory of creativity offered by Carl Rogers (1962). His theory is primarily aimed at explaining the creative process. He stated the following:

> My definition, then, of the creative process is that it is the emergence in action of a novel relational product, growing out of the uniqueness of the individual on the one hand, and the materials, events, people, or circumstances of his life on the other. (p. 65)

He linked the need for creativity to societal demands, laid out inner and environmental conditions that foster creativity, and identified a series of hypotheses that would put the theory to work. As with many other theories of creativity, Rogers (1962) places creativity at the intersection of the individual with his or her environment and emphasizes the role of process.

One family or category of creativity theory is referred to as cognitive, rational, and semantic. It includes those theories that outline certain cognitive skills and abilities associated with creativity (Guilford, 1959; Mumford & Gustafson, 1988; Ward, Smith, & Vaid, 1997), theories of mental association (Koestler, 1964; Mednick, 1962; Rothenberg, 1971), how language is linked to thinking and problem solving (Lakoff & Johnson, 1999; Ogden & Richards,

1927; Upton, 1941), and those who put forward a phasal notion of the creative process (Hadamard, 1945; Rossman, 1931; Wallas, 1926). This family of creativity theory is most closely associated with the main purpose of this chapter.

Summary

We can draw a number of conclusions about learning and creativity from these multilevel theoretical perspectives. First, learning involves continuous dynamic interaction and experience between individuals and their environments. The interaction is both external and internal to the individual via acquisition and elaboration among other developmental and cognitive activities (MacKinnon, 1970). Second, learning can be conceived as a dynamic process capable of a conceptual link to problem-solving. Finally, learning, by itself, is value neutral. It can be derived through both success and failure. Each of these conclusions is dealt with in more detail in the following sections of this chapter.

Learning Is Linked to Problem-Solving and Creativity

The definitions and theories summarized earlier provide clear conceptual support for including problem-solving as related to both learning and creativity. For example, Torrance and Torrance (1973) illustrated the close conceptual link between problem-solving and creativity by emphasizing the process of

> ...becoming sensitive to problems, gaps in knowledge, missing elements, disharmonies, and so on; identifying the difficulty; searching for solutions, making guesses or formulating hypotheses about the deficiencies; testing and retesting these hypotheses and possibly modifying and retesting them; and finally communicating the results. (p. 6)

Guilford (1977) defined problem-solving as facing a situation with which you are not fully prepared to deal. Problem-solving occurs when there is a need to go beyond the information given; thus, there is a need for new intellectual activity. Creativity and problem-solving were closely related since both demand novel responses. Newell, Shaw, and Simon (1967) added further support for linking problem-solving to creativity. They put creativity as a special class of problem-solving characterized by novelty and difficulty in problem formulation.

Both Learning and Creativity Often Start with the Individual

A great deal of research and practice focuses on understanding and nurturing learning and creativity at the individual level of analysis. Even at this level,

ABILITIES
- Domain Relevant Knowledge
- Talent in the Domain
- Level of Education
- Reasoning and Intelligence

MOTIVATION
- Level of Commitment
- Intrinsic Interest
- Attitude

CREATIVE BEHAVIOR

SKILLS
- Interpersonal Skills
- Generative/Divergent Skills
- Focusing/Convergent Skills

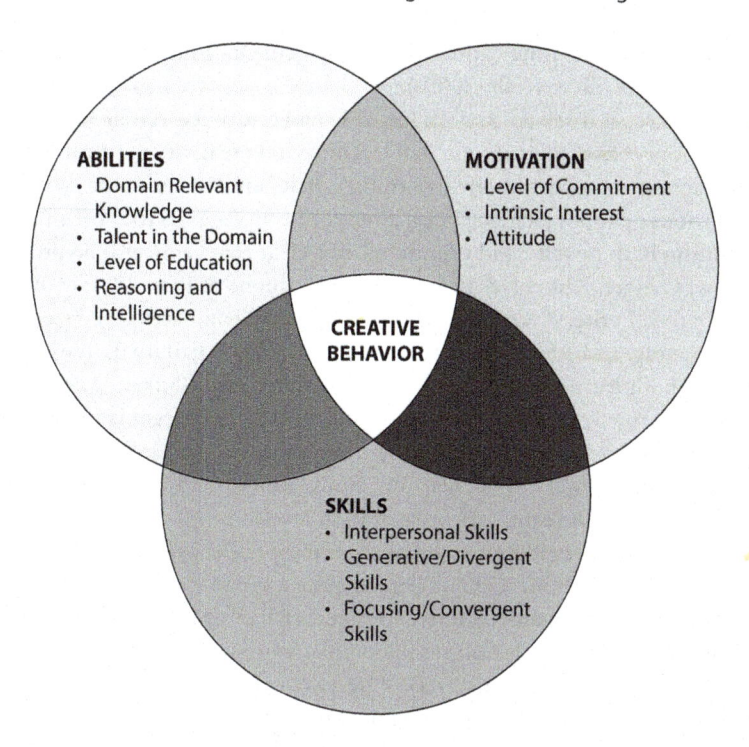

FIGURE 14.1 A model for predicting creative behavior.

conceptualizing, developing, and predicting creative behavior are multidimensional and have multilevel implications. For example, both Amabile (1983) and Torrance (1979) proposed multidimensional models for predicting creative behavior (see Figure 14.1).

Abilities include domain-relevant knowledge, talent in the domain, level of education, as well as reasoning ability and intelligence. Motivation includes the level of commitment to the task, intrinsic interest, appropriate extrinsics, and attitude. Creativity-relevant skills include generative or divergent skills, focusing or convergent skills, as well as interpersonal or collaborative skills. The best way to view creative behavior is as an interaction among these areas – for the individual, group, or team, and at the organizational level of analysis.

Learning and Creativity Stem from Experience: Including Failure

Creativity and learning occur at the intersection of the individual and the environment. We can consider creativity and learning as continuous, iterative, and dynamic processes that integrate experience, cognition, and behavior (Kolb, Boyatzis, & Mainemelis, 2001). Experiential learning transforms experience into learning (Akella, 2010) and creativity (Gundy & Kickul, 1996) and has important implications for management and leadership within organizations (Kolb & Kolb, 2009a).

Experience, as it relates to both learning and creativity, can be perceived as positive or negative. Some argue that learning and creativity are stimulated by dissatisfaction or frustration by things that are inconsistent with our expectations or hopes (Schein, 1996). Since creativity applies to those situations demanding both novelty and usefulness, it is clear that error will be prevalent (Bledow, Carette, Kühnel, & Bister, 2017; Hammond & Farr, 2011; Mumford, Blair, Dailey, Leritz, & Osburn, 2006). In fact, trial and error are inseparable from learning and creativity (Reason, 1990, 2013). Failure is inextricably linked to both learning and creativity at the individual (Sitkin, 1992), group or team (Carmeli, Tishler, & Edmondson, 2011), and organizational levels (Cannon & Edmondson, 2005). Although failure is intricately linked to an organization's creative efforts, learning from failure can be challenging at the individual, group or team, and organization levels.

Failure can be considered any deviation from expected and desired results (Cannon & Edmondson, 2005). There is quite a broad range of failure within organizations: preventable failures in predictable operations that may be blameworthy, unavoidable failures in complex systems, and intelligent failures at the frontier (Edmondson, 2011). The two latter forms of failure require something other than locating blame and taking immediate short-term corrective actions.

A range of emotions can be felt by individuals who fail, including denial, anger, personal pain and embarrassment, sadness, dismay, worry, anxiety, frustration, and depression (Shepherd, Patzelt, & Wolfe, 2011). The emotions associated with failure can lead to defensiveness and denial. Numerous factors can mitigate these negative emotions. Shepherd, Patzelt, and Wolfe (2011) found that an individual's level of affective commitment or identification with and involvement in an organization can decrease the negative emotions associated with failure. They also found that individuals learned more from project failures if they had more time following the event to engage in learning. Finally, they found that learning from failure was more likely, and negative emotions were less apparent, if the work environment normalized failure.

How individuals receive feedback about their failures can impact their learning (Cannon & Witherspoon, 2005). For example, He, Yao, Wang, and Caughron (2016) found that feedback from supervisors can actually increase creativity when the recipients have a strong learning-goal orientation. Learning can be stimulated when both the giving and receiving of failure feedback are effective and take place within an organization that is developmental (Kegan, Lahey, & Fleming, 2014).

Of course, there are many factors within the individual and context that influence the readiness and ability to learn from failure (Zhao, 2011). Politis and Gabrielsson (2009) examined why some entrepreneurs had more positive attitudes toward failure than others. They found that entrepreneurs' favorable attitudes toward failure were a function of earlier life experience – particularly with start-ups and having to close down a business earlier in their career. These experiences may have increased individual levels of self-efficacy, which has been shown to affect creative performance over time (Tierney & Farmer, 2011).

Amabile and Pratt (2016) reported that a high degree of psychological safety can lead to increased intrinsic motivation and reengagement in the creative process in the face of project failure. Psychological safety was a shared sense that it was acceptable to fail and make mistakes because they are treated as opportunities to learn and improve – and did not include derision of the individuals involved.

Bledow, Carette, Kühnel, and Bister (2017) pointed out the importance of high error orientation in learning from stories of managerial failure. High error orientation was defined as a complex attitude toward failure in which individuals can acknowledge that failures are negative but also have positive learning consequences. Failure stories produced deeper levels of information processing and higher levels of learning transfer than success stories. Error orientation moderated this relationship such that those with higher error orientations (those who saw the learning potential of failures) showed more elaboration and learning transfer when listening to failure stories.

Experience occurs at a group or team level through collaboration and interaction, and the nature of this experience can affect the ability of groups to learn from mistakes and failures. Cannon and Edmondson (2001) found that teams within the same organization held different beliefs about failure, and these beliefs were associated with levels of performance. They found that those groups that had clear direction for their efforts, and proximal leaders who were effective coaches, had more constructive beliefs about learning from failure and higher levels of performance.

The nature of the collaboration and interaction at a group or team level can also influence the level of learning from mistakes. Tjosvold, Yu, and Hui (2004) found that team-level learning from mistakes can be encouraged by psychological safety, shared mental models, as well as sharing a problem-solving orientation and working within a cooperative goal structure. Cooperative goal structures for teamwork were compared against competitive goal structures and found to be a better foundation for the problem-solving interaction that helped teams learn from mistakes. They indicated the following:

> Problem solving where team members recognize that mistakes can help them improve and together analyze, discuss, and plan how to correct them, was found to be an important antecedent of learning from mistakes from both the perspective of group members and their managers. (p. 1238)

One of the most dramatic differences between innovative and stagnated organizations is their tolerance of ambiguity and uncertainty, referred to as a climate dimension of risk-taking (Ekvall, 1996). In fact, Garcia-Granero, Llopis, Fernandez-Mesa, and Alegre (2015) demonstrated that a risk-taking climate among employees mediated the relationship between managers' risk-taking and innovation performance of the organization. This suggests that establishing this kind of organizational climate may also encourage learning from failure.

Cannon and Edmondson (2005) differentiated small from large failures. They argue that small failures provide early warning signs that if detected and addressed may be instrumental in avoiding larger and more catastrophic failures in the future.

If the aim is to learn from failure, Cannon and Edmondson (2005) outline three main organizational strategies. The first of these is actually and deliberately identifying failure rather than denying, distorting, or covering up the reality of failure. Systematically and proactively identifying failures – small and large – is the first step in learning from failure. The second strategy is analyzing the failure requiring a spirit of inquiry and openness, patience, and a tolerance for ambiguity. Examples include the U.S. Army's use of after-action reviews or morbidity and mortality conferences in healthcare. Analyzing failure can be encouraged through formal processes for discussing, analyzing, and applying the lessons of failure more broadly within the organization. Cannon and Edmondson (2005) recommend that these formal processes should be conducted by skilled facilitators who have skills and tools for effectively managing group processes.

Cannon and Edmondson (2005) describe their third active organizational process for learning from failure as deliberate experimentation. They acknowledge that this may be provocative as organizations may actually increase their chances of experiencing failure by experimenting. Of course, this implies that leaders in organizations accept that failure is a necessary by-product of experimenting and that they are able to manage the risks to acquire the benefit of learning (Edmondson, 2011).

Although individuals and teams appear to be influenced most directly by proximal leaders (i.e., direct supervisors), top management teams (TMTs) and chief executive officers (CEOs) often set the tone for the entire organization. Carmeli, Tishler, and Edmondson (2011) studied how CEOs and TMTs improved the quality of strategic decision-making by creating trust and facilitating learning from failure. Strategic decision-making is often uncertain and ill structured and conducted by diverse senior teams. Carmeli et al. (2011) found that CEOs who encouraged collaboration and open communication established top-team trust that, in turn, increased team learning from failure. As senior teams invested in learning from failure, their strategic decision-making improved.

Collaboratively and deliberately framing problems and opportunities for improvement, cooperatively generating ideas and suggestions for addressing these, and ultimately taking actions to implement these ideas, can lead to more productive individuals, teams, and organizations. Doing this within a supportive work environment and with relational leaders and facilitators can help organizations learn more productively from both success and failure (Kvalnes, 2017). CPS offers one productive framework and approach for doing so.

Creative Problem-Solving

If you were to Google the term *creative problem-solving*, you would find nearly 45 million results. This search would include a wide variety of conferences, organizations, tools and techniques, methods and processes, journals, books, and other resources. In keeping with the purpose of this chapter, we focus on one main family of work – starting with the foundational work of Alex Osborn (1948, 1952, 1953). The versions of CPS upon which we focus include those starting with Osborn's initial description, and the later modifications provided by Parnes (1966a, 1967) and Parnes, Noller, and Biondi (1977). These versions are referred to as the Buffalo-based CPS approach.

CPS is a broadly applicable process providing an organizing framework for specific generating and focusing thinking techniques to help design and develop new and useful outcomes for meaningful and important challenges, concerns, and opportunities (Isaksen, Dorval, & Treffinger, 1994). CPS is an operational model for a particular kind of problem-solving where creativity is applicable for the task at hand, particularly a task that is novel, complex, and ambiguous.

Noller (1977) defined CPS by offering a definition of each of the three main words: creative, problem, and solving:

> By creative we mean: having an element of newness and being relevant at least to you, the one who creates the solution. By problem we mean: any situation which presents a challenge, offers an opportunity, or is a concern to you. By solving we mean: devising ways to answer or to meet or satisfy the problem, adapting yourself to the situation or adapting the situation to yourself. Creative Problem Solving or CPS is a process, a method, a system for approaching a problem in an imaginative way resulting in effective action. (pp. 4–5)

Foundational Work on CPS

Although Osborn was a well-known businessman, his initial formulation of CPS was informed by the work of early scholars who attempted to outline an explicit creative process (1948, 1952, 1953). As a part of his graduate studies in psychology, Osborn studied the works of James Conant, Robert Crawford, John Dewey, Ernest Dimnet, Johnson O'Connor, Charles Spearman, and Graham Wallas, among others. He outlined stages of the CPS process and procedures for both individuals and groups to engage in the process. His most well-known procedure was brainstorming, which he positioned as creative collaboration in groups.

Parnes and colleagues (Noller, Parnes, & Biondi, 1976; Parnes, 1966a, 1967; Parnes, Noller, and Biondi, 1977) built on Osborn's original work and created an eclectic experimental instructional program to see if it was possible to deliberately develop creative abilities and skills. The results of this two-year experimental program were quite promising (Noller & Parnes, 1972; Parnes, 1987; Parnes & Noller, 1972a,b; Parnes & Noller, 1973; Reese, Treffinger, Parnes, & Kaltsounis, 1976). This instructional program has become known as the Osborn-Parnes approach to CPS and is well established in the research activities of other scholars (Basadur, Graen, & Green, 1982; Buijs & Nauta, 1991; Cramond, Martin, & Shaw, 1990).

Lessons from Experience

The Osborn-Parnes approach was widely disseminated through publications, conferences, and training programs (Parnes, 1977). Numerous organizational consultants and trainers applied CPS, and some modifications (Basadur, Graen, & Green, 1982), to organizational challenges. However, based on a variety of impact studies and experiences within diverse organizations, several major developments were made to the Osborn-Parnes approach. There were clear benefits derived from sustained collaboration, blending research and practical applications in organizational contexts that challenged some aspects of early work on CPS. Many of these are well documented in the literature (Isaksen & Treffinger, 2004; Puccio, Murdock, & Mance, 2005; Puccio & Cabra, 2009; Treffinger & Isaksen, 2005). A few of these key lessons are summarized next.

Balancing Generating with Focusing

One of the first lessons from experience was that the preponderance of CPS tools and techniques were divergent, helping people to generate many, varied, and unusual alternatives. This focus helped to shore up a common misconception that CPS was equivalent to idea generation or brainstorming. There was a clear need to move beyond generating and include tools and techniques to help people screen, select, and support options (Gibson & Mumford, 2013). We undertook efforts to develop a balanced set of focusing tools to complement the generating tools (Isaksen & Treffinger, 1985). Further, there were clear guidelines for generating – the four basic rules for brainstorming. Yet, there were no guidelines for effective focusing or convergent thinking. Parallel focusing guidelines were developed and integrated into the CPS development programs (Treffinger, Isaksen, & Firestien, 1982).

Moving from Prescription to Description

The Osborn-Parnes approach presented the CPS process as a linear, predefined series of stages. Impact studies within organizations challenged this notion (see Isaksen & Treffinger, 2004, for a summary). Instead, the clear feedback was that real-life application of CPS was much more flexible and iterative. People used the stages and tools that were needed for specific applications, rather than "running through" the entire prescribed process. When they described their most frequent applications, they fell into three broad categories: seeking clarity, generating ideas, and planning for action.

Navigating the Open System

When CPS was considered a prescribed series of stages with clear starting and ending points, there was no need to consciously choose where to start. Once the stages were clustered and broken into three major components, we needed a way to consciously plan our approach – link the particular need with the appropriate parts of CPS and design its specific application. This resulted in the development of a management component of CPS called Planning your Approach (Isaksen, Dorval, & Treffinger, 2000).

Clarifying Social Roles

Experience in applying CPS within large, complex organizations challenged the notion that you could train everyone involved, and then simply apply the CPS process. Osborn (1953) had already pointed out that effective application of CPS required someone who was trained in the approach and prepared to manage group dynamics. Three major social roles were defined to guide the effective application of CPS (Isaksen, 1983, 1992, Treffinger, 1983). Process-oriented leadership is provided by a trained facilitator (Parnes, 1985). The person who owns the task is called the client. Others who may be involved in a CPS session are referred to as resource-group members and bring diverse expertise to the task.

Current CPS Framework

As a contemporary framework, CPS integrates learning, creativity, and problem-solving. Creativity emphasizes the search for newness and the

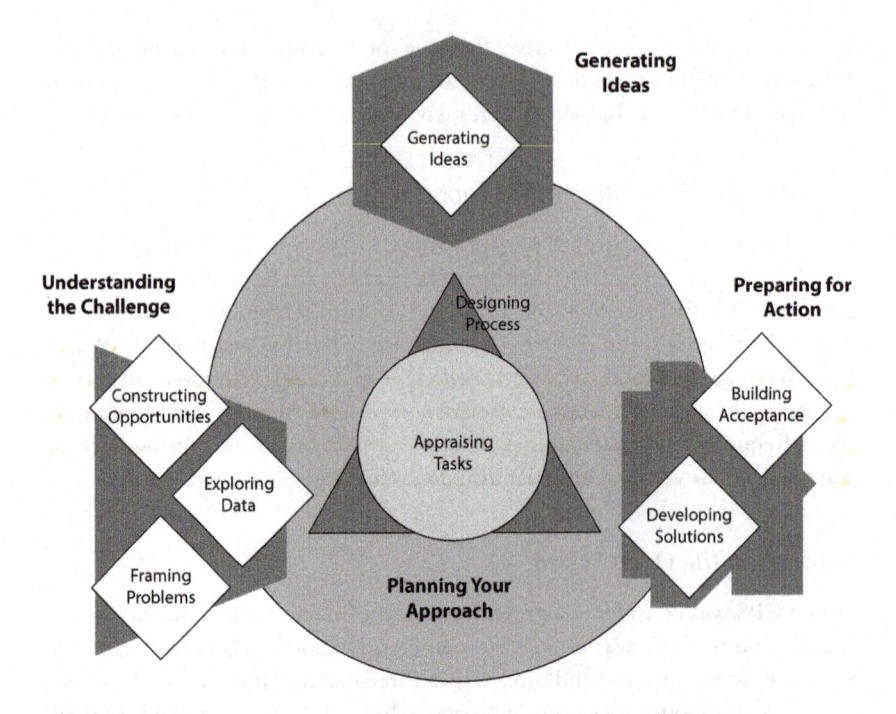

FIGURE 14.2 The current creative problem-solving model.

deliberate generation and development of many and varied alternatives. Problem-solving emphasizes the development of useful and relevant solutions.

The current CPS framework helps to achieve clarity, generate ideas, and take action (Isaksen, Dorval, & Treffinger, 2011). Since these are three distinct choices and areas into which the tools, guidelines, and language of CPS coalesce, you need to be able to navigate your way through its various components and stages. Navigation is obtained by a component called Planning your Approach. Clarity is achieved by Understanding the Challenge. Many, varied, and original ideas are obtained by a component called Generating Ideas. The Preparing for Action component includes strengthening potential solutions and developing plans of action. These main components of CPS are described in more detail in the following sections (see Figure 14.2).

Planning Your Approach

The current version of CPS includes a unique management component called Planning your Approach, that focuses on producing the desired results, as well as considering the people involved, considering the climate within the organization, and designing the appropriate process approach (Isaksen, Dorval, & Treffinger, 2000; Treffinger, Isaksen, & Stead-Dorval, 2006). The purpose of this component is to help you navigate your way through the application of the CPS process.

Planning Your Approach contains two main stages: *Appraising Tasks* and *Designing Process*. These stages deal with the deliberate management of the other components within CPS. Since we need to be able to personalize and customize CPS for many different applications, these stages help you to determine if CPS is an appropriate method and, if it is, to design an effective application of the components, stages, language, and tools.

Appraising Tasks

Task appraisal involves determining whether or not CPS is appropriate for a given task, and whether modifications of your approach might be necessary. During task appraisal, you consider the key people, the desired outcome, the characteristics of the situation, and the possible methods for handling the task. Task appraisal enables you to assess the extent to which CPS might be appropriate – the method of choice, as it were – for addressing a given task or for managing creativity in appropriate ways.

When appraising a task, we consider the following:

People: A key part of the system is to ensure that the proper level of ownership (interest, influence, and imagination) and sponsorship are in place. Engaging people in CPS without clear and legitimate ownership can be a waste of time, energy, and resources. A key decision point when appraising a task is to ensure that you are working with a client – someone who owns the task. It is also helpful to understand the abilities, motivations, skills, and styles of the people who will be involved in CPS.

Place: The climate, working atmosphere, and culture are important factors influencing your approach to CPS. Considering the context can help you understand if the context is ready, willing, and able to use a particular method. Since CPS takes an investment of energy, appraising tasks helps to determine the level of priority that should be assigned to a specific task. A great deal of research has been done to understand the climate that supports creativity and innovation, and climate assessments can be used to supplement your understanding of the context (Ekvall, 1996; Hunter, Bedell, & Mumford, 2007).

Desired Outcomes: Having a clear image of the desired results is key to successful application of CPS. Attention is focused on the domain-relevant knowledge of the current reality when appraising a task. This is where having a client with appropriate content expertise is important. By understanding the desired outcome or need, you are in a much better position to validate the need for novelty. After all, if there is no real need for newness, there is no need to apply CPS.

The current approach to CPS requires the development of a written task summary that clearly points out the need for originality and the requirements for the outcomes, including key background information. This statement guides the specific application of the tools and language and helps everyone understand the purpose of the session, project, or initiative. Task summaries act as springboards for effective problem-solving and ensure delivery of desired outcomes.

Methods: Since CPS is an open system, it allows for the integration and use of a number of alternative methods. The information gained from an improved understanding of the people, context, and outcomes guides the choice to use CPS or integrate other methods within your approach. CPS is best applied when you are approaching a novel, complex, and ambiguous situation for which there is no solution currently available.

Designing Process

As a result of appraising tasks, you are in the position to design your process approach. This stage includes considering the scope of your work. Will it be a single session, a longer-term project, or an even larger and longer-term initiative? Is the level of your application targeted to an individual, group or team, or at an organizational level? And then, which of the components or stages of CPS will be most helpful?

Once you have determined the scope and level of application for CPS, you need to decide if the need is for clarity, ideas, or action. These are the main purposes of the three main process components of CPS. You may sense a gap between current reality and the desired future but not have a clear understanding of the opportunity or problem. In this case, you may benefit from the clarity component: understanding the challenge. If you have a clear statement of the problem but do not have ideas to address the problem, then the generating ideas component would be a good fit. If you have a tentative solution that needs to be strengthened for implementation and acceptance, the planning for action component would be appropriate.

Sample Application of Planning Your Approach

A large, global consumer products company had developed a very clear screening process for new product concepts. The competition was developing and launching new products much faster in key market segments. We were invited to be the lead and coordinating consultants on Project Discovery. The goal was to obtain new and different concepts for the laundry, soap, and paper sectors. The project was designed using appraising tasks and a designing process allowing the use of five alternative methods to obtain consumer insight. Within 18 months, the company went from having just 25 product concepts (developed over seven years) to 76 new and fundamentally different product concepts that were capable of being tested in the market. The project proved to be so successful that the methods are being taught to everyone who works in product development and research.

Understanding the Challenge: Clarity

The *Understanding the Challenge* component includes a systematic effort to define, construct, or focus your problem-solving efforts. This component deals with the natural structural tension (Fritz, 1993) that arises when there are discrepancies between what you want or desire, and what you have – or current reality.

Understanding the challenge includes the three stages of *constructing opportunities*, *exploring data*, and *framing problems*. Constructing opportunities involves generating broad, brief, and beneficial statements that help set the principal direction for problem-solving efforts. We use invitational stems like "Wouldn't it be great if…" or "Wouldn't it be awful if…" These statements are framed at a rather high level of abstraction to point out the boundaries of the domain (Ogden & Richards, 1927; Upton, 1941). This stage focuses on helping to identify broad goals at a strategic level phrased as both opportunities and obstacles. This helps you identify your vision, as well as key barriers or discrepancies to accomplishing it.

Exploring data includes generating and answering questions that bring out key information, feelings, observations, impressions, and questions about the task. This emphasis on information processing helps problem-solvers to develop an understanding of the current situation. Exploring data helps you obtain a deeper understanding of the current reality within the context of the opportunity or problem space.

Framing problems involves seeking specific or targeted questions (problem statements) on which to focus subsequent efforts. The questions are framed using language like "How to…" or "In what ways might we…" as invitational stems. Framing problems is related to the concept of problem finding, which is well described in the creativity literature (Dillon, 1982; Getzels & Csikszentmihalyi, 1976; Runco, 1994).

Sample Applications of Understanding the Challenge

A global university publisher needed to focus their efforts on increasing sales and market share for one of their major divisions. By applying constructing opportunities, the division was able to generate more than 200 opportunity statements and ended up focusing these down to seven key areas for investment and development. By prioritizing these initiatives, they were able to develop specific action plans much faster and more cheaply and to involve many more stakeholders in the process than in earlier efforts.

A global consumer products company needed to develop some fundamentally new products within one of their major divisions. By applying a Deep Dive Discovery approach to exploring data, they were able to obtain very original insights into consumer needs, and a deeper meaning of what these needs implied, resulting in a significantly improved use of their technology and marketing efforts.

One of our clients produces high-tech medical solutions. By applying framing problems tools to acquire consumer insight, the client was able to redefine their initiative to reengineer their anesthesia equipment. The company ended up with a substantial cost savings and was able to develop a new add-on piece of equipment usable on new and existing machines.

Generating Ideas

When you have a well-defined problem space but lack ideas to address the issue, the *Generating Ideas* component and stage help you come up with many, varied, or unusual options for responding to the problem. During the generating phase of this stage, problem-solvers produce many options (fluent thinking), a variety of possible options (flexible thinking), novel or unusual options (original thinking), or a smaller number of detailed or refined options (elaborative thinking). The focusing phase of generating ideas provides an opportunity to examine, review, cluster, and select promising ideas. Although this stage includes a focusing phase, its primary emphasis rests in generating or the commitment of extended effort to seek creative possibilities (Basadur & Thompson, 1986; Parnes, 1961).

CPS has often been equated with generating ideas and brainstorming. As I have pointed out, brainstorming is only one tool within the CPS framework. Although there was some early evidence that supported the use of brainstorming (Parnes & Meadow, 1959; Parnes, Meadow, & Reese, 1959), one early study (Taylor, Berry, & Block, 1958) compared nominal versus real groups and concluded that group participation inhibited creative thinking. For Osborn (1953) brainstorming was never meant to exclude individual ideation. In fact, he encouraged participants who were to be involved in brainstorming sessions to generate ideas before joining the group.

Brainstorming research that followed provided insight into the barriers for the effective use of the tool. Numerous studies pointed out the negative influence of uniformity pressure and evaluation apprehension (Diehl & Stroebe, 1987; Vroom, Grant, & Cotton, 1969). Social loafing, matching of effort, or the sucker effect also limited the effectiveness of brainstorming (Henningsen, Cruz, & Miller, 2000; Paulus, 1983). A third key barrier was the structure of the interaction, production blocking, or procedural mechanism effect (Bouchard, 1972; Gallupe, Bastianutti, & Cooper, 1991; Mullen, Johnson, & Salas, 1991).

Brainstorming research has focused on two key ways to mitigate these barriers. The first is the use of technology such as group decision support systems or electronic brainstorming (Cooper, Gallupe, Pollard, & Cadsby, 1998; Thompson & Coovert, 2002). Nunamaker, Briggs, Mittleman, Vogel, and Balthazard (1997) shared lessons from their experience in using technology to support brainstorming and concluded that it: "can make a well-planned meeting better, and it can make a poorly planned meeting worse…any tool is only as good as the artisan who wields it" (pp. 171–172). The use of technology does not replace the need for group leadership.

The second major way to overcome these barriers is to use trained facilitators. CPS groups using trained facilitators did better than groups without one, and facilitated groups can actually match or exceed the productivity of nominal groups (Offner, Kramer, & Winter, 1996). Oxley, Dzindolet, and Paulus (1996) reported similar findings when studying the level of training of the facilitator. They found that the groups having the benefit of a highly trained facilitator outperformed nonfacilitated groups and those helped by facilitators with less training. They concluded that groups with a highly trained facilitator may achieve the productivity of nominal groups without foregoing the advantages of interaction. Isaksen and Gaulin (2005) confirmed these findings.

So much work within organizations must be done in teams and groups. Sutton and Hargadon (1996) critiqued brainstorming research based on the heavy use of non-sense tasks, ideas not actually being used, no appropriate training in the tool, and the use of average quality as a key metric. Real groups engaged in productive brainstorming should actually produce many low-quality ideas, as well as a larger number of higher-quality ideas. Average quality should be replaced or supplemented by assessing the number of high-quality ideas.

Sample Application of Generating Ideas

A global direct marketing/publishing company has applied tools for generating ideas to "turbocharge" their use of focus groups, resulting in substantially better insights from consumers. In addition, they have used these tools to help a major global division generate fundamentally different product ideas, to help them generate hundreds of new media and marketing channel ideas, and to generate ideas for consideration in their three-year planning process. All were aimed at helping them grow their core business.

Preparing for Action

Problem-solvers use the *Preparing for Action* component to make decisions about, develop, or strengthen promising alternatives, and to plan for their successful implementation. The two stages included in the component are called *developing solutions* and *building acceptance*.

During developing solutions, promising options may be analyzed, refined, or developed. If there are many options, the emphasis may be on compressing or condensing them so that they are more manageable. If there are only a few promising options, the challenge may be to refine, strengthen, or develop each one to make them as strong as possible. This stage can involve ranking or prioritizing a number of possible options, generating and selecting specific criteria for evaluating promising options, or selecting the most promising options from a larger pool. The emphasis in this stage is primarily on focusing options and developing promising ideas into plausible solutions. This stage of CPS transforms the potential solutions into more workable and implementable concepts.

The building acceptance stage involves searching for potential sources of assistance and resistance and identifying possible factors that may influence successful implementation of solutions. The aim is to help prepare solutions for improved acceptance and greater value. This stage helps the problem-solver identify ways to make the best possible use of assisters and avoid or overcome possible sources of resistance. By considering these factors, problem-solvers can develop and evaluate a plan of action. Preparing for implementation also provides opportunities to consider alternative possibilities, contingency plans, or feedback loops.

Sample Application of Preparing for Action

A major manufacturing company needed to obtain more value from their research and development (R&D) investment decisions. The senior management team worked with CPS tools for developing solutions in order to generate and then prioritize the criteria for new product development investment projects. This diverse management team reached a clear consensus on their top 10 criteria for investment and made swift changes to the projects currently under consideration.

A global professional services consulting firm needed to speed up the development and launch of new services. The firm was able to decrease its time to market from 18 to 3 months by applying CPS building acceptance tools to a new suite of service offerings. This resulted in creating and maintaining increased market share.

Learning and Applying CPS

There are a number of key issues relating to learning and applying CPS. One of these is the role of expertise. It is possible, and perhaps even more desirable, to see expertise from both content and process perspectives. People can have

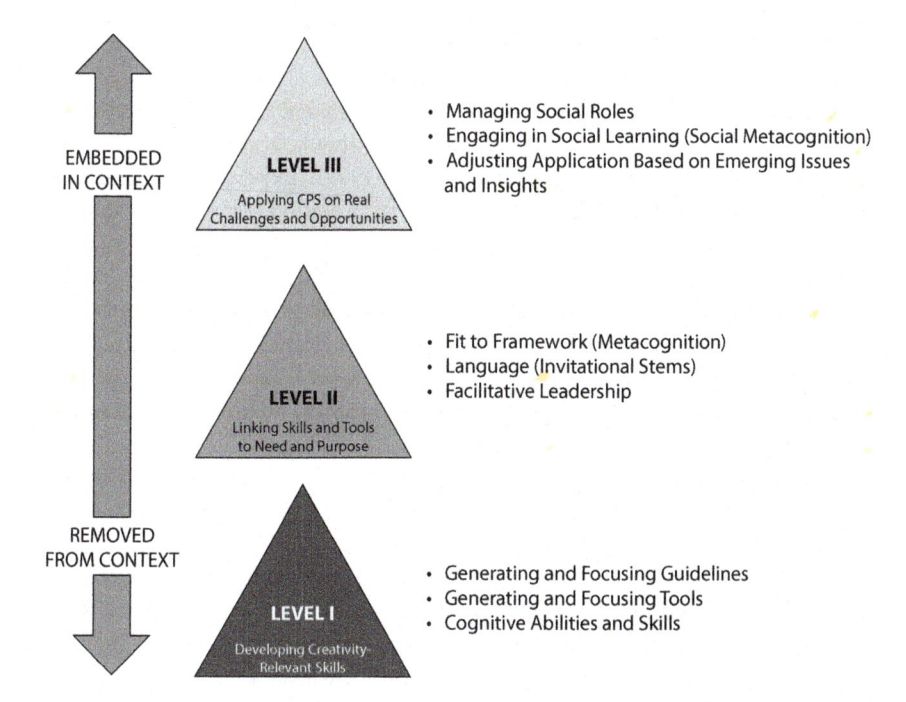

FIGURE 14.3 A model for learning and applying creative problem-solving.

extensive knowledge or ability based on research or experience in both a content domain and a managing process. Second, when engaging in CPS, both cognitive and affective issues matter. Further, since CPS requires conscious attention to thinking and planning problem-solving activity, it requires metacognition and social metacognition. Building CPS process expertise to unleash the creative talent within organizations is generally undertaken at multiple levels of activity (see Figure 14.3). In order to apply CPS to real challenges and concerns, we have found two additional and foundational levels of learning beneficial. The first of these focuses on learning creativity-relevant guidelines, skills, and tools. The next involves linking these to need and purpose, and using the language that best fits these. The next few sections elaborate on these and outline the dynamics involved in learning and applying CPS.

Expertise: Content and Process

Some creativity theorists argue that creative performance is domain specific, rather than being rooted in general domain-transcending traits or skills (Baer, 1998, 2012a,b). One implication of this domain-specific approach is that general cognitive-creative skills may not transfer to other task or content domains (Baer, 2011). Other theorists argue for the existence of general creativity-relevant skills that can be broadly applied at the individual, group, and organizational levels (cf. Amabile & Pratt, 2016).

There is no question that having domain knowledge that is organized in a way that is accessible and integrated enables experts to excel in numerous memory and problem-solving tasks (Wiley, 1998). Experts can recognize relevant features within tasks, infer missing information, represent problems better, and impose constraints to narrow the search for solutions. These aspects of expertise manifest across a variety of domains (Chi, Glaser, & Farr, 1998), and the acquisition of expertise has been explicitly linked to problem-solving (Ericsson, 2003). Yet, there are conditions in which domain-relevant expertise may inhibit creative thinking. In certain circumstances, expertise can function as a preconceived mental set and promote fixation, particularly in unstructured and ambiguous problem spaces (Wiley, 1998).

Groups and teams are more likely to generate novel and useful ideas when they have access to and share diverse knowledge, expertise, and information through interaction with team members with dissimilar expertise – as in cross-functional teams. Yet, there are difficulties and nuances when it comes to teams that contain highly dissimilar expertise (Huang, Hsieh, & He, 2014). Individuals with unique expertise may not be able to understand and use the expertise of others unless they engage in team-level knowledge-sharing practices. These practices involve expertise coordination such as socially shared cognitive processes, collaborative problem-solving, and team-level integration processes (De Church & Mesmer-Magnus, 2010a,b; Faraj & Sproull, 2000).

Content and domain-relevant expertise plays a key role in CPS. Many of our most impactful CPS applications have involved experts within their domains. Since these applications have been conducted across a variety of content domains, it seems reasonable that domain-relevant expertise could be complemented by general, process-relevant expertise. The debate between domain-specific and domain-general skills continues, yet the CPS framework and tools are ultimately applied within a domain – on real content.

Starting with the foundational work of Lewin (1947), Maier (1967), and others (Benne & Sheats, 1948; Zajonc, 1965), there has been recognition of the need of an integrative or facilitative function within groups. There is expansive literature that points out the importance of a facilitative role when working with problem-solving groups (Bostrom, Anson, & Clawson, 1993; Chilberg, 1989; Nelson & McFadzean, 1998; Wardale, 2013). There is also general consensus that a facilitator is a process-oriented leadership role requiring expertise in managing group dynamics and experience in methods and techniques that help groups function more effectively.

Osborn (1953) recognized this need for learning and applying CPS, as did Parnes (1985). Parnes (1985) defined the CPS facilitator as one who "draws out, reinforces, and thus facilitates the creative learning, development, and problem solving of the people with whom he or she is working" (p. 1). He went on to elaborate on the desired qualities and specific responsibilities of the CPS facilitator. The majority of these deal with managing group dynamics and the CPS process. Research has supported the positive effects of trained facilitators on CPS performance (Isaksen & Gaulin, 2005; Kramer, Fleming, & Mannis, 2001; Offner, Kramer, & Winter, 1996; Oxley, Dzindolet, & Paulus, 1996). It seems reasonable to conclude that both content and process expertise can be valuable for learning and applying CPS.

Role of Metacognition

Cognition is the mental action or process of acquiring knowledge, understanding through thought, experience, and through the senses. It includes a variety of mental processes such as attention, memory, working memory, comprehension, judgment, evaluation, reasoning, and problem-solving.

The term *metacognition* means, literally, cognition about cognition or thinking about thinking (Flavell, 1979). Metacognition is related to a family of constructs called theory of mind (Flavell, 2004; Papaleontiou-Louca, 2008) and includes self-regulated learning (Donker, de Boer, Kostons, van Ewijk, & van der Werf, 2014), learning strategies (Weinstein & Mayer, 1986), and mindfulness (Langer, 2000; Weick & Putnam, 2006), among others.

Cognitive skills are required to perform a task, while metacognitive skills are required to understand how the task was accomplished. There are a variety of components to metacognition. Schraw (1998) outlines two major sets of activities within metacognition: knowledge of cognition and regulation of cognition. Knowledge of cognition includes three types of knowledge. The first is *declarative,* which is knowledge about oneself as a learner and the factors that influence one's performance. The second is *procedural* and includes knowledge about doing things such as heuristics and strategies. The third is called conditional metacognitive knowledge and includes knowing when and why to apply declarative and procedural knowledge.

Regulation of cognition includes three sets of skills that help individuals control their learning. The first is planning, which includes selecting appropriate strategies and allocating time and attention that affect performance. The second set of skills is called monitoring and includes one's conscious awareness and comprehension of task performance. The third is evaluating, which is when learners appraise the outcomes and efficiency of their learning.

Knowledge and regulation of cognition are interrelated, and they span a wide variety of subject areas and domains. Further to the domain specificity of creativity debate, there is some evidence that both components of metacognition are domain-general in nature (Donker et al., 2014; Scott & Berman, 2013; van der Stel & Veenman, 2010).

Metacognition has been linked to productive experiential learning (Kolb & Kolb, 2009b) and to successful problem-solving (Berardi-Coletta, Buyer, Dominowski, & Rellinger, 1995). The explicit integration of metacognitive skills into efforts to deliberately develop creativity has been sparse. Two exceptions are the work of Mumford and colleagues investigating mental models when engaged in CPS (Mumford et al., 2012) and Hargrove and Nietfeld (2015) who specifically investigated the impact of metacognitive instruction on CPS.

Setting the Stage for CPS

McCluskey (2000) pointed out that there are many factors that affect ability, willingness, and readiness to learn and apply CPS. Although CPS is based primarily on the cognitive, rational, and semantic theories of creativity, other factors influence its learning and application from both personal and situational points of view.

A variety of individual differences, beyond domain-relevant knowledge, are salient when learning and applying CPS. For example, problem-solving style has been shown to influence preferences and use of CPS skills (Basadur, Graen, & Wakabayashi, 1990; Isaksen & Geuens, 2007; Puccio, 1999). Personality factors such as creative self-beliefs (Karwowski, 2014), openness to experience (Karwowski & Lebuda, 2016), and creative self-efficacy (Puente-Diaz & Cavazos-Arroyo, 2017) will also have an effect. Affective factors (Isen, 1999) such as mood (Davis, 2009), psychological safety (Kark & Carmeli, 2009), and levels of passion and persistence (Grohman, Ivcevic, Silvia, & Kaufman, 2017) can also make a difference.

Individuals engaged in learning and applying CPS do not exist in a vacuum. Numerous situational factors have an influence. For example, the nature and quality of the work environment or climate will influence the degree to which people engage in creative behavior (Amabile, Conti, Coon, Lazenby, & Herron, 1996; Isaksen, 2017). Their physical location, such as geographical region, can also influence creative behavior (Van der Vegt, Van de Vliert, & Huang, 2005). Tellis, Prabhu, and Chandy (2009) identified national culture as having an influence as well.

CPS is often applied within groups and teams. There are numerous assets and liabilities to working in groups (Hargadon & Bechky, 2006; Kozlowski & Ilgen, 2006; Reiter-Palmon, Wigert, & deVreede, 2012). Part of setting the stage at the group level includes managing group dynamics, establishing trust and clear guidelines for creative collaboration, as well as clarifying roles to be taken during the collaboration (Bezrukova & Uparna, 2009) – the key responsibilities of a trained facilitator.

The model we use to guide the learning and use of CPS (see Figure 14.3) depicts the transition from cognitive learning of foundational tools and guidelines that occur at a distance from a specific context, to metacognitive learning and social metacognitive learning – which are ultimately embedded within a domain-specific context or task.

Developing Creativity-Relevant Skills

Learning and applying CPS starts with developing creativity-relevant skills, guidelines, and thinking tools. The current approach to CPS is built on a foundation incorporating both creative and critical thinking (Treffinger, 2007). Creative thinking stems from encountering gaps, opportunities, and obstacles requiring the generation of meaningful new connections. Critical thinking stems from the need to examine these possibilities constructively, and then focus to refine, develop, and decide. These two kinds of thinking and behaving are considered mutually important and complementary. On this foundation, we provide clear guidelines that establish the basic conditions or group norms for both kinds of thinking.

The generating guidelines are to defer judgment, strive for quantity, build on each others' suggestions, and freewheel – share highly unique options. The focusing guidelines include the following: use affirmative judgment, be deliberate, consider novelty, and stay on course. The emphasis to deliberately consider novelty is important when focusing during CPS due to the natural tendency to select options that are immediately feasible (Rietzschel, Nijstad, & Stroebe, 2010). The rationale and application of these guidelines are detailed in Isaksen, Dorval, and Treffinger (2011).

This first level includes learning generating (divergent) and focusing (convergent) thinking tools. These tools tend to promote certain kinds of cognition for individuals and procedural metacognition for groups (Vernon, Hocking, & Tyler, 2016). Tables 14.1 and 14.2 present a description of these tools. Each of the CPS tools can be applied within groups, and by individuals with slight technique modification. The tools are also capable of being applied within entire organizations, particularly through their idea-management systems.

A great deal of research now informs us about the specific cognitive processes and skills that undergird each of these tools (Barrett et al., 2013; Mumford, Medeiros, & Partlow, 2012; Puccio & Cabra, 2009; Ward, Smith, & Vaid, 1997). Many aspects of CPS depend on a complex set of cognitive processes (Mumford, 2001; Mumford & Gustafson, 2007; Mumford, Mobley, Reiter-Palmon, Uhlman, & Doares, 1991; Puccio, Murdock, & Mance, 2005). Further, these creativity-relevant cognitive skills predict CPS performance beyond creative ability (Mumford, Supinski, Baughman, Costanza, & Threlfall, 1997).

For generating tools, some are more likely to produce exploratory or innovative outcomes, while others are more likely to produce developmental

TABLE 14.1 Creative problem-solving tools for generating options

Brainstorming: During Brainstorming, individuals think of options that address the topic (stated as an open-ended question) and share them aloud for the group. An individual records the options as stated in a visible place. In contrast to group discussion (where generating and focusing often happen together), during Brainstorming, critical analysis and development are temporarily suspended.

Brainstorming with Post-its: As in Brainstorming, group members generate options by sharing them aloud. However, instead of one person recording the options, group members record their own options on Post-it notes. An individual then collects the Post-it notes and places them on a flipchart or other visible space. This allows for a greater flow of options because you do not have one person attempting to write each option generated by the group. Also, because the Post-its are movable, options do not need to be rewritten, thereby increasing the efficiency of subsequent focusing activities.

Brainwriting: Brainwriting provides quiet time to group members as they generate options. Group members work individually and quietly to record their options on a Brainwriting worksheet. After generating three options, each group member exchanges the worksheet for another one lying in the middle of the workspace. The group member reads these options silently and uses them as stimuli to generate three additional options. Members can build on the options previously written or generate entirely new options. Repeat the exchange of the Brainwriting worksheets until they are completely filled, or until a stated time period has elapsed.

Brainstorming Enhancers: SCAMPER and Forced Fitting are tools to help people shift their perspectives and think about things from new directions. Forced Fitting requires an individual to force a relationship between a random object (e.g., a toy) and the task at hand. SCAMPER is a mnemonic device for a menu of thought-provoking questions that can be used to stimulate a shift in thinking.

Imagery Trek: The goal of Imagery Trek is to create new connections by taking a mental or physical journey, first away from a task and then connecting back to it. First, a list of words is generated. One word is selected and used to create an image. The image is used to stimulate "fuzzy" connections back to the task at hand. Finally, more concrete connections are made, which relate to the task.

Ladder of Abstraction: As the name Ladder of Abstraction suggests, this tool consists of moving up and down different levels of abstraction in a systematic way. Asking the question "Why," about a task, helps to identify a broader view or a higher level of abstraction. Asking "How," leads to a more specific or concrete view of the task, and moves down the ladder. Asking "Why else" or "How else" stimulates a search for other options or views at the same (or parallel) level of abstraction. Moving up and down the Ladder of Abstraction, viewing many possibilities at different levels, helps to determine the most appropriate and useful level of abstraction at which to pose and work with the task.

Morphological Matrix: The Morphological Matrix uses three to five key parts or parameters of the task as a framework for creating new options. Each parameter is listed as a column heading in the matrix. Below each parameter are placed specific examples of possible values that parameter might have. New options are generated by selecting one item from each column. These items are combined to make a composite option. A matrix containing four parameters with ten values for each parameter yields 10,000 possible combinations.

Visually Identifying Relationships (VIR): VIR uses visual images to help group members distance themselves from an issue in order to develop fresh and novel perspectives. After an initial relaxation exercise, group members look at three to four pictures and record several observations or reactions to each on a worksheet (individually and quietly). Group members then connect their observations and reactions back to the task to generate highly original or unusual possibilities. By stepping away and then reengaging, there is an increased probability of finding new perspectives on the task.

TABLE 14.2 Creative problem-solving tools for focusing options

Advantages, Limitations, Unique, Overcoming Limitations (ALUo): ALUo provides a structured approach to analyzing and developing promising options. To use this tool, identify the Advantages (strengths), Limitations (concerns or possible weaknesses), and Unique Qualities (novel or useful elements) of an option. In addition, you will develop and strengthen the option by identifying and overcoming the key limitations (overcome limitations). The tool's structure helps avoid the common idea slaughtering that often occurs when groups confront novel or unusual options.

Criteria: Criteria are used to make the process of evaluation and decision-making explicit and deliberate. First, develop a list of possible criteria using the generating guidelines. Then, use the focusing guidelines to select the key criteria to act as "yardsticks" for evaluation. These yardsticks are used to screen, select, and support options under consideration. When creating the list of criteria, use the phrase, "Will it...." Once the criteria are chosen, they may be applied informally or in conjunction with other structured focusing tools (e.g., Evaluation Matrix).

Evaluation Matrix: The Evaluation Matrix provides a structure for evaluating promising options against key Criteria. Write specific Criteria across the top and options to be evaluated down the left side of the matrix. Complete the matrix by evaluating each option against the Criteria, column by column. A rating scale is used to determine how well each option meets each specific criterion. The results of the matrix are then used to evaluate, develop, and strengthen the options.

Selecting Hits: By Selecting Hits, an individual uses internal or implicit criteria, experience, and personal judgment to identify and select promising options from a list of alternatives. Review the options and ask, "Which ones are on target, intriguing, or intuitively seem to be the best possibilities?" Selecting Hits is often used as an initial or preliminary focusing tool, particularly when considering a large number of options.

Highlighting: Highlighting is a tool commonly used to compress options. First, options considered important, called Hits, are selected from a list. The Hits are then clustered into groupings called "hot-spots," based on emerging themes. The theme for each Hot Spot is identified and used as a title for the grouping. Finally, the titles for each Hot Spot are restated in a format that accurately captures the meaning of the hot-spot.

Paired Comparison Analysis (PCA): The PCA uses a simple grid to develop an understanding of the relative priority of a group of options. Individuals list the options under consideration on the PCA form. Options are then compared to each other, one pair at a time. Two decisions are made for each comparison: First, which option is most important? Next, how much more important is one option over the other? A rating is then assigned. Total scores are calculated for each option and used to understand their priority. Individual results can be placed on a flipchart and used to help groups come to consensus about priority.

Musts/Wants: Sorting options into "Musts" and "Wants" provides an informal but effective approach to focusing options. A person selects, evaluates, and places promising options into categories of priority called Musts and Wants. Musts are the most important options that most certainly need to be addressed in order to reach a sound or effective choice or decision. Failing to consider the Musts may jeopardize the success of subsequent efforts or actions. Wants are options that you would like to consider for selecting, refining, polishing, or strengthening, although they may not be "critical factors" influencing the success or failure of future efforts or actions. The Musts are what you *have* to consider; the Wants are what it would be *nice* to consider.

Short-Medium-Long (SML): This tool is used to focus options by arranging them in a meaningful way based on time. Short-, medium-, and long-range time frames are defined, and then promising options are placed into groups based on these time frames.

or adaptive options (Gryskiewicz, 1987). Knowing the kind of outcome you desire (more radical or incremental) can help you to choose, organize, and sequence the use of generating tools. For focusing tools, you can make choices based on how many alternatives you have. If you have been successful in generating many, varied, and unusual options, you may suffer from cognitive overload (Elsbach & Hargadon, 2006; van Merrienboar & Sweller, 2005). For larger numbers, you may need tools that help to organize or sort options down to a more reasonable number for further consideration. For small numbers, you may need to apply tools that develop and strengthen options.

The learning dynamics at this stage are primarily cognitive, acquiring knowledge through thought and experience. The best way to introduce the tools and guidelines is through experiential learning (Smart & Csapo, 2007) based on adult learning theory (Knowles, 1984). For example, we often begin by asking participants (working in groups) to generate as many ideas as they can for a well-known object. We record the number of ideas each group generates and debrief the activity. They often identify what they did as brainstorming. We then ask them to identify the four guidelines for brainstorming. We often need to help groups correctly identify the guidelines, and then ask them to think about what may have kept them from generating even more ideas. They will often identify the fact that the facilitator was working on a flipchart, and they had to wait until he or she were finished before offering additional ideas. We then introduce them to the idea of brainstorming with Post-its to overcome this production-blocking effect. We then ask them to go back to that object and do another round of generating using Post-its and working to follow the four guidelines. The results usually show a dramatic improvement in group fluency.

When it comes to focusing tools, we follow a similar approach. We ask participants to provide comments on a relatively unknown and novel product. They generally provide negative judgments. We debrief this with the participants, and then introduce the guidelines for focusing, along with the ALUo (advantages, limitations, unique, and overcoming limitations) tool. We go back to the object and practice the application of the ALUo tool and debrief the differences in behavior from the first round of comments.

Once participants are comfortable with the two sets of guidelines and kinds of thinking, we introduce them to the other tools in the toolkit (and described in more detail within Tables 14.1 and 14.2). We apply the tools on prepared tasks so they experience how the tools actually work and the unique value each tool provides. The general learning dynamics are providing participants with a briefing about the tool, engaging them on its actual use (doing), debriefing its use (how did it work), and then developing insights for their future individual or group use of the tool.

Linking Skills and Tools to Need and Purpose

There is no shortage of creativity tools. The key is to know how to apply these tools appropriately. The first level of preparation is to know if you are at a point where generating many, varied, unique options is needed, or are you at a place where you have the options and now need to screen, select, and strengthen selected options. During CPS, these two kinds of thinking are kept distinct (Parnes, Noller, & Biondi, 1977) and referred to as maintaining a dynamic balance. This dynamic balance between judgment and imagination is reflected within each stage of CPS (Parnes & Biondi, 1975).

There are many models of the creative process and some convergence on the core processes involved (Funke, Fischer, & Holt, 2018; Kaufmann, 1988; Mumford & McIntosh, 2017; Mumford, Mobley, Reiter-Palmon, Uhlman, & Doares, 1991). The CPS framework provides one model of three basic clusters of these processes (need for clarity, ideas, or to plan for action). Linking the tools and guidelines to these components of CPS is based on the need within the task. Putting the tools to work within the right component also ensures that the appropriate language is applied.

The language we use influences our thinking and problem-solving (Sapir, 1929; Whorf in Carroll, 1956). Although the Sapir-Whorf hypothesis and the concept of linguistic relativity created some controversy in cognitive science, there is some consensus that the language we learn, speak, and write is a guide to the language in which we think and solve problems (Hunt & Agnoli, 1991; Hussein, 2012; Lakoff & Johnson, 1999; Pourcel, 2002). The integration of general semantics within the Buffalo-based approach to CPS was deliberate (Noller, 1971).

For example, brainstorming could be applied to framing a problem within the understanding of the challenge component. What you would generate would be problem statements that would start with invitational stems like "How to…" or "In what ways might we…." If you had a clear statement of the problem but needed ideas, you could use one of the problem statements to generate ideas. If you had a solution and wanted to involve others in helping to evaluate it, you could use brainstorming to generate a variety of criteria. Then you could use the invitation stem: "Will it…?"

The point is that the CPS framework is applied based on the task and need under consideration. In a sense, the framework is an open system that helps to provide the most appropriate cognitive activity and language for tasks that require creative thinking. This level of activity demands the use of metacognition (Coutinho, Wiemer-Hastings, Skowronski, & Britt, 2005).

This phase of learning involves declarative knowledge of cognition, encouraging participants to understand their problem-solving preferences, yet focusing more on the needs within the task and the people involved. Participants build on their procedural knowledge of cognition regarding the guidelines and tools, and now move to determining the best fit to the CPS framework – and learn to apply conditional metacognition to determine when and why to apply the guidelines and tools.

Participants then move to the regulation of cognition by engaging in purposeful planning. For example, based on their understanding of the task at hand, if the need is for clear direction for future opportunities or understanding potential obstacles, constructing opportunities may be the appropriate CPS stage. If the need is to obtain an improved understanding of the key data within a task, the exploring data stage may be appropriate. If the task need is for a clear statement of the problem, framing problems may be the best fit. All three of these needs would locate the task within the understanding the challenge component. If the task contains a clearly defined problem statement that needs many, varied, and original ideas, the generating ideas component and stage would be the best fit to the CPS framework. If the need is to narrow down, evaluate, or analyze options, then the developing solutions stage would be the best location within the CPS framework. Finally, if the need is developing actions and understanding sources of assistance and resistance, then the building acceptance stage would be appropriate. These final two stages would place the focus of work within the preparing for action component.

When learning and applying CPS at this level, learners first practice their regulation of cognition by practicing the diagnosis on a series of presented tasks that clearly call for specific needs within the CPS framework. Then, they work with their own or another's real task to locate themselves within CPS. This provides them with insight into what language or invitational stems to apply to their problem-solving efforts and builds their conditional metacognitive knowledge.

Applying CPS on Real Challenges and Opportunities

Once you know which part of the CPS framework fits the need of the task, the focus turns to application and use of the process. This activity is grounded within the context surrounding the task. The planning of the process approach is the main responsibility of the CPS facilitator. The facilitator has worked with the client – the person who owns the task – to prepare the appropriate level of application, determine which part of the framework provides the best fit to the need, and decide on the tools and language to be deployed. The facilitator and client can also determine the level of involvement of other people for the session (a single group meeting), project (coordinated series of sessions), or initiative (a larger and longer-term project). These others take the role of resource-group members and use their knowledge, expertise, and perspectives in service of the client's need.

A session is the actual working meeting for a real group to interact to engage in the tools, follow the guidelines, and work to both generate and focus options. Small group sessions usually last two to three hours. The facilitator takes the process-leadership role and manages the client's interaction with the resource group. Specifically, as a result of facilitator-client interaction, the group is provided a visible summary of the task, including key background, the desired session outcome, and a working statement that uses the appropriate language to guide the generating and focusing. The facilitator would have chosen CPS tools, briefed the group on the guidelines, and prepared the session logistics. During the session, the facilitator will check with the client to ensure the outcomes are being met and make adjustments to the tools as needed. When the session concludes, the facilitator ensures that clear next steps are identified and that the outcomes are recorded.

The learning dynamics at this level depend on social learning (Bandura, 1977), social metacognition (Chiu & Kuo, 2009), and shared mental models (De Church & Mesmer-Magnus, 2010a,b; Lim & Klein, 2006) or schemas (Georgeon & Ritter, 2012; Shea & Wulf, 2005). While applying CPS, the facilitator engages in metacognitive monitoring and evaluating to ensure that the social collaboration is working well – making adjustments along the way. As a result of the planning between the facilitator and client, a shared mental model is developed, and then the resource group is engaged within this approach. Shared mental models have generally demonstrated a positive impact on team performance (Mohammed, Ferzandi, & Hamilton, 2010; Van den Bossche, Gijselaers, Segers, Woltjer, & Kirschner, 2011).

Applying the CPS framework in this manner enables social metacognition (Levine & Smith, 2013; Salonen, Vauras, & Efklides, 2005). As CPS tools are introduced and guidelines are reinforced, the group can focus their thinking and problem-solving on the task at hand – and consciously reflect on how they are contributing. Having an explicit task and process allows for a level of transparency that can be monitored and evaluated at a collective level (Frith & Frith, 2012).

Needed Future Research

It is well beyond the scope of this chapter to review the general research on creativity. There are many recent and comprehensive resources aimed at addressing that challenge (Feist, Reiter-Palmon, & Kaufman, 2017; Glăveneanu, 2016; Plucker, 2017; Shiu, 2014; Thomas & Chan, 2013; Zhou & Hoever, 2014). Instead, this section focuses on the various needs for further research surrounding the current approach to CPS.

There is a great deal of evidence supporting the learning, application, and impact of the Buffalo-based approach to CPS (Basadur, 1993; Buyer, 1988; Puccio, Firestien, Coyle, & Masucci, 2006; Rose & Lin, 1984; Scott, Leritz, & Mumford, 2004a,b; Sousa, Monteiro, Walton, & Pissarra, 2014). We are well beyond the fundamental question: Can we deliberately develop creative talent?

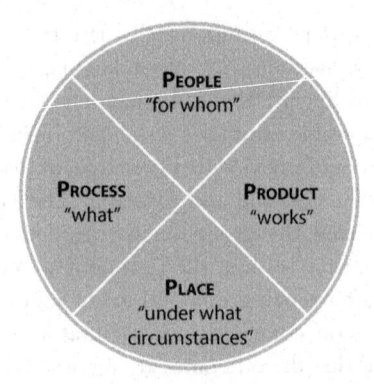

FIGURE 14.4 A model for future research on creative problem-solving.

A more challenging question is: What works, for whom, and under what circumstances (see Figure 14.4)?

Many creativity scholars have argued for a more sophisticated methodology to future CPS research by taking a systemic (Csikszentmihaly, 1999; Hennessey, 2017), ecological (Harrington, 1990; Isaksen, Puccio, & Treffinger, 1993), or interactionist (Mumford & Gustafson, 1988) approach. Woodman and Schoenfeldt (1990) promoted this more interactionist approach by asserting that it would allow appropriate levels of complexity to better understand creative behavior. This research framework, although focused on CPS, is an attempt to take a systems approach for future research.

What works?

The current thrust of most impact studies already links method (process) to product (results). Much of this research focuses on the impact (often effect sizes) of various training methods. This is certainly a good place to start. Future research could make even more targeted comparisons among alternative methods for various kinds of impact in specific domains. For example, studies could compare the current approach to CPS versus design thinking for efficacy in new product development in a specific targeted industry. This comparative research could be conducted at a specific tool level, rather than on a process or framework level. This sort of research would be invaluable to practitioners trying to unleash creative talent.

Comparing Various Process Frameworks

Since there are many models of the creative process, future research should be conducted to determine their efficacy by comparing outcomes derived by various models. Despite wide usage of CPS methods within organizations, there is a paucity of comparative research regarding methods and models of

CPS (Stein, 1975). The majority of research supporting the effects of deliberate training and learning of CPS methods usually examines those trained in a method versus a control group (i.e., Basadur, Graen, & Green, 1982). Only two notable exceptions were found. Ekvall (1981) conducted an experiment to compare four different methods (brainstorming, analogical problem-solving via Synectics [Gordon, 1961], morphological analysis [Zwicky, 1969], and the discussion method) within the product development context. He found mixed results on novelty, originality, and usefulness on real-world solutions generated by these methods. Ekvall and Parnes (1984) followed up on Ekvall's first study using real-life criteria to compare four methods, including brainstorming, brainstorming combined with analogical thinking, morphological analysis, and leaderless discussion (Maier, 1963). They found that brainstorming combined with Synectics-like analogical thinking produced the highest-quality solutions.

Given the proliferation of models and methods for CPS, we would be well-served to conduct and design comparative studies using a clear vocabulary. For example, brainstorming is a tool or technique. Synectics, CPS, and design thinking are methods. Future research should be conducted using fair comparisons: tool against tool, full method against full method.

Assessing Impact of Diverse Training Designs

Impact research needs to go well beyond single-shot courses and examine various durations of training, content, and delivery systems (Mumford, 2003). What is the optimum amount and kind of training required to produce novel, useful, and elegant outcomes? Again, there is a paucity of research that addresses these issues. An example of this type of research is proved by Parnes (1966b). He examined training in CPS by comparing programmed instruction versus programmed instruction with direct teacher-led instruction. Three randomly selected groups, matched on IQ, were assigned to the two experimental conditions along with a control group. On the basis of numerous creative ability assessments, the results from the instructor-led group were consistently superior to the control group and the group that used only programmed instruction.

Similar kinds of studies should be conducted comparing more current delivery technologies, differing training designs and durations. This line of research should follow the three main guidelines suggested by Valgeirsdottir and Onarheim (2017). These include assessing creativity both pre- and post-training, using control groups, and ensuring a sufficient sample size. These studies would provide insights to guide training and development design within organizations.

Strengthening Impact Criteria

How we determine the increase in value derived from learning and applying CPS needs some attention. Much of this work is descriptive, uses samples of convenience, or focuses on increases in cognitive ability or potential. Many studies use measures of divergent thinking to assess the impact of creativity training (Runco & Acar, 2012). Runco (2008) argued for going beyond divergent thinking and differentiating among creative potential, creative products, creative performance, and creative problem-solving. Future research must focus more on real-life criteria that are more relevant to organizational applications (see Montag, Maertz, & Baer, 2012).

For Whom?

If the goal is unleashing creative talent, then we need a good understanding of talent – particularly the talents required to solve creative problems. A preponderance of creativity research has been aimed at understanding the characteristics associated with high-level creativity in people (Kaufman, Pumaccahua, & Holt, 2013; MacKinnon, 1978). Making a distinction between level (capacity, ability, degree) and style (preference, predilection) of creativity is a more recent trend within creativity research (Isaksen, 2004; Kirton, 2003). Separating the question, "How creative are you?" from "How are you creative?" offers insights into individual differences when learning and applying CPS. It is likely that everyone brings something different to the creative process and may benefit differently from the creative process (Treffinger, Selby, & Isaksen, 2008). In fact, emerging research is beginning to provide some specific ways style of creativity interacts with CPS (Basadur, Gelade, & Basadur, 2014; Isaksen & Geuens, 2007; Puccio, Wheeler, & Cassandro, 2004).

This research is focused on linking personal style with the CPS process. Further research needs to focus on linking these insights with outcomes. Wang and Horng (2002) provided an example of this approach. They examined the impact of CPS training on R&D productivity and considered style as well. They found an increase in fluency and originality skills, improvement in R&D performance, and implications for creativity style. Namely, they found stronger effects for those with extroverted and feeling cognitive-type orientation. Another example was provided by Sitar, Cerne, Aleksic, and Mihelic (2016). They found that independent and collaborative learning styles were associated with higher levels of creativity, yet the relationships were mediated by other individual difference variables like self-efficacy and enjoyment of learning.

Determining Key Individual Differences

Style differences could be more salient in different stages or phases of CPS. Future research could examine more deeply how individual differences play out along the full creative process. Aptitude-treatment-interaction (ATI) is a research approach that examines how the quality of outcomes depends on the fit between peoples' aptitudes and the treatments they receive (Cronbach, 1967; Cronbach & Snow, 1977; Snow, 1991). Puccio, Wheeler, and Cassandro (2004) provided a typical example of a CPS impact study. They examined whether participants' styles interacted with their reactions to training on CPS. Problem-solving style was the aptitude; the treatment was 40 hours of instruction on CPS. They found significant interaction; however, they did not make any comparison regarding an alternative delivery system or approach, did not examine impact through a pre- or posttest, and did not include a control group. Future impact research should follow these suggestions outlined by Valgeirsdottir and Onarheim (2017) and take advantage of the ATI approach to further our understanding of what works for whom.

Although much current research focuses on problem-solving style as a key individual difference variable, other constructs should be included in this approach. For example, the level and kind of expertise and domain relevant knowledge required for successful application of CPS could contribute to the ongoing debate regarding the general versus content-specific issue.

Determining Effects of Social Roles

The emergence of the roles of client(s), facilitators, and resource-group members in CPS offers new ground to be addressed by future research. What are the effects of differentiating these roles? The notion of ownership for change and the role of sponsor are well established in the literature on organizational change and innovation (Amezcua, Grimes, Bradley, & Wiklund, 2013; By, 2005; Goodman, 1983; Kelly & Amburgey, 1991). Applying CPS also requires ownership for the task under consideration. Otherwise, the outcomes have minimal or no likelihood of implementation. The social role of client can be held by a single individual or by multiple individuals. Questions to be addressed through future research include the following: What are the desired characteristics of clients? Does shared clientship influence the impact of CPS? How much expertise in the task domain is required from the client for successful application of CPS?

Those who join a group application of CPS to offer their perspectives and input on the task are referred to as resource-group members. How much diversity of expertise, both content and process, is required for what types of tasks? How does both process and content diversity affect the outcomes and impact of CPS? This line of inquiry would require attention to the group performance (Dayaram & Fung, 2012) and team cognition (De Church & Mesmer-Magnus, 2010a,b) literature.

The process-oriented leadership role of the facilitator plays an important part in managing group CPS. Although there is abundant practical literature on the topic, there is scant empirical research to guide practice (Gregory & Romm, 2001). An exception can be found in the field of group support systems

(GSSs). Bostrom, Anson, and Clawson (1993) provided an extensive review of group facilitation within a GSS. This was followed by numerous studies of the effect of this role in GSS groups. For example, Anson, Bostrom, and Wynne (1995) examined the impact of facilitation on the performance of 48 GSS groups and found that facilitated groups experienced improved group processes and greater cohesion. They also found that the quality of facilitation moderated the impact on the quality of group outcomes. These results were confirmed by Miranda and Bostrom (1999).

The literature then turned to examination of the desired competencies of facilitators (McFadzean, 2002; Nelson & McFadzean, 1998). For example, Wardale (2013) interviewed managers across five industry sectors regarding their best and worst facilitation experiences in order to identify stages and strategies of effective group facilitation. She found four stages of group facilitation, including preparation, the event, satisfactory outcomes, and transfer. She also found clear strategies and tactics for the first three phases, but the participants identified frustration when the results and outcomes of group work were not implemented. The participants lacked well-developed facilitative processes or systems for maximizing the implementation or transfer of their results to the workplace. This suggests that future research should be aimed at improving our understanding of specific facilitator skills and abilities to encourage impact of creative results. Baer (2012a,b) provided an example of this kind of research. He found that implementation of creative ideas can be enhanced when participants are highly motivated to realize their ideas and when they are also highly skilled networkers.

Understanding and Appreciating Style

There is preliminary experimental evidence that providing feedback to participants engaged in CPS regarding their preferred problem-solving styles enhanced problem-solving performance (Main, Delcourt, & Treffinger, 2017). These findings seem to support the value of providing participants declarative knowledge of cognition – metacognitive knowledge about oneself as a problem solver. Much more research needs to be done to confirm and extend these findings. Further, the Main et al. (2017) study included students engaged in the Future Problem-Solving program. We need to conduct future experimental research with adults and professionals on real challenges within organizations.

Under What Circumstances?

Unleashing creative talent does not happen in a vacuum – it occurs in a specific context (Shalley & Gilson, 2004). It is quite probable that people can learn the very best CPS skills and tools but work in a context that would not provide them the opportunity to apply this learning. Progress has been made in understanding the context, climate, and culture that support creativity (Amabile, Conti, Coon, Lazenby, & Herron, 1996; Ekvall, 1996; Hunter, Bedell, & Mumford, 2007) and how leadership plays a key role in creating this climate (Isaksen, 2017).

Understanding the people-place-process interactions would enhance our ability to establish appropriate conditions for learning and applying CPS and for deeper impact within organizations. Future research along these lines could be done along multiple levels (work-unit, divisions, functions, industries, and national cultures) of analysis. Robinson-Morral, Reiter-Palmon, and Kaufman (2013) provided an example study that explored the linkages among people (self-efficacy), place (requirements for creativity in the workplace), and CPS. Their findings suggested that quality and originality of CPS solutions were highest when people have requirements for creativity at work, as well as the belief that they are creative.

Creating Conditions to Sustain Learning

What factors or dimensions within a team or organization are most important for sustained creative behavior in specific contexts and domains? We need to go well beyond the single facilitated CPS session that produces novel and useful outcomes to focus more on the stimulants and obstacles to the implementation and diffusion of the outcomes. Baer (2012a,b) pointed out some of the attributes of the participants, but we need to go further into how to prepare them to take their ideas forward and continue their learning. This future research should be informed by the expansive organizational innovation literature (e.g., Isaksen & Tidd, 2006; Tidd & Bessant, 2009). Moving from an "event" orientation to a "journey" orientation may help create conditions that support learning from success and failure. Future research could inform us about the most productive balance in disseminating previous learning from both positive and negative CPS experiences.

Determining Dimensions of Organizational Climate

Understanding the work environment is key to establishing the circumstances that support the learning and application of CPS within organizations (Oldham & Baer, 2012; West & Sacramento, 2012). Hunter, Bedell, and Mumford (2005) provided a review of the literature and identified 14 dimensions of a creative climate. Hunter, Bedell, and Mumford (2007) conducted a meta-analysis and concluded that climate was strongly related to creative achievement across contexts and criteria. However, we lack consensus on which dimensions of the climate for creativity are most salient for both learning and applying CPS. The climate or work environment for creativity can have differing levels of influence on type of outcome (exploratory or exploitative). Further, you may have the best-trained facilitators and CPS tools, but if the climate does not support their effective use, little productivity or transfer will result. Future research must help us determine which dimensions are more important for different kinds of tasks, people, and stages of CPS.

Linking People and Place

We sometimes artificially separate aspects of people (style, competence, personality) from place (climate, context). We need to better understand the integration of people and place – as this interaction is key to both learning and creativity. There is support in the literature for the importance of linking style as a people-oriented construct and climate as a work-environment construct (Armstrong, Cools, & Sadler-Smith, 2011; Kozhevnikov, Evans, & Kosslyn, 2014). Within the creativity literature, studies have shown that the effect of leadership behaviors on organizational creative performance is moderated by climate (Ekvall & Ryhammer, 1999; Isaksen & Akkermans, 2011; Jung, Chow, & Wu, 2003; Jung, Wu, & Chow, 2008). Are certain climates or contexts likely to interact with individual style preferences and then impact CPS performance? Isaksen and Aerts (2011) found that problem-solving style did influence perceptions of best and worst-case climate for creativity. Are there other individual difference variables (i.e., level of expertise, gender, etc.) that should be considered to better understand the linkages between people and place? The linkages between people and place could be explored further via the individual, group or team, and organization, as these are central to linking learning and creativity.

Conclusion

Learning and creativity are linked through the process of discovering and defining problems and opportunities, generating ideas, and putting those ideas to work. CPS is a natural outgrowth of the intersection of learning and creativity. The Buffalo-based approach to CPS provides a comprehensive system that has been subjected to more than 60 years of continuous research, development, and application. As such, it offers potential to help organizations, teams, and individuals to nurture and release their creative talent. Much more research and development remain to be done in order to focus on its productive organizational use.

References

Akella, D. (2010). Learning together: Kolb's experiential theory and its application. *Journal of Management and Organization*, 16, 100–112.

Amabile, T. M. (1983). The social psychology of creativity: A componential conceptualization. *Journal of Personality and Social Psychology*, 45, 357–377.

Amabile, T. M., Conti, R., Coon, H., Lazenby, J., & Herron, M. (1996). Assessing the work environment for creativity. *Academy of Management Journal*, 39, 1154–1184.

Amabile, T. M., & Pratt, M. G. (2016). The dynamic componential model of creativity and innovation in organizations: Making progress, making meaning. *Research in Organizational Behavior*, 36, 157–183.

Amezcua, A. S., Grimes, M. G., Bradley, S. W., & Wiklund, J. (2013). Organizational sponsorship and founding environments: A contingency view of the survival of business-incubated firms, 1994-2007. *Academy of Management Journal*, 56, 1628–1654.

Anson, R., Bostrom, R., & Wynne, B. (1995). An experiment assessing group support system and facilitator effects on meeting outcomes. *Management Science*, 41, 189–208.

Archambault, R. (1966). Philosophical bases of the experience curriculum. In R. Archambault (Ed.), *Dewey on education: Appraisals* (pp. 160–179). New York, NY: Random House.

Argyris, C. (1983). *Reasoning, learning, and action: Individual and organizational.* San Francisco, CA: Jossey-Bass.

Argyris, C. (1999). *On organizational learning* (2nd ed.). Oxford, UK: Blackwell Publishing.

Argyris, C., & Schon, D. A. (1995). *Organizational learning II: Theory, method, and practice.* New York, NY: Addison-Wesley.

Armstrong, S. J., Cools, E., & Sadler-Smith, E. (2011). Role of cognitive styles in business and management: Reviewing 40 years of research. *International Journal of Management Reviews*, 14, 238–262.

Ayman-Nolley, S. (1988). Piaget and Vygotsky on creativity. *Laboratory on Comparative Human Cognition Quarterly*, 10, 107–111.

Baer, J. (1998). The case for domain specificity in creativity. *Creativity Research Journal*, 11, 173–177.

Baer, J. (2011). Why grand theories of creativity distort, distract, and disappoint. *The International Journal of Creativity and Problem Solving*, 21, 73–100.

Baer, J. (2012a). Domain specificity and the limits of creativity theory. *Journal of Creative Behavior*, 46, 16–29.

Baer, M. (2012b). Putting creativity to work: The implementation of creative ideas in organizations. *Academy of Management Journal*, 55, 1102–1119.

Bandura, A. (1977). *Social learning theory.* New York, NY: General Learning Press.

Barley, S. R., Bechky, B. A., & Milliken, F. J. (2017). The changing nature of work: Careers, identities, and work lives in the 21st century. *Academy of Management Discoveries*, 3, 111–115.

Barrett, J. D., Peterson, D. R., Hester, K. S., Robledo, I. C., Day, E. A., Hougen, D. P., & Mumford, M. D. (2013). Thinking about applications: Effects on mental models and creative problem solving. *Creativity Research Journal*, 25, 199–212.

Basadur, M. (1993). Impacts and outcomes of creativity in organizational settings. In S. G. Isaksen, M C. Murdock, R. L. Firestien, & D. J. Treffinger (Eds.), *Nurturing and developing creativity: The emergence of a discipline* (pp. 278–313). Norwood, NJ: Ablex.

Basadur, M., Gelade, G., & Basadur, T. (2014). Creative problem solving process styles, cognitive work demands, and organizational adaptability. *Journal of Applied Behavioral Science*, 80, 80–115.

Basadur, M. S., Graen, G. B., & Green, S. G. (1982). Training in creative problem solving: Effects on ideation and problem finding in an industrial research organization. *Organizational Behavior and Human Performance*, 30, 41–70.

Basadur, M. S., Graen, G. B., & Wakabayashi, M. (1990). Identifying individual differences in creative problem solving style. *Journal of Creative Behavior*, 24, 111–131.

Basadur, M. S., & Thompson, R. (1986). Usefulness of the ideation principle of extended effort in real world professional and managerial creative problem solving. *Journal of Creative Behavior*, 20, 23–34.

Beghetto, R. A., & Kaufman, J. C. (2007). Toward a broader conception of creativity: A case for "mini-c" creativity. *Psychology of Aesthetics, Creativity, and the Arts*, 1, 73–79.

Beghetto, R. A., & Kaufman, J. C. (2009). Intellectual estuaries: Connecting learning and creativity in programs of advanced academics. *Journal of Advanced Academics*, 20, 296–324.

Beghetto, R. A., & Kaufman, J. C. (2017). Theories of creativity. In J. A. Plucker (Ed.), *Creativity and innovation: Theory, research, and practice* (pp. 35–48). Waco, TX: Prufrock Press.

Benne, K., & Sheats, P. (1948). Functional roles of group members. *Journal of Social Issues*, 4, 41–49.

Bennett, N., & Lemoine, G. J. (2014). What VUCA really means for you. *Harvard. Business Review*, 92, 27.

Berardi-Coletta, B., Buyer, L. S., Dominowski, R. L., & Rellinger, E. R. (1995). Metacognition and problem solving: A process-oriented approach. *Journal of Experimental Psychology: Learning, Memory, and Cognition*, 21, 205–223.

Bezrukova, K., & Uparna, J. (2009). Group splits and culture shifts: A new map of the creativity terrain. In E. A. Mannix, M. A. Neale, & J. A. Goncalo (Eds.), *Creativity in groups: Research on managing groups and teams – Volume 12* (pp. 163–193). Bingley, UK: Emerald Group.

Bledow, R., Carette, B., Kühnel, J., & Bister, D. (2017). Learning from others' failures: The effectiveness of failure stories for managerial learning. *Academy of Management Learning and Education*, 16, 39–53.

Bostrom, R. P., Anson, R., & Clawson, V. K. (1993). Group facilitation and group support systems. In L. M. Jessup & J. S. Valacich (Eds.), *Group support systems: New perspectives* (pp. 146–167). New York, NY: Macmillan.

Bouchard, T. J., Jr. (1972). Training, motivation, and personality as determinants of the effectiveness of brainstorming groups and individuals. *Journal of Applied Psychology*, 56, 324–331.

Buijs, J., & Nauta, K. (1991). Creativity training at the Delft school of industrial design engineering. In T. Rickards, P. Clemont, P. Grøholt, M. Parker, & M. Tassoul (Eds.), *Creativity and innovation: Learning from practice* (pp. 249–252). Delft, The Netherlands: Innovation Consulting Group – TNO.

Buyer, L. (1988). Creative problem solving: A comparison of performance under different instructions. *Journal of Creative Behavior*, 22(1), 55–61.

By, R. T. (2005). Organizational change management: A critical review. *Journal of Change Management*, 5, 369–380.

Cannon, M. D., & Edmondson, A. C. (2001). Confronting failure: Antecedents and consequences of shared beliefs about failure in organizational work groups. *Journal of Organizational Behavior*, 22, 161–177.

Cannon, M. D., & Edmondson, A. C. (2005). Failing to learn and learning to fail (intelligently): How great organizations put failure to work to innovate and improve. *Long Range Planning*, 38, 299–319.

Cannon, M. D., & Witherspoon, R. (2005). Actionable feedback: Unlocking the power of learning and performance improvement. *Academy of Management Executive*, 19, 120–134.

Carmeli, A., Tishler, A., & Edmondson, A. C. (2011). CEO relational leadership and strategic decision quality in top management teams: The role of team trust and learning from failure. *Strategic Organization*, 10, 31–54.

Carroll, J. B. (Ed.). (1956). *Language, thought, and reality: Selected writings of Benjamin Lee Whorf*. Cambridge, MA: MIT Press.

Chi, M. T., Glaser, R., & Farr, M. J. (1998). *The nature of expertise*. Hillsdale, NJ: Erlbaum.

Chilberg, J. C. (1989). A review of group process designs for facilitating communication in problem solving groups. *Management Communication Quarterly*, 3, 51–70.

Chiu, M. M., & Kuo, S. W. (2009). From metacognition to social metacognition: Similarities, differences, and learning. *Journal of Educational Research*, 3, 1–19.

Cole, M., John-Steiner, V., Scribner, S., & Souberman, E. (1978). *L. S. Vygotsky mind in society: The development of higher psychological processes*. Cambridge, MA: Harvard University Press.

Cooper, W. H., Gallupe, R. B., Pollard, S., & Cadsby, J. (1998). Some liberating effects of anonymous electronic brainstorming. *Small Group Research*, 29, 147–178.

Coutinho, S., Wiemer-Hastings, K., Skowronski, J. J., & Britt, M. A. (2005). Metacognition, need for cognition and use of explanations during ongoing learning and problem solving. *Learning and Individual Differences*, 15, 321–337.

Cramond, B., Martin, C. E., & Shaw, E. L. (1990). Generalizability of creative problem solving procedures to real life problems. *Journal for the Education of the Gifted*, 13, 141–155.

Cronbach, L. J. (1967). Instructional methods and individual differences. In R. Gagne (Ed.), *Learning and individual differences* (pp. 23–39). Columbus, OH: Charles E. Merrill.

Cronbach, L. J., & Snow, R. E. (1977). *Aptitudes and instructional methods: A handbook for research on interactions*. New York, NY: Irvington.

Crossan, M. M., Lane, H. W., & White, R. E. (1999). An organizational learning framework: From intuition to institution. *Academy of Management Review*, 24, 522–537.

Csikszentmihaly, M. (1999). Implications of a systems perspective for the study of creativity. In R. J. Sternberg (Ed.), *Handbook of creativity* (pp. 313–335). Cambridge, UK: Cambridge University Press.

Davis, M. A. (2009). Understanding the relationship between mood and creativity: A meta-analysis. *Organizational Behavior and Human Decision Processes*, 108, 25–38.

Dayaram, K., & Fung, L. (2012). Team performance: Where learning makes the greatest impact. *Research and Practice in Human Resource Management*, 20, 28–39.

De Church, L. A., & Mesmer-Magnus, J. R. (2010a). Measuring shared team mental models: A meta-analysis. *Group Dynamics, Theory, Research, and Practice*, 14, 1–14.

De Church, L. A., & Mesmer-Magnus, J. R. (2010b). The cognitive underpinnings of effective teamwork: A meta-analysis. *Journal of Applied Psychology*, 95, 32–53.

De Houwer, J., Barnes-Holmes, D., & Moors, A. (2013). What is learning? On the nature and merits of a functional definition of learning. *Psychonomic Bulletin and Review*, 20, 631–642.

Dewey, J. (1933). *How we think: A restatement of the relation of reflective thinking to the educative process*. Lexington, MA: D.C. Heath.

Diehl, M., & Stroebe, W. (1987). Productivity loss in brainstorming groups: Toward the solution of a riddle. *Journal of Personality and Social Psychology*, 53, 497–509.

Dillon, J. T. (1982). Problem finding and solving. *Journal of Creative Behavior*, 16, 97–111.

Donker, A. S., de Boer, H., Kostons, D., van Ewijk, D. C. C., & van der Werf, M. P. C. (2014). Effectiveness of learning strategy instruction on academic performance: A meta-analysis. *Educational Research Review*, 11, 1–26.

Drazin, R., Glynn, M. A., & Kazanjian, R. K. (1999). Multilevel theorizing about creativity in organizations: A sensemaking perspective. *Academy of Management Review*, 24, 286–307.

Edmondson, A. C. (2011). Strategies for learning from failure. *Harvard Business Review*, 89, 48–55.

Ekvall, G. (1981). *Creative problem solving methods in product development: A comparative study*. Stockholm, Sweden: The Swedish Council for Management and Organizational Behavior.

Ekvall, G. (1996). The organizational climate for creativity and innovation. *European Journal of Work and Organizational Psychology*, 5, 105–123.

Ekvall, G., & Parnes, S. J. (1984). *Creative problem solving methods in product development: A second experiment*. Stockholm, Sweden: The Swedish Council for Management and Work Life Issues.

Ekvall, G., & Ryhammer, L. (1999). The creative climate: Its determinants and effects at a Swedish University. *Creativity Research Journal*, 12, 303–310.

Elsbach, K. D., Barr, P. S., & Hargadon, A. B. (2005). Identifying situated cognition in organizations. *Organizational Science*, 16, 422–433.

Elsbach, K. D., & Hargadon, A. B. (2006). Enhancing creativity through "mindless" work: A framework of workday design. *Organizational Science*, 17, 470–483.

Ericsson, K. A. (2003). The acquisition of expert performance as problem solving. In J. E. Davidson & R. J. Sternberg (Eds.), *The psychology of problem solving* (pp. 31–83). Cambridge, UK: Cambridge University Press.

Faraj, S., & Sproull, L. (2000). Coordinating expertise in software development teams. *Management Science*, 46, 1554–1568.

Feist, G. J., Reiter-Palmon, R., & Kaufman, J. C. (Eds.). (2017). *The Cambridge handbook of creativity and personality research*. Cambridge, UK: Cambridge University Press.

Flavell, J. H. (1979). Metacognition and cognitive monitoring: A new area of cognitive-developmental inquiry. *American Psychologist*, 34, 906–911.

Flavell, J. H. (2004). Theory of mind development: Retrospect and prospect. *Merrill-Palmer Quarterly*, 50, 274–290.

Frawley, W. (1997). *Vygotsky and cognitive science: Language and the unification of the social and computational mind*. Cambridge, MA: Harvard University Press.

Frith, C. D., & Frith, U. F. (2012). Mechanisms of social cognition. *Annual Review of Psychology*, 63, 287–313.

Fritz, R. (1993). *Creating: A practical guide to the creative process*. New York, NY: Fawcett Columbine.

Funke, J., Fischer, A., & Holt, D. V. (2018). Competencies for complexity: Problem solving in the 21st century. In E. Care, P. Griffin, & M. Wilson (Eds.), *Assessment and teaching of 21st century skills: Research and applications* (pp. 41–53). Cham, Switzerland: Springer International Publishing.

Gallupe, R. B., Bastianutti, L. M., & Cooper, W. H. (1991). Unblocking brainstorms. *Journal of Applied Psychology*, 76, 137–142.

Garcia-Granero, A., Llopis, O., Fernandez-Mesa, A., & Alegre, J. (2015). Unraveling the link between managerial risk-taking and innovation: The mediating role of a risk-taking climate. *Journal of Business Research*, 68, 1094–1104.

Georgeon, O., & Ritter, F. (2012). An intrinsically-motivated schema mechanism to model and simulate emergent cognition. *Cognitive Systems Research*, 15, 73–92.

Getzels, J. W., & Csiksentmihalyi, M. (1976). *The creative vision: A longitudinal study of problem finding in art.* New York, NY: John Wiley and Sons.

Gibson, C., & Mumford, M. D. (2013). Evaluation, criticism, and creativity: Criticism content and effects on creative problem solving. *Psychology of Aesthetics, Creativity, and the Arts*, 7, 314–331.

Glăveneanu, V. P. (Ed.). (2016). *The Palgrave handbook of creativity and culture research.* New York, NY: Palgrave Macmillan.

Goodman, P. S. (Ed.). (1983). *Change in organizations: new perspectives on theory, research, and practice.* San Francisco, CA: Jossey-Bass.

Gordon, W. J. J. (1961). *Synectics: A new method of directing creative potential to the solution of technical and theoretical problems.* New York, NY: Harper & Row.

Gregory, W. J., & Romm, N. R. A. (2001). Critical facilitation: Learning through intervention in group processes. *Management Learning*, 32, 453–467.

Grohman, M. G., Ivcevic, Z., Silvia, P., & Kaufman, S. B. (2017). The role of passion and persistence in creativity. *Psychology of Aesthetics, Creativity, and the Arts*, 11, 376–385.

Gryskiewicz, S. S. (1987). Predictable creativity. In S. G. Isaksen (Ed.), *Frontiers of creativity research: Beyond the basics* (pp. 305–313). Buffalo, NY: Bearly Limited.

Guilford, J. P. (1959). Three faces of intellect. *American Psychologist*, 14, 469–479.

Guilford, J. P. (1977). *Way beyond the IQ.* Buffalo, NY: Bearly Limited.

Gundy, L. K., & Kickul, J. R. (1996). Flights of imagination: Fostering creativity through experiential learning. *Simulation and Gaming*, 27, 334–349.

Hadamard, J. (1945). *An essay on the psychology of invention in the mathematical field.* Princeton, NJ: Princeton University Press.

Hammond, M. N., & Farr, J. L. (2011). The role of errors in the creative and innovative process. In D. A. Hoffman & M. Frese (Eds.), *Error in organizations* (pp. 67–96). London, UK: Routledge.

Hargadon, A. B., & Bechky, B. A. (2006). When collections of creatives become creative collectives: A field study of problem solving. *Organization Science*, 17, 484–500.

Hargrove, R. A., & Nietfeld, J. L. (2015). The impact of metacognitive instruction on creative problem solving. *The Journal of Experimental Education*, 83, 291–318.

Harrington, D. M. (1990). The ecology of creativity: A psychological perspective. In M. A. Runco & R. S. Albert (Eds.), *Theories of creativity* (pp. 143–169). Beverly Hills, CA: Sage.

He, Y., Yao, X., Wang, S., & Caughron, J. (2016). Linking failure feedback to individual creativity: The moderation role of goal orientation. *Creativity Research Journal*, 28, 52–59.

Hennessey, B. A. (2017). Taking a systems view of creativity: On the right path toward understanding. *Journal of Creative Behavior*, 51, 341–344.

Henningsen, D. D., Cruz, M. G., & Miller, M. L. (2000). Role of social loafing in pre-deliberation decision making. *Group Dynamics: Theory, Research, and Practice*, 4, 168–175.

Huang, X., Hsieh, J. P., & He, W. (2014). Expertise dissimilarity and creativity: The contingent roles of tacit and explicit knowledge sharing. *Journal of Applied Psychology*, 99, 816–830.

Hunt, E., & Agnoli, F. (1991). The Whorfian hypothesis: A cognitive psychology perspective. *Psychological Review*, 98, 377–389.

Hunter, S. T., Bedell, K. E., & Mumford, M. D. (2005). Dimensions of creative climate: A general taxonomy. *The Korean Journal of Thinking and Problem Solving*, 15, 97–116.

Hunter, S. T., Bedell, K. F., & Mumford, M. D. (2007). Climate for creativity: A quantitative review. *Creativity Research Journal*, 19, 69–90.

Hussein, B. A. (2012). The Sapir-Whorf hypothesis today. *Theory and Practice in Language Studies*, 2, 642–646.

Illeris, K. (2009). A comprehensive understanding of human learning. In K. Illeris (Ed.), *Contemporary theories of learning* (pp. 7–20). New York, NY: Routledge.

Isaksen, S. G. (1983). Toward a model for the facilitation of creative problem solving. *Journal of Creative Behavior*, 17, 18–31.

Isaksen, S. G. (1992). Facilitating creative problem solving. In S. S. Gryskiewicz & D. A. Hills (Eds.), *Readings in innovation* (pp. 91–135). Greensboro, NC: Center for Creative Leadership.

Isaksen, S. G. (2004). The progress and potential of the creativity level-style distinction: Implications for research and practice. In W. Haukedal & B. Kuvaas (Eds.), *Creativity and problem solving in the context of business management* (pp. 40–71). Bergen, Norway: Fagbokforlaget.

Isaksen, S. G. (2017). Leadership's role in creative climate creation. In M. D. Mumford & S. Hemlin (Eds.), *Handbook of research on leadership and creativity* (pp. 131–158). Cheltenham, UK: Edward Elgar Publishing.

Isaksen, S. G., & Aerts, W. S. (2011). Linking problem-solving style and creative organizational climate: An exploratory interactionist study. *The International Journal of Creativity and Problem Solving*, 21, 7–38.

Isaksen, S. G., & Akkermans, H. J. (2011). Creative climate: A leadership lever for innovation. *Journal of Creative Behavior*, 45, 161–187.

Isaksen, S. G., Dorval, K. B., & Treffinger, D. J. (1994). *Creative approaches to problem solving*. Dubuque, IA: Kendall Hunt.

Isaksen, S. G., Dorval, K. B., & Treffinger, D. J. (2000). *Creative approaches to problem solving: A framework for change* (2nd ed.). Dubuque, IA: Kendall/Hunt.

Isaksen, S. G., Dorval, K. B., & Treffinger, D. J. (2011). *Creative approaches to problem solving: A framework for innovation and change* (3rd ed.). Thousand Oaks, CA: Sage.

Isaksen, S. G., & Gaulin, J. P. (2005). A reexamination of brainstorming research: Implications for research and practice. *Gifted Child Quarterly*, 49, 315–329.

Isaksen, S. G., & Geuens, D. (2007). Exploring the relationships between an assessment of problem solving style and creative problem solving. *The Korean Journal of Thinking and Problem Solving*, 17, 5–27.

Isaksen, S. G., Puccio, G. J., & Treffinger, D. J. (1993). An ecological approach to creativity research: Profiling for creative problem solving. *Journal of Creative Behavior*, 27, 149–170.

Isaksen, S. G., & Tidd, J. (2006). *Meeting the innovation challenge: Leadership for transformation and growth*. Chichester, UK: John Wiley and Sons.

Isaksen, S. G., & Treffinger, D. J. (1985). *Creative problem solving: The basic course*. Buffalo, NY: Bearly Limited.

Isaksen, S. G., & Treffinger, D. J. (2004). Celebrating 50 years of reflective practice: Versions of creative problem solving. *Journal of Creative Behavior*, 38, 75–101.
Isen, A. (1999). On the relationship between affect and creative problem solving. In S. Ruaa (Ed.), *Affect, creative experience and psychological adjustment* (pp. 3–18). Philadelphia, PA: Brunner/Mazel.
Jost, J. T., Kruglanski, A. W., & Nelson, T. O. (1998). Social metacognition: An expansionist review. *Personality and Social Psychology Review*, 2, 137–154.
Jung, D. I., Chow, C., & Wu, A. (2003). The role of transformational leadership in enhancing organizational innovation: Hypotheses and some preliminary findings. *The Leadership Quarterly*, 14, 525–544.
Jung, D., Wu, A., & Chow, C. W. (2008). Towards understanding the direct and indirect effects of CEOs' transformational leadership on firm innovation. *The Leadership Quarterly*, 19, 582–594.
Kagan, J. (1967). *Creativity and learning.* Boston, MA: Houghton Mifflin.
Kark, R., & Carmeli, A. (2009). Alive and creating: The mediating role of vitality and aliveness in the relationship between psychological safety and creative work involvement. *Journal of Organizational Behavior*, 30, 785–804.
Karwowski, M. (2014). Creative mindsets: Measurement, correlates, consequences. *Psychology of Aesthetics, Creativity, and the Arts*, 8, 62–70.
Karwowski, M., & Lebuda, I. (2016). The big five, the huge two, and creative self-beliefs: A meta-analysis. *Psychology of Aesthetics, Creativity, and the Arts*, 10, 214–232.
Kaufman, J. C., & Beghetto, R. A. (2009). Beyond big and little: The four C model of creativity. *Review of General Psychology*, 13, 1–12.
Kaufman, J. C., Pumaccahua, T. T., & Holt, R. E. (2013). Personality and creativity in realistic, investigative, artistic, social and enterprising college majors. *Personality and Individual Differences*, 54, 913–917.
Kaufmann, G. (1988). Problem solving and creativity. In K. Grønhaug & G. Kaufmann (Eds.), *Innovation: A cross-disciplinary perspective* (pp. 87–137). Oslo: Norwegian University Press.
Kazanjian, R. K., & Drazin, R. (2012). Organizational learning, knowledge management and creativity. In M. D. Mumford (Ed.), *Handbook of organizational creativity* (pp. 547–568). New York, NY: Elsevier.
Kegan, R., Lahey, L., & Fleming, A. (2014). Making business personal. *Harvard Business Review*, 92, 45–52.
Kellogg, W. N., & Britt, S. H. (1939). Structure or function in the definition of learning? *Psychological Review*, 46, 186–198.
Kelly, D., & Amburgey, T. L. (1991). Organizational inertia and momentum: A dynamic model of strategic change. *Academy of Management Journal*, 34, 591–612.
Kim, D. H. (1993). The link between individual and organizational learning. *Sloan Management Review*, 35, 37–50.
Kirton, M. J. (2003). *Adaption-innovation in the context of diversity and change.* New York, NY: Routledge.
Knowles, M. (1984). *Andragogy in action.* San Francisco, CA: Jossey-Bass.
Koestler, A. (1964). *The act of creation.* New York, NY: Macmillan.
Kolb, A. Y., & Kolb, D. A. (2009a). Experiential learning theory: A dynamic, holistic approach to management learning, education, and development. In S. J. Armstrong & C. V. Fukami (Eds.), *The SAGE handbook of management learning, education and development* (pp. 42–68). Thousand Oaks, CA: Sage.

Kolb, A. Y., & Kolb, D. A. (2009b). The learning way: Metacognitive aspects of experiential learning. *Simulation and Gaming*, 40, 297–327.

Kolb, D. A., Boyatzis, R. E., & Mainemelis, C. (2001). Experiential learning theory: Previous research and new directions. In R. J. Sternberg & L-F. Zhang (Eds.), *Perspectives on thinking, learning and cognitive styles* (pp. 227–247). London, UK: Routledge.

Kozbelt, A., Beghetto, R. A., & Runco, M. A. (2010). Theories of creativity. In: J. C. Kaufman & R. J. Sternberg (Eds.), *The Cambridge handbook of creativity* (pp. 20–47). New York, NY: Cambridge University Press.

Kozhevnikov, M., Evans, C., & Kosslyn, S. M. (2014). Cognitive style as environmentally sensitive individual differences in cognition: A modern synthesis and applications in education, business, and management. *Psychological Science in the Public Interest*, 15, 3–33.

Kozlowski, W. J., & Ilgen, D. R. (2006). Enhancing the effectiveness of work groups and teams. *Psychological Science in the Public Interest*, 7, 77–124.

Kramer, T. J., Fleming, G. P., & Mannis, S. M. (2001). Improving face-to-face brainstorming through modeling and facilitation. *Small Group Research*, 32, 533–557.

Kvalnes, Ø. (2017). *Fallibility at work: Rethinking excellence and error in organizations.* Cham, Switzerland: Palgrove Macmillan.

Lakoff, G., & Johnson, M. (1999). *Philosophy in the flesh: The embodied mind and its challenge to Western thought.* New York, NY: Basic Books.

Langer, E. J. (2000). Mindful learning. *Current Directions in Psychological Science*, 9, 220–223.

Lave, J. (2009). The practice of learning. In K. Illeris (Ed.), *Contemporary theories of learning* (pp. 200–208). New York, NY: Routledge.

Levine, J. M., & Resnick, L. B. (1993). Social foundations of cognition. *Annual Review of Psychology*, 44, 585–612.

Levine, J. M., & Smith, E. R. (2013). Group cognition: Information search and distribution. In D. E. Carlston (Ed.), *The Oxford Handbook of Social Psychology* (pp. 616–636). Oxford, UK: Oxford University Press.

Lewin, K. (1947). Frontiers in group dynamics: Concept, method and reality in social science; Social equilibria and social change. *Human Relations*, 1, 5–41.

Lim, B. C., & Klein, K. J. (2006). Team mental models and team performance: A field study of the effects of team mental model similarity and accuracy. *Journal of Organizational Behavior*, 27, 403–418.

Lindqvist, G. (2003). Vygotsky's theory of creativity. *Creativity Research Journal*, 15, 245–251.

Lubart, T. (2008). Connecting learning, individual differences and creativity. *Learning and Individual Differences*, 18, 361–362.

MacKinnon, D. W. (1970). Creativity: A multi-faceted phenomenon. In J. D. Roslansky (Ed.), *Creativity: A discussion at the Nobel conference* (pp. 17–32). Amsterdam: North-Holland Press.

MacKinnon, D. W. (1978). *In search of human effectiveness: Identifying and developing creativity.* Buffalo, NY: Bearly Limited.

Maier, N. R. F. (1963). *Problem solving discussions and conferences.* New York, NY: McGraw-Hill.

Maier, N. R. F. (1967). Assets and liabilities in group problem solving: The need for an integrative function. *Psychological Review*, 74, 239–249.

Main, L. F., Delcourt, M. B., & Treffinger, D. J. (2017). Effects of group training in problem-solving styles on future problem-solving performance. *Journal of Creative Behavior, Early View*, 1–12.

Maitlis, S., & Christianson, M. (2014). Sensemaking in organizations: Taking stock and moving forward. *The Academy of Management Annals*, 8, 57–125.

McCluskey, K. W. (2000). Setting the stage for creative problem solving. In S. G. Isaksen (Ed.), *Facilitative leadership: Making a difference with creative problem solving* (pp. 77–101). Dubuque, IA: Kendall-Hunt.

McFadzean, E. (2002). Developing and supporting creative problem solving teams: Part II – Facilitator competencies. *Management Decision*, 40, 537–551.

McLeod, G. (2003). Learning theory and instructional design. *Learning Matters*, 2, 35–43.

Mednick, S. A. (1962). The associative basis of the creative process. *Psychological Review*, 69, 220–232.

Miranda, S. M., & Bostrom, R. P. (1999). Meeting facilitation: Process versus content interventions. *Journal of Management Information Systems*, 15, 89–114.

Mohammed, S., Ferzandi, L., & Hamilton, K. (2010). Metaphor no more: A 15-year review of the team mental model construct. *Journal of Management*, 36, 876–910.

Montag, T., Maertz, C. P., & Baer, M. (2012). A critical analysis of the workplace creativity criterion space. *Journal of Management*, 38, 1362–1386.

Moran, S., & John-Steiner, V. (2003). Creativity in the making: Vygotsky's contemporary contribution to the dialectic of creativity and development. In R. K. Sawyer, V. John-Steiner, S. Moran, R. J. Sternberg, D. H. Feldman, J. Nakamura, & M. Csikszentmihalyi (Eds.), *Creativity and development* (pp. 61–90). Oxford, UK: Oxford University Press.

Mullen, B., Johnson, C., & Salas, E. (1991). Productivity loss in brainstorming groups: A meta-analytic integration. *Basic and Applied Psychology*, 12, 3–23.

Mumford, M. C., & Gustafson, S. B. (1988). Creativity syndrome: Integration, application, and innovation. *Psychological Bulletin*, 103, 27–43.

Mumford, M. D. (2001). Something old, something new: Revisiting Guilford's conception of creative problem solving. *Creativity Research Journal*, 13, 267–276.

Mumford, M. D. (2003). Where have we been, where are we going? Taking stock in creativity research. *Creativity Research Journal*, 15, 107–120.

Mumford, M. D., Blair, C., Dailey, L. E., Leritz, L. E., & Osburn, H. K. (2006). Errors in creative thought? Cognitive bias in a complex processing activity. *Journal of Creative Behavior*, 40, 75–109.

Mumford, M. D., & Gustafson, S. B. (2007). Creative thought: Cognition and problem solving in a dynamic system. In M. A. Runco (Ed.), *Creativity research handbook* (pp. 33–77). Cresskill, NJ: Hampton.

Mumford, M. D., Hester, K. S., Robledo, I. C., Peterson, D. R., Day, E. A., Hougen, D. F., & Barrett, J. D. (2012). Mental models and creative problem solving: Relationship of objective and subjective model attributes. *Creativity Research Journal*, 24, 311–330.

Mumford, M. D., & McIntosh, T. (2017). Creative thinking processes: The past and the future. *Journal of Creative Behavior*, 51, 317–322.

Mumford, M. D., Medeiros, K. E., & Partlow, P. J. (2012). Creative thinking: Processes, strategies, and knowledge. *Journal of Creative Behavior*, 46, 30–47.

Mumford, M. D., Mobley, M. I., Reiter-Palmon, R., Uhlman, C. E., & Doares, L. M. (1991). Process analytic models of creative problem solving. *Creativity Research Journal*, 4, 91–122.

Mumford, M. D., Supinski, E. P., Baughman, W. A., Costanza, D. P., & Threlfall, K. V. (1997). Process-based measures of creative problem solving skills: V. Overall prediction. *Creativity Research Journal*, 10, 73–85.

Nelson, T., & McFadzean, E. (1998). Facilitating problem-solving groups: Facilitation competencies. *Leadership and Organization Development Journal*, 19, 72–82.

Newell, A., Shaw, J. C., & Simon, H. A. (1967). The processes of creative thinking. In H. E. Gruber, G. Terrell, & M. Wertheimer (Eds.), *Contemporary approaches to creative thinking: A symposium held at the University of Colorado* (pp. 63–119). New York, NY: Atherton Press.

Noe, R. A., Clarke, A. D. M., & Klein, H. J. (2014). Learning in the twenty-first century workplace. *Annual Review of Organizational Psychology – Organizational Behavior*, 1, 245–275.

Noller, R. B. (1971). Some applications of general semantics in teaching creativity. *Journal of Creative Behavior*, 5, 256–266.

Noller, R. B. (1977). *Scratching the surface of creative problem solving: A bird's eye-view of CPS*. Buffalo, NY: D.O.K. Publishers.

Noller, R. B., & Parnes, S. J. (1972). Applied creativity: The creative studies project, Part III – The curriculum. *Journal of Creative Behavior*, 6, 275–294.

Noller, R. B., Parnes, S. J., & Biondi, A. M. (1976). *Creative actionbook: Revised edition of creative behavior workbook*. New York, NY: Charles Scribner's Sons.

Nunamaker, J. F., Briggs, R. O., Mittleman, D. D., Vogel, D. R., & Balthazard, P. A. (1997). Lessons from a dozen years of group support systems research: A discussion of lab and field findings. *Journal of Management Information Systems*, 13, 163–207.

Offner, A. K., Kramer, T. J., & Winter, J. P. (1996). The effects of facilitation, recording, and pauses on group brainstorming. *Small Group Research*, 27, 283–298.

Ogden, C. K., & Richards, I. A. (1927). *The meaning of meaning: A study of the influence of language upon thought and of the science of symbolism*. New York, NY: Harcourt, Brace.

Oldham, G. R., & Baer, M. (2012). Creativity and the work context. In M. D. Mumford (Ed.), *Handbook of organizational creativity* (pp. 387–420). New York, NY: Elsevier.

Osborn, A. F. (1948). *Your creative power: How to use imagination*. New York, NY: Charles Scribner's Sons.

Osborn, A. F. (1952). *Wake up your mind: 101 ways to develop creativeness*. New York, NY: Charles Scribner's Sons.

Osborn, A. F. (1953). *Applied imagination: Principles and procedures of creative thinking*. New York, NY: Charles Scribner's Sons.

Oxley, N. L., Dzindolet, M. T., & Paulus, P. B. (1996). The effects of facilitators on the performance of brainstorming groups. *Journal of Social Behavior and Personality*, 11, 633–646.

Pagano, A. L. (1979). Learning and creativity. *Journal of Creative Behavior*, 13, 127–138.

Paletz, S. B., & Peng, K. (2008). Implicit theories of creativity across cultures: Novelty and appropriateness in two product domains. *Journal of Cross-Cultural Psychology*, 39, 288–304.

Papaleontiou-Louca, E. (2008). *Metacognition and theory of mind*. Newcastle, UK: Cambridge Scholars Publishing.

Parnes, S. J. (1961). Effects of extended effort in creative problem solving. *Journal of Educational Psychology*, 52, 117–122.

Parnes, S. J. (1966a). *Manual for institutes and programs*. Buffalo, NY: Creative Education Foundation.
Parnes, S. J. (1966b). *Programming creative behavior*. Buffalo, NY: State University of New York at Buffalo.
Parnes, S. J. (1967). *Creative behavior guidebook*. New York, NY: Charles Scribner's Sons.
Parnes, S. J. (1977). CPSI: The general system. *Journal of Creative Behavior*, 11, 1–11.
Parnes, S. J. (1985). *A facilitating style of leadership*. Buffalo, NY: Bearly Limited.
Parnes, S. J. (1987). The creative studies project. In S. Isaksen (Ed.), *Frontiers of creativity research: Beyond the basics* (pp. 156–188). Buffalo, NY: Bearly Limited.
Parnes, S. J., & Biondi, A. M. (1975). Creative behavior: A delicate balance. *Journal of Creative Behavior*, 9, 149–153.
Parnes, S. J., & Meadow, A. (1959). Effects of brainstorming instructions on creative problem solving by trained and untrained subjects. *Journal of Educational Psychology*, 50, 171–176.
Parnes, S. J., & Noller, R. B. (1972a). Applied creativity: The creative studies project, Part I – The development. *Journal of Creative Behavior*, 6, 1–22.
Parnes, S. J., & Noller, R. B. (1972b). Applied creativity: The creative studies project, Part II – Results of the two-year program. *Journal of Creative Behavior*, 6, 164–186.
Parnes, S. J., & Noller, R. B. (1973). Applied creativity: The creative studies project, Part IV – Personality findings and conclusions. *Journal of Creative Behavior*, 7, 15–36.
Parnes, S. J., Noller, R. B., & Biondi, A. M. (1977). *Guide to creative action*. New York, NY: Charles Scribner's Sons.
Parnes, S. J., Meadow, A., & Reese, H. (1959). Influence of brainstorming instructions and problem sequence on a creative problem solving test. *Journal of Applied Psychology*, 43, 413–416.
Paulus, P. B. (1983). Group influences on individual task performance. In P. B. Paulus (Ed.), *Basic group processes* (pp. 97–120). New York, NY: Springer-Verlag.
Plucker, J. A. (2017). (Ed.), *Creativity and innovation: Theory, research, and practice*. Waco, TX: Prufrock Press.
Politis, D., & Gabrielsson, J. (2009). Entrepreneurs' attitudes toward failure: An experiential learning approach. *International Journal of Entrepreneurial Behavior and Research*, 15, 364–383.
Popova-Nowak, I. V., & Cseh, M. (2015). The meaning of organizational learning: A meta-paradigm perspective. *Human Resource Development Review*, 14, 299–331.
Pourcel, S. (2002). Investigating linguistic relativity: A research methodology. *Durham Working Papers in Linguistics*, 8, 125–138.
Puccio, G. J., & Cabra, J. (2009). Creative problem solving: Past, present, and future. In T. Rickards, M. A. Runco, & S. Moger (Eds.), *The Routledge companion to creativity* (pp. 327–337). London, UK: Routledge.
Puccio, G. J., Firestien, R. L., Coyle, C., & Masucci, C. (2006). A review of the effectiveness of CPS training: A focus on workplace issues. *Creativity and Innovation Management*, 15, 19–33.
Puccio, G. J., Murdock, M. C., & Mance, M. (2005). Current developments in creative problem solving for organizations: A focus on thinking skills and styles. *The Korean Journal of Thinking and Problem Solving*, 15, 43–76.
Puccio, G. J., Wheeler, R. A., Cassandro, V. J. (2004). Reactions to creative problem solving training: Does cognitive style make a difference? *Journal of Creative Behavior*, 38, 192–216.

Puccio, G. P. (1999). Creative problem solving preferences: Their identification and implications. *Creativity and Innovation Management,* 8, 171–178.

Puente-Diaz, R., & Cavazos-Arroyo, J. (2017). Creative self-efficacy: The influence of affective states and social persuasion as antecedents and imagination and divergent thinking as consequences. *Creativity Research Journal,* 29, 304–312.

Reason, J. (1990). *Human error.* Cambridge, UK: Cambridge University Press.

Reason, J. (2013). *A life in error: From little slips to big disasters.* Boca Raton, FL: Taylor and Francis Group.

Reese, H. W., Treffinger, D. J., Parnes, S. J., & Kaltsounis, G. (1976). Effects of a creative studies program on structure of intellect factors. *Journal of Educational Psychology,* 68, 401–410.

Reiter-Palmon, R., Wigert, B., & deVreede, T. (2012). Team creativity and innovation: The effect of group composition, social processes, and cognition. In M. D. Mumford (Ed.), *Handbook of organizational creativity* (pp. 547–568). New York, NY: Elsevier.

Richards, R. (2007). *Everyday creativity and new views of human nature.* Washington, DC: American Psychological Association.

Rietzschel, E. F., Nijstad, B. A., & Stroebe, W. (2010). The selection of creative ideas after individual idea generation: Choosing between creativity and impact. *British Journal of Psychology,* 101, 47–68.

Robbins, P., & Ayded, M. (Eds.). (2009). *The Cambridge handbook of situated cognition.* Cambridge, UK: Cambridge University Press.

Robinson-Morral, E. J., Reiter-Palmon, R., & Kaufman, J. C. (2013). The interactive effects of self-perceptions and job requirements on creative problem solving. *Journal of Creative Behavior,* 47, 200–214.

Rogers, C. R. (1962). Toward a theory of creativity. In S. J. Parnes & H. F. Harding (Eds.), *A sourcebook for creative thinking* (pp. 63–72). New York, NY: Charles Scribner's Sons.

Rose, L. H., & Lin, H. T. (1984). A meta-analysis of long-term creativity training programs. *Journal of Creative Behavior,* 18, 11–22.

Rossman, J. (1931). *The psychology of the inventor.* Washington, DC: Inventors Publishing.

Rothenberg, A. (1971). The process of Janusian thinking in creativity. *Archives of General Psychiatry,* 24, 195–205.

Roweton, W. E. (1970). *Creativity: A review of theory and research: Report from the Task and Training Variables in Human Problem Solving and Creative Thinking Project – Theoretical paper number 24.* Madison, WI: Wisconsin Research and Development Center for Cognitive Learning.

Runco, M. A. (Ed.). (1994). *Problem finding, problem solving, and creativity.* Norwood, NJ: Ablex.

Runco, M. A. (2008). Commentary: Divergent thinking is not synonymous with creativity. *Psychology of Aesthetics, Creativity, and the Arts,* 2, 93–96.

Runco, M. A. (2014). *Creativity: Theories and themes: Research, development and practice* (2nd ed.). San Diego, CA: Academic Press.

Runco, M. A., & Acar, S. (2012). Divergent thinking as an indicator of creative potential. *Creativity Research Journal,* 24, 1–10.

Runco, M. A., & Albert, R. S. (Eds.). (1990). *Theories of creativity.* Newbury Park, CA: Sage.

Salonen, P., Vauras, M., & Efklides, A. (2005). Social interaction – What can it tell us about metacognition and co-regulation in learning? *European Psychologist,* 10, 199–208.

Sapir, E. (1929). The status of linguistics as a science. *Language*, 5, 207–214.
Sawyer, R. K. (2012). *Explaining creativity: The science of human innovation*. Oxford, UK: Oxford University Press.
Schein, E. H. (1996). Kurt Lewin's change theory in the field and classroom: Notes toward a model of managed learning. *Systems Practice*, 9, 27–47.
Schraw, G. (1998). Promoting general metacognitive awareness. *Instructional Science*, 26, 113–125.
Scott, B. M., & Berman, A. F. (2013). Examining the domain-specificity of metacognition using academic domains and task-specific individual differences. *Australian Journal of Educational and Developmental Psychology*, 13, 28–43.
Scott, G., Leritz, L. E., & Mumford, M. D. (2004a). Types of creativity training: Approaches and their effectiveness. *Journal of Creative Behavior*, 38, 149–179.
Scott, G., Leritz, L. E., & Mumford, M. D. (2004b). The effectiveness of creativity training: A quantitative review. *Creativity Research Journal*, 16, 361–388.
Sefton-Green, J., Thomson, P., Jones, K., & Bresler, L. (Eds.). (2011). *The Routledge international handbook of creative learning*. New York, NY: Routledge.
Shalley, C. E., & Gilson, L. L. (2004). What leaders need to know: A review of social and contextual factors that can foster or hinder creativity. *The Leadership Quarterly*, 15, 33–53.
Shea, C. H., & Wulf, G. (2005). Schema theory: A critical appraisal and reevaluation. *Journal of Motor Behavior*, 37, 85–101.
Shepherd, D. A., Patzelt, H., & Wolfe, M. (2011). Moving forward from project failure: Negative emotions, affective commitment, and learning from the experience. *Academy of Management Journal*, 54, 1229–1259.
Shiu, E. (Ed.). (2014). *Creativity research: An interdisciplinary and multi-disciplinary research handbook*. New York, NY: Routledge.
Simonton, D. K. (2014). *The Wiley handbook of genius*. Chichester, UK: Wiley.
Simonton, D. K. (2017). Big-C versus little-c creativity: Definitions, implications, and inherent educational contradictions. In R. A. Beghetto & B. Sriraman (Eds.), *Creative contradictions in education: Cross disciplinary paradoxes and perspectives* (pp. 3–19). Basel, Switzerland: Springer International.
Sitar, A. S., Cerne, M., Aleksic, D., & Mihelic, K. K. (2016). Individual learning styles and creativity. *Creativity Research Journal*, 28, 334–341.
Sitkin, S. B. (1992). Learning through failure: The strategy of small losses. *Research in Organizational Behavior*, 14, 231–266.
Smart, K. L., & Csapo, N. (2007). Learning by doing: Engaging students through learner centered activities. *Business Communication Quarterly*, 70, 451–457.
Smith, E. R., & Semin, G. R. (2004). Socially situated cognition: Cognition in its social context. *Advances in Experimental Social Psychology*, 36, 53–117.
Smith, E. R., & Semin, G. R. (2007). Situated social cognition. *Current Directions in Psychological Science*, 16, 132–135.
Snow, R. E. (1991). Aptitude-treatment interaction as a framework for research on individual differences in psychotherapy. *Journal of Consulting and Clinical Psychology*, 59, 205–216.
Sousa, F. C., Monteiro, I. P., Walton, A. P., & Pissarra, J. (2014). Adapting creative problem solving to an organizational context: A study of its effectiveness with a student population. *Creativity and Innovation Management*, 23, 111–120.
Stein, M. I. (1975). *Stimulating creativity: Volume 2 – Group procedures*. New York, NY: Academic Press.

Supratman, A. M. (2013). Piaget's theory in the development of creative thinking. *Journal of the Korean Society of Mathematical Education, Series D*, 17, 291–307.

Sutton, R. I., & Hargadon, A. (1996). Brainstorming in context: Effectiveness in a product design firm. *Administrative Science Quarterly*, 41, 685–718.

Taylor, D. W., Berry, P. C., & Block, C. H. (1958). Does group participation when using brainstorming inhibit creative thinking? *Administrative Science Quarterly*, 3, 23–47.

Tellis, G. J., Prabhu, J. C., & Chandy, R. K. (2009). Radical innovation across nations: The preeminence of corporate culture. *Journal of Marketing*, 73, 3–23.

Thiel, C. E., Bagdasarov, Z., Harkrider, L., Johnson, J. F., & Mumford, M. D. (2012). Leaders ethical decision-making in organizations: Strategies for sensemaking. *Journal of Business Ethics*, 107, 49–64.

Thomas, K., & Chan, J. (Eds.). (2013). *Handbook of research on creativity*. Cheltenham, UK: Edward Elgar.

Thompson, L. F., & Coovert, M. D. (2002). Stepping up to the challenge: A critical examination of face-to-face and computer-mediated team decision making. *Group Dynamics: Theory, Research, and Practice*, 6, 55–64.

Tidd, J., & Bessant, J. (2009). *Managing innovation: Integrating technological, market, and organizational change* (5th ed.). Chichester, UK: John Wiley and Sons.

Tierney, P., & Farmer, S. M. (2011). Creative self-efficacy development and creative performance over time. *Journal of Applied Psychology*, 96, 277–293.

Tjosvold, D., Yu, Z., & Hui, C. (2004). Team learning from mistakes: The contribution of cooperative goals and problem solving. *Journal of Management Studies*, 41, 1223–1245.

Torrance, E. P. (1979). *The search for Satori and creativity*. Buffalo, NY: The Creative Education Foundation.

Torrance, E. P., & Myers, R. E. (1970). *Creative learning and teaching*. New York, NY: Dodd, Mead, & Company.

Torrance, E. P., & Torrance, P. (1973). *Is creativity teachable?* Bloomington, IN: Phi Delta Kappa.

Treffinger, D. J. (1983). George's group: A creative problem solving facilitation case study. *Journal of Creative Behavior*, 17, 39–48.

Treffinger, D. J. (2007). Creative problem solving (CPS): Powerful tools for managing change and developing talent. *Gifted and Talented International*, 22, 8–18.

Treffinger, D. J., & Isaksen, S. G. (2005). Creative problem solving: The history, development, and implications for gifted education and talent development. *Gifted Child Quarterly*, 49, 342–353.

Treffinger, D. J., Isaksen, S. G., & Firestien, R. L. (1982). *Handbook of creative learning – Volume I*. Honeoye, NY: Center for Creative Learning.

Treffinger, D. J., Isaksen, S. G., & Firestien, R. L. (1983). Theoretical perspectives on creative learning and its facilitation: An overview. *Journal of Creative Behavior*, 17, 9–17.

Treffinger, D. J., Isaksen, S. G., & Stead-Dorval, B. (2006). *Creative problem solving: An introduction* (4th ed.). Waco, TX: Prufrock Press.

Treffinger, D. J., Schoonover, P. F., & Selby, E. C. (2013). *Educating for creativity and innovation: A comprehensive guide for research-based practice*. Waco, TX: Prufrock Press.

Treffinger, D. J., Selby, E. C., & Isaksen, S. G. (2008). Understanding individual problem-solving style: A key to learning and applying creative problem solving. *Learning and Individual Differences*, 18, 390–401.

Upton, A. (1941). *Design for thinking: A first book in semantics*. Palo Alto, CA: Pacific Books.
Valgeirsdottir, D., & Onarheim, B. (2017). Studying creativity training programs: A methodological analysis. *Creativity and Innovation Management*, 26, 430–439.
Van den Bossche, P., Gijselaers, W., Segers, M., Woltjer, G., & Kirschner, P. (2011). Team learning: Building shared mental models. *Instructional Science*, 39, 283–301.
Van der Stel, M., & Veenman, M. V. J. (2010). Development of metacognitive skillfulness: A longitudinal study. *Learning and Individual Differences*, 20, 220–224.
Van der Vegt, G. S., Van de Vliert, E., & Huang, X. (2005). Location-level links between diversity and innovative climate depend on national power distance. *Academy of Management Journal*, 48, 1171–1182.
van Merrienboar, J. G., & Sweller, J. (2005). Cognitive load theory and complex learning: Recent developments and future directions. *Educational Psychology Review*, 17, 147–177.
Vernon, D., Hocking, I., & Tyler, T. C. (2016). An evidence-based review of creative problem solving tools: A practitioner's resource. *Human Resource Development Review*, 15, 230–259.
Vroom, V. H., Grant, L. D., & Cotton, T. S. (1969). The consequences of social interaction in group problem solving. *Organizational Behavior and Human Performance*, 4, 77–95.
Wallas, G. (1926). *The art of thought*. New York, NY: Harcourt, Brace and Company.
Wang, C-W., & Horng, R-H. (2002). Effects of creative problem solving training on creativity, cognitive type, and R&D performance. *R&D Management*, 32, 35–45.
Ward, T. B., Smith, S. M., & Vaid, J. (Eds.). (1997). *Creative thought: An investigation of conceptual structures and processes*. Washington, DC: American Psychological Association.
Wardale, D. (2013). Towards a model of effective group facilitation. *Leadership and Organizational Development Journal*, 34, 112–129.
Washburne, J. N. (1936). The definition of learning. *Journal of Educational Psychology*, 27, 603–611.
Weick, K. E. (1969). *The social psychology of organizing*. Reading, MA: Addison-Wesley.
Weick, K. E. (1995). *Sensemaking in organizations*. Thousand Oaks, CA: Sage.
Weick, K. E., & Putnam, T. (2006). Organizing for mindfulness: Eastern wisdom and Western knowledge. *Journal of Management Inquiry*, 15, 275–287.
Weick, K. E., Sutcliffe, K. M., & Obstfeld, D. (2005). Organizing and the process of sensemaking. *Organizational Science*, 16, 409–421.
Weinstein, C. E., & Mayer, R. E. (1986). The teaching of learning strategies. In M. Wittrock (Ed.), *Handbook of research on teaching* (pp. 315–327). New York, NY: Macmillan.
West, M. A., & Sacramento, C. A. (2012). Creativity and innovation: The role of team and organizational climate. In M. D. Mumford (Ed.), *Handbook of organizational creativity* (pp. 359–386). New York, NY: Elsevier.
Wiley, J. (1998). Expertise as mental set: The effects of domain knowledge in creative problem solving. *Memory and Cognition*, 26, 716–730.
Woodman, R. W., & Schoenfeldt, L. F. (1990). An interactionist model of creative behavior. *Journal of Creative Behavior*, 24, 279–290.
Zajonc, R. B. (1965). Social facilitation. *Science*, 149, 269–274.

Zhao, B. (2011). Learning from errors: The role of context, emotion, and personality. *Journal of Organizational Behavior, 32,* 435–463.

Zhou, J., & Hoever, I. J. (2014). Research on workplace creativity: A review and redirection. *Annual Review of Organizational Psychology – Organizational Behavior, 1,* 333–359.

Zwicky, F. (1969). *Discovery, invention, research – Through the morphological approach.* Toronto, Canada: Macmillan Company.

INDEX

Note: **Bold** pages indicate tables. *Italic* pages indicate figures

abductive reasoning 10, 228, 232, 234; *see also* firm strategy
absorptive capacity 288
activation 113
activities facilitating innovation 227; adapting to help expertise meet 230–231; connecting multiple entities 228–230; legitimate peripheral participation 229; practice within organizations 229, 230; routine approach 231; searching for avenues 227–228; thinking together 230; *see also* firm strategy
adaptive creative ideas 19
ADHD *see* attention deficit hyperactivity disorder
adoption decision-making 323
affect 109, 112–115
affiliation motives 124
agile method 203
algorithmic tasks 18
alternative and objective creativity 31; customer satisfaction 31; forward patent citations 32; objective and macro innovation factors 31; patent applications and patents 32
ALUo tool (advantages, limitations, unique, and overcoming limitations tool) 366
amateurs 100

Amazon 22
ambidexterity: architectural 224; contextual 224, 326; leaders of 209; reaching 325
aptitude-treatment-interaction (ATI) 372–373
architectural ambidexterity 224
aspirin 22
ATI *see* aptitude-treatment-interaction
attention deficit hyperactivity disorder (ADHD) 95
attribution errors 99

Big C creativity 342
Big Five 93–95
Big Three 91–93
bipolar disorder 95–96
Boston Consulting Group 26
boundary objects 230
brainstorming 371; methods 74; research 356–357; *see also* divergent thinking
breakthrough ideas 25
briefing 203–204; -debriefing learning cycle 203–204

California Personality Inventory (CPI) 91
case-based knowledge 51; *see also* knowledge
causal analysis 54–55; *see also* cross-process strategies

CCQ *see* creative climate questionnaire
CEOs *see* chief executive officers
champions breeders 201
chief executive officers (CEOs) 196, 223, 287, 348
chief operating officers (COOs) 287
Clean Air Act 296
climate 137, 140–141, 274–275; dimension of risk-taking 348; elements of 145; leaders as designers of 198–199; as mediator 146–147
codified knowledge 328
cogent theory of thinking 72; *see also* divergent thinking
cognition, situated 342
cognitive: hyperspace 73; skills 361; variables 91; *see also* divergent thinking
collaborative communication 173
collaborative idea generation 166; epistemic motivation 168; information processing capacity 167–168; meetings and experience 167; social processes and 168–169; *see also* team cognitive and social processes
commercial creatives 93–94
communication, contentious 173
concept selection strategies 47
conceptual category 75
conceptual knowledge 51, 79; *see also* knowledge
conflict: drivers of creative performance 147–148; effect on creativity 165; during idea evaluation 171; task and relationship 165
conscientious individuals 93
consensual assessment technique 30
consensus 174
consequences measures 48
constraints 253; analysis 57–58; external 256; internal 253–256; *see also* cross-process strategies
content-based approaches 121; affiliation motives 124; intrinsic motivation 122–123; regulatory focus 124; *see also* creativity and motivation
content-based theories 109
contentious communication 173
context: -based approaches 124–125; -based theories 109; and teams 9–10; *see also* creativity and motivation
contextual ambidexterity 224, 326
convergent thinking (CT) 72
COOs *see* chief operating officers
corporate: culture 99; vision 272–273

cost-leadership strategies 221
counterproductive work behavior (CWB) 19
CPES *see* Creative Process Engagement Scale
CPI *see* California Personality Inventory
CPS *see* creative problem-solving
creative: achievement 5; behavior predicting model *345*; behaviors and intrinsic motivation 106; complex 69; outcome effectiveness 21; person 100; process 100; product 100; self-efficacy 9, 116–117; situation 100
creative and innovative contributions 22; advance forward incrementation 23; forward incrementation 22–23; reconstruction 23; redefinition 22; redirection 23; reinitiation 23–24; replication 22; Sternberg's propulsion model 22; synthesis 24; type-based model 24; types of 22, 24–25
creative climate 137, 140, 141–142; dimensionality and 142–144; elements of 145; evolution of *143*; exploratory factor analyses 142; five-factor solution 144; focused climate 140; intrinsic motivation and creative behaviors 106; KEYS measure of 141; levels of analysis and 145–146; psychological climate 144, 146
creative climate and CPS integration 137, 146, 156; capacity and support 151; climate as mediator 146–147; conflicting drivers of performance 147–148; five-dimensional taxonomy 154; future directions 155–156; heuristic model *148*; information organization 149; integration and extension 151–152; leadership direction 150–151; limitations 154; meta-analysis 137–138; monitoring process 151; positive peer exchange 149; practical implications 152–153; theoretical implications 153–154; work autonomy 148–149; *see also* creative climate; creative problem-solving
creative climate questionnaire (CCQ) 142
creative environments 99–100; attribution errors 99; corporate culture 99; group dynamics 99; physical environment 99; reward system 100

creative idea generation 197; leaders as designers of climate for 198–199; leaders' task engagement approach to 198; transformational leadership behaviors 197–198; *see also* leadership in CPS and innovation
creative ideas 19
creative organizations 137
creative performance 8; behaviors 21
creative problem-solving (CPS) 7–8, 52, 60, 193, 339, 349; balancing alternatives 350–351; brainstorming 356–357; challenges and opportunities 368–369; clarifying social roles 351; impact of conceptual knowledge on 51; consensus 174; and creative process 138; creative thinking processes *43*; critical processing activities 42; current model *352*; developing creativity-relevant skills 363, 366; expertise 359–361; face-to-face discussion 174; facilitators 140, 360–361; factors in 42; foundational work on 349–350; framework 351; future research on *370*; idea evaluation and selection 175–176; idea generation 175, 178, 356–357; ideation sessions 176; impact of implementation planning strategies 49; integrated model *194*; leadership role in 191; learning and applying 358; lessons from experience 350; linking personal style 372; linking skills and tools 367–368; literature on 191; metacognition 361–362; model for future research *370*; model for learning and applying *359*; models 193, *352*; navigating open system 351; Planning your Approach 351, 352–355; preparing for action 357–358; prescription to description 351; problem construction 174; process-oriented leadership role 373; Sapir-Whorf hypothesis 367; setting stage for 362–363; teams for effective 173–174; tools for focusing options **365**; tools for generating options **364**; understanding challenge 355–356; *see also* learning and creativity; team cognitive and social processes
creative problem-solving and innovation 193–194

Creative Process Engagement Scale (CPES) 27
creative thinking 42, *43*, 59–62, 363; activities 43; concept selection strategies 47; consequences measures 48; cross-process strategies 53, 54–59; evidence supporting process model 43–44; execution strategies 46–50; go-no-go framework 49; idea evaluation 48; individual 10; information gathering 42, 47; knowledge 50–54; model 42–46; modified think-aloud protocol 45; impact of planning strategies 49; planning techniques 50; problem definition 42; problem redefinitions 46; requirements 41; studies on 44–46
creative work behaviors 18
creativity 2–5, 18–19, 25, 41, 69, 70, 89, 138, 192, 272, 342–343; appraisal 4; attributes of people and 5; Big C creativity 342; conflict effect on 165; creative achievement 5; imaginativeness and 98; impact on firm 2; learning linked to 344; measurement 17; mental illness and 95–96; models of 139; motivation for creative work 8–9; observing and assessing 26–27; persistence of effort and 120–121; impact of personality on creative work 8; psychopathology and 91; and schizophrenics 91; self-efficacy 9; study of 105; theory of personal 83–84; *see also* alternative and objective creativity; creative problem-solving; innovation; personality and creativity at work
creativity and innovation assessment 17, 33; algorithmic tasks 18, 19; alternative and objective measures 31–33; heuristic tasks 18; ideas 19, 22–25; incremental ideas 19; observing and assessing creativity 26–27; performance vs. outcome effectiveness 21; person-based measures 27, 29; practical implications 34–35; process-based measures 27, 29; product-or evaluation-based measures 27; routine vs. creative performance 19–22, 25; survey-based measures 26, 28–30; *see also* creativity and innovation at work

creativity and innovation at work 1, 11–12, 25; abilities contributing to 69; appraisal for creativity 4; attributes of people 5; constraints 11; context and teams 9–10; creative achievement 5; creative self-efficacy 9; impact of creativity on firm 2; declarative knowledge 79; divergent thinking 3, 72–77; evaluative skills 79–80; expressions of intelligence 78; forecasting 80–81; imaginativeness and productive obsessionality 9; innovation and cost-benefit trade-offs 6; innovation and CPS 6; IQ tests 79; key creative thinking 10; multiple intelligences 78; noncreative vs. creative behaviors 18; organizational applications 81–82; people and performance 7–9; personal creativity 83–84; problem construction 83; psychological safety 83; qualifiers and context effects 82–84; relationship of creativity and innovation 70–72; impact of strategy on 10–11; threshold theory 78; traditional intelligence 78; triangular theory 77; value of 12; *see also* creativity; creative problem-solving; organizational creativity and innovation

creativity and motivation 105, 128; content-based approaches 121–124; content-based theories 109; context-based approaches 124–125; context-based theories 109; discussion and future research 125–128; intrinsic motivation–information gathering relationship 107; proactivity 125; process-based approaches 109–118; processed-based theories 109; psychological empowerment 125; self-efficacy and performance 107; state-of-the-science review 108; studies on **110–111**; within-person level of analysis 106; within-person perspective on 105–108

creativity in arts, sciences, and business 96; Game Changers in Business 98; imaginativeness 98; intelligence, personality, and creativity **97**; Obsessive Imagination 99; productive obsessionality 98–99; Repertory Grid 98

creativity-relevant skills 345, 363, 366
criterion problem 17
cross: functional integrations 271; -industry fusion 219
cross-process strategies 53, 54; causal analysis 54–55; constraint analysis 57–58; error analysis 56–57; forecasting 55–56; wisdom 58–59; *see also* creative thinking
CT *see* convergent thinking
culture 234, 274–275; open innovation and strategy 235; supporting searching, connecting, and adapting 234–235; *see also* firm strategy
cumulative learning episodes 204
customer: expectations and product development 204–205; satisfaction 31
CWB *see* counterproductive work behavior

debriefing 204
decision-making: adoption 323; centralization of 275–276
declarative knowledge 50, 60, 61, 79; *see also* knowledge
departmental management teams 298–300; *see also* organizational creativity and innovation
Dewey's theory of reflective thinking 340
differentiation strategies 221
direction of effort 121
disruptive ideas 25
divergent thinking (DT) 72, 93; brainstorming methods 74; cogent theory of thinking 72; cognitive hyperspace 73; and CT 73; extra-cognitive influences 74; Guilford, J. P. 72; ideational flexibility 75; ideational fluency 73, 74; measures 3; open nature of DT tasks 76; originality 74–75; scores 76–77; SOI model 72; SWOT test 73, 75; theoretical advances 73; Torrance Tests of Creative Thinking and data 76; virtual brainstorming 75; *see also* creativity and innovation at work
domain: separation 326–327; -specific knowledge 330
DT *see* divergent thinking

Edwards Personal Preference Schedule 91

effective leadership behaviors 195; challenge, problem, need, or opportunity identification 195–196; Erez's model 208; evaluating ideas 199–200; idea generation phase 195, 197; idea implementation 202–203; idea mobilization 200–202; integrated model *194*; reaching customers 205–208; *see also* leadership in CPS and innovation
effort 119
empathy in leaders 204
entrepreneurial leaders 207
epistemic motivation 168
Erez's model 208
error analysis 56–57; *see also* cross-process strategies
errors, attribution 99
evaluative skills 79–80
evocation 115
experience 345–349
experiential: knowledge 51; learning 345; *see also* knowledge
expertise 52, 329, 359–361; of source 30
expert knowledge *see* expertise
exploration and exploitation 223–224
exploratory factor analyses 142
expressions of intelligence 78
external firm constraints 256; markets 257; resources 258–259; social demands 259
external stakeholders 259
extra-cognitive influences 74
extraversion 91, 94
extraverted 94
Eysenck, H. 91; hypothesis 91; theory of creativity 91–92
Eysenckian measures 91

face-to-face discussion groups 174
failure 346
feasibility 24
felt obligation for constructive change (FOCC) 124
finance department 281, 285–286; finance availability 281–283; finance integration 285; firm finance differences 283–284; institutions and financial systems 283; role of institutions and financial systems *284*; *see also* organizational creativity and innovation
finance-marketing integration 292

firm: finance differences 283–284; flexibility in manufacturing operations 256; history elements 253; operational structures of 256; product-based 256; service 254; technological resources 255; *see also* external firm constraints
firm innovation planning 243, 259–261; cognitive operation evaluation of strategies 251; constraints 253–259; facilitative effects of 245; investment strategies 244; model of *248*; radical innovations 244; strategic planners 245; strategic planning 244–247; strategic planning processes 247–253
firm strategy 219; abductive reasoning 227–228; activities facilitating innovation 227; adapting to help expertise meet 230–231; basics of 221; communities of practice 229, 230; connecting across multiple entities 228–230; cost-leadership strategies 221; cross-industry fusion 219; culture 234–235; differentiation strategies 221; discussion and future research 236–237; exploration and exploitation 223–224; innovation 219, 222, 224–225, 226; legitimate peripheral participation 229; organizational culture 227; organizational structure 226–227; resources and capabilities 221–222; routine dynamics approach 231; strategic decision-making 222–224; strategies for innovation failure 235–236; strategy foundations 220; strategy-making process 223; structures 231–234; thinking together 230; value innovation 221
five-dimensional taxonomy 154
five-factor solution 144
FOCC *see* felt obligation for constructive change
focused climate 140
forecasting 55–56, 80–81, 195–196, 251; *see also* cross-process strategies; leaders in challenge identification
formalized innovation processes 321
forward patent citations 32
four P's of marketing 256
functional diversity 167

Game Changers in Business 98
Generating Ideas 352

global competitive work context 191
go-no-go framework 49
group: decision literature 170; dynamics 99
group support systems (GSSs) 373–374
GSSs *see* group support systems
Guilford, J. P. 72, 77; *see also* divergent thinking

heuristic tasks 18
high error orientation 347
HR *see* human resources
HRM *see* human resources management
Hudson book 96
human resources (HR) 271; department 277, 281; *see also* organizational creativity and innovation
human resources management (HRM) 272, 278; culture 278; innovation-oriented 277; knowledge base 280–281; knowledge management capabilities 279–280; practices and innovation performance *279*

ICTs *see* information and communication technologies
idea evaluation and selection 169–171, 175–176; activities 169; conflict during 171; evaluation 48, 171; group decision literature 170; for implementation by leaders 199–200; MIP-G theory 172; pro-social motivation 172; social processes and 171–172; *see also* team cognitive and social processes
idea generation 175, 178, 199, 356; brainstorming 356–357; breakthrough of idea 25; in groups 166; idea types 24–25; mad genius 95; sample application of 357; social processes and 168–169
idea implementation stage 202–203; agile method 203; cumulative learning episodes 204; empathy in innovation leader 204; learning cycle 203–204; minimizing time to market 203–204; product development 204–205; *see also* leadership in CPS and innovation
idea mobilization 200–202; ill-defined problem 202; issue-selling efforts 201; leaders' behavioural change 202; *see also* leadership in CPS and innovation

ideation: flexibility 75; fluency 73, 74; sessions 176, 193; *see also* divergent thinking
imaginativeness 8, 98
individual differences 372
information and communication technologies (ICTs) 294
information gathering 42; collaborative communication 173; contentious communication 173; creative strategies of 47; and knowledge sharing 172; *see also* creative thinking
information organization 149
information processing: capacity of groups 167–168; patterns 92
innovation 5–7, 18–19, 89, 219, 272, 315; base of 316; and capabilities 222; constraints on 11; cost-benefit trade-offs 6; and creative problem solutions 6; creativity and 90; cycle 207; empathy in leader 204; factors 31; failure 235–236; and firm strategy 219; generation 320; ideation phase 193; implementation phase 193; leadership role in 191; management process research literature 191; marketing-R&D integrations and *293*; models of 193, 316; objective and factors 31; social impact of 41; strategy 276, 317; theoretical base of 316; value 221; *see also* activities facilitating innovation; alternative and objective creativity; creativity; institutional supports for innovation; processes in innovation
innovative firms 10, 318, 319
inspiration 115–116
institutional supports for innovation 315, 322–324; ambidexterity 324–328; funding 317; future research 331–332; implications for management 332–333; innovation models 316; innovation strategy 317; innovative organizations 318, 319; knowledge management 317; mechanistic organizations 318; organic organizations 318; organizational knowledge 332; organizational structure 318–322; overarching factors 317; process domain 317; resources and creativity 328–331; structural elements 317; Triple Helix model 316

institutions and financial systems 283, *284*
integrated model *194*; *see also* leadership in CPS and innovation
intellectual property (IP) 255, 296
intelligence: declarative knowledge 79; expressions of 78; IQ tests 79; theory of multiple 78; threshold theory 78; traditional 78; triangular theory 77
intensity 119–120
interactive groups 299
internal boundary crossing 233
internal constraints 253; history 253–254; resources 254–256; structures 256
internal organizational boundaries 233
interpersonal processes 180
intrinsic motivation 106, 122–123; content-based approaches 122–123; and creative behaviors 106; -information gathering relationship 107
investment strategies 244
IP *see* intellectual property
IQ tests 79
issue-selling efforts 201

job requirements 20

KEYS measure 141
KMCs *see* knowledge management capabilities
knowledge 50–54; base 280–281, 329; boundaries 230; codified 328; of cognition 361; conceptual 51; cross-process strategies 53; declarative 50, 60, 61; experiential 51; expertise impact on creative achievements 52; management 317, 328; mental models 52–54; sharing 233, 279; types of 50; *see also* conceptual knowledge; creative thinking
knowledge management capabilities (KMCs) 279

leader: ambidextrous 209; cost-leadership strategies 221; task engagement approach 198
leader-member exchange (LMX) 273
leadership 273–274; behaviors 197; direction and encouragement 150–151; paradoxical 192, 209; transformational 197–198, 209; visionary 196; *see also* effective leadership behaviors; leaders in challenge identification

leadership in CPS and innovation 191; complementary processes 193–194; discussion and integration 208–210; paradoxical leadership 192; *see also* effective leadership behaviors
leaders in challenge identification 195–196; forecasting 195–196; scanning the environment 195; visionary leadership 196; *see also* leadership in CPS and innovation
learning 340; climate dimension of risk-taking 348; cognitive development 340; creative behavior prediction model *345*; creativity 342–343; Dewey's theory of reflective thinking 340; experience 345–349; failure 346; high error orientation 347; individual 340–341, 344–345; linked to problem-solving and creativity 344; little c 343; metacognition 341; organizational level 341–342; Pro-C 343; schemas 342; sensemaking perspective 342; social development theory 341; social learning theory 341; social metacognition 341; team level 341; theory of situated cognition 342
learning and creativity 339; aptitude-treatment-interaction 372–373; assessing impact of training designs 371; comparing various frameworks 370–371; conceptual and theoretical foundations 340; creating conditions to sustain learning 375; current CPS framework 351–358; future research 369; individual differences 372; learning 340–349; learning and applying CPS 358–369; linking people and place 376; linking personal style with CPS 372; organizational climate 375–376; process-oriented leadership role 373; social roles 373–374; strengthening impact criteria 371–372; style differences 372; understanding and appreciating style 374; *see also* creative problem-solving
learning cycle 203–204
legal department 295, 298; legal integrations 295–297; *see also* organizational creativity and innovation
little c 343
LMX *see* leader-member exchange

mad genius idea 95
management 332–333; departmental teams 298–300; see also organizational creativity and innovation
marketing and sales department 291, 294–295; finance-marketing integration 292; ICTs 294; marketing and sales integrations 291–294; marketing-manufacturing integration 292; marketing-R&D integrations 293; see also organizational creativity and innovation
Market Opportunity Navigator 205
market penetration 205–208; innovation cycle 207; Market Opportunity Navigator 205; SodaStream 207–208; strategic leadership literature 207; technophiles or technology enthusiasts 206; theories 206; see also leadership in CPS and innovation
Mattel 23
mechanistic organizations 318
mental illness and creativity 95–96
mental models 52–54; about causal relationships 163–164; types of 164; see also knowledge
metacognition 108, 341, 361–362
mid-level leaders 244
mini-c 343
minimizing time to market 203–204
MIP-G see Motivated Information Processing in Groups
momentary psychological empowerment 125
mood: fluctuation 92; valence and creativity 112
Motivated Information Processing in Groups (MIP-G) 168, 172
motivation 105; constructs 108; -information gathering relationship 107; intrinsic 106, 122–123; measure of 106; variation in 106; within-person level of analysis 106; see also creativity and motivation
motives, affiliation 124
multiple intelligences, theory of 78

new product development (NPD) 246, 272, 289–290
NGOs see nongovernmental organizations
nominal groups 299
noncreative work behaviors 18
nongovernmental organizations (NGOs) 316
NPD see new product development

objective and macro innovation factors 31
OBSE see organization-based self-esteem
obsessive-compulsive disorder (OCD) 98
Obsessive Imagination 99
OCBs see organizational citizenship behavior
OCD see obsessive-compulsive disorder
Oldham and Cummings's three-item scale 30
open innovation and strategy 235
Openness 93, 94
Open-to-Experience 94
opportunity recognition 257
organic organizations 318
organization 171; actions 153; assessing creativity in 26–27; capacity and support 151; climate 375–376; communities of practice 229, 230; creative 137; culture 141, 227; integration and extension 151–152; knowledge 332; learning 341; norms 171; reflectively structured 229; routines 230; separation 325; see also firm
organizational ambidexterity 224, 324, 325; contextual 326; domain separation 326–327; issues in 327–328; reaching 325; structural 325
organizational citizenship behavior (OCBs) 19
organizational creativity and innovation 271, 300–301; cross-functional integrations 271; departmental management teams 298–300; finance department 281–286; human resources department 277–281; legal integrations 295–297, 298; legitimacy and support for 301; marketing and sales department 291–295; purchasing department 286–291; strategic alignment and collaboration 272; top management teams 272–276, 277
organizational structure 226–227, 231–234, 318; cross-level conflicts 322; cross-level effects on innovation 321–322; formalized innovation processes 321; functional

differentiation 319; intensive communication 319; knowledge resources 318–319; organizational units 11; positive attitude to change 319; product vs. process innovation 320; radical and incremental innovations 320; structural factors and innovation type 320
organization-based self-esteem (OBSE) 124
originality 70; in context of DT 74–75
overdetermination 69

Palo Alto Research Center (PARC) 236
paradoxical leadership 192, 209
PARC *see* Palo Alto Research Center
patent 32
people and performance 7–9
personal computers 22
personal creativity, theory of 83–84
personality: factors 362; measures 90; variables 91
personality and creativity at work 89, 101–102; Big Three and power of psychoticism 91–93; bipolar disorder 95–96; caveat 89–90; commercial creative 93–94; creative environments 99–100; creatives and schizophrenics 91; creativity and innovation 90; creativity and psychopathology 91; creativity in arts, sciences, and business 96–99; extraversion 91, 94; extraverted 94; Eysenckian measures 91; implications for practice 100–101; information-processing patterns 92; mad genius idea 95; mental illness and creativity 95–96; Openness 93, 94; Open-to-Experience 94; personality traits and creativity 90; psychosis 92; research using Big Five 93–95; schizophrenia 95
Personal Preference Schedule 91
person-based measures 27, 29
physical environment 99
Piaget's theory of cognitive development 340
Planning your Approach 351, 352; appraising tasks 353–354; designing process 354; framing problems 355; sample application of 354–355
Polaroid 243, 257
positive: moods 114; peer exchange 149
proactivity 125

problem: construction 83, 174; definition 42; of organizations 161; redefinitions 46; -solving 344
problem identification and construction 162–164; effect of conflict on creativity 165; ill-defined problems 162; mental models about causal relationships and relationships 163–164; representational gap 163; research on 162; social processes and problem construction 164–166; task and relationship conflict 165; types of mental models 164; *see also* team cognitive and social processes
Pro-C 343
process: -based measures 27, 29; -based theories 109; domain 317; innovations 320; models of creativity 139
process-based approaches 109; activation 113; affect 109, 112–115; creative self-efficacy 116–117; direction 121; effort 119; evocation 115; inspiration 115–116; intensity 119–120; mood valence and creativity 112; persistence 120–121; positive moods 114; qualitative study of preprofessional dancers 117–118; self-efficacy 116–119; transcendence 115; *see also* creativity and motivation
processes in innovation 322–324; adoption decision-making 323; management systems 323; ongoing innovation projects 323–324
product: -based firms 256; -based measures 27; innovations 320; vs. process innovation 320
production loss 74
productive obsessionality 8, 98–99
Project Discovery 354
pro-social motivation 172
psychological: climate 144, 146; safety 83
psychopathology 92; creativity and 91
psychosis 92
psychoticism 91–93
PsycINFO and Business Source Premier 108
purchasing department 286, 290–291; new product development 289–290; strategic sourcing 288–*289*; structure and responsibilities 287; supplier market intelligence 287–288; *see also* organizational creativity and innovation

R&D *see* research and development
radical: ideas 19, 25; and incremental innovations 320; innovations 244
reaching ambidexterity 325
reasoning, abductive 10, 228, 232, 234; *see also* firm strategy
reflective thinking theory 340
regulatory focus 124
Repertory Grid 98
representational gap (rGaps) 163
research and development (R&D) 92, 243, 271, 358
resources and capabilities 221–222
resources and creativity 328–331; codified knowledge 328; domain-specific knowledge 330; expertise 329; knowledge 328, 329
return on investment (ROI) 317
reward system 100
rGaps *see* representational gap
Rockefeller, J. D. 1
ROI *see* return on investment
role requirements 20
routine: dynamics approach 231; performance 19

Sapir-Whorf hypothesis 367
scanning the environment 195; *see also* leaders in challenge identification
schemas 342
schizophrenia 95; creatives and schizophrenics 91
schizotypy 91
seaplanes 24
self: -concordant strategies 120; -efficacy 107, 116–119; -management strategies 120; -reported creativity 28; -reported innovative work behavior 28; -report measures 28
sensemaking perspective 342
service firms 254
shared mental models (SMMs) 164
situated cognition 342
16 Personality Factor (16PF) 96
16PF *see* 16 Personality Factor
SMI *see* supplier market intelligence
SMMs *see* shared mental models
social: development theory 341; learning theory 341; loafing 74; metacognition 341
SodaStream 207–208
SOI model *see* Structure of Intellect model
solution monitoring process 151

Sternberg's propulsion model 22
strategic: alignment and collaboration 272; decision-making 222–224, 348; leadership literature 207; sourcing *289*
strategic planning 244–247; facilitative effects of 245; for firm innovation *248*; goal specification 247, 249–250; implementation plans 252; planners 245; strategy evaluation 251–252; strategy generation 250–251; strategy implementation 252–253
strategy foundations 220; abductive reasoning 227–228; activities facilitating innovation 227; adapting to help expertise meet 230–231; basics of strategy 221; communities of practice 229, 230; connecting multiple entities 228–230; cost-leadership strategies 221; culture 234–235; differentiation strategies 221; exploration and exploitation 223–224; firm innovation and strategy 224–226; innovation activities 226; innovation and capabilities 222; legitimate peripheral participation 229; organizational structure 226–227; resources and capabilities 221–222; routine dynamics approach 231; strategic decision-making 222–224; strategies for innovation failure 235–236; strategy-making process 223; structures 231–234; thinking together process 230; value innovation 221; *see also* firm strategy
strategy making 222; process model 223
structural elements 317
Structure of Intellect model (SOI model) 72; *see also* divergent thinking
structures 231, 275–276; internal boundary crossing 233; investment in technological structures 232; organic 231; supporting, connecting, and adapting 231–234; *see also* firm strategy
style differences 372
supplier market intelligence (SMI) 287–288
survey-based measures 26; advantages and disadvantages 28; consensual assessment technique 30; expertise of source 30; facets 29; issues with 28; self-report measures 28; survey content 29–30; survey source 28–29
SWOT test 73, 75

tacit knowledge 328
task: algorithmic 18; vs. creative performance distinct 19–22, 25; performance 19
TCI *see* team climate inventory
team climate inventory (TCI) 146
team cognitive and social processes 161; collaborative communication 173; collaborative idea generation 166–168; contentious communication 173; design thinking 176–178; effective CPS team 173–174; epistemic motivation 168; future directions 178–180; idea evaluation 169–172; idea generation 166, 168–169; information processing capacity 167–168; information sharing 172–173; meetings and experience 167; problem construction 164–166; problem identification 162–164; problems of organizations 161; research on team innovation implementation 180; team size 180
team creativity 161; *see also* team cognitive and social processes
technological: resources 255; turbulence 257
technology enthusiasts *see* technophiles
technophiles 206
temporal: monopoly 315; separation 325–326
theory of; multiple intelligences 78; personal creativity 83–84; situated cognition 342
think: -aloud protocol 45; room 232
thinking: cogent theory of 72; convergent 72; together 230; *see also* divergent thinking
3-D holographic television 43, 47
three-item scale 30

threshold theory 78
TMTs *see* top management teams
top management teams (TMTs) 272, 277, 348; centralization of decision-making 275–276; corporate vision 272–273; culture and climate 274–275; innovation strategy 276; leadership 273–274; structure 275–276; *see also* organizational creativity and innovation
Torrance Tests of Creative Thinking and data 76
traditional intelligence 78
transcendence 115
transformational leadership 209; behaviors 197–198
triangular theory 77
Triple Helix model 316
type-based model 24

value innovation 221
video rentals 23
virtual brainstorming 75
vision 196
visionary leadership 196; *see also* leaders in challenge identification
VUCA (volatile, uncertain, complex, and ambiguous) 339
Vygotsky's social development theory 341

wisdom 58–59; *see also* cross-process strategies
within-person: level of analysis 106; predictors 112
work autonomy and stimulation 148–149
World Economic Forum 17
worthless follies 25

Xerox 236